ALSO BY BOB WOODWARD

The Secret Man
(with a Reporter's Assessment by Carl Bernstein)

Plan of Attack

Bush at War

Maestro: Greenspan's Fed and the American Boom

Shadow: Five Presidents and the Legacy of Watergate

The Choice

The Agenda: Inside the Clinton White House

The Commanders

Veil: The Secret Wars of the CIA 1981–1987

Wired: The Short Life and Fast Times of John Belushi

The Brethren
(with Scott Armstrong)

The Final Days
(with Carl Bernstein)

All the President's Men
(with Carl Bernstein)

STATE

SIMON & SCHUSTER

OF DENIAL

Bob Woodward

NEW YORK · LONDON · TORONTO · SYDNEY

SIMON & SCHUSTER
Rockefeller Center
1230 Avenue of the Americas
New York, NY 10020

Copyright © 2006 by Bob Woodward
All rights reserved,
including the right of reproduction
in whole or in part in any form.

SIMON & SCHUSTER and colophon are registered trademarks
of Simon & Schuster, Inc.

For information about special discounts for bulk purchases,
please contact Simon & Schuster Special Sales at
1-800-456-6798 or business@simonandschuster.com.

Designed by Jaime Putorti

Manufactured in the United States of America

10   9   8   7   6   5   4   3   2   1

Library of Congress Cataloging-in-Publication Data is available.

ISBN-13: 978-0-7432-7223-0
ISBN-10:   0-7432-7223-4

To Mary Walsh

AUTHOR'S NOTE

TWO PEOPLE HAVE HELPED me at every stage of this book, working out of third-floor offices in my home in Washington, D.C.

Bill Murphy Jr., a former reporter and an attorney who practiced in the Army Judge Advocate General's Corps and the Department of Justice, saw that I needed to do a third book on President Bush with the focus on the Iraq War. Honest, straightforward and insistent on fairness and the truth, he is a natural reporter, winning the trust of a number of key sources. Focused and incredibly resourceful, Bill became my partner. Authors only rarely get such maturity, skill and wise counsel from one person. Without him, I never would have finished this book, which is as much his as mine.

Christine Parthemore, a 2003 Phi Beta Kappa political science graduate of The Ohio State University, is a kind of Wonder Woman of the Information Age, capable of finding any information or any person. She has never let me down. Meticulous and diligent in every task from transcribing hundreds of hours of interview tapes to editing the manuscript, she is learned, frank, and smart. A natural editor, she knows how to get to the heart of matters. As she demonstrated every day, Christine has the energy of half a dozen and an endless capacity for work.

PROLOGUE

I N LATE DECEMBER 2000, less than a month before his inauguration, President-elect George W. Bush was still debating who should be his secretary of defense. Former Senator Dan Coats, an Indiana Republican who had served on the Armed Services Committee, had been at the top of Bush's list and had the backing of his conservative base. But Coats had not been impressive in his interview with Bush and Vice President–elect Dick Cheney, who was heading the transition team for the new government. Coats knew the top generals mostly from a distance and was lukewarm on the national missile defense system Bush had promised in the campaign. He had never run a large organization and he acknowledged he would need a strong, experienced number two at the Pentagon.

It wouldn't work. Bush needed someone who could not only battle things out with the generals but who also had as much gravitas as the rest of his new national security team. Cheney had been secretary of defense under Bush's father; Colin Powell, Bush's pick for secretary of state, had been chairman of the Joint Chiefs of Staff and Reagan's national security adviser. He needed a secretary of defense with more stature, grit and experience.

What about Donald Rumsfeld? Cheney suggested. Rumsfeld, 68, Cheney's old boss and mentor, had the dream résumé. He had been secretary of defense once before, under President Ford from 1975 to 1977. He had been a Navy pilot in the 1950s, elected to four terms in Congress, served as Ford's White House chief of staff, and been the CEO of two Fortune 500 companies. They'd been talking about making Rumsfeld

CIA director, but maybe that wasn't right. Maybe they needed him back at Defense.

Three days before Christmas, Bush, Cheney and Rumsfeld had a long meeting and lunch. Wiry, cocky, confident with a boyish intensity, Rumsfeld seemed only half his age. He blew into the meeting like a tornado, full of excitement and vision. He knew the Pentagon; he had recently headed commissions on the use of space and the ballistic missile threat. He seemed to know everything.

Bush was surprised to be so impressed. Afterward, he spoke with his incoming White House chief of staff, Andrew H. Card Jr.

Bush had selected Card, 53, because his father said there was no more loyal person. Back in 1988, Card had been instrumental in his father's win in the critical New Hampshire primary. Later, Card had been Bush senior's deputy White House chief of staff and transportation secretary.

After the 2000 election, Card thought he would be asked to run the transition team. "No, I'm not talking about that job," Bush told him. "I'm talking about the big one." They would have to have a completely candid, unique relationship, Card insisted, setting out his conditions for becoming chief of staff. Access to all people, meetings and information. "I also can't be a friend," Card said.

"Of course," Bush said.

In November, weeks before the Supreme Court settled the election in his favor, Bush announced Card's appointment, intentionally sending the strongest signal: Besides the vice president, Andy Card would be first among equals in the Bush White House, on all matters, at all times.

COATS SEEMED LIKE a good man, Bush told Card, but the contrast with Rumsfeld was stunning. Rumsfeld understood what military transformation meant—making the weapons and troops more mobile, swifter, higher-tech and more lethal. He was so impressive, Bush said. *This is what has to be done. This is how to do it. These are the kinds of people it takes.* It was as if he already had a plan. Rumsfeld was 43 when he had the job a quarter century ago. It was as if he were now saying, "I think I've got some things I'd like to finish."

There was another dynamic that Bush and Card discussed. Rumsfeld and Bush's father, the former president, couldn't stand each other. The two had been the young GOP stars in the 1970s, and there was a lingering animosity between them. Bush senior thought Rumsfeld was arrogant, self-important, too sure of himself and Machiavellian. He believed that in 1975 Rumsfeld had maneuvered President Ford into selecting him to head the CIA. The CIA was at perhaps its lowest point in the mid-1970s. Serving as its director was thought to be a dead end. Though things had turned out differently, Bush senior didn't trust Rumsfeld. Rumsfeld had also made nasty private remarks that Bush was a light-weight, a weak Cold War CIA director who did not appreciate the Soviet threat and was manipulated by Secretary of State Henry Kissinger.

Card could see that overcoming his skepticism about Rumsfeld added to the president-elect's excitement. It was a chance to prove his father wrong. And Rumsfeld fit Cheney's model.

Cheney had been in charge of the search for Bush's running mate. He'd said he was looking for someone with a broad range of experience. An ideal candidate would know the White House and Congress, have held elected office, have run a large federal executive department. He also had to be someone who wasn't just a creature of Washington. He had to have experience in the real world, the corporate world perhaps. A CEO, for example. Perhaps it was not surprising that Cheney, who had been a congressman, White House chief of staff, secretary of defense and Fortune 500 CEO, would value his own experience and model the ideal candidate after himself. Bush got the message and picked Cheney as his running mate. Now, Cheney seemed to have done it again. He had set up a model for secretary of defense that mirrored his own résumé. Cheney thought Bush needed a Cheney at the Pentagon. Nobody resembled Cheney more than Rumsfeld. On paper, at least, they looked almost perfect.

Bush would nominate Rumsfeld, he told Card. Cheney had been selected for his national security credentials. He was the expert, and this was the sort of decision that required expertise. Still, Bush wondered privately to Card about pitfalls, if there was something he didn't see here. After all, his father had strong feelings.

Is this a trapdoor? he asked.

A MOVIE OF THE George W. Bush presidency might open in the Oval Office a month later, on January 26, 2001, six days after the inauguration, when Rumsfeld was sworn in as defense secretary. A White House photographer captured the scene. Rumsfeld wears a pinstripe suit, and rests his left hand on a Bible held by Joyce, his wife of 46 years. His right hand is raised. Bush stands almost at attention, his head forward, his eyes cocked sharply leftward, looking intently at Rumsfeld. Cheney stands slightly off to the side, his trademark half smile on his face. The man in the black robe administering the oath is Judge Laurence H. Silberman, a close friend of both Rumsfeld and Cheney dating back to the Ford days, when he was deputy and then acting attorney general. It is a cold, dry day, and the barren branches of the trees outside can be seen through the Oval Office windows.

The White House photograph captures a moment tying the past with the future. Back in the days of the Ford presidency, in the wake of Watergate—the pardon of Nixon, the fall of Saigon—Cheney and Rumsfeld had worked almost daily in the same Oval Office where they once again stood. The new man in the photo, Bush, five years younger than Cheney and nearly 14 years younger than Rumsfeld, had been a student at Harvard Business School. He came to the presidency with less experience and time in government than any incoming president since Woodrow Wilson in 1913.

Well into his seventh decade, many of Rumsfeld's peers and friends had retired, but he now stood eagerly on the cusp, ready to run the race again. He resembled John le Carré's fictional Cold War British intelligence chief, George Smiley, a man who "had been given, in late age, a chance to return to the rained-out contests of his life and play them after all."

"Get it right this time," Cheney told Rumsfeld.

1

—————

IN THE FALL OF 1997, former President George H. W. Bush, then age 74 and five years out of the White House, phoned one of his closest friends, Prince Bandar bin Sultan, the longtime Saudi Arabian ambassador to the United States.

"Bandar," Bush said, "W. would like to talk to you if you have time. Can you come by and talk to him?" His eldest son and namesake, George W. Bush, who had been governor of Texas for nearly three years, was consulting a handful of people about an important decision and wanted to have a private talk.

Bandar's life was built around such private talks. He didn't ask why, though there had been ample media speculation that W. was thinking of running for president. Bandar, 49, had been the Saudi ambassador for 15 years, and had an extraordinary position in Washington. His intensity and networking were probably matched only by former President Bush.

They had built a bond in the 1980s. Bush, the vice president living in the shadow of President Ronald Reagan, was widely dismissed as weak and a wimp, but Bandar treated him with the respect, attention and seriousness due a future president. He gave a big party for Bush at his palatial estate overlooking the Potomac River with singer Roberta Flack providing the entertainment, and went fishing with him at Bush's vacation home in Kennebunkport, Maine—Bandar's least favorite pastime but something Bush loved. The essence of their relationship was constant contact, by phone and in person.

Like good intelligence officers—Bush had been CIA director and Bandar had close ties to the world's important spy services—they had recruited each other. The friendship was both useful and genuine, and the utility and authenticity reinforced each other. During Bush's 1991 Gulf War to oust Saddam Hussein from Kuwait and prevent him from invading neighboring Saudi Arabia, Bandar had been virtually a member of the Bush war cabinet.

At about 4 A.M. on election day 1992, when it looked as if Bush was going to fail in his bid for a second term, Bandar had dispatched a private letter to him saying, You're my friend for life. You saved our country. I feel like one of your family, you are like one of our own. And you know what, Mr. President? You win either way. You should win. You deserve to. But if you lose, you are in good company with Winston Churchill, who won the war and lost the election.

Bush called Bandar later that day, about 1 P.M., and said, "Buddy, all day the only good news I've had was your letter." About 12 hours later, in the early hours of the day after the election, Bush called again and said, "It's over."

Bandar became Bush's case officer, rescuing him from his cocoon of near depression. He was the first to visit Bush at Kennebunkport as a guest after he left the White House, and later visited him there twice more. He flew friends in from England to see Bush in Houston. In January 1993 he took Bush to his 32-room mansion in Aspen, Colorado. When the ex-president walked in he found a "Desert Storm Corner," named after the U.S.-led military operation in the Gulf War. Bush's picture was in the middle. Bandar played tennis and other sports with Bush, anything to keep the former president engaged.

Profane, ruthless, smooth, Bandar was almost a fifth estate in Washington, working the political and media circles attentively and obsessively. But as ambassador his chief focus was the presidency, whoever held it, ensuring the door was open for Saudi Arabia, which had the world's largest oil reserves but did not have a powerful military in the volatile Middle East. When Michael Deaver, one of President Reagan's top White House aides, left the White House to become a lobbyist, First Lady Nancy Reagan, another close Bandar friend, called and asked him to help Deaver. Bandar gave Deaver a $500,000 consulting contract and never saw him again.

Bandar was on hand election night in 1994 when two of Bush's sons, George W. and Jeb, ran for the governorships of Texas and Florida. Bush and former First Lady Barbara Bush thought that Jeb would win in Florida and George W. would lose in Texas. Bandar was astonished as the election results poured in that night to watch Bush sitting there with four pages of names and telephone numbers—two pages for Texas and two for Florida. Like an experienced Vegas bookie, Bush worked the phones the whole evening, calling, making inquiries and thanking everybody—collecting and paying. He gave equal time and attention to those who supported the new Texas governor and the failed effort in Florida.

Bandar realized that Bush knew he could collect on all his relationships. It was done with such a light, human touch that it never seemed predatory or grasping. Fred Dutton, an old Kennedy hand in the 1960s and Bandar's Washington lawyer and lobbyist, said that it was the way Old Man Kennedy, the ambassador Joseph P. Kennedy, had operated, though Kennedy's style had been anything but light.

BANDAR PLANNED HIS 1997 VISIT with the Texas governor around a trip to a home football game of his beloved Dallas Cowboys. That would give him "cover," as he called it. He wanted the meeting to be very discreet, and ordered his private jet to stop in Austin.

When they landed, Bandar's chief of staff came running up to say the governor was already there outside the plane. Bandar walked down the aisle to go outside.

"Hi, how are you?" greeted George W. Bush, standing at the door before Bandar could even get off the plane. He was eager to talk.

"Here?" inquired Bandar, expecting they would go to the governor's mansion or office.

"Yes, I prefer it here."

Bandar had been a Saudi fighter pilot for 17 years and was a favorite of King Fahd; his father was the Saudi defense minister, Prince Sultan. Bush had been a jet pilot in the Texas Air National Guard. They had met, but to Bandar, George W. was just another of the former president's four sons, and not the most distinguished one.

"I'm thinking of running for president," said Bush, then 52. He had hardly begun his campaign for reelection as governor of Texas. He had been walking gingerly for months, trying not to dampen his appeal as a potential presidential candidate while not peaking too early, or giving Texas voters the impression he was looking past them.

Bush told Bandar he had clear ideas of what needed to be done with national domestic policy. But, he added, "I don't have the foggiest idea about what I think about international, foreign policy.

"My dad told me before I make up my mind, go and talk to Bandar. One, he's our friend. *Our* means America, not just the Bush family. Number two, he knows everyone around the world who counts. And number three, he will give you his view on what he sees happening in the world. Maybe he can set up meetings for you with people around the world."

"Governor," Bandar said, "number one, I am humbled you ask me this question." It was a tall order. "Number two," Bandar continued, "are you sure you want to do this?" His father's victory, running as the sitting vice president to succeed the popular Reagan in the 1988 presidential election was one thing, but taking over the White House from President Bill Clinton and the Democrats, who likely would nominate Vice President Al Gore, would be another. Of Clinton, Bandar added, "This president is the real Teflon, not Reagan."

Bush's eyes lit up! It was almost as if the younger George Bush wanted to avenge his father's loss to Clinton. It was an electric moment. Bandar thought it was as if the son was saying, "I want to go after this guy and show who is better."

"All right," Bandar said, getting the message. Bush junior wanted a fight. "What do you want to know?"

Bush said Bandar should pick what was important, so Bandar provided a tour of the world. As the oil-rich Saudi kingdom's ambassador to the United States, he had access to world leaders and was regularly dispatched by King Fahd on secret missions, an international Mr. Fix-It, often on Mission Impossible tasks. He had personal relationships with the leaders of Russia, China, Syria, Great Britain, even Israel. Bandar spoke candidly about leaders in the Middle East, the Far East, Russia, China and Europe. He recounted some of his personal meetings, such as his contacts with Mikhail Gorbachev working on the Soviet withdrawal from Afghanistan. He spoke of Maggie Thatcher and the current British prime minister, Tony Blair. Bandar described the Saudi role working with the Pope and Reagan to keep the Communists in check. Diplomacy often made strange bedfellows.

"There are people who are your enemies in this country," Bush said, "who also think my dad is your friend."

"So?" asked Bandar, not asking who, though the reference was obviously to supporters of Israel, among others.

Bush said in so many words that the people who didn't want his dad to win in 1992 would also be against him if he ran. They were the same people who didn't like Bandar.

"Can I give you one advice?" Bandar asked.

"What?"

"Mr. Governor, tell me you really want to be president of the United States."

Bush said yes.

"And if you tell me that, I want to tell you one thing: To hell with Saudi Arabia or who likes Saudi Arabia or who doesn't, who likes Bandar or doesn't. Anyone who you think hates your dad or your friend who can be important to make a difference in winning, swallow your pride and make friends of them. And I can help you. I can help you out and complain about you, make sure they understood that, and that will make sure they help you."

Bush recognized the Godfather's advice: Keep your friends close, but your enemies closer. But he seemed uncomfortable and remarked that that wasn't particularly honest.

"Never mind if you really want to be honest," Bandar said. "This is not a confession booth. If you really want to stick to that, just enjoy this term and go do something fun. In the big boys' game, it's cutthroat, it's bloody and it's not pleasant."

Bandar changed the subject. "I was going to tell you something that has nothing to do with international. When I was flying F-102s in Sherman, Texas, Perrin Air Force Base, you were flying F-102s down the road at another Texas base. Our destiny linked us a long time ago by flying, without knowing each other." He said he wanted to suggest another idea.

"What?"

"If you still remember what they taught you in the Air Force. I remember it because I spent 17 years. You only spent a few years. Keep your eye on the ball. When I am flying that jet and my life is on the line, and I pick up that enemy aircraft, I don't care if everything around me dies. I will keep my eye on that aircraft, and I will do whatever it takes. *I'll never take my eye off.*"

FORMER PRESIDENT BUSH continued in his efforts to expand his son's horizons and perhaps recruit future staff.

"George W., as you know, is thinking about what he might want to do," he told Condoleezza Rice, the 43-year-old provost of Stanford and one of his favorite junior National Security Council staffers from his White House years. "He's going to be out at Kennebunkport. You want to come to Kennebunkport for the weekend?"

It was August 1998. The former president was proposing a policy seminar for his son.

Rice had been the senior Russia expert on the NSC, and she had met George W. in a White House receiving line. She had seen him next in 1995, when she had been in Houston for a board meeting of Chevron, on which she served, and Bush senior invited her to Austin, where W. had just been sworn in as governor. She talked with the new governor about family and sports for an hour and then felt like a potted plant as she and the former president sat through a lunch Bush junior had with the Texas House speaker and lieutenant governor.

The Kennebunkport weekend was only one of many Thursday-to-Sunday August getaways at Camp Bush with breakfast, lunch, dinner, fishing, horseshoes and other competitions.

"I don't have any idea about foreign affairs," Governor Bush told Rice. "This isn't what I do."

Rice felt that he was wondering, Should I do this? Or probably, Can I do this? Out on the boat as father and son fished, the younger Bush asked her to talk about China, then Russia. His questions flowed all weekend—what about this country, this leader, this issue, what might it mean, and what was the angle for U.S. policy.

Early the next year, after he was reelected Texas governor and before he formally announced his presidential candidacy, Rice was summoned to Austin again. She was about to step down as Stanford provost and was thinking of taking a year off or going into investment banking for a couple of years.

"I want you to run my foreign policy for me," Bush said. She should recruit a team of experts.

"Well, that would be interesting," Rice said, and accepted. It was a sure shot at a top foreign policy post if he were to win.

BUSH RAISED AN IMPORTANT ISSUE with his close adviser Karen Hughes, then 43, a former television reporter who had worked for five years as his communications czar in Texas.

He said he needed to articulate why he wanted to be president. "You know, there has to be a reason," he said. "There has to be a compelling reason to run."

Hughes set out to come up with a central campaign theme. She knew Bush had three policy passions. First, there were the so-called faith-based initiatives—plans to push more government money to social programs affiliated with religious groups. That enthusiasm was real, but it couldn't be the backbone of a presidential campaign.

Second, Bush cared about education. But America's schools are run at the state and local level. It would be tough to run for president on a national education platform.

Bush's third belief, in tax cuts, held promise. It could provide the rationale. The campaign autobiography Hughes wrote with Bush—*A Charge to Keep*, released in November 1999—included 19 provisions about "education" and 17 entries under "taxes." "Faith-based organizations" are mentioned three times. The phrase "foreign policy" occurs twice, both in the context of free trade. There was a single reference to Iraq, no mention of Saddam Hussein, terrorists or terrorism.

During one of the 2000 primaries, Bush called Al Hubbard, a former deputy chief of staff to his father's vice president, J. Danforth Quayle, and one of a group of advisers the elder Bush had recruited to tutor his son on economic issues.

"Hubbard," Bush exclaimed. "Can you believe this is what I'm running on! This tax cut!"

BUSH INVITED RICHARD L. ARMITAGE, a former assistant secretary of defense in the Reagan administration, to join his team of foreign policy advisers. Armitage, 54, was Colin Powell's best friend. Barrel-chested with a shaved head, a weight-lifting addict who could bench-press 330 pounds, Armitage was a 1967 graduate of the Naval Academy. He signed on because he believed that the Clinton administration had no theory or underlying principle for its foreign and defense policies. It was ad hoc. The Republicans had a chance of getting it right. Armitage was an admirer of Bush senior, who he felt understood the necessity of a strong foreign policy tempered by restraint.

The U.S. military was preeminent in the world and could dominate or stabilize any situation, in Armitage's view. Clinton and his team had failed to develop adequate exit strategies for getting out of foreign entanglements such as Bosnia or Kosovo in the Balkans.

A big job for the next president, he thought, was no less than figuring out the purpose of American foreign policy. Rice's team called themselves the Vulcans. The name started out in jest because Rice's hometown, Birmingham, Alabama, known for its steel mills, had a giant statue of Vulcan, the Roman god of fire and metal. But the group, which included Paul Wolfowitz, the undersecretary for policy in Cheney's Pentagon, liked the image of toughness, and Vulcans soon became their self-description.

In 1999, Armitage attended five meetings with Bush and various Vulcans. He found good news and bad news. The best news was that Bush wanted Powell to be his secretary of state.

At the first Vulcan meeting in February 1999, Bush had asked, "Is defense going to be an issue in the 2000 campaign?" The advisers said they didn't think it would. Bush said he wanted to make defense an issue. He said he wanted to transform the military, to put it in a position to deal with new and emerging threats.

To do that, the advisers said, the military would need new equipment to make it more mobile and modern, and more advanced training and intelligence gathering. This might take 15 to 20 years before the real advantages would be realized. It would certainly be beyond a Bush presidency, maybe not in their lifetimes.

Bush indicated he was willing to make that investment. Armitage and the others worked on a speech that Bush gave at The Citadel, the South Carolina public military university, on September 23, 1999.

"I will defend the American people against missiles and terror," Bush said, "And I will begin creating the military of the next century. . . . Homeland defense has become an urgent duty." He cited the potential "threat of biological, chemical and nuclear terrorism. . . . Every group or nation must know, if they sponsor such attacks, our response will be devastating.

"Even if I am elected, I will not command the new military we create. That will be left to a president who comes after me. The results of our effort will not be seen for many years."

Armitage was pleased to see realism in a presidential campaign. He thought that terrorism, and potential actions by rogue states such as Iraq, Iran and North Korea, could be trouble, but not lethal. The big issues in defense policy were the great power relationships with Russia, China and India.

But there was also bad news about Bush. "For some reason, he thinks he's going to be president," Armitage told Powell. It was like there was some feeling of destiny. Bush talked as if it was a certainty, saying, "When I'm president . . ." Though not unusual for candidates to talk this way in speeches, Bush spoke that way privately with his advisers. It was as if Bush were trying to talk himself into it.

And there was Bush's smirk, Armitage said.

The big problem, Armitage thought, was that he was not sure Bush filled the suit required of a president. He had a dreadful lack of experience. Armitage told his wife and Powell that he was not sure Governor Bush understood the implications of the United States as a world power.

2

<hr />

Among the Vulcans was another veteran of the Cheney Pentagon, Stephen J. Hadley, who had been assistant secretary of defense for international security policy. It was the post Armitage had held in the Reagan administration—a kind of State Department within the Pentagon focusing on foreign relations. Hadley, 52, was as quiet and soft as Armitage could be vocal and hard. Raised in Ohio, Phi Beta Kappa from Cornell and with a Yale Law degree, Hadley was a student of national security with early service on the National Security Council staff in the Ford administration.

Hadley had helped in the preparation of Bush's Citadel speech. When Bush said he wanted a reform or transformation agenda for the Pentagon, several Vulcans demonstrated their knowledge of Army hardware by reeling off the names of some of the lighter vehicles that could be used to replace the heavy tanks. Bush began asking questions about the kinds of lighter vehicles and their various merits.

"You really don't want to go there," Hadley told Bush, "because if you start proposing an alternative to the tank, there are 200 specialists in Washington all ready to jump on what you're saying and say, 'This guy doesn't know what he's talking about.' So stay away."

"Let me tell you how I think about elections," Bush replied. "I want to reform the Defense Department. Now, I run and don't mention it, when I'm elected and go to the Joint Chiefs and say, 'By the way, I want to reform the Defense Department,' they'll say, 'Who are you? You've been elected. You'll be gone in four years. We'll be here. Thank you very much.'

"If I go to the American people and say, 'I'm going to reform the Defense Department. Here's why. Here's what I'm going to do.' And when I get elected and I go to the Joint Chiefs and I say, 'The American people have just elected me to reform the Defense Department. Where do we start?' That makes a big difference." He apparently didn't know that the Joint Chiefs, the heads of the services, serve only four-year terms. He clearly thought of them as a monolith.

At another meeting during Bush's early candidacy, the Vulcans were discussing arms control. Bush had lots of questions and he was getting lots of answers. Hadley told Bush, "They're very good on this stuff. You don't need all the technical stuff. You've got great instincts. If I could urge you to do one thing, it would be 'Trust your instincts.' "

Bush had no problem trusting his instincts. It was almost his second religion. In an interview with me several years later, on August 20, 2002, he referred a dozen times to his "instincts" or his "instinctive" reactions as the guide for his decisions. At one point he said, "I'm not a textbook player, I'm a gut player."

IN ADDITION TO SEEKING foreign policy tutors for his son, the former president spent his post-presidential years defending his decisions in the 1991 Persian Gulf War. The United Nations had authorized the use of force to oust Saddam Hussein's army from neighboring Kuwait, which Saddam had invaded the previous summer. It was a specific mission, endorsed by most of the world's nations. Saddam's army had been driven out of Kuwait, but because he survived the war and stayed in power, a number of critics, many Republican conservatives, said Bush had screwed up and should have pushed on to overthrow the Iraqi dictator.

On February 28, 1999, the former president was the honored guest at a gathering of some 200 Gulf War veterans at the Fort Myer Army base, just across the Potomac River from Washington.

It burned him up when people said they hadn't finished the job, he said. "Had we gone into Baghdad—We could have done it. You guys could have done it. You could have been there in 48 hours. And then what? Which sergeant, which private, whose life would be at stake in perhaps a fruitless hunt in an urban guerrilla war to find the most-secure dictator in the world? Whose life would be on my hands as the commander-in-chief because I, unilaterally, went beyond the international law, went beyond the stated mission, and said we're going to show our macho? We're going into Baghdad. We're going to be an occupying power—America in an Arab land—with no allies at our side. It would have been disastrous."

As GEORGE W. BUSH locked up the Republican presidential nomination, Prince Bandar kept in touch. Over the weekend of June 10, 2000, Bandar attended a surprise party for Barbara Bush's 75th birthday at the family retreat in Kennebunkport. Bandar thought it was quaint and old-fashioned, complete with the Bush family members putting on a 45-minute variety show with comic skits. The effort put into these family spoofs astounded him but he found the show hilarious.

George W. pulled Bandar aside.

"Bandar, I guess you're the best asshole who knows about the world. Explain to me one thing."

"Governor, what is it?"

"Why should I care about North Korea?"

Bandar said he didn't really know. It was one of the few countries that he did not work on for King Fahd.

"I get these briefings on all parts of the world," Bush said, "and everybody is talking to me about North Korea."

"I'll tell you what, Governor," Bandar said. "One reason should make you care about North Korea."

"All right, smart aleck," Bush said, "tell me."

"The 38,000 American troops right on the border." Most of the U.S. 2nd Infantry Division was deployed there, along with thousands of other Army, Navy and Air Force personnel. "If nothing else counts, this counts. One shot across the border and you lose half these people immediately. You lose 15,000 Americans in a chemical or biological or even regular attack. The United States of America is at war instantly."

"Hmmm," Bush said. "I wish those assholes would put things just point-blank to me. I get half a book telling me about the history of North Korea."

"Now I tell you another answer to that. You don't want to care about North Korea anymore?" Bandar asked. The Saudis wanted America to focus on the Middle East and not get drawn into a conflict in East Asia.

"I didn't say that," Bush replied.

"But if you don't, you withdraw those troops back. Then it becomes a local conflict. Then you have the whole time to decide, 'Should I get involved? Not involved?' Etc."

At that moment, Colin Powell approached.

"Colin," Bush said, "come here. Bandar and I were shooting the bull, just two fighter pilots shooting the bull." He didn't mention the topic.

"Mr. Governor," Bandar said, "General Powell is almost a fighter pilot. He can shoot the bull almost as good as us."

BANDAR FOLLOWED W.'s 2000 campaign like a full-time political reporter and news junkie. He appreciated the focus and the method. The candidate's father promised to come to Bandar's estate outside London for pheasant shooting after the election. Bush senior told Bandar, "By the time I come to shoot with you, either we will be celebrating my boy is in the White House, or we'll be commiserating together because my boy lost."

A man with his own addictions and obsessions, Bandar spent immense amounts of time studying the psychology of individual human beings and he developed a theory about what drove George W. Bush's ambition. First, W. had rejected the key figure in his father's rise in politics to the presidency, James A. Baker III, his father's chief political operative and secretary of state. In W.'s opinion, Baker had not done enough in the 1992 reelection campaign, had left his father alone. Barbara Bush thought Baker was out for himself.

But when W. was faced with the Florida recount battle in 2000, he swallowed his pride and named Baker to head the recount effort. Who played the big boys' bloody and cutthroat game better than Baker?

"I think Bush came into office with a mission," Bandar said. "Many people are confusing it with his faith—religious faith. I think he had a mission that is agnostic. That he was convinced that the mission had to be achieved and that he is the only one who is going to achieve it. And it started with: Injustice has been done to a good man, George Herbert Walker Bush, a man who was a hero, who served his country, who did everything right." His father had been a decorated World War II pilot, congressman, United Nations ambassador, Republican National Committee chairman, envoy to China, CIA director, vice president. All the things that W. did not do. Then as president, his father went to war in 1991 to oust Saddam Hussein from Kuwait. "And he wins," Bandar continued, "and a charlatan—in his mind—draft dodger, etc., beats him. There is no justice."

Clinton's victory in 1992 was the catalyst. "So from 1992, this young man who was a wild young man in his youth, matured, but with a focus on one mission. There's injustice. There's something not right. I am going to correct it."

After the 2000 election, Bandar visited President Bush in the White House regularly, and kept in touch with Bush senior all the time. On occasion, he saw the father and son together. There was a bonding, an apparent emotional connection, and yet there was a standoffishness, a distance that was not explainable. Many times Bush senior commented to him about policies being pursued by his son.

"Why don't you call him about it?" Bandar asked.

"I had my turn," Bush senior replied. "It is his turn now. I just have to stay off the stage. For eight years I did not make one comment about Clinton. I will not make any comment vis-à-vis this president, not only out of principle but to let him be himself."

IN A SMALL FIFTH-FLOOR corner office of his international consulting firm three blocks north of the White House, Brent Scowcroft, one of the few men as close to former President Bush as Bandar, viewed the fledgling presidency of Bush's son with mixed emotions. A small-framed Mormon with a doctorate in international relations and 29 years of military service, a three-star general in the Air Force, Scowcroft had served as national security adviser to both Presidents Gerald Ford and George H. W. Bush.

He and the elder President Bush were contemporaries, born just nine months apart. And they were policy soul mates, so close that instead of writing a presidential memoir, Bush had teamed up with Scowcroft to co-author a 566-page book in 1998 called *A World Transformed.* It was a sort of semimemoir, one of the most unusual books to emerge from a 20th-century presidency. Bush and Scowcroft wrote alternating, dueling sections with occasional snippets of narrative sandwiched between. It demonstrated both men's immersion in the events of the Bush presidency from 1989 to 1992, including revealing though carefully manicured inside accounts of the collapse of the Soviet Union and the Gulf War.

Scowcroft communicated with Bush senior as much as Bandar did. He knew the father did not want to leave the impression that he was looking over his son's shoulder. If it were even suggested that Bush senior had any hidden-hand presence in his son's administration, in Scowcroft's view it would demean the son and reduce the respect and support for his presidency, even undermine it.

But Scowcroft also knew that it was very personal—a textbook case encompassing more than half a century of subtle and not-so-subtle father-son tensions, love, joy, rivalries and disappointments. After all, Scowcroft knew that here was the father who had done everything—and done everything quite well in his view.

As best Scowcroft could calculate, George W. Bush didn't know who he was until he was about 45. And now he was president? It was astonishing. Now, Scowcroft knew, the father did not want to injure the son's self-confidence. He and Barbara had given the world not only a son but a president of the United States. The father desperately, passionately, wanted him to succeed. The best way to help was to stay out of his way.

"AS SOON AS I take my hand off the Bible, I want a plan of action," George W. Bush told Karl Rove, his chief political strategist, immediately after the Supreme Court declared him the winner on December 12, 2000. "I saw what happened to my old man, whom I love more than life itself, and he got into office and had no plan." He said he'd watched Clinton quickly plunge into controversies of the moment over gays in the military and cabinet appointments. Bush said he wanted to focus on big-agenda items.

"Time is our ally at the beginning of the administration," Bush told Rove. "It will at some point turn against me." He wanted momentum, and he wanted the focus and political debate in the Congress and the country to be on his agenda. "So I want a plan."

Bush had known Rove for 28 years. As one of their most senior Texas political associates explained, "Karl has got a somewhat split personality in that he can be your loyal, dear friend—and cut your throat the next day without thinking about it if he perceives that you're a threat to him." Rove could get paranoid, the Texas associate said, and he never really got the paranoia out of his system. But Bush knew that paranoia—especially Rove's version of it—was useful in politics.

When Bush had decided to run for president, he had asked Rove to divest himself of Karl Rove & Company, his direct mail and political consulting firm. "If you're going to be my guy, you've got to sell your business and be full-time for me. If you're going to be my guy, you're going to be *my* guy." Rove had strong views and wanted to control many things, and Bush had to cut him off at the knees, at times nicely, at other times quite forcefully.

Now, Bush wanted to make sure "my guy" was right there by his side in the White House. Rove was given no line responsibility but instead a broad and open-ended license to look after two matters: first, Bush's immediate political well-being that day, that week, that month; and second, Bush's long-term political health, positioning him for reelection in 2004.

Rove, 50, set himself up in a second-floor West Wing White House office that had last been used by Hillary Clinton. He believed Bush's reelection prospects would hinge on a successful first term, and in the first months of the Bush presidency that meant one issue: tax cuts, the centerpiece of Bush's domestic agenda. In a debate during the Republican primaries, Bush had said, "This is not only 'no new taxes,' " quoting the campaign pledge his father had made and later broken. "This is 'Tax cuts, so help me God.' "

So Rove threw himself into tax cuts, which he thought would define the Bush presidency. In contrast, and despite all the tutoring, Bush had no plan for foreign affairs. He held no "so-help-me-God" convictions.

3

IN HIS FIRST PENTAGON TOUR, Donald Rumsfeld had acquired a disdain for large parts of the system he was to oversee once again. He had found the Pentagon and the vast U.S. military complex unmanageable. One night at a dinner at my house a dozen years after he had left the Pentagon the first time, he said that being secretary was "like having an electric appliance in one hand and the plug in the other and you are running around trying to find a place to put it in." It was an image that stuck with me—Rumsfeld charging around the Pentagon E-ring, the Man with the Appliance, seeking an elusive electrical socket, trying to make things work and feeling unplugged by the generals and admirals.

This time he was going to get control. He would not be distracted by outside events. The military services—Army, Navy, Marines and Air Force—were special pleaders, narrow-minded. Though a former congressman, he thought Congress also was narrow, unhelpful, wedded to habit and protocol. Foreign visitors and officials chewed up too much time, and the routine of ceremonies and meetings was a pain in the ass. No, he had big things to do. That meant focus. He was going to change the entire U.S. military, transform it into a leaner, more efficient, more agile, more lethal fighting machine. It was not just important to the military, he felt; it was important to the credibility of the United States.

Shortly after Rumsfeld settled into his office, the chairman of the Joint Chiefs of Staff, Army General Henry H. "Hugh" Shelton, who had been appointed the nation's senior military officer by President Clinton, asked for a private meeting.

"When President Bush took the oath of office, my loyalties immediately shifted to him as commander in chief," Shelton said. "I want to be considered a member of your team."

Shelton, 59, was a paratrooper with 37 years in the military, including two tours in Vietnam. Tall, amiable, never considered one of the Army's intellectuals, Shelton had a direct manner. He knew the value of political loyalty, and how contentious the 2000 presidential election had been. He was making a peace offering to the new regime.

Under recent defense secretaries for the last 15 years, the chairman acted as the link and communications channel between the secretary and the combatant commanders. The model was the 1991 Gulf War, when JCS Chairman Colin Powell had been the main conduit of information and orders between then Secretary of Defense Cheney and General H. Norman Schwarzkopf, the commander of Operation Desert Storm.

The JCS chairman had potential power and influence, as a go-between and adviser, but he was not in the chain of command.

"What precisely are your duties?" Rumsfeld asked Shelton. Since his first time as defense secretary in the Ford administration, the Goldwater-Nichols reform legislation of 1986 had enhanced the chairman's role, at least on paper.

"I'm the principal military adviser to the president, you and the National Security Council," General Shelton answered, citing his authority from the 15-year-old Goldwater-Nichols law in Title X of the U.S. Code.

"Oh, no," Rumsfeld said, "not the NSC."

Yes, sir, Shelton quietly repeated. The law was clear.

"Not the NSC staff," Rumsfeld said. He had found NSC staffers in the Ford administration troublesome, puffing themselves up as if they spoke for the president.

Not the staff, Shelton agreed. But as the principal military adviser to the NSC, he dealt with the NSC principals—the president, vice president, secretary of state, secretary of defense, the president's national security adviser and the CIA director. Though the law said that the chairman's role was limited to advice, communications and oversight, he had a seat in the White House Situation Room when policy and war were discussed.

Rumsfeld was uncomfortable with a system that interfered with a strict chain of command from the president as commander in chief to him as secretary of defense and then to the military combatant commanders out around the world from the Pacific to the Middle East.

A week later, Rumsfeld told Shelton he had an idea to cut staff. Colin Powell had built the Joint Staff into a powerhouse of hundreds of ambitious middle-level and senior officers. Powell called it an "action staff," organized and dedicated to getting things done. With two- and three-star generals and admirals heading the directorates, the Joint Staff was still often considered the most potent staff in Washington.

It's too big, Rumsfeld said. He wanted Shelton to pare it down, get rid of the people who handled public relations, legislative liaison and legal matters for the chairman. Shelton could use Rumsfeld's civilian staff for those matters.

"Sir, I'm supposed to give independent military advice," Shelton replied. He pointed out that he had probably fewer than 30 people in those three sections while Rumsfeld had over 200. Maybe the civilian side would be the best place to cut? he suggested.

Rumsfeld dropped the matter for the moment.

SHELTON WAS WORRIED about trust between himself and the new secretary. Before Rumsfeld had been confirmed, he had received a chilling warning. A retired Navy captain who had worked for Air Force General George S. Brown, the chairman of the Joint Chiefs during Rumsfeld's first tour as secretary of defense, had sent him a personal letter. It was damning. The captain claimed that Rumsfeld could not be trusted, that he despised the uniformed military.

"You are not going to enjoy this relationship," he wrote. "He will be in control of everything." Shelton shared the letter with several senior generals and admirals.

"God, I hope this isn't true," Shelton said, noting that he had only nine months left to serve as chairman. "I don't want to spend my last year in this kind of environment."

Other retired senior military officers had chilling stories of being dressed down by Rumsfeld. Admiral James L. Holloway, the chief of naval operations from 1974 to 1978, said Rumsfeld had chewed him out in front of 40 other senior military officers and civilians. Rumsfeld was concerned about some congressional testimony and Holloway had attempted to explain.

"Shut up," Rumsfeld said, according to Holloway, "I don't want any excuses. You are through and you'll not have time to clean out your desk if this is not taken care of."

Shelton was concerned as Rumsfeld built a kitchen cabinet of special assistants and consultants within the Office of the Secretary of Defense. It was growing into a fortress, old friends and retired military officers. First was Stephen Cambone, a 6-foot-3 defense intellectual who had worked closely on Rumsfeld's space and missile defense commissions in the 1990s. Cambone was named Rumsfeld's top civilian assistant. Second was Martin Hoffman, who had been Rumsfeld's roommate and fellow member of the Princeton Class of 1954, and who had been secretary of the army during Rumsfeld's first Pentagon tour. The two men had been close friends for nearly 50 years. Third was M. Staser Holcomb, a retired Navy vice admiral who had been Rumsfeld's military assistant in the 1970s.

The fourth and perhaps most important member of the kitchen cabinet was Steve Herbits, 59, a lawyer and longtime Rumsfeld friend going back to 1967. Herbits had been one of Rumsfeld's civilian special assistants during the first Pentagon tour, and ran the Defense transition and personnel search for Caspar Weinberger in 1981 and for Cheney in 1989 when each became secretary of defense. Herbits became a top executive at the Seagram Company, the giant liquor business. Probably no one had more longevity or credibility with Rumsfeld on basic military management and issues. Rumsfeld made Herbits a consultant with a license to analyze current problems, and he functioned as a management fix-it man somewhat as Karl Rove did for President Bush.

Herbits, who was also a gay rights activist and occasional contributor to Democratic candidates—and thus highly unusual among Republican defense experts—was known for his incisive, provocative, slashing dissections of personnel and institutions. Rumsfeld appreciated his style and skill at cutting through the normal fog of Pentagon paperwork and lowest-common-denominator analysis.

RUMSFELD AND CAMBONE were looking for a senior military assistant, a key post on Rumsfeld's team. Previously, the position had been held by a three-star general or admiral. Nope, Rumsfeld said. He wanted to demonstrate what downsizing was about. The Pentagon bureaucracy was bloated, and the military kept putting officers of higher and higher rank in key positions, a kind of rank inflation. Rumsfeld wanted to go down two full ranks to not even a two-star but a one-star officer—a junior flag officer.

They thought of a Navy rear admiral named J. J. Quinn, who had headed the Naval Space Command and had given candid testimony the previous year to Rumsfeld's space commission. Quinn, a 1974 Naval Academy graduate, had testified in secret that the small Navy space program should ideally be increased to assist the war-fighting commands. If it wasn't expanded, maybe the Navy should get out of the space business altogether. It was almost unheard of to have a military commander suggest that his command be eliminated.

Rumsfeld and Hoffman called Quinn in for an interview. Quinn, 48, 6-foot-2, had been the captain of the baseball team at the Naval Academy. Rumsfeld, a former Navy pilot, delved into Quinn's career.

Quinn was a naval aviator though not a pilot. He had flown in the back seat of F-14 fighter jets as the radar interceptor officer and later as a Top Gun instructor. He had served in the White House as a military aide to President Reagan for 19 months, and to President Bush senior for five months, carrying the so-called football, or codes for nuclear war.

Rumsfeld asked Quinn about his service as commanding officer of an F-14 squadron on the USS *Ranger* during the 1991 Gulf War. Quinn described flying 51 strike escort and photo reconnaissance missions in 43 days. After the war, he went to the grueling 20-month nuclear power school founded by the late Admiral Hyman Rickover in preparation for command of a nuclear-powered aircraft carrier.

Rumsfeld asked about his time as commanding officer of the USS *Abraham Lincoln*.

"The best time of my life," Quinn said. He'd commanded a crew of 5,000 and some $12 billion worth of ship and equipment. Command at sea was the emotional pinnacle for a Navy officer, as Rumsfeld knew. "That's what we live for," Quinn said.

Marty Hoffman grabbed a piece of blank paper and asked Quinn to write something to see if Rumsfeld could read his handwriting.

Quinn wrote, "Mr. Secretary, I really want this job."

"I can read that," Rumsfeld said chuckling. Within two weeks, Quinn was sitting at the desk in a small office adjacent to Rumsfeld's beneath a framed picture of several Civil War generals' aides standing around holding the reins of their bosses' horses. Called *The Horse Holders,* the picture had been signed by the previous senior military assistants to the secretaries of defense. Among the signatures was that of Colin Powell, who had held the post for Secretary of Defense Weinberger and was now Bush's secretary of state.

. . .

ON FRIDAY, FEBRUARY 16, Rumsfeld's 21st day in office, two dozen U.S. and British planes bombed 20 radar and command centers inside Iraq, enforcing the no-fly zones the United Nations had put in place after the 1991 Gulf War. These were the largest strikes in two years. A general from the Joint Staff informed the White House about the bombing, but Rumsfeld felt he had not been fully brought up to speed and he was livid. Information from the commanders in the field was being routed to him through Shelton. It could take six to ten hours before he learned what had happened.

"I'm the secretary of defense," he said. "I'm in the chain of command." He—not the generals, not the Joint Staff—would deal with the White House and the president on operational matters.

Rumsfeld demanded that Shelton do a detailed reconstruction of the process. Why had those targets been selected? Who had approved them? Who had briefed? Who knew? Who was thinking? The attacks had been against Iraqi long-range search radars outside Baghdad. The explosions were heard in the Iraqi capital. So there was CNN coverage, and it looked like an air strike on Baghdad, grabbing international attention. For a brief moment it had looked like the new Bush administration had launched a war against Saddam Hussein in its first month.

Rumsfeld felt he had been misled, not warned, not given the full story in advance.

Vice Admiral Scott A. Fry, the director of the Joint Staff and General Shelton's right-hand man, thought Rumsfeld had a point. They should have made it clearer. They had failed to anticipate and they had violated the no surprise rule—don't surprise the boss.

Fry, a 51-year-old, 1971 graduate of the Naval Academy, was one of the Navy's most promising officers. As a junior officer he had read about the careers of some of the top admirals, and he had dreamed about being director of the Joint Staff. In his view it was the greatest job in the U.S. military for a three-star officer. He had previously served as executive assistant to the chief of naval operations, been the deputy in the Joint Staff plans and policy directorate (J-5), and gone on to command an aircraft carrier battle group—the USS *Eisenhower*, two cruisers, four destroyers and two submarines—the backbone of the Navy. He was then made director for operations (J-3), and finally given the most coveted position, director.

Rumsfeld's attitude was one of fundamental distrust, Fry realized. So that meant they would have to prove themselves. One day he took two slides classified confidential on a minor operational issue up to Rumsfeld's office. He was going over them with Steve Cambone when Rumsfeld came in.

Why are they classified confidential? Rumsfeld asked.

Fry wasn't sure. It was the lowest level of classification. Most matters that came to the secretary had much higher classifications—SECRET, TOP SECRET, code word special access programs, special compartments to limit distribution of sensitive information. Soon Rumsfeld, Cambone and Fry were in a discussion about classification. It turned out, Fry conceded, that these particular slides didn't really need to be classified at all. He wanted to review the substance.

No, Rumsfeld said. Please go down and get new slides and bring them back properly marked unclassified.

Fry talked to Shelton, who unloaded about the nonstop questions from Rumsfeld: Why did the chairman have a special assistant who traveled with Secretary of State Powell on trips abroad? What was that all about? Rumsfeld wanted to know. Who did he report to? What was the information flow? When would he, Rumsfeld, learn about what Powell was doing? Tell me again why you have a lawyer.

Rumsfeld sent short notes all around the building, called "snowflakes," asking questions, seeking detail and asking for reconstructions when it was unclear to him what had happened. He'd developed the snowflake system early in the Nixon administration, when he led the Office of Economic Opportunity. Though unsigned, everyone knew they represented orders or questions from the boss. But if a snowflake leaked, it provided deniability—no signature, no clear fingerprints. He was quite proud of his new management tool. When Rumsfeld had been ambassador to NATO from 1973 to 1974, his memos were on yellow paper, called "yellow perils." Now they were once again on white paper, and "snowflake" was resurrected.

Rumsfeld either scribbled out his notes or dictated them, and Delonnie Henry, his confidential assistant, then typed them out. Rear Admiral J. J. Quinn, the new military assistant, became the keeper of the snowflakes. There were roughly three kinds—administrative ("call and arrange a lunch with Fed Chairman Alan Greenspan"—an old Rumsfeld friend from the Ford days), simple thoughts or personal reflections, and calls for information or action. Some were quite broad and asked for a lot. Quinn delivered them, often by hand if they were urgent and important. Rumsfeld kept copies of the snowflakes in files on his desk. He had a file for Shelton, another for Quinn, one for Cambone and others for his top aides.

In an interview later, Quinn said, "It was a simple, efficient way for him to keep track of what he had asked for and what he wanted to get done. It was a way for him to get his arms around this big behemoth called the United States military."

Rumsfeld was into everyone's business. No one was immune. Many in the Pentagon looked at the snowflakes as an annoyance. Others found them intrusive and at times petty. For some, there was no way to keep up.

Vice Admiral Fry told the Joint Staff this was an opportunity to examine what they were doing and why. Soul-searching and introspection were good, it would be good for the Joint Staff. "We need to do this," he said. "We'll get through this. We'll gain his confidence. He'll get comfortable with us."

UNDER THE OLD SYSTEM, as practiced by Secretary of Defense William S. Cohen and General Shelton, when there was a significant incident—a ship collision, violation of the no-fly zones in Iraq, or in the extreme an outbreak of war—the duty general or admiral in the National Military Command Center (NMCC), which was part of the Joint Staff and manned around the clock, would call Shelton. Rumsfeld wondered to Shelton why he didn't get called first. He was in the chain of command, not Shelton. He, Rumsfeld, reported to the president. Shelton replied that he often had to get answers from the duty general or admiral. He had to anticipate the secretary's questions so that when he called Rumsfeld, he'd have answers.

Oh, no, Rumsfeld said. He wanted to know first. Suppose it was serious and he had to call the president? Since the command center monitored the world, the duty officer called Shelton regularly. Whenever this happened, Rumsfeld demanded a full reconstruction of the timeline— when Shelton got called, when Rumsfeld got called, what information each received, and explanations for the delays and discrepancies in the reports. It was almost a daily occurrence. Rumsfeld brought in another retired admiral to do a study of the NMCC. As the overseer of the NMCC and the duty officers, Fry was in the middle.

ON THURSDAY, MARCH 15, 2001, the 53rd day of the Bush presidency, Prince Bandar went to the Oval Office with his loyal aide-de-camp, Rihab

Massoud. Condoleezza Rice, who was now Bush's national security adviser, attended. It was highly unusual for an ambassador to have Bandar's kind of direct access to the president.

Bandar complained about a remark Secretary of State Powell had made in congressional testimony a week earlier. The United States planned to move its embassy from Tel Aviv to "the capital of Israel, which is Jerusalem," Powell had said. Since Arabs claimed that part of Jerusalem is Palestinian, it was outrageous.

Bush said he knew how sensitive Jerusalem was to the Saudis. Powell had probably misspoken.

In a message from the Crown Prince, the de facto leader of Saudi Arabia, Bandar said that moving forward on the peace process between the Palestinians and Israel, which had just elected Ariel Sharon its new leader, was critical to building a coalition of moderate Arabs to pressure Saddam Hussein. He asked how much longer the enforcement of the United Nations no-fly zones over Iraq would continue. Two years? Five years? Ten years? "This is costing us militarily, financially, but much more importantly politically," he said. "And it is not hurting Saddam Hussein."

Bush seemed to agree. "If there is any military action, then it has to be decisive. That can finalize the issue," the president said. "The Iraqi opposition is useless and not effective." They discussed the difficulty of using covert action to overthrow Saddam. The president expressed concern about increases in worldwide oil prices, something the Saudis influenced heavily. He said he would like to see Bandar at least once a month. He wanted honest talk.

Bandar was elated. He sent a secret message to the Crown Prince: "Many positive signs as far as relations and issues that are of concern to both countries. Loyalty and honesty are sensitive issues for this president. It is important that we invest in this man, in a very positive way."

RUMSFELD WAS TRYING to define the task before him and get everything down on paper. His dictations, memos, drafts, redrafts and snowflakes reveal his conviction that he faced huge obstacles. On March 20, he dictated a four-page memo, "Subject: The Challenge—the Importance of Succeeding."

"After two months on the job, it is clear that the Defense establishment is tangled in its anchor chain," he dictated. Congress required hundreds of reports. The Pentagon couldn't construct a $500,000 building without congressional approval. There were so many auditors, investigators, testing groups and monitors looking over their shoulders at the Pentagon, more perhaps, "at 24,000 on any given day, than the U.S. Army has deployable front-line troops with weapons." The military's personnel policies "were designed to manage a conscript force of single men" and had not been changed for "a volunteer force with families." Military officers were transferred "from assignment to assignment every 20 to 25 months or so, to the point that successful officers skip across the tops of the waves so fast that even they can't learn from their own mistakes." The military fringe benefits "mindlessly use the failed Soviet model centralized government systems for housing, commissaries, healthcare and education, rather than using the private sector competitive models that are the envy of the world."

Distrust between Congress and the Defense Department was so great, he said, that "from a practical standpoint, the DOD no longer has the authority to conduct the business of the Department.

"The maze of constraints on the Department force it to operate in a manner that is so slow, so ponderous and so inefficient that whatever it ultimately does will inevitably be a decade or so late."

Without changing and fixing the relationship with Congress, Rumsfeld concluded, "transformation of our armed forces is not possible."

Six days later, he snowflaked Wolfowitz, Cambone and two others asking for their edits and ideas. This "Anchor Chain" memo became notorious among Rumsfeld's staff as they watched and tried to help him define the universe of his problems. By April 10 he had dictated a 10-page version, and by May 1 it had grown to 12 pages. By then he had found that Congress required 905 reports a year. The 1962 Defense Authorization Act had been a single page; in 1975 when he'd been secretary it was 75 pages. "Today the Act has ballooned to 988 pages."

It sounded like he had almost given up fixing the Pentagon during the George W. Bush presidency. The task was so hard and would take so long, he dictated, that "our job, therefore, is to work together to sharpen the sword that the next president will wield."

"I'VE GOT FOUR DRAFTS OF IT," I told Rumsfeld in a 2006 interview.

"Do you really?"

"Yes, sir," I said, handing him copies. "I wanted to give you copies."

"It got better," he said.

"It did," I agreed. "It almost looks like you're struggling, if I may be frank with you."

"This is a difficult job here," he said. "This is not easy, this department. And I can remember having been here a month or two and standing at my desk at night, reflecting over this whole thing and saying, Okay, I was asked to do this job. I've accepted. And what is it? How do you define the job and what are the problems you're facing and what are the obstacles to getting it done? And what's doable and what isn't doable?"

I quoted from the last draft of the memo: "We'll have to do it for the next president."

"You know," he said, "in a place this big that's almost true of everything." He noted that back in 1975 as secretary of defense the first time he had approved the M1 tank that was used in the first Gulf War and the recent invasion of Iraq. He also had approved the F-16, which was still being used in air operations over Iraq. He spoke almost wistfully. "These decisions you make play out over a long period time, either to the benefit of the country, or conversely to the detriment of the country if you fail to do something."

4

On April 1, China forced down a U.S. Navy EP-3E spy plane and took its 24 crew members hostage, the first major foreign policy crisis of the new Bush administration. The White House was determined to keep President Bush away from the delicate hostage situation. Presidents Jimmy Carter and Ronald Reagan had given hostage-takers leverage by becoming emotionally involved in trying to get back Americans held in Iran and Lebanon. In Carter's case, it had led to a general sense of impotency and fear in the country, with ABC News running a nightly show called *America Held Hostage* and prominently reminding viewers each day how long the Americans had been held. Under Reagan, the hostage crisis had led to secret arms sales to Iran and the biggest scandal of his presidency, Iran-contra. The image of powerlessness his predecessors had endured would not be allowed to develop in the George W. Bush administration.

Secretary of State Powell was given the assignment of negotiating a settlement with the Chinese. Powell enlisted Prince Bandar, who had special relations with the Chinese through various deals to purchase arms and missiles. China was also beginning to rely on Saudi oil.

Bandar eventually got the Chinese to release the 24 hostages. Never modest about his influence, Bandar considered it almost a personal favor to him. The Chinese wanted a letter from the United States expressing regret. It was the kind of diplomatic gobbledygook that was Bandar's specialty. As the Chinese wanted, the United States would say it was "very sorry" the spy plane had entered Chinese airspace to make an emergency landing, while the United States would not apologize for what it considered a legitimate intelligence-gathering mission. The National Security Agency was monitoring Bandar's calls with the Chinese, and sending reports to Powell about the various negotiations, including the final deal Bandar arranged. Powell called Bandar with congratulations.

"Hey, it's great!" he said.

"How the hell do you know?" Bandar asked.

Having jumped the gun, Powell sheepishly tried to get out of explaining. Bandar knew his calls were monitored, but he and Powell couldn't really talk about one of the most sensitive and classified intelligence-gathering operations of the U.S. government involving communications among foreign governments. So for a year Powell and Bandar laughed and half joked about *it* without ever really defining *it*.

Rumsfeld demanded a full reconstruction of the timeline of the EP-3 flight from the first moment. He didn't like any aspect of it. The EP-3 was being followed closely and harassed by a Chinese fighter, and there had been a collision. One question was whether the U.S. pilot had made the right decision to land in China. As Rumsfeld dug deeper, he was asking what these intelligence missions accomplished. Who authorized them? Who assessed the value of the intelligence that was gathered? What about the risks versus the rewards? That led to more questions and a top-to-bottom evaluation of intelligence-gathering missions from all U.S. military airborne platforms.

"Painful, but important," Fry told the Joint Staff and the intelligence experts. Such potentially high-risk missions had been going on for years and were on a kind of automatic pilot. They needed to be reexamined, Fry thought, but as Rumsfeld turned over rocks, he was finding too many worms.

The question was when to resume the EP-3 missions off the Chinese coast. A few days later Rumsfeld convened a secure conference with Vice Chairman of the Joint Chiefs Richard B. Myers and Admiral Dennis Blair, the commander in chief of Pacific Command, the combatant commander in the region. General Shelton was traveling so Myers represented the JCS. The gentlemanly, 6-foot-3½-inch Air Force general had been Shelton's deputy for just over a year. A Vietnam combat pilot who flew F-4 Phantom fighter jets, the soft-spoken Myers had served as the commander in chief of the U.S. Space Command before becoming the vice chairman in March 2000.

Rear Admiral Quinn took notes as Rumsfeld, Admiral Blair and General Myers conferred.

Blair recommended that they restart the spy missions soon. The Chinese alleged the flights violated their airspace, but the U.S. recognized a 12-nautical-mile limit and did not want to concede anything or cave in to Chinese intimidation. Blair outlined a rough schedule for resumption of flights.

"Denny," Rumsfeld said, "that sounds like a good plan. Send me a one-page message that outlines the exact details so I can show it to Condi Rice and Colin Powell tomorrow morning." He had a secure conference call with Rice and Powell at 7:15 A.M. each weekday.

Aye aye, sir, Blair said.

The next morning Quinn was in by 6 A.M. looking for Blair's message when Rumsfeld called.

"I don't see the message from Denny Blair," he said.

"Mr. Secretary, I'm searching for it too and can't find it."

Quinn popped into Fry's office before 7 A.M. Fry was in a meeting. His executive assistant, a Navy captain and stickler for the chain of command, looked kind of funny at Quinn when he asked about the message from Admiral Blair. Apparently Blair had addressed the message the old way—only to Shelton and the JCS, not to Rumsfeld.

Fry's executive assistant said that since it was addressed only to the JCS, his hands were tied. "I can't give it to you."

When Fry returned, his executive assistant held up a copy of Blair's message. "Oh, by the way," the captain said, "I'm telling J. J. Quinn that the secretary can't see this until the chairman has seen it."

Quinn remembers also asking Fry for the message and maintains that Fry also refused to hand over a copy of the message. Fry places the responsibility on his executive assistant.

Whatever the case, Quinn returned to Rumsfeld's office to report. "Mr. Secretary, the message is in the Joint Staff director's office and they refuse to give it to me."

Rumsfeld picked up the phone. Shelton was still traveling, so he summoned Vice Chairman Myers.

Myers came rushing up to Rumsfeld's office. "What's the problem, Mr. Secretary?"

"What the hell are you guys thinking down there?" Rumsfeld exploded. "I can't believe this."

Quinn was standing on the other side of the room. Rumsfeld was about as furious as he had ever seen a human being.

"Where is the loyalty here?" Rumsfeld shouted, and proceeded to give Myers a royal ass chewing. It had been months of being tangled in the anchor chain. Frustration came pouring out. In his own quarter of a century in the Navy, Quinn had never seen anything quite like it as he froze in place.

Myers insisted they were not trying to keep anything from the secretary. That would be absurd. They had both been on the conference call with Blair. Obviously, there had been some routing mistake. Yes, clearly Rumsfeld was the boss. He tried to defend the Joint Staff.

Rumsfeld would not hear of it, as he continued to rip Myers up one side and down the other. Quinn looked at the clock and recalls it registered 7:02 A.M. The Powell-Rumsfeld-Rice conference call was coming up in 13 minutes.

When it was over, Myers walked out and turned to Quinn. "What the hell is going on?"

Quinn filled him in, and Myers flew down to get a copy of the message, which he brought back to Rumsfeld's office in time for the conference call.

After the call, Rumsfeld came on the squawk box in Quinn's office. "Can you come in?"

Quinn went in and Rumsfeld asked his opinion about what had happened.

"Mr. Secretary, next time you have to dress down a four-star officer like that, I think I'll make myself disappear."

"No, you won't. I want you there as a witness." He asked Quinn to get the Pentagon general counsel. He wanted to inquire about his legal authority over the Joint Staff and his power to fire people.

Rumsfeld was beside himself. Most of his key civilian appointees had not yet been confirmed. He complained that he felt like he was running the Pentagon alone. He didn't have his team. "I'm here and I don't have anybody working for me," he said. Edgy and fed up after weeks of feeling that the chain of command was not being enforced, he leaned on his consultant Steve Herbits.

"I want to talk to the combatant commanders," Rumsfeld told Herbits. "They report to me. That's what the law says." He told Herbits he was learning things too late from the Joint Staff time and time again. He was furious with Shelton and Fry.

"You've got to fire somebody," Herbits proposed. "You've got to let people know who's boss here. Here's a perfect example." Fry seemed incompetent. "Fire Fry."

Word soon reached Shelton, who was back, that Rumsfeld was planning to do precisely that. Shelton and Myers thought they had explained the screwup about the message from Admiral Blair, and had promised it would not happen again. Shelton wasn't sure if it was that or if it was a new problem, so he stopped by Fry's office to see what snowflake answers might be due Rumsfeld.

Steve Cambone had issued an edict that all snowflakes would get a response within 24 hours, and Fry explained that he was trying to keep up. At times he felt that he had most of the Joint Staff working on Rumsfeld's queries. "There aren't enough people in the Pentagon to respond to all the snowflakes that are coming down from the third deck"—the third floor, where Rumsfeld had his office.

Shelton could see that Fry, a tireless worker with a real leadership future ahead of him, was exhausted, working weekends and staying up half the night trying to answer snowflakes.

Shelton bolted up to Rumsfeld's office and barged in, forcing a confrontation.

"If you're not happy with Scott Fry," the chairman said, "he works for me, and if you're not happy with him, it means you're unhappy with me. You can have two for the price of one," Shelton said.

Rumsfeld seemed to jump back and heatedly denied that he had any plan to fire Fry.

Shelton went back down to Fry's office.

"You've never had any leave," Shelton said. "You've never had a day off. You've been here every day that I've been here. Why don't you take a couple of days off?"

"Ah, bullshit," Fry responded. "We're doing fine."

"Take a couple of days off," Shelton ordered. "I'll see you Thursday."

FRY'S DAY BEGAN about 6 A.M. when he would go to the National Military Command Center to get briefed on overnight developments, review messages, and make phone calls around the world to get updated. At 7 A.M. he briefed Shelton for the chairman's own 8:30 A.M. meeting with

Rumsfeld. Fry then represented the Joint Staff at a larger meeting Rumsfeld had later in the morning. At that meeting, Rumsfeld went around the table and asked if anyone had something to offer. "Nothing this morning, Mr. Secretary" was Fry's usual refrain because everything he knew of significance that morning he had passed to Shelton, who had already informed Rumsfeld.

"Fry comes to my meeting," Rumsfeld told his staff. "He never has a goddamn thing to say."

ON APRIL 25, 2001, ABC television ran an interview with Bush about his first 100 days. The interviewer, Charles Gibson, asked Bush whether the U.S. had an obligation to defend Taiwan.

"Yes, we do. And the Chinese must understand that," Bush replied.

"And you would . . ."

"Yes, I would."

"With the full force of the American military?"

"Whatever it took to help Taiwan defend herself."

It was one of the strongest statements the U.S. had made about the delicate issue of Taiwan. The Chinese were very upset.

Condoleezza Rice called Brent Scowcroft, who had had her job under Bush's father, and asked him to come see the president. Scowcroft met privately with Bush and Rice.

How do I get out of this? Bush essentially asked.

After listening to Scowcroft, Bush asked him to go on a secret mission to China to meet with President Jiang Zemin and explain U.S. policy. Scowcroft, who was going to China on private business, agreed to talk with Jiang on the president's behalf. He told the Chinese leader that Bush's policy was to defend Taiwan if the island was attacked unprovoked, but if the Taiwanese took action to change the status quo on their own, the United States would not defend them. Jiang and Bush seemed satisfied, and Scowcroft's secret mission never became public.

Scowcroft was delighted to see the administration recover from its misstep. Getting off on a balanced, moderate footing was the key ingredient, in Scowcroft's and Bush senior's view, of a strong and sensible foreign policy. It was good news.

RUMSFELD'S DAILY 7:15 A.M. secure phone call with Powell and Rice was causing trouble. With all his contacts from his 35 years of previous military service, as Reagan's national security adviser, and now as Bush's chief diplomat, Powell gathered more intelligence than perhaps any single other individual in the U.S. government. His best friend, Richard Armitage, now the deputy secretary of state, conducted an aggressive daily sweep during his meetings and phone calls—"Feed the Beast," he would say. He wanted something good to pass to Powell. "Give," he often said emphatically.

In the morning Rice-Powell-Rumsfeld phone calls, Powell often had something new from abroad or the Washington information chain. He relished these moments when he could drop a little item involving the military that Rumsfeld had not heard about. At the later morning meeting with Shelton, a frequent Rumsfeld question was "Why is it that Powell knew this and I didn't?" This often led to reconstructions of the information flow. How was it that someone out there in the vast U.S. military enterprise knew something potentially or obviously important and it didn't make its way to the secretary of defense? One of Rumsfeld's favorite questions for Shelton was: How come the combatant commanders talk to you, when they work for me?

The snowflakes came fast and furious. At one point Fry realized he couldn't create a tracking system that could adequately monitor all that impacted the Joint Chiefs and the Joint Staff. This was because Rumsfeld sent snowflakes to almost everyone, whatever their rank or position in the Pentagon. Snowflakes sent to others often got rerouted to Fry in whole or in part, and suddenly there would be a massive request and only hours to answer. Rumsfeld, however, had his own tracking system, which led to more queries and follow-on snowflakes about what had happened to the unanswered snowflakes.

ONE DAY CAMBONE got chewed out by Rumsfeld and came whimpering into Quinn's office. "Am I doing that badly?" he asked.

Another day, Quinn approached Vice President Cheney at a Pentagon reception and asked for any advice. "Here's what I can tell you about Don Rumsfeld," Cheney said. "You're never going to get any credit. And you'll only know how well you're doing if he gives you more work. If that happens, you're doing fine."

As Quinn saw it, Rumsfeld was on a necessary and noble mission. For eight years under Clinton the chairman of the Joint Chiefs and the Joint Staff had taken control of the Pentagon. Rumsfeld was trying to wrest the power back from them and put it under proper civilian control. Quinn's relations with Fry and the other senior flag officers on the Joint

Staff were awful. They wore their superior rank, and Quinn found he was not able to transmit Rumsfeld's requests and orders with the authority and urgency with which they had been issued. One day Fry complained to Quinn that Rumsfeld and his civilians were not cooperating with *them*—the Joint Staff—as if they were in charge.

Quinn's wife and two young daughters were living about an hour and a half away in Maryland where the Naval Space Command was located, so Quinn got home for only part of each weekend. He tried to arrange for housing at one of the local bases closer to the Pentagon, and got in a horrendous fight with the Army. Cambone intervened, but it seemed to be a little harassment campaign, and Quinn never got local base housing. Fry thought it was consuming an inordinate amount of Quinn's time and emotional energy, and began complaining that Quinn was underperforming.

For Quinn, the housing issue was incidental. He felt he couldn't do his job, so he took matters into his own hands and went to Rumsfeld.

"You've got to make a change here in your military assistant," he said. "I am a one-star. The three- and four-stars won't listen to me. They go around me. They go through me. The culture doesn't allow me to pass on orders."

"No," Rumsfeld said. "Our chemistry is good. We'll work through this."

But Rumsfeld complained to Herbits about the disorder in his own office. Everything moved too slowly and he didn't like the way the uniformed military was responding to him. So Herbits packed up his things from the transition offices downstairs in the Pentagon and moved up to Rumsfeld's suite, so he could keep an eye on the traffic of people and paper. He took over a desk between Admiral Quinn and Rumsfeld's civilian special assistant, Steve Cambone.

After several weeks of watching Quinn's performance, Herbits walked into Rumsfeld's office.

"This isn't going to work," he said, echoing Quinn's self-evaluation.

"Why?" Rumsfeld inquired.

Quinn was a competent, decent officer, but in the rank-conscious military, his single star gave him insufficient clout. He was just one step above a Navy captain or Army colonel, and he couldn't really pass on orders or talk as a peer with the three-stars on the Joint Staff and elsewhere. Quinn was being ignored by Fry and the others. The link between the secretary's military assistant and the director of the Joint Staff was critical to the functioning of the Pentagon, Herbits said. It was one of the most important relationships in the building. In some respects it was the most important, and it wasn't working.

THAT SPRING THE NAVY announced that it was going to resume bombing exercises on a small island off Puerto Rico called Vieques. There was a long history of controversy. Two years earlier a civilian security guard had been killed during one bombing run; protesters occupied the range and in 2000 the successful candidate for governor of Puerto Rico made expelling the Navy from Vieques the centerpiece of her campaign.

"I need to get smart about Vieques," Rumsfeld told Quinn. "Call down to the Navy. Tell them I want a briefing. No more than five to 10 charts." He hated the 60-slide, show-and-tell, death-by-PowerPoint briefings renowned in the Pentagon. "A 10-minute briefing and then 20 minutes of discussion," he ordered.

Quinn passed the instructions to the senior Navy operations admirals in the Pentagon and to the four-star admiral in charge of the Atlantic Fleet. He was explicit—no more than five or 10 slides, 10 minutes of briefing followed by a serious 20-minute discussion of the issues. The discussion was always the part Rumsfeld's active mind liked.

The Atlantic Fleet four-star soon showed up in Rumsfeld's office with eight people and 60 slides. The admiral got through 15 slides in the allotted half hour with Rumsfeld rolling his eyes and jumping in his seat.

"I'm going to have to stop this briefing," Rumsfeld said, made some excuse and shooed everyone out.

"Didn't you tell them what I wanted done?" he later complained to Quinn.

It had all been repeated and repeated—everything but an engraved invitation, Quinn said.

"They don't listen, do they?" Rumsfeld said.

"The culture doesn't allow a one-star to do this," Quinn repeated.

On the Vieques problem, Rumsfeld told Quinn, "We'll give them the island back and buy another one. It's a political and media nightmare." But Rumsfeld was deeply concerned about the Navy, his old service. During his first days back at the Pentagon, a Navy submarine, the USS *Greeneville*, was practicing an emergency surfacing off the coast of Hawaii and struck a Japanese fishing boat, killing nine, including some Japanese students. Then there was the EP-3 spy plane incident, and now Vieques.

At 7:51 A.M. on April 27, Rumsfeld dictated a snowflake summarizing his own thoughts and feelings.

"Subject: Navy

"The problems in the Navy may be systemic. It is one thing if you make mistakes when you are pushing the envelope. It's another thing if you make mistakes walking to work."

5

SHELTON WAS GROWING DESPONDENT. Rumsfeld was suggesting that Shelton should give his military advice to the president through Rumsfeld. Shelton reiterated that since Title X made him the "principal military adviser" to the president, he didn't see how that could work. He had to give his advice directly.

"You are not providing added value," Rumsfeld said once during a visit to the Tank, the Joint Chiefs' conference room.

Admiral Vern Clark, the chief of naval operations, 56, bespectacled and studious, pushed back. We can't even get copies of all the studies your consultants are doing, Clark said. There was one document in particular he hadn't been allowed to see. "How can you ask us to comment on this when we have never even seen the document?"

Rumsfeld hotly disputed this. "Well, that's not true. That document's wide open for all of you."

"Mr. Secretary," Clark said, "I called your office myself 30 minutes ago to get a copy of that document and I was told by your office that I was not authorized to see it."

Rumsfeld said he had the studies done because the Joint Staff was essentially useless. They specialized in thick studies that took months or more, didn't cut to the essential issues, and were basically unreadable. "I can't get a product out of these guys," he said.

Clark disagreed. He had been director of the Joint Staff earlier in his career, and he said they did some great work. Rumsfeld ought to appreciate it, Clark said; if he didn't yet, he'd learn to.

Rumsfeld scoffed. Afterward, he went back to his office with Quinn.

"Did you see your CNO down there?" Rumsfeld asked.

"Yes sir," Quinn replied. "First time I ever saw a four-star throw some mud back at you."

QUINN MADE ANOTHER RUN at getting himself relieved. "Mr. Secretary, you need to find the biggest, baddest three-star in the building and make him your senior military assistant. And somehow you need to signal that this is your guy, that this is the next chairman of the Joint Chiefs. Then the other admirals and generals will take him seriously."

All Rumsfeld did was smile.

In interviews later, Quinn said that the uniformed military believed that Rumsfeld was engaged in a hostile takeover. "I was considered a traitor," Quinn said.

Herbits discovered that probably the best candidate to replace Quinn was the deputy chief of naval operations for resources, warfare requirements and assessments, Vice Admiral Edmund P. Giambastiani, a nuclear power submariner. Often called "Admiral G" because many people had trouble pronouncing his name, Giambastiani was a 1970 Naval Academy graduate. He had skippered the Navy's only nuclear-powered, deep-sea research submarine, NR-1, and later commanded a fast-attack nuclear-powered submarine, the USS *Russell*, that conducted some of the most sensitive and high-risk covert Cold War missions, spying on the Soviet Union. He'd been a special assistant to the deputy CIA director in the 1980s, and had most recently commanded the Navy's entire Atlantic submarine fleet.

Vern Clark, the Navy CNO, was on the third hole of a golf course at Nags Head, North Carolina, soon afterward, when he received a call telling him to phone Secretary Rumsfeld at a specific time that would be right about when he would finish the first nine holes. Clark was one of the most improbable men to head the Navy. Unlike 25 of his 26 predecessors, he was not a "ring-knocker," a graduate of the U.S. Naval Academy in Annapolis, Maryland. A person of deep Christian faith, Clark had graduated from Evangel College, a small church-affiliated school in Missouri. He had gone to officer candidate school in 1968 at the height of the Vietnam War. He had quit in 1972 after his first tour of duty because he did not respect most of the officers who were making the Navy a career, but rejoined the following year, believing the Navy was something he should do for a while.

An at-sea commander, Clark had served General Shelton in the premier Joint Staff billets: director of operations, or J-3, overseeing all actual military operations, then later as his director of the Joint Staff. Some 25 years earlier Clark, as a Navy lieutenant, had been the commanding officer of a patrol gunboat, the USS *Grand Rapids* (PG-98). His executive officer had been a lieutenant junior grade named Scott Fry, now the Joint Staff director.

Though Rumsfeld had profound doubts about the Navy and Fry, he believed that CNO Admiral Clark was on the road to fixing the Navy.

"I've got an issue here that's developed with my military assistant," Rumsfeld said when he reached Admiral Clark. "You know, it's just not working out."

"Well, I can understand," Clark said. He knew about Rear Admiral Quinn's struggles. "Anything we need to do. You need to have the best support up there that we can get you."

"Well, I don't want him to get hurt," Rumsfeld said.

"Mr. Secretary, I can do something about that," Clark said. "I can assure you that I will order him to command of a carrier battle group, which is the premier thing that could be done in his grade. It will be no harm, no foul. And it will be up to him to make the rest of his future. I can do this in a matter of minutes. So this is done. We've got to protect you and the office, and obviously the people leaving there must do well. So this is a done deal."

"Okay, Vern. Great. Well, thanks."

Clark was about to hang up.

"Whoa, Vern. Wait a minute. I've got to have a replacement."

"Yes."

"They are telling me about an Admiral G that works for you."

"You've got to be kidding, Mr. Secretary."

"Is he any good?"

"Of course, he's good. He ran my transition team. He's fabulous."

Clark said that Rumsfeld didn't have a three-star billet for his military assistant but it could be worked out. "Same rules apply," he said, "You've got to be taken care of."

Admiral G was in his office when he received the call.

"The secretary of what?" Giambastiani asked.

"The secretary of defense."

"I don't know the secretary of defense."

"Well, he wants to see you."

• • •

"I'VE WRITTEN THESE TWO THINGS," Rumsfeld said to Giambastiani. "Would you read them and critique?"

The first document was just a page but the other was about five pages reflecting on the differences in the Pentagon between Rumsfeld's first tour in 1975–77 and 2001, the latest version of the "Anchor Chain" memo. Critiquing the papers was just the kind of little test Giambastiani loved, the meticulous nuclear-power-trained mind forced to pry apart the exact meaning and discover what had been left out and what questions were unasked. He spent about 45 minutes reading and critiquing. Rumsfeld asked him to stay for lunch and the next day called and asked him to become his military assistant.

In early May, Rear Admiral Quinn left to command the USS *Truman* carrier battle group, and three-star Admiral G moved to Rumsfeld's office as senior military assistant. One distinct advantage he immediately had was that as a 1970 Naval Academy graduate he outranked the 1971 Naval Academy graduate Scott Fry.

THE PREVIOUS MONTH, Rumsfeld had sent a two-sentence snowflake to the deputy defense secretary, Paul Wolfowitz. "A person in Illinois sent me this interview from 22 years ago, where I talk about government. You might want to read it." A photocopy of an article from a 1979 *Fortune* magazine was attached. Rumsfeld was opining on what it was like to be a former top government official in the world of business. He talked about setting up task forces, getting rid of underperforming businesses, and management style.

"I was a flight instructor in the Navy," Rumsfeld had said. "The first thing a fledgling pilot usually does, when he climbs into a plane, is to grab hold of the stick and squeeze it so hard that he gets a sore arm. With a grip that tight, every movement is jerky. When government officials get into a tight situation, they have a tendency to do the same thing. They get jerky, over-control, micromanage."

Some of the senior civilians Rumsfeld appointed were astonished and alarmed at how hard he was now squeezing the Pentagon controls. He micromanaged daily Pentagon life and rode roughshod over people. Rumsfeld had picked Powell A. Moore, 63, a Georgia native with more than four decades in Washington, to be his assistant secretary of defense for legislative affairs, the key link between the Pentagon and the Congress. Moore had a long and colorful history in Washington, including serving as one of the spokesmen for the Nixon reelection committee who had had the unenviable task of issuing categorical denials to Watergate stories. He knew how to work for difficult people. Moore had accepted the job as congressional liaison with an agreement that he would have direct access to Rumsfeld. They had many discussions about the care and feeding of the elected representatives.

Few better understood the Congress or how to oil the machine to make it work than Moore. But former Congressman Rumsfeld was not interested. Moore was surprised at Rumsfeld's contempt for Congress. He did not attempt to disguise his feelings.

In one public confrontation at a hearing with Senator Susan Collins, the earnest Maine Republican, Rumsfeld had put her down in a manner that was stunning even for him. Collins's voice had quivered at one point. Later, Moore suggested to Rumsfeld that he call her, try to smooth things over.

"Hell," Rumsfeld said, "she needs to apologize to me."

Another time Moore saw a draft of a harsh letter Rumsfeld had dictated to Representative Ike Skelton of Missouri, the senior Democrat on the House Armed Services Committee. Tone it down, Moore recommended.

"If you let people kick you around," Rumsfeld told him, "they'll do it again and again and again."

Rumsfeld's micromanaging was almost comic. On one occasion, he led a delegation from Congress to the funeral in Columbia, South Carolina, for Representative Floyd Spence, a Republican who had been a pro-Pentagon hawk for three decades. Moore had arranged the seating on Rumsfeld's plane the way everything was done in Congress, by seniority.

"I don't want this," Rumsfeld declared and personally rearranged the seating, putting Representative Duncan Hunter, the California Republican who would soon become the House Armed Services Committee chairman, in the back.

In May, Mississippi Senator Trent Lott, the majority leader, wanted one of his former aides named assistant secretary of the Navy for acquisitions. There was a big shipbuilding installation at Pascagoula, Mississippi, so for Lott it was home-state politics.

Steve Herbits had another candidate in mind, someone he thought had more experience, and he was trying to get the appointment through. Herbits had planned to leave the Pentagon to go home to Florida by mid-

May. According to some of the arcane rules for government contractors, it wasn't even clear he could legally stay at the Pentagon beyond May 15.

Lott apparently didn't know about Herbits's impending departure, and put a hold on many confirmations from Defense.

"If you want your people confirmed, send Herbits back to Florida," Lott told Rumsfeld.

The secretary was in a bind. "If I cave in to that blackmail, I'll be blackmailed all the time," he told Moore. He called Herbits in.

"You can't leave," he said.

"Why?"

"Because I can't be looking like I'm bowing to Lott."

Eventually Herbits's time was up, though, and he went back to Florida for a while. Senior Pentagon civilians were soon being confirmed by the Senate.

Rumsfeld had been a champion wrestler at Princeton in the 154-pound class, and Moore found that nearly every conversation with him was a wrestling match. Who's going to get on top? Who's going to take the other person down? Once Moore asked Rumsfeld about his golf game. "I play it like I wrestle." Moore took that to mean that Rumsfeld gripped too tight and swung too hard at the ball, classic mistakes in golf.

THE SECRETARY WAS NEVER satisfied with what came out of the building, so he sent over a draft of upcoming congressional testimony on a new defense strategy to one of his best friends, Kenneth Adelman.

Adelman had first worked for Rumsfeld in 1970 when Rumsfeld headed the Office of Economic Opportunity, a federal anti-poverty agency, under President Richard Nixon. Another of Rumsfeld's assistants at OEO had been Dick Cheney. Adelman had also been Rumsfeld's civilian special assistant during his first tour as secretary of defense, and later served as head of the Arms Control and Disarmament Agency during the Reagan administration. Adelman had a doctorate in political theory and was an outspoken, pro-military hawk.

Before every "good" inauguration—meaning inaugurations of Republican presidents—Adelman and his wife hosted a black-tie dinner at their home. Rumsfeld and Cheney regularly attended, but in 1981, Rumsfeld wanted to have a brunch at the Jockey Club before the inauguration of Ronald Reagan, and instructed Adelman, "Invite someone new, and just make sure that he's interesting." Adelman brought a 38-year-old professor at Johns Hopkins University named Paul Wolfowitz, who had been a deputy assistant secretary of defense during the Carter administration. After the brunch, both Cheney and Rumsfeld reported that they had been very impressed. They wondered where Wolfowitz had come from and how he knew so much.

Afterward, the Rumsfeld and Adelman families often vacationed together, staying at Rumsfeld's homes in Taos and Santa Fe, and his apartment in Chicago. In 1986, Rumsfeld took the Adelmans to his vacation home in the Dominican Republic.

"I'm running for president," Rumsfeld told Adelman. "I want you to run it."

"It's a specialized field," Adelman protested. He wouldn't know the first thing about managing a presidential campaign.

"You'll learn it," Rumsfeld said.

No way. Rumsfeld didn't need an amateur.

"You can do the issues."

Adelman laughed. "No, you know you'll do that yourself."

"You can write speeches then."

"No, I've already done that." He would of course support his old friend's candidacy and help out, but he wouldn't run the campaign.

Rumsfeld's presidential ambitions sputtered early the next year when he couldn't raise the money, but the friendship flourished.

Now, Adelman, 54, read the planned testimony for the big rollout of Rumsfeld's new national defense strategy. "The testimony is getting there nicely," he wrote in a three-page snowflake of his own to Rumsfeld, "but still needs labels for the Secretary's new approach." He proposed "A MARGIN OF SAFETY FOR AMERICA."

He also offered two warnings. "After our democracies defeated the twin totalitarian monsters of Nazism and Communism," Americans expected an era of peace. Not so fast, Adelman said, noting that in 1914 the same expectation had prevailed. He quoted the "young but ever-wise Winston Churchill," who sarcastically summed up such optimism: "War is too foolish, too fantastic, to be thought of in the twentieth century. . . . Civilization has climbed above such perils. . . . The interdependence of nations . . . the sense of public law. . . . have rendered such nightmares impossible." Adelman noted that "Churchill delivered the punch line in his most ironic voice: 'Are you quite sure? It would be a pity to be wrong.' "

Adelman added, "It was a pity, with the First World War breaking out that very year, only to be followed by an even more disastrous Second.

Unimagined wars become unimaginable tragedies. Some sixty million deaths showed what a huge pity it was to be so wrong."

Rumsfeld wrote "use" in the margin by the Churchill quote.

The last paragraph of the Adelman memo said: "ADD IN SOME-WHERE: On not knowing where the threat will come—surprise element. My successor and then predecessor, Dick Cheney, when taking office, could not have imagined that his main military confrontation would be the then-friendly country of Iraq. The country was never mentioned in Cheney's confirmation testimony and no senator thought to ask him any question about Iraq."

Rumsfeld's May 16 snowflake on Adelman's comments remarked that they were "first-rate" and should be incorporated. "I think this Churchill quote definitely should be used."

Twelve days later, in a Memorial Day speech at Arlington National Cemetery, Rumsfeld used the Churchill quote in full and then added that to expect the end of wars in the 21st century, "would be much more than a pity."

Ten days later Rumsfeld used the Churchill quote at a NATO meeting in Brussels. At his Senate testimony on Defense strategy, he noted that Cheney had not mentioned Iraq in confirmation testimony in 1989, and used Adelman's "margin of safety" language to define the strategy.

IN MAY, CROWN PRINCE ABDULLAH of Saudi Arabia publicly refused an invitation to the White House, saying the United States was blind to the plight of the Palestinians. "Don't they see what is happening to Palestinian children, women, the elderly—the humiliation, the hunger?" the Crown Prince said.

On June 1, a suicide bomber attacked a Tel Aviv nightclub, killing 21, the largest attack in nine months. "I condemn in the strongest terms the heinous terrorist attack in Tel Aviv this Sabbath evening," Bush said in response. "There is no justification for senseless attacks against innocent civilians." Two days later, Prince Bandar and Rihab Massoud had dinner in the White House residence with Bush, Powell and Rice.

Bandar brought a lengthy outline of a paper on how the Arab world viewed the United States. It was all part of Bush's education on the ways of the world—as seen through Saudi eyes—a remarkable, five-hour session that started at 7 P.M. and kept Bush up well past his bedtime.

The situation in the Middle East was getting worse, Bandar said. "This continuous deterioration will give an opportunity for extremists on both sides to grow and they will be the only winners. The United States and the Arab *mutethila*"—friendly moderates—"will pay a very high price." He continued, "There is no doubt that moderate Arab countries, as well as the United States, have lost the media war and the Arab public opinion. What the average Arab person sees every day is painful and very disturbing. Women, children, elderly are being killed, tortured by the Israelis."

Israeli military units, often armed with U.S.-made weapons, were making raids into Palestinian territory as reprisals for attacks. The previous year a Palestinian boy had been killed by Israeli troops while his father tried to shield him—an image played over and over on Arab television.

Bandar said it added up to an image that the U.S. stood behind the Israelis, with the goal of destroying the Palestinian Authority and the Palestinian economy. "The continuous use of American-made weapons against civilians, against Palestinian institutions and entities confirms to public opinion that resisting Israeli occupation by all possible means is then considered legitimate in the mind of the Arab Street."

Bush, Powell and Rice tried to rebut, but Bandar went on. He was not necessarily talking about facts but impressions. "Such impressions become fact in the Arab minds," Bandar said, and that "will have a total devastating and extremely dangerous impact on U.S. interests in the region. And unfortunately, the impression the Arab world has now of the United States, the only superpower in this world, isn't of a just and fair country but as one totally on the side of the Israelis."

Bandar cited examples of the United States condemning violence when Israelis were killed—as Bush had done two days before—"and at the same time, total silence when something similar happens that caused the killing of Palestinians." This jeopardizes the "work of the countries that are too close to the United States, such as Saudi Arabia, Egypt and Jordan."

Bandar said these countries realized the special relationship between the U.S. and Israel, but it looked one-sided. "The United States has to find a way to separate the actions of the Israeli government and its own interests in the region."

Overall regional deterioration had, he said, "even threatened the internal situation in Jordan and therefore King Abdullah's position internally is shaken. President Mubarak is also having a very difficult situation." In a highly unusual but careful admission, he said that even in Saudi Arabia, "for the first time in 30 years we are facing a very questionable internal situation."

Bandar knew which buttons to push. "The continuous deterioration is creating a golden opportunity for Saddam Hussein: one, to create an artificial petroleum crisis and disturb the market." Second, he said, "Saddam's continuous calling for jihad against the Zionist enemy and the imperialist America will create a very fertile ground." The Arab Street will act, he said, particularly "in the absence of real, genuine American involvement and balanced policies."

The collapse of the Palestinian Authority, he said, "as well as the loss of hope among the Palestinians will create a very dangerous situation and not only difficulty for the United States and the moderate Arab states but *even for Israel.*"

Bandar launched into a searing critique of Israel's policy of destroying the homes of anyone involved in terrorism against Israel. "How would you, Mr. President, think the American people would react if McVeigh who did the Oklahoma City bombing, you go and destroy all the McVeigh family's homes?"

Bandar was imploring. "Mr. President, you've got to do something. You've got to do something. I mean, you're killing us basically. We are being slaughtered right and left, and you're not doing anything."

Bush had vehemently criticized Palestinian leader Yasser Arafat and his decision at the last minute to walk away from a settlement with Israel at the end of the Clinton administration. "Arafat is a liar," Bush said. He was impossible to work with, to trust. He would not negotiate with him.

"Fine," Bandar said, "he's a liar. We know that. You know that. He's a schmuck. But he is the only schmuck we have to deal with." The problem was larger than one man.

Bandar's final message was: "The region is boiling and it's building and it's building."

ON JUNE 16, Bush was in Slovenia for a meeting with Russian President Vladimir Putin, part of his first major overseas presidential trip. The president stood waiting for Putin's arrival with Donald B. Ensenat, an old fraternity buddy who had been sworn in just 10 days before as the chief of protocol at the State Department. Both men were members of the Yale Class of 1968, and had been members of Delta Kappa Epsilon, known as "Deke." Bush's first mention in The New York Times, in November 1967, had been as a former Deke president defending the practice of branding new fraternity pledges with a hot coat hanger.

In an interview in 2002, Bush gave me the following account of his conversation with Ensenat as they waited in the 16th-century Slovenian castle for a foreign head of state.

"It's amazing, isn't it, Enzo?" Bush said, calling Ensenat by his fraternity nickname.

"Yes, Mr. President."

"It's a long way from Deke House at Yale."

"Yes, Mr. President."

6

ON JULY 10, 2001, CIA Director George Tenet met with his counterterrorism chief, Cofer Black, at CIA headquarters to review the latest on Osama bin Laden and his al Qaeda terror organization. Black laid out the case, comprised of communications intercepts and other TOP SECRET intelligence, showing the increasing likelihood that al Qaeda would soon attack the U.S. It was a mass of fragments and dots that nonetheless made a compelling case, so compelling to Tenet that he decided that he and Black should go to the White House immediately. Tenet called Condoleezza Rice from the car, and said he needed to see her now. There was no practical way she could refuse such a request from the CIA director.

For months Tenet had been pressing Rice to set a clear counterterrorism policy, including specific presidential orders called findings that would give the CIA stronger authority to conduct covert action against bin Laden. Perhaps a dramatic appearance—Black called it an "out of cycle" session, beyond Tenet's regular weekly meeting with Rice—would get her attention.

Tenet had been losing sleep over the recent intelligence he'd seen. There was no conclusive, smoking-gun intelligence, but there was such a huge volume of data that an intelligence officer's instinct strongly suggested that something was coming. He and Black hoped to convey the depth of their anxiety and get Rice to kick-start the government into immediate action.

Tenet, 48, the husky, gregarious son of Greek immigrants, had been head of the CIA for four years. He was the only Clinton administration holdover to serve on George W. Bush's National Security Council, and thus the only NSC member who had been serving in November and December 1999, just before the Millennium, when a series of worldwide al Qaeda plots had been disrupted. The current situation seemed reminiscent to Tenet.

Back in 1999, the National Security Agency had intercepted a phone call by a bin Laden ally saying, "The time for training is over." The intercept had led to the breakup of attacks in Jordan and Israel. A 32-year-old Algerian jihadist, Ahmed Ressam, had been caught trying to enter the United States from Canada before Christmas 1999 with explosives for an attack on Los Angeles International Airport. Tenet had called the CIA to battle stations. "The American people are counting on you and me to take every appropriate step to protect them during this period," he said in a cable before the turn of the Millennium. There could be 15 or 20 attacks, he warned President Clinton. He spoke with the chiefs of 20 key friendly foreign intelligence services, triggering anti-terrorist operations and arrests in eight countries.

Now, Tenet thought he was seeing something similar, possibly much worse. The NSA was intercepting ominous conversations among bin Laden's people—more than 34 in all—in which they made foreboding declarations about an approaching "Zero Hour," and a pronouncement that "Something spectacular is coming." Ten days earlier, on June 30, Tenet had ordered all his station chiefs to share al Qaeda intelligence with friendly local governments abroad and argue that their intelligence services should disrupt suspected terrorist cells in their countries. As he'd done in 1999, Tenet followed up on July 3 with personal calls or contacts with the chiefs of the same 20 friendly foreign intelligence services, asking them to detain named al Qaeda suspects in their countries and harass members of other terrorist cells affiliated with al Qaeda.

They did not know when, where or how, but Tenet felt there was too much noise in the intelligence systems. Two weeks earlier, he had told Richard A. Clarke, the NSC counterterrorism director, "It's my sixth sense, but I feel it coming. This is going to be the big one."

But Tenet had been having difficulty getting traction on an immediate bin Laden action plan, in part because Rumsfeld had questioned all the NSA intercepts and other intelligence. Could all this be a grand deception? Rumsfeld had asked. Perhaps it was a plan to measure U.S. reactions and defenses. Tenet had the NSA review all the intercepts. They concluded they were genuine al Qaeda communications. On June 30, a TOP SECRET senior executive intelligence brief contained an article headlined, "Bin Laden Threats Are Real."

Tenet hoped his abrupt request for an immediate meeting would shake Rice. He and Black, 52, a veteran covert operator with thinning hair and an improbably soft voice and manner who resembled a taller version of Karl Rove, had two main points when they met with her. First, al Qaeda was going to attack American interests, possibly within the United States itself. Black emphasized that this amounted to a strategic warning, meaning the problem was so serious that it required an overall plan and strategy. Second, this was a major foreign policy problem that needed to be addressed immediately. They needed to act right now, that very moment, to undertake some action—covert, military, whatever—to thwart bin Laden.

The U.S. has human and technical sources, and all our intelligence is consistent, the two men told Rice. Black acknowledged that some of it was uncertain "voodoo," but said it was often this "voodoo" that was the best indicator.

They both felt they were not getting through to Rice. She was polite, but they felt the brush-off. Bush had said he didn't want to swat at flies. As they all knew, a coherent plan for covert action against bin Laden was in the pipeline, but it would take some time. In recent closed-door meetings the entire National Security Council apparatus had been considering action against bin Laden, including the use of a new secret weapon: the Predator unmanned aerial vehicle, or drone, that could fire Hellfire missiles to kill him or his lieutenants. It looked like a possible solution, but there was a raging debate between the CIA and the Pentagon about who would pay for it and who would have authority to shoot. Besides, Rice had seemed focused on other administration priorities, especially the ballistic missile defense system that Bush had campaigned on. She was in a different place.

Tenet left the meeting feeling frustrated. Though Rice had given them a fair hearing, no immediate action meant great risk. Black felt the decision to just keep planning was a sustained policy failure. Rice and the Bush team had been in hibernation too long. "Adults should not have a system like this," he said later.

Black calculated that if they had given him $500 million of covert action funds right then and reasonable authorizations from the president to go kill bin Laden, he would have been able to make great strides if not

do away with him. Bin Laden operated from an unusual sanctuary in
Afghanistan, which was ruled by the extremist Taliban. Possible covert
action was no mere abstraction. Over the last two years—and as recently
as March 2001—the CIA had deployed paramilitary teams five times
into Afghanistan to work with the anti-Taliban Northern Alliance, a
loose federation of militias and tribes in the north. The CIA had about
100 sources and subsources operating throughout Afghanistan. Just give
him the money and the authority and he might be able to bring bin
Laden's head back in a box.

THE JULY 10, 2001, meeting with Tenet, Black and Rice went unmentioned in the various reports of investigations into the September 11,
2001, terrorist attacks on the United States, but it stood out in the
minds of both Tenet and Black as the starkest warning they had given the
White House on bin Laden and al Qaeda. Though the investigators had
access to all the paperwork about the meeting, Black felt there were
things the commissions wanted to know about and things they didn't
want to know about. It was what happened in investigations. There were
questions they wanted to ask, and questions they didn't want to ask.

Philip Zelikow, the aggressive executive director of the 9/11 Commission, which investigated the terrorist attacks, and a University of Virginia professor who had co-authored a book with Rice on Germany,
knew something about the July 10 meeting. Indeed, Tenet and Black had
demanded action that day, but it was not clear to Zelikow what immediate action really would have meant. The strategic warning Tenet and
Black gave lacked details. When? Where? How?

Besides, Zelikow concluded, the planning for covert action to go after
bin Laden in his sanctuary in Afghanistan actually did go forward at a
pretty fast clip—quite fast for a national security bureaucracy, he felt, although the plan was not approved before the September 11 attacks. In
fact, Rice had a National Security Presidential Directive to launch a new
covert war against bin Laden set to go to Bush on September 10, 2001. It
was NSPD-9, meaning eight other foreign policy matters had been formally debated, agreed on and signed by the president as administration
policy before the plan to go after bin Laden.

RUMSFELD WORKED WEEKENDS. One Saturday in early August 2001 he
summoned Shelton, the operations director, and all the section chiefs involved in the 68 war plans on the shelf, including the major war plans for

Iraq and North Korea. It was a grueling session. Rumsfeld wanted to examine the assumptions. "I sat there and these people couldn't believe it," he told me in an interview. "It took most of the day. And then one colonel would pop up and he'd go through the assumptions and I'd discuss them and talk about them. And then the next guy would come up and we went through one after another after another." The formal guidance for these plans from the secretary of defense and the president was in some cases four or five years old. "Yet it had never been even discussed here," in the secretary's office, Rumsfeld recalled with disdain.

"We are going to be here for about a week if we keep up this pace," Admiral Giambastiani told Rumsfeld during the Saturday session.

Rumsfeld was not going to give up. The plans seemed to be stymied by the technical problem of matching objectives with force levels. This was the grunt work, in his opinion, that the colonels solved just by throwing more and more troops into the war plans. They were risk-averse. He wasn't. He was willing, even eager, to assume risk.

SHELTON HAD BEEN CHAIRMAN since 1997. His four-year term would be up in the fall. Rumsfeld assigned the sensitive task of helping find a successor to Staser Holcomb, the kitchen cabinet consultant and retired vice admiral who had been his military assistant 25 years earlier. Holcomb started with a staggering list of 150 officers. He interviewed half himself, culled the list and consulted about 40 active and retired military and civilians—people he called "trusted old hands." The list included some retired officers and some three-stars who were technically not eligible. He listed a dozen characteristics the new chairman should have, including "candor and forthrightness—willingness to disagree, then effectively support the decisions reached."

The prospect that a three-star or a retired officer might jump to the chairmanship sent shock waves through the senior, four-star ranks of the active military.

Holcomb had been asking to see Marine Commandant General James L. Jones, a tough, 6-foot-5 Marine who had a cosmopolitan side. Jones, who had grown up in Paris and was fluent in French, had graduated from Georgetown University in 1966 with a degree in international relations. He had joined the Marines through officer candidate school the next year and served as a platoon leader in combat in Vietnam. He'd had all the right assignments—chief aide to the Marine commandant, Marine division commander and then, in 1997, military aide to Secretary of Defense

William Cohen. Cohen and Jones were close friends, going back nearly two decades when Cohen was a U.S. senator from Maine and Jones, then a major, had been the Marine liaison in the Senate. Cohen had seen that Jones was appointed commandant, the senior Marine and member of the Joint Chiefs. Jones knew that the Cohen connection made him suspect in the Rumsfeld Pentagon.

When Holcomb went to see Jones, he said part of his work for Rumsfeld was to identify bright two- and three-stars who thought the right way on transformation. Holcomb said he was going to be there only six weeks.

"Admiral," Jones said, "everyone who has been in here has said that."

Jones thought that was part of the problem with the Rumsfeld model. The U.S. military was not a think tank where consultants, moving in and out with big, new, bold ideas, could really help.

Still, Jones was on Holcomb's list as a possible chairman. He was called with no advance warning on a Saturday morning for an interview with Rumsfeld about the JCS chairmanship. During Rumsfeld's first months back at the Pentagon, Jones had found himself largely in the dark about what the secretary was doing. As the top Marine—counterpart to Vern Clark at the Navy—he also couldn't get copies of some of the studies Rumsfeld assigned to his civilian staff and consultants.

Jones always had time and showed respect for anyone, whatever their rank or station in life, and he was surprised by Rumsfeld's curt manner. The secretary at times didn't even say hello. Jones felt that Rumsfeld was mostly concerned with his own ideas. He gave the appearance of being deliberate and thoughtful but he often shot from the hip. Rumsfeld's self-importance and arrogance infected everything, Jones concluded. Who would want to be his chairman and senior military adviser, given that it appeared Rumsfeld didn't really want military advice? He wanted voluminous information and detail from others, but then he would only follow his own advice.

Jones took the unusual step of declining the interview, saying he wanted to remain Marine commandant.

SHELTON, AN ARMY MAN, had concluded that the best person to succeed him was the chief of naval operations, Admiral Clark. Though Clark had only been the CNO for about a year, his performance as Joint Staff operations director and overall staff director meant he knew the system. In Shelton's view, Clark was unusual: a team player with fierce independence. If Clark disagreed, he said so. But his style was straightforward and not threatening. Clark was the one officer who might survive Rumsfeld and preserve some sense of dignity and independence for the uniformed military. This had to be done before Rumsfeld changed the system forever.

With an MBA from the University of Arkansas, Clark tried to keep up with best-selling business books. One favorite was Jim Collins's bestseller, *Good to Great*, about businesses with average performances that suddenly experience high growth. Collins's book stresses the importance of humility, discipline and how an individual's core beliefs help define a corporate culture. It had a lasting impact on Clark.

"What does this person really believe?" became Clark's frequently asked question as he evaluated the Navy's senior officers. It created problems when an individual's beliefs did not align with the culture and values of an organization.

As the sweepstakes to replace Shelton opened in the summer of 2001, Clark received a message that he was to see President Bush in several days.

Clark called his former deputy, Admiral G, in Rumsfeld's office.

"What is this all about?"

"This is about you interviewing to be the chairman," Giambastiani said.

"Well, bullshit, I'm not going to be interviewed to be chairman without at least talking to Don Rumsfeld. Nobody's talked to me about that."

Sir, you're kidding! Giambastiani replied. Rumsfeld and Clark had met recently. "What did you do in there the other day?"

"We talked about all the candidates and who the players were and who the leaders were in the department and their qualities."

"You never talked about you?"

"No."

"You're on the short list," Giambastiani said.

Clark felt that preferably the next chairman should not come from among the current heads of the four individual military services. Ideally the new chairman should be selected from the combatant commanders—the CINCs, short for commanders in chief—who controlled operational forces, such as Admiral Blair in the Pacific or Army General Tommy Franks in the Middle East.

Under the Goldwater-Nichols legislation, power had shifted from the service chiefs to the CINCs. Service chiefs, himself included, were too parochial. They simply recruited, equipped and trained their individual services. The CINCs, on the other hand, used the forces and fought the wars. These were joint commanders—a Navy admiral or Air Force general might lead Army and Marine ground forces—and the future of the military was in jointness, the services working together. In Clark's view they needed a sitting CINC who had done it, practiced jointness, to move up to the chairmanship. Clark had been a CINC—head of the Atlantic Command, but only for five months before becoming the CNO. As CNO he had no real operational role, but he had an important job as the top Navy admiral. And Clark believed he was on the road to improving the Navy.

"I'm not going to see the president," Clark told Giambastiani, "until I've at least talked to Don Rumsfeld about this."

7

ADMIRAL GIAMBASTIANI squeezed in an appointment for Clark to see Rumsfeld at 6:45 P.M. on a Friday. Rumsfeld was in a hurry that night, and they agreed to meet on Sunday after church.

Clark opened strong. "I'm not going over there to talk about this. You and I have never even had the discussion about this." Clark told Rumsfeld they needed to discuss all the issues to see what their priorities and goals and beliefs were. Were they the same? What did Rumsfeld want? They needed an understanding. There was lots of confusion about the chairman's role. Clark believed in setting priorities; in the Navy, he focused on five top priorities. If you had 100 priorities, nothing got done. What were Rumsfeld's priorities for the entire United States military?

Rumsfeld waved away the questions.

"You don't trust us," Clark said, going to the heart of the matter, realizing that it was the first time he had a chance to get his true feelings about Rumsfeld off his chest.

"Well, of course I trust you," Rumsfeld said with his best bedside manner. "You're the leader of the United States Navy." Then he turned on a dime. "How could you say that?" he asked sounding both confrontational and hurt. Then back to the Dr. Rumsfeld routine, saying, "I have great confidence," and laying it on pretty thick.

Clark realized that the effusive praise was an astonishingly effective way of pushing away the issue of trust. He didn't want to be picky and small in this interview but he brought up all the studies and reports that

Rumsfeld kept from the Joint Chiefs. "Mr. Secretary," he said, "you have locked us out of this process. As a result, I have read everything that I'm allowed to see, and at this stage still some of the things have not been released to us.

"I don't know that you and I, Mr. Secretary, are on the same page for us to be able to lead the United States military and for me to be your senior military adviser. If I'm going to be your senior military adviser, you have to know what I think and I have to know what you think."

Rumsfeld indicated that Clark was making too much of a bunch of paper. "We'll have other times to talk about this," he assured Clark.

"More than anything else, sir, I do not want to go to the White House tomorrow and have a meeting with President Bush where the first thing he asks is, 'Vern, do you want to be chairman?' We are not ready for that kind of conversation."

"Okay, no problem," Rumsfeld said. "The president will not offer you the job tomorrow. It will not be handled like this. This is a preliminary interview."

In that case, Clark agreed. "Sir, I'm on for tomorrow."

BEFORE HIS MEETING WITH BUSH, Admiral Clark pulled out a copy of the Title X Goldwater-Nichols law on the Joint Chiefs and the chairman. In addition to designating the chairman as the "principal military adviser" to the president, defense secretary and NSC, the law said that the other service chiefs were also military advisers, and if they disagreed with the chairman their views should be presented as well. On the way to the White House, Clark reminded himself to stress that the Joint Chiefs were not a one-man band.

Clark's only real interaction with Bush had been six months earlier on January 20, 2001, at Bush's inaugural parade. When a large Navy contingent walked by the reviewing stand in front of the White House, Clark, as the top admiral, was escorted up. He saluted Bush and stood by his side, describing the various Navy units. As the last one passed by, Clark squared his heels and saluted again.

"Mr. President," he said, "it's a pleasure to be here today and be part of this significant event. And the men and women of the United States Navy are prepared to serve under your leadership. And on a personal basis I want you to know I'll be praying for you."

Bush had blanched.

•   •   •

CLARK WAS GREETED in the Oval Office by Bush, Cheney and Rumsfeld. After a few moments of small talk the president said, "Well, Vern, what would you think about being chairman of the Joint Chiefs?"

Clark shot a glance over at Rumsfeld, and realized he was going to have to tap-dance his butt off. He went into his Rotary Club ramble to keep from saying anything. He said how honored he was to serve as chief of the Navy, and how jointness—the services operating together—was the future.

Bush asked some general questions about the Navy.

Clark had his stock speech down pat and he went into an account of his top five priorities to change the Navy, with a focus on people, readiness and new shipbuilding.

In a little set piece that he hoped would be music to Bush's ears, Clark said that in the 1990s the nation had stopped talking about service, including the military. "My Navy's part of it," he said. "It was all 'I, I, Me, Me!' I'm not getting this and I'm not getting that—pity party feeling about life." Clark continued, "You know, I am a person of faith."

The president just nodded.

"My dad was a preacher," Clark continued. Before his first meeting as CNO with all his subordinate admirals, he said, an aide told him, "We need a revival meeting." Clark recounted how he then spoke to the admirals and said, "We are a people of service. And quality of service doesn't just mean quality of life"—medical care, base housing and other fringe benefits. Service meant "We're going to start talking about quality of work." Service meant giving of yourself for a higher purpose.

"Mission is number one," Clark said. "The Continental Congress did not create a Navy so we could cut a fine silhouette on the horizon. Our business is about taking it to the enemy."

Clark mentioned that Rumsfeld liked to talk about "transformation," meaning modernization and change in the military. He said that he had been doing "transformation" before the word was used, certainly before Bush became president and Rumsfeld became secretary of defense.

Cheney said hardly a word, and after the meeting Rumsfeld said nothing to Clark. Clark felt the meeting had been ho-hum, and he didn't think anyone learned much.

Several weeks later, Clark got word that Cheney wanted to meet with him alone. The meeting was scheduled to last 20 minutes, clearly a pro forma effort. The White House was checking the boxes and Clark felt he was not a serious candidate. However, he had time to prepare.

"I don't know if you remember, but I was the guy standing over your shoulder during the Gulf War," Clark said. "I was the guy that shoved the stack of deployment orders over to you."

Cheney didn't pretend to remember. Clark had been a Navy captain then.

On the overall military situation, Clark indicated that it was a time of difficult adjustment but he felt the principles of transformation being pursued by Rumsfeld were correct.

Cheney wanted to know how he'd risen to become the Navy chief.

Clark said that in 2000 Secretary of Defense William Cohen's civilian chief of staff had asked him, "Vern, how did this get so screwed up?" referring to the Navy. Clark said his answer was "They picked the wrong people." Only one of the top five admirals in the Navy had ever commanded a carrier battle group. There were too many desk admirals. Picking the right leaders with the right operational experience was critical. "Whatever you do, don't let it get like that again," he told the vice president.

Clark said that he had started "stupid study" or "stupid school" for the new admirals. Instead of the old indoctrination for new flag officers built around etiquette, how to hold a knife and fork at foreign embassies or the White House, they now had a two-week course focused on core issues. "Admirals didn't know anything about finance," he said. They only knew how to spend money, not how to manage budgets. So they taught real finance to the admirals. From his studies about how to be a CEO, he tried to get the admirals to spend their time according to the modern business model: one third of the time on the top priorities, one third on executive placement and development, and the final third on evaluating the product or results.

"You know," Clark added, "in this town we never do the last one third. We just build a new budget. That is wrong. We have got to figure out how to do this better. That's what I'm teaching my guys to do. This was part of my agenda. It wasn't Don Rumsfeld's agenda. This was what we came here to do."

Cheney was receptive, so Clark turned to goings-on during the Clinton administration. It was clear that the vice president liked to hear these old war stories.

"Make sure you have people around that will tell the president exactly what the facts are and not like we did in Kosovo," Clark said. Clark recounted how as the Joint Staff's operations director, or J-3, he had attended the White House meetings in 1999 when Clinton decided to deal with Yugoslav leader Slobodan Milošević's ethnic cleansing. Whether it was a miscalculation or simply sugarcoating, President Clinton's advisers first told him that Milošević would fold if he were threatened. When he didn't fold, Clinton was told bombing would do the trick.

"It was all supposed to be over in 48 hours and then in 72 hours," Clark said. Instead it took 78 days of bombing to get Milošević to cave. "You needed a roomful of psychiatrists to counsel all the cabinet members to make sure none of them slit their wrists, because they had so grossly misrepresented what was going to happen and the way they cased this for the president." Some of the Clinton national security team had been selling hope and had lost their sense of realism, Clark said.

"And you want to make sure you never, ever get caught in that situation," Clark said.

In Kosovo, the optimism was so deep, Clark said, that they had a 72-hour strike plan but there was nothing planned to follow it. "Zero," he said. No plan if the optimism didn't turn out, so they really had to scramble. "With your background here," he told the former defense secretary, "you'll be able to play a role in this that will be different than has happened around here in a long time. And for goodness sake, pick a chairman that won't ever let that happen."

Cheney seemed all grins, taking it all in, seeming to want to listen. So Clark went on, saying that General Shelton had insisted that the chiefs read *Dereliction of Duty: Lyndon Johnson, Robert McNamara, the Joint Chiefs of Staff, and the Lies That Led to Vietnam*, the 1997 book by H. R. McMaster, a 1984 West Point graduate. The military leaders during Vietnam were weak and failed to give their best military advice, Clark said. The chiefs had not worked together and they did not have rapport with the civilian leadership.

Clark said the Vietnam-era military leaders had lost their ability to affect the process in a way that kept the president from doing things that were detrimental to the nation. They lost their voice, didn't talk straight, and McNamara manipulated the system. The country and the military paid a price for it. "Mr. Vice President, whatever you do, you've got to make sure you pick a military leader who will never let that happen again."

Clark went back to when he'd been a Navy captain during the Gulf War. He had watched the relationship between Cheney as secretary of defense and Powell as JCS chairman. As far as he could tell, Clark said, it was the ideal model—an independent-minded chairman who was nonetheless close to the secretary of defense. There was a strain between Rumsfeld and Shelton, Clark noted. "You know," Clark continued, "this connection, getting the right guy really is a big deal. It's going to be a big challenge with Rumsfeld." He added, "I've got a fabulous job. I want you to understand that. And I've got it rolling in the Navy." And that was something he, the president and Rumsfeld might want to keep in mind when making a selection.

"Well," Cheney said, "I can see that you'd be a great resource in this job."

The meeting lasted one hour and 20 minutes—an hour longer than scheduled. Clark left thinking, "Wow. I wonder how this plays." He had laid it on the line, but felt it had been a very warm meeting. He believed he had connected with Cheney and that the tide was turning in his favor.

Soon Clark was summoned back to the White House to meet for another 30 minutes with both Bush and Cheney. He was given no advance notice.

"Mr. President," Clark said, "you know I've got a terrific job here. This is not something I covet doing."

"Yeah," Bush said, "that's what they tell me. You don't really care if you get the job, do you? Why is that?"

"Well, Mr. President," the admiral responded, "first of all, I consider it an honor of a lifetime to be able to serve." And, he said, it could be difficult for a service chief, steeped in his own program and service problems, to move up to the chairmanship, which required total jointness. "But there's one other really important reason. You know, ambition is important in people. But too much ambition, my observation, in senior military leaders is a dangerous thing."

Clark let the point just hang, but he thought, be careful with this notion of ambition, dummy. No one could become president without being pretty ambitious. "Of course," Clark attempted to recover, "there are places and positions that you couldn't possibly seek unless you had ambition. But the military positions are first positions of service. And I think when ambition gets in the way of service that it's a dangerous thing."

"Vern and I had a great meeting a couple of days ago," Cheney said. "Vern's got a lot of things going on in the Navy, things that I think it's important that he share with you. Why don't you tell him in more detail what you're doing in the Navy."

Clark summarized his five priorities and stressed the importance of people and the need for a new definition of service. He said retention of officers and enlisted men in the Navy was going up because of programs to improve not only the quality of life but the quality of service. Retention was so high that he was soon going to have to create a new program to start forcing people out of the Navy.

Before the meeting Clark had been escorted to wait in the Roosevelt Room, instead of the normal holding place for visitors in the West Wing lobby, and he knew that Vice Chairman of the Joint Chiefs Richard Myers had seen Bush and Cheney just before him. He wanted to display a little inside knowledge, so he said to the president he understood the choice was probably between Myers and himself. "I wanted to tell you Dick Myers will be a fine chairman," Clark said. His choice of "fine" was intentional. Not "great" or "perfect." Just "fine."

Clark said it was vital that Bush pick a chairman whose announcement would make the whole military stand up and cheer. It was critical, he said, that the men and women in the military from down in the ranks up to the top commanders have confidence in their leaders. That was a key issue not only in recruitment and retention, but in performance. "A military that does not respect its own leaders will not flourish," he said.

The president asked Clark about his understanding of the role of a JCS chairman.

Principal military adviser to the president, the secretary of defense and the National Security Council, Clark said, noting he had been the Joint Staff director and knew the law. But the chairman "principally and first works for the secretary of defense," Clark said, adding that Goldwater-Nichols required the chairman to represent the views and opinions of the other chiefs.

"Tell him about your experience with Kosovo," Cheney said to Clark. "The one you shared with me."

"I wasn't a four-star, I was a three-star," Clark told the president. "I was the guy who worked for the chairman. I got to watch the chairman up close and personal." He recalled how he came to the White House with Shelton in 1999 for what he called the "getting-ready-to-go-shoot talks," and was sometimes sitting at the table in the Cabinet Room or Situation Room, sometimes sitting right behind the chairman. It was important that President Clinton get the facts, realistic evaluations, he said. "When you get ready to pull the trigger," Clark said, "you have got to have a chairman that you have absolute total confidence that you've gotten the whole story from."

Overselling was a big problem, Clark said, recounting the Kosovo bombing story and the need for shrinks in the Clinton Cabinet Room.

Bush chuckled.

"So, this relationship with the president and the chairman is important. What's really important here is the relationship between the secretary and the chairman. Now being that guy on the sidelines, coming up through my career, I've been able to observe this. And the model you want to emulate is the model that existed when that guy"—he pointed to Cheney—"was the SecDef and Colin Powell was the chairman."

Cheney said nothing, but he knew that his relationship with Powell had not been nearly as perfect and seamless as it was being portrayed.

"It's flattering that I'm over talking to you," Clark went on. "But, you know, in a crunch that's not nearly as important as what's going to come over here to you via the SecDef. That's the guy you're going to be talking to."

He continued, "This interview's really interesting." Clark looked right at Bush. "And a connection between you and I, if I were to be the chairman, is important but not nearly as important as the connection between the chairman and the secretary of defense. So of utmost importance is that you get a chairman who has a great connection with the secretary of defense."

"Do you have that relationship with Don Rumsfeld?" Bush asked.

"Not yet," Clark replied.

"Hmmm, okay," Bush said.

CLARK BELIEVED IN divine intervention. He left the meeting hoping that he might get the job but also thankful for the chance to tell the president what the military really needed, what the president needed to do, and how he ought to think about the military matters. Many of his colleagues would have killed for the opportunity.

In addition, Clark believed that he brought few if any of the trappings that bound so many of his peers, especially from the service academies. He felt that he had not had to kiss ass along the way to get there.

SHELTON HAD BEEN TALKING with Rumsfeld regularly, trying to keep his hand in the selection process for his successor. Since it was now down to Clark or Myers, Shelton thought he owed Rumsfeld his recommendation.

"Vern is the best by far," he said. Clark would push hard against Rumsfeld, which Shelton felt was exactly what Rumsfeld needed. But Myers was the exact opposite. He would state his view, but if Rumsfeld disagreed, would withdraw and acquiesce. Shelton had seen it happen.

Rumsfeld smiled and merely said, "Okay."

Shelton did not tell Clark or Myers about his recommendation. He wasn't at all sure which way it would go, and he didn't want any acrimony.

AROUND THIS TIME, Steve Herbits had lunch alone with Rumsfeld, who said the choice was indeed down to Clark or Myers.

"If you want transformation to happen in this building," Herbits said, "then Vern Clark's your man. He is brilliant analytically, he is a leader of change, he knows how to get people moving." Clark had taken on the most hidebound of military cultures—the U.S. Navy. "He knows how to pick change agents. He changed the Navy. He's done an unbelievable job."

But, there was one argument to be made for Myers, Herbits said. "If you think there's a chance that you're going to war, you better pick Dick."

"Why?"

"Because Dick has more war-fighting experience," Herbits replied. Myers had flown 600 hours in combat over Vietnam. Though it had been three decades ago, it might have symbolic importance. "And the military will trust him more in a military situation than they will Vern, who has got all the credentials but he doesn't have the war-fighting experience."

8

TWO DAYS AFTER CLARK'S INTERVIEW, he was summoned by Rumsfeld. Clark was looking for some affirmation that he was Rumsfeld's guy, but when he walked into the room, he could feel it was all edge. It wasn't that he and the secretary did not have a cordial working relationship or that they did not get along, it was that the meeting immediately went to the heart of the matter.

"Well," Rumsfeld said, "you had the meeting with the president."

Clark said it had been a good, healthy exchange, but it had reinforced his concern. "My reservations remain the same," Clark said. "I told the president the most important thing about this selection was not the relationship between the military guy and the president, but the relationship between the military guy and the secretary of defense. And I held as the model what I had observed between Colin Powell and Dick Cheney. And the president asked me if I had such a relationship with you and I said not yet."

Rumsfeld seemed less impatient than usual, so Clark asked about beliefs. What did Rumsfeld actually believe? "I'm not going to be able to be your chairman and stand up in front of the world as your senior military adviser arm in arm with you until I know what you believe."

Rumsfeld had all these studies floating around—on weapons systems, strategies, war plans, personnel—you name it. There were 18 task forces doing studies. Clark felt some of the studies were ridiculous, but he inquired more gently about them, particularly one that suggested all wars could be won from Whiteman Air Force Base in Missouri, home of the B-2 bomber, which, with airborne refueling, could fly 50-hour round-trip bombing missions nonstop to the other side of the world. Another Rumsfeld study similarly suggested that war could be conducted from over the horizon, hundreds if not thousands of miles away, without forward deployment of forces. The Navy was about forward deployment, having the aircraft carriers and fleets on station out in the oceans near and in the face of trouble. Did Rumsfeld think that everything could be fixed by putting crosshairs on targets from great distances?

Rumsfeld didn't respond. He seemed really dumbstruck. Clark thought all the studies—the beehive of activity, the tyranny of the urgent—had overwhelmed Rumsfeld. He did not know the details or did not have enough of a strategic understanding to engage comfortably in a discussion about shaping the military.

"Do you think you're going to change the face of history and deal with every potential enemy the nation has and never get any dirt under your fingernails? If that's what you believe in," Clark challenged, "you and I are not going to be able to work together because we don't believe the same things."

"We haven't done any of that stuff yet," Rumsfeld said dismissively. He was knee-deep in studies and plans. Transformation meant new thinking, and he wanted to make sure he cast a broad net, went deeply into matters and "wirebrushed" everything.

Clark asked about the chiefs and their role, particularly the role of the Joint Staff. The Joint Staff is a national treasure, Clark said, and the secretary tended to undervalue it, even malign it. Clark said that he believed Rumsfeld was dead wrong on that score.

Rumsfeld scoffed again. What they provided was not worth the paper it was written on, he said, and it wasn't timely or useful. Why does the chairman need a head of policy, or a spokesman, a liaison to the Congress or a lawyer? Rumsfeld asked repeating his earlier comments to Shelton. "Why shouldn't he use my lawyer?"

Clark said that the chairman was interfacing with the military leaders of the world. The chairman by law was a member of the National Security Council. "He is asked to put forward opinions on policy questions every time you guys go to a principals meeting," the meetings of the NSC principals without the president.

Rumsfeld bristled.

"If you select me as chairman," Clark said, "I will fully embrace the responsibilities to be the military adviser to the president." The job included providing independent advice. "If we disagree, of course I'll want my position to be made known because that's the way the law's written."

Rumsfeld wasn't really responding and he clearly did not want to have this discussion. Clark started to push his chair back.

"Well, I would have to be the secretary of defense for four years and write my book," Rumsfeld replied sarcastically, "before I'd know the answers to all those questions."

"Well," Clark answered, "you and I both know that that's not what I'm talking about." He stood up.

"I guess there's no use talking about it much further," Rumsfeld said.

"I agree," Clark said, turned on his heels and left. He immediately went to see Shelton.

"I burned my bridges today," the Navy chief said, and described the meeting in its full agony and glory. "I'll never be chairman."

"Yep," Shelton said with a chuckle, "I guess you won't."

LATER I ASKED RUMSFELD about Clark. "Terrific guy," he said. But the question of Clark becoming chairman was apparently a touchy subject, because when I said that I understood General Shelton had recommended Clark, Rumsfeld said, "I don't know that."

We then got into a verbal wrestling match.

"You don't believe he made that—" I began.

"I didn't say I believed it or didn't believe it," Rumsfeld said. "I said I don't know that. I'm very precise. If you say something that I don't remember, I'm not going to say it's wrong and I'm not going to say it's right. I'm going to say I don't know that."

"Okay."

"And I don't," he said.

"You don't recall, so you—"

"I don't recall it," he finally said, answering the question. Of Clark he said, "He didn't seem to want it. He was very engaged in the Navy, doing a terrific job, and I didn't have the feeling that he was leaning forward, anxious to do that." Clark was high on his list and the president knew that, he said, "but I kind of like someone who wants to do something, because these are tough jobs and you take a lot of stuff. And it strikes me that someone needs to be leaning forward and want to do it. And I had the sense that maybe Vern didn't."

I inquired if Clark had said that under the law as chairman he would have to give independent military advice to the president.

"Oh sure," Rumsfeld said. "That comes up always, and I obviously agree with that. That's what the law is. Absolutely. Not just to the president, but to the National Security Council."

"Do you remember a real clash with him?"

"Oh, not at all."

ABOUT FOUR DAYS after Clark's bridge-burning meeting with Rumsfeld, on Saturday, August 11, *The Washington Times*, the conservative daily newspaper in the nation's capital, ran a front-page story headlined, "Admiral Called Front-Runner for Joint Chiefs; Clark Is Said to Impress Bush."

The report by Rowan Scarborough, who had good contacts in the Bush administration, went so far as to say, "One well-placed source said last night that Adm. Clark is Mr. Bush's pick." Noting that Clark is "deeply religious," a source was also cited saying that Clark resembles Vice President Cheney "in appearance and businesslike demeanor."

Clark was playing golf that morning at Andrews Air Force Base. He was on the ninth hole and one under par, one of the best games of his entire life, when his wife, Connie, called his cell phone. "I went out and bought this paper and the headline says you are the front-runner to be the chairman," she said, adding that their home phone was ringing off the hook.

Clark promptly hooked his drive out of bounds, took another shot, sliced it out of bounds and wound up with a triple-bogey.

ON AUGUST 24, 2001, outside his ranch in Crawford, Texas, President Bush introduced his selection to be the next chairman. The president's remarks focused on training, equipping, manning and transforming the military. "Secretary Rumsfeld and I thought long and hard about this important choice, and we enthusiastically agree"—Air Force General Richard B. Myers. Bush promised that he would work closely with Myers, "who will make sure the military's point of view is always heard in the White House."

Rumsfeld had told Bush and Cheney that in the end Clark wanted to remain Navy CNO, so they picked Myers.

Clark was on leave with his wife when they heard Bush's announcement live. Rumsfeld reached him in the car to tell him the news firsthand and thank him for going through the process. It was a very cordial conversation.

"Wow," Clark said to his wife. "That was nice."

MYERS, 59, with president-of-the-student-council good looks, was gentlemanly and controlled. Raised in Kansas, he had graduated from Kansas State with a mechanical engineering degree before joining the Air Force in 1965 as the Vietnam War was escalating. He flew F-4 Phantom fighter jets in combat on dangerous low-level missions over North Vietnam attacking ground targets. On a second tour, he flew so-called Wild Weasel missions against North Vietnamese surface-to-air missile systems. He had spent four years as head of the Space Command and then served one and a half years as vice chairman of the Joint Chiefs. To friends, he acknowledged that he coveted the chairman job.

Shelton was disappointed. As he had long suspected, it looked like Rumsfeld wanted a chairman in name only. The selection meant that when it came to the hardest of decisions there would be no one in the uniformed military positioned and supported by law to provide alternative advice to the president and stand up to Rumsfeld. From all the debates during the first months of the new administration, it looked like the most important issues were how to build a missile defense system, what military hardware to buy, and how to reorganize and modernize the force. Time and energy were almost exclusively directed at those problems, and they had been the focus of Bush's remarks introducing Myers.

But Shelton knew better. He had served in Vietnam and been the assistant division commander for operations of the 101st Airborne during the 1991 Gulf War. The really hard decisions were about the use of military force—under what strategy and plan, what types of force, when, how much, against what enemies or threats. The decision to go to war defined a nation, not just to the world but to the nation itself. War was the core reason for the military's existence. Those decisions could mean the death of thousands. The 1.4 million men and women of the United States armed forces counted on the chairman of the Joint Chiefs as their representative at the table when the president and the National Security Council weighed and debated such matters. With Myers, Shelton worried, the voice would be muted, silenced.

General John P. Jumper, a fighter pilot who had been military assistant to two secretaries of defense, was sworn in as the Air Force chief of staff—the equivalent Air Force position to Admiral Clark at the Navy and General Jones in the Marines—on September 6, 2001.

"Welcome to the most disappointing group you'll ever be associated with," Jones told Jumper as he took his seat on the Joint Chiefs of Staff. "Military advice is compromised by the political leadership. It doesn't emerge."

THE MYERS ANNOUNCEMENT came 18 days before September 11, 2001. He had been truly surprised to be picked. He had met with Bush and Cheney several times for 15- or 20-minute interviews, where the subjects had been transformation and whether he could work with Rumsfeld. Bush and Cheney had asked questions to make sure he could step outside his Air Force uniform. To his recollection, they did not discuss war or what might have gone wrong in Kosovo or Vietnam.

Myers got along with Rumsfeld, but they had had several heated exchanges. He believed that Rumsfeld overstated to make his points. One day Rumsfeld had gone after the Pentagon procurement system. He wouldn't stop. "We've got to reform this. This is just terrible," Rumsfeld said.

"Time out," Myers interjected. "That's wrong. You're wrong." But then he had the Myers way of softening the blow by half agreeing. "Okay, Mr. Secretary, that may all be true, and certainly our system isn't very good. In many respects it needs to be fixed." Then he shifted to the good side of the system, adding, "On the other hand, we produce the world's best military equipment. Everybody wants our stuff, so there's got to be something inherently good about the way we develop things, our whole system that develops things from the concept and the operational requirements to the time it comes out the hangar door or the plant door."

Myers's selection had leaked to cable television news, but he didn't really believe it, telling reporters who called, "What do you guys know?" But a couple of hours later Rumsfeld called and said, "We've selected you to be chairman. The president selected you to be chairman." He gave no reason why they had chosen him and Rumsfeld immediately jumped into a discussion about who should be the new vice chairman. They quickly decided on Marine General Peter Pace, a low-key 1967 Naval Academy graduate and veteran of Vietnam and Somalia.

As chairman, Myers found Rumsfeld so hands-on that he would con-
fide to one of his senior aides at times that he wondered why he was even
there. When they went to the White House, it had all been rehearsed.
They achieved what Myers called a "mind meld," which meant that
Myers adapted his mind to match Rumsfeld's. Many senior officers, including some service chiefs, saw Myers functioning as the senior military assistant to Rumsfeld.

Andy Card, who attended all the principals and NSC meetings, was
struck that Rumsfeld and the chairman tended to opine in the same
voice. It was an echo, and he could not recall an instance when the chairman's advice challenged Rumsfeld's. There were a few times he found
himself thinking to himself that it was significant that the chairman of
the Joint Chiefs wasn't saying anything. The silence might mean the
chairman disagreed but they would never know.

At the end of a long interview with Myers in his office at the Pentagon
on January 9, 2002, four months after the 9/11 terrorist attacks, I asked
him for help in decoding Rumsfeld.

"If I could do that, my blood pressure would be a lot lower," he said.
Maybe it had been a particularly difficult day, but Myers put both his
arms on the small table and then laid his head down on top of them. I
could not tell if it was a sign of exasperation or despair or something in
between. I had not seen this before—a senior officer cradling his head in
his arms.

Myers quickly stood up. The storm, whatever its cause or intensity,
had passed. But it was a statement I would remember, a snapshot of life
as it really was in the Rumsfeld Pentagon.

I wrote a book on the Afghanistan War and the response to 9/11, and
another on the decision to invade Iraq. In the course of the research I interviewed dozens of the key players, including the president, and reviewed notes of many of the highest-level internal deliberations and
National Security Council meetings. Myers is there, making an occasional comment, at times even briefing, only to have his points embar-
rassingly repeated by Rumsfeld. It was as if the secretary hadn't listened
to what the chairman had said.

At times Myers inquired of close aides if they thought it possible
Rumsfeld might leave. The answer was always no. Myers would just
shake his head or put his head down.

Rumsfeld was intimately involved in filling the key positions on the

Joint Staff. If Rumsfeld wanted someone and Myers said he couldn't live with the choice, Rumsfeld generally would drop the candidate and find someone else he wanted. But he insisted on a veto over the choice assignments. At one point, Myers wanted someone on the Joint Staff, and Rumsfeld had his own candidate. It frustrated Myers to death as they went to their separate corners and there was a little standoff.

The dispute lay dormant for about three weeks. Out of the clear blue while riding the escalator up in the Pentagon one day, Rumsfeld brought it up.

"If you could just give on this one, I'd appreciate it," Rumsfeld said.

Myers realized he was saying, "I'm not going to budge, and I'm the boss." Of course, Rumsfeld got his way. And Myers later explained, "We serve the civilian masters and the chain of command. Unless it's illegal or immoral or unethical, you do it. If you can't stand it, then you've got other options. You can retire."

During the first year Rumsfeld gave Myers a copy of an article dating from the Nixon administration. JCS Chairman Admiral Thomas H. Moorer's representative to the NSC staff had been caught spying on the White House and passing secret documents back to the Pentagon.

"Hey," Rumsfeld said, "this is something that might be interesting to you."

Myers couldn't believe it. He felt trapped in Rumsfeld's process, endless meetings and discussions. Once he came into the Tank for a meeting with the chiefs looking absolutely destroyed.

"Had to do two hours up there," Myers said in near despair, "and listen to all that bullshit all over again. And I've got to go back up there. I'm sorry, guys, but I got to go back up there again at five minutes till, and we just don't have long here."

Myers took to undoing his cuffs and scratching his arms compulsively, and he became so oblivious that some of the chiefs thought he didn't even know he was doing it. At times he would stare off in the corner of the Tank like he wasn't there and he didn't care what they were doing or talking about.

When Myers was exasperated he called Rumsfeld "that son of a bitch" or "that asshole." Half a dozen times people saw him just put his head down on the conference table in the Tank in frustration, much as I had seen him do in his office.

It was an irony that Rumsfeld had set up a system that did not ensure that he receive warnings from the uniformed military about rosy scenarios like those that had been promised from Vietnam to Kosovo. Strong, forceful military advice was bleached out of the system. The uniformed military was now just staff, its voice a polite whisper. Rumsfeld thought he had won. He was in control.

9

OVER THE SUMMER OF 2001, Israeli-Palestinian cease-fires had been declared, then broken. In August, the Saudi Crown Prince watched on television as an Israeli solider pushed and then stepped on an elderly Palestinian woman. According to the Saudi version of the story, he called Bandar to carry a message to the White House. Bandar went to see Bush on August 27.

"Mr. President," Bandar began, "this is the most difficult message I have had to convey to you that I have ever conveyed between the two governments since I started working here in Washington in 1982." He recounted at length the many meetings Bush or Cheney or Powell had had with the Crown Prince.

"Mr. President," Bandar read with a straight face, "leadership in Saudi Arabia always has to feel the pulse of the people and then reflect the feeling of its people in its policies."

Saudi Arabia was one of the last monarchies in the world. The leadership—King and Crown Prince—did what it wanted.

Bandar invoked the Saudi partnership with "your father" in the Gulf War and the time "your father" stopped loan guarantees to Israel when the Israelis broke their promise on settlements. In the past, it had been a balanced policy. "The Crown Prince has tried to find many excuses for this administration and we couldn't." The president had allowed Israeli Prime Minister Sharon to "determine everything in the Middle East." The Israeli policy of occupation and killing was like Britain with the

American colonies in the 18th century, France with Algeria, America with Vietnam, and the Soviet Union in Afghanistan. All failures.

"What pained the Crown Prince more is the continuance of American ignorance of Israel upholding policies as if a drop of Jewish blood is equal to thousands of Palestinians' lives."

Then came the action line: "Therefore the Crown Prince will not communicate in any form, type or shape with you, and Saudi Arabia will take all its political, economic and security decisions based on how it sees its own interest in the region without taking into account American interests anymore because it is obvious that the United States has taken a strategic decision adopting Sharon's policy."

Bush seemed shocked. "I want to assure you that the United States did not make any strategic decision," he said.

Powell cornered Bandar later. "What the fuck are you doing?" he demanded. "You're putting the fear of God in everybody here. You scared the shit out of everybody."

"I don't give a damn what you feel," Bandar shot back. "We are scared ourselves."

Whether this was all careful histrionics, or genuine concern, or a combination of show and sincerity, the Saudi threat worked. Two days later, August 29, Bush sent the Crown Prince a two-page letter: "Let me make one thing clear up front: nothing should ever break the relationship between us. There has been no change in the strategic equation.

"I firmly believe the Palestinian people have a right to self-determination and to live peacefully and securely in their own state, in their own homeland, just as the Israelis have the right to live peacefully and safely in their own state." It was a much bigger step than President Clinton had taken. Even as Clinton had tried to fashion a Middle East peace agreement as his legacy, he had never directly supported a separate Palestinian state.

Bandar immediately flew back to Saudi Arabia with the letter. On September 6, the Crown Prince replied: "Mr. President, it was a great relief to me to find in your letter a clear commitment confirming the principle in which the peace process was established. I was particularly pleased with your commitment to the right of the Palestinians to self-determination as well as the right to peace without humiliation, within their independent state." The formal reply added, "First it is very essential that you declare your position publicly which was stated in your letter. Such a declaration at this level will eliminate the common impression prevailing in the region of the U.S. bias to Israel."

Bush agreed to come out publicly for a Palestinian state. A big rollout was planned for the week of September 10, 2001.

NEARLY 3,000 PEOPLE were killed in the al Qaeda terror attacks on America on September 11, 2001. The details of the attacks and Bush's response are well chronicled. Bush had been in a Florida elementary school when the first planes hit. Within hours after the attacks, as Bush was flying around the southern U.S. on Air Force One, staying away from Washington because of the potential for more attacks, he reached Rumsfeld. "It's a day of national tragedy," Bush told him, "and we'll clean up the mess and then the ball will be in your court and Dick Myers's court."

But Rumsfeld and the Pentagon were empty-handed. His efforts at transformation had not taken hold. General Tommy Franks, commander of Central Command (CENTCOM), which includes the Middle East, had no plan to attack Afghanistan, where bin Laden and his network had found sanctuary. He told Rumsfeld it might take months before they could put forces on the ground in the country. At an NSC meeting the day after the attacks, Bush asked what the military could do immediately. Rumsfeld replied, "Very little, effectively."

Later that day, at another NSC meeting, Rumsfeld asked Bush, Why shouldn't we go against Iraq, not just al Qaeda? Rumsfeld was among those who thought Bush's father had failed by not taking out Saddam. One night in 1995, on a trip to Vietnam with his friend Ken Adelman, Rumsfeld kept Adelman up until 3 A.M., giving him an earful on how badly the elder Bush had screwed up. He never should have agreed to a cease-fire that let Saddam survive in power, Rumsfeld said, and he should have destroyed more of the Iraqi military while they still had the cover of war.

The president put Rumsfeld off, wanting to focus on Afghanistan, al Qaeda and Osama bin Laden.

THE CIA STEPPED IN to fill the void left by the secretary of defense and the uniformed military. Within 48 hours, Tenet and Cofer Black briefed Bush on their plan. They could bring to bear all the resources of the intelligence community, combined with U.S. military power and Special Forces, harness the factional opposition known as the Northern Alliance, defeat the Taliban and close out the al Qaeda sanctuary. As disquieting as Rumsfeld's admission of the Pentagon's impotence was, Black was just as reassuring. "Mr. President, we can do this," he said. "No doubt in my mind."

Tenet dispatched the CIA's covert paramilitary team, code-named Jawbreaker, into Afghanistan 15 days after the attacks. Bombing began 11 days later, on October 7, 2001. The campaign represented some of the CIA's finest moments after 9/11, and it was a frustrating time for Rumsfeld. General Franks had only 31 Taliban and al Qaeda targets for the first day of bombing and Rumsfeld was all over target selection, insisting they also destroy some four dozen Taliban airplanes.

Air Force Lieutenant General Charles F. Wald, the Saudi Arabia–based CENTCOM air component commander, told his boss, General Franks, that they had bombed and destroyed the runways. The Taliban aircraft weren't a threat because they could not conceivably take off.

"I'm going to get fired!" Franks told him. The first day of bombing, Franks and his staff appeared on the secure video conference from CENTCOM's Tampa, Florida, headquarters wearing golf shirts. Franks let loose with a torrent of profanity insisting that the "fucking airplanes" be hit.

Wald ordered the strikes. Under the military's rules, however, they could not confirm for Franks that the attacks had been successful and the airplanes destroyed until they got satellite pictures of the targets. When it was delayed, Rumsfeld went ballistic. Franks insisted to Wald that he was going to be relieved. Finally, Wald got the validation from the Defense Intelligence Agency.

Jawbreaker and other CIA paramilitary teams were doing just as Tenet had promised, leading the way in toppling the Taliban from power, and denying bin Laden much of his sanctuary, forcing him into hiding. In all a small team of approximately 110 CIA officers and 316 Special Forces operators, in many ways similar to the more mobile military Rumsfeld desired, combined with massive airpower, were getting the job done.

And Rumsfeld sat uneasily on the sidelines. At an NSC meeting on October 16, his frustration boiled over. "This is the CIA's strategy," he declared. "They developed the strategy. We're just executing the strategy."

CIA Deputy Director John McLaughlin, who was taking Tenet's place that day at the NSC meeting, insisted the agency was just supporting Franks.

"No," Rumsfeld retorted, "you guys are in charge."

Armitage, who was there in place of Powell, stuck it into Rumsfeld. "I think what I'm hearing is FUBAR," Armitage said, using an old military term meaning "Fucked Up Beyond All Recognition." How could they prosecute a war if they couldn't agree who was in charge?

The president ordered Rice, "Get this mess straightened out."

After the meeting Rice took Rumsfeld aside. "Don, this is now a military operation and you really have to be in charge."

Steve Hadley, Rice's deputy, even weighed in, telling Rumsfeld he needed to design a strategy. "It's yours for the taking."

Later Powell also told Rumsfeld he was in charge whether he wanted to be or not.

Rumsfeld had been humiliated by McLaughlin, Armitage, the president, Rice, Hadley and Powell.

Never again. The next month, when the president ordered him to look seriously at the Iraq war plan, Rumsfeld made it his personal project. This would be his.

AFTERWARD, TENET LOOKED BACK on his July 10, 2001, meeting with Rice, two months before 9/11, as a tremendous lost opportunity to prevent or disrupt the 9/11 attacks. It framed his and the CIA's relationships with Rice and the NSC. On paper Tenet reported to Bush, but practically speaking the CIA director works for the national security adviser on a day-to-day basis.

Tenet had been briefing Bush regularly in the first six months of his presidency, and was developing a personal relationship with him. But it was nothing like Rice's. She lived alone, regularly spent weekends at Camp David with the president and first lady, and traveled often to Bush's Texas ranch. She was almost part of the family.

Rice could have gotten through to Bush on the bin Laden threat, but she just didn't get it in time, Tenet thought. He felt he had done his job, laid it on the line very directly about the threat, but Rice had not moved quickly. He felt she wasn't organized and didn't push people as he tried to do at the CIA.

When the multiple 9/11 investigations came in full force, Tenet's CIA was picked apart—failure to do this, failure to do that, failure to connect this dot with that dot. Tenet thought the CIA had been working flat out, and that comparatively the FBI got a free pass. If the FBI had done a simple credit card check on the two 9/11 hijackers who had been identified in the United States before 9/11, Nawaf al-Hazmi and Khalid al-Mihdhar, they would have found that the two men had bought 10 tickets for early morning flights for groups of other Middle Eastern men for September 11, 2001. That was knowledge that might conceivably have stopped the attacks.

A month after the July 2001 meeting, in a TOP SECRET President's Daily Brief on August 6, 2001, that later became famous, the CIA warned again: "Bin Laden Determined to Strike in U.S." Tenet would later say of that period, "The system was blinking red." But the pivot point when they might have shifted from all the dire talk to action had been July 10. Rice had perhaps denied him his biggest moment. U.S. intelligence had pieced enough together and had been on the verge of a significant, even a giant, breakthrough. Tenet's initial angst about Rice after the July 2001 meeting turned to distress, and then disdain. If the White House, Bush, the CIA and all the others—including Tenet himself, he acknowledged— had moved, perhaps, just perhaps, the years that followed would have been about success.

Every intelligence officer, all the way up to the CIA director, wants to be an oracle, to see deeply into the future, dig out the hard data and intelligence, mix it with the voodoo, and predict what will happen. Tenet believed he had done it. His first duty was to avert catastrophe, the bolt-out-of-the-blue event or attack. He had seen it, he believed, and he felt he had sounded the loudest warning he could. But it hadn't been heeded. The July meeting with Rice had been the culmination. As Cofer Black later put it, "The only thing we didn't do was pull the trigger to the gun we were holding to her head."

THE ELDER GEORGE BUSH was concerned about his son after 9/11, and he called Prince Bandar. "He's having a bad time," Bush told Bandar. "Help him out."

On September 13, two days after the attacks, Bandar met again with the president at the White House. The two men, with Cheney, Rice and Bandar's aide, Rihab Massoud, gathered on the Truman Balcony off the second floor. In a photograph of the meeting, both Bush and Bandar have cigars.

The Saudis had arrested and detained some key al Qaeda suspects immediately before and after 9/11. The president told Bandar, "If we get somebody and we can't get them to cooperate, we'll hand them over to you."

With those words, the president casually expressed what became the

U.S. government's rendition policy—the shifting of terrorist suspects from country to country for interrogation. The United States Constitution provides rights and protections that prohibit unrestricted interrogations of its citizens. But in countries like Saudi Arabia, there was nothing like the U.S. Constitution. Terrorist suspects in Saudi custody had few rights. Though the Saudis denied it, the CIA believed the Saudis tortured terrorist suspects to make them talk. In the immediate wake of 9/11 Bush wanted answers from those who had been detained.

AFTER 9/11, BUSH'S APPROVAL RATING soared from 55 to 90 percent, an unprecedented surge. The president pretended not to be interested when Rove showed him the numbers, but it was understood that Rove's job was to make sure the broad support was used effectively. In the past, when the public rallied around the president in times of crisis, the boost in popularity lasted seven to 10 months, Rove calculated.

Bush made it clear that his presidency was now going to be about 9/11. Just like my father's generation was called in World War II, now our generation is being called, he told Rove. Bush's father had enlisted in the Navy in 1942 on his 18th birthday and flown fighters in the Pacific. He'd been shot down and had seen some of his friends killed. It had been a formative experience.

The younger Bush and Rove had never fought in a war, but now they felt that they were being called, in their 50s.

"I'm here for a reason," Bush told Rove, "and this is going to be how we're going to be judged." This was the new plan.

ON NOVEMBER 21, the day before Thanksgiving, 71 days after the 9/11 attacks, Bush asked Rumsfeld to start updating the war plan for Iraq.

"Let's get started on this," Bush recalled saying that day. "And get Tommy Franks looking at what it would take to protect America by removing Saddam Hussein if we have to." He also wondered if this planning could be done so it would be kept secret. Rumsfeld said it could, because he was "refreshing" all the U.S. war plans.

On this day, Bush formally set in motion the chain of events that would lead to the invasion of Iraq 16 months later. In dozens of meetings, many with the president and the war cabinet, the Iraq war plan went through many changes, which I recounted in *Plan of Attack*.

The Iraq war plan was the chessboard on which Rumsfeld would test, develop, expand and modify his ideas about military transformation.

And the driving concept was "less is more"—new thinking about a lighter, swifter, smaller force that could do the job better. Rumsfeld's blitzkrieg would vindicate his leadership of the Pentagon.

He was the main architect, driving the meetings and the changes. His chief implementer was General Franks. General Myers worked from the sidelines, if that. Though Myers believes he was kept abreast and informed of all decisions, he was not a real participant. In Franks's memoir, *American Soldier*, Myers is mentioned in the Iraq war-planning sessions only as being present several times or taking notes. Franks, 58, a tall, hot-tempered Texan who had a reputation as an officer who screamed at his subordinates when he grew impatient, referred openly to the Joint Chiefs as the "Title Ten Motherfuckers." He believed that Myers and the other chiefs were largely irrelevant to the process.

An important contrast to this process can be found in the record of the war planning for the 1991 Gulf War. My own book, *The Commanders*, and memoirs by Powell, who was chairman of the Joint Chiefs, and H. Norman Schwarzkopf, who was the CENTCOM commander in that war, illustrate the difference.

Schwarzkopf describes how Powell as chairman was his intermediary, counselor, regular contact, adviser and psychiatrist. After Saddam invaded Kuwait in 1990, the first President Bush ordered Operation Desert Shield, which involved the deployment of some 250,000 troops to the Middle East to defend Saudi Arabia. By late October 1990, Bush and Cheney, his defense secretary, wanted to know how many troops it would take to provide an offensive option—the capacity to drive Saddam's army out of Kuwait. They did not ask Schwarzkopf; they asked Powell. Powell flew to Saudi Arabia, where Schwarzkopf was headquartered. Schwarzkopf said he needed two more divisions. Powell added two more on top of that. In his memoir, Powell recounted the conversations. "Aircraft carriers? Let's send six." The concept was "Go in big, and end it quickly. We could not put the United States through another Vietnam." The plan to use overwhelming force to guarantee victory became known as the Powell Doctrine.

Powell had then told Bush and Cheney they needed an additional 200,000 troops, which would essentially double the force defending Saudi Arabia. The first President Bush said, "If that's what you need, we'll do it."

In 2001, things were very different. This President Bush wanted an option to invade Iraq and depose Saddam, but he had campaigned promising military transformation. He and Rumsfeld wanted a new way to wage war. The Powell Doctrine was out. Over the next year, the two great Pentagon ideas—a new, "refreshed" Iraq war plan, as Rumsfeld called it, and military transformation—converged.

WELL INTO THE AFGHANISTAN bombing campaign, Paul Wolfowitz, the deputy secretary of defense, called an old friend, Christopher DeMuth, the longtime president of the American Enterprise Institute, the conservative Washington think tank. Just before coming to the Pentagon, Wolfowitz had been the dean of the Paul H. Nitze School of Advanced International Studies at Johns Hopkins University in Washington, known as SAIS. AEI and SAIS, just blocks from each other, were the forum for lots of intellectual cross-pollination.

The U.S. government, especially the Pentagon, is incapable of producing the kinds of ideas and strategy needed to deal with a crisis of the magnitude of 9/11, Wolfowitz told DeMuth. He needed to reach outside to tackle the biggest questions. Who are the terrorists? Where did this come from? How does it relate to Islamic history, the history of the Middle East, and contemporary Middle East tensions? What are we up against here?

Wolfowitz said he was thinking along the lines of Bletchley Park, the team of mathematicians and cryptologists the British set up during World War II to break the ULTRA German communications code. Could DeMuth quickly put together a skilled group to produce a report for the president, Cheney, Powell, Rumsfeld, Rice and Tenet?

Asking a think tank if it would be willing to strategize for the top policy-makers in a time of extraordinary crisis was like asking General Motors if they would be willing to sell a million more cars. DeMuth, a smooth, debonair lawyer trained at the University of Chicago Law School and expert on government regulation, readily agreed. AEI was practically the intellectual farm team and retirement home for Washington conservatives. Among its scholars and fellows were former House Speaker Newt Gingrich and Lynne Cheney, the wife of the vice president. Cheney himself had been an AEI fellow between his stints as secretary of defense and president and CEO of the giant defense contractor Halliburton.

DeMuth recruited a dozen people. He later said they agreed to serve only "if I promised it would all be kept secret."

Included in the group were Bernard Lewis, a Cheney favorite and a scholar of Islam who had written extensively on Middle Eastern tensions with the West; Mark Palmer, a former U.S. ambassador to Hungary who specialized in dictatorships; Fareed Zakaria, the editor of *Newsweek International* and a *Newsweek* columnist; Fouad Ajami, director of the Middle East Studies Program at SAIS; James Q. Wilson, a professor and specialist in human morality and crime; and Reuel Marc Gerecht, a former CIA Middle East expert. Rumsfeld assigned his consultant and general fix-it man, Steve Herbits, to participate. Herbits, who had devised the original idea and encouraged Wolfowitz to push it, called the group "Bletchley II."

On Thursday night, November 29, 2001, DeMuth assembled the group at a secure conference center in Virginia for a weekend of discussion. They passed around some of the participants' various writings. DeMuth was surprised at the consensus among his group. He stayed up late Sunday night distilling their thoughts into a seven-page, single-spaced document, called "Delta of Terrorism." "Delta" was used in the sense of the mouth of a river from which everything flowed.

In an interview, DeMuth declined to provide a copy of "Delta of Terrorism," but he agreed to describe its conclusions.

"What we saw on 9/11 and the less dramatic attacks of the '90s like the USS *Cole*"—which killed 17 Navy sailors—"manifest that a war was going on within Islam—across the region. It was a deep problem, and 9/11 was not an isolated action that called for policing and crime fighting."

It was a different kind of terrorism than the 1970s version, with locally disaffected groups such as the Red Brigades in Italy. Overall, the report concluded, the United States was likely in for a two-generation battle with radical Islam.

"The general analysis was that Egypt and Saudi Arabia, where most of the hijackers came from, were the key, but the problems there are intractable. Iran is more important, where they were confident and successful in setting up a radical government." But Iran was similarly difficult to envision dealing with, he said.

But Saddam Hussein was different, weaker, more vulnerable. DeMuth said they had concluded that "Baathism is an Arab form of fascism transplanted to Iraq." The Baath Party, controlled by Saddam Hussein, had ruled Iraq since 1968.

"We concluded that a confrontation with Saddam was inevitable. He was a gathering threat—the most menacing, active and unavoidable threat. We agreed that Saddam would have to leave the scene before the problem would be addressed." That was the only way to transform the region.

Copies of the memo, straight from the neoconservative playbook, were hand-delivered to the war cabinet members. In at least some cases, it was given a SECRET classification. Cheney was pleased with the memo, and it had a strong impact on President Bush, causing him to focus on the "malignancy" of the Middle East. Rice found it "very, very persuasive."

Rumsfeld later said he remembered the general plan but didn't recall the details of the memo. His design, he said, was to "bring together some very fine minds on a highly confidential basis and provide intellectual content" for the post-9/11 era.

Herbits was very happy with the way Bletchley II had worked out, although Rumsfeld decided not to make the group permanent. Summarizing their conclusions, Herbits said, "We're facing a two-generation war. And start with Iraq."

10

B USH DECIDED on January 18, 2002, that the protections of the Geneva Conventions would not apply to terrorist suspects detained from al Qaeda and the Taliban. They would be declared "unlawful combatants," not entitled to the Geneva protections of prisoners of war.

General Myers had not been involved in the decision. He disagreed with it because it would open the door for mistreatment of U.S. personnel taken as POWs. He argued to Rumsfeld, but he couldn't get the secretary on his side. Worse, he didn't know where Rumsfeld stood.

Secretary of State Powell asked the president to reconsider. At a later NSC meeting with Bush and Cheney, Myers and Rumsfeld were not in agreement. It was one of the few times they had not coordinated ahead of time to bring Myers's position in line with Rumsfeld's.

"Mr. President," Myers said, "you may notice I'm the only guy here without any backup. I don't have a lawyer." The other NSC principals had their legal advisers there. "I don't think this is a legal issue. And I understand technically why the Geneva Conventions do not apply to these combatants." They weren't all fighting in organized national armies or wearing uniforms, as the conventions required. "I got that. But I think there is another issue we need to think about that maybe hasn't gotten enough light."

Myers said he worried about the impact on U.S. POWs. "You have to remember that as we treat them, probably so we're going to be treated." That was the best-case scenario, the going-in hope. "We may be treated worse, but we should not give them an opening." Terrorists or other future enemies could easily use the U.S. policy against the Taliban as an argument that they too could ignore the Geneva Conventions.

By February, the president had decided to compromise. The Taliban would be covered by the Geneva Conventions, although they would not be classified as prisoners of war who had the highest levels of protection and who could not, for example, be physically coerced during interrogations. The administration would not consider al Qaeda terrorists covered at all, although detainees would be treated humanely.

Press Secretary Ari Fleischer was supposed to read the decision to the press on February 7, but Steve Hadley, Rice's deputy, had sent a copy to Rumsfeld giving him a heads-up. Rumsfeld had a last-minute objection—as was often the case—and Hadley told Fleischer not to read it.

Bush was watching Fleischer's briefing that day. When it ended at 1:28 P.M., the president was surprised that Fleischer had not announced the decision.

Bush called Fleischer. "I cleared that statement," the president said, and instructed the press secretary to go out and read it. At 1:40 P.M.—just 12 minutes after he'd walked off the podium—Fleischer appeared again in the press room for an unusual, unscheduled second daily briefing.

"The Geneva Convention will apply to the Taliban detainees, but not to the al Qaeda international terrorists," Fleischer announced, and pointed out the important distinction that "Taliban detainees are not entitled to POW status.

"The President has maintained the United States' commitment to the principles of the Geneva Convention, while recognizing that the Convention simply does not cover every situation in which people may be captured or detained by military forces, as we see in Afghanistan today."

PRESIDENT BUSH HAD SPENT most of August 2002 on vacation at his ranch in Crawford, Texas. Bandar joined him there for a visit on Tuesday, August 27, 2002, a year to the day after the 2001 meeting in which Bandar had delivered the Crown Prince's message and successfully pressured Bush to declare explicit U.S. support for an independent, sovereign Palestinian state. The two had hours to talk that morning. Bandar had met personally with Saddam four times in the five years from 1985 to 1990, and he shared his own reactions, along with those of King Fahd, who had met with Saddam many times.

Bandar recalled for Bush a conversation King Fahd had with Saddam after the November 20, 1979, takeover of the Grand Mosque in Mecca by hundreds of militants who claimed the Saudi government was becoming too liberal and friendly to the West. Saddam had been vice president and acting leader for some time, but he had just become president and was attending his first Arab summit meeting.

"Kill those people," Saddam advised Fahd.

Fahd said when the militants were arrested, their leaders would be executed and the others would go to jail.

"Oh, my, I'm worried," Saddam said. "I'm embarrassed by your comments."

Fahd asked Saddam what he meant.

"In my mind there is no question you are going to kill all 500. That's a given. Listen to me carefully, Fahd. Every man in this group who has a brother or father—kill them. If they have a cousin who you think is man enough to go for revenge, kill him. Those 500 people is a given. But you must spread the fear of God in everything that belongs to them, and that's the only way you can sleep at night."

According to Bandar, Saddam required his bodyguards to do two things to prove themselves: kill somebody else from within their own tribe and kill somebody from another tribe. So there would be a double vendetta.

Bandar explained: "This is smart evil because if you take the evil out of it, it makes sense. If I want to trust you with my life, I want to make sure nowhere else you are safe except with me."

At another time Saddam pointed to the people around him—high and low—and told Fahd, "They are the most loyal to me."

"It is nice to be surrounded by the most loyal people," Fahd replied.

"Oh, no, no, I didn't say that, Your Majesty," Saddam corrected. "I told you they are very loyal to me because every one of them, his hand is bloody. Every one of them knows that when I die, you will never find a piece this big from my body." Saddam indicated the smallest piece of flesh between his fingers. "I'll be cut to pieces, and if that happens to me, they're all finished."

From his personal meetings with the Iraqi dictator, Bandar said, "The most amazing thing about Saddam is how confident he looks, how relaxed he looks, and how charming he is—and how deadly. And each of these attributes are clear and at the same time."

Saddam could make his most senior generals shake, Bandar said. Once, while Bandar met with Saddam in the 1980s while trying to broker an end to the Iran-Iraq War, Saddam told him, "Bandar, all those people are loyal to me. I know a man by looking into his eyes. I can tell you if he is loyal or not. And if his eyes start blinking, I know he is a traitor and then I exterminate him."

Bandar said that Saddam was excited to show his power, and said it in such a gentle voice and in such a genteel manner that it took five seconds to realize he was serious.

"You are a man with presence," Bandar told the Iraqi dictator. "I would not be surprised that some poor young officer or minister might panic, which is natural. Are you going to tell me you are going to kill somebody because he panicked only because he is in awe of you?"

"Ha, ha, ha, ha, HA!" Saddam replied with the most deadly laugh. He then tapped Bandar on the shoulder. "I'd rather kill somebody, not sure if he is a traitor, than let one traitor get by."

IN THE FALL OF 2002, Tenet and Bush had a 30-second conversation in which Bush made it clear that war with Iraq was necessary and inevitable. Tenet was extremely surprised, but the president's short remarks were made with such conviction that Tenet suddenly realized they were on a march to war. There was something about the hard resolve in Bush's body language that made Tenet realize that all the TOP SECRET talk and war planning had a specific purpose. Bush said that the risks presented by Saddam would grow with time.

"We're not going to wait," he said.

On November 4, 2002, Rob Richer, a veteran covert operator and former CIA chief of station in Amman, Jordan, took over as head of the Near East and South Asia Division of the CIA operations directorate, overseeing the entire Middle East. It was the key operations billet with hands-on management of clandestine work in the region. Within a month, as his Iraq Operations Group was moving two CIA paramilitary teams secretly into northern Iraq, Richer attended his first meeting on Iraq and asked Tenet if it really looked like war.

"You bet your ass," Tenet said bluntly. "It's not a matter of if. It's a matter of when. This president is going to war. Make the plans. We're going."

Tenet refined some of his thoughts in discussions with John O. Brennan, one of his closest confidants. Brennan, a veteran of 22 years with the agency, had been the White House daily intelligence briefer for two years during the Clinton administration, and later served as CIA station chief in Saudi Arabia, and as Tenet's chief of staff for two years. He was now the deputy executive director at CIA headquarters.

Tenet told Brennan he believed war was coming and Bush was determined. He said he found that there was a part of Bush that might still be deliberating while some others under him, like Cheney and Wolfowitz, had absolutely decided that war was coming.

Tenet told Brennan that in his gut he didn't think invading Iraq was the right thing to do. Bush and the others were just really naive, thinking they would just be able to go into Iraq and overturn the government.

"This is a mistake," Tenet finally told Brennan.

But Tenet never conveyed these misgivings to the president. Bush had never asked him directly for his bottom-line counsel, although Tenet felt that Bush had nevertheless opened the door in their conversations to the point where Tenet could have said, "No, this is crazy, this won't work, you shouldn't do this." But Tenet never said it.

What held him back was complex. Despite his doubts, Tenet assured Bush on December 21, 2002, that the case that Saddam had weapons of mass destruction (WMD), the prime articulated reason for the looming invasion, was "a slam dunk." For Tenet, the temptation to invade was real because there was no doubt the U.S. could overthrow Saddam and totally defeat the Iraqi military with some ease. And there was all that great momentum, all the CIA and military planning, including getting a few other countries such as Great Britain to commit to action. It was hard to step back. As Tenet said once afterward, "If you get up on your toes, you can't walk away. We sucked in all of these allies—the Saudis, the Jordanians—and we just couldn't pull the plug on them. They were giving us all this sub rosa support."

Lastly there was Cheney. Was the vice president putting all his experience and surface coolness behind a strong push? Had he told Bush, "Yes, you've got to do it"? Tenet had never been in the room when that had happened, but he believed Cheney was privately pressuring Bush, arguing strongly for war as the only solution to the Saddam Hussein problem.

IN LATE SEPTEMBER 2002, Rumsfeld met with General Franks, his operations director, Air Force Major General Victor E. "Gene" Renuart Jr. and Douglas J. Feith, the Pentagon's undersecretary for policy. Feith, 49, was a protégé of Richard Perle, the former Reagan defense official who was one of the most outspoken Iraq hawks.

Rumsfeld said that Defense was better set up to run postwar Iraq than the State Department, and he believed that Defense should and would be put in charge.

Feith agreed and said he wanted his policy operation to lead the postwar effort. Over the past months, he had been attending secret interagency luncheon meetings of the deputies run by Steve Hadley. They had discussed the issues at length, and Feith had pulled together a five-inch-thick notebook outlining the discussions and the planning.

"Make a copy of this for Condi," Rumsfeld said, seeming impressed with the book. If there was war with Iraq, he stressed, he wanted to make sure that it was not another Bosnia. In Iraq he wanted the reconstruction and political issues worked out in advance. "We do not want to be in a position where the failure of somebody to do those things ties our forces down indefinitely the way they seem to be tied down in Bosnia indefinitely." Rumsfeld had been pushing to cut the number of NATO troops still serving in Bosnia, which had recently been as high as 18,000.

Feith would handle the job for Defense, Rumsfeld said. His goal was very precise: "Unity of effort and unity of leadership for the full range of reconstruction activities that need to be performed in order to say that mission is over and the troops can leave."

"Boss, did you just hear what I think I heard?" Renuart said to Franks as they left the meeting.

"What did you think you heard?" Franks inquired.

"Well," Renuart, a fighter pilot, who took notes in a book nicknamed the "Black Book of Death," said, "it sounds to me like OSD Policy"—Feith's office—"has responsibility for planning post-conflict and our responsibility is security. And we don't own the reconstruction stuff."

"That's the way I look at it too," the Central Command commander said.

"I think we just dodged a big bullet," Renuart said.

"Well you may be right," Franks said. "I've got my marching orders. The secretary wants us to focus on security."

Feith and his deputies began drafting policy guidance, establishing working groups and creating specific cells to examine issues such as energy, stability and sovereignty. Rumsfeld agreed to create a new office specifically for reconstruction and humanitarian assistance.

"You're going to be responsible for this," Feith said to Rumsfeld. "Let's get the office created."

"Yes," Rumsfeld agreed, "let's get the office created." Then he said no, then he said yes, then no again. They discussed it repeatedly. Feith spoke to Hadley, who explained that a diplomatic settlement with Saddam was still an option, so they didn't want to create a postwar office.

IN LATE SEPTEMBER, 49-year-old Army Major General James "Spider" Marks was preparing for the assignment of a lifetime: top intelligence officer for the U.S.-led forces planning to invade Iraq. For Marks it was the culmination of 27 years in the Army. Nicknamed "Spider" since his high school days as a 6-foot-1, 150-pound football player, Marks was third-generation West Point, graduating in 1975, a month after the fall of Saigon, perhaps the low point for U.S. military morale. Marks was one of only seven out of the 875 in his class to reach two-star rank, and he was determined not to screw up this critical assignment.

Still rail-thin, handsome in a youthful way, mildly dashing and totally gung ho, Marks would serve directly under the ground commander, Lieutenant General David D. McKiernan. Both men knew accurate, timely intelligence would be crucial, perhaps defining success or failure.

On August 26, Vice President Cheney had given a speech that Marks believed *must* have been cleared by U.S. intelligence. "Simply stated, there is no doubt that Saddam Hussein now has weapons of mass destruction," Cheney said. "There is no doubt that he is amassing them to use against our friends, against our allies and against us." The rhetoric was very strong, and Marks took it as an article of faith that the intelligence behind it was equally strong. Saddam had WMD.

Marks immediately realized the invading ground forces would probably come from Kuwait, the oil-rich desert country that shared a 100-mile border with Iraq and blocked most of its access to the Persian Gulf. That meant he'd be sent there probably months ahead of war, a sitting duck with the rest of the ground force generals. What better target for Saddam to hit with a preemptive chemical or biological attack? It would be an awful way to go, he thought, but it was all too possible. Odds were he would not be coming home. Marks, a Catholic, kept his fatalistic conclusions from his wife and daughters, but he went to confession and put his affairs in order.

For the eleven years since the 1991 Gulf War, the United States had been engaged in what amounted to a low-grade undeclared war to keep

Saddam in a box. U.S. warplanes enforced two no-fly zones in Iraq, where Saddam was not permitted to fly any aircraft. U.S. pilots, permitted by U.N. resolution, had entered Iraqi airspace 150,000 times in the last decade. The Iraqis had attacked hundreds of times but not a single U.S. pilot had been lost, mainly because the U.S. had unsurpassed technical intelligence. Overhead satellite photos, other imagery and extensive communications intercept operations by the National Security Agency provided an astonishing edge. If Iraqi pilots or air defense used their radios, NSA picked it up. The Iraqi skies were an open book, a "glass ball theater," in military and intelligence slang. U.S. intelligence graded its performance based on its ability to penetrate Iraq in support of the Northern and Southern Watch Operations, and gave itself an A plus.

But in studying the Iraq intelligence, Marks found that this superior technical intelligence had become a crutch—a *wait for the next satellite pass* culture. It could be invaluable in pinpointing the location, disposition, strength and movement of Saddam's forces during an invasion. The downside was that it was collection from a distance. They had almost no on-the-ground intelligence, the sort they'd need to find the WMD they were sure Saddam was hiding.

Marks arranged to meet with the top experts on Iraq and WMD at the Defense Intelligence Agency. He thought of these experts at DIA—the brainchild of Kennedy-Johnson-era Defense Secretary Robert S. McNamara and the military's premier, all-source intelligence service—as "the smart guys."

On October 4, 2002, he settled into a conference room at the Pentagon with a dozen or so DIA smart guys. There were the overhead satellite smart guy, the chemical, biological and nuclear weapons smart guys, the Middle East regional smart guys, and the overall intelligence collection systems smart guys.

What do we really know about Saddam's WMD? he asked them.

They presented him with their highly classified WMD database on Iraq, called the Weapons of Mass Destruction Master Site List (WMDMSL). It was a list of 946 locations where intelligence indicated there were production plants or storage facilities for chemical, biological or nuclear-related material in Saddam's Iraq.

The first issue, Marks wrote in his notes, would be "SSE—Sensitive Site Exploitation." What would the invading U.S. ground forces do with each WMD site? Destroy it? Test it? Guard it? Render it useless?

Who physically will be doing that? Marks asked.

"Well, we don't have their names," one of the guys answered.

"Why not?" Marks asked. "What units are doing that?"

"Oh, we've got units who do that."

"Have you notified them?"

"Of course not."

"Well, then how's this all going to come together?" Marks asked. "I hate to be a jerk here, guys, but I'm the guy who's going to be—I and about 400 to 500 guys—are going to be holding the bag on this thing. Can you throw me a bone?"

The precise details on each of the 946 suspected sites—location, type of WMD, what kind of security was there—were more important to the forces on the ground than to anyone else, including the president. Bush might be staking his political capital, but the troops were staking their lives.

The truth was that the civilian Pentagon experts in their suits, shirts and neckties didn't have much to tell Marks on these points. "We haven't done anything," one of them said. Those were operational considerations, several of the smart guys indicated, to be decided by the military commanders, not by them.

The gap between intelligence and operations doesn't exist in combat, Marks said. "The ops guy and the intel guy are as tight as Siamese twins. You are co-joined," he said, dependent on each other. In the heat of warfare, the two had to work together because everything happened instantly in real time. Survival and success depended on it.

For example, when the WMD exploitation teams would arrive at a suspected site in Iraq they were going to have to do triage, and assign priorities based on urgency and threat. There wouldn't really be a hard-and-fast line between intelligence—what they needed to know—and operations—what they needed to do.

It will be a function of experience and equipment, he explained. Does this WMD sample have to go back to the lab to be tested? Would it even be possible to get samples? Is this sample benign? Can this be bagged and marked to be examined later?

The faces of the intel smart guys seemed to say, Not my problem.

Marks looked over the WMDMSL printout. "Are they prioritized?" he asked. Was Site Number 1 more important than Site Number 946?

"Of course, General," one of the people at the table said dismissively. "Why wouldn't it be?"

"No, my point is this: Where physically is 946?" Marks asked. "Is the prioritization based on the likelihood of WMD being there?" Were these all certain sites? Some more certain than others?

No one had an answer.

He tried to dig deeper. If site Number 946 was less important than Number 1, he wanted to know why.

Again, nobody had a real answer.

Was the first site listed first because they thought it had the most WMD? Or was it because of the type of WMD—chemical, biological, nuclear or missile-related activity or another category? Was it related to the overall threat from the site? Or was it a matter of how quickly or easily Saddam could use the WMD? "How are these things racked and stacked?" Marks asked.

The experts indicated that Number 1 was by some measure more valuable.

Okay. Let's try to define valuable, Marks said.

They eventually said that 120 of the 946 were "top priority," and Marks wrote it in his notes.

"Operationally," Marks began. He stopped for a second as he looked around the table. The lack of interest in the room seemed to grow. Most of these guys have never served in uniform, he surmised. He drew a rough map on a piece of paper.

"Iraq kind of looks like this. We're probably going be down here in Kuwait," Marks said. "There are going to be a bunch of kids in Bradley Fighting Vehicles and tanks that are going to be the very first guys that run across these sites that are scattered across the country." As they crossed the border, Marks said, a hypothetical private would have many missions. "He's got to kill bad guys. He's got to protect himself. He's got to protect his buddies. He has got to run his equipment." Now they were going to give him another mission: Secure nearly a thousand suspected WMD sites.

A lot of the smart guys were rolling their eyes at him, Marks thought. Too much detail, too many practical operational issues and questions.

"The very first site might be right here, right across the border," Marks said. "But it might be Site 833. So, does he blow by it? Do you want him to stop? Is it important? I mean, there's an operational requirement, and I need you to kind of give me a sense." He added that he was not asking them to tell him what specifically the ground troops should do. That wasn't their job. "But I've got to be able to give the operators a sufficient sense of the importance and priority of that site. And just by putting it 833 on the list tells me nothing."

Marks left the meeting very disturbed. "I was shocked at the lack of detail," he said later. These were supposed to be some of the smartest, most dedicated men and women working on WMD intelligence in Iraq. The Pentagon was not going to be much help on this critical issue, he realized.

Marks dug into the underlying evidence that suggested each of the 946 sites on the Weapons of Mass Destruction Master Site List actually had WMD. It was thin. There were very old satellite images—five years or more in some cases—and some signals intelligence. These were snippets of intercepted conversations, but nothing conclusive relating to a specific site or to specific WMD. There was nothing even remotely like an intercept of an Iraqi officer saying, "The VX nerve gas is stored on the first floor of 1600 Saddam Avenue." The WMD list was all on a computer network, but if he printed out the total information on any one site file or folder, he'd get at most 15 or 20 pages, much of which was of doubtful value.

The U.S. isolation of Iraq since the Gulf War had been nearly complete, and there was no routine commerce, no interchange, no political dialogue—and thus, no real ground intelligence. Technical intelligence had been great for enforcing the no-fly zones, but it was almost useless for the mission of finding, neutralizing or destroying WMD at nearly a thousand sites around the country before it could be used.

What Marks was confronting was a decade of intelligence blindness. In fact, he realized, of the 946 sites on the WMD site list, he couldn't say with confidence that there were any weapons of mass destruction or stockpiles at a single site. Not one.

"We're on our ass," became a Marks catchphrase, something he repeated to the DIA staff and his own people in meeting after meeting. He would have to galvanize everyone. And yet he kept wondering, "Why are we the only guys doing this? I don't get it."

11

B USH WAS TO GIVE A PRIME-TIME SPEECH in Cincinnati on October 7 spelling out the case against Saddam. The CIA kept tabs on what Bush was going to say, and at one point realized that the president planned to make an alarming claim about a potential Saddam nuclear program, by charging that Iraq had been caught trying to buy uranium oxide in Africa.

"You need to take this fucking sentence out because we don't believe it," Tenet told Hadley when he read the draft. Hadley pulled the reference. Instead, Bush said, "Many people have asked how close Saddam Hussein is to developing a nuclear weapon. Well, we don't know exactly, and that's the problem." It was a modest claim that accurately reflected the National Intelligence Estimate (NIE), the collective judgment of all U.S. intelligence agencies, that had been issued five days earlier. The TOP SECRET NIE said with "moderate confidence" that "Iraq does not have a nuclear weapon or sufficient material to make one but is likely to have a weapon by 2007 to 2009."

But instead of saying a nuclear Iraq was probably five years off, the president pulled out the stops. "Facing clear evidence of peril," he warned, "we cannot wait for the final proof—the smoking gun—that could come in the form of a mushroom cloud."

IN A SECURE VIDEO CONFERENCE October 9, General Franks explained that President Bush, the war cabinet and he himself were still focused on the war plan for invading Iraq.

"The president is not fulfilled with the plan we have," Franks said. Bush was worried that Saddam and his forces would retreat to the capital and hunker down in a kind of "Fortress Baghdad," leading to prolonged urban warfare. This concern had been voiced by Rice and Card in secret war-planning meetings for months. Now the first priority was to find a strategy to counter it.

The president's second priority, Franks said, after "Fortress Baghdad," was the "WMD problem."

That was Marks's problem.

Marks called in favors as he trolled the Army's promotion lists, building up his staff until it reached 400 military officers and others from the civilian intelligence agencies. He selected as his deputy Colonel Steve Rotkoff, 47, a senior military intelligence officer with 25 years in the Army who had been two years behind Marks at West Point. Marks thought Rotkoff was one of the most gifted officers in the Army, his absolute first choice to be the number two officer on the intelligence staff.

Rotkoff was an atypical officer in some ways—a Jewish intellectual, a bookish, irreverent New Yorker with distinctive, thick, bushy eyebrows. He was also a real bulldog who knew how to get things done. Marks knew that Rotkoff was getting ready to retire from the Army. That was a bonus; he might be especially willing to break some crockery and make things happen. His initial orders to his new deputy: "You have complete authority to be strident and border-line disruptive and insubordinate."

Rotkoff decided to keep a daily war journal, and over the next six months he filled six volumes. Pressed for time on many occasions, he summarized his thoughts and emotions with three-line haiku.

One of his early observations:

> *Rumsfeld is a dick*
> *Won't flow the forces we need*
> *We will be too light.*

By the time General McKiernan moved his headquarters to Kuwait to prepare for war, during October and November 2002, Rotkoff could see that the top generals and planners weren't very focused on WMD. But Marks, Rotkoff and their staff spent time on it. As a practical matter, if Saddam launched even a small chemical or biological attack on U.S. forces as they crossed from Kuwait into Iraq, he might slow or even stop the advance.

Marks and Rotkoff together drove their staff. It became a kind of sweatshop. They made an individual target folder for each of the 946 sites, and they went to work trying to improve and update the intelligence for the main sites. This entailed requests for new satellite passes and other overhead imagery.

Air Force Lieutenant General Michael V. Hayden, the head of the National Security Agency, had ordered that $300 million to $400 million of the NSA's money be redirected to "Iraq unique" operations and targets. Most of that was for battlefield intelligence, but NSA was picking up intercepts about WMD. In Hayden's view they were collecting a massive but circumstantial amount of evidence of WMD. Marks didn't consider it "massive," just more and more snippets, and it was indeed circumstantial.

Beginning in late November 2002, when Saddam permitted the United Nations weapons inspection team headed by Swedish lawyer Hans Blix back into Iraq, Marks noticed suspicious activity in a number of new satellite photos. U.N. inspectors were seen coming in the front gate of a suspected WMD site, while Iraqis were seen taking some sort of material out the back and loading it on trucks.

Are they just a step ahead of the hounds? he wondered. Are they that lucky? How did they know the inspectors were coming to that site? He ordered his staff to see if they could track the trucks to the Syrian border.

The big problem, though, was that no one knew for sure if they were looking at WMD. They could only guess or assume that was what it was.

"I don't know if there are bicycles in there from Toys R Us," Marks lamented after looking at the trail of one truck to Syria. He repeated an old military expression about not being able to decipher the real meaning: "You're a pig looking at a watch."

It was a paradox. On the one hand, he was troubled that he still couldn't say with conviction that he could prove any particular site had WMD. On the other, he still harbored no real doubt that they were there—somewhere. The intelligence had conditioned him to expect it.

Unbeknownst to Marks, Rumsfeld was wrestling with the same worries about WMD intelligence. In a classified three-page memo dated October 15, 2002, Rumsfeld listed 29 things that could go wrong in an Iraq war. He reviewed it with the president and the NSC. In the middle, item Number 13 said, "U.S. could fail to find WMD on the ground."

He obviously had some serious doubts and I asked him about it in 2006.

"I was very worried about it," he said. "I worry about intelligence. I have to." At the same time, intelligence was the responsibility of Tenet and others. "I developed confidence over time and conviction, and I think everyone did."

Did he know about a two-star general named Spider Marks who was in charge of ground intelligence and had had doubts about WMD?

"No," Rumsfeld said. "I mean, we dealt with the combatant commander's people. I may have met him, but I don't know him."

In October Congress voted overwhelmingly to authorize war with Iraq. Three weeks later, in the midterm elections, the Republicans retained control of the House and took control of the Senate—picking up two Senate seats and eight in the House. It was exceedingly rare for a president's party to make gains in midterm elections. "How They Aced Their Midterms (And Now for the Big Tests)" was the headline on the cover of *Time* magazine, with an Oval Office photo of a smiling George W. Bush, his arm draped around a laughing Karl Rove.

At State, Armitage worried that the drive to invade Iraq had received a significant boost. Bush, he said, "really believes that his role is to change the face of the world and that attack, 9/11, did it. Combined with the '02 elections, where he became the mighty president of all the people, that's the effect of the off-year victory. He finally became the popularly elected president."

Armitage and Powell received reports from foreign leaders who met with Bush that the president was acting as if he had received validation and vindication. He was saying, "We got to seize this moment. This is an opportunity given us." Armitage thought Rice was running more and more interference for Bush. "Condi, in my view, anytime someone wasn't ready to do immediately exactly what the president wants, it was almost disloyal."

"No one knows the pressure I will put on you to get to Baghdad. You will assume risk," General Tommy Franks told his generals on December 7, remarks that Spider Marks recorded in his diary. That was the point of the plan, right there. Get to Baghdad, and fast. It echoed Rumsfeld's desire—"assume risk." The Powell Doctrine of trying to guarantee success was out. Rapid, decisive warfare was in.

Marks was still asking for help on the WMD list and site folders, and on the teams that would have to do something about the weapons during and after war. He routinely questioned the validity of using only technical methods of looking at the suspected WMD sites. He wanted to increase what he called the Fingerspitzengefühl—German for an instinctive sense and understanding—of Iraq, through human collection. But it was too late to develop human sources, and the CIA and DIA had almost none inside Iraq.

Marks tried to energize the DIA back in Washington, with little success.

"I can't get DIA to move," he told General McKiernan one day. "You need to fire me."

McKiernan wouldn't hear of it. Marks was eventually even more direct.

"Sir, I can't confirm what's inside any of these sites," he said. He amplified his concern about a particular site on the list, a suspected chemical production plant. "There is no confirming intelligence that that's what it does. It's labeled as such and it's got a bunch of signs on it that we can see from overhead imagery, and we've got some architectural designs and that's what it's designed to do. But I can't confirm that that's what it's doing today in the Year of Our Lord 2002."

"Got it," McKiernan replied. "Let's move on."

Marks took that as further reinforcement that it was up to him to solve the problem. Top military officers like Marks were trained to be can-do people. "Can't" was a word not to be uttered. He was in the solutions business, not the whining business or the excuses business. The boss was busy and had his own problems. It was almost a principle of Army leadership, and Marks developed a motto: "Don't visit your personal hell on your boss." His deputy, Colonel Rotkoff, heard it so often he recorded it in his diary as a classic Spider Marks catchphrase: "Don't share your personal hell."

MONDAY WAS ALWAYS the scariest day of the week for Colonel Rotkoff in Kuwait. Like nearly everyone else, he spent days at a time wearing his charcoal-lined chemical weapons defense jumpsuit. A nylon pouch containing a gas mask and hood was strapped to his leg for ready use. Even the lighter, more modern version of the suit, called a J-LIST, was uncomfortable and awkward. Still, he was scared half to death each time he took it off.

Monday was the one day that Rotkoff could find 15 minutes in his schedule to shower. Every time he did, he was sure that would be when

Saddam would attack with chemical or biological weapons. Saddam had fired 88 Scud missiles, with a range of several hundred miles, at American troops in the first Gulf War and 39 more at Israel in an attempt to goad that nation into the fight and fracture the U.S.-Arab coalition that existed at the time. Now, everyone expected he would attack again, only this time he would top the Scuds with chemical or biological warheads. Everyone absolutely *knew* it was coming.

Day after day, WMD scares provided inspiration for the haiku Rotkoff wrote in his diary:

> *Anthrax + smallpox*
> *Gas masks, J-Lists at all times*
> *Scary being here*

> *Yikes—SCUD exercise*
> *Mask four hours avoiding work*
> *Sweat pours down my face*

> *This is not a drill . . .*
> *Mask + chem suit on quickly*
> *Try not to panic*

That was the visceral reaction, but the continuing problem was that there was a real absence of convincing intelligence.

"They were every morning getting up and putting on their chemical suits," Rumsfeld later recalled. "Not for the heck of it, because they were worried about having their troops killed by chemical weapons. We never—none of us ever believed that they had nuclear weapons. The only real worry that we had was chemical."

THE FULL WRITTEN VERSION of the Iraq war plan, called Op Plan 1003 V, included an annex devoted to the task of WMD exploitation. That was the good news, Marks thought. The bad news was that there had never actually been a military unit assigned to the task. This was the operational problem Marks had been grappling with for months, since his first visit with the DIA "smart guys" at the Pentagon in October.

After much wrangling, Franks's Central Command agreed to assign the job to a battalion, designated the "Sensitive Site Exploitation Task Force." But a battalion was a small force of several hundred, and the lieutenant colonel in command was a relatively low-ranking officer to lead the mission, given that weapons of mass destruction were the most often cited reason for war. It seemed odd to Marks, even negligent. "There is no more important or critical mission for the nation," he wrote in his diary at the time, "& DOD keeps wire brushing us/pushing back on our requests—Incredible!"

He searched for a larger unit, and in December 2002 he worked out a solution with a general at the Army's III Corps at Fort Sill in Oklahoma.

"You've got an artillery brigade coming over here," Marks said. "We're thinking about having them leave their big guns at home and come over here to handle the WMD instead." The brigade, about 400 people strong, was commanded by a stocky colonel named Richard McPhee. It was soon rechristened the 75th Exploitation Task Force and given the job of finding the WMD once the U.S. forces entered Iraq. It was what the military called a "field expedient solution," making do with what they had. Finally, at least, somebody was assigned to the WMD job.

AT THE PENTAGON, on Thursday, December 5, 2002, in the middle of the most intense invasion planning for Iraq, Steve Herbits walked into Rumsfeld's office.

"You're not going to be happy with what I'm going to tell you," he said, "but you are in the unique position of being the sole person who could lose the president's reelection for him if you don't get something straightened out."

Rumsfeld flushed.

Herbits continued. "Now that I've got your attention, you have got to focus on the post-Iraq planning. It is so screwed up. We will not be able to win the peace."

Later I asked Rumsfeld if he recalled the conversation with Herbits. "No," Rumsfeld said. "Doesn't mean it didn't happen."

Rumsfeld was under instructions from President Bush to oversee a massive deployment of hundreds of thousands of U.S. forces to the region around Iraq without telegraphing to the world and Saddam Hussein that war was inevitable. The president was still engaged in United Nations diplomacy. So Rumsfeld personally took charge of the mobilization and deployment system called the TPFDD (pronounced TIP-fid) for Time-Phased Force and Deployment Data. He believed he had lifted a big rock and found a system that was totally screwed up. Soon he was personally deciding which units would deploy and when. It was an extraordinary degree of micromanagement that frustrated and enraged the military.

Herbits warned Rumsfeld that policy undersecretary Feith was screwing up. The fighting between State and Defense was so bad that interagency meetings were at times little more than shouting matches. Postwar planning was so fiercely off track that it required the secretary's personal intervention.

Rumsfeld didn't say much but soon called one of his surprise Saturday meetings with Feith and others involved.

"What's going on here?" he asked. "We've got to get this on track."

IN EARLY JANUARY 2003, Marine Commandant General Jones was alone with Rumsfeld in his office. Jones had declined to be interviewed for the JCS chairmanship 18 months earlier, but Rumsfeld was now giving him another important four-star post—the dual assignment of both NATO supreme allied commander and U.S. combatant commander for Europe.

Rumsfeld's ruminations turned to life in Iraq after the battle. Saddam Hussein had effectively and brutally sealed off the country. What was it like there? What were the people really thinking and doing? It was hard, Rumsfeld mused to Jones, to find anyone anywhere who really knew something about Iraq, who knew facts.

"I worked for someone who is a hero in Kurdistan," Jones said, referring to the northern Iraqi region. "Jay Garner."

"I know him!" Rumsfeld said, bolting up at the mention of Garner's name. Garner had worked on Rumsfeld's space commission during the Clinton administration.

Garner, a retired three-star Army general, had led Operation Provide Comfort after the 1991 Gulf War, coming to the rescue of thousands of ethnic Kurds in northern Iraq. Over the years Provide Comfort had become the gold standard of military humanitarian missions.

Jones explained that as a colonel, he had commanded the contingent of 2,200 Marines assigned to Provide Comfort. Garner deserved the lion's share of the credit for the operation's success, he said, setting up critical water purification systems and providing other humanitarian assistance. Overall, Garner was in charge of a U.S.-led force of 20,000 troops who systematically drove Saddam's forces from northern Iraq. Finally, one Sunday morning in 1991, Colin Powell, then chairman of the JCS, had drawn a line on a map establishing a southern Kurdistan border.

After Provide Comfort, the Kurds in northern Iraq set up a semiautonomous enclave. They were regularly threatened by Saddam, but they
were also a real thorn in his side and a conspicuous exception to his iron
rule.

Provide Comfort was considered a great success for another important reason: Garner and the U.S.-led forces had done their job and come
home in a matter of months.

GARNER'S NAME lodged in Rumsfeld's mind. The more he thought
about it, the more sense it made. He told Feith he had decided on Garner
to head a postwar office.

On Thursday, January 9, Garner, then the head of a division of L-3, a
multibillion-dollar defense contractor specializing in high-technology
surveillance, intelligence and reconnaissance equipment, was in New
York for a company meeting. He picked up an incoming call on his cell
phone from Feith's policy office at the Pentagon.

"We want to talk to you. Can you come over?" asked Ron Yaggi, an Air
Force one-star general who was Feith's military assistant.

What do you want to talk about? Garner asked.

"It's a little sensitive on the phone," Yaggi said.

"Look, General," Garner said a little irritably. "This is the only way
we're going to talk about it." Age 64, an intense, 5-foot-7 fireplug of a
man, Garner had retired from the Army half a dozen years earlier after 33
years of service, including two tours in Vietnam.

"We're putting together an organization to do some postwar work.
I'm sure you know where it is," Yaggi explained, trying to be cryptic on
the nonsecure phone line. "We'd like for you to run that, at least to put it
together."

Yaggi explained that Garner would set the organization up, but he
might not go with it into Iraq after combat operations. Garner got the
impression that he might not remain the senior civilian once things really got going.

"I probably can't do this," Garner said. "I'm running a company with
over 1,000 people in it and they depend on me and I just can't take off
like that."

THE FOLLOWING MONDAY, January 13, Feith called Garner. "The secretary of defense said to tell you that if you turn this job down you have to
come in and personally explain it."

Neither man had to state the obvious: It would be almost unthinkable for someone in Garner's business position, dependent on Pentagon contracts, to refuse the secretary of defense. Retired officers working for major defense contractors were in a kind of unofficial standby reserve for special assignments. To no one's astonishment, the CEO of L-3 found it possible to grant a leave of absence.

"By the end of June, I'll be home," Garner promised Connie, his wife of more than 40 years. "I'll be home for our Fourth of July cookout." *

THAT SAME DAY, January 13, President Bush summoned Secretary of State Colin Powell for a 12-minute Oval Office meeting to say he had decided on war with Iraq.

"You're sure?" asked Powell.

Bush said he was.

"You understand the consequences," Powell offered in a half question. For nearly six months, Powell had been hammering on the theme of the complexity of governing Iraq after the war. "You know that you're going to be owning this place?"

Bush said he realized that.

"Are you with me on this?" the president asked his secretary of state. "I think I have to do this. I want you with me."

"I'm with you, Mr. President," Powell replied.

In case there was any doubt—and there really couldn't be any for Powell, the good, obedient soldier—the president explicitly told the former chairman of the Joint Chiefs: "Time to put your war uniform on."

The president very reluctantly confirmed to me that he had asked Powell directly for his support but added testily a rather obvious point. "I didn't need his permission."

THE DIRECTOR OF MIDDLE EAST AFFAIRS on the National Security Council staff, Elliott Abrams, was one of the most controversial, driven, hard-line conservatives. During the Reagan administration he had been

---

* From documents, talking points, chronologies, letters, transcripts, his personal notes and the notes of his executive assistant, Garner's role is presented here in detail and at length because he was the first person given full-time responsibility for postwar Iraq. This is the most complete, documented account of his experience yet available, as he decided not to write his own book or speak to others at such length. Garner was interviewed extensively on the record on September 19, 2005, October 16, 2005, December 13, 2005, and April 22, 2006. Members of his postwar planning office were also interviewed and some supplied additional documents and notes.

the assistant secretary of state and had avidly and energetically supported the covert CIA war in Nicaragua. He pled guilty to withholding
information from Congress in the Iran-contra affair. Bush senior par-
doned him in 1992.

Rice had brought Abrams to the NSC, where he was a workhorse. He
was assigned the humanitarian relief account for Iraq. For months
Abrams had been working with General Franks's Central Command,
drawing up elaborate no-strike lists and trying to keep Iraqi hospitals,
water plants and electrical grids from being bombed when the war
started.

On January 15, two days after Bush informed Powell it would be war,
the president met with the NSC for a secret Abrams presentation on the
plans for humanitarian relief. Two months before the war would start,
the president received his first major briefing on postwar plans.

War might displace two million Iraqis, Abrams said. The U.S. was
stockpiling food, tents and water. Money had to be moved quietly to
United Nations agencies and other nongovernmental organizations
(NGOs) so they would be ready.

Abrams said that the precise number of refugees and displaced per-
sons would be determined by interethnic tensions among the Kurds,
Shiites and Sunnis, the level of violence and reprisals, and weapons of
mass destruction—whether they were used or even if people just
thought they might be. One PowerPoint slide explained how Saddam
might blow up dams and flood parts of the country. In all it was not a
pretty picture, a disturbing forecast for possibly one of the worst humanitarian crises of recent times.

"This is an opportunity to change the image of the United States,"
Bush told the war cabinet. He saw a public relations opportunity. "We
need to make the most of these humanitarian aid efforts in our public
diplomacy. I want to build surge capability." He began issuing orders. "I
want loaded ships ready to provide food and relief supplies so we can go
in very promptly." Then he added, "There are a lot of things that could go
wrong, but not for want of planning."

GARNER, WHO WAS ABOUT to take over the postwar humanitarian mission, had not been invited to Abrams's presentation. The next day, he sat
with both Rumsfeld and Feith at a little table in Rumsfeld's office.

"Look, Jay," Rumsfeld began, "regardless of what you're told, there's
been an awful lot of planning throughout the government for this." But

it had all been done in the "vertical stovepipe" of each of the federal agencies, including the Defense Department. "I recommend that you try to horizontally connect the plans and find out what the problems are and work on those problems and anything else you find."

Feith was very upset with the aftermath of the Afghanistan War of 2001–02. He thought the State Department—which he at times called "the Department of Nice"—had botched it by not stabilizing the country fast enough. He wanted the Pentagon to have control of postwar Iraq until State could stand up an embassy. Until then, State would be subordinate to Defense.

Garner was worried about the lack of time. In World War II, Garner told Rumsfeld, the United States had started planning for postwar Europe years before the war ended. "You're taking on this problem to solve what will need a solution in somewhere between five and 10 weeks."

"I know," Rumsfeld said. "We'll get somewhere. We'll get somewhere on this. Just maximize the time available."

FRANK MILLER, a 22-year veteran of the Pentagon bureaucracy who had served under seven secretaries of defense in some of the most sensitive and senior civilian positions, was now working for Rice as the NSC's senior director for defense. He headed the Executive Steering Group, which was to coordinate the Iraq issues among the different federal agencies. Heavyset with glasses, Miller was the kind of serious, invisible middle manager who can make an organization work, the equivalent of a timing belt in an automobile engine: vital, but barely noticed until gone.

By the start of 2003, Miller felt that Rumsfeld had made his job almost impossible. There was constant tension between the NSC and Rumsfeld's Pentagon, and Rumsfeld went to extra lengths to keep control of information. Often, when Rumsfeld came to the White House with General Franks to brief the president and the NSC and some of the staff on the Iraq invasion plans, he would see that the slides and handouts were distributed just before the meeting, and taken back immediately after. Sometimes there would be a handout for the president with 140 pages, and the lesser beings like Miller would be allowed to see only 40 of them. On one occasion, Rumsfeld came for a meeting without enough briefing packets for all the principals, so Rice wound up looking on with the person next to her. It was all so petty. Miller and a few others allowed in the meeting would scramble, trying furiously to write down the important points.

Sometimes, Rumsfeld would point across the room in the middle of a briefing. "People shouldn't be taking notes," he scolded. "People should not be taking notes in here."

It was absolutely crazy, Miller thought. How could he advise Rice and Hadley or the president if he couldn't keep notes on information from the Pentagon? Miller had handled the most sensitive nuclear war plans issues for Cheney when he was defense secretary, and had been awarded the Defense Department's highest civilian award, the Defense Distinguished Civilian Service Medal, five times. He was deeply insulted that Rumsfeld would treat him and others from the NSC staff like third-class citizens of dubious loyalty, sometimes not even acknowledging their presence. Besides, he thought, it was self-defeating. Weren't they all on the same side?

When the generals came over to the White House with him, Rumsfeld spoke first, introducing everyone, and explaining what they were going to talk about. Miller thought it sounded unnecessarily self-centered, as if Rumsfeld were the conductor leading his orchestra. It was worse for General Myers. Miller and Myers were longtime friends, and Miller could see his friend was suffering.

Miller was also de facto chief of staff for the NSC deputies committee, which included the number two officials such as Wolfowitz, Armitage and McLaughlin. But there had been such chaos that he also had a weekly offline meeting with Card, Rice, Hadley and Vice President Cheney's chief of staff, I. Lewis "Scooter" Libby, to blow the whistle on the Pentagon and get them to nudge Rumsfeld. With the difficulties in getting information, Rice's orders to Miller were to work around it. If you can't do it through the front channels, call someone you know, and use the back channel. Miller thrived on his contacts in the Pentagon and among deployed forces. During his Pentagon years, Miller had known lots of officers who now wore three and four stars, and he counted many among his friends.

Get it done any way, Rice ordered regularly. "Fix it."

Incredibly Rice found that Rumsfeld at times would not return her phone calls when she had questions about war planning or troop deployments. She complained to Rumsfeld, who reminded her that the chain of command did not include the national security adviser.

Rice complained to the president.

Bush's response was to try to be playful with Rumsfeld.

"I know you won't talk to Condi," Bush once teased Rumsfeld, "but you've got to talk to her."

Card was astonished.

The whole scene would have been comic, Miller thought, if the issues hadn't involved war, life and death.

12

HADLEY HAD BEEN WORKING for several months on the transition of power in post-Saddam Iraq. There had been a lot of talk about making General Franks the proconsul for Iraq, and having everybody work for him. But the drawback was that it would put an occupation face on the U.S. presence. They didn't need a General MacArthur; they needed a civilian face for the leadership. Rice was appalled at the idea that they'd tell the Iraqis that their new president was going to be Tommy Franks. "Create a MacArthur?" she asked. She knew it wouldn't be tolerated by Bush or the Iraqis.

But how to structure things, then? Hadley knew that Rumsfeld—and, of course, Feith—thought postwar Afghanistan was a failure. Rumsfeld would say that they had failed because they broke up responsibility for the postwar period in Afghanistan by parceling it out to individual countries. Germany was supposed to do police training. Italy was supposed to do the judiciary. Even within the U.S. government, they had parceled things out—State had its responsibilities, Treasury had other responsibilities—and the result was that Afghanistan was nobody's first priority.

It was out of that experience, Hadley felt, that the idea of Garner's fledgling team had been born. The military term for postwar operations was Phase IV—"stability operations"—but the president wanted more than just stability in postwar Iraq. He wanted democracy, so Hadley pushed for a comprehensive postwar plan covering everything.

The State Department had been working for a year on what was called the "Future of Iraq" project—thousands of pages of reports and recommendations on government, oil, justice and agriculture. Despite this effort, and contrary to his later assertions, Powell agreed that it was logical to give postwar responsibility to Defense. Rumsfeld would have the tens of thousands of troops on the ground, the money and resources. Powell, the military man, was instinctively drawn to a plan that respected the principle of unity of command. There had to be somebody— one somebody—ultimately in charge. It had to go to Defense. To Powell this was not out of the ordinary. It was what had been done after World War II in Germany and Japan.

Hadley, the NSC staff and Feith had about a week to prepare a legal document laying out the Defense Department's authority.

On January 20, 2003, President Bush signed a secret National Security Presidential Directive, NSPD-24. The subject: setting up an "Iraq Postwar Planning Office" within the Defense Department.

Garner didn't have any input. A few days later when he went to work in a Pentagon office near Rumsfeld's, he read the four-page document, which was classified SECRET. It took his breath away.

"If it should become necessary for a U.S.-led military coalition to liberate Iraq," the directive began, "the United States will want to be in a position to help meet the humanitarian, reconstruction, and administration challenges facing the country in the immediate aftermath of the combat operations. The immediate responsibility will fall on U.S. Central Command; overall success, however, will require a national effort."

The new postwar office, Garner's office, would have responsibility for "detailed planning across the spectrum of issues that the United States Government would face with respect to the postwar administration of Iraq." Included among these were all the security, economic and political issues.* Garner had thought he'd been recruited to play the role of a glorified chief of staff, but the presidential directive now gave him responsibility for all the tasks normally run by national, state and local governments in post-Saddam Iraq.

The directive ordered that 10 federal agencies—everything from the CIA and the State Department to the Agriculture and Education Depart-

---

* The list included: (a) Assisting with humanitarian relief; (b) Dismantling weapons of mass destruction; (c) Defeating and exploiting terrorist networks; (d) Protecting natural resources and infrastructure; (e) Facilitating the country's reconstruction and protection of its infrastructure and economy; (f) Assisting with the reestablishment of key civilian services, such as food supply, water, electricity and health care; (g) Reshaping the Iraqi military; (h) Reshaping the other internal security institutions; and (i) Supporting the transition to Iraqi-led authority over time.

ments—begin detailing experts to his office. They had to be sufficiently high-ranking—colonels, one-star generals and the highest levels of career civilian officials—to have the clout necessary to "coordinate issues throughout their agencies when required."

In the event of war, the directive stated, "the Planning Office shall be deployed to Iraq to form the nucleus of the administrative apparatus that will assist in administering Iraq for a limited period of time."

GARNER WENT TO SEE RUMSFELD after he'd had some time to absorb the NSPD.

"Here's what I think we have to have," he said. They needed people who would coordinate efforts in three large areas: reconstruction, civil administration and humanitarian affairs. Then they needed an operations group—something almost totally military—that would handle logistics: food, housing, physical security and transportation. Finally, they should divide the country into three divisions—a northern team, a southern team and a central team covering Baghdad and its outskirts.

"Do you think you can live with this?" Garner asked. Rumsfeld agreed, although Garner could see his mind was on the upcoming invasion, not the aftermath.

Garner found himself waking up at 2 A.M., dictating to-do lists. He realized he had been given an impossible task but the military man's can-do attitude prevailed over doubt. "I thought this was going to be superhard," he told me later. But, he added, "I never failed at anything."

ON SATURDAY NIGHT, January 25, 2003, President Bush attended the 90th annual Alfalfa Club dinner, an old-world, black-tie ritual named after the plant species that would do anything for a drink. The dinner, held at the Capital Hilton Hotel three blocks north of the White House, was a gathering of hundreds of the usual suspects from the top of the political and business worlds, including the president's mother and father.

In brief remarks, President Bush told the audience that his mother had warned him not to joke about U.N. weapons inspectors in Iraq, and not to say anything about North Korea.

"So I finally said, 'Well, why don't you just give the darn speech?' So ladies and gentleman, I give you my mother."

Barbara Bush, the Silver Fox, as her husband called her, then 77, took the floor. "People never believe this, but he was the perfect child," she said. "He'd put on his cowboy outfit and . . . entertain himself for hours fighting the bad guys, or as he called them, 'The Axis of Evil.' " Bush had memorably referred to Iran, Iraq and North Korea as an "Axis of Evil" in his 2002 State of the Union speech.

"I'll never forget the paper he wrote in fourth grade where he explained that in 1519 Ferdinand Magellan set out 'to circumcise the world.' " She got a standing ovation.

Later, mingling in the large crowd, the former first lady reached out to an old family friend, David L. Boren, the centrist former Democratic senator from Oklahoma who had been the chairman of the Select Committee on Intelligence during the presidency of George H. W. Bush. Boren was now the president of the University of Oklahoma but he was still plugged into Washington, not least through George Tenet at the CIA, who had worked for Boren on the Intelligence Committee. Tenet had impressed Boren greatly, and Boren became his patron, recommending him to President Clinton in 1992 and again to George W. Bush in early 2001.

Boren and the elder George Bush had known each other for decades and were close friends.

"You always told me the truth," Barbara Bush opened, drawing Boren aside for a private chat.

"Yes, ma'am," Boren replied.

"Will you tell me the truth now?"

"Certainly."

"Are we right to be worried about this Iraq thing?"

"Yes. I'm very worried."

"Do you think it's a mistake?"

"Yes, ma'am," Boren replied. "I think it's a huge mistake if we go in right now, this way."

"Well, his father is certainly worried and is losing sleep over it. He's up at night worried."

"Why doesn't he talk to him?"

"He doesn't think he should unless he's asked," Barbara Bush said. It was the father-son distance, she said, and he didn't think he should volunteer.

"Well," Boren responded, "I understand the feeling of a father but he's a former president of the United States and an expert in this area."

Barbara Bush shook her head solemnly, almost woefully.

Later, Boren greeted Bush senior.

"Do you ever see our mutual friend, Colin?" the former president asked.

"Just sometimes."

"Be sure to tell him I sure think he's doing a good job."

Both men knew Powell was the reluctant warrior, trying to solve the Iraq problem with diplomacy.

Yes, Mr. President, Boren said. "I certainly will and I certainly think he is too."

LIEUTENANT GENERAL JOHN ABIZAID, General Franks's deputy, was the U.S. military's senior Middle East expert. A member of the 1973 West Point class that just missed Vietnam, Abizaid, whose combat experience in Grenada was dramatized in the 1986 Clint Eastwood movie, *Heartbreak Ridge,* had done postgraduate sabbaticals at Harvard and the University of Jordan in Amman. He had learned Arabic, and his first visit to Iraq had been in the late 1970s.

As director of the Joint Staff succeeding Vice Admiral Fry in 2001–02, Abizaid had felt the full blast of Rumsfeld's impatience, and often he just had to take the ass chewing. "Sometimes he was nice about it, sometimes he wasn't nice about it," Abizaid told a colleague. "I admire the man greatly even though I don't necessarily like him. . . . He's got a weakness in wanting to have his hands around everything. Okay?"

In early 2003, Abizaid was chatting informally with Spider Marks at the U.S. base in the Kuwaiti desert. The subject turned to the WMD master site list.

"What do you think, Spider?" Abizaid asked. He put his arm around the ground forces intelligence chief's shoulders. "What do you really think about these weapons of mass destruction sites?"

"Sir, I don't give a shit," Marks said. It was a flippant reply to the higher-ranking general, but Marks had known Abizaid since they were both cadets at West Point, and sensed he wanted an honest opinion. "Whether it's there or not—and I need to tell you, I can't confirm it's there—but whether it's there or not I still have to do something with that site. I'm going to have to put American men and women at risk to get in there and do something with that site."

It was a stark reframing of the problem. With neither the time nor the resources to figure out with confidence whether there really were any WMD at the 946 sites on the list, Marks had to operate on the presumption that they were there. For the pragmatist generals on the ground who were poised to launch a war over Saddam's alleged WMD, ironclad proof that the weapons were there was getting less and less relevant.

• • •

IN 1991, WHEN ABIZAID was a lieutenant colonel, he had commanded an infantry battalion under Garner during Operation Provide Comfort. Garner thought that Abizaid knew both the military mind and the Arab mind so well that he called him early for advice. He took notes on what his former subordinate said. *"What we've got to do is provide an opportunity for the Iraqi army to emerge with some honor."* The army was largely Sunni and they couldn't be allowed to feel they were losing everything.

Later, in an interview, Rumsfeld said he agreed with Abizaid's approach. "He felt that way about the Sunnis, that we're losing control of the country, and constantly was looking to see that decisions" were "fair and representative of them."

Garner agreed. The idea was to use the defeated Iraqi army for reconstruction, from rebuilding bridges to handling border and building security. Keep them busy. An idle army would be trouble.

Abizaid warned him that the hard part would come after they defeated the Iraqi army. In the aftermath, Abizaid said, "There's going to be a lot of terrorism. There's going to be a lot of things we have to put up with—disgruntled people, pockets of resistance and guerrilla activity."

NEAR THE END OF JANUARY, Garner and his chief of staff, fellow retired three-star Army General Jared Bates, met with General Franks at the Pentagon. The three men were contemporaries. All had served as battalion commanders in Germany in the 1980s. They agreed it made sense for Garner and Franks both to report directly to Rumsfeld.

"You and I both work for the same boss," Franks told Garner, adding that he was concerned about the National Security Council process where the various departments and agencies tried to hammer out a consensus. "What you've got to do is keep the interagency off my back for a while," Franks said, "but keep them wired together where they're not destructive." He promised that after the major combat was over he would get Garner and his team into Iraq. But he offered a sobering assessment. "I don't think you guys will be in there before about 60 to 90 days." Both Garner and Bates felt this was way, way too long to wait, but neither said anything.

On January 28, Garner met with Zalmay M. Khalilzad, the NSC's senior director for the Gulf region, in the Eisenhower Executive Office Building next to the White House. Khalilzad had been born and raised in

Afghanistan and had a Ph.D. from the University of Chicago. He was considered a neoconservative, having worked for Wolfowitz in the Reagan and Bush senior administrations.

"We need to form an advisory group of wise men who advise us on what needs to be done in order to turn the running of the Iraqi government over to the Iraqi people," Khalilzad told him. From all his conversations with everyone else so far, Garner had the strong impression that the U.S. plan was to set up a provisional government. Khalilzad was the first in the administration who was basically saying to him: No, we don't need one. What we need to do is get the Iraqis governing themselves as fast as possible.

"I agree with you," Garner said. He was encouraged by the conversation, as it squared with his idea of rapidly turning over power directly to Iraqis. Here was an ally.

IN THE FIRST FULL WEEK of February 2003, Garner and Bates flew to Doha, Qatar, where Central Command was headquartered, to meet at greater length with Franks and Abizaid. This was Army old-home week for all. Bates felt particularly close to Abizaid. He'd been his superior in the 75th Ranger Regiment, serving as second in command of a Ranger battalion when Abizaid was a relatively young lieutenant in the same unit. Colonels and majors are the mentors to captains and lieutenants in the Army, and a former senior officer has enduring status in the military club.

Franks routinely denounced Doug Feith as the "dumbest bastard, dumbest motherfucker on the face of the earth." He told Garner and Bates, "I'm very comfortable with you two being in charge." Again, he repeated that he wanted them to keep Washington off his back. "We understand trucks and ROWPUs," he said, referring to the Reverse Osmosis Water Purification Units, which could suck polluted water from a river and spew out thousands of gallons of fresh water. Franks was focused on the basic humanitarian issues.

Bates saw that Abizaid understood precisely what the hard part would be. The Army Arabist was focused on Iraq after the war—what had to be done and how quickly it had to be done.

A government had to be put in place, Abizaid said. "We've got to get an Iraqi face on it. It's got to be a multiethnic face." A new government had to involve all Iraqis, not just Sunnis, Shiites and Kurds, but tribes and factions, he explained. Iraqis don't like us, he said, and they are not going to like us in their country. Bates appreciated the fact that Abizaid did not want to reduce the problem to a simple bumper sticker.

But Abizaid expressed unhappiness with the way Washington was thinking its way through the postwar period. One rumbling he kept hearing was how much the Pentagon did not like Saddam's Baath Party. Fair enough. But if someone in Saddam's Iraq wanted a decent job, especially in government, that person almost had to be a member of the Baath Party. The United States, he said, was going to need Baath Party members to be involved in a new government.

AT A MEETING WITH ABIZAID and many senior staffers at the Central Command headquarters in Qatar that week, Garner explained that he planned to follow right behind the combat units as they moved into Iraq.

Oh, really? thought one of the staff officers, Colonel Carol Stewart, the head of Central Command's intelligence plans division. She wondered whether Garner understood that the war plan didn't include taking and holding cities. We're not planning on taking Basra and Nasiriyah. We're going straight to Baghdad.

"Who's providing security in Iraq?" Stewart asked. Garner said he expected the Iraqi police would still be on the job. That didn't sound right at all to Stewart, but she held her words since there were so many higher-ranking officers in the room.

Over the previous month or so, Stewart's intelligence plans division had tried to project how many troops would be needed to accomplish a peacekeeping mission in Iraq, based on the Army's experience in Bosnia and Kosovo. Their estimate was 450,000. But nobody was thinking about troop levels that high, so they worked through some other options. What if, instead of trying to occupy the entire country, they instead focused on the key Iraqi cities? On the low end, they concluded, if the situation in Iraq awaiting American forces was completely peaceful, with the total consent of the Iraqis to an American occupation, they would need at least 60,000 troops. At the other extreme, with lots of opposition and fighting among the Iraqi ethnic groups, an estimated 180,000 to 200,000 troops would be required to secure just the 26 or 27 most important cities.

Later that day, in a smaller meeting with Garner and other senior officers, Stewart spoke a little more freely. The Central Command intelligence estimate said there would be no Iraqi police on the job once the U.S. passed through, she stressed.

"What do you mean, no police?" one of the generals asked.

"It's like Panama," she replied, referring to the 1989 U.S. invasion of that country with some 24,000 troops. When the Americans had toppled the government and the local army, the police force had ceased to exist. In Iraq, the same thing was likely to happen.

She turned to Garner. "You just told us that you'd follow the combat forces. That is not a good idea."

There was more difficult news. One officer pointed out that if they wanted to keep the police and other civil servants on the job after the invasion, somebody had to come up with a way to keep paying them.

Garner turned to Bates. "We're going to have to go back to D.C. and get a checkbook," he said.

BATES KEPT IN TOUCH with Abizaid in the coming months and they had more than a handful of meetings. Abizaid continued to express dismay about Washington. It was more than the field man expressing the classic gripe about headquarters. After one formal meeting, Bates and Abizaid talked as old friends. "You know," Abizaid said, "these bastards in Washington have got no idea what they're doing, and I think I'm going to retire. I don't want any more part of this."

13

VICE PRESIDENT CHENEY was seized with what he thought was a connection between Saddam and al Qaeda, but the CIA disagreed. Tenet and his people had gone over the intelligence as completely as they could. There was no proof, he said plainly. True, a Jordanian named Abu Musab al-Zarqawi, who had strong al Qaeda ties, was involved in various terrorist activities inside Iraq. He had been given sanctuary there by the Saddam regime. But there was no evidence to show that Saddam himself, someone on his behalf, or someone in the Iraqi intelligence or security services was involved with Zarqawi.

"I can't take you to authority, direction and control," Tenet said. That was the high standard that had to be met to make a case for a Saddam–al Qaeda link.

Powell was set to go before the United Nations on February 5, 2003, to make the WMD intelligence case for war, and Cheney wanted him to look at the argument his chief of staff, Scooter Libby, had assembled charging a link between Saddam and al Qaeda. The case included an allegation that Mohammed Atta, the leader of the 9/11 attacks, had met in Prague with an Iraqi intelligence officer as many as four times. Tenet's CIA had chased down some indications about one or two meetings, but nothing had been confirmed. In the end they had concluded there was no evidence of even a single meeting.

Powell thought the Atta link didn't exist and he refused to include it in his speech. He also toned down the references to Zarqawi in his forthcoming U.N. speech. He planned to talk only about the potential for an Iraq–al Qaeda link.

Spider Marks's deputy, Colonel Rotkoff, watched on TV from the Kuwaiti desert on February 5 as Powell addressed the U.N. Despite his firsthand knowledge of the state of the WMDMSL target folders, Rotkoff hadn't really doubted that Saddam had the prohibited weapons. Seeing Powell, the retired four-star who was widely respected in the military, put his credibility on the line and make the case only added to Rotkoff's conviction. They had everything but ironclad evidence.

Every Sunday in Kuwait, as they waited for war, Rotkoff organized informal, invitation-only gatherings for the smartest officers in Spider Marks's intelligence shop. These meetings, which soon took on the nickname "Sunday Afternoon Prayer Sessions," were relaxed working sessions where they'd scrounge pizza and near beer and try to encourage a freewheeling, informal discussion with fresh ideas. Spider Marks and the other generals were never invited so that the officers would not be afraid of taking a chance, thinking out loud or saying something stupid in front of their bosses.

One Sunday in early 2003, Colonel Steve Peterson, a brainy Army officer with a reputation for creative thinking, asked Rotkoff if he could lead a Prayer Session.

"Saddam Hussein's 'Black Hawk Down' Strategy," Peterson's Power-Point presentation began. The reference was to Mark Bowden's celebrated book *Black Hawk Down* about the 1993 Somalia debacle when 18 U.S. servicemen were killed in close-encounter urban warfare, leading President Clinton to withdraw U.S. troops. Somalia had come to symbolize America's apparent unwillingness to incur casualties.

Peterson proposed that their operating premise about Saddam's strategy of retreat to a Fortress Baghdad might be all wrong. What if Saddam instead planned to have his units melt away, only to resurface periodically and randomly attack U.S. forces, creating a long-term insurgency? Saddam would have to know that U.S. forces had far superior equipment, men and tactics. Eventually they would break through a Fortress Baghdad. But what if Saddam got smart, and saw that his better strategy was a campaign of small, sophisticated attacks by Iraqis—a kind of continuous, random, urban terrorism? That way U.S. forces would have to contend with unending violence, with little knowledge of who was carrying it out, or where or when they might strike.

Peterson said his hypothesis derived from the following:

First, some U.S. intelligence showed that Saddam had commissioned an Arabic translation of *Black Hawk Down* and issued copies to his senior officers. We've always assumed this was supposed to buck up his senior leaders' morale, Peterson said, to show that if you kill a few Americans, the United States will go home. But what if the real lesson Saddam takes from *Black Hawk Down* is that insurgents can have local tactical successes against a far superior military force?

Second, in October 2002, Saddam had opened Iraq's prisons, freeing tens of thousands of inmates—both political prisoners and common criminals. What if the idea was that they'd form bands of troublemakers or be individual agents of disruption?

Third, there was evidence of widespread conventional weapons caches all over Iraq—firearms and explosives, the types of weapons that would be especially useful to insurgents.

Fourth, Saddam's Baath Party organization in each town somewhat resembled the classic Communist cell structure, built on loose, informal and personal relationships quite effective for communications in guerrilla insurgencies.

Add it all up, Peterson said, and a logical strategy for Saddam might be to run and hide, and use the Baathist cell structure to develop an insurgent army that would have weapons and explosives for a prolonged fight until the Americans grew exhausted and lost their political will.

Peterson's theory was radical. It flew in the face of all the war planning predicated on a quick defeat of Saddam's army. Rotkoff recognized that it took a lot of confidence to push a contrary possibility, especially this late in the planning game. Everyone else in the room at the Prayer Session seemed to think it was not very feasible. The "Black Hawk Down Strategy" was just another theory.

ON FEBRUARY 14, the president met with the NSC and Franks. A question arose about protecting the Iraqi oil wells during and after the invasion.

"How do you determine if you keep local policemen?" the president asked.

Franks was reassuring. According to the notes of one person at the NSC meeting, the general told Bush, "I have created lord mayors for each Iraqi city. I have the forces in place to do this tomorrow." The implication was that he had Iraqis ready to run the police.

• • •

GARNER SPOKE WITH Lieutenant General George Casey, the director of the Joint Staff, to request 94 people for his postwar operations. In 2004–06, as a four-star, Casey would be the commander of U.S. forces in Iraq.

"That's a lot of people," Casey said. "Let me look at it."

Garner and his chief of staff, Bates, pressed Casey.

"Look, George," Bates said. "Time's running out on us. We have to have these people. Have you requisitioned them?"

"No," Casey replied. "I haven't done that because you guys are trying to convince me this is a 24/7 operation and I don't believe it."

"George," Garner said. "You're out of your mind. You don't think this is 24/7?"

"No," Casey replied.

Garner called Casey again. "Hey, George. This is hardball time now." He proposed a meeting in Rumsfeld's office at 5 P.M. that day. "We'll battle this out in front of him, because I've got to have these people."

About an hour later, the head of personnel for the Joint Staff called Garner. "How many people do you need?"

Garner, with responsibility for all of postwar Iraq, the most important matter being undertaken by the U.S. government, was essentially being forced to assemble a pickup team of several hundred and go beg, cajole and threaten to get his players.

IN 2006, I MENTIONED to Rumsfeld that I thought "for some reason the government assigned a pickup team the most important thing that they were doing," and asked, "Is that fair?"

"Oh, I wouldn't think so," he said, noting that many talented people volunteered, went to Iraq, and did the tough jobs. "You can be pejorative and say it's a pickup team. But it wasn't a pickup team at all." He suggested that I would be embarrassed in history if I drew such a comparison. "As your old friend says," he added, attempting to imitate Nixon's voice, "That would be wrong."

GARNER ALSO RECRUITED Gordon Rudd, a retired Army colonel who had been the official military historian for Provide Comfort in 1991. Rudd had a Ph.D. in history and lived near the Marine Corps Base at Quantico, Virginia, where he was a professor at the command and staff college. Working for Garner, he would hit the road about 5 A.M. each day to beat the snarled Virginia traffic to the Pentagon, work as many as 14 hours a day, and basically let the assignment take over his life.

"Gordon," Garner called out to him in a Pentagon hallway. "Write me a paper on what we should do with the Iraqi army."

Rudd took a day, went to the library, and read everything he could find about what the U.S. had done with the German and Japanese armies at the end of World War II. He also researched how the U.S. had used its own military during the New Deal, developing things such as the Civilian Conservation Corps. He wrote a paper theorizing that if the Iraqi army had armor and artillery units, it must also have engineering and maintenance units. That meant it must have military schools—an engineering school, a transportation school, maybe even a medical school.

What they should do, he wrote, was run the Iraqi infantry units through schools that taught specific reconstruction tasks—mine-clearing school, or explosive-ordnance-disposal school.

But Rudd soon found out that nobody knew where the Iraqi military schools were, which meant it was almost impossible to put together a practical plan. He worked with an Army intelligence colonel and put in requests for more information to the DIA and the CIA, but the response they got back was simply, "We just don't know."

PEOPLE BEGAN FLOWING from various federal departments and agencies into Garner's Pentagon B-ring offices. It resembled one of those stock, rushed preparation scenes in the old World War II movies with everyone hyperactive, focused and knowing their assignments. But Garner could see that it was chaotic. Few knew who was working on what. Everyone was moving but it was not clear where anyone was going.

"What we're going to do is, we're going to do a rock drill," Garner said, using an old Army term for a field commander's technique of diagramming a military plan on the ground using rocks to represent the various units.

The weekend of February 21–22, Garner gathered some 200 people at the National Defense University at Fort McNair in southwest Washington, D.C., for a massive rehearsal and planning conference.

Throughout the weekend, two questions went unanswered during all the presentations, PowerPoint slides and discussions: Who was going to be in charge of Iraq the day after the serious combat ended? And, was there an Iraqi political process that could be tapped to help recruit peo-

ple who could provide the basics—security, water, electricity—matters
that are normally the responsibility of a mayor in an American city?

Shortly after the rock drill, one participant who had spoken with Garner and other key staffers analyzed the conference in a 20-page report.
The analysis identified numerous planning problems a month before the
war. In retrospect, it provides stark and contemporaneous warnings:

- "Current force packages are inadequate for the first step of securing all the major urban areas, let alone for providing interim police. . . . We risk letting much of the country descend into civil
  unrest [and] chaos whose magnitude may defeat our national
  strategy of a stable new Iraq, and more immediately, we place
  our own troops, fully engaged in the forward fight, in greater
  jeopardy."
- "It seems likely that we will begin military action before we
  know whether sufficient Phase IV funds will be available. If
  fewer funds are available than required, we risk leaving behind a
  great unstable mess with potential to become a haven for terrorists."
- "In field after field, the ideas, as briefed, suggest a heavy-handed
  imperial take-over. Danger, danger!"
- "The conference did not take up the most basic issue: What sort
  of future government of Iraq do we have in mind, and how do we
  plan to get there?"
- With no sufficient plan for police from U.S. troops or a civilian
  government of Iraq, "What happens to law and order in the
  meantime?"

The memo went on to explain that Garner himself had introduced at
the rock drill the notion of what he called "Show Stoppers—problems, if
not solved, place mission at risk."

This "Danger, danger!" memo identified several such Show Stoppers.

"Security," was one. "This is far and away the greatest challenge, and
the greatest shortfall. If we do not get it right, we may change the
regime, but the national strategy will likely fall apart and our troops on
the ground will be in jeopardy.

"This complete dearth of needed forces, coupled with the security ex-
igencies we will no doubt face on the ground, make for a very disturbing
picture indeed. Fortunately, Gen. Garner is as aware as anyone of the se-

riousness and urgency of this issue. He stated flatly that the issue is crucial and that we do not have enough forces, and he added he will be taking the issue up this week with SECDEF and NSA Dr. Rice. . . . This should help, particularly should Dr. Rice choose to take the most serious matters—security and cost—to POTUS." POTUS stood for President of the United States.

Garner and his team emerged from the rock drill very troubled. His second in command in the postwar planning group, another retired Army three-star, Ron Adams, wrote in his notes: "Faulty assumptions. Overly optimistic. Lack of reality." Later, Adams recalled, "I personally came out of the rock drill far more concerned than when I went in, and I was uneasy right from the get-go."

DURING THE FIRST MORNING of the rock drill, Garner had noticed one person who found fault with everything. A real "spring-butt," Garner thought, someone who kept popping up out of his seat with something to say on every topic. When they took a break, Garner walked up to him.

"Let me talk to you," he said.

"I'm Tom Warrick," said the man, a 48-year-old State Department civil servant.

"How do you know so damn much?"

"Well, I've been studying this stuff for the last year and a half," Warrick said.

Oh yeah? Who've you been studying it for?

The State Department, Warrick replied, and said he'd written a long report on postwar Iraq. "It's called the 'Future of Iraq' study."

That was very interesting, Garner thought. He had heard vaguely about the study.

"Why aren't you over here working for me?"

"I'd like to work for you," Warrick said.

"You're hired," Garner told him. "Be there Monday morning and bring all your stuff."

The Monday after the rock drill, Warrick showed up at the Pentagon. By noon, Garner noticed that half the people working with Warrick were mad at him. Garner was delighted. They needed someone like that, challenging everyone, keeping them on their toes and engaged. "He runs around and sandpapers everyone," Garner recalled later. Garner read much of the "Future of Iraq" study, didn't agree with all of it, but felt it was sufficiently provocative to be useful.

A few days later, Garner was summoned to Rumsfeld's office for a big get-together with Wolfowitz, General Myers and the vice chairman of the JCS, Marine General Pete Pace.

"Hey, Jay"—Rumsfeld leaned over at one point—"when it's all over, how about staying? I have a couple of things I need to go over."

When everyone else left, the secretary of defense walked to his desk and started shuffling through his papers. It took a while, and Rumsfeld started to get exasperated, unable to find what he was looking for. Finally, he picked up a small piece of paper.

"Jay," he said, looking up. "Do you have a couple people on your team named Warrick and O'Sullivan?"

"Yeah," Garner replied. "I've got a guy named Tom Warrick who did the 'Future of Iraq' study and I got a gal named Meghan O'Sullivan, who's a real talented young lady."

O'Sullivan, also from the State Department, had come over to Garner's team recently. She was 33, indisputably bright, had a doctorate in political science from Oxford University, and had written extensively on rogue states and Iraq.

"I've got to ask you to take them both off the team," Rumsfeld said.

"I can't do that. Both of them are too valuable."

Rumsfeld stared at Garner briefly. "Look, Jay. I've gotten this request from such a high level that I can't turn it down. So I've got to ask you to remove them from your team."

"There's no negotiation here?" Garner asked.

"I'm sorry. There really isn't," Rumsfeld replied.

A level so high that the secretary of defense couldn't turn it down? Garner thought. That could mean only Bush or conceivably Cheney.

Back in his office, Garner couldn't locate Warrick or O'Sullivan. He told Tom Baltazar, an Army colonel who was working as his operations officer, what had happened. "That's crazy," Baltazar said.

"Look, just find them," Garner said. "Tell them to go back to where they came from, and I'll get them back. Tell them it's just temporary."

Garner later tracked down Steve Hadley, the deputy national security adviser.

"I really, really want these two back," he told Hadley.

"Yeah," Hadley replied. "I don't know that we can help you here."

Garner pressed his case. Warrick and O'Sullivan knew what they were talking about. There wasn't much time before they would likely be deploying to the Middle East, and he needed them.

"Well, the man is just too hard," Hadley said. It would be impossible to get Warrick back on the team, but it sounded like he was leaving the door open for O'Sullivan.

That night, Baltazar called Garner at his apartment to report that Warrick and O'Sullivan were gone.

"Tom," Garner asked, "where in the hell do you think this came from?"

"I don't know, but I've got a buddy who works at the White House. I'm going to call him tonight on his phone at home. I don't want to call him on the official line."

Baltazar called his friend, P. J. Dermer, an army colonel who worked for Scooter Libby, the vice president's chief of staff, and who had a secure telephone at home. The bottom line, Dermer said, had to do with Ahmed Chalabi, an Iraqi expatriate and head of the Iraqi National Congress, a group based in London and funded by the U.S. Cheney's office was pushing the idea that Chalabi was the answer to everything, and Warrick was not a fan of Chalabi. Dermer described the opposition to Warrick as coming from "a group of about five people" in Cheney's office—"a cabal," he said.

The next morning, Baltazar told Garner, "It was the vice president. The vice president can't stand either one of them."

Warrick had been in the Clinton administration, and had been a strong advocate of indicting Saddam Hussein as a war criminal. He had worked on regime change issues for State, met with lots of Iraqi exiles, and had discovered that other exiles weren't exactly enamored of Chalabi. In fact, there had been a conference of Iraqi opposition leaders he'd worked on in 2002 when many of them said they wouldn't come if Chalabi and his Iraqi National Congress were put in charge.

O'Sullivan had worked at the Brookings Institution, a left-of-center think tank, and she was seen as a protégé of Richard N. Haass, the director of policy planning at Powell's State Department. She and Haass had co-authored a paper urging the use of economic, political or cultural incentives as levers to influence countries such as Iraq instead of military force or covert action. In another paper O'Sullivan had questioned U.S. support to Iraqi exiles.

Garner thought the whole maneuver was a bad sign. He was repelled that personalities and apparently ideology would play a role in such vital postwar planning. Losing Warrick, clearly a top expert on the issues, was a blow, though Garner's team kept his "Future of Iraq" study, and a lot of

Iraqis who had worked on it wound up working with Garner's organization. The incident demonstrated the depth of the infighting between Defense and State.

At the State Department, Powell got word of what Rumsfeld had done. "What the hell is going on?" he asked Rumsfeld in a phone call.

Rumsfeld said that they needed people who were truly committed and who had not written or said things that were not supportive.

Powell took that to mean that his State Department people didn't support exiles like Chalabi. Soon the secretary of state and secretary of defense were into a giant row. "I can take prisoners too," Powell said.

GARNER WENT BACK to Rumsfeld. "Let me have these two people back," he said.

"I can't do that," Rumsfeld said. "I told you I was asked at a high level to remove these people. I asked you to do it. You've done it. I can't go back on that now." Finally Rumsfeld said, "Look, bring the woman back." Garner could have O'Sullivan. "Nobody will know that."

Powell quickly learned of the half resolution, and he asked himself if things could get any weirder. He found seven senior State officials he thought would be useful to Garner, but Doug Feith wanted outsiders instead of representatives from "the Department of Nice." Powell said it was bullshit. He and Rumsfeld got into another big fight, but Powell got five of the seven approved and on Garner's team after a week of more silliness.

THE OVERRIDING PROBLEM was that there was not one, single plan, thought Paul Hughes, an Army colonel on Garner's staff. There was no single document spelling out, *This is your objective. This is who's in charge. These are the priority tasks. These are the coordinating steps we will take to bring these all together.* Garner had tried to synchronize things at the rock drill, but they clearly weren't there yet, not even close.

Hughes, a tall, trim 50-year-old officer who had served 28 years on active duty, had been in charge of national security studies at the National Defense University until he was assigned to Garner's group. He and another officer on Garner's staff, Colonel Thomas Gross, were known as "The Law Firm," and had wide latitude. Even on some of the official office phone lists, where their colleagues were identified by the division in which they worked, Hughes and Gross were listed simply as "Law Firm."

Hughes had spent six months thinking about what postwar Iraq would look like, and had put together a two-day conference on the issue in November 2002. The National Defense University had done a 41-page report on their findings, which wound up in the hands of Jim Thomas, a special assistant to Paul Wolfowitz.

Hughes continued to push for an omnibus plan. The word from Feith's office was a simple "no." Hughes saw that such a document would almost inevitably involve the interagency process, including State and the CIA. That wouldn't fly because NSPD-24, which had set up Garner's office, had specifically put the authority and responsibility for postwar planning for Iraq in the Defense Department.

RUMSFELD INVITED an outside group of experts to the Pentagon to discuss postwar Iraq. Among the group was James F. Dobbins, who probably knew as much about managing modern post-conflict situations as anyone. A courtly, 60-year-old veteran diplomat, Dobbins was Mr. Postwar. He had been the U.S. envoy for Kosovo, Bosnia, Haiti and Somalia, overseeing both the celebrated and controversial stabilization and reconstruction missions of the 1990s. Now he was at RAND Corporation, the think tank, as the head of international and security policy.

In 2001, Powell had named Dobbins to head the negotiations among the Afghanistan opposition groups to find a leader after the fall of the Taliban. It was a classic brokering assignment, requiring as much negotiating among the various U.S. agencies and departments as with foreign governments. At the CIA several officials proposed Hamid Karzai, a moderate Afghan leader who had been a junior minister under the Taliban but had defected and joined the opposition. General Franks approved and others in the CIA, State and Defense Departments signed off. Having gathered consensus within the U.S. bureaucracy, Dobbins headed to a U.N. conference in Bonn, Germany, where the Afghan factions were engaged in all-night negotiating sessions, trying to settle on a leader. Dobbins persuaded the key regional players—the Russians, the Pakistanis and even the Iranians—to agree on Karzai, who took the oath of office as Afghanistan's president on December 22, 2001—just 102 days after 9/11.

At the Pentagon, one of Feith's deputies briefed Dobbins and several other outside experts on a postwar plan that seemed to envision a full-scale occupation of Iraq. Dobbins thought of it as Plan A—a sort of General Douglas MacArthur viceroy. The United States would prepare the country for elections, after which sovereignty would be given back to the Iraqis.

After the briefing, Rumsfeld came in to meet with Dobbins and the others.

"I thought we did it just fine in Afghanistan," Rumsfeld said, acknowledging Dobbins and his role, "and I would hope that we'll be able to do the same thing in Iraq—that is, bring together a representative group of Iraqis and find Iraq's Hamid Karzai."

Rumsfeld said later, "I tilted to the latter, to the quicker handover, and the president did . . . Clearly you needed somebody who people could recognize as providing leadership in the country. And I've always felt that foreign troops are an anomaly in a country, that eventually they're unnatural and not welcomed really. There's also the concept of declining consent."

Dobbins was happy to see that there was a Plan B—a Bonn conference equivalent with quick transfer of power to an Iraqi government. He wondered which model—MacArthur or Karzai—would be used. There seemed to be no well-devised plan for either, and clearly there was no consensus within the administration. It was also evident to him that the administration did not comprehend the massive undertaking before them—not only the security, governing and economic issues but the task of trying to heal some of the old wounds from the dictatorship, and the hatred between the Sunnis, who ruled Iraq under Saddam, and the Shiites, who were a majority of the population.

Bush had disparaged nation building in the 2000 presidential campaign. But now his administration was going to be in that business big-time.

SIX WEEKS INTO his assignment, Garner went to the White House, mid-morning on Friday, February 28, 2003, to meet President Bush for the first time and brief him on what his team had been doing. Waiting outside the Situation Room, where the president and the war cabinet were meeting, Garner recognized Attorney General John Ashcroft.

Looks like we're both out of the loop, Garner said nervously, trying to break the ice.

Ashcroft responded with what Garner thought was a "go to hell" look.

In the Situation Room, Garner took a seat at the far end of a small,

well-polished table. The president was at the other end, with the principals seated alongside, including Powell, Rumsfeld, Rice and Tenet.
General Franks was there, and Cheney was on the secure video teleconference screen. Frank Miller, director of the NSC staff for defense, was in
the middle of a briefing. Garner was nervous. He could see the president
had no idea who the hell he was.

As Miller talked, Bush shifted his attention between Miller and Garner, staring intently at Miller, and then glancing quickly at Garner, before
turning back to Miller. Then again, a quick look at Garner before turning
back to Miller. Then a third time.

This is going to be a long day, Garner thought. Somewhat out of the blue,
Bush flashed a high-in-the-air thumbs-up sign at Garner. Garner instantly felt better. He thought the president sensed his discomfort and
was trying to put him at ease.

"Okay, what's next?" the president asked when Miller finished.

"General Garner's in the postwar planning group," Rice said, "and
he's going to brief you on that."

"Before you do that," the president said, "tell me about yourself."

"No, I'm going to tell you about him," Rumsfeld interrupted, and
summarized Garner's Army service, his success in Operation Provide
Comfort, and his service on Rumsfeld's space commission.

"That's fine," Bush said. And then to Garner: "Go ahead."

Garner passed around copies of his handout, an 11-point presentation, and dove right in. Addressing his nine basic assignments in NSPD-
24, Garner said essentially that four of them shouldn't be his because
they were plainly beyond the capabilities of his small team. The four
tasks included dismantling WMD, defeating terrorists, reshaping the
Iraqi military and reshaping the other internal Iraqi security institutions.
In other words, four of the really hard ones. Those would have to be handled by the military, Garner said.

The president nodded. No one else intervened, though Garner had
just told them he couldn't be responsible for crucial postwar tasks—the
ones that had the most to do with the stated reasons for going to war in
the first place—because his team couldn't do them.

No one asked the follow-up question of exactly who would be responsible, if Garner wasn't. Were the issues going to be left hanging in the
air? Were they important? Maybe Garner was wrong. Maybe he could or
should have those issues. The import of what he had said seemed to sail
over everyone's heads.

Garner next described how he intended to divide the country into regional groups, and moved on to the interagency plans.

"Just a minute," the president interrupted. "Where are you from?"

"Florida, sir."

"Why do you talk like that?" he asked, apparently trying to place Garner's accent.

"Because I was born and raised on a ranch in Florida. My daddy was a rancher."

"You're in," the First Rancher said approvingly. His brother Jeb was governor of the state, and the president visited regularly.

Garner went on, explaining that each department and agency had to "operationalize" its plan and have a "vision" about its end state, particularly for the first 30 days to one year.

He raised his notion of Show Stoppers, problems that might jeopardize or even stop the mission in its tracks. They were struggling for money, he said.

The president listened.

Referring to the rock drill, Garner explained how they planned to maintain stability in Iraq after combat.

Garner's talking point said, "Postwar use of Iraqi Regular Army." He said, "We're going to use the army. We need to use them. They have the proper skill sets."

How many from the army? someone asked.

"I'm going to give you a big range," Garner answered. "It'll be between 200,000 and 300,000."

Garner looked around the room. All the heads were bobbing north to south. Nobody challenged. Nobody had any questions about this plan.

Next, Garner said he wanted to internationalize the postwar effort. Immediately, he noticed some discomfort in the room. Not from Powell, but from most of the others. He thought there was a lot of squirming going on, and Garner figured most of the others were thinking, *Don't you get it? We're not trying to internationalize this thing. It's a U.S. operation.*

He continued, saying that he would send his advance party to the region in about 10 days, with the rest to follow 10 days later. The president didn't say anything. No one indicated when the war might start, but it was obvious it was coming soon.

"Thank you very much," Bush said when Garner was done. Rice started talking about something else, so Garner figured he was dismissed. As he started to walk out of the room, the president caught his eye.

"Kick ass, Jay," Bush said.

Garner waited for Rumsfeld outside. Soon, Bush and Rice came out and walked three or four steps past Garner. Suddenly Bush turned back.

"Hey, if you have any problem with that governor down in Florida, just let me know," he said.

14

A FTER POWELL HAD TONED DOWN the idea of a Saddam–al Qaeda connection in his address to the U.N. on February 5, Cheney wanted to give his own speech making the charge. Tenet was upset. It was bullshit. He wondered to his associate John Brennan if he should step down. At the same time, Tenet did not want to be the disloyal intelligence director who folded in a national crisis or on the eve of war.

He went to the president. The CIA intelligence does not support the conclusion of Cheney's proposed speech, he said. There is no proof that Saddam had "authority, direction and control" of any al Qaeda aid coming from Iraq. If Cheney gives the speech, Tenet told the president, the CIA cannot and will not stand behind it.

Bush backed Tenet. He told Cheney not to give the speech.

WITHOUT INFORMING ANYONE in the White House or Pentagon, Garner went to the United Nations headquarters in New York City on March 3. He and his deputy, Ron Adams, felt strongly that the more the war was a coalition effort, the better for all. Garner decided to see if he personally could get the U.N. stamp on as much of the postwar effort as possible.

The outreach was dangerous because the White House and the Pentagon had scant interest in the United Nations. Garner's comment about "internationalizing" the effort had not gone over well at the NSC meeting just a few days before.

Louise Fréchette, the deputy secretary general of the U.N., chaired their meeting.

"The U.N.'s working hard on immediate relief on humanitarian affairs and not seeking a role beyond that," Fréchette said.

Garner asked if he could at least have a U.N. liaison officer assigned to him.

No, Fréchette said.

Bang, thought Garner. Shot down. So much for help from the U.N.

Garner next met with Jeremy Greenstock, the British ambassador to the U.N., who looked physically exhausted, overwrought, worn out. The stress of trying to get a second U.N. resolution on weapons inspections in Iraq—an effort that would soon fail—was obviously taking its toll.

"We're in this with you," Greenstock said. "We're together in this, but internationalizing this effort will make everything a lot easier for all of us." He meant especially for British Prime Minister Blair, who had promised his Labour Party at home he'd seek a second U.N. resolution. By tradition Labour paid homage to the United Nations.

Afterward, the American U.N. ambassador, John D. Negroponte, came by. "Lots of luck," he told Garner, and left. He looks a hell of a lot more rested than Greenstock, Garner thought. Negroponte did not have to spend time paying homage to the U.N.

The next day, March 4, Doug Feith gave a secret briefing to the president and the NSC, including a PowerPoint presentation on "U.S. and Coalition Objectives" for an Iraq war. It was rosy, pie-in-the-sky political science—everything from visibly improving quality of life for Iraqis to moving toward democracy and obtaining "international participation in the reconstruction." It was a wish list of high hopes with no how-to.

Garner had not known anything about Feith's meeting with the president. A day later, March 5, he updated Rice in her West Wing office, a cozy, high-ceiling room decorated in blue with an impressively thick door. The office had been the national security adviser's for decades.

Garner revealed that he had gone to the United Nations on Monday, had asked for a liaison officer and been turned down.

Rice sat in silence.

"They're not seeking additional roles," Garner continued. "They're willing to help but they need to understand our concept. And that's why they kept saying, 'We don't understand your concept. Why are you going it alone?' "

Rice continued to sit in silence.

Proceeding with his written agenda, Garner said he needed the "start-up funding" for such basics as food, law enforcement and energy.

"Okay," Rice said, turning to Hadley and Frank Miller. "Let's work on this. Let's get this going. Let's have it by the time they need it."

Hadley and Miller seemed to be taking notes, but Garner got the impression that Rice's directions were just sort of floating up in the ether. He didn't sense that there was a follow-up system in place.

We need money to pay for public servants in Iraq, for the police and the military, Garner told Rice. "I'm still planning on paying all these people just as soon as I can when I get there."

There was about $1.6 billion in frozen Iraqi assets in the United States, Garner had learned. If they could tap into that money, their back-of-the-envelope calculation was that they could afford to bring back the civil servants—especially the police and about 200,000 Iraqi military—and keep them working for about 90 days.

Rice seemed to agree.

"Ministries" was the next agenda item. Who would be the designated American official to go in and run the Ministry of Agriculture in Iraq? Or Interior? He needed to fill out all the people who were going to be responsible, Garner said, and he hadn't finished that yet.

Garner moved on to a crucial issue: They all knew they didn't have enough forces and that they needed more security.

"Well, where are we on that?" Rice inquired.

They both knew part of the answer was that Rumsfeld and Franks were still working out the final war plan. Garner believed that Franks's latest plan called for a force level dramatically below the 500,000 in the initial war plan for Iraq—perhaps as low as 160,000. But with another 100,000 U.S. forces that could flow in after combat began, plus some 200,000 to 300,000 from the Iraqi army who could be turned to work with the U.S. forces, it was possible to have some measure of security and stability.

On the issue of contracts for economic development and reconstruction, Garner said it might be possible to require that all contractors have one or more Iraqi subcontractors—a kind of set-aside that would get money flowing to ordinary Iraqis.

What about the numbers of police and other law enforcement officials? Garner wanted a lot, but Frank Miller wanted only $70 million devoted up front. Garner thought it would cost hundreds of millions, but he urged that they wait. "Let's don't decide on a lower number now or a larger number, but let's leave this open so that if I'm right you can jump in and help me as fast as you can. And if he's right then we haven't lost anything. But I don't think he's right."

The next item was funding. "Who's got the money is in control," Garner said. "Where is the money? I need the money."

Rice seemed supportive, but Garner still didn't have any solid assurances about funding. He realized the president, Rice and the others were being told how easy the war was going to be—perhaps even a "cakewalk," to use a term offered in a hawkish prewar *Washington Post* op-ed by Ken Adelman, the longtime friend to Cheney and Rumsfeld. The money issue, like most others, was left hanging.

"Governance" was the final item. How would they put together a postwar government for Iraq? Garner asked. This was the overriding question of political power. Who would have it after the war? Someone would. But who?

Rice never answered.

On Friday, March 7, Garner and Ron Adams met with Wolfowitz. They were frustrated, and complained that they had no sense even of when they were expected to fly to Kuwait. They barely knew how they would move their people to the region, or where they would stay while they waited for war. Nobody would tell them when the war was planned to start.

"You should already be there," said Wolfowitz, who as the number two Pentagon official presumably had a good idea of the timing.

HUNKERED IN THE KUWAITI DESERT, Spider Marks was outspoken, even strident with what he called his "technical" chain of command among intelligence officers, including Franks's senior intelligence officer, Brigadier General Jeff Kimmons. The intelligence they had on the WMDMSL just wasn't good enough.

"This is unsat, unsat, unsat," Marks told Kimmons, lopping off the last four syllables of "unsatisfactory." "Jeff, you need to move this forward, buddy. I'm not going to call Rumsfeld's office. I'm not going to call Cambone," who was now the Defense Department undersecretary for intelligence. "He doesn't know me from Adam. But this is not working."

It vividly illustrated the breakdown. The general whose job was to find and exploit Saddam's WMD had looked at the fruits of more than a decade of intelligence work and found it wanting. Bush and others in the administration had been escalating the rhetoric. White House spokesman Ari Fleischer said on December 5, 2002: "The president of the United States and the secretary of defense would not assert as plainly and bluntly as they have that Iraq has weapons of mass destruction if it was not true, and if they did not have a solid basis for saying it." Fleischer announced again on January 9, 2003: "We know for a fact that there are weapons there." In his weekly radio address February 8, Bush said, "We have sources that tell us that Saddam Hussein recently authorized Iraqi field commanders to use chemical weapons—the very weapons the dictator tells us he does not have."

Marks understood Kimmons's predicament. It resembled his own. They were just junior generals looking at the same unfulfilling jumble of data. Kimmons was dealing with his own personal hell. He wouldn't want to go to Franks for fear of triggering one of General Franks's notorious and profane explosions, Marks thought. Kimmons could end up with a hole in his chest and, more important, be no closer to a solution.

But the intelligence wasn't getting any better. If Cambone and Rumsfeld didn't know Marks from Adam, maybe that was a problem. Marks had told McKiernan, Abizaid and Kimmons about his concerns, but was there anything else he could have done from the Kuwaiti desert to raise hell up the chain of command until he was heard? For that matter, shouldn't Rumsfeld or Franks—or even Bush—have reached down the chain a link or two, found the general handling WMD intelligence for the invading forces and asked him what he thought? There was too much riding on the answer.

"Still some confusion," Marks wrote in his journal on March 3. "Do we secure as we progress thru zone, or treat like an obstacle and mark, cover, bypass?" He was still waiting for a complete answer to another of the questions he'd hammered on at the DIA "smart guys" meeting back on October 4: How do we prioritize the 946 suspected WMD sites in Iraq?

WAR WAS CLEARLY IMMINENT, but Garner was still at the Pentagon. He believed the nagging question of governance still had to be addressed, and he wanted to stand up the Iraqi ministries immediately. But again the question had not been answered: Who was going to be in charge? At one point Rumsfeld had asked him a key question in a Rumsfeldian way. "By the way, what are you going to do about de-Baathification? Do you have a de-Baathification process?" Garner was going to have to get rid of the members of Saddam's Baath Party, much like the de-Nazification in Germany after World War II.

"You can't do de-Baathification of the ministries," Garner answered. "There won't be anybody left." Most of the jobs were filled by party members. "So what we'll do is take out the top guy. We'll take out the personnel guy." Maybe a few others. "We'll let everybody else return and over time the people in the ministry will begin to point out the bad guys."

"Well, that sounds reasonable to me," Rumsfeld replied.

GARNER WALKED DOWN to see Wolfowitz again.

"You know, probably the most important function we have, we don't have covered," Garner said.

"What's that?"

"It's governance. We have to have a team that's putting together the government." They needed an Iraqi face. "What I'm asking you to do," he continued, "is let's go out and get the smartest minds in America, and go to Harvard or go to wherever you want to go, and put together a world-class governance team that we can bring over there that begins immediately putting together a government for us."

"Let me think about that," Wolfowitz replied to Garner.

Later that afternoon, Wolfowitz called Garner back.

"I thought about what you said," he began. "What do you think about Liz Cheney?"

"I don't know who Liz Cheney is," Garner replied.

"The vice president's daughter."

Cheney, a 36-year-old lawyer and mother of three, had held several posts in the State Department and was now serving as deputy assistant secretary of state for Near East affairs. Steeped in conservative politics since childhood, she had worked on the Bush-Cheney 2000 campaign.

"I don't care, as long as I know it's somebody who knows what they're doing and knows how to do this."

"Well, she'll be over here in the morning, so you can come in and explain to her what you want," Wolfowitz said.

The next day, Garner came to Wolfowitz's office and met with Liz Cheney.

"What we need is a face of Iraqi leadership for the Iraqi people," Garner told her. "I think we need to put together a group that is capable of governance. And we also need to immediately start writing a constitution. We have to start having elections. We need to start having elections in the provinces. And so we need to start all this immediately and let them be involved in what happens."

Leaders, a constitution, elections—it was a tall order.

"Let me work on this," Liz Cheney said. Neither she nor Wolfowitz added much or offered any objections. Later that afternoon, she came back over to the Pentagon with a few people from State. One was Scott Carpenter, a balding but boyish-looking deputy assistant secretary of state who had worked on the "Future of Iraq" study.

Garner outlined his broad, ambitious plan for governing. Carpenter took some notes and said, "Okay, I'll start to put this together. When will we go over there?"

Garner still didn't know when he was leaving. "The best thing for you to do is to stay over here and put the team together and then join me when I go to Baghdad."

"Okay, I'll do that."

After Liz Cheney and Carpenter left, Garner had a private discussion with Wolfowitz.

"You know, he seems like a good guy," Garner said, meaning Carpenter. "He's a little young. I don't know how experienced he is. She would have been okay."

"Yeah, but we can't send her over there because she's too high-risk being the vice president's daughter."

"That makes sense," Garner responded.

IN ROOM 666 in the prestigious E-ring of the Pentagon on the third floor, just several outer corridors from Rumsfeld's office, General John M. Keane, the vice chief of staff of the Army, got wind of Garner's new role. Bizarre, thought Keane.

An old bear of a man with 37 years in the Army, Keane had been stunned by the lack of trust Rumsfeld had shown the uniformed military leaders in the first years. The secretary was abrasive, curt and dismissive of other people's thoughts and ideas. But Keane found that Rumsfeld was right most of the time about the need for change in the military, especially the Army.

Setting aside emotions and personality, Keane had become a Rumsfeld favorite and for practical purposes was running the Army, because Rumsfeld had battled with Keane's boss, General Eric K. Shinseki, the Army chief of staff. In late 2000 and early 2001, there had been a big imbroglio over Shinseki's decision to issue a black beret to every soldier in the Army. Black berets had long been the trademark of the elite Army Rangers. Rangers, ex-Rangers and some members of Congress were offended. A couple of former Rangers even marched from Fort Benning, Georgia, to Washington to protest the change. But Shinseki dug in his heels. Bush talked to Rumsfeld twice about the controversy, which dragged on for months. So Rumsfeld, who came back to the Pentagon wanting to focus on big priorities, had to quell a big fight over the kind and color of hat the Army would wear.

In April 2002, Rumsfeld had asked Keane to become the next Army chief. Keane had agreed but more recently had reconsidered, saying he was leaving the Army because his wife was seriously ill. He told Rumsfeld that his married life had been about him for 37 years and now it had to be about his wife. Of all the top people in the Pentagon, Keane had found Rumsfeld to be by far the most understanding and instinctively compassionate.

Keane asked Garner to come give him a briefing. He thought Garner was smart and he had lots of wonderful ideas. Garner was painting on the broadest of canvases—everything from water, food and electricity, to a new government, a constitution and elections—trying to do quickly what American entrepreneurs and the Founding Fathers had needed decades to accomplish.

"Who are you working for?" Keane asked.

"I'm working for the secretary of defense," Garner replied.

"Jay, that's the wrong answer. I mean, God Almighty, you've got to be working for General Franks, and de facto for General McKiernan. You can't be working for the secretary. There will be a separate channel. I mean, your staff will immediately become dysfunctional from the military command. I mean, you can see it coming. They're not going to want to deal with you. You're not going to—"

"No," Garner protested. "We'll make it work somehow."

Keane reminded Garner of the principle of unity of command. One person had to be in charge in each theater or operation. Franks should be in charge of Phase IV and held accountable for stability. Early on, everything would be military anyway. "Jay, if we've learned one thing in the last fifteen years, it's this. Come on. Every time we've screwed up we've had problems with this. We don't have to relearn this lesson."

"I will make it work," Garner said, reminding Keane he was a military man and very sensitive to the problem. In addition, he added, decisions had already been made.

Keane was aware of that. Perhaps worse were the decisions that had not been made. Soon, he heard Abizaid too pressing Rumsfeld on the governance questions.

"Mr. Secretary," Abizaid said, "I'm concerned about who is going to be in charge when we take the regime down. What is the political apparatus going to be?" Abizaid had four or five variations of the same question. "Who is going to be in charge of the country?" he asked another time.

Once Rumsfeld said, "Well Doug is working on that." That meant Feith, who Keane believed to be a very weak link in Rumsfeld's team and completely underqualified for his post. Feith had lots of paper and documents outlining elaborate plans. Garner, for example, was technically supposed to be under General Franks. But Garner was already reporting directly to Rumsfeld, who not only liked it that way, but insisted on it.

SEVERAL DAYS BEFORE DEPLOYING, Garner and Bates went to the State Department to see Powell and Armitage. Powell and Bates gave each other a hug. It wasn't only the long Army affiliation; in September 1994 Bates and Powell had been part of the small team President Clinton dispatched to avert a hostile U.S. invasion of Haiti. Former President Carter, Powell and former Senator Sam Nunn, who had been chairman of the Armed Services Committee from 1987 to 1995, had been the trio in charge of the mission. Bates had been the military representative from the Joint Staff.

"You know, sir," Bates said to Powell, "we could solve this if you and I just take another trip over there with President Carter and Sam Nunn."

Powell laughed and made some remarks about the eternal and escalating warfare between State and Defense. It was extraordinarily dysfunctional, the four former military men agreed.

"You know," Powell said, "the problem with these guys is they've never been in a bar fight." He was referring to Bush, Cheney, Rice, Rumsfeld and others in the administration who had never served in the military or never seen actual combat. Among the four in Powell's office, including Armitage's six years in the Navy, they had over 100 years of military experience. There was a feeling among them that they were the old hands who knew the ropes.

"Whatever you need that I can give to you, I'll give to you," Powell told them. "You know that.

"It really pissed me off when Don had you get rid of Warrick and O'Sullivan," Powell said.

"You know, I don't think he did that. I think he was just following orders," Garner replied.

"Well, let me tell you something. I picked up the phone and said, 'Hey, look. I can take prisoners too.' I started to pull everybody in the State Department off your team, but after taking a brief moment thinking about that, I thought, well, that won't do anybody any good. That just damages what you're doing. It'll ruin what you're doing. It'll ruin what the nation's trying to do. Somebody has to be the big guy about this, and I've tried to be it."

As they were getting up to leave, Armitage stopped Garner.

"Hey, Jay. Let me tell you one thing. You've got a bunch of goddamn spies on that team of yours. They're talking about you. They're reporting on you, so you better watch your back."

"Well, yes, sir," Garner replied, "I'll do that. But you've got some spies over here too."

"We know who they are," Armitage said. "We call them bats."

"Bats?" Garner asked.

"Yeah. Because those sons of bitches hang upside down all day long with their wings covering up their eyes. But as soon as we close the door in the evening they part their wings and they look around and they flap around all goddamn night long, calling everybody."

Bates and Garner liked the nickname, and they bestowed it on the people they thought had been funneled onto their team by Feith to keep an eye on them. One of their Pentagon bats had four cell phones—later confirmed by the phone bills. When they deployed to Kuwait, this person seemed to be constantly on one of the phones. One day while deep in concentration on his cell phone, the man walked into a swimming pool. "It was the highlight of the day," Bates recalled later. "It made everyone's day."

AROUND THIS TIME Powell had one of his semiprivate meetings with the president. As usual, Rice was there.

Powell raised the question of unity of command. There are two chains of command, Powell told the president. Garner reports to Rumsfeld and Franks reports to Rumsfeld.

The president looked surprised.

"That's not right," Rice said. "That's not right."

Powell thought Rice could at times be quite sure of herself, but he was pretty sure he was right. "Yes, it is," Powell insisted.

"Wait a minute," Bush interrupted, taking Rice's side. "That doesn't sound right."

Rice got up and went to her office to check. When she came back, Powell thought she looked a little sheepish. "That's right," she said.

"Yeah," Powell said, pocketing the small victory and addressing Bush. "You have got a military chain of command that correctly goes to the secretary of defense, to you. But you have also created this alternative, which goes through Garner or whoever the civilian guy is, which also goes to the secretary."

Continuing his little lecture, Powell expanded. "There's nothing fundamentally wrong with this as long as you understand what you've done. But you have to understand that when you have two chains of command and you don't have a common superior in the theater, it means that every little half-assed fight they have out there, if they can't work it out, comes out to one place to be resolved. And that's in the Pentagon. Not in the NSC or the State Department, but in the Pentagon."

What Powell didn't say was that he believed the Pentagon wouldn't resolve the conflicts because Wolfowitz and Feith were running their own little games and had their own agenda to promote Chalabi.

Rice thought it was all a rather theoretical discussion. If they put Garner under Franks, that would mean Franks was the viceroy. Bush would never allow that, she knew.

But it was the way Rumsfeld wanted it. Both Franks and Garner reported to him, giving him the most control—always his goal.

GARNER WAS HOLDING regular meetings with Rumsfeld, trying to keep him informed, get decisions and convey his growing sense of the magnitude of the task.

The issue of money was omnipresent. Garner felt that almost nobody in the Bush administration thought there was going to be a big bill for the Iraq aftermath. One budget document Garner had prepared, dated February 27, 2003, showed that he had just over $27 million for his group. The numbers required for the basics of running the country were huge by comparison. He projected humanitarian assistance at over $1 billion including the next year, reconstruction at $800 million and running the government at $10 billion—nearly $12 billion, all told. Where would it come from?

He was seeking guidance. "Hey, Mr. Secretary," Garner recalls asking Rumsfeld one day before deploying, "We've got three options. What do we want to do in reconstruction? Do you want to take everything back to where it was pre–first Gulf War? Do you want to take it back to where it was before this war? Or do you want to build all new?" The budget document also listed proposals to do a percentage of one of those periods or just repair everything. Yet no actual numbers—the important kind, with dollar signs in front of them—had been proposed.

"What do you think that will cost?" Rumsfeld inquired.

"It will cost billions of dollars," Garner answered. "Any of them will."

"Well, if you think we're spending our money on that, you're wrong," Rumsfeld said, in his most sweeping, assertive way. "We're not doing that. They're going to spend their money rebuilding their country."

15

THE "FIELD EXPEDIENT" ARTILLERY BRIGADE that was going to search the 946 locations on the WMD Master Site List started to assemble in Kuwait. Experts from other Pentagon agencies such as the Defense Intelligence Agency started flowing in, but the Exploitation Task Force, or XTF, didn't have enough people, equipment or vehicles to field all the teams they'd planned to send on site inspections. They scaled back, allocating troops and trucks as best they could.

On March 10, Rotkoff got word that he was to embed a *New York Times* reporter with the WMD-hunters. The order came straight from the top, he was told. He didn't recognize the reporter's name, but he scribbled it down in his daily notes, with the abbreviations and scratchy handwriting of a man in a hurry: "Judith Miller. Write chem bio stuff. Secdef wants her embedded in XTF—gets here Wednesday."

Formally embedding reporters with military units was a fairly new Pentagon idea, and the troops on the ground were still getting used to it. War was now a 24-hour business, and Rotkoff knew only too well how, thanks to instantaneous, worldwide, secure video transmissions, military officers could spend half the day compiling information and assembling briefings for the bosses back in Washington.

Rotkoff would follow the order, but he was predisposed to dislike *The New York Times* after his experience with another *Times* reporter, Michael Gordon, who had been embedded at the ground forces' headquarters. Gordon was a skilled and experienced military affairs reporter but had a reputation for aloofness and self-importance. He inspired a Rotkoff haiku:

> *Gordon N.Y. Times*
> *Demonstrates Media Ethics*
> *It's all about him*

ON TUESDAY, MARCH 11, Garner held a press briefing in the Pentagon. It was on background so he could be quoted only as an unnamed "senior Defense official."

In case there was any doubt about his plans, Garner told the reporters, "What we need to do up front is pay the people in the ministries, be able to pay the army and be able to pay the law enforcement agencies and the court system." He said he planned to stay only for a few months. Iraq was in better shape than Afghanistan had been, he said. "In Iraq you do have a somewhat more sophisticated country and a somewhat more structured country than you do in Afghanistan . . . it has the structure and mechanisms in there to run that country and run it fairly efficiently."

A reporter asked about the INC, the Iraqi National Congress, the group headed by Ahmed Chalabi.

"We're not trying to hire any of them right now. Okay?" Garner said. He added later, "We haven't gone out to hire people from the INC."

That night, Feith called Garner, distraught. You've damaged the credibility of both Chalabi and the INC, he said.

"Doug, number one, I don't have a candidate" for who should run Iraq after the invasion, Garner replied. "And by the way, your boss doesn't have one either. I've heard Rumsfeld say two or three times, 'I don't have a candidate. The best man will rise.' "

Feith wasn't subdued. He struck Garner as a bright guy, but very, very disorganized, and he seemed really worried, almost in shock. You've really screwed up here, was his message. You've really created problems for us, and everybody at the Pentagon is really displeased with you.

"Look, Doug, there's an easy answer to your problem. Fire me. Hell, I'll go back to my company tomorrow. You don't have to settle for me. Go get somebody else."

"We can't do that now," Feith said.

Wolfowitz also called Garner. He was smooth, in contrast to the excitable Feith, but Garner realized that he was being reprimanded by the deputy secretary of defense.

"We're really going to have to be careful now," Wolfowitz said, "because there's a lot involved with the INC and Chalabi, and we have to be careful how we frame our remarks."

That night, the word came down to Garner: Don't talk to the press again until you leave. A day or two later, Garner's public affairs officer, a captain in the Navy Reserve, got another official word: He was not to speak to the press, even after he got to Kuwait.

At some point afterward, the official Department of Defense transcript of Garner's press conference was amended to add three highly unusual "clarifications," interrupting the text of Garner's remarks, and praising the INC.

"The INC has played an important role over the years in getting various Iraqi opposition groups to cooperate with one another," one such "clarification" stated in bracketed text. "The U.S. government admired the INC's successes in organizing the endorsement by those groups of principles that the U.S. Government favors for the creation of a new democratic government in Iraq."

LARRY DIRITA, a former Navy officer who had served on the Joint Staff and was now Rumsfeld's special assistant and right-hand man, called Garner on March 13.

"The SecDef wants to be briefed before you leave," DiRita said.

The next morning, Garner and his group met with Rumsfeld, Wolfowitz, Feith and the top military men from the Joint Staff—Chairman Myers, Vice Chairman Pace, General Casey and a dozen others.

Rumsfeld seemed a little stiff and distracted. Unknown to Garner, Bush was about to issue an ultimatum to Saddam: Leave Iraq or it will be war. Rumsfeld was pushing hard that Saddam be given 48 hours.

"I'm the mayor of Baghdad," said Barbara Bodine, a controversial former ambassador on Garner's staff.

"Well, that's interesting, isn't it?" Rumsfeld replied sarcastically.

Garner thought Bodine's comment was stupid and ill advised, but he said nothing.

That night Larry DiRita called Garner. "SecDef wants to meet you in the morning at eight."

The next morning, Rumsfeld saw Garner alone.

"Look, Jay," Rumsfeld began. "I accept responsibility for all of this, because I haven't given you the time I should have given you." It was an unusual admission from Rumsfeld. "Quite frankly, I just have been so engulfed in the war that I just didn't have time to focus on everything that you're doing. I tried to keep abreast of it, but I wasn't able to give it the time it needed.

"I'm really uncomfortable with all these people you have running the ministries," he said. Iraq had 23 main ministries. Most were similar to the cabinet departments in the United States government—Agriculture, Labor, Health, Education, Justice, Foreign Affairs and Defense. Other ministries reflected the Iraqi economy or special problems—Electricity, Irrigation, Culture and Religious Affairs. Less than half the people designated to run the ministries were from Defense. "I think they all should be from DOD," Rumsfeld said.

"Mr. Secretary," Garner replied, "we can't do that. There are clearly functions that belong to other agencies more than DOD." Bush's directive, NSPD-24, made it an interagency planning office.

"No," Rumsfeld insisted. "I think they all ought to be DOD." The same directive had put Defense in charge.

"We just can't agree on this," Garner said.

They went back and forth, but Rumsfeld held all the cards. He was the boss. He was polite, but insistent.

"Okay," Garner said, trying another tack. "Give me your nominee for the Ministry of Agriculture." Garner had recruited Henry Lee Schatz from the USDA's Foreign Agricultural Service. Schatz had been working internationally on behalf of the Department of Agriculture for nearly three decades.

"Look, we'll find the right people," Rumsfeld said. "I'm going to put together a good team for you."

"I don't want that," Garner said. "Let's look at health." He had designated Dr. Frederick "Skip" Burkle, yet another veteran of Operation Provide Comfort. "He's been on every operation like this—he's been in charge of health—everything like this since about 1986, and he's never failed. He knows what he's doing."

"We have competent people too," Rumsfeld protested.

"You don't have anybody as competent as Burkle," Garner said. "None of us do. Let's take the best there is, and the best are not all in DOD."

"I could probably go along with someone like Robin Raphel because I know her and I respect her a lot and I know that she's a hard worker." Raphel, a former ambassador to Tunisia, was going to be in charge of the Iraqi Ministry of Trade. She and Rumsfeld had worked together when he had been the U.S. special envoy to the Middle East in 1983 and 1984. But, Rumsfeld added, "I'm just not comfortable with the rest of these people." He obviously did not have alternatives and he proposed a compromise of sorts, or at least a delay. "Look. You think about this on the way over and call me as soon as you get to Kuwait."

"I'll do that," Garner agreed.

Garner left incredulous. All he could do was make sure he brought all the people he had designated and assigned.

THREE DAYS BEFORE THE START of the war, Sunday, March 16, Vice President Cheney was on NBC's *Meet the Press*. "My belief is we will, in fact, be greeted as liberators," he predicted.

The host, Tim Russert, pointed out that General Shinseki had testified to Congress that the postwar phase in Iraq would likely require several hundred thousand troops.

"To suggest that we need several hundred thousand troops there after military operations cease, after the conflict ends, I don't think is accurate. I think that's an overstatement," Cheney said.

About the same time as Cheney's television appearance, Garner and the roughly 150 members of his team responsible for Iraq "after the conflict" gathered in a parking lot outside the Pentagon. Rumsfeld came outside to see them off. For most of Garner's people, it was the first time they'd seen the secretary in person. The team headed to Andrews Air Force Base in Maryland, and left on a chartered US Airways jet for Kuwait.

Emotions were running high. "What went through my mind all the time was, I hope we pull this off," Garner recalled. He was thinking, "I just need a little more time. Just need a little more time."

Within hours after they landed in Kuwait on March 17, Lieutenant General McKiernan, the commander of the ground forces, asked Garner and Bates to come to a meeting of his senior staff officers.

"These are the two new members of the team," McKiernan told his staff, with his arms on Garner's and Bates's shoulders. "Your ticket home is to make these guys feel comfortable."

McKiernan had said there was no space available for Garner's team at the military camp, so the group found space at a brand-new Hilton hotel complex outside Kuwait City. The resort had been leased by the defense contractor Kellogg, Brown and Root, a subsidiary of Cheney's old company, Halliburton, in anticipation of war. It was an hour's drive away.

That same day, Garner and his deputy, Ron Adams, phoned Rumsfeld to go over the ministry list. Rumsfeld continued to press for Defense people.

"Okay, maybe we can take a DOD guy here," Garner said at one point, then, at another, "Maybe we can take one there." It looked like Rumsfeld might get more, maybe enough to have a majority.

"Trust me," Rumsfeld said. "I'm going to put together a good team for you. It'll be a great team."

"Mr. Secretary, you can't get them here in time," Garner said. War was going to start any day.

"Jay, we're going to give you a much better team than you have now," Rumsfeld promised.

"Okay, that's fine," Garner said.

When he hung up, Garner turned to Adams. "We're not going to do a damn thing," he said. "We're going to go with what we got. Don't say a word to anybody. They'll never know."

THE WAR BEGAN ON MARCH 19 with a target-of-opportunity strike on Dora Farm, a complex southeast of Baghdad on the bank of the Tigris River, where Saddam was incorrectly thought to be hiding.

As a pure military operation, the invasion seemed to go astonishingly well. On Day 3, the 3rd Infantry Division was 150 miles into Iraq, and Saddam's army was either being defeated or dissolving. Still, some of the former Iraqi soldiers were coming back dressed in civilian clothes or in the black-and-white garb of the Saddam Fedayeen, the militia commanded by Saddam's son Uday. Unprotected Iraqi civilian fighters were throwing themselves on armored formations. Mostly, they were being slaughtered. They tried insane, impossible, suicidal tactics, attacking tanks on foot, or trying to ambush Bradley Fighting Vehicles with small arms.

Rotkoff wrote a haiku:

> *Saddam Fedhayeen*
> *Where the hell did they come from?*
> *Everyone missed it*

Spider Marks concluded that Saddam loyalists were pointing guns at the civilians' backs: You either attack the Americans or you die right here. The Iraqi people were simply and deeply fearful. A few days after the invasion, Marks, McKiernan and a couple of others were talking it over with Tenet in Kuwait.

"So, what do you think?" Marks asked the CIA director. "You know, these guys are fighting. They're coming at us."

"I can't fucking figure it out," Tenet said.

ON MARCH 21, 2003—the second day of the war—Rice and Hadley gave the president and the NSC a formal briefing on the nine U.S. and coalition war objectives. The point was to make sure everyone agreed about what they planned for Iraq after the shooting stopped. One goal was stated as: "Iraq is seen to be moving towards democratic institutions and serves as a model for the region." In addition, they had to "place as many Iraqi faces in positions of visible authority as quickly as possible. . . . Accomplish the above urgently."

It was consistent with what Garner had told the president the only time they had met. His efforts had been approved yet again by the principals, including Rumsfeld.

GARNER SPOKE WITH RUMSFELD via secure video teleconference from Kuwait just about every day. Usually many others were in the rooms on both ends. On March 22, they renewed their firefight over who was going to run the ministries. Rumsfeld still wanted to handpick each one. Soon they were arguing, and Garner tried another dose of reality, telling Rumsfeld again that he could not possibly get new people over there on time.

"You know, it doesn't seem like you're on our team," Rumsfeld said, according to a note-taker.

"Okay, that's it," Garner replied. The teleconference was over. Garner then sent a longhand note by fax to Rumsfeld insisting they had the same goals. "I am a team player," he wrote. He was deeply offended. It was the worst kind of bullying tactic—if you don't agree with me you are disloyal.

NO WMD HAD BEEN USED or found in the first days of the invasion. The intense pace of Marks's intelligence team only got more frantic. The quality of the intelligence on the hundreds of remaining sites on the WMD site list was still unsatisfactory, and the unanticipated Iraqi opposition was jarring. It had been part of the intelligence shop's job to figure these things out, and they hadn't done it.

Marks had to give himself a pep talk at one point. One of the CIA station chiefs he was dealing with, he wrote on March 29, had "been watching this region for his entire professional life and he did not understand the depth of the people's fear. Don't beat yourself up Marks." Everybody was worn out. "This is the most fulfilling but most difficult and frustrating job I have ever endeavored to do," Marks continued in his diary. "The scope of responsibilities, the compressed timelines for execution, little time for anything other than execution, no time to think. Substance does matter, but the process is what is killing me. Just keeping the engine room stoked is monumental."

Rotkoff put it succinctly, baring his exhaustion, frustration and doubt:

> *Mental bone tired*
> *Hard to stay not wanted*
> *Can't rest—men will die*

"THOUSANDS ARE JUST taking off their uniforms and going home," Bush told British Prime Minister Blair on the phone.

"Yes, they are just melting away," Blair added.

"Just melting away," Bush echoed.

Bush didn't really have a lot to do once the fighting started. Notes of his conversations and meetings show he spoke repeatedly about victory, but they also reveal a president concerned that the U.S. could win the ground conflict but still lose the propaganda battle.

"We need to remind people why we are here," Bush said in a Pentagon meeting on March 25. He told Rumsfeld: "You will remind the world of who we are fighting."

The Air Force had three giant, four-engine Commando Solo transport planes in the air—flying TV and radio stations—broadcasting over Iraq.

"How does this look to the average Iraqi?" Bush asked at an NSC meeting on March 28. The answer was that the broadcasts were reaching Baghdad for five hours a day, from 6 to 11 P.M. They weren't broadcasting video, just still photographs.

Not enough, was Bush's reply. "You have to calibrate it. You have to market programs. People don't turn on television if there's nothing to watch."

Three days later, he had General Franks on a secure video teleconference. "Are you pleased with our information ops?" he asked. "Can you broadcast our message into Baghdad?"

Franks said he wasn't pleased that Iraqi TV was still on the air, and he needed more translators "to turn up the quality and volume of Arab language broadcasts."

Bush said, "If you need help from the States, we'll give it to you."

On April 4, toward the end of another NSC meeting, somebody mentioned that the electricity was off in Iraq's capital city, which U.S. forces had not yet reached.

"Who turned out the lights in Baghdad?" Bush asked.

"Most probably the regime to reposition its forces," Franks said on the video screen. "But we don't know for sure."

"Well, then, if it's the regime, put the word out that we didn't do it," Bush said.

Still, the president appeared confident. "Only one thing matters: winning," he said at one NSC meeting, as he dismissed "second-guessing regarding the post-Saddam world." In a private moment, Hadley asked him how he was doing.

"I made the decision," Bush said. "I sleep well at night."

16

"I DON'T KNOW HOW LONG it's going to last, and I don't know how much it's going to cost," Rumsfeld told his staff often. On April 2, he sent a one-page memo to the service secretaries, the chairman of the Joint Chiefs, Feith, Franks and other key people in the Pentagon. He directed them to support Garner "as required," and said Garner's mission was "to help create the conditions for transition to Iraqi self-rule and the withdrawal of coalition forces upon completion of their military objectives." In Kuwait, Colonel Tom Baltazar on Garner's staff got a copy. The memo had been written because Garner's group just couldn't get cooperation from the military commands. Amazing, he thought. The president's signature on the National Security Presidential Directive of January 20, saying, in effect, "support them," isn't good enough for these guys. We've got to get Rumsfeld's signature as well.

BESIDES BEING THE HEAD of the Iraqi National Congress, Ahmed Chalabi was the head of a group of exiled Iraqis who had received some American-sponsored military training. But everything about the military group had been a bust. Besides training only a tiny fraction of the number who were supposed to be armed and ready, there had even been a fight over what the group should be called. Chalabi's band was eventually given the alliterative but redundant name Free Iraqi Freedom Fighters.

By early April, Chalabi was clamoring to get into Iraq. Despite the support of his patrons at the Pentagon and in Washington, the American generals in the Middle East had little use for him. The last thing they wanted to do was drop Chalabi with his small army in the middle of the war zone, but there was pressure to do just that.

Abizaid finally relented. "Okay, let's put the son of a bitch in there and see if he can do what all of them think he can do," he told Garner. "And I'll tell you he can't."

The U.S. flew Chalabi, the Free Iraqi Freedom Fighters and other Chalabi associates into Nasiriyah aboard one of its durable, take-off-and-land-anywhere C-130 Hercules transport planes. Spider Marks was there when Chalabi landed. He thought the INC leader was trying to emulate MacArthur's return to the Philippines. Chalabi was wearing a black sport shirt with a bush hat, leading a group of his people. So these are the Free Iraqi Freedom Fighters, Marks thought. "Check your wallets. Boy, that's a nasty crowd."

Reports started to come in that the Free Iraqi Freedom Fighters were carrying out reprisals, stealing and looting.

Marks and another intelligence officer, Colonel Jon "Jake" Jones, were riding in an open-air Humvee one night with their weapons pointed outward, wondering whether they might get into a firefight with some unknown enemy.

"Slow down," Jones said, spotting four or five bearded Iraqis gathered around a fire at the side of the road. They were cooking some kind of animal on a spit—a sheep or a dog maybe—and dancing around. It looked as if they were smoking dope, the officers thought. It was almost a scene out of *Lord of the Flies.*

Jones and Marks looked at each other and reached the same conclusion, in stereo. "Free Iraqi Freedom Fighters," they both said, before hitting the gas.

CHRISTOPHER "RYAN" HENRY had gone to work in February as principal undersecretary of defense for policy, making him Doug Feith's top deputy. A retired Navy captain and a former top official at the defense contractor SAIC, Henry had a unique connection to the secretary of defense. His wife, Delonnie Henry, was Rumsfeld's confidential assistant and chief secretary, the woman who typed his snowflakes and kept his files. Rumsfeld was still pressing on control of the Iraqi ministries, and on April 6, Henry called Garner with Defense's new list of people.

"Ryan, that's great," Garner said. "When are they going to get here?"

"Well, we don't know. We haven't even notified some of them yet."

"Ryan, let's be reasonable on this. You'll never get them here on time." Major combat would soon be over. U.S. troops were nearing Baghdad.

"No," Henry said, "we're going to work this hard."

Garner and Bates knew the problem was soon going to be in Baghdad. As they'd been saying for months, the question was going to be who was going to be in charge. Garner had an idea. "Here's what you have to do to be successful," he told Rumsfeld. "You bring John Abizaid in the country and you promote him." As Franks's deputy, Abizaid was too much out of the real action. "Make him a sub–unified commander, because you need a four-star. And put me in charge of all the reconstruction, civil administration. Put McKiernan in charge of all the security and military operations."

Rumsfeld balked, but he wouldn't say why he didn't think it was a good idea. Garner persisted. He felt it was the solution, ensuring unity of command in the theater, with both McKiernan and him reporting to Abizaid.

"I'm not talking about this anymore," Rumsfeld said in another phone call.

About the third or fourth time Garner raised the suggestion, Rumsfeld said, "Look, Jay. We've discussed this before and you know my position." He slammed down the phone. Bush and Rice had made it clear that no military man was going to get the job. Imagine, Rice thought: "President John Abizaid."

RICE THOUGHT GARNER was sitting in Kuwait too long. All the important things—running the government, getting the ministries up and running in Iraq—were not getting done. She understood that Iraq had a pretty good civil service, and she assumed it would still be there. But several days into the war, she received reports that the government workers, including oil workers, could not be found.

"What do you mean you can't find the oil workers?" she asked.

There was a brittleness in the country, she concluded. As a Soviet expert she had studied what happens to totalitarian systems when they collapse. She recalled reading about the 1953 death of Joseph Stalin. For five weeks the Soviet Union ceased to function. Nobody could do anything because everybody counted on direction from the very top. Iraq seemed to have cratered in the same way or worse. But history predicted it would be temporary. In the end, she was confident, order would re-assert itself, as had happened in the old USSR.

THE XTF—the artillery brigade turned WMD-hunting unit—had to scale back. The plan had been to send five teams to travel with the combat forces and catalogue or quickly deal with whatever WMD they came across, and to field three more teams with greater expertise to systematically visit the sites on the WMD master list. With too few people and vehicles, they pulled back to four teams with the invading units, and two teams of between 12 and 25 people—called MET units, for "mobile exploitation team"—to do the most intensive inspections.

On April 8, Colonel Richard McPhee, the XTF commander, rolled into Iraq with one of the two MET units, on their way to its first inspection in a small town south of Baghdad, where the WMD intelligence suggested they would find a form of chemical weapons agent. There was nothing. Buried where they thought they were supposed to look, they found only 55-gallon drums of gasoline.

Part of the team hurried on to another suspected site at Karbala, about 60 miles southwest of Baghdad, where they heard a rumor about an Iraqi man who had passed a note to U.S. forces saying he was a scientist who had worked on WMD, had information for the coalition, and wanted to turn himself in. After a 24-hour chase through the Iraqi desert, the unit tracked down the soldiers who had the note, and then found the Iraqi scientist.

Colonel McPhee left the team and flew quickly back to Kuwait by helicopter to meet with Marks. Tension was growing over whether the teams should keep going down the list of WMD suspect sites, or if the better idea was to follow new leads, such as the site the scientist suggested.

"I've got to tell you, this is as important as it gets," McPhee told Marks, and described the Iraqi scientist, who didn't ask for anything from the Americans. McPhee wanted clearance to dedicate a significant effort to focus on this one assignment.

"Rich, you don't have to do that, man," Marks replied, meaning McPhee didn't have to fly back to Kuwait and ask for permission to do his job. "Absolutely. Got to go for it."

Marks wrote briefly about the meeting in his daily diary. "WMD testing—keep expectations low." Even with his chagrin at the quality of the intelligence, Marks had been thinking: 946 sites! They couldn't be wrong about all of them, could they? Even if they were right on only 30 percent of the sites, that would still be a heck of a lot of WMD. Batting .300 was enough to get a ballplayer into the Hall of Fame. "We're all going to Cooperstown," Marks thought. But news of the Iraqi scientist was still a welcome relief.

McPhee went back to Iraq, and the MET unit spent about a day and a half with the scientist, first searching exactly where he'd thought the WMD materials had been buried, and then spreading an arc around the area and continuing the search.

McPhee contacted Marks by secure radio and classified e-mail. "No joy," he reported.

It was a watershed moment for Marks. "No joy" said it all.

GENERAL FRANKS was on a secure video line on April 9, piped into the National Security Council meeting at the White House. The war was going well, he said. "In the south all the enemy formations are destroyed. There are small groups operating with no threat. The Marines and the Brits are squeezing the Iraqi divisions."

In the Baghdad region, they'd destroyed 90 percent of the Iraqi forces' equipment, Franks reported.

"Are we picking up the bad guys?" Bush asked.

"We've distributed pictures of the top 55. There aren't a lot of refugees yet. Some bad guys will slip through but we're doing everything we can to cut the main routes."

The humanitarian crisis, the burning oil fields, and the WMD attacks hadn't happened, Franks said. Nine hundred of the 1,000 southern oil wells were under control, and the last 100 would be under control within 48 hours. "The population of Umm Qasr"—Iraq's largest deepwater port, just over the border from Kuwait—"in a week has gone from 15,000 to 40,000. Water is better than prewar, electricity is restored, food's available," Franks said. There were some problems in other cities, but they were mostly under control.

Bush told him to make sure that somebody was compiling statistics on what prewar Iraqi life was like under Saddam.

"We cannot have people coming into one of these cities and say, the conditions here are appalling, and measure it against an American city. You have to measure it against the city prewar, the way it was," Bush said. "This guy's spent 20 to 30 years ruining this country. It's going to take a while to rebuild it."

We're moving McKiernan's headquarters up to Baghdad, Franks said. Eventually Garner's team would follow. "Sensitive site exploitation will continue." So far there had been no WMD stockpiles found.

In a few days, Franks said, there would be a conference of Iraqi representatives in Tallil, outside Nasiriyah, about 100 miles southeast of Baghdad. "It'll be an organizational meeting without commitment," meaning it was preliminary.

"Very wise," Bush replied. "It'll be a focal point for the world to see that we're not parachuting our own choice in. You know, 'Do we believe in democracy? Yes.' We're bringing these guys together."

"We've got to win the story in the peacetime era," Bush told British Prime Minister Blair. "We've won the war. We cannot have people define the peacetime era for us."

RUMSFELD DISPATCHED LARRY DIRITA, his special assistant, to Iraq. DiRita was in Qatar that same day, April 9, waiting to catch a plane to Kuwait, where he would link up with Garner.

In the airport, DiRita watched on television as an amazing scene unfolded in downtown Baghdad, broadcast live throughout the world. A team of U.S. Marines who had swept into the city were helping a group of Iraqis topple a 20-foot statue of Saddam, using an armored vehicle with a chain. It marked the symbolic end of Saddam's regime.

That night, after DiRita landed in Kuwait, Garner's people gave him a series of briefings in a small dining room in one of the villas at the Kuwait City Hilton. One discussion turned to the benefits that the Iraqis would enjoy as a result of American reconstruction plans.

As Colonel Paul Hughes remembers, DiRita slammed his fist on a heavy oak table, and said, "We don't owe the Iraqis anything! We're giving them their freedom. That's all we should give them. We don't owe them any other benefit."

DiRita does not recall the remarks, but says his point was that the U.S. had to help the Iraqis do it for themselves. If the United States came in with large amounts of cash flowing out of everyone's pockets, it would tell the Iraqis to stand back. Rumsfeld wanted them to stand up.

A few days later, DiRita met with Garner's senior staffers at the Kuwait City Hilton.

"We went into the Balkans and Bosnia and Kosovo and we're still in them," Hughes recalls DiRita saying. "We're probably going to wind up in Afghanistan for a long time because the Department of State can't do its job right. Because they keep screwing things up, the Department of Defense winds up being stuck at these places. We're not going to let this happen in Iraq."

The reaction was generally, Whoa! Does this guy even realize that half the people in the room are from the State Department?

DiRita went on, as Hughes recalled: "By the end of August we're going to have 25,000 to 30,000 troops left in Iraq."

DiRita had heard Rumsfeld talk privately many times about foreign occupations. "It's like a broken bone," Rumsfeld said. "If you don't set it right at first, it is always somewhat broken." Rumsfeld said later, "I think I used the characterization of a broken arm. If you don't set it, everything grows around the break and you end up with that abnormality there." Too many occupations like Kosovo and Bosnia had been approached as if they would be permanent; and sure enough, that was what they became.

Others in the room that day don't recall DiRita's words being quite so stark, but most of the State Department people there instinctively knew there was no way they could run Iraq the way Defense envisioned. Invading and quickly departing didn't seem just physically impossible, it was morally dubious. Robin Raphel's eyeballs were on the ceiling, as she thought to herself: *What is Larry DiRita smoking? The poor baby. He just doesn't get it.*

THE NEXT DAY, APRIL 10, Ryan Henry called Garner again.

"Hey, we've got a real problem in the ministries," Henry said.

"What's that?"

Well, Henry explained, the White House had learned about the Defense Department list of people for the Iraqi ministries. "And they want to know why they're not appointing people and why are we doing it. So we've got to send the list to the White House, and we think they're going to redo it, so it will be a little while longer."

"Fine," Garner said sarcastically. "Whenever you get them together and go get them trained and ship them over here, we'll welcome them with open arms."

Rumsfeld just didn't think Garner's group was the A team. It hardly mattered, though. In Garner's opinion, Rumsfeld and Henry didn't have a clue what was going on.

• • •

SEVERAL DAYS AFTER Saddam's statue fell, Prince Bandar went to the White House to see the president. Rumsfeld was leaving as he arrived.

"We'll accelerate the withdrawal," he told Bandar. "Don't worry."

Bandar expressed concern about stability in Iraq to Bush. The United States military had occupied the country, but Rumsfeld was talking about a fast withdrawal. Bandar repeated what he had told Bush before the war. There would be a power vacuum in Iraq for sure. The Baath Party and the military, including the Iraqi intelligence and security services, had run the country.

"Take the top echelon off because of their involvement and their bloody hands," Bandar said. "But keep and maintain the integrity of the institutions. What you should do, announce all of the military report back to their barracks and keep, let's say the colonels on down. Somebody has to run things." And do the same thing with the Iraqi intelligence and security services. "Look, their intel service was the most efficient. Take off the top echelon and keep the second line and let them find those bad guys, because those bad guys will know how to find bad guys." They could find Saddam.

"That's too Machiavellian," someone said. The Saudi notes of the meeting indicate it was either Bush or Rice.

"Let bad people find bad people, and then after that you get rid of them," Bandar said. "What's the big deal? Double-cross them. I mean, for God's sake, who said that we owe them anything?"

No one responded.

Saudi Arabia shared a 500-mile border with Iraq, and stability in the aftermath was a major concern. Chaos or an extremist, pro-Iranian Shiite regime would be a nightmare for the Saudis, conceivably worse than the relative stability provided by Saddam.

The Saudis estimated that there were some 3 million retirees in Iraq, sitting at home, getting about the equivalent of $6 a month. "Go and pay them for six months, for God's sakes," Bandar advised. "Each of them supports a family, mind you. So from 3 million you could get the support of literally 10 million people. Suddenly you have a major constituency for you because you have paid them off."

It was the Saudi way. Paying 3 million retirees would amount to about $100 million. Bandar proposed doing the same with the Iraqi military. Chop off the top echelon, and then pay the rest for three to six months. That might be another $100 million. After liberation, people in Iraq were going to have high expectations, Bandar said. Don't disappoint them. "You have to make people feel that their life is going to get better."

Saddam's party and army—the instruments of repression—could be instruments of stability. The total cost of the buyout program would be about $200 million. It might be the best $200 million the U.S. ever spent, he said.

Bush indicated it was up to Rumsfeld.

AMIDST THE JUBILATION of the swift military victory, the news in the U.S. was increasingly filled with images of looting and chaos. Robin Raphel, who had 28 years of diplomatic experience, chiefly in South Asia and the Middle East, was the senior State Department official among the ministry advisers. As she and others watched television in Kuwait, waiting for their chance to move up into Iraq, they grew increasingly concerned about the state of affairs. Was Garner's team, only about 200 strong, supposed to run the entire country? It was pure fantasy.

"Don't worry," Raphel said to some of the more junior members of Garner's team. "The truth is we can't actually do this. So don't worry. We really just have to kind of put our finger in the dike, get there, and within weeks we're going to be on our knees to the U.N. and the international community." She meant to be reassuring.

"I PICKED UP a newspaper today and I couldn't believe it," Rumsfeld exclaimed during a Pentagon news conference on April 11. "I read eight headlines that talked about chaos, violence, unrest. And it was just Henny Penny—'The sky is falling.' I've never seen anything like it! And here is a country that is being liberated, here are people who are going from being repressed and held under the thumb of a vicious dictator, and they're free."

Rumsfeld's remarks were punctuated by a PowerPoint presentation of photographs shown to the journalists. The images bore captions or file names such as "Iraqis share a laugh with a U.S. Army soldier"; "Jubilant Iraqis cheer U.S. Army soldiers"; "Happy Iraqis pose with a U.S. Army soldier"; and "Two young Iraqis give the thumbs-up sign to coalition soldiers."

"Let me say one other thing," Rumsfeld continued. "The images you are seeing on television you are seeing over, and over, and over, and it's the same picture of some person walking out of some building with a vase, and you see it 20 times, and you think, 'My goodness, were there that many vases?' "

Both Rumsfeld and the press corps laughed. "Is it possible that there were that many vases in the whole country?" he asked.

Bush echoed the comment in a press conference two days later. "You know, it's amazing," he said, "the statue comes down on Wednesday and the headlines start to read: Oh, there's disorder. Well, no kidding. It is a situation that is chaotic because Saddam Hussein created conditions for chaos."

"FRI. APR. 11, D+23," Spider Marks wrote in his war diary. "No WMD."

The next day, he flew to Baghdad with McKiernan. Even with the euphoria of setting foot in Iraq for the first time and the hundreds of things on his mind, WMD kept percolating to the top. It wasn't just the failure to find the weapons; it was the concern that they might fall into someone else's hands. "Think about the worst thing that could happen," Marks wrote on April 13 after a session with General Franks. His shorthand answer: "Foreign Jihadists w CBW," meaning chemical or biological weapons.

On April 19, "D+31," after a meeting with General McKiernan, Marks recorded the coalition's two top objectives: "maintain integrity of Iraq's borders," and "WMD—id/elminate."

But they weren't finding anything. Part of the problem seemed to be the intense looting and the "limited number of forces available to secure sensitive sites," according to a report later written by Chief Warrant Officer Richard "Monty" Gonzales, the officer in charge of one of Colonel McPhee's MET units.

"Targeted destruction of specific items was evident at nearly every site," the report continued. "On one occasion, at an Iraqi Intelligence Services headquarters in Baghdad, the team was amazed to find Iraqis actively attempting to destroy materials, even while U.S. forces were scouring the area. In an urban environment—without adequate security—the tasks of eliminating looters, stopping deliberate destruction efforts, and safeguarding the team became a nearly impossible task."

17

WITHOUT MENTIONING IT TO GARNER, Rumsfeld was working on a plan to replace him with a new presidential envoy to Iraq, a significant upgrade over Garner's position. The new envoy would be more like a super-administrator or even a viceroy. On April 8, Rumsfeld gathered a group in his Pentagon office so Ryan Henry could brief them on a list of potential candidates. Steve Herbits, who had set up a formal system for Rumsfeld on major personnel decisions that required that the jobs and goals be defined precisely, was present. "By the end of this meeting," Rumsfeld said, "I want Herbits to take this presentation and redo it."

Henry's list of possible envoys included 100 names. It included former Tennessee Senator and Reagan White House Chief of Staff Howard Baker, former Secretaries of Defense James Schlesinger and Harold Brown, former California Governor Pete Wilson, former Oklahoma Governor Frank Keating, and former Federal Reserve Chairman Paul Volcker. There were some Brits on the list—former U.K. Foreign Secretary Lord Carrington was one—as well as a couple of Democrats—Clinton Treasury Secretaries Robert Rubin and Larry Summers. Herbits knew the Democrats were not serious options. Absent from the list were the people who had experience in postwar stabilization operations, such as Richard Holbrooke, the former Clinton U.N. ambassador who had negotiated a peace agreement among warring factions in Bosnia in 1996, and James Dobbins, Mr. Postwar, the former State Department official who had the most experience in post-conflict situations. They were not considered because of their association with Clinton nation building.

After listening for about an hour, Rumsfeld told Herbits privately, "I want you to do this, but understand that this is for the president."

Over the next 48 hours Herbits rewrote the job description. It boiled down to security, reconstruction and politics. He cut the list of candidates down to the top 10.

He wrote that the best candidate was former Secretary of State George Shultz, who had once headed Bechtel Corporation, a major government contractor. Shultz, 83, had stature as one of the world's most respected statesmen. Herbits called him "an international adult." Upsides included, "Capable of holding ground against all comers in press and in negotiations," and "Prevents DOD from being blamed for acts committed or omitted."

The downsides included: "Not known for taking direction. . . . Older—may falter if stressed too long. . . . may be more tolerant of State's viewpoints than DOD person. . . . May be accused of taking on the duties in order to further Bechtel's interests."

But Herbits had a dark-horse candidate for the job. In his view the perfect person to run Iraq was Paul Wolfowitz. He composed a separate four-page memo that would eventually be sent to President Bush and find its way into the hands of Vice President Cheney.

"Getting Post-Iraq Right," Herbits typed as the heading on April 10, 2003. "Since the diplomatic first phase has fallen short in achieving a broadly-based consensus for action," he wrote, firing a shot at the State Department, it was critical to get the phase after military action right. Herbits, who had been part of the Bletchley II group 16 months earlier and had concluded that the U.S. was in for a two-generation war with Islamic extremists that had to start with Iraq, wrote that success could mean Bush would have "a model for the creation of a Palestinian state" and even eventual "Iranian overthrow."

Under the heading, "Benchmarks to Measure Success," Herbits wrote, "In the months after the shooting stops, it is essential that there be no civil war. Civil wars, rightly or wrongly, hearken back to Vietnam. The president's strategy will die in the embrace of such a comparison.

"An orderly and healthy life for Iraqis must quickly be established on a self-sustainable basis." The interim domestic civilian government had to become a "cherished model for the rest of liberty-desiring peoples and governments."

The presidential envoy had to have absolute authority "on all Iraq questions outside of military activity . . . report to the president if possible and the SecDef as only other option."

"Why the Presidential Envoy Should Be DepSecDef Wolfowitz," Herbits typed, starting a new section. Wolfowitz's appointment would provide "clarity to the world" about the president's vision of freedom and thwart "traditional Department of State resistance to seeking change in the region."

Because he was already the deputy defense secretary, Wolfowitz "has all the necessary authority in his current position.

"But perhaps most important and exclusive to Paul personally are the facts that he enjoys the widest support among Iraqis." In this context, of course, "Iraqis" meant "Iraqi exiles," especially Chalabi. "To say that *he* is not essential could be seen as saying that *they* are not important." His selection "would unequivocally demonstrate the importance of the Iraqi Diaspora is, indeed, central. He is the best long-term symbol of the overall strategy."

Then Herbits added, "His being Jewish is a plus: It is a reminder that this is not a war against religion, it is a clear signal that the position is temporary, that the former ambassador to the world's largest Muslim nation for three years"—Wolfowitz had been ambassador to Indonesia from 1986 to 1989—"has experience in being culturally sensitive."

The next afternoon, Herbits took the memo to Rumsfeld. The proposal was the kind of jolting, out-of-left-field thinking that greatly appealed to the secretary. He called in Delonnie Henry.

"Take off Herbits's name," Rumsfeld instructed her. "Put the following cover on it, and send it over the president's private fax." He wrote out a brief note saying that a good friend and associate had written this excellent paper, adding, "I'm available all weekend if you'd like to discuss."

Over the weekend, Herbits was at Cheney's house for lunch to brief him on a conference at the American Enterprise Institute. He took a copy of his Wolfowitz memo.

"I'd like you to see this," Herbits told the vice president, handing him the copy, "because it might come your way."

Cheney looked at the paper. "I've seen it."

"Oh."

"I went over to Rumsfeld's house for dinner last night and he wouldn't let me eat until I read it." He paused. "Good paper," Cheney added, giving one of his half smiles.

. . .

STEVE HADLEY read the Herbits memo and agreed with it. Wolfowitz was his candidate. But Rumsfeld was sending lots of memos, papered everyone including the president with snowflakes. Picking Wolfowitz would be seen as tantamount to endorsing Chalabi, and the president was adamant that the United States not be seen as putting its thumb on the scales. In addition, the president knew that Wolfowitz did not have a strong reputation as a manager. The deputy secretary of defense was a thinker, but he could barely run his office.

Both Herbits and Rumsfeld told Wolfowitz that he was being proposed as the Iraq envoy.

"If that's what they want," Wolfowitz told Rumsfeld, "I'd be happy to do it."

Rumsfeld's recollection is different. "Paul came to me and said he'd like to be considered. He asked me to do that and I did it."

Notwithstanding Herbits's suggestion that Wolfowitz's Jewish background was a plus, both Rumsfeld and the White House worried that putting a Jewish viceroy in the middle of the Arab world would be difficult.

Rumsfeld never told Wolfowitz why he had not been selected. "Probably the Jewish factor weighed heavily in their minds," Wolfowitz later told an Iraqi-American friend.

GARNER WANTED DESPERATELY to get to Baghdad. He believed the only way to reconstruct the country was through contractors. They had to get the American and Iraqi civilians who would be doing the rebuilding hired so they could start work. But only three of the 13 main contracts had been signed. Franks's plan said that Garner and his team should not go into Iraq until the invasion was over and Phase IV stability operations began.

Garner flew to the Qatar headquarters of Central Command to make a personal plea to Franks. His mission was in jeopardy. Chaos was the mother of all Show Stoppers.

"You have got to get me in there," Garner implored his old friend.

"Jay," Franks said, "there's still fighting in there." Baghdad was still a hot combat zone. Back in January he had promised only to get Garner in after major combat was over. "Think about this. It isn't going to do either of us any good to get a bunch of your civilians killed in Baghdad."

"Look, Tommy. Baghdad has vacuums in it that are being filled up with things you and I don't want it to be filled up with, and we're not going to be able to get rid of those things unless we get in there now." The violence and looting were beyond the scale anyone had expected. "If you don't get me in there we're going to have more problems than a few civilians shot up."

"Okay, damn it," Franks finally said. "I'll call McKiernan and see if he can support this." They both knew that in the middle of a war the last thing the ground commander needed was a handful of civilians. "Jay, he's got his hands full right now."

"I know that," Garner said sympathetically, "and I'll try to be as easy on him as possible but you've got to get me in there."

Franks called Garner that night. "You've got a green light. I've talked to McKiernan. He said he's going to have a hard time supporting you, but he's willing to give it a try. God bless you. Be careful."

On April 21, Garner and eight of his people flew into Baghdad. Everything was filthy. Basic supplies were low. Electricity was on, then off. Garner went to the sewage plant, and found that it was not running. The heat was unbearable. His chief of staff, Bates, set off with the rest of the team in a caravan of nearly 150 new Chevrolet Suburbans in a 400-mile road march from Kuwait to Baghdad. Garner and his pickup team took over a 258-room palace-like former government building located near the center of the city.

THE PRESIDENT WAS STILL CONCERNED that the U.S. was losing the propaganda war. Whatever it was called—public affairs, global outreach, public diplomacy, strategic communications—they were losing.

One of Rice's NSC staffers, Jeffrey Jones, a retired Army colonel, had presented a SECRET briefing to the NSC principals called "Phase IV Iraq Information Strategy" full of charts, tasks, organization schemes, objectives and themes. It went nowhere. Karen Hughes, Bush's information czar and White House counselor, believed the State Department was not aggressive enough in explaining Bush's foreign policy. She persuaded Margaret Tutwiler, the grande dame of Republican communications strategy during the Reagan and Bush senior years, to take the top job in the State Department as the undersecretary for public diplomacy.

Tutwiler, 52, described in a *Washington Post* article as a "one-woman psychological operations team," was born and raised in Birmingham, Alabama, and had a deep, confiding southern accent. She had worked nonstop as communications and political adviser to Jim Baker for 12 years while he served as White House chief of staff and treasury secretary for Reagan and then as secretary of state for George H. W. Bush. She had one interest and focus: Baker's image and success.

Tutwiler was serving as U.S. ambassador to Morocco when she received her Iraq assignment—Do for Garner what you did for Baker.

When Tutwiler arrived in Baghdad, she was overwhelmed by the government and societal meltdown—no showers, no reliable electricity. She was being eaten alive by mosquitoes. Garner personally taught her how to cook military field rations—MREs, or "Meals, Ready to Eat." Chicken tortellini number 19 turned out to be her favorite. Mess and gunk and garbage and waste were everywhere. There was no privacy in the rooms, if it was possible to call them "rooms," with no doors or windows. Sleep was almost impossible.

"It's just so damn hot," she told Garner. "I'm just burning up."

"Here, Margaret," he said, proposing an old soldier's solution. "Here's what you do. Take your clothes off, as much of them as you're comfortable with. If you've got enough bottled water, just pour it all over and rinse your body and then lie on top of your bed inside the mosquito net. It's going to evaporate off of you and you'll be cooler."

The next morning Garner asked her if it had worked.

"I drenched my body," Tutwiler said, "and I got in and I was soaking wet and I closed my eyes and I went to sleep. When I woke up I was choking and I couldn't stand it. We had that big sandstorm. I was nothing but a mud ball."

Iraq was such a catastrophe, Tutwiler concluded, that even Jim Baker would not have been able to fix it. The country had neither a functioning society nor a functioning government. But she knew from experience that every White House wanted total control and instant results. Soon she was getting calls from the White House and Pentagon complaining about the pictures of the looting and chaos on television and in the newspapers. Get those pictures off, they said.

Tutwiler told everyone in Washington that the political power and infrastructure vacuums were of unimaginable magnitude. This surpassed anything she had ever seen.

Tutwiler liked Garner. He was a genuine patriot, she thought, without a personal agenda. But he was no Jim Baker. Garner did not know how to line up all the players in the Washington game, the interagency process—how to make the Pentagon, the State Department, the CIA, the White House and Treasury all happy. Garner seemed to have the right ideas, but he just didn't have the contacts or clout in Washington, and he didn't have the manpower in Baghdad.

Garner complained to Tutwiler that he'd been under orders not to talk to the press since he'd left Washington, when he'd shown indifference toward Chalabi and the INC at his press conference. It was ridiculous. Communicating and explaining were part of his job. The press was suspicious, madder than hell that he would not talk.

Tutwiler tried and failed to get the embargo lifted. She talked to her own contacts in the White House, the Pentagon and State Department. No one wanted Garner talking to the press. They didn't want him making policy statements. He seemed too quick on the draw. Tutwiler even received complaints that Garner wasn't showing proper respect for the Iraqis because he went around the country without a coat and tie.

Garner finally called Rumsfeld to complain.

"You're not embargoed," Rumsfeld said, "you can talk to whoever you need to talk to."

Tutwiler immediately arranged a press conference, but about 45 minutes later she told Garner, "You've been reembargoed."

"I'll call Rumsfeld," Garner said.

"It won't do any good," she replied. "It's from the White House." That meant from Karen Hughes.

Tutwiler then set up a partial solution. She would tip off reporters when Garner was moving so he could be "ambushed" by one news organization or another about once a day and give brief comments. She then would handle Washington, telling them, "He just got ambushed and he had to say something. The cameras were going. It would just be worse if he didn't say anything."

But the little snippets of news or comments were terribly unsatisfying for both Garner and the media.

Tutwiler became friendly with Hero Talabani, the wife of Kurdish leader Jalal Talabani. In one discussion, Hero turned to her and said something that Tutwiler remembered for years: "We expected more from you Americans."

WEEKS INTO THE WAR, more and more paper was flying around Rumsfeld's office and the Pentagon about how to organize the aftermath. One classified SECRET draft chart was titled "Restoration: Civil Primacy," with SecDef at the top and everything flowing down through the Central

Commander, General Franks. Another had the president at the top, then Rumsfeld and then a new "Coalition Administrator." Garner was listed as the deputy for civil affairs, and General Abizaid was proposed as the deputy for security and support. Both would report to the new "Coalition Administrator." Another chart listed a deputy for security and support, but did not name Abizaid.

HERBITS WAS STILL SEARCHING for the perfect envoy. By April 22, more than a month after the invasion, he'd completed a list of necessary characteristics: commitment to the president's mission, responsiveness to the president's and Rumsfeld's direction, judgment, stature, presence and ability to communicate, empathy, political negotiation skills, bipartisan respect, ability to work with senior military officers, interagency skills, availability and stamina. The organization chart had Garner reporting to the new, unnamed special envoy, separate from the military chain.

Under the section concerning key tasks for the transition to an interim Iraqi government, all the economic and political issues were listed under the heading "Not Currently Addressed." That was everything from debt, credit and oil policy to the tasks of reform, rule of law and political process for the new government. This was two weeks after the fall of Baghdad.

Since anyone associated with the Clinton administration was automatically disqualified, one name kept popping up on Herbits's short list: L. Paul "Jerry" Bremer, a 61-year-old terrorism expert who had 23 years in the foreign service. A protégé of Henry Kissinger, Bremer had been U.S. ambassador to the Netherlands from 1983 to 1986, and then the State Department's ambassador-at-large for counterterrorism, but he had retired from the foreign service so he had not been tainted by serving in the Clinton State Department. He had been managing director of Kissinger Associates, the former secretary of state's consulting firm, for more than a decade before heading the 2000 National Commission on Terrorism. Before the 9/11 terrorist attacks he had publicly predicted that the U.S. homeland would be struck. Boyish with a thick head of hair, Bremer projected utter self-confidence and a toughness that bordered on smugness.

On April 24, Rumsfeld called Powell to propose Bremer. Powell said he would have to think about it. He and Armitage reviewed Bremer's

23-year foreign service career and his close association with Kissinger and the State Department. "Yeah!" cheered Armitage. Bremer was a likely ally. But they didn't want to express too much enthusiasm. That would kill the appointment for sure.

RUMSFELD WAS A LITTLE DEFENSIVE about his role in selecting Bremer when I interviewed him in 2006.

"Jerry Bremer, of course, was a presidential envoy, and as such he reported to the president and to Condi and the NSC staff," Rumsfeld said.

"You picked him," I said.

"Just a minute," Rumsfeld said. "We all agreed on him, that he was the guy. I think I've forgotten where his name came from, but it might have been George Shultz had recommended him."

"That is not correct," Shultz said later when I told him of Rumsfeld's recollection. "Don called me and had a list." Shultz said he told Rumsfeld he thought well of Bremer. "But he also had on his list Howard Baker, and he would be the ideal person because he was a politician and could reach out to others."

I mentioned to Shultz that he initially was at the top of the Pentagon list to be the Iraq envoy.

"That's the first I heard of that!" Shultz said, almost gasping. Neither Rumsfeld nor anybody else ever raised the possibility with him, he said.

The Pentagon apparently felt he might lean too much to the State Department and could not be controlled, I said.

"I was never able to be controlled," Shultz said.

THE TWO KURDISH LEADERS, Massoud Barzani and Jalal Talabani, long-time rivals and leaders of the semiautonomous Kurdish region in northern Iraq, had largely set aside their differences in a pragmatic effort to promote the Iraqi Kurds' future. In April 2003, the two men put out word that they wanted to form an interim government in Baghdad.

Garner was alarmed. Certainly it was part of the U.S. strategy to put an Iraqi face on an interim government, but Iraq was majority Shiite. The Kurds were a minority like the Sunnis. A new government would have to have more of a Shiite face. On April 22, just after arriving in Baghdad, Garner and Larry DiRita flew up north to see Barzani and Talabani. Both men were old acquaintances of Garner from Provide Comfort, though he had not seen them in more than a decade. "This day, for me, is like coming home," Garner said to a crowd of Iraqi Kurds who greeted his arrival.

Barzani and Talabani welcomed him with hugs and kisses. Garner took the two leaders aside. "One of the reasons I came up here is, number one, I wanted to see you," Garner said warmly. "But number two, I understand you're planning to form a government in Baghdad. I've got some problems with that."

"We're not forming a government," Talabani said.

"That's what I was told," Garner replied.

"No. We're going to put together an advisory group, a face of leadership for you. Don't you think you need it?"

"Absolutely," Garner said. "I want to do that. Who will that be?"

Well, Talabani said, "it will be all of us that worked with Zal." Zalmay Khalilzad of the NSC had been working with them for about a year and a half, and had been designated the "ambassador-at-large for the Free Iraqis." Talabani listed three of the Iraqis he thought should be involved. There was Adnan Pachachi, a Sunni octogenarian who had been Iraq's foreign minister and ambassador to the U.N. before Saddam Hussein had taken power. Next, there was Ayad Allawi, the Shiite leader of a London-based exile opposition group called the Iraqi National Accord. Finally, inevitably, there was Ahmed Chalabi.

"Look, here's the problem I have with that," Garner said. "All those guys except you two are expatriates, and you two are Kurds. What about someone from inside the country who's been here who's an Arab?"

"We're going to bring in Hakim," Talabani said, referring to Mohammed Bakir Hakim, the spiritual leader of the biggest Shiite party in Iraq, the Supreme Council for the Islamic Revolution in Iraq (SCIRI). "We thought we'd bring in Jafari"—Ibrahim al-Jafari, a Shiite exile and vehement Saddam opponent—"and we'll bring in a Christian."

"Okay, that will work out," Garner said, but added, "the one thing I'm uncomfortable with is Hakim. He's too Iranian."

"Jay," Talabani said, putting his hand on Garner's leg, "it's better to have Hakim inside the tent than outside the tent."

"That's pretty damn good advice," Garner said. "Let's go along with that. I want you in Baghdad in a week, all of you. I want you to bring your deputies. I want you to set up a deputies committee." It would work directly with Garner's team.

"We'll do that," Talabani said.

"Look, if this works I'll make you a provisional government," Garner told the two leaders. "You'll still work for me but I'll make you a provisional government."

He turned to some practical considerations. "What are we going to do about a constitution, because we've got to get people involved," Garner asked.

"We already thought about that," Talabani answered. "We'll have a big-tent meeting and we'll bring in somewhere between 200 and 300 people. Jay, this will be a mosaic of Iraq. It will be all the ethnic groups, all the religions, all the professions . . . the genders. We'll write this constitution. We'll give you the list of people and you can take off anybody you don't want and you can add anyone you want to it."

"How quick can we do this?" Garner asked, mindful that he'd promised his wife he'd be home by July Fourth.

"We'll have it started on the first of July," Talabani promised.

Immediately after the meeting, Garner called General Abizaid to explain the plan.

Abizaid wondered if it would work.

"I don't think we have a choice," Garner said.

"I don't think we do either. Let's go ahead and go with it."

"I want you to get safe passage for Talabani and Barzani from the north down into Baghdad," Garner said.

GARNER TOLD DIRITA to call the Pentagon and let them know what was happening. He called Powell himself.

"What are you doing down there?" the secretary of state asked.

Garner described the plan for a provisional government, bringing in everyone under a big tent.

"Interesting," Powell said. It sounded like one of those tent-event sale-a-thons advertised on television by big car dealers. He knew the issue was vastly more complicated. There were so many competing efforts. The Pentagon and Cheney obviously were promoting Chalabi. At one point, Khalilzad had presented "Megabrief Two," a secret plan on the Iraqi political process, to the principals—Powell, Rumsfeld, Rice, Cheney, Myers and Tenet. It was a scheme about organizing Iraqis at the local level, taking a census, beginning the effort to build political parties, then establishing local governments and working up from there to the national level.

By modest estimate this would entail years of work. The principals quickly sidelined both the idea and the "Megabrief." They decided that it should not be presented to the president.

Bush had agreed to put a super-administrator in charge over Garner.

But the president wanted to see the organization chart on the U.S. side and also how the government in Iraq would be put together.

Hadley called a deputies committee meeting, but they did not come up with the final organization chart. He indicated that the president was antsy, and said that he wanted key people from each department and agency to stay behind and work, such as Frank Miller, Elliott Abrams, someone from State and a CIA representative. Hadley quipped that he was going to keep them locked in the Situation Room until they finished.

Doug Feith, who was representing Defense, got up to leave. Feith's deputy, William Luti, a retired Navy captain who had been an aide to Newt Gingrich and to Cheney, rose also. "Well," Luti said, "I've got to go back with Doug. He's my ride."

"You heard what Steve said," Frank Miller interjected, "We're going to sit here and work."

"We will try and send someone back," Luti replied and left, but no one came back from the Pentagon.

For about two hours, the group struggled to come up with a chart with the U.S. administrator at the top. An Iraqi Council of Elders and a United Nations representative would consult with the administrator, but the chain of command went from the American administrator to the Iraqi ministries, which would at first be headed by a U.S. official with Iraqi advisers. Over time Iraqis would take over and the U.S. representatives would become advisers. Some of the less important ministries would transition to Iraqi control quickly, but the crucial ones like Defense and Interior would stay under U.S. control for a long time.

The scheme envisioned a long occupation.

The next day the chart and diagram were presented to a principals meeting. Rumsfeld came in swinging. "This isn't an interagency product," he said. "My people weren't involved."

"Mr. Secretary," Miller said, "Hadley said to do it. Your people left and said they might send somebody back. There was no other option. Your people left the game."

Rumsfeld didn't respond, but charts and diagrams were only so much abstraction. Under the president's directive, NSPD-24, he was in charge.

18

Though technically outside the government since 1999, former House Speaker Newt Gingrich threw himself into the mix, publicly blaming the State Department for the failed diplomacy and for the ideological warfare within the administration. "The State Department is back at work pursuing policies that will clearly throw away all of the fruits of hard-won victory," he said on April 24 in a speech at the American Enterprise Institute.

Armitage responded for Powell: "It's clear that Mr. Gingrich is off his meds and out of therapy."

A few days later, the staff threw a small party in Armitage's seventh-floor office for his 58th birthday. Tenet sent a large poster depicting a cartoon version of Armitage lifting weights, straining and dripping sweat. The caption read: "Off His Meds and Out of Therapy. Happy Birthday."

Garner knew little about all the meetings and squabbling in Washington. As far as he knew, the postwar responsibilities were his. On his arrival in Baghdad, a reporter had asked how long the U.S. would be in Iraq and whether he was the country's new ruler.

"I don't think I would put 90 days as a mark on the wall, but we will be here as long as it takes. We'll leave fairly rapidly," Garner replied, adding, "The new ruler of Iraq is going to be an Iraqi. I don't rule anything."

The situation in Iraq was clearly different from what they had anticipated. The worst-case scenarios they had anticipated hadn't happened:

oil fires, displaced people, refugees, epidemics, mass casualties from chemical warfare. But in many ways the problems were more insidious because they were so widespread and deep. On April 23, Garner sat down and made a list of nine things he wanted to accomplish before the July 1 "big-tent meeting" and his planned departure. It was basically an ambitious good-government agenda, covering everything from police to sewers.*

In Baghdad on April 24, Garner met with General McKiernan to go over the nine objectives.

There's a 10th you've got to add on there, McKiernan pointed out—security. There was still some fighting going on but no huge outbreak of violence. Garner agreed and added security as the 10th objective. Neither pointed out that McKiernan, who was in command of roughly 150,000 American and British troops, was subtly shifting responsibility for security to Garner, whose organization numbered only about 200.

The looting was intense. Colonel Tom Baltazar on Garner's staff later recalled watching "a freaking boat, a 25-foot boat, being dragged by a car down the middle of a main street there in Baghdad. Not on a trailer." Some guy had chained it to the back of a car, and was pulling it, completely wrecking the hull as he drove along. Another car drove past, pulling an antique cannon, one of two that the British had left as ceremonial decorations outside an Iraqi military academy in 1924.

Baltazar implored McKiernan: "You have got to stop this," he said. "Our mission is to reestablish the government, and we can't do it if everything's being destroyed."

"Tom, I don't ever want to hear that from your lips again," Baltazar recalled McKiernan saying. "This is not my job."

Nevertheless, Garner felt he was working exceptionally well with McKiernan. McKiernan's staff was the best Garner had ever seen, with one- and two-star generals heading sections that might have had only a colonel in charge in a comparable organization. They agreed to put a flag

---

* Garner's to-do list of things to accomplish before July 1 included: (1) Bring all Iraqi government ministries back to a functioning level. (2) Pay the salaries of all the public servants across the country, including the army and the police. (3) Restore the police, the courts and the prisons. (4) Ensure basic services to Baghdad—water, electricity, sewage and so forth. This would have an added benefit, Garner reasoned, because most of the foreign reporters who covered Iraq were centered in Baghdad. They'd be happier—and might write better stories—if they had air-conditioning and hot showers. (5) End the Iraqi fuel crisis. (6) Purchase the Iraqi harvest—tons of barley and wheat. (7) Reestablish the food distribution system. (8) Restore interim local governance by arranging for the election of town councils in each of Iraq's 26 cities with 100,000 or more people. (9) Ensure the public health system was working, and continue to avoid epidemics.

officer—at least a one-star general or admiral—in charge of each of Garner's 10 objectives, and Garner would assign a senior civilian from his group to each, creating a military-civil team. Junior flag officers got things done in part because they wanted to become senior flag officers. There was no more conspicuous bundle of energy than a one-star general with a mission.

In Baghdad, Garner noticed that U.S. forces were deployed all about in tanks and armored personnel vehicles. He wanted them to reduce the visibility of the force. He called the tanks "sidewalk crushers" and at one point he suggested to one unit, "Quit riding your goddamn tracks and tearing up the sidewalks and curbs." He even spoke with one of McKiernan's deputies and said they ought to do more dismounted patrols, get out of the body armor and Kevlar helmets. Garner refused to wear a flak jacket or travel in armored vehicles. It would send the wrong signal.

But there was a tension in the city, and the U.S. forces were spring-loaded for action. They generally stayed in full armor and in combat mode.

"YOU HAVE A CALL in from SecDef," Air Force Colonel Kim Olson, Garner's executive assistant, told him about 6 P.M. on April 24.

"Hey, you're really doing great," Rumsfeld said when he got on the phone. "We're proud of what you're doing." He said he understood that Garner's team was arriving in full, and it really looked good from what Rumsfeld could tell.

"Yes, sir," Garner replied.

"By the way," Rumsfeld said, "one of the reasons I'm calling is to let you know that the president has selected Jerry Bremer to be the presidential envoy." He didn't know when this would be announced, but he wanted to make sure Garner knew beforehand.

"Well," Garner said, taken by surprise, "if he's already selected somebody then I'll come home."

"No," Rumsfeld objected. "I don't want you to come home."

"It doesn't work that way," Garner said. "You can't have the guy who used to be in charge and the guy who's now in charge there, because you divide the loyalties of the people. So the best thing for me is just to step out of here."

"Don't do anything until I come to Iraq. You and I will talk," Rumsfeld said. He was planning to arrive in a few days. "Jay, this has always been the plan. You know that. This has always been our plan."

"Well, that's true. I have to give you that," Garner said. It was happening earlier than he'd thought.

"I want you to call Jerry Bremer," Rumsfeld said, and gave him the phone number.

"I'll do that."

After hanging up, Garner recalled in an interview, he felt betrayed. "I was thinking: Those sons of bitches. I busted my ass. I dropped everything I had. I walked away from everything I was doing. I thought I had done an incredibly good job at that time. In my head I thought I had." He said he felt cheated. "I was naive enough to think that I could get all this started and there would be such a groundswell among the Iraqis . . . I thought, 'I've got everything going.' And all they were going to have to do is wait and see it come to fruition and it's not going to take long for that to happen.

"What really got me," he said, "is they never really announced what they were doing. Suddenly Bremer's coming and it looks like they fired me, which they may have.

"I think to the outside world I was seen as the envoy to Iraq, whatever you want to call it, the first governor and all that. Inside the administration, inside Defense, I was seen as a mechanic. 'We hired this guy.' I certainly never had the status I had to the outside world."

A FEW HOURS AFTER Rumsfeld called Garner, he made another call. The president had traveled to Lima, Ohio, that day for a campaign-style appearance at a factory that makes the M1 Abrams Main Battle Tank, where Bush had singled out Jay Garner for praise. "We've followed up with a team of people, headed by this man Garner who's got one overriding goal, to leave a free nation in the hands of a free people," he said. He also praised the $4.3 million, 70-ton Abrams tank as "the most safe vehicle for our fighting personnel, precise enough to protect innocent life." Nine hundred M1 tanks had crossed the borders the previous month in the Iraq invasion.

Rumsfeld called Andy Card to complain that the Lima Abrams tank plant had been picked for a presidential visit. The Abrams tank was a thing of the past, not the light, quick, transformational weapon of the future. The president was sending the wrong message. They should speak with one voice: Transformation! This would not have happened when he had been chief of staff, he told Card.

Unbelievable, Card thought. Rumsfeld was out of control. Not only was the secretary in the military chain of command by law, but he played it for all it was worth.

Card found he could pretty much call the other cabinet secretaries— Powell, for example—and get them to play ball and carry out presidential orders and requests. But not Rumsfeld.

BREMER HAD STRONGLY SUPPORTED the decision to invade Iraq. He believed it was the only moral course, that the alleged WMD were an incontestable, imminent threat. In April, he later wrote, he'd been contacted by both Wolfowitz and Scooter Libby, asking if he'd be interested in taking over in postwar Iraq. Garner was never intended to be the permanent head of the reconstruction effort, they told him. They needed someone who knew diplomacy and politics.

Bremer got his wife's blessing and was quickly brought in to talk with Rumsfeld, whom he'd known since they worked in the Ford administration. Soon after, he met with the president.

"Why would you want this impossible job?" Bush asked him, according to Bremer's account.

"Because I believe America has done something great in liberating the Iraqis, sir. And because I think I can help."

IN BAGHDAD, Bremer's impending arrival was greeted with shock.

"What the hell are they doing that for?" Abizaid said when Garner told him.

"John, I don't know."

McKiernan was surprised. Tutwiler said she was stunned. "Can you believe this?" Robin Raphel exclaimed.

"Come on, you're kidding," DiRita said when Garner told him. He was concerned not so much by the decision to switch to a more experienced diplomat, but by the left-footed way it was being handled. "That can't be right."

"Paul, this is not good," DiRita told Wolfowitz. The message being sent was that Garner had failed. "I mean, it's a problem. Somebody needs to go out today and explain what the hell's going on."

But the decision had already been made and no one was stepping up to explain.

Garner ran into Khalilzad, the presidential envoy. "Bremer's coming over here and I'm leaving," he said.

"Who?"

"Jerry Bremer."

"What do you mean he's coming over here?"

"He's coming over here to be the presidential envoy."

"Then I'm quitting."

"I don't think you can quit, Zal," Garner replied. "You've got too much invested here. You're too important a guy. You can't quit."

Khalilzad just walked off. He would return two years later as U.S. ambassador to Iraq.

Garner called Rumsfeld to see if Bremer's arrival could be delayed for several months.

"I have a lot of things on the fire and I think I can get them all done by the first of July," Garner pleaded.

"I can't do that," Rumsfeld said. "That's not my call."

WHEN GARNER WENT to his office the next morning to call Bremer, the phone was ringing.

"You're doing a great job over there," Bremer said, echoing Rumsfeld, but with the skill of a diplomat.

"The optics are pretty bad over here in the newspapers," Bremer said on a later call. The television and newspapers were filled with images of looting and chaos.

"Jerry," Garner replied, "if you're going to try to run Iraq based on what's in *The Washington Post*, you're in for a long haul." He added that he didn't know what was in the newspaper. At that moment, he said, he didn't even have electricity.

"Yeah, but you've got to manage the optics," Bremer repeated. "You've still got to be wary of what's being said about you."

"When you get here you can do that."

Garner's team was trying to function in buildings that had been torn apart; 17 of the 23 ministry buildings were virtually destroyed. Doors, doorjambs, windows, windowsills, plumbing and electrical wiring had been ripped out. In some cases, looters had set the empty husks of buildings on fire. Soot, dirt, filth and human waste littered the floors. Ministry workers had fled. Some of Garner's people had gone out into Baghdad to look for them, asking almost at random, "Do you know anybody that was in the Ministry of Transportation?" or "Do you know anybody in the Ministry of Health?"

• • •

IN LATE APRIL, a Lebanese translator who had been working for the CIA approached Colonel Paul Hughes, one half of Garner's two-man "Law Firm."

"Have you seen this?" he asked.

He showed Hughes a one-page document, an English translation of a directive that had been issued by the headquarters of the Mukhabarat, Saddam's intelligence service.

The memo listed 11 things that the Mukhabarat would do "in the event, God forbid, of the fall of our beloved leader." Each local Baath cell, each squad of Fedayeen, and each individual Mukhabarat agent would be responsible for assassinating collaborators, burning the ministry buildings, looting, burning public documents—doing things that would lead to chaos. It said nothing about sectarian violence, nothing about exploiting the divisions among Shiites, Kurds and Sunnis. It said that it would be up to all the independent agents of the Baath Party to figure out how to raise hell if Saddam's government fell.

Hughes was stunned. He saw that the U.S. and coalition forces were up against a lot more than they had imagined.

In his book, Bremer recalled being shown a similar document, but not for another three months, in late July or early August. Dated January 23, 2003, the Mukhabarat memo Bremer was shown was addressed "To All Offices and Sections," and offered a contingency plan for what to do if the country were invaded. "Burn this office," the memo began, and continued on to describe a strategy of "sabotage and looting" and ordering subordinates to "scatter agents to every town. Destroy electric power stations and water conduits. Infiltrate the mosques, the Shiite holy places."

"I CAN'T BELIEVE that son of a bitch, what he has done," General Myers said in the Tank at the Pentagon. Myers couldn't get General Franks to answer questions, couldn't even get him on the phone. Now, he heard, Franks wanted to leave the combat zone and come to Washington for the White House Correspondents Dinner on April 26. Leave a combat zone for a party? Myers was dumbfounded. Rumsfeld had to pass the word to Franks that he should not attend.

SPIDER MARKS was now living the challenge that he had outlined to the DIA smart guys at the Pentagon more than six months earlier. It no

longer mattered whether failure to find WMD was an intelligence problem or an operational problem. The simple fact was that they weren't
finding anything. In a moment of frustration, he put the blame squarely
on the shoulders of General Franks's Central Command. If he couldn't
share his personal hell with his boss, he had to express it somewhere.

"They are completely asleep at the switch. No one anticipated or executed on the req. to get details of WMD," Marks wrote in his war journal
on April 28, abbreviating "requirements" as "req." "How idiotic are
these guys! Incredible."

That same day, Marks learned that DIA would be taking over the
WMD hunt. The Iraq Survey Group, as the effort was going to be called,
would be commanded by a two-star general named Keith Dayton, the
head of DIA's human intelligence section.

Marks got in touch with Dayton. You're going to have a massive coordination program, Marks said, but maybe if you have the authority of the
secretary of defense's office, you'll be able to move things around and
find some WMD. "When you come," he said, "make shit happen."

Dayton said he was delaying his arrival in Iraq to attend his son's college graduation. It meant that Marks and Dayton would barely overlap.

RUMSFELD FLEW TO IRAQ on April 30. All the ambiguity on the ground
was there for him to see. It was over but it was not over. He addressed
1,000 troops of the 3rd Infantry Division in a large aircraft hangar at the
airport.

"You've rescued a nation," he told them. "You've liberated a people.
You've deposed a cruel dictator and you have ended this threat to free nations. You've braved death squads and dust storms, racing across hundreds of miles to reach Baghdad in less than a month." He could not
resist a dig at those who had written or said that the war had moved
slower than the administration had predicted. "Some people called that
a quagmire."

Traditionally in war, taking the enemy's capital meant the end. So
Rumsfeld and the others—even Garner—were feeling very muscular.
Garner made some remarks to reporters that were totally unrealistic.
"There's not much infrastructure problems here," he said, "other than
connecting some stuff back together."

Rumsfeld videotaped an optimistic message to be broadcast to the
Iraqis from the military's Commando Solo psychological operations aircraft: "Let me be clear: Iraq belongs to you. We do not want to own or

run it," Rumsfeld said, perhaps trying to refute Powell's warning that the U.S. would own Iraq. He added, "We will stay as long as necessary to help you do that—and not a day longer."

In an interview later, Rumsfeld said he realized that "the Iraqi infrastructure had been neglected for decades. I went over and looked at an electric power plant, I can remember. It was being held together with chewing gum, bobby pins and baling wire. And I looked at [it] myself and said, My Lord, this took 30 years to get there." Saddam had ruled for over 30 years. "It's going to take 30 years to get out of here, to get that—not us out—for them to get back to looking like Kuwait or Jordan or Saudi Arabia or Turkey or their neighbors. And I said, My goodness, that's going to be their job over a long period of time, because it just takes that long. You can't—and they have wealth. They've got water. They've got oil. They've got industrious people. They clearly are going to be the ones that are going to have to do that."

Rumsfeld also met privately with Garner to talk about Bremer's impending arrival.

"I want you to stay here, keep working," he said. "You're doing a great job and I want you to transition Jerry in and all that."

"I'll stay for a short time," Garner promised, "but it won't be a long time."

BUSH AND HIS STAFF were borderline giddy. The president's speechwriters, including Michael Gerson, drafted an address that echoed the formal surrender of Japan on the deck of the battleship USS *Missouri* at the end of World War II. The draft borrowed General MacArthur's memorable remarks—"the guns are silent"—and according to Rumsfeld included the line "Mission Accomplished."

The *Missouri* was not available—it was now a memorial at Pearl Harbor in Hawaii—but the aircraft carrier *Abraham Lincoln* was at sea off the coast of San Diego.

"I took 'Mission Accomplished' out," Rumsfeld recalled. "I was in Baghdad and I was given a draft of that thing and I just died. And I said, it's too inclusive. And I fixed it and sent it back. They fixed the speech but not the sign."

On May 1, Bush, the former Texas National Guard pilot, landed dramatically on the *Lincoln*, riding in the second seat of a Navy anti-submarine warplane. Later, after trading his military flight suit for a suit and tie, he addressed the nation and the world, standing before 5,000 of the crew under a huge banner reading "Mission Accomplished." The *Lincoln*'s crew had been told over the ship's public address system that after the president officially came aboard, "you'll be allowed to cheer as loudly as possible, and you'll be encouraged to show your affection." The White House later claimed the "Mission Accomplished" sign had been the Navy's idea. Rumsfeld is the first to say "Mission Accomplished" was in the White House speech draft.

Giving the revised, Rumsfeld-approved version of the speech, Bush declared that "major combat operations in Iraq have ended." He stopped just short of formally declaring victory in Iraq, not only because of Rumsfeld's objection, but also in part because of the implications that declaration would have under international law. "In the battle of Iraq, the United States and our allies have prevailed," he said. "And now our coalition is engaged in securing and reconstructing that country."

The president signaled that a new phase of work was beginning. "We have difficult work to do in Iraq. We are bringing order to parts of that country that remain dangerous. We are pursuing and finding leaders of the old regime, who will be held to account for their crimes. We have begun the search for hidden chemical and biological weapons, and already know of hundreds of sites that will be investigated. We are helping to rebuild Iraq, where the dictator built palaces for himself, instead of hospitals and schools for the people. And we will stand with the new leaders of Iraq as they establish a government of, by, and for the Iraqi people. The transition from dictatorship to democracy will take time, but it is worth every effort. Our coalition will stay until our work is done. Then we will leave and we will leave behind a free Iraq."

IN BAGHDAD, one of Garner's team's computer printers was humming, churning out copies of a new *Ministry Teams Newsletter* dated May 2. It was an internal update on the ministries.

A major project was to "requisition and provide plastic sheeting and tape for use in covering over broken windows and holes in buildings." The Interior Ministry—the organization in charge of intelligence, security and police forces—was completely out of control. "HQ building occupied by 'family' or tribe," the newsletter said. "Need to remove occupiers and return to police control." The Agriculture Ministry was devoid of any security and could not be opened until someone could post guards. "Islamist faction in bldg that needs to be evicted; workers will not return without the eviction and guard." Even the National Library was "occupied by religious group; ministry officials request removal of group and posting of security."

A report to Garner on May 4 begins: "Security continues to be the top concern of all ministry and senior advisors. . . . Scheduled trips to ministries continue to be canceled due to insufficient numbers of military police escorts; advisors have stressed that such cancellations undermine their credibility with ministry staff, particularly given that advisors rarely can contact staff to let them know of changed events." U.S. advisers reached the Ministry of Defense building for the first time, nearly a month after the collapse of Saddam's government, to find that it had been heavily looted. There was gunfire in the streets as they arrived. The team carted off a thousand pounds of highly classified documents, the report said, but there were still many more documents left behind, uncollected and unguarded.

"MEMORANDUM FOR Director," begins another document, this one dated May 6 and written by Colonel Paul Hughes in the formal style of official military correspondence. "Subject: Meeting with Iraqi Military Officers—INFORMATION MEMO."

The day before, Hughes had met with a group of senior Iraqi military officers who claimed to represent about 30,000 army officers, soldiers and Iraqi civilians from the Ministry of Defense. A colonel with the group named Mirjan Dhiya translated.

"Before and during the war," Hughes wrote, these Iraqi officers and others "removed computers and files from the MOD and placed them in their homes." They'd now heard that the coalition was going to give a $20 emergency payment to every government worker in the other ministries, and they hoped they could get the same deal for the former soldiers. Among the officers was a brigadier who had been the comptroller of the Iraqi army. They had all the pay records, and the group was "willing to turn all of its information over to the Coalition."

Hughes wrote that he'd explained to the group that they could not be paid salaries, but that the $20 emergency payment might be possible. "I also informed them that this money was originally Iraqi money being returned to them, something that overwhelmed all of them with a deep sense of gratitude."

Hughes met with the Iraqi officers again two days later, and the list of Iraqi soldiers they claimed to be able to organize had grown to 137,000. On May 8, a document was prepared for the signature of another member of Garner's team, Major General Carl A. Strock, who was acting as the interim senior adviser to the Ministry of Defense, authorizing the Iraqi generals to work with the coalition at the Baghdad building where Garner's team was headquartered. The computers began printing out page after page of records of Iraqi soldiers. Hughes was very excited, believing he had stumbled on an opportunity to get the former Iraqi army on the coalition's side and help them retain some honor. It was what General Grant had done in the Civil War after Lee's surrender at Appomattox, he thought. For $20 a head—less than $3 million for all 137,000 soldiers on the lists—they could offer parole to part of the Iraqi military, and get them invested in the post-Saddam society.

He just needed the money.

19

—————

J ERRY BREMER HAD JUST OVER TWO WEEKS from the first time he met
with Bush in the Oval Office until he left for Iraq. While he had a long
career in foreign policy and counterterrorism, he was not a Middle East
expert. In essence, he was putting together a new pickup team to take
the place of Garner's pickup team. The issue that would likely define the
Bush presidency was being handled by a series of pickup teams.

At one point, James Dobbins, the post-conflict expert and former
State Department official who worked for the RAND Corporation,
brought Bremer a draft of a study estimating that 500,000 troops were
needed in postwar Iraq, three times as many as currently deployed.

Bremer sent a summary of the draft to Rumsfeld with a cover memo
saying, "I think we should consider this." He never heard back, and Bremer never followed up.

AFTER 1 P.M. ON MAY 6, with Bremer by his side in the Oval Office,
Bush formally announced his appointment as presidential envoy to Iraq.
"He's a can-do type person," Bush said, bestowing one of his greatest
compliments. "The ambassador goes with the full blessings of this administration and the full confidence of all of us in this administration
that he can get the job done." The press generally described Bremer as a
buttoned-down, conservative organization man who contrasted with the
informal, unbuttoned Garner.

Four days before his departure, Bremer had lunch with Bush alone at the White House. He raised the "unity of command" issue, but not about the military, as Powell and others had done. "I could not succeed if there were others in Iraq saying they too represented the president," Bremer later wrote—meaning especially Zalmay Khalilzad, the NSC staffer who still bore the title "presidential envoy."

Bush said he understood and agreed. By Bremer's account he also mentioned the RAND study calling for 500,000 troops, but got no response, and he never pursued it with the president.

After their lunch, Bush led Bremer into the Oval Office for a meeting with Rumsfeld, Powell, Rice and Card. As they filed in, "Bush waved me to the chair beside him and joked, 'I don't know whether we need this meeting at all. Jerry and I have just had it.'

"His message was clear," Bremer wrote. "I was neither Rumsfeld's nor Powell's man. I was the president's man."

On May 9, Bush put it in writing, appointing Bremer as his envoy, "reporting through the Secretary of Defense." He was in charge of everyone except Rumsfeld and General Franks.

That day, Bremer met with Feith and his deputy, William Luti, a retired Navy captain and veteran of Cheney's office.

"I have my letter," Bremer said, referring to his appointment letter from the president. He proudly patted the breast pocket of his suit jacket.

Feith had a draft de-Baathification order, and Bremer recalls that Feith was going to have Garner issue it.

According to Bremer, he replied, "Hold on a minute. I agree it's a very important step, so important that I think it should wait until I get there." Bremer later recalled that Feith agreed and said it was to be carried out "even if implementing it causes administrative inconvenience." For his part, Feith has recalled that it was Bremer pushing a de-Baathification order and another order to disband the Iraqi army.

GARNER'S DEPUTY, RON ADAMS, had come down with severe pneumonia in early April, and was evacuated back to the U.S. to recover. As he recuperated, he resumed work at the Pentagon as Garner's liaison.

"Everything's changed here," Adams told Garner in one of their daily phone conversations. "They don't like us."

After a month, Adams finally got clearance to return to the Middle East, and he flew to Kuwait on May 6. It took four frustrating days for the retired three-star general and deputy director of the organization still officially in charge of postwar Iraq just to get a seat on a military airplane to travel the 350 or so miles from Kuwait to Baghdad.

"SUNDAY 11 MAY D+53," begins another entry in Spider Marks's war diary. "No WMD," he wrote again.

It was almost too late to worry about it. There was no such thing as un-invading Iraq. They still had to drive on, and check all 946 sites on the list, even if he was now nearly as sure there was nothing to find as he had previously been positive that the weapons were there.

Colonel Rotkoff summed up the situation:

> *Where is WMD?*
> *What a kick if he has none*
> *Sorry about that*

ON MAY 11, Garner flew to Qatar to meet Bremer at Franks's headquarters. The two shook hands briefly, and after a routine military briefing, Garner handed Bremer a copy of his list of the 10 major objectives to be accomplished before July 1.

"Okay," Bremer said. "Thanks."

General Myers had flown with Bremer to Qatar en route to Iraq. He had been out of the loop on the Bremer decision, and thought Garner should have stayed in place as a kind of civilian number two to General Franks.

Myers and Garner later talked privately. Garner pushed his idea of making Abizaid the military commander in Baghdad, but giving him a fourth star so he would have greater authority.

"Bring Abizaid in here as the sub–unified commander," Garner said. "Let Bremer do the civilian stuff. Keep McKiernan here. He's got a great staff." Abizaid could then arbitrate the inevitable disputes between Bremer and McKiernan. Franks was heading for retirement, and had left Iraq. Abizaid was the man for the job.

"I agree with you, but I can't get any headway on that," Myers told Garner. He'd made the same proposal to Rumsfeld. The chart in the Pentagon that showed the transition from military to civilian control never had a timeline on it, and that was for a reason. This new idea of putting Bremer in control was happening too abruptly in Myers's view. "We've had that discussion," Myers added in obvious frustration. Rumsfeld "just won't listen."

Bremer and Garner spent a day in Basra before flying on to Baghdad. Bremer later recalled his feeling on arriving in the Iraqi capital. "I was driving down the muddy road in a fog at 100 miles per hour," he said. That night, he and Garner gathered about 30 senior staff members into a small conference room at the so-called palace. Bremer was gracious, thanking Garner and his team and emphasizing that they knew the challenges better than he did.

"The media coverage of the unchecked looting makes us look powerless," Bremer said. "When the American-led forces occupied Haiti in 1994, our troops shot six looters breaking the curfew and the looting stopped. I believe we should do the same thing here, even if it means changing the military's Rules of Engagement." But he never got the rules changed to allow that kind of shooting.

ABOUT 7 A.M. ON MAY 14, Bremer's first full day in Baghdad, Robin Raphel ran up to Garner.

"Have you read this?" she asked.

"No," Garner replied. "I don't know what the hell you've got there."

"It's a de-Baathification policy," she said, handing him a two-page document.

Garner read quickly: "Coalition Provisional Authority Order Number 1—De-Baathification of Iraqi Society." The Baath Party was organized by rank, and the order said that all "full members"—those in the top four ranks—would be immediately removed from their posts and banned from future government employment. Additionally, the three top layers of management in the ministries would be investigated for crimes and as possible security risks.

"We can't do this," Garner said. He still envisioned what he had told Rumsfeld would be a "gentle de-Baathification"—eliminating only the number one Baathist and the personnel directors in each ministry. "It's too deep," he added.

"That's exactly why you can't go home," Raphel said.

Garner ran into Charlie, the CIA station chief.

"Have you read this?" Garner asked.

"That's why I'm over here," Charlie said.

"Let's go see Bremer." The two men got in to see the new administrator of Iraq around 1 P.M. "Jerry, this is too deep," Garner said. "Give Charlie and I about an hour. We'll sit down with this. We'll do the pros and cons and then we'll get on the telephone with Rumsfeld and soften it a bit."

"Absolutely not," Bremer said. "Those are my instructions and I intend to execute them."

"Hell," Garner answered, "you won't be able to run anything if you go this deep."

Garner turned to Charlie. The experienced CIA man had been station chief in other Middle East countries.

"Charlie, what's going to happen?"

"If you put this out, you're going to drive between 30,000 and 50,000 Baathists underground before nightfall," Charlie said, according to notes taken by Kim Olson, Garner's assistant. Charlie said the number was closer to 50,000 than 30,000. "You will put 50,000 people on the street, underground and mad at Americans." And these 50,000 were the most powerful, well-connected elites from all walks of life.

"I told you," Bremer said, looking at Charlie. "I have my instructions and I have to implement this."

Garner called Rumsfeld and tried to get the depth reconsidered and the language of the order softened.

"This is not coming from this building," he replied. "That came from somewhere else."

Garner presumed that meant the White House, NSC or Cheney. According to other participants, however, the de-Baathification order was purely a Pentagon creation. Telling Garner it came from somewhere else, though, had the advantage for Rumsfeld of ending the argument.

The next day, May 15, Robin Raphel brought Garner another draft order. This was Order Number 2, disbanding the Iraqi ministries of Defense and Interior, the entire Iraqi military, and all of Saddam's bodyguard and special paramilitary organizations.

Garner was stunned. The de-Baathification order was dumb, but this was a disaster. Garner had told the president and the whole National Security Council explicitly that they planned to use the Iraqi military—at least 200,000 to 300,000 troops—as the backbone of a corps to rebuild the country and provide security. And he'd been giving regular secure video reports to Rumsfeld and Washington on the plan.

Moreover, Colonel Hughes had been meeting with his former Iraqi generals with their lists of some 137,000 who wanted to rejoin their old units or sign on with new units if they each received a $20 emergency payment. The CIA had also compiled lists and was meeting with generals and arranging for a reconstitution of the Iraqi military. The former Iraqi military was making more and more overtures, just waiting to come back in some form.

Garner went to see Bremer for the second day in a row. "We have always made plans to bring the army back," he insisted. This new plan was just coming out of the blue, subverting months of work.

"Well, the plans have changed," Bremer replied. "The thought is that we don't want the residuals of the old army. We want a new and fresh army."

"Jerry, you can get rid of an army in a day, but it takes years to build one." Garner tried to explain that it was not just about a soldier in the field, or getting a bunch of riflemen. "Any army is all the processes it takes to equip it and train it and sustain it and make it last." Bremer shook his head.

"You can't get rid of the Ministry of Interior," Garner said.

"Why not?"

"You just made a speech yesterday and told everybody how important the police force is."

"It is important."

"All the police are in the Ministry of the Interior," Garner said. "If you put this out, they'll all go home today."

Bremer, looking surprised, asked Garner to go see Walter B. Slocombe, Bremer's director of defense and national security. Slocombe, 62, had been the defense undersecretary for policy during most of the Clinton administration, Feith's predecessor. A Rhodes Scholar, a former clerk for Supreme Court Justice Abe Fortas and a prominent tax attorney, Slocombe felt that as a matter of international law the U.S. invasion meant Iraq was under military occupation. It was not an elective status and the U.S. should not be shy about asserting authority. The governmental system had imploded and the Iraqi army had dissolved, he believed. Everyone—the Iraqis and the United States—needed there to be a new government and a new army in Iraq. Saddam's army had been a principal instrument of repression. In Slocombe's opinion it could hardly be used as the shield for a new democracy.

But Slocombe agreed to excise the Ministry of Interior from the draft so the police could stay. Bremer soon signed the order, which canceled all military "rank, title or status." In his book published in 2006, Bremer did not recount his exchanges with Garner over disbanding the Iraqi army, but he made clear his belief that by the time he got to Iraq, there no longer was an Iraqi army—it had "self-demobilized." Signing the order abolishing the old regime's military services "would not send home a single soldier or disband a single unit," he wrote. "All that had happened weeks before." He was also convinced that the Kurds, who hated and feared the old army, would secede if it was brought back.

But over the next year, every one of the officers and sergeants who made up the new Iraqi army came from the old Iraqi army.

BREMER HUDDLED IN A TINY OFFICE in the Republican Palace with four of his aides: Scott Carpenter from State, whom Liz Cheney had put in charge of the Iraqi governance issue; Meghan O'Sullivan, the State Department official who had come over to Garner's team with Tom Warrick, only to be chased out by Cheney's office and sneaked back in with the tacit approval of Rumsfeld and Hadley; Ryan Crocker of the State Department; and Roman Martinez, a 24-year-old Harvard graduate who had worked for Feith at the Pentagon. Each of the five had a copy of the de-Baathification order.

"The White House, DOD, and State all signed off on this," Bremer said. "So let's give it one final reading and, unless there's some major screwup in the language, I'll sign it."

THE NEXT MORNING, MAY 16, Bremer signed the de-Baathification order. Later that day, he wrote in his book, he e-mailed his wife back home in the United States, as he tried to do each day, to tell her about the response he'd heard from the Americans on the ground. "There was a sea of bitching and moaning with lots of them saying how hard it was going to be. I reminded them that the president's guidance is clear: de-Baathification will be carried out even if at a cost to administrative efficiency. An ungood time was had by all."

ABOUT 4 P.M. THAT DAY, Abizaid, the likely successor to General Franks as CENTCOM commander, flew to Baghdad to meet with Garner. Both men were worried about the combat continuing north of Baghdad. Some Iraqis weren't giving up, but they were so ill equipped for the fight that they were being slaughtered. One way to stop the pointless resistance and carnage, Garner and Abizaid agreed, was to show the Iraqis convincingly that there would be a new government, and Saddam's rule was over.

They turned to the policies on de-Baathification and disbanding the army.

Garner told Abizaid, "John, I'm telling you. If you do this it's going to be ugly. It'll take 10 years to fix this country, and for three years you'll be sending kids home in body bags."

Abizaid didn't disagree. "I hear you, I hear you," he said. He asked Garner to stay on in Iraq.

"I can't stay," Garner said.

On Friday, May 16, Bremer and John Sawers, Britain's ambassador to Egypt, who had been sent to Iraq as the top U.K. representative to Bremer's organization, officially called the Coalition Provisional Authority (CPA), hosted a dinner meeting with the Iraqi leadership group that Garner had put together. Bremer had resisted meeting with the leadership group earlier in the week, he later recalled, in part because he "wanted to show everybody that I, not Jay, was now in charge."

Bremer explained he was dedicated to fighting terrorism. Brimming with self-confidence, he conveyed a sense that the Iraqis were almost superfluous. He then said it explicitly: "One thing you need to realize is you're not the government. We are. And we're in charge."

At least it was candid, no cat-and-mouse pretense. But Garner realized that the imperial takeover that he had been warned about and worried about at his rock drill three months earlier had come to pass.

The next day Garner's interim group went home. The face of Iraqi leadership was now an empty room.*

Hadley first learned of the orders on de-Baathification and disbanding the military as Bremer announced them to Iraq and the world. They hadn't been touched by the formal interagency process and as far as Hadley knew there was no imprimatur from the White House. Rice also had not been consulted. It hadn't come back to Washington or the NSC for a decision. But Rice didn't find the order surprising. After all, the Iraqi army had kind of frittered away.

One NSC lawyer had been shown drafts of the policies to de-Baathify Iraq and disband the military—but that was only to give a legal opinion. The policy-makers never saw the drafts, never had a chance to say whether they thought they were good ideas or even to point out that

---

* Over the months, Bremer would set up his own interim governing council and it would be made up mostly of the same people Garner had in his group. The first two interim Iraqi prime ministers, Allawi and Jafari, would come from Garner's initial attempt at putting an Iraqi face on the government, as President Bush had approved two days into the war.

they were radical departures from what had earlier been planned and briefed to the president.

Instead, from April 2003 on, the constant drumbeat that Hadley heard coming out of the Pentagon had been "This is Don Rumsfeld's thing, and we're going to do the interagency in Baghdad. Let Jerry run it."

General Myers, the principal military adviser to Bush, Rumsfeld and the NSC, wasn't even consulted on the disbanding of the Iraqi military. It was presented as a fait accompli.

"We're not going to just sit here and second-guess everything he does," Rumsfeld told Myers at one point, referring to Bremer's decisions.

"I didn't get a vote on it," Myers told a colleague, "but I can see where Ambassador Bremer might have thought this is reasonable."

Rumsfeld later said he would be surprised if Wolfowitz and Feith gave Bremer the de-Baathification and army orders. He said he did not recall an NSC meeting on the subject. Of Bremer, Rumsfeld said, "I talked to him only rarely. And he had an approach that was different from Jay Garner's. No question."

Bremer was swamped. De-Baathification and disbanding the military were only part of his first five days, according to his notes. Within hours after he landed in Baghdad, someone wanted to know if they should let Baghdad University hold its elections for university officers. Bremer said to go ahead. He rescinded one of Saddam's laws that prohibited professors from foreign travel. He set up a television station and newspaper. They were trying to arrange cell phone service. Bremer visited the Baghdad children's hospital, and ordered emergency generators for all of the city's hospitals. He made arrangements for emergency deliveries of gasoline and propane to Baghdad. None of the Iraqi civil servants had been paid since before the war, now going on three months. "It'll take us three months to design a coherent pay grade system," one of his advisers said.

"You've got three days," Bremer replied. They put together a radically simplified wage structure with four levels of pay. It amounted to $200 million every month.

It was a staggering to-do list, and decisions had to be made on the tightest deadlines. There was no time to set up a system, to farm decisions back to the U.S. or to delegate. Besides, Bremer thought, no one in their right minds who had any experience with the U.S. government bureaucracy would refer crucial decisions back to Washington.

Robin Raphel, who was a Bremer contemporary in the State Department and had known him for years, said they needed to raise $150 million to buy Iraqi farmers' wheat and barley. "We've got to do something right away, because the crop is already being harvested," she said. She and Bremer went to the U.N. lead officials in Baghdad, who could release money from the U.N. Oil-for-Food program—commonly known as OFF—to buy the national grain crop.

"Mr. Ambassador," the U.N. official told him, "the OFF money belongs to the Iraqi government, and I can't release it without the approval of their government."

"I am the Iraqi government for now," Bremer said. "And on behalf of that government, I am asking the United Nations to release these funds immediately." He eventually got the money.

Everywhere there were problems. "My God," he said to himself, "this place needs fixing. Let's get on with it."

Electricity flickered on and off. "Go fix the electricity," Bremer told Clay McManaway, one of his most trusted deputies. "Go find out why we can't get it back up."

McManaway, 70, was one of the first people Bremer had coaxed into joining him. He'd brought him along for just this kind of mission. McManaway had spent 30 years in the foreign service, along with time in the Defense Department and the CIA. He'd been all over the world, including five years in Vietnam. He knew how to function in dysfunctional places.

Things were even worse with the Baghdad sewer system, another portfolio Bremer gave McManaway. Raw sewage was backing up all over the place. They could see it and smell it everywhere. Literally going down into the system, McManaway found things were a total mess. There were two or three separate sewage systems under the streets of Baghdad. They weren't connected, and none of them was working. They had only one American trying to fix the problem, a sanitation engineer from Pennsylvania.

"Aw, shit," McManaway said.

GARNER AWAKENED ON SATURDAY, May 17, thinking about Sun Tzu, the ancient Chinese general and military strategic thinker. In *The Art of War*, Sun Tzu cautioned that you don't want to go to bed at night with more enemies than you started with in the morning. By Garner's calculation the U.S. now had at least 350,000 more enemies than it had the day before—the 50,000 Baathists, the 300,000 officially unemployed soldiers from the army, and a handful from the now defunct Iraqi leadership group.

Later that day he hosted a major meeting with Abizaid, McKiernan and the flag officer–civilian teams dealing with his top 10 issues. It was hot and the room was full, with lots of people crowded around a large table. One entrance led directly outside to a courtyard; across the courtyard were Bremer's offices.

The first of the staff generals was beginning his report when McManaway came through the doorway from the courtyard.

"Bremer wants to see you," McManaway said, indicating Abizaid.

"As soon as we finish this meeting," Abizaid said.

McManaway indicated, "Now."

Abizaid looked at Garner as if to say, What do I do?

"Go on in there," Garner said. "Look, he called for you."

Several minutes later McManaway came in and said Bremer wanted to see McKiernan.

"Do you want me to go?" McKiernan asked Garner.

"Yeah."

"Well," another general inquired, "do you think we ought to go on with this meeting or is it over?"

"Let's go ahead and finish it because everybody's put a lot of work in it," Garner said. After all, he realized, the issues on the table were only the ministries, back pay, police, water, electricity, sewage, fuel, food, governance, health and security. Just the essence of Iraq's future. Who could possibly give a shit?

"I was disgusted," recalled Ron Adams. "We were being marginalized."

When the meeting was over, Garner marched into Bremer's office. He shut the door behind him with a gentleness and control he did not feel.

"Don't you ever do that to me again."

"What do you mean?" Bremer asked.

"If you ever have me in a meeting and you start pulling people out of it—" Garner began. He cut himself off, and added, "You give me more respect than that. I'll tell you what. I'll make it easy on you, Jerry. I'm going home."

Bremer jumped up. "You can't go home."

"I can't work with you, and I'm leaving. What you just did in there—I've never had anybody do something like that to me before, and I'll never let you do something like that again."

"I didn't know what was going on," he said.

"That's bullshit. You knew exactly what was going on."

They went back and forth for a minute or two.

"Look, Jay," Bremer said, stopping them both. "You and I may not agree on anything, but we both have the same objective."

"I don't think so," Garner interrupted.

"Yes, we do. Our objective is to make our nation successful in this endeavor."

"You're right," Garner agreed. "You're right about that."

"Well, if you believe in that strongly enough, as I do, then you need to stay for a while. You've got to help me do that."

"I'll tell you what I'll do, Jerry. I'll work on a day-to-day contract with you. The next time you piss me off, I'm gone. There's a couple of things that I'd like to finish, and I don't think it'll take me long. And once I finish with those things then I'll come shake your hand and leave."

"Okay, let's try to work that way," Bremer agreed.

"You've got to make the staff available to me," Garner said.

Bremer thought for a moment, and finally said, "I don't think I can do that."

"Why?"

He and Garner would give conflicting guidance, Bremer said, but he said he would think about it.

"I don't think I can get anything accomplished if I don't have a staff," Garner said.

"Let me think about that."

"I'll tell you what I'm going to do. The one thing that has to happen immediately is we've got to get the public servants and the police paid. It's a very complicated and difficult process. I'm going to stay here until I'm sure that process is in place. And when I'm sure of that then I'll either make a decision to stay a little longer or to leave."

"Okay," Bremer said. "And I'll get back to you on staff."

Later, Bremer said that while he recognized he needed a smooth transition from Garner's group to his own, he was already growing angry at people—he assumed they were Garner's people—who had leaked details of his plans and meetings to the media. One such leak had sparked a news story about Bremer's suggestion that the military start shooting looters. "I wanted Jay's expertise in logistics," Bremer wrote, "but I wouldn't be sorry to see the leakers go."

Within hours after the confrontation, Garner and his executive assistant, Colonel Olson, got the heck out of Baghdad and headed south to the city of Hillah. Olson thought that if Bremer just stroked Garner some or gave him some assignments, especially away from Baghdad, Garner would stay and help. But, she felt, Bremer was making a classic leadership mistake: not figuring out how to use the talent that was sitting there at his disposal.

Robin Raphel wanted Garner to stay. She thought he had a better sense than Bremer about what needed to be done. Garner and his core group had worked hard to get a foothold in Iraq, but politically they were in way over their heads. In one of her few criticisms of him, she agreed with the White House about Garner's habit of not wearing a jacket and tie. He didn't seem to understand that Iraqis liked formality.

Bremer was wired. He dressed every day in a suit with a white shirt and a tie. The tan Timberland boots he wore with his dark suit were already a trademark. He surrounded himself with an entourage of energetic 20-somethings. Some of them ridiculed Garner because he didn't have an official daily schedule. Garner's group had nicknamed themselves the "Space Cowboys," after a Clint Eastwood movie in which retired astronauts get together for one final mission. Bremer's young staff was referred to as the "Neocon Children's Brigade," or even more derisively by some military officers, in a play on the CPA's initials, as "Children Playing Adults."

Bremer recognized that the challenges were immense. "I'd settle for MacArthur's problems," he later recalled saying. "Conditions weren't this complicated for him." But still, he just seemed so confident that he would succeed. Was it his nature, Raphel wondered, or did it stem from the religious faith he shared with the president?

IN LATE MAY, the day before Larry DiRita left to return to Washington, a report came that an explosion had gone off on the road to the Baghdad airport—called the BIAP highway—as a Humvee passed by. No one was killed, but DiRita thought to himself, "Wow, that's kind of interesting. I wonder what that was all about." It seemed out of the ordinary, since the airport road was almost like an American superhighway, where everyone traveled without security, armor or escorts.

It was his last day in Baghdad, and that night, around 11 P.M., he and several of Bremer's staff piled into a car and drove halfway across Bagh-dad to have dinner at a packed restaurant. Everyone else there seemed to be Iraqi, and DiRita's group ate dinner and had a few beers. A couple of U.S. soldiers came walking down the street, and people in the restaurant ran out to greet them and thank them. It was a memorable evening, very pleasant, almost a scene from liberated Paris after World War II.

When DiRita returned to the Pentagon he reported to Rumsfeld on the way Iraqis felt and described his last-night-in-Baghdad restaurant outing.

This thing, Rumsfeld said, is on the right track.

20

E ARLY IN MAY 2003, terror attacks rocked Riyadh, Saudi Arabia, targeting a U.S.-linked business and three housing compounds used mainly by Westerners. Eight Americans were among the 34 killed. Hundreds were wounded. It was one of the worst terror attacks since September 11, 2001. Bush sent Tenet to warn the Crown Prince.

Al Qaeda is here in the Kingdom, Tenet told Crown Prince Abdullah in Saudi Arabia. They will kill you. They are using your country as a launching ground for attacks on the United States. If that happens, it is all over with U.S.-Saudi relations, he warned.

Abdullah agreed to massive joint intelligence and police security operations within the Kingdom. Soon, the CIA was giving the Saudis access to more and more sensitive U.S. intelligence, including transcripts of NSA intercepts inside Saudi Arabia and the region.

Saudi intelligence said that was not good enough. The Saudis did not trust the American translations. The Arabic spoken in Saudi Arabia, Morocco, Tunisia, Yemen, wherever, was all different. Eventually, the NSA started giving the Saudis actual audio voice cuts of some of the intercepts so that more accurate translations could be made, and some of the voices might be traced or recognized by Saudi security forces, informants or detainees.

GARNER MOSTLY STAYED out of Baghdad and away from Bremer after their row. He encountered a British lieutenant colonel in southern Iraq who said he had about $1 million in discretionary funds to spend in his sector. Garner couldn't move a dime on his own. He went to Babylon, the ancient city once known for its wealth and extravagance, about eight miles from Hillah on the lower Euphrates River.

"We're just never going to get this right," he said, according to Kim Olson's notes.

BREMER WROTE A MEMO to President Bush, sending it through Rumsfeld a week after he'd arrived in the country. Reflecting his new tough line, Bremer said, "We must make it clear to everyone that we mean business: that Saddam and the Baathists are finished." He claimed, "The dissolution of his chosen instrument of political domination, the Baath Party, has been very well received." This accompanied "an even more robust measure dissolving Saddam's military and intelligence structures to emphasize we mean business."

On the other hand, Bremer wrote, "we must show the average Iraqi that his life will be better. We face a series of urgent issues involving the resolution of basic services. We have made great progress under Jay Garner's leadership. There has been an almost universal expression of thanks to the U.S. and to you in particular for freeing Iraq from Saddam's tyranny. In the northern town of Mosul yesterday, an old man, under the impression that I was President Bush (he apparently has poor TV reception) rushed up and planted two very wet and hairy kisses on my cheeks."

"WHY WOULD WE WANT to pay an army we just got through defeating?" Walt Slocombe asked Jerry Bates, Garner's chief of staff.

"Because we don't want them to suddenly show up on the other side," Bates answered. "We need to get control of them."

Slocombe and Bates had worked in the Pentagon together during the Clinton years. Bates liked Slocombe and thought he was smart. But on this issue they vehemently disagreed, and Bremer was clearly of the same mind as Slocombe. The army had melted away, Bremer said. "They don't exist, so we're not paying them."

On May 19, 2003, Bremer sent Rumsfeld a two-page memo informing him that he was going to issue the order disbanding the Iraqi military. He was not really recommending it or asking permission. "In the coming days I propose to issue the attached order."

• • •

IN THE DAYS AFTER the order disbanding the military, vehicles traveling the road between Baghdad and the airport started coming under attack more regularly. Crowds began to gather to protest the order, although reports differed greatly as to how many people turned out each time. On May 19, about 500 people demonstrated outside the Coalition Provisional Authority's gates. A week later, on May 26, a larger crowd gathered to demonstrate. Some Arab media reports that were later translated and given to Bremer's team said there were as many as 5,000 protesters.

"We demand the formation of a government as soon as possible, the restoration of security, rehabilitation of public institutions, and disbursement of the salaries of all military personnel," said one of the leaders of the protest, an Iraqi major general named Sahib al-Musawi. His speech was carried over the Arabic-language television network Al Jazeera, and later translated for the CPA. "If our demands are not met, next Monday will mark the start of estrangement between the Iraqi army and people on the one hand and the occupiers on the other."

PAUL HUGHES now had to deal with the former Iraqi officers who wanted their soldiers to be given the $20 emergency payments, but who were now shut out under the Bremer order. Hughes stalled for a while but finally went to see the officers.

"Colonel Paul, what happened?" asked Mirjan Dhiya, their English-speaking spokesman.

"I don't know," Hughes said. "I can't tell you what happened. I'm as shocked as you are."

"Colonel Paul, we have men who have families. They have no food. They are running out. We need to do something."

Hughes finally got Slocombe's chief of staff to meet with the former Iraqi military representative. There was still a possibility that they might get the $20 each, but things were moving very slowly.

GARNER WAS OUT at Baghdad International Airport to meet with a visiting congressional delegation on May 26. He drove back on the BIAP highway in his unarmored Chevy Suburban to the so-called palace where his team had been working, for a little going-away party in his honor. It was a bit of a joke among some of the staffers whether Bremer would show up, but he was there, and was gracious.

That same day, three American cavalry scouts whose job was to escort or go ahead of convoys of supply trucks were also on the BIAP highway, riding in the first of a team of two armored Humvees. They drove over what looked like a backpack in the middle of the road.

The backpack exploded, tearing into their Humvee and throwing one of the soldiers from the vehicle. Ammunition started to cook off, causing more explosions.

The soldiers in the second Humvee slammed on the brakes and manned their machine gun, looking frantically for the enemy. One soldier got out and ran quickly to the fallen man, Jeremiah D. Smith, a 25-year-old Army private from Missouri, one of the first American soldiers confirmed to have been killed by hostile fire in Iraq in weeks.

Paul Hughes was at the palace at Garner's farewell party. He heard a report: "We just lost two Humvees on the BIAP highway."

"I was pissed," Hughes later recalled. He presumed Iraqi soldiers were behind the attack, and was equally sure that the U.S. had missed its best opportunity to keep the Iraqi army under control by working with the Iraqi generals and colonels. "I had them by their balls. They would have stood on their head in the Tigris River for me as long as we were dealing fairly with each other. It was just so tragic, so needless."

The next day, one of the U.S. intelligence agents at the palace had a stark, matter-of-fact assessment. "These guys all have munitions in their garages," he said. "They're pissed off. This is the beginning."

ON MAY 27, Garner wrote a formal memorandum to the president. A copy later turned up with a stamp on the first page reading "SECDEF HAS SEEN."

"As I near the end of my service," he said, "I want to thank you for allowing me to serve the country and you in this important mission. I believe we have set a baseline that will bring stability to Iraq, although there will certainly be ups and downs in the period ahead. We have assembled a wonderful team of professionals, and Jerry Bremer is a fine choice to take the team to the next level and help create the conditions for true political and economic reform in Iraq."

He listed some of the main tasks ahead—from food to security—putting the most positive possible spin on the accomplishments. Garner did not mention or even hint that he had concluded that Bremer had already made three huge mistakes—broad de-Baathification, disbanding the military, and rejecting the Iraqi council Garner had set up. Instead, the ex-general closed simply, by thanking the president again for the chance to serve. "It was challenging, exhilarating, and rewarding. Thank you, too, for your inspired wartime leadership."

It was ironic, Garner thought, that though Rumsfeld had been eager to ensure that the Defense Department controlled the postwar effort, almost everyone in a position of power within Bremer's new CPA came from the State Department. Bremer, who had been an ambassador but had otherwise never managed a large organization, had wrested control of the effort from Rumsfeld.

But Bremer didn't know how to delegate, Garner thought. Every decision had to come to him, which meant that nothing moved quickly.

RUMSFELD'S CONSULTANT and personnel expert Steve Herbits wrote a scathing, four-page confidential memo to Rumsfeld on Doug Feith's performance as undersecretary for policy.

"After nearly two years, Doug's leadership has not improved; his style and approach to his job continue to produce a significantly under performing team. His negatives continue to accumulate. Six months of post-Iraq planning is now widely regarded as a serious failure, both in substance, personnel selection, cooperation within Department of Defense and in interagency relations."

Within the interagency process at the NSC, he continued, "Policy's nickname is 'The lunatic Feith and his evil spawn.' " He reported that Victoria A. "Torie" Clarke, the Pentagon spokesperson, said that Feith lacked "respect and trust."

Herbits suggested to Rumsfeld that confirmation of these views could be provided by Wolfowitz, Pace and other consultants.*

At the NSC, Hadley knew that Feith was much criticized, but he thought Feith had a few things in his favor. He was one of the few Rumsfeld trusted, one of the few who could get a decision from Rumsfeld and get it to stick. He generated an enormous number of good ideas and provided the interagency with intellectual leadership, Hadley thought, and he could prepare briefings and memos in a form that Rumsfeld would sign off on rather than sending them back 10 to 15 times. And finally, he was loyal to Rumsfeld.

---

* In an interview in 2006, Pace said he did not agree at all with Herbits's assessment, and that he thought Feith was "super-smart" and had done a good job. Feith later sent me a letter saying that Rumsfeld and Wolfowitz also strongly disavowed the Herbits assessment, which Feith called "a piece of gutter name-calling" that should not be in my book. "His memo is just libelous musings from a marginal figure," Feith wrote. "It harms me without shedding any true light on anything."

When Feith got in trouble publicly, Hadley concluded, it was always because he was carrying out Rumsfeld's policy. Hadley felt strongly that Feith went undefended, hung out to dry. The problem was not Feith. It was Rumsfeld.

Feith was practically pulling his hair out, Frank Miller of the NSC staff could see. Bremer wouldn't speak to him. He had his deputies answer Feith's memos. His message was very clear: "I work for the President of the United States," skipping over Feith and therefore Rumsfeld.

Miller found the decision to disband the Iraqi army jarring. They'd been telling Bush for months about the plan to use 300,000 Iraqi troops for reconstruction. Miller counted Walt Slocombe, Bremer's point man on the military, among his close friends, but he thought it was silly when Slocombe and others justified the decision by saying that the Iraqi army had disbanded itself. That's what we told them to do, he thought—the CIA had dropped leaflets over Iraqi positions saying, "Go home. Put down your weapons and go home."

But with Bremer on the scene, Miller's interagency group working on postwar Iraq plans, the Executive Steering Group, had disbanded. The feeling at the White House was the same as it was at the Pentagon—Bremer didn't need them looking over his shoulder. But reports flowed into the NSC, from the British and through the media, and from Frank Miller's military contacts, although not from Bremer himself. Looting was still going on. Iraqi civil servants weren't getting paid. There was a report that 40,000 teachers had been fired because they were Baathists.

Bremer was making statements and holding press conferences suggesting he expected to be in Baghdad for a long time.

"Occupation is an ugly word, not one Americans feel comfortable with, but it is a fact," Bremer told a reporter from *The Washington Post*, as they flew together in a C-130 transport plane from Baghdad to the southern city of Umm Qasr on May 28. "President Bush has always said that we will be here as long as it takes to do the job, and not a day longer. At the same time, we should make sure we don't leave a day earlier."

"WE FOUND THE WEAPONS of mass destruction," President Bush declared in an interview with a Polish television reporter on May 29. "We found biological laboratories. You remember when Colin Powell stood up in front of the world, and he said, Iraq has got laboratories, mobile labs to build biological weapons. They're illegal. They're against the United Nations resolutions, and we've so far discovered two. And we'll find more weapons as time goes on. But for those who say we haven't found the banned manufacturing devices or banned weapons, they're wrong. We found them."

Bush was on a whirlwind, seven-day trip through Europe and the Middle East, and he made similar remarks about finding WMD in an interview in France. The only problem was that the weapons hadn't actually been found. The military's 75th Exploitation Task Force was running into massive problems in the Great Hunt for Saddam's WMD, not the least of which was a series of highly publicized false positives. Each time they seemed to have found something that could be portrayed as a smoking gun—an alleged stockpile, a vat or even a small vial of biological weapons—it would soon be discredited.

Unknown to the president, four days before his TV interview, the DIA had dispatched a nine-member team of civilian experts to Iraq to examine the two mobile labs that had been found. The team had sent back a three-page field report the day before Bush's statement with their conclusion that the labs were not for biological weapons. Their secret 122-page report, finished the next month, said the labs had nothing to do with WMD. All the evidence was that the labs were most likely for manufacturing hydrogen to be used in weather balloons.

A day after Bush's remarks, at a Pentagon press conference, Rumsfeld's undersecretary of defense for intelligence, Steve Cambone, and Army Major General Keith Dayton, the head of the human intelligence service at DIA, officially announced the creation of the new Iraq Survey Group. Now, Dayton said, his new, 1,400-member group would take over the hunt, but they would have other tasks such as gathering intelligence on terrorism and war crimes. His unit would be based in Qatar, some 400 miles south of Iraq on the other side of the Persian Gulf, where the military's Central Command had sophisticated communications systems in place for sending information back to the U.S.

SPIDER MARKS WAS READY to go back to the U.S. Colonel Rotkoff was exhausted. He was ready to retire from the Army, and he'd arranged for a desk job in Washington for a few months while he figured out what to do in the civilian world. Just before he left the Middle East, he summarized his thoughts on the war, the fear, the stunning military victory, the failure to find any weapons of mass destruction, and the chaotic aftermath—in one of the final haiku in his journal.

We knew how to fight
Not so; building a NATION
We may lose the PEACE

ON JUNE 2, ABOUT 1,000 ex-soldiers gathered in Baghdad outside the gates of the CPA headquarters to protest the army's disbanding. An internal CPA memo recounted the event, focusing on the widespread coverage in Arabic-language media like the Al Jazeera and Al Arabiya television networks, and in the English-language Reuters news service.

"There have been public statements by some former MOD [Ministry of Defense] members that they will resolve to suicide attacks if their grievances are not addressed," the memo said. "Other protesters have continued to state that they will organize armed units to fight against the CPA and occupation."

"The entire Iraqi people is a time bomb that will blow up in the Americans' face if they don't end their occupation," one protest leader told reporters after he'd met with an official from the CPA.

"All of us will become suicide bombers," declared another protester, a former military officer. "I will turn my six daughters into bombs to kill the Americans."

"We're not going to be blackmailed into producing programs because of threats of terrorism," Bremer said in response. Besides, he noted, the demonstrations marked the first time in decades that anyone had dared protest outside Saddam's presidential palace. Wasn't that progress?

BUSH FLEW TO QATAR for a stopover on the Middle East leg of his trip, and Bremer came down from Baghdad to meet him. The two men talked in the back of Bush's limousine as they headed from Central Command headquarters near the airport to the Ritz-Carlton hotel.

"How's the overall situation?" Bush asked, Bremer recalled in his book.

"I'm optimistic for two reasons, Mr. President," Bremer began, and gave an explanation that sounded as if it came from *Encyclopaedia Britannica*. "First, Iraq has excellent resources, plenty of water, and it's fertile, besides the huge oil reserves. And, the Iraqis are energetic and resourceful folks."

At the same time, Bremer added, the Iraqi people were "psychologically shattered" after living so long under Saddam.

Without mentioning the de-Baathification policy or disbanding the military, which had left hundreds of thousands of Iraqis without work, Bremer told the president, "Our most urgent problem is unemployment. We think it's about 50 percent, but who really knows? Also, Iraq's got a young population, with about half of them under the age of nineteen. That's an explosive combination."

IN A DISCUSSION with Rumsfeld and Bremer, Bush had asked the two men point-blank who was in charge of finding the WMD. Who had the hunt as their primary, exclusive mission? Given that it was one of the main reasons for war, there was a heck of a lot riding on the outcome.

Bremer indicated it was Rumsfeld's responsibility.

Rumsfeld said Bremer was in charge.

Bush just about exploded. He said the task would go to someone else. He wanted someone in charge, someone for whom it would be his one mission in life. Since the CIA had insisted Iraq had WMD, the agency could go find the weapons. So finally, two and a half months into the war, the administration was going to give some focus to the hunt.

Although Bremer technically was to report to Bush through Rumsfeld, Rice could see that the Pentagon did not have that much influence over Bremer, let alone control.

"It's not going well," she told Frank Miller. He'd been the NSC's point man on Iraq in the run-up to the invasion, with his Executive Steering Group, and now she wanted him to reprise his role in the postwar era. "Reconstitute the ESG," she said.

21

THE AFTERNOON OF THURSDAY, JUNE 5, David Kay, one of the world's foremost experts on nuclear weapons inspections, was at CIA headquarters at Langley, Virginia. Kay, 63, a short, intense, outspoken Texan with a Ph.D. in political science, had been the chief United Nations nuclear weapons inspector inside Iraq after the 1991 Gulf War and had led the successful effort to uncover Saddam's secret nuclear program, which was six to 18 months away from building a bomb. It had been one of the major intelligence shocks of the 1990s.

As a member of a so-called Gray Beards panel of old hands, Kay was now at Langley to review a highly classified report on North Korea's clandestine efforts to reprocess plutonium for nuclear weapons. The initial report was pretty poor in Kay's view because the U.S. surveillance flights close to North Korea had been halted for fear of losing a plane. Kay had recommended that the CIA report be up front and say the data was not reliable. Just say you simply don't know, he advised, because the technical data was open to any interpretation.

Afterward, John McLaughlin, Tenet's deputy at the CIA, asked Kay to stop by his office. "George would like to see you," McLaughlin said.

Kay had just returned from Iraq, where he had spent a month working as an expert analyst for NBC News, following the work of the military's WMD-hunting task force. He'd even tagged along on some of their searches. Once he'd gone with them to search a chicken farm where the WMD Master Site List suggested there were banned substances. It turned out to be just a chicken farm.

"What do you think?" Tenet asked. "Why aren't they finding anything?"

"These guys probably couldn't find it if it was in front of them," Kay said bluntly. "They're not organized, equipped or led to do it."

"Okay. If you were king, what would you do?"

"First of all, you've got to have a group that is dedicated to the task that has the expertise necessary," he said. The 75th Exploitation Task Force did not have a clue. "You're not going to get there with the military leading it because the military has shown a massive lack of interest. They were interested in deterring their use, and they didn't view finding WMD as a military task."

Second, it was a mistake to start the search based on the WMD Master Site List, with its 946 locations, some of which had been labeled suspect sites for more than a decade. It was a catch-all catalogue of maybes. Kay had seen the list in Baghdad in May. A large number of the sites were places he'd inspected himself in 1991 and 1992, and found nothing.

"You simply cannot find weapons of mass destruction using a list," he said. "You have to treat this like an intelligence operation. You go after people. You don't go after physical assets. You don't have enough people in the country. It's too big a country. You can't dig up the whole country. So you treat it by going after the expertise, the security guards that would have been there, the movers, the generals that would have seen it, the Special Republican Guard."

Instead of looking for stockpiles or warheads, it was more important and easier to look for the capability—find the scientists who made the weapons, those who worked at the production facilities, the guards who provided security, the truck drivers who transported the weapons. If Iraq had WMD, then they had to have either produced them or bought them somewhere.

"Yeah, that makes sense," Tenet said.

Kay knew names, and he rattled off a list of key Iraqis, explaining how he thought they should find and question them. He thought Spider Marks had been pushing the WMD Master Site List, thinking they would find it if they only went to every site. Kay had been told that when the CIA station chief in Baghdad had tried to set up a meeting for Kay to talk to General McKiernan, McKiernan had declined, saying, "I don't have any interest in WMD. Why should I talk to Kay?"

The things that Kay had seen going wrong with the 75th XTF didn't seem to be any better with General Dayton's new group, the Iraq Survey

Group, he said. They were already off to a bad start. What were they doing in Doha, Qatar, hundreds of miles away from Iraq? Why were they talking about missions besides WMD?

"You don't start the search from Doha. You put people in the field. If they aren't, you've got to move them there. You need to focus on a single mission," Kay said.

"Fucking military can never get anything organized," Tenet said. "We need to find them. We don't want this job. The military should have done it. But we're going to be stuck with it. I know we're going to be stuck with it. The president's unhappy with what's happening." Tenet added, "The military has screwed this up so much. I don't want it now." Left unmentioned was that most of the intelligence and conclusions about the "slam dunk" intelligence about WMD had come from or through Tenet's CIA.

That weekend, Kay and his wife were on a getaway in Virginia when he got a call on his cell phone from Stu Cohen, the 30-year-veteran CIA analyst who had been acting chairman of the National Intelligence Council when the October 2002 National Intelligence Estimate on WMD in Iraq had been approved.

"The White House has agreed to put George in charge," Cohen said. "And he wants you to do it. George wants to know if you'll take the job."

Kay was surprised that the CIA would look outside its ranks for someone to run the WMD hunt, but he wanted the job.

"Yeah," Kay agreed, but added a caveat—"if all the conditions that I talked about with George were to hold true."

Kay was convinced that Saddam had WMD stockpiles. His experience after the Gulf War had seared itself into his head. When he had gone to Iraq for the U.N. after the Gulf War in 1991, he did not expect to find a nuclear program. Israeli intelligence, for example, was convinced that their strike in 1981 on the Osirak nuclear reactor about 10 miles outside Baghdad had ended Saddam's program. Instead Kay had uncovered the covert funding for a nuclear program code-named "PC3" involving 5,000 people testing and building ingredients for a nuclear bomb such as calutrons, centrifuges, neutron initiators, high-explosive lenses and enriched-uranium bomb cores. Saddam was on a crash program to build and detonate a crude nuclear weapon in the desert as a demonstration to the world, to say, "Now we've got one."

Kay vividly recalled how shocking it had been to Cheney, then secretary of defense, and Wolfowitz, the policy undersecretary. "I don't know what we would have done, if we had known," Wolfowitz had said. There might have been no Gulf War to eject Saddam from Kuwait. The Saudis might have tried to buy their way out of the problem as was their habit. In 1991 Kay's fellow U.N. inspectors also had uncovered hundreds of gallons of VX nerve gas, the deadliest known nerve agent, and biological weapons, including hundreds of liters of anthrax and some botulinum toxin.

Leading the new inspection effort in 2003 meant that Kay would have to become an official CIA employee. On Tuesday, June 10, he took a lie detector test and underwent a psychological evaluation. "Anyone who could take this job obviously fails the psychological test," Kay said, "so just flunk me."

He passed, and since he had the security clearances from his previous work, that afternoon Tenet swore him in as special adviser to the director on WMD and head of the Iraq Survey Group. Tenet was crowing about getting someone through CIA personnel in 12 hours—an apparent record for the agency—and he said the plan was for Kay to fly that evening for Baghdad, the next day at the latest.

"George, I can't do that," Kay objected. "I haven't been read in to all your evidence. I've got to talk to the analysts. I've got to talk with the people that are doing collection. I need to talk to Defense. Look, I can't just jump on a plane and go do this."

Over the next week or so, Kay embarked on a crash course in WMD intelligence. Since he had not worked the Iraq WMD case since the 1990s, he expected some new treasure trove as he spent 15- to 18-hour days reading and sitting through CIA and Defense Department briefings. He was shocked at what was not there.

"It was nothing new," he recalled. Anything with a strong or reasonable factual basis came from before 1998, when the U.N. inspectors had left. "Everything after that either came from a defector or came through a foreign intelligence service in an opaque sort of way."

For example, Kay found that all the prewar intelligence about the mobile biological weapons labs that Powell had described at the U.N. in February, and that the president had declared had been discovered on May 29, had come from a single source, the Iraqi defector used by German intelligence code-named Curveball.

Powell had told the U.N. and the world there were four sources for the allegation, based on the CIA information, but in truth three of the sources only provided information about Curveball's career or about an alleged mobile lab facility of some kind. "They had no knowledge of the biological program," Kay said later.

The surprises kept coming. Kay was aghast to realize that the CIA had never even independently interviewed Curveball, but relied instead on the Germans' reports of 112 interrogations they conducted. Worse still, it appeared that the Germans had warned that Curveball was an alcoholic, although this had been downplayed in the U.S. files.

On the alleged Iraqi effort to restart its nuclear program, Kay found that the conclusion hinged on only one piece of physical evidence— "high-specification aluminum tubes" Powell had told the U.N. that Saddam kept trying to acquire. "Most U.S. experts think they are intended to serve as rotors in centrifuges used to enrich uranium," Powell said.

The CIA file on the aluminum tubes ran hundreds of pages, and contained information from foreign sources suggesting that Iraq had tried to purchase 60,000 such tubes to be used as artillery shells. That was a lot by any standard, Kay agreed. But he had learned back in the 1990s that the Iraqis would overspend and buy much more of what they thought they needed. It was a far more serious offense under Saddam for someone in a government program to fail to procure enough than to buy too much.

After several days, the lyrics to an old Peggy Lee song began running through Kay's head: *Is That All There Is?* He said later, "The more you look at it, the less is there. It was an eye-opening experience. But realize, (a) I still believed they were there. And (b) I thought the answer was not going to be found in Washington or Doha. It was going to be found in Baghdad, in Iraq. So I was anxious to get out in the field and see what I can do."

AT THE END OF THE WEEK of Kay's WMD crash course, Tenet arranged a lunch for the two of them with Rumsfeld at the secretary's Pentagon office. Generals Myers and Franks were there, along with Steve Cambone.

Tenet proposed that they share responsibility for Kay, and have him report to both Rumsfeld and himself.

"Absolutely not," Rumsfeld said. It was Tenet's responsibility now.

Kay could see that Rumsfeld deserved respect as one of the best bureaucratic infighters of all time. Presuming Kay found WMD, it would validate the CIA estimates. If he didn't find WMD, no good could come from being associated with the unsuccessful search. It was not a winnable proposition, so Rumsfeld opted out.

Franks was still on his victory lap. He was to retire later in the month and his replacement, General Abizaid, had been announced.

"I want to be sure you and Keith Dayton get along," Rumsfeld said, "and you don't fight over this."

"You don't have to worry," Kay promised, "because if we don't get along, I tell you, we will be there longer than either of us wants to be."

"I like that attitude," Franks said, bursting into laughter.

"I understand that attitude," Rumsfeld added.

Before leaving for Baghdad, Kay expressed a final concern to Tenet. "Look, I don't have any base in the CIA," Kay said. "I don't want to have to fight people for resources once I'm out there."

"Don't worry," Tenet said. "You'll get whatever you want. You have any problems, John and I will take care of it." Putting his arms around Kay in a big Greek hug, Tenet said, "Don't fuck up."

It was his standard farewell to those going into the field.

ON JUNE 12, 2003, *The Washington Post* ran a front-page story by Walter Pincus reporting that an unnamed "retired U.S. ambassador" had been sent to Africa in 2002 to see if Iraq had tried to get uranium from Niger. The retired ambassador disputed that there was any evidence of a deal. This ran contrary to President Bush's assertion in his State of the Union address before the war, in 16 words that would become famous: "The British government has learned that Saddam Hussein recently sought significant quantities of uranium from Africa."

The next day, a Friday, I interviewed a senior administration official, someone who did not work in the White House, for my book *Plan of Attack*. Near the end of the one-hour-and-30-minute background interview, our conversation drifted to a gossipy interchange that is common after a long, substantive discussion. I said I knew the "retired U.S. ambassador" on the CIA mission was Joseph C. Wilson, who had been ambassador to the African country of Gabon under George H. W. Bush, and who had worked on the Clinton National Security Council.

"His wife works in the agency," the official said. "She is a WMD analyst out there."

He said Wilson's wife had proposed him for the mission because Wilson knew Africa. We moved on to another subject.

After the interview, I told Pincus what I had heard about Wilson's wife working as a WMD analyst at the CIA, without saying who I had learned it from. Pincus later said he did not recall our conversation.

A few weeks later, on July 6, Wilson wrote an op-ed piece in *The New York Times* and said it was "highly doubtful" that any Iraq-Niger deal had taken place. Eight days after that, syndicated columnist Robert Novak wrote that "two senior administration officials" had told him that Wilson's wife, Valerie Plame, was a CIA "operative on weapons of mass destruction" and had been instrumental in his going to Africa. The Justice Department launched a criminal investigation into how Wilson's wife's CIA ties were revealed to the press and whether it meant an undercover agent had been revealed. A special prosecutor was soon named to take over the investigation, U.S. Attorney Patrick Fitzgerald of Chicago.

JAY GARNER BASICALLY hid out for a couple of weeks when he returned to the U.S. in the beginning of June, not wanting to see anyone at the Pentagon or talk about his experience in Iraq. Larry DiRita called several times. "You've got to get over here and see Rumsfeld," DiRita implored. Finally, Garner agreed to go over on Wednesday, June 18.

When he was alone with Rumsfeld around the small table in the secretary's famous office, where they had met back in January, Garner felt he had an obligation to state the depths of his concerns.

"We've made three tragic decisions," Garner said.

"Really?" Rumsfeld said.

"Three terrible mistakes," Garner said, laying out what he'd omitted from his May 27 memo to the president. He cited the extent of the de-Baathification, getting rid of the army, and summarily dumping the Iraqi leadership group. Disbanding the military had been the biggest mistake. Now there were hundreds of thousands of disorganized, unemployed, armed Iraqis running around. It would take years to rebuild an army. They'd taken 30,000 or 50,000 Baathists and sent them underground, Garner told Rumsfeld. And they'd gotten rid of the Iraqi leadership group. "Jerry Bremer can't be the face of the government to the Iraqi people. You've got to have an Iraqi face for the Iraqi people."

Garner made his final point: "There's still time to rectify this. There's still time to turn it around."

Rumsfeld looked at Garner for a moment with his take-no-prisoners gaze. "Well," he said, "I don't think there is anything we can do, because we are where we are."

He thinks I've lost it, Garner thought. He thinks I'm absolutely wrong. Garner didn't want it to sound like sour grapes, but facts were facts. "They're all reversible," Garner said again.

"We're not going to go back," Rumsfeld said emphatically. Discussion over. "Come on. Let's go in the other room."

In 2006, I asked Rumsfeld if he recalled Garner's warning about the three mistakes.

"Vaguely," Rumsfeld answered. "I remember having a very good discussion with him. I felt that he had not been properly recognized for what he had done. I think he's a fine retired officer and a very talented guy who cares a lot about Iraq."

After their discussion, Rumsfeld and Garner walked into the large conference room where most of Rumsfeld's top people were assembled—Wolfowitz, Feith, Ryan Henry, DiRita and Torie Clarke, General Pace and General Casey.

In a small ceremony, Rumsfeld pinned the Defense Department Medal for Distinguished Public Service on Garner, who didn't want the medal.

Afterward, Rumsfeld and Garner held a press conference.

"I do want to thank Jay for the absolutely superb job that he has done," the secretary said, "laying the foundation for the Iraqi people to begin this process of rebuilding from the rubble of decades of Saddam Hussein's tyranny and to put themselves on a path towards democratic self-government."

Rumsfeld told the press corps that the water system in Iraq was now operating at 80 percent of its prewar level, and that close to 2 million Iraqi civil servants were being paid. He read off a list of impressive statistics: Basra had 24-hour electricity, and Baghdad's power was on 19 or 20 hours a day. Lines to buy gasoline were disappearing, there was no health crisis, and Iraqi children were returning to school. Eight thousand police officers were back on the job, he said. Two thousand of them were patrolling. As for the security situation, Rumsfeld said, "In those regions where pockets of dead-enders are trying to reconstitute, General Franks and his team are rooting them out. In short, the coalition is making good progress. It was made possible by the excellent military plan of General Franks and by the terrific leadership of the stabilization effort by Mr. Jay Garner and his team."

When Garner finally had a chance to speak, he was more sober. "To all of you, I'd like to just say one thing. There are problems in Iraq and there will be problems in Iraq for a while. There's always problems when you've been brutalized for 30 years and you take people out of absolute darkness and put them in the sunshine. So I think there's more goodness, far more goodness than there is badness, and the glass absolutely is half full."

At the end of his remarks, Garner completely contradicted what he had privately told Rumsfeld, saying of Bremer, "I think all the things he's doing are absolutely the right things."

NEXT, RUMSFELD AND GARNER went to the White House to see Bush. It was Garner's second time with the president.

"Mr. Secretary, who's that famous man you have with you?" the president called out, coming through the doorway from the Oval Office. He reached out his hand. "Hi, Jay."

"Mr. President," Garner said, "you've got more important things to do for this nation today than take time out to talk to me, so all I want to do is shake your hand and thank you for the chance to serve."

Bush took Garner's hand and in one of his trademark moves pulled Garner in close physically.

"I do have time for you," Bush said, "and I'm going to take time. I want to be with you." Bush put his arm around Garner and propelled him into the Oval Office, stopping by one of the windows. "Look out here, Jay. Look out here on the lawn. If I wasn't spending this time with you, I'd probably be out there with the press corps or somebody kissing their ass. Or if I weren't with the press corps I'd probably be up there on Capitol Hill with a bunch of congressmen kissing their asses."

Bush led Garner over to the main pair of chairs in the Oval Office. "You sit here and I'll sit here," the president said, taking his usual position and offering the other chair to Garner. "Why wouldn't I want to be in this comfortable office in these two nice chairs sitting here with you kissing your ass?"

Cheney and Rice joined them.

"Mr. President, let me tell you a couple of stories," Garner said. It was his turn.

Garner had an overly long story and he recalls telling it this way to Bush: Buck Walters, a retired Air Force one-star who was Garner's man in charge of the southern Iraq region, called him one day when he was visiting Hillah, near Babylon. Malcolm MacPherson, a reporter for *Time* magazine, and Mike Gfoeller, a State Department officer who had a reputation for being an even better Arabic speaker than most Iraqis, were there. "Before you leave," Walters said, "I've got to take you up to see Darth Vader."

"Who's that?" Garner asked.

"He's the leading cleric here."

"Why do you call him Darth Vader?" Garner asked.

"Well, you'll understand that when you see him."

So Garner told Bush and the others that he went to meet the man. Out comes this giant guy, a Shiite cleric the size of basketball great Shaquille O'Neal dressed all in black. Black turban. Big black beard. He was said to be a direct descendent of the Prophet Muhammad. Everybody sits down. He speaks good English.

"Your Excellency," Garner began, "as you know we've been here several weeks now and we've done some things that were good and we've done some things that weren't good. And we've not done a lot of things because we didn't know to do them. And so what I'd like during this period of time is I'd like your evaluation on what we've done right and on what we've done wrong, and then I'd like your guidance on what we should do next."

"Good," said Darth Vader. "I've thought about this a while. Let me talk to you. Do you mind if I speak in Arabic? Do you have a translator?"

Garner told Bush and the others: I had the best translator in the United States with me. So Darth Vader talked in Arabic for the next hour.

"I've taken so long and I apologize for being this long," finished Darth Vader (later identified as Sheik Farqat al-Qizwini), switching back to English. "I shouldn't have taken this much of your time."

"No, this has been wonderful," Garner recalled. "I'm going to go back and we're going to work on these things that you brought up."

But Darth Vader said, "Let me summarize. What we need to do now is get a working government. But that working government has to be based on a constitution. That constitution has to be written by all the Iraqi people. It has to be founded on the democratic principles, and it must take care of everyone regardless of their religion, of their ethnic background.

"Once we have this, then we can have an Iraqi government. We can begin to be a democratic state. We can be a beacon of light in the Middle East."

Darth Vader began to raise his voice. "So we must follow these principles and we must put a democracy together and we have to write a constitution built on the principles of Jesus Christ."

Bush and the others loved it.

Garner continued quoting the cleric: "We'll have this government. Once we have this government you bring us in as the 51st state."

Garner then said he replied, "Your Excellency, that is a terrific idea. It's going to take me a little longer to work on this one than the other things, but I will come back to you and talk to you about that."

After the session, Garner said he and the *Time* reporter got in the car to drive away.

"Wow," the reporter said. "What are you going to do about that?"

"Hey, that's not my problem. The question is what are you going to do about that? Because no one is going to believe it when you put this in *Time* magazine."

"For Christ's sake, I'll never put this in *Time*. Nobody would believe it."

True story, Garner said. He was on a roll.

Every third day or so, Garner told Bush, he would try to go to the market, because that's where Iraqi people would recognize him and come up and talk to him. For the first 20 or 25 minutes, people would raise hell and bitch at him, Garner said, but then they'd start to run out of steam, and Garner would have a minute or so to make an "elevator speech," to rattle off all of their accomplishments. "You've got this many megawatts of electricity coming in now. We project this many more by next week. We're going to open schools at this time. We think we're going to be able to have provincial elections around this time. We'll start writing the constitution. Got this much water that we're bringing in. I know the fuel crisis is bad so we're bringing this many tankers of fuel every day. We are going to start buying the harvest next week."

If they had specific problems, Garner said, he would promise that the next day at 10 A.M. he would have some general come by there to work on their problems. And as he'd get ready to wind up, Garner said, he'd thank the crowd for their time.

"I'd get ready to leave," Garner said, "and this is true—as I leave they're all thumbs-up and they'd say, 'God bless Mr. George Bush and Mr. Tony Blair. Thank you for taking away Saddam Hussein.' That was in 70 meetings. That always was the final response."

"Oh, that's good," Bush said.

Garner told him about how the Baathists tried to take over the first post-Saddam elections at Baghdad University. That had led to some negative press. The Americans had felt forced to let elections at the school proceed so that there would be somebody in place and the school year could finish on time. But the Baathists on campus, unpopular as they were, were more organized than anyone else, and they won. The university had been plunged into chaos.

"That was bad," Bush said, indicating he knew about it.

"Mr. President, the one thing I'll tell you, I've had three weeks to work with Ambassador Bremer and he's one of the hardest-working men I've ever seen. He's a very bright guy. He's articulate and he'll get the job done. You made a good choice."

"I didn't choose him," Bush said. "Rumsfeld chose him just like he chose you."

Garner looked over at Rumsfeld. The secretary of defense had told him explicitly in late April that Bush had selected Bremer, and had added later that even the timing of Bremer's arrival was not his call. But now Rumsfeld didn't say a word.

As Garner go up to leave, Rice stopped him and extended her hand. "Jay, you've got to stay in touch with us," she said.

"I'd like to," Garner said, thinking to himself, *How the hell am I going to do that?* After all, he only talked with Rumsfeld.

On the way out, Bush slapped Garner on the back. "Hey, Jay, you want to do Iran?"

"Sir, the boys and I talked about that and we want to hold out for Cuba. We think the rum and the cigars are a little better . . . The women are prettier."

Bush laughed. "You got it. You got Cuba."

OF COURSE, WITH ALL THE STORIES, jocularity, buddy-buddy talk, bluster and confidence in the Oval Office, Garner had left out the headline. He had not mentioned the problems he saw, or even hinted at them. He did not tell Bush about the three tragic mistakes he believed that Bremer, supported by Rumsfeld, had made—de-Baathification, disbanding the army and dumping the Iraqi governing group. Instead, he had said Bremer was great and had painted a portrait of an Iraq where a Shiite cleric envisioned an Iraq governed on the principles of Jesus Christ and joining the union as the 51st state. On top of that, he told Bush that everyone on the Iraqi street loved him. Once again the aura of the presidency had shut out the most important news—the bad news.

Later, I asked Rumsfeld about the obligation to make sure the person at the top knows the bad news. "Oh, I think the president knew that there were big disagreements over de-Baathification. And big disagreements over the military. There's no question that the president was aware of those issues."

But I could find no evidence that was the case.

On October 16, 2005, during a four-hour interview at Garner's home on a lake outside Orlando, Florida, I asked him about his decision not to mention the three tragic mistakes.

"Didn't you owe the president that?"

"I didn't work for the president," Garner answered. "I worked for Rumsfeld. I'm a military guy."

I recalled for him my time as a junior officer in the Navy. "I reported to the operations officer on the ship I was on. And if I thought we were making even half a tragic mistake, I'd tell my boss, but I'd make sure the captain knew."

"No," Garner said.

I said that was perhaps why I didn't do so well in the Navy.

"No," Garner repeated, "my view was I did my job. I told my boss in what I thought were pretty stern terms on the mistakes we'd made."

"Now suppose you said, 'Mr. President, I just told the secretary the following and I want you to hear it from me, because when he reports it to you I want it to be—' "

Garner interrupted. "I'd have no idea how he'd have reacted, but I think he would have said, 'Well, you know, Rummy's in charge of that' or something like that."

"Three tragic mistakes," I said.

"Yeah," Garner said softly, exhaling.

"Because the three tragic mistakes we're living with now two-plus years later. You realize that?"

"Absolutely," Garner replied.

"You watch the news."

"Yeah," he said.

"You don't feel you should have kind of, particularly at the upper levels there . . ."

"I think Rumsfeld's the upper level. No, if I had that to do over again I'd probably do that the same way." He said that he did not know of anything that Rumsfeld had done that had been overturned by the president. "I'm not the only one who thought that," he added.

"If you'd said it to the president, and you could save one life—" I stopped, leaving the second half of my question unasked. "Because you're a pretty smart guy. You've been around—"

"Yeah. You know you put it—" Garner started, but he didn't finish his sentence. "But you've got to remember, I didn't look at in that context. I looked at it like, I, Jay Garner, do not think this was the right thing to do. I, Jay Garner, said this over there to the guy in charge and I've said it to the guy that I work for. I've done that. I didn't even really think of bringing that up" to President Bush.

Two months later, on December 13, 2005, at a long breakfast at my home in Washington, D.C., I again raised the question of what he did not tell the president.

"That was more of a happy-glad than it was a business meeting," Garner said.

I asked, "Do you wish now that you said, 'Mr. President, as I just told the secretary of defense, in my view, I've been there and I need to make sure you understand what I think I understand. We've made three tragic mistakes.' Boom, boom, boom."

"You know, I don't know if I had that moment to live over again I don't know if I'd do that or not. But if I had done that—and quite frankly, I mean, I wouldn't have had a problem doing that—but in my thinking, the door's closed. I mean, there's nothing I can do to open this door again. And I think if I had said that to the president in front of Cheney and Condoleezza Rice and Rumsfeld in there, the president would have looked at them and they would have rolled their eyes back and he would have thought, Boy, I wonder why we didn't get rid of this guy sooner?"

I laughed and started to ask another question.

"They didn't see it coming," Garner added. "As the troops said, they drank the Kool-Aid."

It was only one example of a visitor to the Oval Office not telling the president the whole story or the truth. Likewise, in these moments where Bush had someone from the field there in the chair beside him, he did not press, did not try to open the door himself and ask what the visitor had seen and thought. The whole atmosphere too often resembled a royal court, with Cheney and Rice in attendance, some upbeat stories, exaggerated good news, and a good time had by all.

22

D AVID KAY LEFT WASHINGTON FOR QATAR on June 18, the same day Garner met with Bush. He quickly realized that his Iraq Survey Group was a pretty typical military organization. There were 1,400 people assigned, but that included a lot of support staff, even a military chaplain and others in charge of morale and recreation. The core people included between 25 and 40 CIA operations officers, and some analysts and other people from the DIA and other intelligence agencies. His missile team had between 12 and 15 people, and there were about a half-dozen experts on biological weapons. There were a few hundred translators with varying levels of skill.

Kay immediately stopped the daily trips to suspect sites. "We're going to be led as an intelligence operation," he told Dayton and the others, "so it means you've got to know something about what you're doing. So we'll divide the teams up into chemical and biological, missiles, and nukes, and a team for procurement."

The contract awarded to the company providing them with translators stipulated that they couldn't be sent into the combat zone. So documents in Iraq had to be shipped back to Qatar for translation. They had developed a list of a couple hundred key Arabic words and phrases, such as "nuclear weapons," "biological weapons," "anthrax" or "botulinum toxin." If any of these words or phrases was found in a quick review of captured documents, they were assigned a higher priority and reviewed carefully.

But it took too long to get the documents back, and then Kay found nothing new in the documents with one major exception—the personnel directory of the Military Industrial Commission.

"We don't have an interest in the personnel record of a ministry," one of the ISG military officers said.

"Well," Kay said, "actually you do." The directory would lead to people. People were the key.

Some of his group resisted going to Iraq until they had permanent facilities set up to eat, sleep and live in.

"No," Kay said again. "We can eat MREs and sleep in tents or whatever, but we're going forward because you can't—you're not going to find the weapons in Doha."

"Stop searching," Kay ordered when they got to Baghdad. Forget about the WMD site list, he repeated. "Start thinking and finding people."

Living conditions had improved since the Garner era. Kay slept in an air-conditioned shipping container at the airport, and they were able to move around the city and eat at restaurants. With nothing else to do, they worked late most nights.

Kay first had his team deconstruct Powell's February 5 U.N. speech to make sure they were pursuing all the allegations Powell had made. Supposedly it was the best intelligence, and he wanted to make sure that nobody could say later, "Well, Powell said this and you ignored him." The group had a list of Iraqis who had been involved in the WMD programs, and who had been interviewed at length by the myriad U.N. inspection teams in the 1990s. Within three weeks, they had tracked down 50 to 60 of them, including scientists, technicians and senior bureaucrats. They questioned them, went through their offices, and dug through documents. A fairly consistent picture began to emerge.

"The nuke story was falling apart," Kay recalled. "We were getting a clear picture of what their nuclear capability had been, and quite frankly it was worse, much worse, than it had been in '91 at the start of the first Gulf War."

More interesting was the state of the chemical and biological weapons program. There was nothing to back up the idea that there had been stockpiles of chemical or biological weapons. They found nobody who had produced, guarded, transported or knew about those kinds of weapons.

ON SUNDAY, JUNE 22, about 2,000 Shiites protested outside Bremer's headquarters, saying they wanted elections so they could form a national government. "No Americans, no Saddam, all the people are for Islam," they chanted. The protesters were strongly supported by Grand Ayatollah Ali Sistani, the revered, infallible spiritual leader and guide to millions of Shiites in Iraq. Sistani refused to meet with Bremer directly, apparently because he would not meet with infidels. Sistani, then 73, had a role roughly equivalent to that of the Pope for Catholics. He was insisting on elections before a constitution was drawn up. How could they have a constitution written by people who were not elected?

In Washington at the NSC meeting the next day, the president was upset.

"How did we get on the wrong side of the question of whether or not the Iraqis ought to have elections?" he asked. Here the United States, this great democracy, has it backward. Maybe elections had to come first, before they tried to write a constitution and organize a new Iraqi society.

For Rice, it crystallized the problem. The majority Shiites were saying that only a legitimate government that had some kind of blessing from the people could write a constitution. After decades of minority Sunni rule, the Shiites didn't want appointed people—Saddam was always appointing people—writing a constitution. It seemed reasonable to her. But others were in charge, namely Rumsfeld and Bremer. Sistani added another dimension. On June 28, he issued a fatwa—an Islamic legal decree—rejecting any U.S.-picked constitutional council, and said Iraqis should elect the drafters of their constitution.

BUSH APPEARED IN THE ROOSEVELT ROOM at the White House on July 2, 2003, to discuss a $15 billion U.S. effort to fight AIDS abroad. When he took a few questions from the press afterward, Iraq was Topic A.

One reporter noted that the number of attacks on U.S. forces and the casualty rate were rising.

"There are some who feel like that if they attack us that we may decide to leave prematurely," the president responded, shaking his head no. "They don't understand what they're talking about, if that's the case."

A reporter started to interrupt.

"Let me finish," Bush said. "There are some who feel like—that the conditions are such that they can attack us there." He swung his arm across his chest emphatically as he spoke. "My answer is, 'Bring 'em on.' We've got the force necessary to deal with the security situation."

It was an ill-advised comment, reflecting little understanding of guerrilla war, taunting and egging on the enemy, almost inviting more attacks.*

ARMITAGE WAS AT THE WHITE HOUSE for a briefing for the president around that time, and Hadley took him aside.

"Some people are saying your body language is very bad at the meetings," Hadley said.

"My body language is bad?" Armitage echoed.

You're telegraphing your discomfort, Hadley said. "You feel really tense."

"Steve, I don't like what the president is being told," Armitage said. "So yeah, I'm very unhappy. I am not unhappy with the president. I am unhappy with the brief we are getting. It is a sophomoric brief."

"I thought that was what it is," Hadley said. He indicated that the real work was being done upstairs in the Oval Office with the president, Cheney and Rumsfeld.

Was that supposed to set him at ease? Armitage realized that once again he and Powell were window dressing, about as influential as a couple of potted plants. In the meetings upstairs, it was mostly Rumsfeld's positive spin, because there was no one to challenge him, and no NSC or interagency review to test his assessments.

IN SADDAM'S IRAQ, possession of a satellite TV dish, which gave unfettered access to uncensored news, had been punishable by six months in prison and a $300 fine. With the regime gone, satellite dishes sprang up like weeds all around the country, even in the poorest areas. Huts and hovels without running water or sewer hookups would have satellite television dishes on the roof or in the yard. It was so sudden, and the U.S. tried to move fast so that the coalition message could get on the air, and at least compete with all the Arabic-language television suddenly being beamed into and enthusiastically watched in Iraq.

The American defense contractor SAIC had been given an $82 million, no-bid contract to build up Iraqi television and radio networks.

---

* At a White House press conference nearly three years later, on May 25, 2006, a reporter asked Bush to name "which missteps and mistakes of your own you most regret." Bush replied: "Sounds like kind of a familiar refrain here—saying 'bring it on,' kind of tough talk, you know, that sent the wrong signal to people. I learned some lessons about expressing myself maybe in a little more sophisticated manner—you know, 'wanted dead or alive,' that kind of talk. I think in certain parts of the world it was misinterpreted, and so I learned from that."

Rice was skeptical: "SAIC doesn't do that kind of thing," she said, and sent a team over to check it out.

Eventually there was a U.S.-sponsored television network set up. To fill out its schedule, it broadcast Arabic-language reruns from elsewhere in the Middle East. As a result, some Iraqis took to calling it the "Lebanese Cooking Channel," especially after one day when most other major networks, like Qatar-based Al Jazeera, covered a significant news event live but the U.S.-sponsored network ran a foreign program on how to cook a rabbit.

Inside the Green Zone, the heavily fortified roughly six-square-mile area where the CPA was headquartered, a group of consultants tried to figure out what kind of television programs Iraqis would like to watch. They talked about capturing the Iraqi stay-at-home mom market segment with some kind of Iraqi version of Oprah Winfrey's show.

"You know, we could go to Hollywood," Bush said later to Rice. "I know people in Hollywood. We can go to Disney. We can get people involved who can do this kind of thing."

"Oh, we've got it, Mr. President," Rice replied. "We've got it."

He kept after her: "Do something."

By summer 2003, Bush realized they were failing at communications. He told Tony Blair, "We're doing a lousy job here. If I haven't solved this by December, I'm going to just give this to the U.K." He probably wasn't serious, but it gave voice to his frustration.

THE CONTROVERSY over the president's reference to the discredited Iraq-Niger uranium deal was gaining steam, and was fast becoming a symbol of both the failure to find WMD, and the suspicion that the president had cherry-picked intelligence to make the case for war.

On Saturday, July 5, Tenet talked to the chief NSC spokesperson, Anna Perez. As best she could tell, the fact that the 16 words about the uranium had made it into the State of the Union address was the result of failures in both the NSC staff and the CIA. "We're both going to have to eat some of this," Perez said. Something should be done to correct the record on what the president had said in his speech.

Tenet had gotten the accusation pulled out of Bush's speech in Cincinnati the previous October, but Hadley, who had reviewed the final State of the Union address, had apparently forgotten the earlier warning. Tenet had not reviewed the final State of the Union draft as he was supposed to do.

Tenet agreed with Perez that all would share the blame. The plan was to work on a joint statement over the weekend that would be put out on Monday. Rice and Tenet spoke next and agreed that they had to put the issue to bed. Rice was with the president traveling in Africa. Hadley and some NSC staffers worked on a draft but they couldn't reach an agreement.

Tenet said he would put out a statement. On Tuesday, July 8, however, after Ambassador Joseph Wilson's *New York Times* op-ed piece cast doubt on the claim, the White House released a statement saying, "Knowing all we know now, the reference to Iraq's attempt to acquire uranium from Africa should not have been included in the State of the Union speech."

Democrats began calling for an investigation.

"What else don't we know?" asked Florida Senator Bob Graham, the former chairman of the Senate Intelligence Committee, in a public comment.

On Friday, July 11, Bush and Rice were in the fourth day of the Africa trip. At the back of Air Force One, Rice engaged reporters in a discussion for nearly an hour about the matter. "I can tell you, if the CIA, the director of central intelligence, had said, 'Take this out of the speech,' it would have been gone without question," she said. "If there was a concern about the underlying intelligence there, the president was unaware of that concern, as was I." She later laid it out more starkly, putting the blame four-square on Tenet's CIA. "The agency cleared the speech and cleared it in its entirety," she said.

Bush adopted Rice's line. "I gave a speech to the nation that was cleared by the intelligence services," he said.

"Condi shoved it right up my ass," Tenet told a colleague. They had an agreement and had been working on a joint statement for two days. Now Rice had dropped a dime on him, blaming only the CIA. The problem was a classic. Two views of the Niger-uranium issue had existed inside his CIA. At the lower level, they believed a connection was possible. But Tenet had access to the highest-level, most sensitive intelligence from a foreign intelligence service that had an agent inside Saddam's government who discounted the Niger-uranium story.

Tenet decided to fall on his sword. The statement was retooled so he would take full responsibility. He released it that night to avoid a second-day story.

His long statement said in part, "First, the CIA approved the President's State of the Union address before it was delivered. Second, I am responsible for the approval process in my agency. And third, the President had every reason to believe that the text presented to him was sound. These 16 words should never have been included in the text written for the president."

The next morning the front-page headline in *The Washington Post* read, "Bush, Rice Blame CIA for Iraq Error; Tenet Accepts Responsibility for Clearing Statement on Nuclear Aims in Jan. Speech."

It was 100 percent public grovel, and Tenet was privately furious. He had the CIA search all its records to see what had been passed in writing to the White House. The CIA found two memos sent to the White House just before the October 2002 Cincinnati speech voicing doubts about the intelligence that Iraq was trying to buy uranium in Africa.

Instead of taking the memos to Rice or Hadley, Tenet took them to Andy Card, effectively dropping his own dime on the president's national security adviser and her deputy. Card heard Tenet out.

"I was not told the truth," Card said ominously. He directed that the White House investigate.

Full war was now on between the CIA and the White House.

Eleven days after Tenet's public mea culpa, Hadley went before the press to take his turn.

"I should have recalled at the time of the State of the Union speech that there was controversy associated with the uranium issue."

It was painful for the meticulous, careful Hadley. He was visibly shaken. "I am the senior-most official within the NSC staff, directly responsible for the substantive review and clearance of presidential speeches," he said. "I failed in that responsibility in connection with the inclusion of these 16 words."

At a long, grueling press briefing, he and Dan Bartlett, the president's communications director, nonetheless said that though the uranium claim did not rise to the high standard for a presidential speech, it was accurate because the statement in the president's speech had been attributed to the British.

"The real failing," Hadley said, "is that we've had a national discussion on 16 words, and it's taken away from the fact that the intelligence case supporting concerns about WMD in Iraq was overwhelming . . . as strong a case as you get in these matters."

It was his own "slam dunk."

"These 16 words affect not one whit the decision he made which was based on the intelligence case," Hadley said.

Armitage was pretty sure that Hadley had taken a figurative bullet not for the president so much as for the vice president. It was Cheney who was the strongest advocate that Saddam had been reconstituting his nuclear program.

In private, Tenet told Armitage he believed that Hadley was a Cheney-Rumsfeld "sleeper agent"—an intelligence term for an undercover agent who lurks dormant without a mission for years, but who can be awakened to do the bidding of his handlers. It was a hyperbolic statement, but it reflected the growing animus between the CIA and the NSC.

First Tenet, and now Hadley, had taken the hit for the president. The public blowup opened up old wounds, such as the Tenet-Rice hostility and charges of basic incompetence at the CIA.

IN JULY 2003 BREMER approved a 25-member Iraqi interim Governing Council, which met for days trying to determine who would be its leader. It was an expanded version of Garner's group. Reflecting the intense divisions of Shiites, Sunnis and Kurds, the council finally reached an agreement: The presidency of the group would rotate among nine people, each of whom would be president for a month. Moreover, all but one of the nine had been exiles who had returned to Iraq after the U.S.-led invasion.

When word reached the White House, even the very controlled Hadley was disbelieving.

"Iraq was an abused child for 30 years," he said. Saddam Hussein had killed many of the elites, and most of those who weren't killed left the country and lived in exile. Now the exiles were back, but the country was so divided no one could agree on much of anything. At one meeting Hadley said sarcastically, "We say, 'Pick your president,' and they say, 'The first month it'll be this guy's president. The second month it'll be this guy's president. The third month it'll be this guy's president. The fourth month it'll be this guy's president.' And at that point you say, 'This is not ready for prime time. Who's going to lead this country?' That is what the president wants to know, 'Who is going to step up and lead this country?' "

For the moment it was Bremer.

DAVID KAY WAS IN almost daily contact with Tenet on video teleconferences, but officials from other intelligence agencies and the

Pentagon—including Cambone, who was against the very idea of Kay's involvement—were always in on the discussions. So Kay e-mailed Tenet and McLaughlin directly once a week or so with his most important, secret, early conclusions.

On chemical and biological weapons, Kay wrote in a secure, private CIA e-mail, it was beginning to look very much like the Iraqis had adopted something like what the Soviets called surge capacity. It meant they would maintain some ability to make chemical and biological weapons, but they wouldn't actually produce and stockpile the weapons until they needed them. "You've got to start to understand that the puzzle may fit together that way," Kay wrote.

"Don't tell anyone this," McLaughlin wrote back, as Kay recalled. "This could be upsetting. Be very careful. We can't let this out until we're sure."

Around 3 A.M. one morning, Kay was asleep in his shipping container when someone from his communications shop banged on his door. "The vice president's office. He's on the phone."

Kay hustled over to the secure phone, where it turned out that it wasn't Cheney, but a staffer in his office. "The vice president wants to know if you've seen this communication intercept," said the staffer, going on to describe information that the NSA had picked up from Syria alleging a location of some chemical weapons. It was a highly classified Executive Signals Intercept that would be circulated only among the most senior officials, and that wouldn't normally be shared with the field in its raw form.

"Honestly, no, I haven't," Kay said, "but I will look at it."

Kay located his team's NSA representative, who dug out the intercept. It was innocuous—particularly innocuous at 3 A.M., Kay thought—and inconclusive. He was surprised that Cheney or his people were getting down to such detail. Kay didn't think intercepts were going to lead them to WMD because the intercepted conversations were almost always vague. It was rarely clear who was talking, or what the "it" might be they were discussing.

IN LATE JULY, Bremer flew back to Washington. He met with George Tenet, and mentioned an issue that he'd raised in a cable he'd sent the Pentagon to be forwarded to the other NSC principals. Tenet had no idea what Bremer was talking about. He said he'd never seen the cable.

Bremer worked it backward. He'd been sending all his reports back to

Rumsfeld through military channels, and counting on Rumsfeld or the Pentagon to disseminate them to the others on the NSC. But it was now evident that Rumsfeld just hadn't done it, and was keeping the reports for himself. Rumsfeld was so wearing. Questions galore, always demanding answers, and here he wasn't even keeping the others informed.

"Rumsfeld's impossible to deal with," Bremer told a colleague. He was really steamed. It was total bullshit. Rumsfeld was throwing his weight around, and the rest of the NSC was just too weak to do anything about it. The whole interagency process was broken down. Where was Rice? Bremer went on the warpath, demanding the kind of diplomatic cable system ambassadors normally used to send messages back to Washington. Get it set up, he told McManaway.

A few days later on his way back to Baghdad, Bremer called his spokesman and close aide, Dan Senor, a tall, young, former Republican congressional staffer who had worked briefly for the White House. Bremer rattled off a to-do list covering some 48 items that had to be taken care of immediately on his return, including issues on medics, the economy, his political team, banks, mobile phones, polling, interrogations, corruption, mercenaries, the museums, an orphanage visit, new laws and various budgets—an overwhelming amount of detail.

KAY FLEW BACK TO WASHINGTON, arriving on July 26. He was already coming to the conclusion that they might not find stockpiles of WMD anywhere in Iraq, and he wanted Tenet to get the CIA stations in the region to see if Saddam might have smuggled WMD out of Iraq before the war. Spider Marks and his team had seen trucks heading toward the Syrian border but they still couldn't improve on Marks's statement that the trucks might, for all they knew, contain Toys 'R' Us bicycles.

"Look, things may have gone across borders, but you're going to have to energize the intelligence community to find out what's in those countries because we can't," Kay told Tenet. His group couldn't operate outside Iraq. "All we can report is evidence of movement toward borders."

"I want you to come with me to the White House tomorrow morning, for the President's Daily Brief," Tenet said. "Come in early and you can get a ride down with the PDB briefer." The President's Daily Brief was the highly classified report of the most sensitive and supposedly important intelligence that went only to Bush, Cheney, Powell, Rumsfeld, Rice and a few others.

The next morning, Kay arrived at CIA headquarters at 5:30. The woman in charge of the PDB told him, "We're glad you're briefing this morning, because it means we can reuse this material. We're getting sort of thin, and we can reuse it."

Kay was surprised to hear that PDB intelligence was not so urgent or relevant that it had to be used immediately. He was more surprised about his presumed role that morning.

"I'm briefing?" Kay asked.

Yes, she said.

Tenet was waiting at the White House, along with Rumsfeld and Andy Card. Kay and the PDB briefer went into the Oval Office, where Bush and Cheney were waiting. She went through her sections of the presentation, and then Kay was asked to report.

"The biggest mistake we made was to let looting and lawlessness break out," Kay said. Iraq was a mess and that made his job vastly more difficult. "Some of this evidence is beginning to shape up as if they had a just-in-time policy," he said, explaining the Soviet surge capability theory. They might have had the equipment, the facilities and the material to make WMD on short notice but they might not have actually produced any.

"We have not found large stockpiles," Kay said. "You can't rule them out. We haven't come to the conclusion that they're not there, but they're sure not any place obvious. We've got a lot more to search for and to look at."

"Keep at it," Bush said. "You understand you're to find out the truth about the program. David, what do you need that we can do for you?"

"Sir, the only thing we need right now is time and patience," Kay said.

"You have the time," Bush said. "I have the patience."

Kay left the meeting almost shocked at Bush's lack of inquisitiveness. Kay had a Ph.D. and had taught at high levels, and he was used to being asked challenging, aggressive questions. A lot of the trauma in getting a graduate degree was surviving the environment of doubt, skepticism and challenge.

"He trusted me more than I trusted me," Kay later recalled. "If the positions had been reversed, and this is primarily personality, I think, I would have probed. I would have asked. I would have said, 'What have you done? What haven't you done? Why haven't you done it?' You know, 'Are you getting the support out of DOD?' The soft spots. Didn't do it."

Cheney had been quiet in the meeting, but on the way out he and Scooter Libby pulled Kay aside. Cheney was now as probing as Bush had been passive. He was particularly concerned about the possible Syrian connection to WMD. What did Kay think? Cheney asked. Was there evidence? Could the weapons have gone to Syria?

"If things went across the border," Kay replied, "we can't go across the borders." He had alerted Tenet to the problem, he added.

Cheney inquired about the possibility that WMD could have been smuggled out and taken to the Bekaa Valley in Lebanon, an area dominated by the Iranian-backed Hezbollah, which had deep terrorist connections.

Again, Kay said, any meaningful assessment or action would have to involve the CIA stations.

Cheney pressed. He seemed to have a conviction that something had gone to Lebanon's Bekaa Valley.

Lebanon? Kay thought to himself. The Israelis and their intelligence services knew the most about the Bekaa. He thought of saying, "Don't ask me, ask the Israelis." But he let it pass.

Libby had a small sheaf of intelligence reports, including some sensitive, raw NSA communications intercepts. Kay hadn't seen them, because like the intercept he'd been called about at 3 A.M. in Baghdad, they were Executive Signals Intercepts or involved individual conversations or snippets. The CIA had analysts whose job it was to take dozens of such intercepts and reports, sift through them and distill them into usable conclusions. As with many intercepts, they were maddeningly vague. They had interesting little tidbits, and sometimes even specific locations were mentioned, but it was as clear as smoke.

Kay was astounded that the vice president of the United States was using such raw intelligence. Here Cheney and Libby were acting like a couple of junior analysts, poring over fragments as if they were trying to decipher the Da Vinci Code. If only the world could be understood that way.

Kay said later, "Cheney had a stock of interpretations and facts that he thought proved a case and he wanted to be sure that you examined them. It was very sort of in the weeds, detailed, evidentiary questions, and not about what I had said, but about what he knew, that he wanted to know a little more. It was almost a doctoral exam. You're worried about someone trying to trip you up. 'Have you read this source?' "

Afterward, Kay had a call from Colin Powell asking him to come to the State Department. He'd known Powell in 1991 and 1992, when he was the U.N. nuclear inspections chief in Iraq and Powell was JCS chairman. Powell had not been included in the White House briefing, and he wanted to hear what Kay was finding. As the public face of the American declaration before the United Nations that Saddam had WMD, Powell had almost as much at stake as Bush.

Kay gave Powell basically the same briefing that he had given to Bush—inconclusive but basically a neutral to negative report.

"This is my personal e-mail address," Powell said, handing Kay a card as he turned to leave. "Write me if you have any concerns or any questions."

Kay looked at the card when he got back to Langley and almost died laughing. Powell had given him a regular, commercial, America Online e-mail address, a communication method about as secure and confidential as spray-painting graffiti on a highway overpass.

"Here I am sitting in the CIA headquarters," Kay thought. "I'm going to send something to an AOL account?"

KAY WENT TO CONGRESS on July 31 to testify in closed session before the Senate Armed Services and Intelligence Committees. Between the two sessions, he spoke briefly to reporters. They had found no smoking gun, Kay said, but added, "The American people should not be surprised by surprises. We are determined to take this apart and every day, I must say, we're surprised by new advances that we're making."

23

RUMSFELD JUST WAS NOT PAYING ATTENTION, Rice and Hadley had concluded by August 2003. He was not showing the same interest in postwar Iraq as he had with the military invasion plans. The only option was for the NSC to step in and manage Bremer more directly.

Rice needed someone dedicated to the task, and she thought of the man who had been her boss on the NSC in George H. W. Bush's administration. Robert D. Blackwill, 63, had recently resigned as ambassador to India to teach at Harvard.

Blackwill had served 22 years in the foreign service and had worked in the upper reaches of the State Department, including a stint as an aide to Henry Kissinger. At 6-foot-3 and heavyset with white hair, he looked like Santa Claus when he smiled. But he was a prickly, demanding boss, who often referred to himself as Godzilla. In India, he had roiled the embassy staff. Two State Department inspector general reports criticized his management style.

Hadley, the consummate staff man, started canvassing people who had worked with Blackwill. The general report: *Don't bring him in. He'll be disruptive. He has a terrible reputation. People don't want to work with him. He's after your job, and he has even let it be known he wants to be Condi's deputy.* Al Kamen's popular "In the Loop" column in *The Washington Post* in July had quoted unnamed officials—"mischief makers," Kamen called them—suggesting that Hadley might move over to the Pentagon to make room for Blackwill.

But Rice wanted Blackwill's brainpower, so she and Hadley called him to the White House. They summarized the rap on him, and said there would be new rules of civility and collegiality if he joined the NSC staff.

"I hear you," Blackwill said. "I understand exactly what you're saying and I tell you that you will not have cause to complain."

In a second tough session, Rice asked Blackwill if he would have trouble working for her, his former subordinate, or for Hadley. He said he would not.

Blackwill was given the exalted title of coordinator for strategic planning on the NSC staff. Soon Rice made him point man for Iraq.

After a couple of weeks Blackwill told Rice and Hadley. "We're losing. We're just losing this whole thing. The public opinion's going against us. This is awful. We're losing the battle for Iraq heart and soul."

Rice's immediate concern was not the situation on the ground in Iraq. The problem, she told Blackwill, was "the dysfunctional U.S. government." He soon understood what she meant. He attended the deputies committee meetings where Armitage and Doug Feith often sat across from each other in the Situation Room. The hostility between them was enormous, and Blackwill watched as Armitage, a mountain of a man, barked at Feith. It was almost as if Armitage wanted to reach across the table and snap Feith's neck like a twig. Armitage's knuckles even turned white.

The principals meetings or NSC meetings with Powell and Rumsfeld were not as coarse but had the same surreal quality, rarely airing the real issues. Blackwill, a veteran of the Kissinger style, was astonished. Rumsfeld made his presentation looking at the president, while Powell looked straight ahead. Then Powell would make his to the president with Rumsfeld looking straight ahead. They didn't even comment on each other's statements or views. So Bush never had the benefit of a serious, substantive discussion between his principal advisers. And the president, whose legs often jiggled under the table, did not force a discussion.

Blackwill saw Rice try to intervene and get nowhere. So critical comments and questions—especially about military strategy—never surfaced. Blackwill felt sympathy for Rice. This young woman, he thought, had to deal with three of the titans of national security—Cheney, Rumsfeld and Powell—all of whom had decades of experience, cachet and strong views. The image locked in Blackwill's mind of Rice, dutiful, informed and polite, at one end of the table, and the inexperienced president at the other, legs dancing, while the bulls staked out their ground, almost snorting defiantly, hoofs pawing the table, daring a challenge that never came.

DAVID KAY'S PEOPLE developed a solid explanation for why Saddam's regime had been so bent on acquiring 60,000 aluminum tubes. Powell had told the U.N. the tubes were for a centrifuge system to be used in Saddam's nuclear weapons program. The evidence now showed that the tubes were meant for conventional artillery shells, just as the Iraqis had maintained before the war. The propellant for the rockets was produced by an Iraqi company run by a close friend of Saddam's son Qusay. The propellant was lousy, but nobody in the Iraqi military had the clout to tell a friend of Qusay's to improve his products or lose the contract. So the artillery scientists came up with a work-around: tighten the specifications on the aluminum tubes, making them smaller and lighter so that the weak propellant would still work.

One of the prisoners the U.S. was holding and interrogating was the former head of the procurement arm of the Iraqi military. "We bought these tubes because we had a contract," he said under interrogation. He explained the bureaucratic process, and how they had felt that tightening the specifications was the only option. Kay's group tracked down some of the military officers involved in the rocket program, who confirmed the story. "We never wanted these," one said. "We kept trying to cancel the contract but they told us we had to honor the contract."

To Kay, it almost sounded like a Washington or Pentagon contracting scandal, with $500 toilet seats and $1,000 hammers.

Kay's team uncovered evidence showing how Saddam spied on and tracked the U.N. inspection programs. At one point, they found a full set of faxes that U.N. inspectors had sent back and forth between Baghdad, New York and Vienna, home of the International Atomic Energy Agency, which oversaw prewar WMD inspections in Iraq. These were not electronic intercepts, but were the actual faxes, which meant that the Iraqis had spies or agents of some kind who could get physical access to the IAEA offices. In one case Kay saw that a fax the Iraqis had taken was an original, with handwritten notes that a member of his inspection team had made on the document years earlier.

Kay had extraordinary incentives to offer Iraqis for proof of WMD, including $10 million from a CIA covert fund that he could use to pay informants. He could also provide green cards to cooperative Iraqis who wanted to live and work in the United States. His group could move people out of Iraq and relocate them to other countries. They put out word of the program on the street hoping to attract genuine informers, and about 100 people came forward with information that seemed good enough to investigate. But virtually nothing panned out, and Kay wound up moving only one person to the U.S. It was all "I didn't see, but my neighbor saw." Others were coming in with pieces of equipment, making up stories and saying, oh, this came from a chemical weapon. There were all sorts of hoaxes.

At another point, Kay's communication teams were able to eavesdrop on a conversation an Iraqi scientist had with his wife, who was pleading with her husband. They were desperate, and she was begging him to go tell the Americans anything so that they could get some of the reward money and leave the country.

"I don't know anything," the scientist said. "We didn't have anything. I can't give the Americans anything. We didn't have it."

Kay had interrogators interview all of the senior Iraqi officials in U.S. custody. It was amazing. None of the Iraqis had actually seen any WMD, but they all believed that such unconventional weapons existed somewhere else in Saddam's arsenal. To a person, they assumed that Saddam Hussein was making a lot of public noise about destroying his weapons stockpiles after the 1991 Gulf War for the benefit of the rest of the world, but that he'd never really be stupid enough to actually follow through. But it looked more and more like that was exactly what Saddam had done.

Through the end of September, Kay's group made lots of ambiguous discoveries—"dual-use" production facilities or chemicals that could be used for either weapons or non-WMD products. Chlorine could be used to make chemical weapons, or it could be used to purify water for swimming pools. Kay never had a Eureka! moment, but he gradually concluded that the reason they weren't finding WMD stockpiles was because they simply didn't exist.

GENERAL JOHN ABIZAID had taken over as commander of CENTCOM in July. Kay started getting hints that he and Rumsfeld wanted to reassign Kay's Iraq Survey Group to additional missions such as counterterrorism. Kay called Tenet. "George, this isn't going to happen," he said. "You know, we had an agreement that they would focus on WMD until I had concluded. I've been around Washington too long. I know when you get multiple objectives you usually don't achieve any of them."

"Absolutely," Tenet said. "You're right. I'll go talk to Rumsfeld."

Soon, they had another conversation.

I told Rumsfeld that if he did this, you would resign, Tenet told Kay.

FROM JUNE TO AUGUST 2003 there had been a change in the nature of violent incidents in Iraq. In June an average of 35 to 38 violent incidents occurred each day, and the U.S. forces would have initiated half of them. In contrast, on one day in August, insurgents initiated 28 out of 33 violent incidents. Consistently, Armitage saw, the insurgents were taking the initiative in two thirds of the violent encounters now. That meant to him that the general Iraqi population was sitting in neutral, waiting to see who would win or lose and whether the U.S. forces would stay or leave. The Iraqis probably knew who some of the insurgents were and where they were, but they weren't telling the United States or other coalition forces ahead of time.

In his office at the State Department, Armitage looked over the data. He felt like he'd already seen this movie during his three tours on the ground in Vietnam. He didn't like the ending.

In the summer doldrums without a lot of news, *The Washington Post* ran a front-page story on August 4, 2003, saying that Powell and Armitage had signaled they would leave the administration even if Bush were reelected. It was something both had indicated in private, reflecting their on-again, off-again, thoroughly schizophrenic attitudes toward being high-level officials in the Bush administration.

With violence mounting in Iraq, Bush did not want to lose his reluctant warrior or leave the impression that there was any distance between him and Powell. He knew that Powell and Armitage operated as a duo, glued together permanently. So he invited both men to his ranch in Crawford.

The first afternoon, Powell and Armitage arrived, changed into casual clothes and went over to the president's ranch house.

"Do you want a drink?" Bush asked.

"A double martini," Armitage replied.

Bush, the former heavy drinker, stared at him in mild surprise.

"Nah, nah," Armitage said. "Actually a nonalcoholic beer."

Bush laughed.

Later they had cigars and Bush drove them on the standard tour of the ranch.

The three had a pleasant dinner with Laura Bush, Rice and Powell's wife, Alma. The next day they sat down for a three-hour discussion of foreign policy.

"Let's get one thing clear so we can truthfully say it never came up," Powell began. "We're not going to talk about this press story about Rich and I leaving."

Bush swept his hand in the air as if to wave the topic away. They went on to have an unremarkable discussion about where they were going in foreign policy.

In a brief session with the press on August 6, Bush said that Powell "has done a fabulous job," and added, "The fact that he is here in Crawford, Texas, talking about issues of importance should say loud and clear to the American people that he's completely engaged and doing what he needs to do, and that is serve as a great secretary of state."

Powell added dutifully, "I don't have a term. I serve the president." What they called "the whispering campaign" against them slowed down, only to be refocused on Tenet.

Former Speaker Newt Gingrich was regularly in touch with the White House, especially Cheney and Rove. There was a simple explanation why Bush would cling to Powell, he said. "Why would you go into a general election getting rid of the guy who has the highest approval rating in the country?"

RICE WAS AT THE GREENBRIER RESORT in West Virginia on August 19, 2003, playing tennis on the last day of her vacation. It was one of those rare four-day periods when not much had happened.

The person on duty as her secure communications operator came running up. "I have to talk to you."

A massive truck bomb had gone off at the U.N. headquarters in Baghdad. Reports were incomplete but there were many killed and injured. Sergio Vieira de Mello, the delegation head, was injured and reportedly buried in the rubble but able to talk to rescue workers. Rice packed up her car and she and her security and communications team headed back to Washington.

Vieira de Mello is dead, the watch officer from the Situation Room said in a call.

Rice felt as if she'd been punched in the gut. She had personally urged Vieira de Mello, a highly respected diplomat who had been with the U.N. for 34 years, to go to Iraq.

What an outrage, Bush told her when they spoke later, that terrorists would go after the U.N.

She said it was apparently the first such attack of this magnitude on a U.N. headquarters. The final death toll was 22, with many more wounded. Hit-and-run attacks had occurred before, but such wholesale barbarity? For Rice, it meant something else was going on here. It was devastating and symbolic at once. What was happening? She felt out of touch.

Bush met with the National Security Council the next day, August 20. "An ugly day for freedom, but it should toughen our resolve to do what we have to do for freedom," he said. "We're at war. It's a different kind of war, but war nonetheless, and we will win it. Terrorists want us to retreat and we cannot. We need to redouble our efforts against terror."

Having set the tone, the president went into some operational matters. "We need to make assessments about what are the soft targets that are in Iraq? How are we going to harden those soft targets? Look, we need to reanalyze the enemy. What's his strategy? We've got to be constantly reviewing our offensive plan to take into account the changes we're seeing." He added, "This is a thinking enemy that changes, and as he changes, we need to change. And attacking the U.N. mission was a change. Now, what has he just told us, this enemy?"

They were facing a host of new questions, and Bush rattled some of them off. "What are we going to do about bad guys coming out of Syria and Iran? We need to counter those. We need better intel and military capabilities to deal with these guys." But he quickly pulled back from the more specific things that needed to be addressed. "Groups that respond by pulling out of Iraq are simply giving in to the killers and rewarding them," he said, back in pep talk mode.

Bremer, who was piped into the meeting over the secure video teleconference, said the U.N. attack needed to be a wake-up call for the Iraqis, and that the temporary Iraqi Governing Council had to take action. They need to get their faces out front, Bremer said, both internationally and with their own people. We need to rally the Iraqi people so they will rally the international community, he said. He wanted the Governing Council to call on the Iraqi people to support the police and the army.

"Do we have the communications strategy to be able to run with Al Jazeera?" Bush asked.

"We have a network. We're using it," someone said.

"We should— Do we have the communications network?" Bush asked.

"Yes," someone said again. "We have our network, and we're also trying to use Al Jazeera and Al Arabiya to the extent we can."

"Our theme should be that the Iraqis should not allow foreign fighters to come into Iraq," the president said. "We need to play on a sense of nationalism that will motivate Iraqis to cooperate with us to exclude the foreigners."

The irony of the commander in chief of an occupation force of approximately 130,000 heavily armed foreign troops saying they should play on Iraqi nationalism and convince the people of Iraq to "exclude the foreigners" seemed to go unnoticed.

"We need to look at all possible sources of attack from all groups," Bush said. "Who did this and who do we worry about? We've learned something. We need to reevaluate who is the enemy, what are his tactics, and how do we adapt to it?"

It was a wake-up call for Bush and his war cabinet, but the president avoided mentioning it publicly. He flew to the Pacific Northwest to give speeches on the environment. Two days after the NSC meeting, a reporter asked him whether the conflict in Iraq was becoming a guerrilla war against the West.

"The way I view this is Iraq is turning out to be a continuing battle in the war on terror," Bush said. "You know, it's one thing to remove the Saddam Hussein regime from power in order to protect America and our friends and allies, which we did. And then there are—we found resistance from former Baathist officials. These people decided that, well, they'd rather fight than work for peaceful reconstruction of Iraq because they weren't going to be in power anymore. I also believe there's a foreign element that is moving into Iraq and these will be al-Qaeda-type fighters. They want to fight us there because they can't stand the thought of a free society in the Middle East. They hate freedom. They hate the thought of a democracy emerging. And therefore, they want to violently prevent that from happening."

He added in a radio address on August 23 that the picture in most of Iraq was rosy, despite the attack on the U.N. "There is steady movement toward reconstruction and a stable, self-governing society. This progress makes the remaining terrorists even more desperate and willing to lash out against symbols of order and hope, like coalition forces and U.N. personnel. The world will not be intimidated. A violent few will not determine the future of Iraq, and there will be no return to the days of Saddam Hussein's torture chambers and mass graves."

RUMSFELD WAS BACK in Baghdad on September 4. He wanted to see if they could reduce the number of U.S. troops. The initial plan had been for the United States to have only 25,000 or 30,000 troops, maybe 60,000 at most, in Iraq by this time. That reduction had been impossible because of the violence, and there were still about 130,000 in Iraq. Though no one was advertising it, there had been nearly 500 attacks against U.S. and coalition forces in July and more than 500 in August. At a small dinner with Bremer and his senior staff that night, Rumsfeld said, "I wonder if all of you working here have a sufficient sense of urgency." Bremer, who was working day and night, was stunned and outraged. He insisted to Rumsfeld that the problem was security.

David Kay had about 30 minutes with the secretary of defense. If there was any doubt that Rumsfeld felt he had successfully shifted responsibility for finding WMD from the military to the CIA, he cleared matters up nicely by telling reporters he had not asked Kay for an update on the WMD search. "I have so many things to do at the Department of Defense," he said. "I made a conscious decision that I didn't need to stay current every 15 minutes on the issue. I literally did not ask. . . . I'm assuming he'll tell me if he'd gotten something we should know."

BREMER WAS MAKING IT CLEAR that as far as he was concerned, the U.S. would likely be in Iraq for years. On September 8, four days after his dinner with Rumsfeld, he published an op-ed piece in *The Washington Post*, "Iraq's Path to Sovereignty." He again used the word "occupation," apparently not understanding that for Iraqis, the word occupation— "IHTILAL" in Arabic—invoked humiliation at the hands of foreigners. Also, in the Middle East, the "occupation" was the Israeli occupation of Palestinian lands. Certainly most Iraqis weren't thinking of the U.S. occupations of Germany and Japan after World War II, with massive infusions of American money and the rebuilding of societies as democracies and economic powerhouses, which the U.S continually pointed to as evidence of its past successes as an occupying power.

Bremer outlined seven steps that needed to take place before sovereignty would be transferred to the Iraqis, including the drafting of a constitution, its ratification and then elections.

Rice had had no idea Bremer was going to publish such a sweeping declaration. "I am not going to lose connectivity with you," she told him afterward. But she already had. Bremer kept a tight hold on the reins. "He's a control freak," Bush began saying in private. Rice agreed that Bremer was a micromanager. But no one did anything about it. Six months earlier, the NSC had agreed that the goal was to get Iraqi faces in the government as fast as possible. Now the face was Bremer, who was using the MacArthur-in-Japan model of occupation. It was a massive redefinition that did not involve the NSC. It was policy drift.

Bremer was telling the Iraqis in no uncertain terms that the coalition held sovereignty over Iraq for now. He reports in his book that he told a group of new Iraqi ministers on September 16, "Like it or not—and it's not pleasant being occupied, or being the occupier, I might add—the Coalition is still the sovereign power here." He did not try to hide his disdain for the Iraqis. "Those people couldn't organize a parade, let alone run the country," he told Wolfowitz.

ON SEPTEMBER 24, Bremer was back in Washington, where he and his wife, Francie, had a private dinner with the president and first lady. He reports that he told the president that he was optimistic about Iraq but was concerned about the growing and sophisticated insurgency. Bush did not respond, he wrote.

Bremer complained about the Congress, the number of U.S. troops, the quality of the intelligence, the new Iraqi army trainees and what he called "bureaucratic spiderwebs." He wrote that he told Bush that it was "misleading" that all the Iraqis in uniform were being counted as if they were equivalent to U.S. troops. At dinner they prayed for one of Bremer's favorite Iraqis who had died, but there was no discussion of Iraqi sovereignty.

One matter Bremer left out of his book about his time with the president was Bush's reaction to Bremer's organization chart that showed about 20 people reporting directly to him.

"Look," the president said, "I know you went to business school, but I went to business school. You've got too many direct reports."

"I know," Bremer replied. "It's crazy, and I'm going to start the process of reorganizing."

He later did some, but nearly everything flowed through him.

Bremer also did not mention one of his conclusions, reached from working in eight presidencies. He felt that presidents really didn't have much power. Other than starting a war, Bremer thought, presidents can only set a vision and choose the right people. In Iraq, he, the Coalition Provisional Authority, had the power.

STEVE HERBITS, still Rumsfeld's unofficial eyes and ears at the Pentagon, was regularly in and out of Washington. He was a hawk on the war, a firm believer that invading had been the right thing to do. But Bremer, he believed, was not working out. Herbits didn't think he could effectively go to Rumsfeld about the situation because he knew the secretary was set on a course. But he might listen if Herbits could build pressure from within the Pentagon and from conservative circles in Washington. Distressed at the situation, he reached out to two of the most influential conservatives he knew: Paul Wolfowitz and Newt Gingrich. He had been close to both men for years, but Wolfowitz and Gingrich didn't know each other very well. The three of us have to get together and talk over dinner, Herbits said.

Herbits made a reservation for a private room at Les Halles, a pricey French restaurant four blocks from the White House on Pennsylvania Avenue, for Tuesday, September 30, 2003. Wolfowitz and Gingrich were almost on time.

The three chit-chatted briefly, and then Herbits stepped in.

"This is the premise of the meeting. The president is losing the peace. He is not going to get reelected unless we get this thing straightened out. There are two things which he has to do, and he has to do now, or it's going to fail. This is the premise, and you guys discuss it," Herbits said. "Item number one is we have to set a date that we are turning over the government to the Iraqis, and we have to set it now. And I pick June 30, 2004."

It was an arbitrary date, Herbits acknowledged, but they needed a date before the presidential election. June 30, 2004, seemed about right, being nine months away, and four months before the November election.

"The reason we have to do that," he said, "is because no one will work towards that date unless the date exists." Herbits was a process person, and there was no process here. He knew how bureaucracies worked, and why they didn't. People don't move unless they have a deadline. A long, indefinite occupation would be a disaster. "The American people won't tolerate it. Mostly the Iraqis will throw us out before then if we don't have a date.

"The second thing I'm arguing is that we have got to put Iraqis in uniform." Bremer and the Pentagon had announced that month that they envisioned a 40,000-soldier Iraqi army by 2005 or later, with another 146,000 people in the police, the border guards and other security forces. So far, there were only 1,000 would-be soldiers training for the new Iraqi army.

"My idea is 300,000 by June of 2004," Herbits said, pausing theatrically. "Gentlemen, discuss."

"You're completely wrong," Gingrich said. The election was going to be about the American economy.

No, Herbits said. The economy would be fine. And even if it wasn't there wasn't much Bush could do about it. But Iraq was important and it was also something that could be influenced. "I'm looking at the process," he said. "It's failing."

Wolfowitz agreed that occupation was the wrong approach and started to make a point to Herbits.

"This isn't about me," Herbits insisted. "This is about you two discussing it."

Wolfowitz, a longtime advocate for dissolving the Iraqi army as a critical element of ridding Iraq of the Saddam legacy, reminded them that the army had just disappeared and melted away.

The army dissolving was not our choice, Herbits agreed. But allowing it to stay dissolved was indeed the doing of the United States and Bremer. And that was the mistake that had to be rectified. Iraq had to have an Iraqi army.

Herbits's final argument was political necessity. "Listen, this president is going to get creamed if you don't change this."

For more than two hours, Wolfowitz and Gingrich went at it, quoting poetry, studies, historians, Greeks, the moderns. But in the end they agreed with Herbits's two main points—deadlines had their virtue and something had to be done about an Iraqi army.

At the end of the dinner, both said they would act. Wolfowitz would talk to Rumsfeld and Hadley. Gingrich was a member of the Defense Policy Board, an outside group that periodically advised Rumsfeld, but his real connection was to Cheney. The two men had first been elected to Congress together in 1978, and had been friends for nearly 25 years. Gingrich said he would go to Cheney and Scooter Libby.

• • •

GINGRICH LATER RECALLED the dinner "vividly."

"It was the first captive moment," he said. "We sat down and compared notes about how bad it was, and the degree to which Bremer was totally outside of the chain of command." According to Gingrich, "Washington was being systematically misinformed."

On the economic front, Gingrich said, "Bremer's model was totally wrong. Totally. His model was you could use peacetime contracting, hire big multinationals. They could do all the planning in Denver, and in two or three years, things would start to happen." The infighting in the National Security Council, he said, was still intense. "The big guys were so tired of fighting each other that they all said, 'I sure hope Bremer solves it.' And when you come in and say this ain't going well, they'd say, 'Well, let's give Bremer time.' "

But Gingrich thought there was no way Bremer was going to solve the problems. "Bremer is the largest single disaster in American foreign policy in modern times," the former speaker said later.

"The most dangerous thing in the world is a confident, smart person with the wrong model because they have enormous enthusiasm in pursuing the wrong model. Bremer arrives thinking he was MacArthur in Japan and that we should have an American-centric system."

He said that if you ask great American businessmen or entrepreneurs, "What's the biggest mistake of your career?" their answer is "Not firing people fast enough."

"Okay," Gingrich said, "Bremer, no later than September, should have been relieved."

But Gingrich added that he and Wolfowitz realized Bremer couldn't be fired. He had been appointed by Bush, and Jay Garner had effectively been fired. Two in one year just wouldn't be possible.

"You have to find specific things to fight over that are measurable," he said. So more than the turnover date or the rebuilding of the Iraqi army, Gingrich said he was upset that the military could not get the emergency money they needed for small projects.

The White House said the money was released, but officers that Gingrich had known for years were telling him it was not. Finally, he said, he called Cheney.

"You and Condi are being lied to," Gingrich said he told the vice president.

"I'll get into it," Cheney said.

It still took 60 days of direct orders to get the money.

Gingrich said he went in to see Rove and Hadley and handed them a memo that said, "Bremer may cost you the election." He said he then told them, "I'm here to tell you it is that bad." Gingrich said that he felt he had to engage Rice and Cheney. "They are going to make a thousand decisions. So it's not just getting a decision made, it's getting them to think differently about what's at stake."

The bottom line, Gingrich said: "Losing a war is bad."

24

THE CIA'S TOP LEADERSHIP met with Condoleezza Rice in September 2003 to argue that the U.S. needed to develop a new Iraqi national intelligence service. Tenet and McLaughlin filed into Rice's White House office, along with Deputy Director of Operations Stephen R. Kappes, Near East Division Chief Rob Richer, and the counterterrorism chief, who was still undercover.

Tenet sat down in the back of the room, chewing on one of his half cigars. The meeting was important, but he would let the others do the talking. His alienation from Rice was nearing a high-water mark.

Both State and Defense were opposed to the idea. Saddam's intelligence service had been a symbol of his brutal despotism. Dissolving it in May had been an important step. They feared any effort to form a new spy service would be received with such trepidation and loathing by the Iraqi people that it would outweigh any benefits.

Kappes outlined the problem. Iraq was the only country in the world where the U.S. was fighting terrorism without a native intelligence service to assist. It was a crippling disadvantage. They needed an internal partner that could provide the CIA with information.

Iraq now has the largest CIA station, Kappes said. That's where we're facing the largest terrorist threat.

In addition, the idea that stepping up a new spy service would send the wrong signal and imply a return to old Saddam-style secret police tactics was simply wrong. The new service could be carefully recruited and monitored. McLaughlin said it had been his experience that after the fall of the Berlin Wall and the collapse of Communism, the intelligence services in Eastern Europe swiveled on a dime and were willing to work with the CIA. In 1990, he had gone to Hungary, where the intelligence people said in effect, "Okay, we used to work for the Soviets, now we're going to work with you guys." Intelligence officials abroad could be bought.

We need better ground intelligence, they argued. A local service could be subsidized and co-opted. "We created the Jordanian intelligence service and now we own it," Tenet said.

"How do you know we will not create another KGB?" Rice asked, referring to the old Soviet intelligence service.

The original KGB wasn't a creation of the CIA, Kappes said.

Tenet shook his head, saying nothing more, barely disguising his disgust. The CIA got some of its best intelligence from foreign intelligence services. It was preposterous that anyone would want them blinded in Iraq.

McLaughlin thought Hadley and Wolfowitz were naive and he spent the next months pushing the deputies committee for approval for an Iraqi service. At one meeting, he told the group, including Wolfowitz and Armitage, "I've been on the deputies committee for four years and never been in such violent disagreement with my colleagues."

For his part, Wolfowitz just didn't trust the whole concept. The CIA would back the wrong people, he thought. So far, the CIA had been sending people in for 90-day Iraq assignments who didn't even speak Arabic. The military was doing a much better intelligence job.

After nine months of arguing and pestering by Tenet and McLaughlin, the CIA finally won authorization for an initial 1,000 Iraqi intelligence officers in July 2004.

ONE OF BLACKWILL'S ASSIGNMENTS was to be the NSC's coordinator for strategic planning, and Rice asked him to do some interagency planning on Pakistan. After Blackwill had some meetings of middle-level officials, Powell called Rice.

"I'm not going to participate in some make-work project on Pakistan," he said. "Our Iraq policy is in more trouble every day. Put Blackwill in charge of Iraq policy. You should assign him full-time to Iraq. Iraq policy is a terrible problem."

Without consulting Blackwill, Rice assigned him to Iraq. It was obvious that Powell wanted Godzilla to come in and step on automobiles that belonged to the Pentagon.

Blackwill went to work, read the files and Pentagon reports, made the rounds and wrote a long memo to Rice in late September. The bottom line: We need more troops in Iraq on the ground, about two more divisions or 40,000 men.

Rice didn't say no or yes.

Since Blackwill had been a friend of Bremer's for decades and they had both served as foreign service officers, Rice sent Blackwill to Baghdad to assist Bremer. They became more and more convinced they needed to make a dramatic pitch to Rice. They asked for a secure video conference with Rice and Hadley with no one else present. To emphasize the importance they asked that all communications and technical people involved in the secure video leave the rooms in both Washington and Baghdad.

When Bremer and Blackwill came up on their end they could see only Rice and Hadley. They went through a methodical presentation about the geography of Iraq, the level of violence, and how the military commanders dealt with the attacks in one area or where suspected insurgents were concentrated and then moved on. After a while the insurgents just moved back into the old areas. From two of Kissinger's protégés, it was what could be called a "full Kissinger." In their minds it was irrefutable proof that at least two more divisions were needed. Hadley took notes furiously.

With the time lag on the security video it looked like neither Rice nor Hadley had a reaction.

"Well, Jerry, Bob," Rice finally began, "thank you so much for these ideas. Let us think about them."

Then the screen went black.

Bremer turned to Blackwill and said, "Swing and a miss."

"Deep space shot," Blackwill replied, forecasting that their proposal was now heading out to Mars and then beyond the outer galaxies and star systems for all of time.

IN TWO INTERVIEWS in July 2006, I asked Rumsfeld about troop levels—a key issue and point of contention. The record showed that the plan for invading Iraq had a top number of 275,000 ground combat forces, including about 90,000 who were scheduled to flow into Iraq in the weeks and months after March 19, 2003, when the war began. Rumsfeld said it is one of the great "canards" that he had decided or unduly influenced the decision to not bring in the 90,000. It was all on General Franks's recommendation. "He made a judgment that he had what he needed, or would have as this played out and that he would not need the additional ones that were in the queue. . . . And he made that recommendation and I made the recommendation to the president, and we agreed with it." So the 90,000 additional ground troops were not sent for the war or stabilization.

The critics or the "opiners," as Rumsfeld called them, "the people who don't have responsibility for making the decisions," don't understand. "Many of them say, 'Oh, it's Rumsfeld,' as though I'm sitting around with a black box figuring all this out. And anyone who knows me or watched me do anything knows that I don't do it that way. I come here to this job knowing that there's no one smart enough to do this job." So he relied on "smart people," he said, and on "advice from multiple sources."

But half a dozen of the generals and civilians who worked most closely with Rumsfeld made it clear in interviews that Rumsfeld drove the train.

By the summer of 2006, Rumsfeld had softened his position on the issue of whether there were enough troops.

"It's entirely possible there were too many at some point and too few at some point, because no one's perfect," he said. "All of us that were trying our best to make these judgments were doing it in a context of concern about having enough to get the job done, and enable a process, political and economic process, to go forward, and not so many that it persuaded people that we were there to steal their oil and occupy their country and disrupt and cause disturbances in the neighboring countries that cause the overthrow of some of those other regimes. And so we made the best judgment we could. In retrospect I have not seen or heard anything from the other opiners that suggests to me that they have any reason to believe that they were right and we were wrong. Nor can I prove we were right and they were wrong. The only thing I can say is they seem to have a lot more certainty than my assessment of the facts would permit me to have."

DAVID KAY RETURNED to Washington in time to give an interim report to Congress on October 2, 2003. "We're not going to give it to the White House until the morning that you're testifying," Tenet told Kay. If the

White House didn't see the testimony beforehand, it would be harder to pressure Kay to shape what he would say.

"We have not yet found stocks of weapons," Kay said in his prepared testimony, "but we are not yet at the point where we can say definitively either that such weapon stocks do not exist or that they existed before the war and our only task is to find where they have gone." The new twist Kay put on his work was to say that he had found "dozens of WMD-related program activities." In essence, Kay was trying to have it both ways: No stockpiles had been found but they might someday be found.

News reports of Kay's remarks correctly focused almost exclusively on his acknowledgment that no weapons had been found. Kay was interviewed by PBS news anchor Jim Lehrer that night. "We found quite a bit of activity in the weapons area, but we have not, again, we have—haven't found the weapons."

Powell, who had much at stake, called up Tenet, outraged that the administration had done such a poor job spinning the report. Facing escalating criticism, Bush tried to spin things himself the next day, saying that Kay's report "states Saddam Hussein's regime had a clandestine network of biological laboratories, a live strain of deadly agent botulinum, sophisticated concealment efforts, and advanced design work on prohibited longer-range missiles." The botulinum was not in a weapon or near one, though the president seemed to imply it was about to be put on a missile.

A MEMO CREATING Rice's Iraq Stabilization Group—the new NSC effort to coordinate Bremer that would be run by Blackwill—wound up in the hands of David Sanger, the resourceful *New York Times* White House reporter. On October 6, the *Times* ran a front-page story headlined "White House to Overhaul Iraq and Afghan Missions."

Bremer read the story online in Baghdad. It was the first time he'd heard of the Iraq Stabilization Group, or that Rice would be taking a larger role.

Rice insisted to Bremer when they spoke that the reorganization was not really a reorganization. It reflected no unhappiness with Bremer, she said, and was designed only to mobilize the bureaucracy.

At a news conference the next day, Rumsfeld was plainly irritated.

"I think you'd have to ask Condi that question," he said when a reporter asked about the Iraq Stabilization Group, insisting he'd not heard of the reorganization before it leaked in the press.

A reporter tried to follow up.

"I said I don't know. Isn't that clear? You don't understand English?" Rumsfeld said. "I was not there for the backgrounding."

Rumsfeld thought it was outrageous that Rice would declare she was in charge. Over the next several days he observed with some satisfaction that she was backpedaling.

His concern was that the stories created the impression there was a new strategy and that somehow the national security adviser, the NSC staff and the president's staff were now responsible for the 130,000 U.S. troops in Iraq, and not he. How many times did he need to remind everyone? The National Security Council was not in the chain of command. The problem was not that there might be a new strategy. The problem was that there was not much of a strategy at all other than to leave Bremer in charge.

IN IRAQ, DAVID KAY had a call from Scooter Libby.

"The vice president wants to know if you've looked at this area," Libby said. "We have indications—and here are the geocoordinates—that something's buried there."

Kay went to the mapping and imagery experts on his team. They pulled up the satellite and other surveillance photos of the location. It was in the middle of Lebanon.

"That's where we're going next," joked one of the imagery experts.

At another point Kay got a cable from the CIA that the vice president wanted him to send someone to Switzerland to meet with an Iranian named Manucher Ghorbanifar.

"I recognize this one," Kay said when he saw the cable. "This one I'm not going to do."

Ghorbanifar had been the Iranian middleman in the Reagan administration's disastrous secret arms-for-hostage deals in the Iran-contra scandal. Though he had been a CIA source in the 1970s, the agency had terminated him in 1983 and the next year issued a formal "burn notice" warning that Ghorbanifar was a "talented fabricator."

This time, Kay read, Ghorbanifar claimed to have an Iranian source who knew all about Iraqi nuclear weapons, but who wanted $2 million in advance, and who would not talk directly to the U.S., only through Ghorbanifar.

Kay discovered that the latest Ghorbanifar stunt involved Michael Ledeen of the American Enterprise Institute, a former NSC colleague of

Oliver North who had been involved with Ghorbanifar in the Iran-contra days.

Kay sent a cable to the CIA saying, "Unless you give me direct instructions to talk to him, I will not have any member of the ISG talk to this guy. The guy is a known fabricator-peddler, and it will ruin someone. If the DCI wants to send me direct instructions to do it, I will of course do it. But it's got to be direct."

The idea was dropped. Cheney was acting as a kind of super-investigator, trying to ferret out the elusive WMD, Kay concluded. But there were always loose ends in intelligence, disparate bits of information that could lead to all kinds of wild conclusions. But by focusing in on only a few items and assigning them great significance, they could wind up with a skewed picture. It continued to remind Kay of the block-buster novel *The Da Vinci Code*, in which a Harvard professor and a French policewoman piece together clues in the Bible and in great works of art and myths that supposedly reveal a giant conspiracy to hide the true nature and life of Jesus Christ.

Kay was going to stick with the basics—human sources, people who might really know something.

BREMER FLEW BACK and forth between Baghdad and the U.S., trying to keep things moving and dealing with what he called the 8,000-mile screwdriver that was twisted by Washington officials and bureaucrats.

On October 27, 2003, he was at the White House to meet with Bush. Rice, Card, Rumsfeld and Myers were in the room.

On the video screen, General Abizaid argued that they needed to bring back officers from Saddam's army.

"There are risks in that," said Bremer, who had signed CPA Order Number 2 formally disbanding the army as one of his first acts in Iraq. "We've got to proceed with great care so we don't give the impression that we're reconstituting the old regime."

"Well, one thing is clear," the president said, according to Bremer's book. "We stay the course in Iraq. We don't show any weakness in the wake of these new attacks. There'll be no loss of resolve."

Doubt was corrosive and would lead only to hand-wringing. The president had been the head cheerleader for the football team in his prep school days. There is little or no evidence that he engaged in much substantive policy debate at this point in the war cabinet meetings. His role was to express confidence and enthusiasm.

At the Pentagon, Rumsfeld presented Bremer with what was being called the "Wolfowitz-Feith Option," a plan to turn over sovereignty as early as April 9, 2004, the one-year anniversary of the fall of Saddam.

Too early, Bremer replied. "We'd risk Iraq falling into disorder or civil war." He wanted to wait until there was an elected government and a constitution. There was no way they could do that by April.

Rumsfeld pushed. The next day, at a principals meeting, he said they had to turn over sovereignty to remove the label that the United States was an "occupier." General Pace, the JCS vice chairman, made the same point to Bremer.

"The most important military strategy is to accelerate the governance track," Pace said. So the generals, responsible for security and a military strategy, were looking for early sovereignty and politics as a solution.

Pace later said it was a comment that Bremer might have taken out of context. "You can kill folks for the next 27 years," Pace said, "and you're not going to have a better environment. What you have to do is provide enough security, inside of which the governance can take place, and that's why the governance piece is so important. They are intertwined."

Powell consistently argued to Bush that all the talk about reconstruction and the political process, oil exploration and electric generation, and economic development and privatization is wonderful, but security is most important.

"This is all great, but there's only one issue," Powell told Bush on one occasion. "And if you solve this one, this is going to look like the greatest thing anyone's ever thought of. That's security. If you don't have security, none of this follows. Everything has to be focused on security, more so than oil or electricity or water or anything else."

"Yeah," Bush said. "I understand."

"It's not going to happen if you don't get the security situation," Powell said.

Classified reports showed that the insurgent attacks had jumped to 1,000 in the month of October, more than 30 a day. Many did not succeed, but it was an extraordinary level of violence. The numbers were kept secret.

To attempt to answer the questions the president had posed after the U.N. headquarters bombing, John McLaughlin put together a briefing entitled "Who Is the Enemy?" that he gave the deputies and principals. He identified four groups: former Baathists with a restoration agenda to bring back Saddam; foreign fighters; Iraqi nationalists who hated the occupation; and tribal members angry over the death of family members and the heavy-handed door kicking of the coalition military.

AT THE FULL NSC MEETINGS Bremer presented the options on sovereignty. He backed off a bit and was now willing to turn over sovereignty by the end of 2004—more than a year away and after the U.S. presidential election.

Bush kept cheerleading, according to Bremer, who said the president closed the meeting almost from his public script. "We are going to succeed in Iraq despite the difficult times we are going through. Nobody should be in any doubt. We will do the right thing irrespective of what the newspapers or political opponents say about it. Success in Iraq will change the world. The American people need to have no doubt that we're confident about the outcome. We may not succeed by the time of the election. So be it."

Afterward, Bush invited Bremer to work out with him in the private third-floor White House gym. Bush asked Bremer about Rumsfeld.

"What kind of a person is he to work for? Does he really micromanage?"

"I like Don, Mr. President. I've known him thirty years, admire him, consider him highly intelligent. But he does micromanage."

Bush looked surprised, according to Bremer's account.

"Don terrifies his civilian subordinates so that I can rarely get any decisions out of anyone but him. This works all right, but isn't ideal."

Bush didn't offer any firm conclusions on the sovereignty issue but his bottom line was obvious. "We are not going to fail in Iraq," the president said again.

Bremer went back to Iraq on October 31. He was reasonably certain he had Bush's backing to hold off on an early transfer of sovereignty.

RICE VOICED CONCERN to Andy Card about Bush's one-on-one meetings with Bremer. What issues were raised? Were any decisions made or instructions given? Such a private meeting gave Bremer incredible latitude to operate. He could invoke presidential authority now for almost anything he did, or at minimum claim he interpreted the president's statements to back his actions.

Card replied that the job of envoy was so important that the president and Bremer needed to get to know each other.

Rumsfeld was furious and spoke with Card about being excluded from a meeting one of his subordinates had with the president.

"He works for me!" Rumsfeld bellowed.

"He's the presidential envoy," Card responded.

AT ANOTHER NSC MEETING with the president, the issue of the Iraqi army came up.

Powell wanted to use some mid-level leaders of the old army to create the new one. "Look," he said, "why don't we get these battalion commanders, and since we need to reconstitute a force, get the battalion commanders, give them a bunch of money, and tell them to go re-create their battalions. These people need money."

Rumsfeld's answer was that they were already recruiting and training police and a new army. Numbers were thrown around. First it was 54,000 and then double that, and at one point 200,000.

Bremer wondered where the hell the numbers were coming from. On the secure video piped into the White House Situation Room, Bremer could be seen shaking his head in disagreement when the last number was floated. Two hundred thousand? It was news to him. At other times he could be seen writing comments on a mound of CPA "paperwork" in front of him.

BUSH AND RICE wanted to cut short the occupation, but now they were caught in Bremer's long political process. "Nobody wants to be occupied. We wouldn't want to be occupied," Bush said time and again. The question was how to get out of occupation.

In Baghdad, Meghan O'Sullivan and Roman Martinez were wrestling with the complex, three-step electoral process that Bremer and the U.N. had put in place. They had been worried for some time that Bremer's objection to direct elections for a group to write the constitution could spark a governance crisis they would not be able to weather. It looked as if Bremer was going to make it a "red line," and that that would cause Sistani to disengage. People close to Sistani told O'Sullivan that he had issued the June 28 fatwa insisting that the constitution be written by properly elected Iraqis because he worried that Iraq would resemble American-occupied Japan after World War II. MacArthur's staff had written most of the nation's postwar constitution, and Japan, which had unconditionally surrendered, had adopted it with only minor changes.

Sistani wanted full elections, but it would take another six to nine months, likely doubling the time the U.S. would occupy Iraq.

At the same time, another looming crisis was that the 25-member interim Governing Council might revolt or dissolve over the issue. Getting on the wrong side of Sistani or losing the Governing Council could be a major blow that would leave them without viable alternatives.

AT ONE NSC MEETING in the fall of 2003, the discussion turned to the role of Grand Ayatollah Sistani. Bremer was piped in on the secure video network.

"Are we going to let a 75-year-old cleric decide what our policy is going to be in Iraq?" he asked.

"Jerry," Vice President Cheney said, "you know, I wonder if there's another way to look at this. I'm beginning to think that we have to deal with Sistani the way you deal in the Congress with a cranky committee chairman if you're in the executive branch. You may not like him. You may not agree with him. But you've got to cultivate him because he can do you a lot of harm."

From that point on Sistani was the certified go-to cleric for the Bush administration. Whether cranky or Iranian or beloved, one thing was for sure: He had power over millions in Iraq.

O'SULLIVAN AND MARTINEZ put together two memos dated November 4 that outlined an alternative plan, and briefed Bremer on it in a bomb shelter during a mortar attack. The idea was to create an interim constitution without calling it that, since Saddam had run the country under an interim constitution and the very idea had a terrible connotation for the Iraqis. Instead, it would be called the Transitional Administrative Law, or TAL. Though it would be drafted and imposed on Iraq in large part by Americans, it would include benchmarks requiring elections and the drafting of a new, permanent constitution by a specific date.

Someone was sent down to Najaf to run the idea by Sistani. He approved.

Hadley and Blackwill told Rice that perhaps they could have interim elections in Iraq and then transfer sovereignty. Rice called Bremer.

"Look," Bremer told her. "We have a new proposal, I think, an emerging consensus." He outlined it for her.

"Don't you think you should come back here and let us all talk about this first, because this is really kind of a presidential-level decision."

"Sure. I'll be on a plane tomorrow."

Hadley breathed a sigh of relief. "Hallelujah," he told Rice. "We just had a real break."

"I told Jerry Bremer he's got to come back," Rice told the president.

"Why'd you do that?" Bush asked.

"Because I think we'd better have this discussion here."

"WE DO NOT HAVE A MILITARY STRATEGY for victory in Iraq," Bremer complained to Cheney in a secure phone call several days later.

"I've been asking the same question," Cheney said. "What's our strategy to win? My impression is that the Pentagon's mind-set is that the war's over and they're now in the 'mopping-up' phase. They fail to see that we're in a major battle against terrorists in Iraq and elsewhere."

He promised to raise the issues on his own at the White House.

ON NOVEMBER 7, Bremer met with General Abizaid. It had been a bad day, with a second U.S. helicopter shot down in a week, and four American soldiers killed.

"I'm concerned that people in Washington might try to drive a wedge between us," Abizaid said. But as they talked it was clear that a wedge already existed. Abizaid said he needed to rehire experienced Sunni army officers from Saddam's old army. He was fed up with public pronouncements against doing so from Walt Slocombe, one of Bremer's senior deputies. "Listen," Abizaid said, "I've always told you that I opposed disbanding the army, but I've never gone to the press with my opinion."

"Bringing back Saddam's army," Bremer replied, "would have set off a civil war here. If you think we've got problems now, imagine what they *would* have been."

BUSH GAVE A LUNCHEON SPEECH at the conservative Heritage Foundation on Veterans Day, November 11, 2003. The war in Iraq was much like the efforts of Presidents Truman and Reagan to thwart Communism, he told the audience. "The will and resolve of America are being tested in Afghanistan and in Iraq. We are not only containing the terrorist threat, we are turning it back."

The claim was contradicted by the facts on the ground in Iraq. Nothing was being turned back. The classified reports showed there had been about 750 enemy-initiated attacks in Iraq in September and the number climbed again to about 1,000 in October. That was still more than 30 attacks each day.

About an hour after his speech, Bush was back at the White House, where he met with his National Security Council.

"Okay," Bush said. "Let's see how it's going in Iraq."

Rob Richer, who had been heading the CIA Near East Division for a year, started with the intelligence briefing.

"We are seeing the establishment of an insurgency in Iraq," he said.

Rumsfeld cut off the CIA man. "That's a strong word. What do you mean? How do you define insurgency?"

"Sir," Richer replied, "according to DOD's own publications there are three characteristics of an insurgency." He rattled them off: popular support, sustained armed attacks or sabotage, and the ability to act at will and move independently.

"I may disagree with you," said Rumsfeld, sitting back and letting it go. It was the Rumsfeldian hedge. He might. He might not.

Richer understood why Rumsfeld would resist the use of the word "insurgency." It meant plainly that those on the other side were a durable, organized and perhaps catastrophic force. But in Richer's view that was the reality, and it needed to be faced. Iraq was now a classic guerrilla warfare scenario in the CIA view, and the military was having to confront the question of not only protecting their own troops but of protecting the Iraqi population. Young men in Iraq were making practical decisions. Should they join the new Iraqi police force or the insurgency?

Bush turned to Bremer.

"Is this how you see it?" Bush asked.

Bremer nodded.

Richer, who had been to Iraq to visit the CIA's seven main bases two months earlier, had found that Bremer would agree in the field, but would not really engage in the debate back in Washington. He would never come clean in front of Rumsfeld.

Richer made his pitch directly to the president for a new Iraqi intelligence service. The CIA's collection efforts are limited in Iraq because there's no Iraqi intelligence service to help get information. The CIA had about 200 case officers and people in Iraq, and Tenet was planning to expand the CIA presence.

"I need more data," Bush said. "I don't want to read in *The New York Times* that we are facing an insurgency. I don't want anyone in the cabinet to say it is an insurgency. I don't think we are there yet."

General Myers mentioned various successes, painting a favorable picture.

"I'm not hearing that," Tenet interjected. He wanted his station chief brought in on the secure video link to state his views.

"I think the generals are best placed to tell us," Rumsfeld said.

"Okay," Tenet said, raising his hands in a signature signal of resignation. He seemed to be not only yielding but giving up.

"I want some clarity," Bush said, but the contradictions were not resolved for him, and he did not insist they be.

Later, Rumsfeld said, he looked up "insurgency" and other related phrases in a military dictionary. "I didn't have conviction that I was the one who ought to use, to set the phrase, as to what we would call it at any given time."

Armitage had concluded that his friend Tenet had stayed too long as CIA director. He felt Tenet should have left in 2002 after the successful Afghanistan War, or more recently in the summer, when Saddam's brutal sons, Uday and Qusay, had been killed on July 22, 2003. He always said that leaving high-level government was not as traumatic as lots of people feared. "When you leave government your IQ goes up 30 points," he said. And there was a tendency for people to believe incorrectly that they were indispensable. "You got to remember when you remove your fist from a pail of water there's no hole," he said.

But the giant problem now was the president's state of mind, Armitage thought. Bush was in denial about Iraq.

25

A T ANOTHER POINT IN THE NSC MEETING, Rumsfeld argued that it
was important to turn things over to the Iraqis to show them that
they could run the country.

"We should accept the reality that we can't get a permanent constitution right away," the president said. He asked Bremer, "Wouldn't cau-
cuses allow for better security? I mean you wouldn't have the spectacle
of lines at polls getting bombed or shot at."

The president ended the meeting declaring, "It's important for everyone to know that we're going to stay the course and that I'm determined
to succeed." Meeting with Bremer later in the Oval Office, he asked,
"What's the real situation on the ground?"

"The intelligence is just not good," Bremer answered. "And I'm personally not persuaded that the military has a strategy to win."

They chatted a little longer. At the end, Bush told his special envoy,
"You're doing a great job. Keep it up."

Confronted with distressing reports from his lead man in Iraq, Bush
seemed to want to use pure willpower to change the situation on the
ground. His public comments around this time stressed similar passion
and optimism.

"The failure of Iraqi democracy would embolden terrorists around
the world, increase dangers to the American people, and extinguish the
hopes of millions in the region," Bush said in a speech November 6.
"Iraqi democracy will succeed, and that success will send forth the

news, from Damascus to Tehran, that freedom can be the future of every nation."

But if success were truly so important, where was the urgency to develop a strategy to win? And if there was no such strategy, as Bremer believed, what was the reason for optimism?

BREMER WORRIED that everyone was getting what he privately called "bug-out fever." Though he kept insisting that early sovereignty—which would end his job at the CPA—was a "lousy idea," it kept coming up.

Bremer could read a calendar. The president was up for reelection in 2004 and reelection campaigns drove every White House. Nobody ever explicitly said anything to Bremer like "You've got to get out of there before the presidential election." But winning would be the most important thing in Bush's life. He would be campaigning almost every day. Iraq was important, but reelection was the prize.

Bremer spoke with Andy Card at the end of October 2003, and argued that they needed to do the right thing for history and for Iraq. "It might make the president's life more difficult next year. It might even cost him the election."

Card urged Bremer to talk to the president.

"Do what's right," Bush said. "Even if we don't get this thing sorted out by the election."

Bremer later said, "This pressure, this early sovereignty pressure, I think part of it was political . . . although nobody spelled it out for me. I could figure it out."

The military was soon arguing that ending the occupation would enhance the security situation because the Iraqis didn't like occupation. At one meeting, Bremer said, "Look, ending the occupation is a good idea. But we are kidding ourselves if we think that it's the silver bullet that's going to end the opposition. It won't, just because the average Iraqi's going to go outside his house and there's still going to be a Bradley tank sitting there, even if you're no longer the occupier."

The president finally decided on November 12 that they should do early sovereignty.

Bremer recalls in his book that he made the point that the decision they had just made to turn over sovereignty should be portrayed as something that the Iraqis had come up with, not the Americans.

Bush laughed. "I agree with that. And I suggest that maybe this can be the one meeting in history where everybody doesn't rush out to tell the press what we decided."

It worked. The front-page headline in *The Washington Post* on November 15 read, "Iraqis Say U.S. to Cede Power by Summer; Town Meetings to Set Process in Motion," and *The New York Times* headline was "U.S. Is to Return Power to Iraqis as Early as June." Just as had been agreed in the White House, it was portrayed in the *Times* and elsewhere as a plan that had been "put forward by Iraqi leaders," couriered to Washington by Bremer, and then "broadly accepted" by Bush.

TWO DAYS AFTER THE ANNOUNCEMENT that sovereignty would be turned over the Iraqis, a group of 17 Iraqi women visited the White House. Dina Powell, Bush's special assistant for personnel, an Egyptian-born Arabic speaker, was taking the women around.

Someone told Bush, and he agreed to see them. Many of the women had horror stories of the brutality of Saddam's regime. One had watched her son tortured to death. Others had been raped. Several of the women declined to go into the Oval Office to see Bush, but five of them went in for a private meeting.

"Muharrir," one of the women said in Arabic to the president upon entering the Oval Office.

What does that mean? Bush asked Dina Powell.

"Liberator," she translated.

The president broke down in tears.

DAN SENOR, the Republican political consultant who was Bremer's spokesman, thought the best assessments of Bremer's situation came from Hume Horan, who had served as U.S. ambassador in five countries—Cameroon, Equatorial Guinea, Sudan, Saudi Arabia and the Ivory Coast. Fluent in Arabic and widely considered the most seasoned Middle East hand, Horan, 68, whose first foreign service assignment had been in Baghdad in the 1960s, was one of the first Arabists Bremer had recruited for the provisional authority. On one long road trip out of Baghdad, Horan told Senor they were doing full-blown nation building now, and estimated that their chance of building a democracy in Iraq was only about 30 percent.

"Those are the highest odds we have ever had or will ever have in trying to pull this off," Horan said, referring to the whole Middle East. But even at 30 percent, they were right to give it a try. "It's worth doing," he said.

In November, just before Horan left the CPA, Senor had dinner with him at Cafe Ranana, a restaurant in the Al Rashid Hotel in Baghdad. It was a pleasant evening, and Horan was in a reflective mood.

When he had been ambassador to Saudi Arabia or had another important job, he said, he would have one decision land on his plate each year that was crucial and hard enough to keep him up at night. "One a year that was sort of huge pressure, no mistakes, major intensity, high stress," he said. Bremer, on the other hand, was making anywhere from 10 to 100 decisions of that magnitude every day. "No diplomat can fully appreciate what Bremer is up against," Horan said.

ONE OF DAVID KAY'S INTERROGATORS in Baghdad went to visit the former head of the Iraqi military procurement commission. Now that he had cooperated with the Americans, the Iraqi was asked, what hopes did he hold for his future?

"As long as you're here, I want to stay right in confinement," the Iraqi man replied. "It's safe."

Kay thought it was disturbing evidence of what Iraqis thought about the security situation in their country.

Just before Thanksgiving, General Abizaid sent word he wanted to meet with Kay. "Alone," came the word from Abizaid's staff, meaning Kay should not bring General Dayton with him.

"I need your help," Abizaid told Kay. He was trying desperately to get better intelligence to help his forces battle the insurgency. Kay's Iraq Survey Group was perhaps the biggest and best intelligence network in Iraq right then. "I need these resources. You've got translators. You've got analysts."

Kay objected. "I have analysts who are experts on WMD. They're not going to help anyone on counterinsurgency. They don't know it. I have exactly two operational officers who are fluent in Arabic." Take them away from me and I might as well close up shop and go home. He would be unable to interview any Iraqi who wasn't in custody.

Abizaid bargained. He'd be willing to take only a dozen of Kay's 60 or so analysts. Then it got down to six or seven.

"No, I can't do it because I got assigned this mission. I have absolutely no problem if you go back to Washington and Washington decides at this point in time counterinsurgency is more important than WMD," Kay said. "Look. I live out here. I travel the BIAP highway four times a day. I've had teams attacked. If you say that and Washington says that's important, I understand. But it's not my decision."

"No. I don't want to go back to Washington. I don't want to ask. I just want us to agree to it," Abizaid replied.

Kay wouldn't budge, and Abizaid called his intelligence staff into the room. He repeated the request, leaving Kay to conclude that Abizaid thought that he wouldn't be willing to stand up to him in front of the staff, or maybe that the general just wanted to demonstrate that he'd made the effort. It grew uncomfortable for the staff, Kay thought, because he was doing something none of them could ever dream of doing: He was telling a four-star general "No."

IN DECEMBER, Tenet called Kay to tell him that he had lost his tug-of-war with the military. Kay's Iraq Survey Group would have to take on other missions besides WMD. Kay flew back to Washington to remind Tenet that part of the deal for him to take the job was that his group would focus solely on the WMD hunt.

"It's just time to go," Kay said.

Tenet didn't stand in Kay's way, though he was concerned about what Kay would say after he left. He didn't want him to go out and trash the CIA.

"No, that's not my intention," Kay said.

Was he planning on writing a book?

"I don't do that. I've never done that. I didn't do it after the first Gulf War." If anything, perhaps a book on his successful search for WMD after the Gulf War would have been more marketable than a book on his 2003 WMD hunt, which was coming up zeroes.

Tenet proposed to Kay that he stay on the CIA's rolls as a consultant. Kay agreed, although he recognized that if he stayed and kept his security clearances, Tenet might think that would restrain him from talking. He had come to see Tenet as a relationship guy, someone who thought he could manage anything or anybody.

Not long afterward, Kay met with Charles Allen, the assistant director of central intelligence for collection, who told Kay about a highly covert operation to gather intelligence about WMD about eight months before the war, so secret that it wasn't even in the files. It was similar to the so-called Dead Souls Program launched after the collapse of the Soviet Union to track down and pay Soviet weapons scientists who were out of the country to find out what had been going on inside.

For Iraq, the CIA had run a two-part clandestine program to try to develop reliable human-source intelligence on WMD. During the United Nations inspection days in the 1990s, the CIA had acquired a very good roster of the Iraqi scientists involved in WMD research and production. The first part of the operation entailed contacting Iraqi scientists who were outside Iraq and paying them to see if they knew anything about WMD programs. The second part, which was more dangerous, involved paying Iraqis in Europe or Asia to go back into Iraq and talk with their relatives who had been involved in WMD programs in the past.

It hadn't turned up any evidence of WMD, but the CIA was so convinced that Iraq had the weapons that absence of evidence was taken as proof that the Dead Souls–style program wasn't working. After some 120 contacts had been made without developments, the program was terminated.

Upon learning of it, Kay was offended that the contrary pieces of evidence hadn't been reported or included in the wide dossier of intelligence he was shown before he'd begun his mission that summer. "I don't think the president was told," Kay later said. "I don't think Powell was told. I don't think Condi ever asked or was told." *

ON DECEMBER 6, 2003, Rumsfeld was on one of his dashes through the Middle East. He stopped in Baghdad, where he pulled Bremer aside at the airport.

"Look," Rumsfeld said, "it's clear to me that your reporting channel is now direct to the president and not through me. Condi has taken over political matters. I think that's a mistake. The last time the NSC got into operational issues, we had Iran-contra. But she seems to have jumped into this with both feet."

It was an extraordinary accusation. Iran-contra was the Reagan administration scandal involving the secret sale of arms to Iran and the illegal diversion of millions of dollars in profits to the anti-Communist contras in Nicaragua. The various Iran-contra investigations concluded unanimously that the National Security Council should be involved only

---

* McLaughlin didn't think the program was very large and certainly not at all conclusive. In his opinion, it was ridiculous to think anything had been suppressed.

in policy and coordination—not operations—and criticized the covert work.

According to Bremer, Rumsfeld added with a tight smile, "I'm bowing out of the political process. Let Condi and the NSC handle things. It might make your life a little easier."

Around this time coming out of the Situation Room one day, Rice asked Rumsfeld to call Bremer to handle some routine matters.

"No," Rumsfeld said, "He doesn't work for me."

"Well, who does he work for?" Rice asked.

"He works for you," Rumsfeld said.

Rumsfeld later confirmed to me in an interview that he felt that Bremer had only "technically but not really" reported to him.

"He didn't call home much," Rumsfeld said of Bremer. "He was out there in a tough environment, making a lot of decisions, calling audibles, and it's a difficult job."

"And he felt he was the president's man," I asked, echoing the language Bremer had used in his book.

"You bet. And he was. It wasn't a matter of feeling it. He was."

IN EARLY DECEMBER, Newt Gingrich decided to create some public pressure with his complaints about Bremer. "I was planting a flag because the things that had started in September weren't happening fast enough," he later explained. He gave an interview to *Newsweek* magazine in which he said the U.S. was going "off a cliff" in Iraq.

"I'm told over there that CPA stands for 'Can't Produce Anything,' " Gingrich told the magazine. He did not attack Bremer personally, but his core argument was that governing should have been placed in the hands of the Iraqis much sooner. Gingrich then went on *Meet the Press* on Sunday, December 7, 2003, and said the postwar model should have been what the U.S. had done in Afghanistan, quickly installing Hamid Karzai.

Iraqis wanted their own government, Gingrich said. "The longer we keep Americans front and center, the greater the danger that Iraqi nationalism will decide it has to be anti-American."

The next day Bremer called Gingrich. "You don't get it," Bremer told him. We're not going off a cliff here. He said he had things under control. "Why don't you come visit?"

"I'll come for a week," Gingrich said. But having been on countless hurry-up, in-and-out briefings as a visiting, gadfly congressman, he added, "I'm not coming over for a one-day dog-and-pony show."

Vice President Dick Cheney, Federal Appeals Court Judge Laurence Silberman, President Bush, Joyce Rumsfeld and Donald H. Rumsfeld on January 26, 2001. Rumsfeld is being sworn in as secretary of defense, a post he had first held in the 1970s during the Ford administration. "Get it right this time," Cheney told Rumsfeld, his old friend and mentor.

Vice President Cheney, Saudi Arabia Ambassador Prince Bandar, National Security Adviser Condoleezza Rice and President Bush meet on the White House Truman Balcony several days after the September 11, 2001, terrorist attacks. "If we get somebody and we can't get them to cooperate, we'll hand them over to you," Bush told Bandar of his plans for handling possible terrorist suspects.

3

4

(left) Steve Herbits, Rumsfeld's former special assistant and long-time friend, was brought back as a consultant during Rumsfeld's second tour as secretary of defense. "In the months after the shooting stops, it is essential that there be no civil war in Iraq," he wrote in a memo to Rumsfeld April 10, 2003. "Civil wars, rightly or wrongly, hearken back to Vietnam. The president's strategy will die in the embrace of such a comparison."

(right) Chief of Naval Operations Admiral Vernon Clark. "If you select me as chairman," Clark told Rumsfeld in a private meeting, "I will fully embrace the responsibilities to be the military adviser to the president."

5

Deputy Secretary of Defense Paul Wolfowitz (right) and General Peter Pace, vice chairman and later chairman of the Joint Chiefs of Staff. As violence escalated in the fall of 2003, Wolfowitz, one of the early advocates for the Iraq War, felt increasingly marginalized by Rumsfeld and concluded that Rumsfeld was blocking early efforts to train Iraqi security forces. Pace, a Vietnam veteran, abhorred enemy body counts, and advised against using them, but President Bush often wanted the numbers, and the U.S. military frequently reported them publicly.

L. Paul "Jerry" Bremer, III *(center)* replaced retired Lieutenant General Jay Garner *(right)* as the head of postwar operations in Iraq just weeks into the occupation. While Bremer wore a formal suit and tie with his Timberland boots, some of his staff ridiculed Garner for his casual dress. Garner told Rumsfeld that Bremer made "three tragic mistakes" within days of his arrival, leaving hundreds of thousands of disorganized, unemployed, armed Iraqis running around. But Rumsfeld never told the president.

Joint Chiefs Chairman General Richard B. Myers, Rumsfeld, Bush and Bremer *(left to right)*. "I was neither Rumsfeld's nor Powell's man. I was the president's man," Bremer wrote of his authority in Iraq.

Dr. David Kay, who headed the Iraq Survey Group that took over the search for weapons of mass destruction in the summer of 2003. After concluding that no WMD would be found, Kay met with Bush, who asked how the CIA could have been so wrong. "One of the problems for a director," Kay said referring to then CIA Director George Tenet, "is if he's inside the political process, he loses his balance. For example, George comes here every day for the briefing. And inevitably that communicates a sense of the political process to the people at the agency . . . there is a cost. Now, please don't tell George I told you."

Undersecretary of Defense for Policy Doug Feith. One of the most controversial figures to emerge from the Iraq War, Feith was in charge of key parts of the postwar planning. In a written evaluation, Rumsfeld's adviser Steve Herbits said early on that Feith's work was "now widely regarded as a serious failure." But Rumsfeld, Wolfowitz, General Pace and Steve Hadley, the first-term Deputy National Security Adviser, strongly defended Feith's performance.

Frank Miller, the senior director for defense on the National Security Council staff who had held senior Pentagon posts for seven secretaries of defense. "Fix it," Rice frequently told Miller, who struggled to move Rumsfeld or the Pentagon on key issues that would help the U.S. troops in Iraq.

Major General Spider Marks, in charge of intelligence for the invading U.S. ground forces, believed Iraq had weapons of mass destruction, but he was shocked that the classified list of 946 suspected WMD sites offered no real evidence. He realized he could not say with confidence that there were WMD at any of the sites on the list.

General John Abizaid, the commander of the Central Command responsible for the Middle East, with Rumsfeld's special assistant and spokesman, Larry DiRita. In a 2006 private meeting with Congressman Jack Murtha of Pennsylvania who had called for the withdrawal of U.S. troops from Iraq, Abizaid held his thumb and forefinger a quarter of an inch from each other and said, "We're that far apart."

John Negroponte, the first American ambassador to Iraq after the invasion, tours his embassy with Chargé d'Affaires Jim Jeffrey. Jeffrey showed him a map of Baghdad locating a week's worth of about a hundred insurgent attacks. The main issue was security, Jeffrey said. "We don't have it." Negroponte later became the first director of national intelligence and by June 2006 concluded that U.S. Iraq policy was in trouble.

Secretary of State Colin Powell, Cheney, Bush, Rumsfeld, and Generals Myers and Pace *(left to right)*. Rumsfeld offered his resignation in the wake of the Abu Ghraib prisoner abuse scandal, but Bush refused to accept it. The president instead gathered many of his national security team for a rare group trip to the Pentagon for a public display of unity.

Deputy Secretary of State Richard Armitage, Bush and Secretary of State Powell *(left to right)* meet at Bush's Texas ranch in 2003. After he and Powell had resigned the next year, Armitage was asked if he would accept a new post in Bush's second term. "I just don't know how I can work in an administration that lets Secretary Powell walk and keeps Mr. Rumsfeld," he said.

Presidential advisers Karl Rove, Karen Hughes, Bob Blackwill, a deputy national
security adviser, and Chief of Staff Andy Card *(left to right)* travel with the president
on the campaign trail in 2004. Blackwill, who had spent months in Iraq and probably
knew as much about the war as anybody in the White House, traveled regularly with
Bush in the last months of the presidential campaign. He was surprised that any
discussion of Iraq was through the prism of the campaign, what Senator John Kerry
might have said, or the impact that events in Iraq might have on the president's
reelection bid. Not once did Bush ask Blackwill what things were like in Iraq, what
he had seen, or what should be done.

(*Above*) George Tenet, retired General Tommy Franks, and Jerry Bremer each receive the Medal of Freedom on December 14, 2004. All three had been criticized for their roles in the war, but Bush stood by them and selected each for the highest civilian award.

(*Below*) Judge Silberman (*right*) and former Senator Chuck Robb, co-chairmen of Bush's commission investigating weapons of mass destruction intelligence. "It was clear and understood that we would not be asked to evaluate the administration's use of the intelligence," Silberman recalled. Among the figures the commission failed to interview were Generals Abizaid, McKiernan and Marks.

Former President George H. W. Bush at his son's second inauguration, January 20, 2005. In a 1999 speech the senior President Bush explained his decision not to extend the first Gulf War and try to overthrow Saddam Hussein. "We're going to be an occupying power—America in an Arab land—with no allies at our side. It would have been disastrous." He at times commented privately to Prince Bandar and other friends about policies being pursued by his son. "Why don't you call him about it?" Bandar once asked. "I had my turn. It is his turn now," the former president replied.

ice and Rumsfeld answer questions from the press on their April 2006 Baghdad trip.
Rumsfeld suggested to Iraqi Prime Minister-elect Nouri al-Maliki that they discuss
U.S. forces. He didn't use the words "drawdown" or "withdrawal," but everyone
knew what he meant. Maliki looked at the American secretary of defense as if he were
crazy. "It's way too early to be talking about that," he said.

Philip Zelikow, the former executive
director of the 9/11 commission, who
became counselor of the State Department
and one of Rice's closest aides. In
September 2005, Rice sent Zelikow to Iraq.
"If pressed, the odds of success are as good
as, say 70 percent," he reported to her.
"Again, that means at least a 30 percent risk
of failure, and a significant risk of
catastrophic failure. Even in the upbeat
assessment, we might optimistically judge
that our efforts are probably just enough to
succeed. Not much room to spare, but
hopefully just enough."

Bush with outgoing Chief of Staff Andy Card in April 2006. "The best way to signal that you are serious about making changes is to change your chief of staff," Card had told the president right after the 2004 election, and waged an unsuccessful 18-month battle to get Bush to replace Rumsfeld, too. Card told his successor, Joshua Bolten, that his job would be, "Iraq, Iraq, Iraq."

Cheney, Bush and Rumsfeld in August 2006. Rumsfeld thought it was "nonsense" that Cheney controlled Bush. "He does not take strong positions when the president's in the room that could conceivably position him contrary to the president," Rumsfeld said. "He doesn't put the president in a corner or take away his options."

...mer Secretary of State Dr. Henry ...singer. "Of the outside people that I talk ...n this job, I probably talk to Henry ...singer more than I talk to anybody ...e," Cheney said in 2005, adding that ...sh was "a big fan" of Kissinger. Bush ...t privately with Kissinger every couple ...months, making the former secretary the ...st frequent outside adviser to Bush on ...eign affairs.

Senator Chuck Hagel, the Nebraska Republican, became an outspoken crit of the handling of postwar Iraq. In June 2005 he privately told Preside Bush, "I believe that you are getting really bubbled in here in the White House on Iraq."

25

26

Senator Carl Levin of Michigan, the ranking Democrat on the Senate Armed Services Committee. Levin believed that in 2003 then-Secretary of State Colin Powell had the power and influence with Bush to stop the Iraq War. "I don't thin he ever realized what power lay in his hands, and that's an abdication," Levin sai "Can you imagine the power of that one person to change the course? He had it."

*(Above)*Condoleezza Rice and President Bush. Rice regularly made unpublicized visits to military hospitals that cared for the wounded from Iraq. "I have to be able to look at those young soldiers and ask myself honestly if I think what they're going through was worth it, and are we making it worth it," she said. "These are not toy soldiers that somebody sent in, you know, little toy soldiers. These are real, living human beings."

(Below) Steve Hadley with President Bush at the president's Crawford, Texas, ranch. As Hadley became national security adviser, he said of the first term, when he was Rice's deputy, "I give us a B minus for policy development and a D minus for policy execution."

On April 24, 2003, a month after the invasion, President Bush spoke at the
Army tank plant in Lima, Ohio, and praised the postwar efforts of retired
Lieutenant General Jay Garner. "We've followed up with a team of people,
headed by this man Garner who's got one overriding goal, to leave a free nation
in the hands of a free people."

Bremer agreed and Rumsfeld and Abizaid signed off.

A week before Gingrich's scheduled trip, however, Bremer sent word through an aide: "We're too busy. You can't come."

"Rumsfeld was not prepared to overrule Bremer," Gingrich later said. "They were not prepared to bring him home in a way that would lead him to be an open enemy of the president." As a result, they were in anguish, "knowing it's not working and not able to figure out how to change it."

For Rumsfeld, the question was why they couldn't do the same thing in Iraq that they'd accomplished in Afghanistan. Clearly they needed some version of Karzai, somebody the Iraqis could recognize as a leader.

ON DECEMBER 13, the U.S. military captured Saddam Hussein. The former dictator was hiding in a spider hole near a farmhouse outside Tikrit, 90 miles north of Baghdad, where he'd been born in 1937.

"Ladies and gentlemen, we got him!" Bremer announced on TV. It underscored to the Iraqis that it was an American show.

"We've got to really run with this success," Bremer told his deputy. "It just might be the tipping point."

He later told one of his aides, "Maybe now, the moderate Sunnis will realize Baathism is finally dead."

It was not. The violence continued, though the attacks dropped to about 800 in December.

GENERAL MYERS THOUGHT the first eight months of the Iraqi occupation had been relatively calm. That only proved he wasn't stationed there. In January 2004, he and Rumsfeld were at the White House briefing Bush on a range of issues.

"Oh, by the way," Rumsfeld mentioned, "we have this incident." There were allegations of prisoner abuse by Army military police at Abu Ghraib, Saddam's old fortress prison. "Apparently there are photos involved." He said an investigation was under way. "We're on it."

On January 16, Lieutenant General Ricardo S. Sanchez put out a press release announcing an investigation of "detainee abuse at a Coalition Forces detention facility." Specific details could hinder the investigation, the release said.

RICE'S FRUSTRATIONS WITH RUMSFELD were mounting, although she tried to conceal them. At one point, the president had determined that the hundreds of suspected terrorists who were detainees at the U.S. base in Guantánamo Bay, Cuba, were unlawful combatants who could be tried in military tribunals and denied access to the U.S. federal court system. This meant that they had been turned over to the Defense Department, but Rumsfeld would not start the tribunal process. The secretary of defense was balking. Rice had overseen an elaborate interagency review that took weeks and involved the senior lawyers in the administration. It was designed to get the president to order Rumsfeld to commence the tribunals.

Attorney General John Ashcroft had become a strong internal advocate for starting the tribunals. One way or another, the detainee cases were going to wind up reviewed by the federal courts. If they didn't have a credible tribunal process up and running, Ashcroft said, the Justice Department would be dead in the water when they tried to defend the system at the federal appeals courts.

At an NSC meeting with the president, Rice began going through a long paper on the issues that everyone was supposed to have read and understood.

Rumsfeld leaned back and made it pretty clear he was not paying much attention. The president also seemed bored. But Rice plowed on.

"Don, what do you think about this?" Bush asked, interrupting Rice.

"They are bad guys," Rumsfeld said. He believed Americans were so oriented to think automatically about the rights of those accused or jailed. The problem was keeping apprehended terrorists off the battlefield and then interrogating them to get useful intelligence. The administration had to find a way to get that story out to the public.

Bush agreed. How? When?

"I'm not a lawyer," Rumsfeld reminded them. He couldn't do it and wouldn't do it.

The discussion drifted off and the decision was left hanging. Some of the backbenchers at the NSC meeting were astonished at the deference the president gave Rumsfeld. It was as if Rice and the NSC had one serious, formal process going on while the president and Rumsfeld had another one—informal, chatty and dominant.

GENERAL ABIZAID vented to Tenet and Rob Richer in January 2004 about Rumsfeld and Steve Cambone, the Pentagon intelligence chief. "The world is not as rosy as Cambone and SecDef say," he said, "and they need to let me run the war." The draconian de-Baathification policy was crazy and self-defeating. "We have got to take the head off the hydra but not the body." Of Bremer, Abizaid added, "I can't talk to him."

At another point Abizaid told senior CIA officials that taking the war to the Sunnis who were leading the insurgency in Iraq would not work. "You can't kill every Sunni in the heartland."

JORDANIAN KING ABDULLAH came to visit the president in January 2004. Jordan shared only a 50-mile border with Iraq, Abdullah said, but "I'm very concerned I have an insurgency on the other side."

"I understand," Bush said. "But my generals tell me that 85 percent of the country is completely calm. Only 15 percent has some problems and those are low-level."

Classified reports showed there were about 800 enemy-initiated attacks that January, roughly the same number as there had been in December.

TENET ASKED DAVID KAY to hold off on announcing his resignation from the Iraq Survey Group until after the president's State of the Union address on January 20. Kay agreed. In that speech, the president carefully parroted the language Kay had used before the Congress in October, sharply backing off the allegations he had made the year before about the state of Iraq's weapons programs. He referred not to "WMD," but to "weapons of mass destruction related program activities."

Kay met with some Republican senators and congressmen privately to urge them to follow the president's lead. Stop talking about WMD, he said. "Be really careful, because you're not going to find that. Doesn't mean it was a regime that shouldn't have been replaced. Doesn't mean it's a regime you can't build a case up on WMD in the U.N. But it's not on the actual weapons."

On January 23, 2004, Kay officially resigned. That night a reporter for the Reuters news agency tracked down his home phone number and called him.

"I don't think they existed," Kay said when asked about the WMD. "What everyone was talking about is stockpiles produced after the end of the last Gulf War, and I don't think there was a large-scale production program in the '90s."

Bill Harlow, Tenet's CIA spokesman, called Kay. He was angry as hell. Kay was supposed to stay on as a consultant and senior adviser. The message was that he was supposed to stay on the reservation.

Tenet went so far as to tell Powell that the CIA would "keep him on the farm."

KAY TESTIFIED PUBLICLY before the Senate Armed Services Committee on January 28, a few days later, and said what would be the headline and make the cover of *Newsweek*. "We were almost all wrong, and I certainly include myself." Kay said 85 percent of the work was done and he had no reason to believe they ever would find WMD stockpiles in Iraq. "It is important to acknowledge failure," Kay said, adding that an outside investigation was needed.

The next day about 10:30 A.M., Kay was at his Virginia home when Rice called to invite him to lunch with the president. Kay had about an hour and a half, so it was a race to shower, dress and drive into town in time from 30 miles away.

The lunch was with Bush, Cheney, Rice and Andy Card in a small dining room off the Oval Office.

How did you reach your conclusions? Bush wanted to know. And how did U.S. intelligence miss all this?

"We missed it because the Iraqis actually behaved like they had weapons," Kay said. "And we weren't smart enough to understand that the hardest thing in intelligence is when behavior remains consistent but underlying reasons change." Saddam didn't have WMD but wanted to appear as if he did. His purpose was deception. Kay said he thought Saddam had decided to get rid of his WMD on the theory that they were too easy to find.

Take the aluminum tubes, he said. The high cost, the secrecy, the tighter specifications, and some intelligence that Saddam himself had been following the purchase of the tubes had led to the conclusion they were for a nuclear program.

But Kay and the inspectors had interviewed engineers, gone through the files and found the contracts. The tubes were for conventional artillery, a rework of an Italian rocket system. He explained that the propellant wasn't powerful enough, but the contract to buy the propellant couldn't be changed because the man who ran the propellant factory was close to Saddam's son. They tried to make the tubes thinner—which required tighter specifications—so that the propellant might work. Everyone involved said that was a good thing because tighter specifications made the tubes more expensive. Those involved made their money on commissions so the more expensive, the better. The contracts were cost-plus, like the contracts for many U.S. weapons systems, so no one took a hit except the government.

All kinds of purchases were made through clandestine channels and the black market, Kay told them, rather than through the U.N. export control mechanism. Intelligence analysts assumed that there must be a reason, and that the reason was that these items were for prohibited weapons programs.

"The flaw in that is that they attempted to procure almost everything clandestinely," Kay said. "They could because the family had a rake-off. The black market was essentially run by Uday Hussein and their friends."

Even bigger and more basic, however, the CIA had not understood the utter corruption within the system and the deterioration of Iraq's society, Kay said. Things had gotten so bad that the regime itself was not capable of purposeful development of WMD programs. Kay's group would ask the Iraqis during investigations, "How could you do this? Why did you lie?" And the response was "Everyone was lying! Everyone was out for their own." The corruption was so acidic and pervasive that it just leached away the government's ability to function.

Bush wanted to know why Kay thought Saddam hadn't just come clean on WMD long ago. Why had he risked his whole life, his government, instead of just throwing the doors open?

Kay said he thought Saddam never believed the U.S. would actually invade. But more important, more than he feared the U.S., he feared the Shiites and Kurds who lived in Iraq. He knew that they in turn feared him because they thought he had WMD.

"You know, as you have to recognize, totalitarian regimes generally end up fearing their own people more than they fear external threats. It's just the history of totalitarian regimes," Kay said. "We missed that." And, he said, they were especially susceptible to missing it because they had so little human intelligence, and instead relied on technical collection.

Cheney kept quiet as Bush plunged on. He wanted to know more about what Kay thought about the U.S. intelligence process.

"The disease of the intelligence community is this over-focus on current intelligence," meaning what was going that day or week, as opposed to longer-term, strategic intelligence. "Look," he said, "current analysis is better if you turn CNN on or read the paper. Quite frankly, the press does a better job."

"A good example of this is the PDB"—the President's Daily Brief. "Do you understand that if you respond positively to anything in it, you're going to get nothing but that stuff for the next month or so?" The president's expression of interest put it at the top of the agenda in the intelligence community. "George takes it back and it drives it and it will keep appearing. They respond to it. If you ever respond to a PDB item, it's going to be there for a very long time with more and more information." Presidential interest suggests it is important and the intelligence flow just snowballs out of control.

Bush turned to Cheney. "That's why they keep telling me about that SOB in Mozambique," he said. "I had to ask a question about it once, and I keep getting stuff on that."

Bush wondered how the CIA and the U.S. intelligence could have been so wrong.

"You know, one of the problems for a director is if he's inside the political process, he loses his balance," Kay answered. "For example, George comes here every day for the briefing. And inevitably that communicates a sense of the political process to the people at the agency."

"Do you think I shouldn't have George here every day?" Bush asked.

Kay felt he might be stepping over a line. "No, but there is a cost," he said. "Now please, don't tell George I told you. Recognize that the problem is current intelligence. It's when you express interest in current events you're going to drive the community."

The questions kept coming. Kay barely had a chance to touch his lunch. Card asked, "You told us about the U.S. intelligence service. Who do you think runs a really good intelligence service?"

"In my experience, it was not the British or the Israelis, despite their reputation," Kay said. MI6 and the Mossad were legends in the intelligence world, but Kay said he was not always impressed with the usefulness of their product. "In my judgment, the best one is the Chinese."

"Yeah, they're always trying to steal our technical secrets," Bush said.

AFTERWARD, KAY REFLECTED on what he had not said. He believed that the president was faced with a larger problem than just the failure of intelligence in Iraq. He was left with an intelligence service that he couldn't and shouldn't rely on for much of anything.

The next day, Rice called Kay back to the White House.

"There was something you said to the president that really hit a nerve," she said. She was struck by a point he'd made about how one of the hardest things to do in intelligence is discern real change, to fig-ure out why someone keeps doing the same thing, but for different reasons.

"I should have been smart enough," Rice said. "When I heard you say this, I realized that was exactly the same thing that had happened in the DDR," the Deutsche Demokratische Republik, or East Germany, which had collapsed in 1988. "I should have recognized it because of that."

"Yeah," Kay replied, "I have a German friend who told me, 'Don't feel bad about what you missed in Iraq, because we couldn't even figure out that the DDR couldn't collect its own garbage until after it fell.' " Intelli-gence services, he said, don't do a very good job trying to understand the soft side of societies—how well the government is working and the fun-damental attitudes of the people.

POWELL WENT TO *The Washington Post* for an interview on February 2, 2004, with a group of reporters and editors that did not include me. He was asked what his position on the war would have been if he had known there were no stockpiles of WMD.

"The absence of stockpiles changes the political calculus," Powell said. "It changes the answer you get."

His remarks were the lead story in the *Post* the next day headlined: "Powell Says New Data May Have Affected War Decision."

In the Oval Office early that morning, Bush vented to Rice and several other aides. The president claimed in public that he didn't read the newspapers, but that morning he had. "I woke up this morning and read the paper and found that I am the only person in Washington willing to defend me," he said.

Rice called Powell. She and the president were "mad," she said. Pow-ell had "given the Democrats a remarkable tool." His remarks were mak-ing headlines throughout the world. Bush's public position was that the jury was still out on WMD. So Powell had to go back out in public and re-tract his remarks, saying five times that the president's decision to go to war had been "right."

MONTHS LATER, Kay ran into Tenet at a conference in Aspen, Colorado. Tenet clearly knew what Kay had told Bush and Rice. Kay tried to explain that he had only been giving his professional opinion on the intelligence. He hadn't set out to trash the CIA.

"George, I really like you," Kay said.

"Well, I really like you too, David," Tenet said. "But some of this has gotten a little personal."

KAY FELT THERE WAS MORE than enough blame on the intelligence failures to go around. Some of it definitely fell on Rice's shoulders. Her job had been to guard the president's backside and she had not done so.

Tenet was at fault too. He had been brought in not as an intelligence professional but as a sort of big-picture leader, someone who boosted morale and rebuilt the clandestine service. He had fallen victim to his greatest weakness, Kay felt, which was a lack of affinity for the detailed drudgery of intelligence analysis.

But the real villain at CIA, Kay thought, was McLaughlin. Tenet had made his way on the political side of the intelligence world, but McLaughlin had been with the agency for more than 30 years. He was the professional, and Kay felt he had also been the one who clung most stubbornly to the belief that Iraq had mobile biological weapons labs. Kay also recalled that McLaughlin at one point had told him it didn't matter what Kay said or found—he would always believe the aluminum tubes had been part of a nuclear program. McLaughlin had taken the aluminum tubes account and made it his own, a big mistake for someone as high up as the deputy.

To an outsider, McLaughlin recognized, it might look like he had taken the aluminum tubes account as his own. But this was because he was engaged. No, he felt people below him whom he had trusted had not been aggressive enough in surfacing their doubts. Whatever the excuses for the WMD intelligence, he, Tenet and the CIA had failed. Tenet would later acknowledge in private that the CIA didn't have a leg to stand on.

26

U P ON THE TOP FLOOR of the Federal Courthouse on Pennsylvania
Avenue in Washington, one of the enduring legacies of the Reagan
Revolution was moving about his expansive chambers. Senior Judge
Laurence H. Silberman of the U.S. Court of Appeals for the District of
Columbia was following the WMD controversy closely in the press. Silberman, 68, sat on the second most important and prestigious court in
the United States, after the Supreme Court. The court had been a liberal
bastion until Reagan made a succession of conservative D.C. Circuit
appointments—Antonin Scalia, who had gone on to the Supreme Court;
Robert Bork, whose Supreme Court appointment was rejected by the
Senate; Kenneth Starr, who later became the independent counsel who
investigated President Clinton's relationship with Monica Lewinsky;
and Silberman, in 1985.

He was still there nearly two decades later in senior status, meaning
he had to work only three months a year.

Silberman considered both Cheney and Rumsfeld his close personal
friends. He had been deputy attorney general during the last months of
the Nixon administration and acting attorney general during part of the
Ford administration, and had worked closely with the current vice president and secretary of defense.

Silberman knew something about intelligence. On the wall of one of
the rooms in his chambers there was a picture of him with President
Ford and Rumsfeld. At the time, Rumsfeld, Ford's White House chief of
staff, had been trying to persuade Silberman, then acting attorney gen-

eral, to come to the White House as intelligence czar. When Rumsfeld vaguely dangled the possibility of becoming CIA director six months after he took the White House job, Silberman declined. He didn't think it was possible to run intelligence from the White House even for six months. More than a quarter century later, it was Silberman who swore Rumsfeld in as secretary of defense in the Oval Office on the sixth day of the Bush presidency, January 26, 2001.

SILBERMAN WAS NOT at all surprised, only days after David Kay's "We were almost all wrong" congressional testimony, when a call came in from the vice president. In an interview, Silberman recalled the conversation.

"We want to have a commission to look at the intelligence community," Cheney told Silberman on the phone, "to determine whether the intelligence community properly evaluated the question of weapons of mass destruction in Iraq." He wanted Silberman to be its co-chair.

Silberman felt comfortable enough to call the vice president of the United States by his first name. "I think that means, Dick, I'd have to resign from the bench."

Cheney said he thought that was the case.

"Let me think about that and talk to Ricky about it," Silberman said. Ricky, his wife who was also a lawyer, had worked with the vice president's wife, Lynne Cheney, on the Independent Women's Forum, a group of conservative women who had supported Clarence Thomas's Supreme Court nomination.

Silberman enjoyed his judgeship, but he said he felt in wartime he had to answer the vice president's call. The next morning, he called Cheney to say he would take the job. A day after that, in his telling, he went over to meet with White House Counsel Alberto Gonzales, and some other lawyers from the White House and the Justice Department. They had some welcome news: A senior judge was not prohibited from accepting appointment to such presidential commissions.

"That makes it rather easy, since I was prepared to resign," Silberman said.

PRESIDENT BUSH CALLED TOM FOLEY, the former Democratic speaker of the House of Representatives, who was now a Washington lawyer. He needed a Democrat to serve as co-chairman of the commission so that it would be bipartisan. Foley agreed to be the co-chairman.

By February 5, Silberman was over at the White House, meeting with Card to work out the particulars.

"I just got the most extraordinary phone call from Tom Foley, saying that he couldn't serve," Card said. News of his participation on the commission had leaked to the press, and Foley had come under pressure from congressional Democrats not to participate. House Minority Leader Nancy Pelosi, the San Francisco Democrat, had convinced Foley to back out, Card said, arguing that the presidential commission was designed to give Bush political cover on the failure to find WMD nearly a year after the Iraq invasion.

"A commission appointed and controlled by the White House will not have the independence or credibility necessary to investigate these issues," wrote Pelosi and two senior Senate Democrats, Minority Leader Tom Daschle and Senator John D. Rockefeller IV, the top Democrat on the Senate Intelligence Committee, in a letter to Bush. "Even some of your own statements and those of Vice President Cheney need independent scrutiny."

Privately, they had convinced Foley not to lend his name to the effort. Card said the president was disappointed.

Bush and Cheney dropped by Card's office.

"What do you think, Larry?" the president asked. "Do you want to be chairman by yourself?"

"I'm not sure that's wise," Silberman replied. "I was appointed as a Republican. I'll be perceived as a Republican. I think there ought to be a co-chairman."

"I think so too," Bush said.

Bush, Cheney, Card and Silberman started to brainstorm for a co-chair who could give the commission some political balance and themselves political cover.

What about Chuck Robb? Bush suggested. Charles S. Robb was a former Democratic governor and senator from Virginia, and son-in-law of Lyndon Johnson. Robb had been a Marine captain in Vietnam, and as a senator for 12 years, from 1989 to 2001, he had served on each of the key national security committees—Foreign Relations, Armed Services and Intelligence.

Robb was viewed as a moderate, even conservative Democrat. He was known in Virginia as an almost-Republican. He had supported the 1991 Persian Gulf War and criticized President Clinton's decision to rule out using ground troops in Kosovo in 1999.

The president called Robb, who agreed to serve.

Bush, Cheney, Card and Silberman then reviewed some lists of names to fill out the commission. Silberman knew they would need at least one real, liberal Democrat and so he suggested Judge Patricia Wald, a Carter appointee with whom he had served on the federal appeals court. The two were ideological opposites, but Silberman said he had enormous respect for her.

"Zeal, intelligence, courage and integrity," he said.

"Well, it's your pick," Card responded.

Later, when Karl Rove heard about the Democrats on the committee, he was taken aback.

"Pat Wald?" Rove joked to Bush in disbelief. "Don't you remember, Mr. President? Back in the antediluvian age, she was a Commie."

Bush told Rice that he didn't want a congressional investigation that resembled the Church and Pike committees after Watergate in 1975–76 that exposed CIA and NSA spying on U.S. citizens, drug testing and assassination plots of foreign leaders including Cuba's Fidel Castro. The president thought those investigations had been witch hunts. They had demoralized the CIA and had wound up limiting presidential power.

THE DEMOCRATIC LEADERS in the House and Senate wanted to model the WMD investigation on the 9/11 Commission created by law, with the president and Congress each appointing half its members. Massachusetts Senator John F. Kerry, who was emerging as the leader in the race for the Democratic nomination for president, called for an independent inquiry into the WMD intelligence.

"It goes to the core of why the nation went to war," he said. "If there is that kind of failure, the kind of separation between the truth of what the CIA tells the White House and what happens, then we have to separate that investigation from the White House so the American people get the truth."

The president was not about to lose control of the investigation. At 1:30 P.M. Friday, February 6, he took the podium in the White House press briefing room to announce that he was signing an executive order appointing nine people to the Silberman-Robb Commission. They would have broad authority not just to look at Iraq WMD intelligence, but to study WMD intelligence worldwide and look at all U.S. intelligence capabilities and organizations.

Bush then added, "Members of the commission will issue their report by March 31, 2005." That would be five months after the presidential election.

"IT WAS CLEAR AND UNDERSTOOD that we would not be asked to evaluate the administration's use of the intelligence," Silberman later recalled. "And frankly, if that had been the charge I wouldn't have wanted the position. It was too political. Everybody knew what the president and the vice president had said about the intelligence. They can make their own judgment as to whether that was appropriate or fair or whatever."

A few Democrats expressed outrage at the limitation. Representative Henry Waxman, a California Democrat and 29-year veteran of the House, said the commission "had been told to ignore the elephant in the middle of the room, which is how the intelligence was used and misused by President Bush, Vice President Dick Cheney and other senior administration officials." Senator Harry Reid, the number two Democrat, said the commission had been designed "to protect the president."

PRINCE BANDAR WAS BACK in the Oval Office on Friday, February 20, 2004, to meet with Bush, Rice and Card. The Saudis had received a message from Saddam's wife, who was in Jordan, asking for permission for herself and her daughters to visit the holy site of Mecca in the Saudi Kingdom. It was going to be approved but the visit would be kept secret.

Next Bandar reported that the Crown Prince was committed to his political and economic reforms. He would expand participation by all Saudis. "But we are asking that America should ease on continuous rhetoric on this issue in order for the Saudi individual not to think that we are doing this because of pressure from the United States," Bandar said.

Bush repeated his appreciation for the Crown Prince's vision and efforts on democratic reform. "Maybe the speed of this process could be sort of expedited," Bush said, agreeing that the reforms had to be homegrown. He then thanked Bandar for what the Saudis were doing on oil— essentially flooding the market and trying to keep the price as low as possible. He expressed appreciation for the policy and the impact it could have during the election year.

On a new and important subject, Bush said that the United States had a program of $3 billion in aid to Pakistan. General Pervez Musharraf, Pakistan's president, was in a precarious position. On December 11 and again on December 25, Musharraf had almost been assassinated.

"Pakistan is in desperate need of 26 helicopters that cost about $250 million," Bush said. "Since putting the program through Congress could take a very long time," he asked his friend, "the Crown Prince, if he could pick up the tab for these helicopters."

The Bell helicopters, model 412EP NVG-compatible, are ideal Special Operations aircraft for tracking terrorists and potential assassins—in other words, Osama bin Laden and Musharraf's violent opponents. They are helicopters with a track record, used by the British and Canadian armed forces.

Bandar said he would have to convey the request to the Crown Prince.

Four days later, the Pentagon gave Bandar a detailed briefing on the helicopter fleet. The written briefing pitched Bandar. "These aircraft will provide operational service and support to further U.S. and allied strategic interests in the region." The Crown Prince soon agreed and Saudi Arabia paid $235 million for 24 of the Bell helicopters for the Pakistan army, including a training and maintenance program, and technical representatives and spare parts, according to Saudi records.

The Saudis had honored special requests from American presidents before. In the 1980s, Reagan's national security adviser had asked Bandar to arrange for about $22 million in covert funding to the Nicaraguan contras, Reagan's favorite "freedom fighters," after Congress had cut off contra funding. Now the request was not, at least in this case, for covert money, but the price of friendship and doing business was higher, 10 times higher.

BREMER HAD FOLDED on the issue of Saddam's old army by February 2004. He told a leading Iraqi, "The Coalition has no principled objection to former army personnel. About 80 percent of the New Iraqi Army and Civil Defense Corps are former soldiers. All officers and NCOs are." The officers and noncommissioned officers were the ones that Bremer and Slocombe had been worried about. Allegedly they had the Baathist connections. Now *all* of the new army's leadership came from the old army.

That same month, General Abizaid proposed at an NSC meeting that he begin embedding U.S. forces in Iraqi military units. The U.S. troops could provide the leadership, intelligence and communications.

"Don, that's great," the president said, turning to Rumsfeld. Bush said they should make a big deal of this publicly because it would show that they were shifting the burden of the war to the Iraqis—exactly the theme he wanted emphasized. "This is terrific." Bush next turned to Dan Bartlett, "Bartlett, I want a—"

"Oh, Mr. President, I haven't approved this yet," Rumsfeld interjected. He was very worried about vetting the Iraqi units who would be getting U.S. troops. In other wars American officers had been "fragged"—killed by their own troops. What kinds of safeguards could they put in place to keep U.S. troops from being fragged by insurgents or other enemies in Iraqi units? "It's a recommendation to me and when I'm happy with it, I'll bring it to you, Mr. President."

"Okay," Bush said. "I understand, but when you approve it, if you do approve it, let me know so that we can take proper advantage of it."

Frank Miller of the NSC staff had been sitting in on the meeting, and afterward he tracked down Hadley.

"Steve," he said, "we are embedding people in Iraqi units." He was in touch with officers in Iraq and it was already being done, even if it wasn't an official program at the Pentagon level.

"No," Hadley said, hoping it wasn't true.

"Steve, trust me. It's Frank. I'm talking to people who know what's going on. We are doing this."

"Okay," Hadley said. "Thank you."

Later, Miller was talking with one of the four-stars in the Pentagon. "Why won't Rumsfeld approve this thing?" the general asked. "Is the president putting his thumb on this and saying, 'Don't do it'?"

"No, quite the contrary," Miller said. "The president wants to go. The president wants to take advantage of this."

Rumsfeld eventually more or less approved of the embedding, quietly. It later became the major U.S. method of upgrading the combat capability of the Iraqi troops. The news slowly made its way into some newspaper stories, but it did not get the rollout or public relations big bang Bush had wanted.

RICE WAS HUNGRY for data and intelligence. She wanted to know what was really happening Over There. She kept telling Frank Miller, "Get me more. Bring me more."

In March 2004, she sent Miller to Iraq to find out what things were really like. He went as her representative, but he tried to downplay his NSC credentials. Not helpful, he thought. He wanted to avoid polished-up presentations calibrated to impress and perhaps mislead visitors from Washington. He never asked to meet with Bremer. He didn't think it would be useful, but also he didn't want to risk being turned down. Such was Bremer's perceived independence from NSC oversight.

Miller was struck by how the Coalition Provisional Authority had become a hermit city, ensconced in the Green Zone. He explained to one CPA official how he planned to fly around the country to visit with the U.S. military division commanders who were in charge of the tens of thousands of U.S. troops.

"Wow," the CPA official said. "I wish we could do that. I wish we could see the country."

It was telling, Miller thought. There was a sense of lethargy, like a bunch of basketball players passing the ball back and forth, back and forth, all reluctant to take a shot. It's March and the turnover is set for June, he thought. Quit passing and launch one at the basket.

Miller and the two people he'd brought with him—retired Army Colonel Jeff Jones from the NSC, and an active-duty Army colonel from the Joint Staff—linked up with the 1st Armored Division in Baghdad, where the deputy commander, a one-star general named Mark Hertling, was an old friend of Miller's from his Pentagon days. The group joined a Humvee patrol through an area just south of the notorious Shiite Baghdad slum, Sadr City. Screaming poverty, Miller thought—no fresh water, few working sewers. People were living in hovels and throwing trash and human waste in their front yards.

American soldiers in Sadr City and elsewhere now seemed to be acting as much as engineers as infantrymen, setting up water distribution points and improving some roads. But the only money to fund these ad hoc projects came from the military's emergency funds, called the Commander's Emergency Response Program (CERP). Miller made a note that they would need to expand and expedite these CERP funds—walking-around money for the battalion and brigade commanders—as they were the only expenditures that seemed to have a visible impact on the population.

It was striking, Miller thought, that the Iraqis he saw seemed generally friendly, or at least not antagonistic. Little kids came running out, smiling, saying hello, and giving them a thumbs-up sign as they moved through. It wasn't the middle finger, he noted, not realizing that in Iraq the thumbs-up sign traditionally was the equivalent of the American middle-finger salute.

Miller went on to Tikrit, where the 4th Infantry Division was operating, and where Saddam Hussein had been captured three months earlier.

The division's senior officers said they believed they had broken or captured much of the senior leadership of the insurgency. The mere fact that Iraqis were talking to the Americans was a promising sign, and they were getting better intelligence from Iraqis, lots of walk-ins with good information. Nobody seemed to want a return to Saddam. The divisions were setting up the Iraqi Civil Defense Corps, using their emergency funds—the CERP money again, Miller noted—to buy weapons and uniforms.

Everywhere, Miller found that the Iraqi units suffered from a desperate shortage of vehicles and communications equipment. And the Civil Defense Corps—whose first mission was to guard valuable infrastructure like banks and other buildings, thus freeing up better-trained forces for more difficult duties—was a creature of the individual U.S. military divisions that parented them. One division had a one-week training program, another a two-week program, and a third had extended it to three weeks. It was ridiculous. Earlier that year, Miller learned, a two-star general had sent a report to Defense practically begging for national standards for the new Iraqi corps, but it hadn't happened.

Miller recorded in his notes the comment of one division commander: "What's wrong with Baghdad?" the commander said, meaning Bremer's CPA. "Why won't they give us money to do this, and to do the reconstruction projects that need to be done?" Building Iraqi units, both police and military, and rebuilding the country's infrastructure were prerequisites to an exit strategy for the U.S. But there was too little money, too little coordination to do the job right.

Iraq looked and felt like a war zone. Attacks had climbed again, to about 1,000 a month. Every soldier Miller saw carried a weapon. A mess hall Miller was eating in was attacked with mortars. When he flew in helicopters, the door gunners kept their weapons pointed down at potential targets. Miller wore a flak jacket, and he and his two aides traveled under the watchful eye of an earnest young lieutenant of field artillery from Kansas who was assigned as his escort officer. When they moved on the ground, it was in convoys with Humvees and big sport utility vehicles, a machine gunner on top of the Humvees and the escort officer with his M-16 pointed out the window. It was good on the one hand—Miller felt pretty safe—but then he thought, "We ain't winning any hearts and minds this way."

From Tikrit, Miller flew on to Kirkuk, where he linked up with a brigade from the Hawaii-based 25th Infantry Division. He checked out an Iraqi police station where the U.S. Army was trying to train Iraqis to become real police. Fairly impressive, Miller thought, but he also heard more about the thousands of Iraqi teachers who had been fired under the de-Baathification order. It was a real catch-22, because in Saddam's Iraq, all teachers had been required to join the Baath Party.

Miller headed down to the city of Basra, at the southeastern tip of Iraq, which was under U.K. control. A British two-star and a lieutenant colonel gave him what he considered a happy-face briefing about their great success teaching the local Iraqi police how to patrol. The local cops couldn't read the English-language maps they got from the British, they said, so they memorized their patrol routes: Come out of the station and turn right, walk 10 blocks to the marketplace, turn right, go 15 blocks to the mosque, turn right, that sort of thing.

The British officers took Miller over to the Iraqi police station for another briefing by a British captain.

"Tell me," Miller asked an overweight, elderly Iraqi police brigadier. "What do your men do when they come to work in the morning?"

The Iraqi said, "Well, they come in and they have a coffee and they sit here until I tell them to go out and arrest somebody."

Miller shot a glance at the British two-star and lieutenant colonel. "Hey, guys, this is what Saddam did," he said. "You give me all this bullshit about how you've reformed the police. You haven't done a goddamn thing."

Miller moved on to meet with the Polish commander of the Multinational Division, made up of troops from 23 nations. This was the shakiest part of the coalition—but an important fig leaf to suggest that the war was a broad international effort.

The Polish division commander told Miller, "I've got 23 separate national units. They have 23 separate rules of engagement. I pick up the phone, I tell the colonel in charge of the Spanish Brigade what to do. He picks up his phone, calls Madrid, and says, 'I've been told to do this. Is it okay?' "

Miller understood that this meant the Multinational Division had little or no fighting capability.

IN THE GREEN ZONE on his way out of the country, Miller tried to locate the CPA bottlenecks. One basic problem was that Bremer and Lieutenant General Ricardo Sanchez, the ground commander who had replaced General McKiernan, were not really speaking. Bremer was trying to deal with the internal Iraqi politics and the reconstruction effort, while Sanchez was supposed to deal with security and the violence. Bremer kept saying that the central problem was the lack of security—Sanchez's job.

Sanchez asked to see Miller for dinner.

There's a big problem in communication, Miller told Sanchez. I've spent a week with your division commanders, and they don't all have the same understanding of what their authority is. One thought he could fire bad cops. Another thought he had the authority to run his own psychological operations. A third thought he had to clear everything with Baghdad. With all these new divisions coming in, Miller suggested, "It might be useful to you if you promulgate your standing orders again for the benefit of the new guys."

Sanchez said they were having trouble getting the money that Congress had authorized for reconstruction projects in Iraq—billions of dollars. He turned to Colonel Jeff Jones, who was accompanying Miller, and said all the talk from Washington had too little follow-through. "Prove to me that Iraq is the number one priority, because I don't see it from here," Sanchez said.

In a week in Iraq Miller figured he'd seen more of the country and had a better sense of what was going on than most of the CPA people who'd been there for months.

27

MILLER REPORTED to Rice and Hadley. "There's a lot of urgency outside the Green Zone, but I did not find a sense of urgency inside the Green Zone. It was slow, it was unresponsive, it was ineffective." He read from his notes: "Bremer didn't delegate and he doesn't have time to do everything." One general summed things up nicely, Miller said: "Bureaucracy kills."

He quoted a commander talking about the Commander's Emergency Response Program. "If I don't do it with CERP it doesn't get done," adding that it was vital to keep the CERP program going after the handover of sovereignty.

Though Bremer tried to control things, on so many issues, Miller said, the staff at CPA was playing to run out the clock. They kept deferring to the Iraqi Governing Council, which was slow or stagnant in making decisions—communications, regulatory policy, police code of conduct, hiring former officers, firing the Kirkuk teachers. It was always the same story. People in the CPA are tired, bitter and defeatist. There are few problem-solvers there, and the Iraqi ministries aren't much help.

"We need to pick our top 10 issues," he advised, things that needed to be accomplished before the handover of sovereignty was scheduled to take place.

He made five additional points. First, they shouldn't underestimate how many Iraqis were watching Al Jazeera on satellite TV. Electricity is a problem, he added, not just because they didn't have enough of it, but because to Iraqis it was seen as something that should be free.

Second, Sanchez and Bremer aren't talking. And Sanchez and his division commanders aren't communicating effectively enough.

Third, CPA never leaves the Green Zone. Their regional offices in all 18 provinces outside Baghdad are worth their weight in gold, but the folks in the Green Zone were not doing anything.

Fourth, de-Baathification is a mess. There are some good people with only tenuous Baathist connections who are not being allowed in, Miller said. He wasn't sure whether it was the CPA or the de-Baathification group run by the nephew of Ahmed Chalabi who was responsible, but Chalabi was hoarding files from the old Iraqi intelligence service—a prime source of information on who had been a true-believer Baathist under Saddam—making it almost impossible to determine levels of involvement.

Fifth, they needed to put contracts on a wartime footing. CPA was sending out requests for proposals with 90-day timelines. That was pointless, bureaucratic busywork. In 90 days, CPA would be nearly extinct.

Miller repeated his briefing to most of the deputies on the NSC, including Armitage and Pace. He talked with Scooter Libby, hoping his most salient points would make their way to the vice president.

At the Pentagon briefing for Wolfowitz, it was standing room only, with lots of straphangers from Feith's policy shop and the CPA-Washington liaison. There's not a single person in this room who will do a thing about what I have to say, Miller thought, even if they believe it. The problem as always was implementation.

He started putting these items on the deputies committee agendas. How do we cut contracting time? How do we get more CERP funds for military commanders? Can't we standardize the training for the Iraqi Civil Defense Corps? How do we weed out the bad apples so we have a better, saner, quicker de-Baathification process?

"I will fix it," Rice told Miller. She called Bremer. "You will give the division commanders more money." The division commanders got another billion dollars in CERP funds.

RICE SAW THEY HAD to get the United Nations reengaged in Iraq. Earlier, she had resisted Jay Garner's push to internationalize the postwar phase, but now she saw it was necessary. The U.N. had pretty much withdrawn from Iraq after the terrorist attack on their headquarters that had killed 22, including their top envoy, Sergio Vieira de Mello.

Bob Blackwill was handed the U.N. task. Not surprisingly he found that Cheney and Rumsfeld were not enthusiastic at all. "We'll get the U.N. in," Rumsfeld warned Blackwill, "and we'll lose control."

"Yeah, but I think we can manage it," Blackwill insisted, and he went on a recruiting drive. He zeroed in on Lakhdar Brahimi, a former Algerian foreign minister who had headed the U.N. mission in Afghanistan for two years. In Blackwill's view, Brahimi, a 70-year-old secular Sunni, was a world-class diplomat, the kind of person who could really help with everything from funding, to stability to elections.

"Absolutely not," Brahimi said, when Blackwill solicited his help. Brahimi detested the American approach and did not want to become an enabler of or spokesman for U.S. Iraq policy.

Still, Blackwill kept up the diplomatic courtship. In January, Brahimi became top adviser to Secretary General Kofi Annan on peace and security. Though he resisted focusing primarily on Iraq in his new job, Blackwill and Rice invited him to the White House to press him to help with Iraq. Powell dropped by during the visit, and Bush made time to talk with Brahimi too.

The wooing worked, and Brahimi and Blackwill went to Iraq. The two men virtually lived together there for three months. As sovereignty was about to be transferred, Brahimi warned Blackwill that something would have to be done for the Sunnis, who had run things under Saddam. They were used to their privileges—the first group of positions in the military academy, the medical schools and just about everything else. "If you got all these exiles," Brahimi said, referring to the Shiites likely to rule, "none of whom have any real political roots in this country, this thing is going to turn into a terrible mess."

Blackwill tried to reach out to the Sunnis, who were really only a fifth of the population, and keep them involved. In one meeting with a key Sunni leader, he said, "I want to reassure you that it's our intent that the Sunnis in this new Iraq have in every dimension a status and privileges consistent with their role and number in Iraqi society."

"Mr. Ambassador," the Sunni said, formally addressing the former envoy to India, "you don't understand. We want to run Iraq."

It was a frightening moment for Blackwill, who sensed that it would take a generation or two to get the Sunnis adjusted to majority Shiite rule.

ON WEDNESDAY, MARCH 31, 2004, insurgents in the Iraqi city of Fallujah attacked a small convoy of sport utility vehicles, killing four Blackwater USA security guards working as independent U.S. contractors. The grotesquely disfigured and blackened bodies of two of the dead Americans were strung up from the steel girders of the main bridge across the Euphrates, nicknamed the Brooklyn Bridge by American troops. The widely broadcast images, with Iraqi crowds jubilantly celebrating in the background, became one of the ugliest symbols of the war, its horrors and the American impotence.

"We still face thugs and terrorists in Iraq who would rather go on killing the innocent than accept the advance of liberty," Bush said in a speech at a Bush-Cheney fund-raiser at the Marriott Wardman Park Hotel in Washington at 6:30 that night, adding, "This collection of killers is trying to shake our will. America will never be intimidated by thugs and assassins. We are aggressively striking the terrorists in Iraq."

Bremer promised, "Their deaths will not go unpunished." Fallujah, a city of about 250,000 on the Euphrates River some 50 miles west of Baghdad, was the heartland of bandit country, a place so rough even Saddam had not bothered to tame it. The city was now the epicenter of the Sunni insurgency. If the U.S. forces could take the city, they would hand the insurgency a major setback. Bush told General Abizaid, "Get ready to go," and said, "If this isn't resolved in 48 hours, you go."

Abizaid in turn passed the order to General Sanchez, the commander of U.S. ground forces in Iraq. The U.S. Marine units around Fallujah were to begin a full assault on the city.

For Bremer, it was unclear what was happening. He did not see the American military's operational messages. Worse, there was personal distance and a real communication breakdown between him and Sanchez. The two were from different worlds. Sanchez grew up poor in the small Texas town of Rio Grande City, on the border with Mexico. He and his five brothers and sisters lived in a one-bedroom house with no indoor plumbing at the end of a dirt road. Many days the only food had been beans and rice. But Sanchez pulled himself up, earning a math degree at Texas A&I and excelling in the Army.

Bremer, raised in tony New Canaan, Connecticut, and a graduate of Yale and Harvard Business School, was from the other side of the tracks. Intentional or not, "Jerry's patronizing elitism," as one person close to him called it, was palpable in his dealings with Sanchez.

Sanchez was the junior three-star general in the Army. He had been given America's most important ground command and had a small and inexperienced staff. In 2006, Rumsfeld acknowledged in an interview that he had not been involved in or even aware that such a junior three-star was being given the critical Iraq ground command. "I've asked people to think about it so that we don't repeat the mistake," Rumsfeld said. For about six months after the completion of major combat on May 1, 2003, Rumsfeld said, there were decisions being made—including the Sanchez appointment—that weren't visible to him. "I felt badly a year or so later when I started looking at all that stuff that had happened so rapidly without my awareness, and I honestly felt badly for General Sanchez. I think he ended up in a position that was difficult."

As the military prepared a full-scale assault on Fallujah, Brahimi issued dire warnings to Blackwill, threatening to pull out the U.N. mission if the Sunni Arab city was attacked. Brahimi was trying to help put together a sovereign government that could take over. An attack on Fallujah, he said, would crush any possibility of that because both the United Nations and the interim Iraqi Governing Council were against it. Losing the U.N. and the Governing Council could mean losing the country.

Rice understood the implications. If there were no government it would mean they could lose the war. The security problem and the political problems had finally converged. Bremer also voiced uncertainty. He couldn't judge whether an attack would blow up the political process, but the Sunni leadership made it clear they would walk, and if that happened they would be transferring sovereignty just to the Shiites. It was a nasty dilemma.

Bremer and Blackwill watched General Abizaid, who was Sanchez's boss, on the secure video conferences seesaw back and forth about whether to continue with a full attack.

"We've got to go do this now in a big way," Abizaid said at one point, "and get this over with because my guys, they're sitting ducks out there." They would lose the war if they did not clean out Fallujah, he said. "Forget the politics. We got to go do this. We're taking casualties." Then at the next secure video conference he shifted, saying "If we clean out Fallujah we're going to have an Arab revolt far beyond Iraq."

Blackwill was struck by how erratic and emotional the combatant commander was, totally schizophrenic.

Also at the NSC, Frank Miller found that Abizaid suddenly was not sounding like the commander in the field. "Maybe I shouldn't get ready," Abizaid told Miller. "Maybe we shouldn't assault the place."

Miller was so worried that Abizaid was losing his nerve that he called on his old friendship with Colin Powell.

"You've got to talk to John Abizaid," Miller said to Powell on the secure phone. "You've got to buck him up." Remind him that he is a soldier
and fighting a war, Miller recommended, and that it would be a terrible
mistake to pull back on Fallujah. It is not clear if Powell ever made the
call to Abizaid.

In Baghdad, Bremer's interim Governing Council started to come
apart. "We're leaving the Government Council for good," Adnan
Pachachi, a Sunni leader, told Blackwill. Brahimi again told Blackwill
that he would go home and pull the U.N. mission out.

Bremer and Blackwill got on the secure video with Washington and
warned the president. "We've got to stop," Blackwill said. They couldn't
hold the Governing Council together. It would shatter. Sovereignty was
supposed to be transferred to the council. Without it there could be no
transfer.

Bush began to backtrack. An attack might be dicey, he said. He began
reeling off questions, unusual for the typically confident Bush. Why
move now? Why not let the political situation develop? What about a
larger backlash against the U.S. elsewhere in Iraq? Bush never said,
"Don't do Fallujah now," but those in the room could read the president's body language and his newfound caution. A president can kill an
operation with questions, Bremer felt, and Bush's were in effect an order
not to attack.

Blackwill was pretty sure Bush was calculating the potential impact
on the presidential election. A cornerstone of his Iraq policy was the
transfer of sovereignty. The June 30 transfer date had been announced as
a sign of great progress. If there was no one to take the reins of government, Bush's policy would be in even more trouble.

The assault was called off, but the Marines were ordered to stay
around the city and lay siege, hopefully trapping the insurgents inside.

"We just can't let them melt away and leave Fallujah," the president
said. "At least they're inside there." It almost became a preoccupation for
him.

At the White House, Frank Miller went over the situation with Blackwill, who told him they were going to keep the Marines in place.

"We're taking wounded," Miller objected. "We're getting people
killed. You cannot maintain the morale of a unit by saying we're going to
encircle the city and just get shot at. You can't do it, Bob."

"Well, show me the numbers of killed and wounded," Blackwill said.
He was extremely skeptical that the casualties were high.

"Bob, you've not served," Miller said, aghast. "I was a naval officer. I have not served on the ground, but I know these guys. You can't expect them to live in the dirt with no showers for weeks at a time and all they're going to be doing is thinking, 'I'm a target.' "

Blackwill singled out some of the generals. "They don't know what they are doing," he complained at one point. "Why are we losing soldiers to IEDs?" Improvised explosive devices, or IEDs, were homemade bombs made from old munitions, artillery shells or other explosives. They were the terrorist weapon of choice. Insurgents camouflaged them ingeniously and hid them on roads, in mounds of garbage and even the carcasses of dead animals. They were the chief killer of U.S. personnel. "Why are we driving around?" Blackwill said. "We ought to get off the roads. What are the missions that these people are on that put them on the roads where they get blown up? Are they just driving from one place to another?"

"Bob, you have a force here, and a force here and a logistics base here," Miller said. "You have to resupply your posts."

"Let's do it all by air," Blackwill suggested.

Miller felt this suggestion betrayed a complete lack of understanding of what the troops needed and what life was like in a violent foreign outpost. A hundred mini–Berlin Airlifts all around the hostile Iraqi countryside would be eminently impractical.

At one point Blackwill and Bremer went out to the Fallujah region. For them the stand-down was a vivid example—the most dramatic example—proving that the United States simply did not have enough troops in Iraq. With more troops, Fallujah could have been taken fairly quickly, they thought, fast enough that they could have held the Governing Council together until it was over.

AROUND THE SAME TIME, the CIA came up with what seemed to be a middle course. A renegade Baathist two-star who had served in the Republican Guard said he could form a Fallujah Brigade of Iraqis and clean out the city. The general, Jassim Mohammed Saleh, appeared on television wearing a dark green uniform and beret. When Rice saw his pictures, she screeched, "Oh, God. He looks like Saddam Hussein! Can't they pick somebody who doesn't look like Saddam?"

The ineffectual Iraqi Fallujah Brigade eventually folded. After a few months, its members largely joined the insurgents.

· · ·

BLACKWILL KEPT IN CLOSE CONTACT with the Kurds in the north. Massoud Barzani, one of the two chief Kurdish leaders, told him that the United States had made a terrible mistake trying to draw the Sunnis into the political process. The Sunnis, so used to ruling in Iraq, had to be defeated and crushed. They had to be told they were going to pay a price for their brutality against the rest—the Kurds and Shiites. After the Sunnis were totally defeated and isolated, then and only then could the United States afford to be magnanimous, Barzani said.

The withdrawal from Fallujah was a serious strategic failure, Barzani said. "That was a disaster because you broadcast to every potential Sunni insurgent that they can wait you out, that if they cause enough casualties to you, you won't go through with it. There was an answer to this."

"Massoud, what was the answer?" Blackwill inquired.

"The pesh merga," he said, referring to the formidable Kurdish militia of some 50,000 or more fighters. "You should have just asked us to send 30,000 pesh merga to Fallujah. If your Marines couldn't do it, let the pesh go."

It was only several hundred miles from the Kurdish north to Fallujah.

"Well," Blackwill replied, "sounds to me like a recipe for civil war, the Kurds clean up Sunni Fallujah."

"Short term that may be a problem," Barzani agreed, "but it's not as serious as the long term—the lesson you're teaching these Sunnis, which is they can beat you."

Blackwill came to believe that the low troop level had another consequence. The professional Iraqi officers—the Sunni majors and lieutenant colonels in their late 30s and early 40s—had been stunned by their defeat and had been completely intimidated by the U.S. blitzkrieg. Rumsfeld's rapid, decisive warfare had worked. But Blackwill felt that the U.S. had not killed enough of the Iraqi officer corps. They had stayed out of the initial insurgency, but Fallujah and the steady growth of the violence and attacks had caused them to think this insurgency might have legs, and might put them back in the saddle. Now those who had been sitting on the sidelines were helping the insurgency or joining up.

"Unless this gets over pretty soon," Bremer told Blackwill, "we're not going to be able to finish."

Back at the White House and the NSC, Blackwill told Rice and Hadley that the NSC needed to do a military review. What was the military strategy? What were the military deployments and troop levels?

Rice voiced agreement and expressed immense frustration at Rumsfeld and the Pentagon, but never said she would force the issue. Blackwill, who still often referred to himself as Godzilla, was no shrinking flower. As Rice's former boss in Bush senior's NSC, he had an opportunity to press. But he didn't want to be so coarse as to ask, "Well, what are you going to do about it?" Rice had put up a slight wall, and Blackwill wanted to be careful not to be seen as trying to penetrate her relationship with the president.

Blackwill also pressed Hadley about the military strategy. "If we have a military strategy, I can't identify it," the deputy national security adviser said. "I don't know what's worse—that they have one and won't tell us or that they don't have one."

AND THEN THERE WAS poor Frank Miller, Blackwill thought, trying to find solutions. Miller was indefatigable, trying to help the troops in Iraq moving electrical generators or guarding pipelines or securing transportation routes. Blackwill figured he wasn't being paid enough to ever go to any of Miller's meetings. They were exercises in frustration and futility.

It had taken Blackwill a while to understand what was really wrong, but now he felt he fully comprehended. There was no way that Rice, Hadley, Miller or he could fix Iraq because they had no control over the real problem: There were not enough troops. Everyone got diverted, trying to solve derivatives of the real problem. But those problems couldn't be solved until somebody fixed the real problem of not having enough troops on the ground.

Instead of the top 10 to-do list he'd wanted after he had come back from Iraq in March, Miller's reconstituted Executive Steering Group now had a list of 90 things that were supposed to be completed by June 30, a few months away, when the transfer of sovereignty was scheduled. That's useless, he said again. We need to pick out the 10 most important. Chairing the ESG was frustrating. Defense was increasingly out of it. Feith sent a different person from his policy staff each time. When Feith came, he'd refuse to discuss issues, saying he hadn't talked with Rumsfeld about them and so, of course, he couldn't engage. Then he'd come back with Rumsfeld's inflexible position.

Miller thought he'd never seen a group of people less able to advance their own interests. In the field the division commanders knew what needed to be done, but they weren't getting support. Where is the chairman of the Joint Chiefs, Dick Myers? Miller wondered. Why wasn't

Myers pounding the table saying, "Why aren't my soldiers being supported?"

MILLER NOTICED THAT Rumsfeld had a short attention span at the White House meetings. Someone droned on about an issue, covering it thoroughly, and then Rumsfeld would suggest that they ought to talk about the same issue.

"He's a bully," Miller said to Rice one day.

"Oh, no."

"Condi, come on. It's me."

"Don's Don. We'll deal with it," she said one time. It was pretty clear to Miller that challenging Rumsfeld was outside her boundaries.

IN APRIL 2004, MY BOOK *Plan of Attack* was published. It reported that three months before the war, Tenet had twice told the president in an Oval Office meeting that the intelligence case on Iraq's WMD was a "slam dunk." The colorful scene of the CIA director raising his hands to mimic the basketball going through the hoop drew lots of attention. I had quoted the president on the record in the book confirming that Tenet had made such assertions.

Tenet called Andy Card and complained bitterly that sensitive Oval Office conversations were being quoted to a reporter.

Tenet shared his anger with Armitage.

"George," Armitage said, "it's over. It's gone. Someone reports it, it's the last thing you have to worry about.

"George," Armitage said, "I'm your friend. I'm not criticizing you. But this is Washington. One 'Aw, shit' wipes out ten 'Atta boys.' Period." It was nasty, mean, unfair, but true, and not something to worry too much about.

Tenet did worry. The trust was gone.

Tenet later claimed he did not remember saying "slam dunk," though he did not dispute it. He asserted that the meeting was to determine what intelligence could be made public to "market" the case for war. That is correct, as I reported in *Plan of Attack*. But a public case for war could hardly be a "slam dunk" if the CIA director did not believe that the underlying intelligence was also a "slam dunk." Obviously, Tenet had believed it was. Since the National Intelligence Estimate of three months earlier had flatly asserted that Iraq possessed chemical and biological weapons, it is not surprising that Tenet was a believer. He has a strong case when he asserts that his "slam dunk" assertion did not cause the president to decide on war. Tenet believes Bush had already made the decision.

A year after *Plan of Attack* was published I attended a public forum in Los Angeles at which Tenet was asked before a crowd of 5,000 about the "slam dunk" comment.

"Those are the two dumbest words I ever said," he replied.

28

I N LATE APRIL, *60 Minutes II* broadcast photographs of naked, hooded and even leashed inmates being piled up or harshly interrogated at Abu Ghraib prison in Iraq, as smiling American military guards watched. Seymour Hersh of *The New Yorker* published details of a secret Army investigation documenting the detainee abuse. Dozens of deranged and despicable prisoner photographs flooded television screens, newspapers and the Internet.

Rumsfeld and General Myers downplayed the importance. Rumsfeld stated publicly he had not looked at the pictures. "I think I did inquire about the pictures and was told that we didn't have copies," he said. Myers, on one of the Sunday shows, was asked if he had seen the Army investigation on Abu Ghraib. "I haven't seen that report," he replied.

"Bush Privately Chides Rumsfeld" was *The Washington Post* front-page headline on May 6, 2004. The story recounted that the president had admonished Rumsfeld over the Abu Ghraib scandal and that he was unsatisfied and unhappy with Rumsfeld's handling of the matter.

Rumsfeld wondered to his staff how in the hell anyone at the White House could possibly think it would help the president to have this kind of chatter and whispering campaign going on. There was always someone at the White House who thought it was high political art to have the president show he was tough with cabinet secretaries and could kick them around. How could it possibly help a war president to have his secretary of defense perceived to be in trouble or weakened, somehow suspect, lacking presidential "full confidence"? The president, and everyone, needed clarity. If it was time for him to go, then he would go, Rumsfeld said. He decided to force clarity.

The next day, May 7, the secretary testified in public before Congress. Asked if he would resign, he answered, "It's a fair question. Since the firestorm started, I have given a good deal of thought to the question." He also told the House Armed Services Committee, "If I thought that I could not be effective, I certainly wouldn't want to serve. And I have to wrestle with that."

The coy suggestion that he hadn't decided triggered calls to Rumsfeld's aides from the White House almost as soon as the words left Rumsfeld's mouth.

The next day *The New York Times* reported in its front-page story that Rice might not be unhappy if Rumsfeld resigned. An unidentified person close to Rice was quoted as saying that Rumsfeld "appears to have become a liability for the president, and has complicated the mission in Iraq."

Two days later, Monday, May 10, Bush went to the Pentagon and met with Rumsfeld, who offered to resign.

Just before noon, Bush appeared in public with Cheney, Powell, Rumsfeld and General Myers.

Turning to Rumsfeld, he said, "You're doing a superb job. You are a strong secretary of defense, and our nation owes you a debt of gratitude."

"I submitted my resignation in writing twice," Rumsfeld recalled in an interview. "He handed the first one back and he said, 'No.' And the second one he handed back and I handed it back to him and I said, 'You ought to keep this.' And he said, 'No.' You know, he did not want me to go. And he says this publicly."

I asked Rumsfeld what was in the two letters. "One was a relatively short letter, and the other was a relatively long letter." He would say no more.

WITH THE APPROACHING TRANSFER of sovereignty to the Iraqis, Powell turned his attention to opening an embassy in Baghdad. It was an opportunity, a treacherous one. Under normal conditions an American embassy means the State Department is the lead agency. But conditions were nowhere close to normal. It was hard to tell what might happen, and Powell wanted to be ready. Months earlier he had called in Armitage and Frank Ricciardone, the U.S. ambassador to the Philippines and a 26-year foreign service veteran.

"Look, this has got to be a full-court press," Powell had ordered, "and a very organized effort because these guys are leaving a mess and they're leaving it for us. And we've got to be ready by the summer to take this over and not screw it up."

Who should be the new U.S. ambassador? The White House, the Pentagon and Powell all began making lists.

John Negroponte, 64, the U.S. ambassador to the United Nations, decided he wanted the job. Negroponte was from the old school of foreign service. There was almost no one like him anymore. His role models were Ellsworth Bunker and Henry Cabot Lodge, the U.S. ambassadors in Vietnam who had slugged it out, fighting an insurgency and civil war. In his twenties, Negroponte had worked in the U.S. embassy in Saigon from 1964 to 1968, and he believed ambassadors were the executors of programs and policies made by others. He had been Powell's deputy when Powell was Reagan's national security adviser almost two decades earlier. Most of his 40-year career had been spent in the Third World. He had been U.S. ambassador to Honduras, Mexico and the Philippines. He was used to bad and ineffective governments. He thought Garner and Bremer had been a little starry-eyed in thinking that they could reconstruct the country quickly. The first order of business had to be reestablishing central authority in the Iraqi government.

He called Powell. "Diana and I have been talking about this," Negroponte said, referring to his wife. "I know you're looking for names, and I would do it if you asked me."

A volunteer! One of the unwritten rules in the Army Powell had served in for 35 years was never to volunteer. But he considered Negroponte a consummate diplomat. Being ambassador to the United Nations was hard duty in the Bush administration. Powell thought Negroponte had performed extremely well, working within the U.N. system, and listening to Powell's instructions. When it had looked to Rice that Powell and the U.N. ambassador were getting too international, she sent Elliott Abrams to watch Negroponte. Powell thought she was aiming to stiffen the spine of the striped-pants set.

"I can't stand this," Negroponte once told Powell. "I don't want it."

"John," Powell replied soothingly, "let him go up there. He'll see that you're doing your job. He'll be an occasional annoyance. But it keeps us from getting rudder checks all day long, which we would, if he wasn't there." Negroponte survived Elliott Abrams.

When Powell floated Negroponte's name at the White House, it was not immediately embraced. But he had done well in over two years at the U.N., and his standing at the White House had improved. The consensus was they had no one better, and besides, he had volunteered.

The president had one question for Negroponte: "Do you believe democracy is possible in Iraq?"

The ambassador gave a diplomat's answer. "I don't believe it's beyond the wit of man."

POWELL AND NEGROPONTE tapped James F. Jeffrey, the U.S. ambassador to Albania, for the number two position in the new embassy— deputy chief of mission—in Baghdad. Jeffrey had been deputy in the U.S. embassies in Turkey and Kuwait. A career foreign service officer, he had served eight years in the Army, including Vietnam. A 6-foot-3-inch Bostonian with a head of thinning white hair, and an amiable, lumbering gait, Jeffrey spoke quickly and directly. He had no love for the slowness of government bureaucracy.

Jeffrey went to Baghdad early so that he would overlap with Bremer for about six weeks before Negroponte arrived. He reported home, "We're standing up an embassy for this crazy goddamn CPA thing in the midst of this burlesque palace, being shelled every day—a really bad nightmare."

He immediately recognized that Bremer had an acrimonious relationship with General Sanchez, who did not want to play defense with the insurgency. The general resisted securing the route out to the airport and he didn't want to establish perimeter defenses. Jeffrey understood the U.S. Army was a highly offense-oriented organism that hated peacekeeping, civil action, training other forces and playing defense.

Jeffrey also recognized that the idea of an Iraqi army was a farce. Wolfowitz came to Iraq for a full review of the training of the Iraqi army. The U.S. had bought equipment packages for dozens of Iraqi battalions—machine guns, trucks, body armor—but the contract had been challenged in a U.S. court and delayed for six months. There was no Iraqi army.

Bremer and Sanchez were on the way out. After more than a year of talk, Rumsfeld had finally decided to put a four-star general in command inside Iraq and had selected General George Casey, the former director of the Joint Staff.

• • •

BY THE SPRING OF 2004, Wolfowitz was frustrated. As perhaps the chief neoconservative intellectual architect of the war, he had been on a yearlong crusade to get Rumsfeld to take the training of Iraqi security forces seriously. The secretary's resistance was maddening.

Rumsfeld said in a later interview that in the Pentagon, too many people thought that only Special Forces could do the training. "Every time I turned around," he said, the elite force was being dispatched for training missions. "There's no reason Marines and Army people can't train people," he added. "Then I said, 'Let's get contractors to do some of it.' " He had insisted that they not try to make the Iraqis as good as the U.S. troops. "It's not that they're going to end up winning the soldier of the year award at Fort Bragg. You've got too little time, too many people to deal with, too fast a turnover."

Wolfowitz had estimated once privately to Rumsfeld that the invasion would take only seven days. But he had suspected that former Saddamists and Baathists would conduct a prolonged guerrilla war. The former regime was pure evil in his view, a form of Middle Eastern fascism.

Wolfowitz made his first trip to Iraq in July 2003, and found security much worse than he had anticipated. The police were in need of a total overhaul. He met with General Sanchez, then the newly installed commander of the ground forces in Iraq. He listened as Sanchez rattled off a list of 10 problems. Number 10 was recruiting the new Iraqi army. Wolfowitz thought it was the most important. He was certain the training would take two to three years.

But Wolfowitz found that he could not get Rumsfeld to focus. As violence escalated in the fall of 2003, he pushed Rumsfeld. "Let's send a study mission out to look for the real requirements for Iraqi security forces," he suggested. Nothing happened. Wolfowitz thought the Iraqi police were as big a problem as the army, but he could get no movement from his boss. He spent about eight weeks trying to persuade Rumsfeld to send the study mission. When Rumsfeld finally agreed, Wolfowitz felt he practically had to hold Rumsfeld's hand when he signed the order sending Army Major General Karl W. Eikenberry, who had helped set up the new army in Afghanistan, to Iraq. In an interview, Rumsfeld denied this. "Oh, that's silly," he commented, adding that the only discussion was what level to train the Iraqis to. "I remember during the Vietnam War, I turned around and we were training people to be doctors instead of medics. And what the Vietnamese people needed were medics. They didn't need U.S.-style hospital care over there at that stage."

Eikenberry's emphatic conclusion was that a unified command had to be established for the Iraqi training mission. In April 2004, Army Major General David Petraeus was sent to Iraq and soon given his third star as head of training of the Iraqi forces. He had to start from scratch more than a year after the invasion.

In May 2004, Negroponte met with Wolfowitz before heading to Iraq.

"I'm afraid we may have made the same mistake that we did in Vietnam, where we didn't start Vietnamization until it was too late," Negroponte said. The Vietnamization strategy had been designed to transfer responsibility for the fight and the internal security to the Vietnamese. It had been adopted only late in the war by President Nixon.

"Well," Wolfowitz replied, "you've certainly put your finger on the right question. I don't think it's too late, but that's the issue."

Wolfowitz felt increasingly marginalized by Rumsfeld, who canceled several of his deputy's trips to Iraq. The reasons were never clear. Rumsfeld would say there was too much work to do. Before one trip, Rumsfeld simply said, "It's not necessary for you to go." His deputy felt he was more or less on his own. The Pentagon responded to the top guy, not the deputy, and that was what the top guy was demanding.

Once after Rumsfeld had canceled a trip, Wolfowitz arranged a virtual Iraq tour, with each of the major division commanders and their staffs giving him two-hour briefings on secure video conference. He came in on a Saturday about 6:30 A.M. and spent the day listening and questioning. The predominant theme was that the commanders were disappointed in the performance of the Iraqi security forces. The new army, police and even the border patrol needed better equipment, improved training and much more money.

In largely overlooked public testimony, Wolfowitz told the House Armed Services Committee that training Iraqis had been the central issue "even before the war." In the struggle with the insurgency, he added, "The key to defeating them all along has been getting Iraqis trained and equipped and capable of fighting them as quickly as possible."

Nobody on the committee asked why it had taken over a year to get this focus. Wolfowitz told close associates it was not just neglect but that Rumsfeld had blocked efforts to get the training up and running earlier.

"I can't understand it," Wolfowitz told one associate.

• • •

THE STAFF OF JUDGE SILBERMAN'S WMD intelligence commission conducted hundreds of interviews in the intelligence community, and also
relied heavily on the interviews of David Kay's Iraq Survey Group. Silberman and Robb agreed that only they would be allowed to see some
very secret intelligence. They would not share it with others on the commission. In an interview in 2005, I asked Silberman if Rumsfeld was
among those the commission interviewed.

"We had trouble getting Don to come over to be interviewed by the
full commission," Silberman said. He had threatened to subpoena him,
believing that Rumsfeld would not know the commission had no such
power, and Rumsfeld gave in. Rumsfeld was "particularly sensitive about
the fact that DIA had not exactly covered themselves with glory," he
said.

I said that some of the generals had doubts about WMD, and realized
before the war they couldn't prove there was any WMD at any one
site.

Silberman wondered who.

I mentioned Generals Abizaid, McKiernan and Marks.

"Interesting," Silberman said. "I'm sorry we didn't talk to them."

Tenet was willingly interviewed three or four times, Silberman said.
He concluded that Tenet had relied too heavily on a few pieces of intelligence from foreign services. "Poor George," Silberman said. "I mean, it
took him a long time in this process to try and figure out what the hell
went wrong, why they were so wrong, and how incredibly stupid some
of their decisions were."

John McLaughlin, the CIA deputy director, insisted that the failure of
the intelligence community on WMD was the result of "a perfect storm,"
that everything went wrong at once but it couldn't have been anticipated. "We thought that was garbage," Silberman said. "There were
some fundamental flaws. The very worst thing was the chemical stuff."
Analysts had looked at satellite photos of large tanker trucks in Iraq and
decided they contained chemical weapons. "It was a guess, a deduction.
It wasn't hard evidence but you could say that it was logical," Silberman
said. But then the analysts "concluded they were accelerating the
process because we saw so many more trucks. Nobody bothered to tell
the analysts that they saw many more trucks because we were running
the satellite more over them. That was almost like *Saturday Night Live*."

• • •

AS BREMER PREPARED to turn over sovereignty to the Iraqis, Powell and Rumsfeld got into another fight. The question was yet again: Who would be in charge? Powell and Negroponte would be standing up the first U.S. embassy in Baghdad since the 1991 Gulf War. Powell wanted State in charge.

Rumsfeld argued that with 130,000 troops in Iraq, this was not a normal situation. Back and forth it went. One contentious issue was the $18.4 billion that Congress had provided in the Iraq Relief and Reconstruction Fund the year before. This was the money for the key economic and infrastructure rebuilding. Rice and Hadley got involved in acrimonious negotiations between Powell and Rumsfeld.

Rice insisted it must be spelled out clearly. For the last eight months of Bremer's time in Iraq she had been his nominal reporting channel, though on paper Rumsfeld and Defense were supposed to be in charge. No more. She was not going to have the question of who was in charge subject to Rumsfeld's whim.

After direct intervention of the president, a three-page order was finalized. On May 11, 2004, Bush signed National Security Presidential Directive/NSPD-36. The three-page directive, classified SECRET, formally shifted responsibility for Iraq from the Pentagon to the State Department after the termination of the Coalition Provisional Authority and transfer of sovereignty to the Iraqis.

"Under the guidance of the Secretary of State," Bush's directive set out, the U.S. would be represented in Iraq by a "Chief of Mission"—an ambassador—who would "be responsible for the direction, coordination and supervision of all United States government employees, policies and activities in country except those under the command of an area military commander."

Though it was pretty standard language, it was a clear, defined shift to State in the midst of the war zone. If the model were to work, the new ambassador, Negroponte, and the military commander, Casey, would have to cooperate. To underscore this and make sure there was some foundation for their relationship, Bush threw a small dinner party for both men and their wives at the White House.

THE IRAQI INTERIM GOVERNMENT was about to be set up. Bremer and Blackwill were on the hunt for a leading Shiite to head it. The criteria included someone who was strong, could get along with the Sunnis and would be approved by Grand Ayatollah Sistani. Blackwill liked Ayad Allawi, 58, a physician, the son of one of the leading Shiite families whose grandfather had helped negotiate Iraq's independence from the United Kingdom in 1932. He had been exiled in Britain since 1971, and had survived an assassination attempt in England in his early 30s that was reportedly directed by Saddam Hussein. He had extensive ties to the CIA.

Blackwill-Godzilla became Allawi's campaign manager.

"The first prime minister of this new Iraq is going to have been a CIA agent for a dozen years?" Brahami asked Blackwill incredulously.

"Yes," Blackwill replied. "You would rather have an Iranian intelligence agent?"

Wolfowitz didn't like Allawi, as he was Chalabi's main rival, but Bremer supported him and persisted. "He's the right guy for Iraq," Bremer told Jeffrey, "but watch it. This guy is not a democrat." The secular Allawi was basically a reformed Baathist and didn't like what he called "the turbans"—the religious leaders. So the new leader of Iraq was to be a CIA man who was skeptical of democracy and had little influence with Sistani and the clerics, who held most of the power.

TRANSFER OF SOVEREIGNTY was scheduled for June 30, and insurgents were thought to be planning a wave of violence to mark the occasion. Bremer was especially worried about information that the attacks would include major sabotage of Iraq's oil pipelines and refineries. On June 1, Scott Carpenter, one of a handful of Coalition Provisional Authority staffers who had stayed with Bremer in Iraq the entire 14 months, proposed a novel idea: How much were they really going to accomplish in the next few weeks that was worth risking all the expected terror and violence on June 30? Why not just transfer sovereignty immediately, and catch the insurgents off guard?

Bremer liked the suggestion, but there were legal problems, the CPA and Pentagon lawyers said. An occupying power couldn't just pack up and leave under international law. Besides, there were all sorts of official events planned for June 30.

On June 17, Rice called Bremer to say the president wanted to go ahead with an early handover. But violence was running at about 60 attacks a day, and they were never quite sure it would be possible. By June 27, Bremer was pushing hard for the handover to take place the following day—two days early, enough to catch the insurgents by surprise. He called the president, who was in Istanbul with Blair and Powell for a NATO summit.

"Sounds good to me. Let's ask Tony," Bush told Bremer, and then turned to Blair. "Tony, what do you think?" Bush came back quickly. "Yeah, sounds good. Okay."

Bremer and Prime Minister Allawi made the official transfer just after 10 A.M. on June 28 in a simple ceremony in Allawi's office. By noon, Bremer had flown out of the country in a camouflaged, four-propeller Air National Guard C-130. The secret had been kept. Most of the CPA staff—many of whom were staying behind to work in the new U.S. embassy—knew nothing about the early transfer before it happened.

29

NEGROPONTE ARRIVED IN BAGHDAD the same day. His working assumption was that the task of bringing democracy was doable and that they had a better than 50 percent chance of defeating the Sunni insurgency. Jeffrey asked the military to make a slide with a map of Baghdad locating precisely one week's worth of insurgent attacks—red dots for rocket-propelled grenade (RPG) attacks, yellow dots for indirect fire, green dots for ground attacks. There were well over 100 dots on the map—just in Baghdad.

"John, this is your embassy compound," Jeffrey told Negroponte, handing him the slide when he arrived. The main issue was security. "We don't have it."

Powell and Rice had instructed Negroponte to take a light touch with the Iraqis. They had sovereignty. Don't play Jerry Bremer's proconsul role. Negroponte agreed and approached his job as a traditional foreign mission—diplomatic relations with a sovereign country. But he quickly found that even though Iraq had the trappings of a modern government and modern society, most things just didn't work. Transportation was a mess. All the basics were corroded. It was a Potemkin village. Agriculture was totally collapsed and the food-rationing system that depended on imports was chaotic. The U.S. embassy had to track letters of credit and soybean accounts through Lebanese and Turkish banks or people wouldn't get fed.

One of Negroponte's first actions was to shift about $3.3 billion of his funds from long-term electricity and water projects to more immediate needs. He gave General Casey $2 billion for security and some $200 million in CERP funds, which had an immediate impact because the American officers could hire Iraqis on the spot.

The shift was a shot in the arm for Casey and Petraeus. The ready money also helped cement the relationship between Negroponte and Casey. Casey decided to have two offices—one at Camp Victory at the airport and the second at the embassy, almost across the hall from Negroponte. Both were determined to avoid the conflict of what the old hands called the "Jerry and Rick Show," Bremer and Sanchez.

The availability of electricity was one of the most visible indicators of progress in Iraq, so during that summer of the American presidential campaign, the shaky electrical system was run hard. Availability steadily increased by some measures. Rice found herself quickly becoming an expert on Iraqi electricity. Preferably, clean natural gas would have been used in the generators. But what natural gas pipelines existed had been hit by the insurgents. Diesel was the fallback fuel and it was in short supply because the refineries were underproducing. So new generators were run on fuel oil, but that required that they be taken offline every few weeks for maintenance. By fall the system would virtually collapse, and one day it lost half its capacity.

ON JULY 15, 2004, Steve Herbits, Rumsfeld's one-man think tank, sat down at his computer and wrote a scathing seven-page report entitled "Summary of Post-Iraq Planning and Execution Problems." Though he discussed the postwar planning and policies, and Bremer, his real target was his friend of 37 years, Don Rumsfeld. The memo listed a series of tough questions:

- "Why didn't Rumsfeld supervise him [Bremer] the way he did Franks?"
- "Who made the decision and why didn't we reconstitute the Iraqi Army?"
- "Did no one realize we were going to need Iraqi security forces?"
- "Did no one anticipate the importance of stabilization and how best to achieve it?"
- "Why was the de-Baathification so wide and deep?"

"Rumsfeld's style of operation," Herbits wrote, was the "Haldeman model, arrogant," referring to Nixon's White House chief of staff, H. R. "Bob" Haldeman.

"Indecisive, contrary to popular image," Herbits wrote of Rumsfeld. "Would not accept that some people in some areas were smarter than he. . . . Trusts very few people. Very, very cautious. Rubber glove syndrome"—a tendency not to leave his fingerprints on decisions.

Rumsfeld was "often abusive" in meetings. "He diminished important people in front of others.

"He had a prosecutor's interrogation style. While he was trying to improve product—and his questioning almost always did—his style became counterproductive. . . . Summary: Did Rumsfeld err with the fundamental political calculation of this administration: not getting the post-Iraq rebuilding process right within 18 months?"

TENET WENT TO SEE BUSH alone in early June. He had to get out. His doctor had told him he was jeopardizing his health. He'd had a heart attack years ago when he'd been on the Clinton NSC staff.

Bush said he didn't want any member of his war cabinet leaving now, in the election year.

Tenet knew he and the CIA were targets. The Senate Intelligence Committee was investigating Iraq WMD, Silberman and Robb were investigating. The 9/11 Commission report was coming out soon. He insisted that he was out.

The president had no choice.

The June 4 *Washington Post* front-page headline read, "Tenet Resigns as CIA Director; Intelligence Chief Praised by Bush, but Critics Cite Lapses on Iraq War." Tenet had given a tearful speech at the CIA headquarters in Langley, Virginia, the day before, saying he was leaving because he wanted to spend more time with his wife and teenage son, who would be leaving for college the following year. He had been director for seven years, under two presidents, and had seen the agency for better or worse through both 9/11 and the Iraq and Afghanistan Wars. On July 11, he officially left office.

Eleven days later, the 9/11 Commission released its report. Among its many recommendations was the creation of a director of national intelligence who would oversee the entire intelligence community, including the CIA.

JUDGE SILBERMAN and some other members of the WMD commission felt they had been preempted by the 9/11 Commission. What was their purpose now? But if the commission pulled the plug on itself, the White

House would lose its political cover on the Iraq WMD intelligence issue just months before the U.S. presidential election.

Card called Silberman. "The president wants you to know that just because the 9/11 Commission came out with a report, he doesn't want you to stop." He suggested, "Can you give us some kind of structural analysis of the 9/11 report, its structural recommendations?"

Silberman and Robb wrote a memo addressed to their fellow commissioners on the 9/11 Commission's recommendations and sent it to Card. Soon afterward, Silberman and his wife were traveling in the western U.S. They stopped to have dinner at Cheney's house in Jackson Hole, Wyoming. "Enormously helpful," Cheney said of the memo.

"WE DON'T IMPLEMENT" was one of Hadley's refrains to Frank Miller. Implementation was the job of the various departments and agencies, like the Pentagon and State Department. The role of the National Security Council was to coordinate. If Miller couldn't get people to implement a solution to one problem or another, Hadley instructed, "Bring it to me, and I'll get it done at deputies," meaning the deputies committee. Miller thought that was a bit of a farce. Nothing ever got done at the deputy level.

Rice's refrain was entirely different. If things weren't happening through normal channels, she told Miller, "You know how to do it. You make things happen."

It was one of the many contradictions of daily life for Miller in the Bush White House.

One of the most inexcusable examples of failure to get things done, Miller felt, had to do with the classified Secret Internet Protocol Router Network (SIPRNET), which was used to store and communicate information about intelligence, operations orders and other technical data. The classified information on the SIPRNET had a caveat— "NOFORN"—meaning no foreigners were allowed access, a restriction that included even the British and Australian troops fighting alongside the Americans in Iraq.

At times it went beyond the absurd. British pilots flying American warplanes, F-117s and F-15Es, weren't allowed to read parts of the classified pilot manuals and maintenance manuals because they were marked NOFORN. In another case, raw intelligence data gathered by British operatives in Iraq was given to the U.S. intelligence fusion center that was supposed to merge all-source intelligence into one product.

The report came out and the British couldn't see it, let alone get a copy, because it was marked NOFORN.

Prime Minister Blair and Australian Prime Minister John Howard complained directly to the president about the issue several times. In July 2004, Bush signed a directive, supported by Rumsfeld and John McLaughlin as acting director of Central Intelligence, that said NOFORN would no longer apply to the British and Australians when they were planning for combat operations, training with the Americans or engaged in counterterrorism activities. Bush told Blair and Howard about the directive, saying, "I've just signed something out." Problem solved.

But Miller soon discovered that instead of giving the Brits and Aussies access, the Pentagon began creating a new, separate SIPRNET for them. The SIPRNET had years of information stored on it and the U.S. military didn't want to give it to the British and Australians. It could take years to sort and comb through it all. The president's orders were to put the British and Australians on the real SIPRNET, not create some new version for them.

The problem dragged on. Months later, it still wasn't fixed.

"WE'VE GOT A REALLY bad situation over here," General Abizaid told Armitage in frustration one day in the summer of 2004. "Can't win it militarily."

Armitage passed this on to Powell. Later, Powell came back from a video conference that included the president and Abizaid.

"He didn't say it here, what he told you," Powell said to Armitage.

"I know," Armitage said. Worse, when he sat in on NSC meetings, the principals were now talking about body counts. The number of insurgents killed was a regular feature of the briefings. Either Bush asked or the military just started telling him. It had a bad and familiar ring to Armitage and the other Vietnam veterans in the meetings.

Abizaid had told the president earlier that there were about 5,000 violent insurgents. "Mr. President, we've killed scads of them here, but I know that I told you at one time that there were 5,000 enemy," he later said, adding, "We've killed well over 5,000 of them and there's a whole bunch still out there." At still another point Abizaid said they had killed three times the 5,000.

When there was a big battle around the Syrian border, the president, looking for any sign of progress, asked, "How many did we kill?"

Wanting to show progress, Abizaid rattled off the number.

In 2003, a year or so before these meetings, I interviewed Vice Chairman General Peter Pace of the Joint Chiefs several times. What stood out during several sessions was his emphatic denunciations of body counts. "Not once in this building have we ever reported a number," he said. "Probably because guys like me from Vietnam know what happens when you start counting. You completely skew the way people think, the way folks on the ground operate. What we want the people on the ground to understand is that we want to get the job done with the least amount of killing, but with whatever is needed to be done to protect our own guys."

Body counts continued to be reported and used as a measure of progress.

IN AUGUST 2004, Frank Miller returned to Iraq, this time traveling with Pace, who was a Rumsfeld favorite.

Miller thought Pace was a wonderful man and officer, but found that he would not stand up to Rumsfeld. For four days the two men went around to Iraq's major cities and combat zones. On August 5, they stopped in at Camp Fallujah, where Pace pinned Purple Heart medals on seven Marines wounded in the seemingly endless siege. Miller kept asking the ground commanders at all levels the same question: What do you need?

The division commanders with between 10,000 to 20,000 men and women said: Translators. The brigade commanders with several thousand said: Translators. The battalion commanders with 600 to 800 troops: Translators. Small teams or platoons were being sent to search homes, seal off areas, knock on and break down doors without translators who could speak Arabic.

The shortage was unconscionable, Miller thought. If American troops and Iraqis couldn't talk to each other, the possibilities for misunderstanding were compounded. Monumental communication failures were occurring every day. Sometimes the troops on patrol might as well go in blind. Nothing could solidify the image of Americans as imperial occupiers more than teams of heavily armed soldiers with helmets and flak jackets careening around the country, unable to communicate, and seemingly uninterested in what the Iraqis thought, felt or wanted.

Miller was once again reminded of the value of ground truth. After they returned to Washington, he watched Pace, who had also got the message, expecting him to get the ball rolling. Nothing happened. Miller called Lieutenant General Walter L. "Skip" Sharp, the director of Strategic Plans and Policy, the J-5, on the Joint Staff.

"Translators," Miller said. "You need translators."

"No, we don't," Sharp said. "We need interrogators." His focus was on higher-skilled linguists who could not only speak Arabic but also knew how to elicit intelligence from captured Iraqis.

"Fine, you need interrogators," Miller said, but added that they also needed more basic translators.

"I'll talk to some of my people," Sharp promised. He reported back later that he had checked with some brigade commanders. "We're fine," he said.

"Goddamn it," Miller said, "you're not fine."

Finally the Joint Staff sent a brigadier general to Mosul to check things out before he was scheduled to become the second in command of the U.S. military in that region.

"I owe you an apology," the general later reported to Miller.

"Great. Why?"

"We need translators."

Miller wondered why an old civilian bureaucrat like himself on the NSC staff had to alert the military that they needed translators at the unit level. Kids were dying because of the shortage. He raised the issue with the commandant of the Marine Corps and the vice chief of staff of the Army, and finally with Rice.

"Fix it," Rice said. Miller was to use his authority, although sometimes he wondered what exactly his authority was. Getting translators was hard; it could take years to train them, years they didn't have. He decided the solution was to get the State Department to hold an international job fair for translators. It didn't have to be in Iraq. They could go to Algeria or Morocco. Translators didn't need security clearances; they just needed people to speak both English and Arabic. Send them to Iraq, he thought, quarantine them at night inside a secure compound, take away their cell phones. Use them for six months and send them home with a big bonus. Money would talk.

Months later, the problem still had not been solved. It was now worse than a scandal, Miller believed. "I think we fucked it up," he said later in growing despair. Still later, at the end of 2005, the "we" became an "I," and he put the blame on himself. "I failed and did not get it done," he said.

• • •

IN AUGUST 2004, Moqtada al-Sadr, the young militant Shiite cleric, decided to challenge the U.S. Grand Ayatollah Sistani, the real Shiite power center in Iraq, was in London for medical treatment, and Moqtada had infiltrated his people into the city of Najaf and eventually into the holiest of Shiite shrines, the Imam Ali Mosque.

Moqtada had always been a troublemaker as far as the U.S. was concerned, and about 4,000 U.S. Marines and Army troops surrounded the area and were getting closer and closer to the Shrine of Ali.

Arab and Muslim leaders called the White House and sent messages that said, in effect, "Whatever you do, do not attack the Shrine of Ali Mosque." Rice realized that an attack on the shrine would create such a problem with the Shiites that the United States would never be able to deliver on a unified Iraq. Her heart was in her throat. If that went bad, they might not be able to win.

Orders from Washington—the White House, the Pentagon and State—flooded into Baghdad. Negroponte was on leave, so General Casey and Jim Jeffrey attempted to juggle the mixed messages, which were variations of "Deal with the guy," "Don't inflame the Shiites," "Work it out—that's why we have embassies and generals."

Jeffrey met every night with Acting Prime Minister Allawi. The secular Allawi, who didn't like the "turbans," didn't want to let Sistani back in the country. Even if it meant storming the mosque, Allawi wanted to solve the problem without Sistani. "We've got to crush them," Allawi told Blackwill.

With clearance from Washington, Jeffrey told Allawi, "You can't do that." Sistani, the leader of millions of Iraqi Shiites, had to be allowed back into Iraq. Period. Please?

Allawi relented. His security adviser, Qasim Dawood, who had better relations with Sistanti, met the ayatollah when he came back through Basra in the south.

Casey ordered nearly every U.S. sniper team in the country to Najaf—Special Forces, Navy SEALs. They were cutting down dozens of Moqtada's men in the citylike compound around the mosque.

"Where the hell is John Negroponte?" asked Jeffrey, who realized it could be the whole ball game. Negroponte, who was in the Aegean Sea on vacation, was trying to get back. Allawi sent a soft ultimatum to Moqtada that Jeffrey thought was essentially a "they-win, we-lose" proposition. His anger was exceeded only by his nervousness.

Sistani then ordered a march on Najaf and the siege of the Shrine of Ali.

"What are you doing out there?" was the question that came in from the White House, Pentagon and State Department.

"We're kind of calling our shots from the huddle," Jeffrey answered, "and we think it's going to be okay. You've got to trust these guys."

In Washington, trust was hard.

Thousands descended peacefully on Najaf. Sistani got Moqtada to come in and talk, and they eventually negotiated a withdrawal from the Shrine of Ali. Jeffrey and Casey had to promise only that they would not kill Moqtada's forces as they moved out from the shrine. It looked a lot like victory to Jeffrey, who was once again reminded of Sistani's power. "As long as I can just urge policies that keep us close to Sistani, I'll look good," Jeffrey half joked. The president got the message. "Where's Sistani on this?" became his frequent question. "We need to find out. Go find out."

Moqtada retired for the moment to his power base in Sadr City, the northeastern quadrant of Baghdad with its 2 million people.

FRANCES FRAGOS TOWNSEND, a 42-year-old former New York federal prosecutor, was appointed head of the Homeland Security Council in mid-2004, making her Bush's top White House adviser on counterterrorism matters. She was holding a number of meetings of the principals to address various sensitive counterterrorism proposals. Rumsfeld sent some second- or third-tier person. A 13-year veteran of the Justice Department, Townsend had learned that surviving meant avoiding unnecessary bureaucratic fights. She decided not to object, and continued with the meetings. About three weeks into her job, she had a meeting of the council with the president at which Rumsfeld laid into her. All these decisions were being made without his input, he said. He claimed that he had never received notice of the meetings. Townsend corrected him, saying that the notices had gone to the regular person in his office who received all such notices, citing the name and contact information.

Shortly afterward, Townsend received an invitation to a cocktail party at Rumsfeld's house. She asked Rice if she had been invited; Rice said she had not. The two women shared a good laugh about the necessity of going mano a mano with Rumsfeld.

Townsend had a more delicate counterterrorism issue to mediate. Over the years, Tenet had negotiated agreements with telecommunications and financial institutions to get access to certain telephone, Internet and financial records related to "black" intelligence operations. Tenet personally made most of the arrangements with the various CEOs of the companies. They were very secret, among the most sensitive arrangements, and based largely on informal understandings. Tenet had been very good at this, playing the patriot card and asking CEOs to help on matters of national security.

After 9/11, as the FBI got more and more involved in counterterrorism operations in the United States, their agents often went to the corporations with subpoenas to obtain the same or similar telephone, Internet or financial records. In addition, the new Department of Homeland Security, which had been created in late 2002 to bring together 22 federal agencies as diverse as Customs, the Coast Guard and the Secret Service, wanted in on this action.

The CEOs began saying, look, we'll do this once but not three times. The FBI's formal subpoenas tended to trump the other efforts.

The main conflict was between the FBI and the CIA. Part of the arrangement Tenet had made involved the CIA's National Resources Division, which had personnel stationed in a dozen major U.S. cities so that the CIA could interview and recruit foreigners visiting the United States. The NRs, as they were called, apparently were involved in making arrangements so other intelligence agencies, such as the National Security Agency, could get access to the information and records the corporate CEOs had agreed to provide.

The conflict was so intense that Townsend called FBI Director Robert Mueller and acting CIA Director John McLaughlin to the White House and asked them to resolve the conflicts. She then met periodically with them until each appointed a senior official to coordinate so that corporations were not bombarded with multiple requests.

It raised a number of serious legal questions. The CIA was forbidden by law from gathering intelligence in the United States. One official I spoke with said that the arrangements made by Tenet gave access only to passive databanks from the American telecommunications and financial institutions. To gather specific information about specific individuals required either subpoenas, court-authorized FISA (Foreign Intelligence Surveillance Act) warrants or operations under the controversial executive order signed by President Bush after 9/11 called the Terrorist Surveillance Program (TSP), authorizing the National Security Agency to eavesdrop on international phone or Internet communications to or from suspected al Qaeda operatives and their affiliates.

Nonetheless, the Tenet arrangements were part of the murky world of intelligence gathering in the 21st century that raised serious civil liberties questions and also demonstrated that the laws had not kept pace with the technology.

POWELL AND ARMITAGE engaged in a private, running commentary about Bush, Cheney, the White House and what was really going on. Both wanted Bush to succeed, and they believed the Iraq War had to be won for the stability of the Middle East. A precipitous U.S. withdrawal would be followed by chaos. But what about adjusting the policy? they were asking. Shouldn't we all be more realistic?

"Don't they have moments of self-doubt?" Armitage asked Powell one day. Didn't Bush within his soul wonder if all this was right?

Powell said he had the same question. They always had self-doubt. They lived on it, mainlined it. If you didn't, Powell said, if you didn't get up in the morning wondering if you're doing a good enough job or if you can still hit the long ball, you're not worth much.

"Not worth a shit," Armitage said.

Doubt never seeped into the president's public rhetoric. And as far as Powell's and Armitage's experience went, he was the same in private.

Powell said Bush and Cheney didn't dare express reservations. Armitage agreed. "They cannot have any doubt about the correctness of the policy because it opens too many questions in their minds."

But the president was at the center. Armitage was baffled. "Has he thought this through?" Armitage asked Powell. "What the president says in effect is we've got to press on in honor of the memory of those who have fallen. Another way to say that is we've got to have more men fall to honor the memories of those who have already fallen."

I HAD EXPLORED THE ISSUE of doubt with Bush in several interviews. In December 2001, three months after 9/11 and several weeks after the apparent success of the first part of the war in Afghanistan, he volunteered at the end of an interview the following: "I know it is hard for you to believe, but I have not doubted what we're doing. I have not doubted what we're doing. . . . There is no doubt in my mind we're doing the right thing."

Rice and others had said that doubt was an essential ingredient in decision making because it forces careful reconsideration and readjustment. I pushed Bush on this again during an August 2002 interview at his ranch in Crawford. The topic was the Afghanistan War but he was, of course, heavily involved in secret planning for the Iraq War, which he would order seven months later.

"First of all," he said, "a president has got to be the calcium in the backbone. If I weaken, the whole team weakens. If I'm doubtful, I can assure you there will be a lot of doubt. If my confidence level in our ability declines, it will send ripples throughout the whole organization. I mean, it's essential that we be confident and determined and united.

"I don't need people around me who are not steady. . . . And if there's kind of a hand-wringing attitude going on when times are tough, I don't like it."

The initial tough times in the Afghanistan War really lasted for only a while. That was the brief time between public discussion of a quagmire and the quick collapse of the Taliban. In Iraq, though, the tough times—the violence, the deaths, the uncertainty, and all the signs of a quagmire—had lasted years, and were continuing.

IN THE RARE MOMENTS Rice had time to read, she read about the Founding Fathers to remind herself that the United States of America should never have come into being. In particular, she was affected by David McCullough's 1776, about the darkest times of the American Revolution. General George Washington wrote a private letter to his brother in which he reflected on the contrast between his public demeanor and knowledge of the dire circumstances. "Many of my difficulties and distresses were of so peculiar a cast that in order to conceal them from the enemy, I was obliged to conceal them from my friends, indeed from my own army," Washington wrote, "thereby subjecting my conduct to interpretations unfavorable to my character."

Rice maintained to colleagues that neither she nor the president felt any equivalent distress. "Tough sledding," she said, but Bush had told her, "I see the path on Iraq."

She often used football analogies to her inner circle. "You're going to get sacked once in a while," she said one time. "Once in a while you might have a fumble. But it's not as if anybody feels that we're down 25 points with no time-outs and one minute, 34 seconds to go."

•　•　•

BUT THE REALITY of Iraq was escalating violence. Enemy-initiated attacks against the coalition and Iraqis had numbered around 200 in June 2003. By the summer of 2004 they were around 1,750 per month, nearly a ninefold increase, according to the classified summaries given to top officials. This information was not necessarily concealed from the public, but it was certainly not emphasized, and the reporting on it was not regular. News reports on TV and in the newspapers tended to focus on the big, spectacular attacks that killed dozens or more. But the disturbing truth was that Iraq had become a country where normal now meant nearly 60 attacks a day.

30

SOON AFTER THE TENET RESIGNATION, Andy Card called Armitage to see if he was interested in taking over the CIA.

No, Armitage replied emphatically.

"Can I ask you the reason? We're disappointed."

Armitage replied that he could give the reason but he would prefer not to because it might hurt Card's feelings.

Card knew the problem for Armitage was Cheney and Rumsfeld. He nonetheless asked Powell if there was a way to persuade Armitage.

"You can ask him again," Powell replied, "but he doesn't fool around." An Armitage no is a no. "My personal view is he won't do it."

In Armitage's view, after "yes," the second best answer anyone could give you in the English language was "no." It was definitive. It would allow you to move on. In Washington, he felt, you were just tempting fate if you hung around very long. The time to leave was when you were at the top of your game, when everyone was saying, "Man, you're the man." By that standard Powell and he had already stayed too long.

Armitage concluded that the penalty for disagreement in the Bush White House was an implied or explicitly stated accusation that you were not on the team. If he or Powell said something might be harder than it looked, Rice or Hadley judged them not on the team. If they said, as they had, "Maybe the Iraqis might not like it if we occupy their country very long," that meant they were not on the team.

Powell was getting about 20 minutes a week with Bush. In theory they were supposed to meet alone, but Cheney was often there. The vice president wouldn't say a word, but afterward, Powell was convinced, Cheney would offer Bush one version or another of "He's not on the team."

Powell and Armitage understood that the White House saw the State Department and its diplomats as appeasers. Cheney, Rumsfeld, and Rice to some extent, would not allow State to engage in diplomacy because diplomacy was considered a weakness.

"Their idea of diplomacy," Armitage said to Powell once, "is to say, 'Look fucker, you do what we want.' "

Nonetheless, because Iraq had consumed so much attention, money, military force and political effort—sucking the oxygen out of everything else, as Powell had warned Bush six months before the war—the result was that the United States had no choice but to engage in diplomacy. It was about the only tool left, for example, in dealing with North Korea and Iran.

ON AUGUST 11, President Bush nominated eight-term Florida Congressman Porter Goss, the 65-year-old chairman of the House Intelligence Committee, as the new CIA director. Armitage ran into him soon afterward. Poor Porter, he was thinking.

"What's a nice guy like you doing sitting in a place like this?" Armitage asked.

"I thought you were going to take this job," Goss replied, "and I could avoid it."

"No way," Armitage said. "I've been on the inside too long. Porter, you never take a job where you don't know who your boss is going to be."

Under the new intelligence legislation, the director of national intelligence would outrank the CIA director. Goss and his successors would report to the DNI—whoever that might be.

DAVID KAY TESTIFIED before Congress on August 18 about the Iraq WMD intelligence. There was plenty of blame to go around, he said, but his most pointed criticism was of the NSC and by implication Rice.

"The dog that did not bark in the case of Iraq's WMD program, quite frankly in my view, is the National Security Council," Kay testified.

The next day, Kay's testimony was in the newspaper. He'd barely read the story when he got a call from Robert Joseph, the NSC staffer for weapons proliferation, who worked for Rice, asking him to come by for lunch. Kay and Joseph had known each other for 15 years.

"This conversation never took place," Joseph said when they sat down. He tore into Kay. How could he have testified about Rice like that? She was the best national security adviser in the history of the United States.

"Well, she could have stopped trying to be the best friend of the president and be the best adviser and realize she's got this screening function," Kay said. When Tenet insisted the WMD case was a "slam dunk," she should have followed up aggressively, demanding a full reexamination of every last shred of the "slam dunk" evidence.

Joseph was adamant. Rice had done all she could. The intelligence community and CIA had befuddled her, he said.

Kay figured Joseph had been sent by Rice, and there was nothing to be gained by shooting the messenger. He was amazed at how sensitive she was.

Kay was unmoved. "She was probably the worst national security adviser in modern times since the office was created," he said.

MEGHAN O'SULLIVAN, the young Oxford Ph.D. who had been temporarily kicked off Jay Garner's team at the urging of the vice president's office, had turned out to be a survivor in both Baghdad and Washington. After her on-again, off-again, on-again experience in Garner's group, she'd made it to Iraq. She, Scott Carpenter and Roman Martinez were among Bremer's closest aides, and among the very few staffers who worked for him in Iraq throughout the entire history of the Coalition Provisional Authority. After the transition of sovereignty, she came back to the White House with Blackwill to work on the NSC staff.

"So," she said to Miller when she arrived, "I understand I'm supposed to take over all of Iraq someday,"

"Maybe," Miller said, chafing a bit, "but I'm still here."

Miller started to get complaints from some of his contacts in the Pentagon, sources he'd cultivated over three decades in government. He confronted her. The DOD was his turf. "I stay out of your business," Miller said. "You stay out of mine." He soon concluded that O'Sullivan was very bright, but that she knew little about security, reconstruction or how the military fights wars. She was another policy person, he thought. With the rise of the Iraqi militias, the private armed sectarian groups, she had an idea: "Let's just draft the militia into the Iraqi army," she proposed.

"Meghan, that's a really bad idea," Miller said. The militias were not controllable. They worked for sectarian leaders or clergy like Moqtada al-Sadr.

Every night, Miller and O'Sullivan put together Bush's Iraq situation report. It was short—a page or two maybe, never more than four—spelling out key developments on Iraq's politics, reconstruction and military issues, and always including the most recent casualties. O'Sullivan had personal relationships with many Iraqi leaders after her time with Bremer, and she would have long phone conversations with some of them. Miller noticed that she included what she'd heard from them in the presidential briefing.

These wily old sheiks are playing her for all she's worth, and it's going directly and unfiltered to the president, Miller thought. He decided to drop the penalty flag and went to Hadley, who seemed to understand his concerns. She's very bright but she has some significant flaws and she needs management, Hadley agreed. He said he'd figure out a way to put someone over her, to keep her in line. But it didn't happen. Soon she was her own boss and the senior NSC staff person for Iraq. Miller was astonished.

IN AUGUST 2004, the number of enemy-initiated attacks jumped by 1,000 over the previous month to 3,000, according to classified reports. Rice hated getting up in the morning and reading the newspaper. It was one bad story after another with the American presidential election just several months off.

"I feel like that little Road Runner character," she told her staff, "hanging on to a branch and spinning my little feet with news stories coming along and chopping at the branch."

In early September, White House communications director Dan Bartlett called a meeting of experts from the various departments and agencies to see what could be done to improve the message on Iraq.

Several suggested that the president carefully acknowledge some mistakes in Iraq, arguing that it is human and powerful to admit a mistake.

No, Bartlett said, closing the door, making it clear the president was not going to talk about mistakes.

"Do you want him to inspire or inform?" one of the generals at the meeting asked.

Both, Bartlett said.

"You probably can't do both," the general said. Informing people is often boring, and an inspiring message is more often rhetorical and not driven by facts. He cited former President Reagan, the so-called Great Communicator, who shied away from facts but could give uplifting speeches.

"Thank you," Bartlett said.

Bush did not have to refashion his message. Though it was his war, the communications spotlight was on his opponent, Senator John Kerry, the Democratic nominee, for his service in Vietnam as a Navy Swift Boat commander, and his votes in the Senate authorizing the war, and voting against $87 billion in war funding.

The president did not have to inspire or inform. He could hide in the fog created by the mismanagement of Kerry's message. Kerry, swimming in the past, defending his Vietnam and Senate service, never explained how he would use the power of the presidency. Bush had made it clear. He had used the power to go to war, and he was not going to back down.

NEWT GINGRICH came to the White House in early fall 2004 to talk with the NSC staff about Iraq. Here's what's wrong, he said, confidently rattling off his litany. Managers don't have flexibility. We're not addressing the root causes of people's concerns. We have not built sufficient inroads into the local populations. We don't have translators.

Translators, thought Frank Miller. There it was again.

Afterward, Gingrich spoke with Miller. "Were you not interested, or did you know everything I said to you? Because usually when I say these things people are surprised and react."

"No," Miller said. "I've been there twice. I've been doing this for eighteen months. You're not telling me anything I don't know."

CARD STARTED GETTING REPORTS that things were not going well at Langley under the leadership of Porter Goss. Goss was too often keeping a congressional schedule—leaving Washington Thursday night and returning Monday. Goss had chaired the House Intelligence Committee for seven years, and he had made his staff director on the committee, Pat Murray, the new CIA chief of staff. Murray was rubbing many experienced people in the agency the wrong way. So Card took the highly un-usual step of making an appointment to go see Goss at CIA headquar-ters.

"The president picked you to run the CIA," Card told Goss. "He didn't pick Pat Murray."

"He's just helping me out," Goss said.

Porter, Card said, you are separated from the building. Everything seemed to be going through Pat Murray. Get out of the office here on the seventh floor, go around and interact with the people in the building, eat in the cafeteria, show the flag, build up morale, slap backs, be a floor walker.

Good suggestions, Goss said.

Reach out to the former CIA directors—Bob Gates, even former Pres-ident Bush, 41. And talk with others such as Admiral William Studeman, who had been NSA director and deputy CIA director. "They're all talk-ing," Card warned. "Call them. Invite them over and solicit." Card felt he was just giving Goss basic leadership advice. Work closely with FBI Di-rector Bob Mueller, and build relationships with the Homeland Security and the Defense crowd.

Card told the president he had gone out to the CIA to give Goss some management training.

"Good, good, good," Bush said. "I'm glad you did that."

IN OCTOBER 2004, interim Prime Minister Allawi wrote to President Bush. Everywhere he traveled in Iraq, he was being ferried by big mili-tary aircraft with "U.S. AIR FORCE" painted on the side, Allawi said. It wasn't exactly the image of a free and sovereign Iraq that he or the U.S. wanted to project. Could he get his own plane?

The issue came up at an NSC meeting, and Bush made it clear he wanted Allawi to have his own planes. Afterward Frank Miller walked outside with the chairman and vice chairman of the Joint Chiefs.

"Make it happen," Myers said to Pace.

Weeks went by, and Miller hadn't heard anything, so he called some of his contacts on the Joint Staff.

"Oh, it's okay," was the response. "The Brits are flying them around now."

I can't make this stuff up, Miller thought. "No, that's not the point," he said. "The point is not the Royal Air Force instead of the U.S. Air Force." The point was to make Allawi's plane an Iraqi plane.

"Oh. Got it."

A few more weeks went by. Now the plan was stalled by the State Department, which was concerned about transferring sensitive U.S. military technology to a foreign government. Finally, at the end of December, they repainted three C-130s with Iraqi flags on the tails.

Myers thought that wasn't too bad a record. Three months was an accomplishment. But Miller thought it was ridiculous that it took this much effort to get a simple presidential order carried out in the spirit in which it was issued. The snail's pace was not because nobody gave a damn—though Miller thought it sure looked that way at times. It was because too often no one was made responsible and then held responsible.

Miller's complaints finally got some attention at the Pentagon.

Myers called to declare, "We've got a master plan."

Hadley went over to the Pentagon for a briefing, taking Miller and O'Sullivan with him. Skip Sharp, who headed the plans and policy directorate, gave them a presentation with 60 or 70 items that he said needed to be accomplished in Iraq. It was another ponderous list of basic infrastructure and security issues. Each item was marked with the familiar stoplight red, yellow or green, marking alleged progress.

At the end of the Pentagon meeting, Hadley said to Miller, "Here, Frank, take it. Keeper of the lists. Take it."

Miller knew that the State Department had a very similar list. So much of it was the same—worthy goals such as getting the electricity working, building sewer lines, and putting Iraqis back to work. Make sure that there are embassy representatives with each of the military commanders, the State Department list said, and that each embassy representative has someone from USAID with them. But the list never really got reduced to eight or 10 priority items.

PRINCE BANDAR AND HIS AIDE, Rihab Massoud, had half a dozen meetings with President Bush in 2004. Bush's deep religious convictions came up time and time again, as he talked about his faith and his relationship with God. The president made it clear that he felt no doubt that a higher authority was looking after him and guiding him. "I get guidance from God in prayer," he said, and mentioned a number of times that he had asked for, prayed for and received such guidance.

The Lord had played an important part in his life, Bush said, and prayer was a significant element of his daily routine. It helped him, he said, and gave him comfort. He made it clear that he felt the burdens that

God had put on his shoulders as president. Bush said he relied on his faith to carry him through.

Whenever Bush saw or talked with the Crown Prince he referred to their shared, deep belief in God. The Crown Prince sent Bush a prayer, which the president told Bandar he used.

"This is the most precious thing I ever got," the president said.

IN THE TWO MONTHS before the presidential election, Bush would be campaigning almost nonstop. Rice decided that either she, Hadley or Bob Blackwill would travel with the president wherever he went.

Since Rice was giving her own speeches around the country—a controversial role for a national security adviser—and Hadley was much more of the nuts-and-bolts NSC manager, the campaign travel duty often fell to Blackwill. He got up at 4:30 each morning so he could go over the President's Daily Brief with the CIA before Bush received it. Blackwill's focus was whether anything in the PDB could cause difficulty in the campaign. What was out there that might suddenly surface as an election issue? He gave special attention to intelligence reports on possible terrorist attacks in the U.S.

The daily campaign routine began after Bush heard the PDB briefing—which took 20 to 25 minutes before 7 A.M. Then he and his entourage headed out to Andrews Air Force Base. There usually were six or seven events scheduled, in as many as three states, with helicopters flying Bush from one event to the next. The stops were often an hour or less. Bush landed, made his speech, and then was back in the air.

Karen Hughes, Bush's longtime aide and communications adviser, spent the travel time writing Bush's remarks and rewriting his stump speech. Karl Rove would be pushing campaign strategy on the president, calibrating the impact of presidential visits in the key battleground states.

"If you go to this stop in Ohio you can catch the tip of West Virginia," Rove told Bush in one such instance.

Blackwill was struck that there was never any real time to discuss policy. In between the stops or in the air, whenever Iraq came up, it was always through the prism of the campaign. What had the Democratic nominee, Massachusetts Senator John Kerry, said that day about Iraq? What had happened on the ground in Iraq that might impact the president's bid for reelection? As the NSC coordinator for Iraq, Blackwill probably knew as much about the war as anybody in the White House.

He had spent months in Iraq with Bremer. But he was with the campaign only as part of the politics of reelection. Not once did Bush ask Blackwill what things were like in Iraq, what he had seen, or what should be done. Blackwill was astonished at the round-the-clock, all-consuming focus on winning the election. Nothing else came close.

In the days and weeks just before election day, violence surged in Iraq. The classified figures showed that the number of insurgent attacks in Iraq had soared over the summer, going from 1,750 or so in June and July to more than 3,000 in August. In September there was some hope, as the number of attacks fell to just over 2,000, but in October they were back up to about 2,500.

The violence was now 10 times worse than it had been when Bush landed on the aircraft carrier in May 2003 and declared that major combat was over. New Iraqi army and police units rolling out of training were being butchered. Insurgents were getting reliable intelligence and acting on it. In Diyala Province, about 100 miles northeast of Baghdad, insurgents dressed as Iraqi police set up a false checkpoint on October 23. They grabbed 49 new Iraqi soldiers off a bus, forced them to lie down, and executed them with bullets to the head. Between 30 and 50 percent of all trained Iraqi units melted away and went home.

It was clear to Blackwill that things weren't going well. For over a year he had been baffled there was no military strategy. Again and again, Bush talked about Iraq strategy in his campaign speeches, but never gave specifics. He talked about goals, expressed his optimism and determination, and gave pep talks. "We have a strategy that says to our commanders, adapt to the ways on the ground," Bush said in a September 23 speech in Bangor, Maine. "The way to prevail, the way toward the successful conclusion we all want, the way to secure Iraq and bring our troops home is not to wilt or waver or send mixed signals to the enemy. We can grieve, but we will not waver."

Blackwill had taught strategy at Harvard. Strategy involves a series of actions to achieve a goal and entails answering questions such as: What is going to be done? By whom? When? Where? How? The president, whom Blackwill liked and respected as a political leader, instead talked about winning and goals. But as Blackwill taught in his class, "Aspirations aren't strategy." The administration had no real strategy, he concluded.

Rice had made it clear that her authority did not extend to Rumsfeld or the military, so Blackwill never forced the issue with her. Still, he wondered why the president never challenged the military. Why didn't he say to General Abizaid at the end of one of his secure video briefings, "John, let's have another of these on Thursday and what I really want from you is please explain to me, let's take an hour and a half, your military strategy for victory."

Lack of a strategy in Iraq and the worsening situation on the ground never quite grabbed hold in the campaign. Part of that had to do with skillful politics. The public learned of specific, spectacular violence through news reports. But the real evidence of just how badly things were going—the data and trends on the violence, the number and the effectiveness of the enemy-initiated attacks—was all kept classified, hidden away from the voting public.

31

NOVEMBER 2, 2004, was one of the most important days of Bush's life. His comments, interactions and behavior on election day were well documented internally in the White House by aides, friends and note-takers. The day shows how Bush processed information, made decisions and responded to both bad news and good news.

BUSH CAST HIS VOTE early that day at the Crawford Fire Station, Precinct 80, near his ranch in Texas. He grabbed a cell phone to call his chief strategist and pollster, Matthew Dowd.

"Matty, what do you think will happen?"

"Mr. President, I think you will win by two to three percentage points."

"Really," Bush said. "As you know, I'm a five-point man." The latest polls had Bush and the Democratic nominee, Senator Kerry, dead even, at 48 percent each. But Bush had been saying he wanted to win by 5 percent. It was his gut sense.

"Yeah, I know," Dowd said. "I like your optimism, but I don't think that's going to happen."

"Well, we'll see," Bush said, ending the call.

On the surface, John Kerry had looked like a formidable opponent. A four-term senator from Massachusetts, two years older than Bush, he had won the Silver Star and three Purple Hearts in combat, commanding a small Navy Swift Boat in Vietnam in 1968 and 1969. But the group called Swift Boat Veterans for Truth had challenged Kerry's heroism and published a book, *Unfit for Command*, that rocketed to number one on the best-seller lists. Kerry and his campaign had failed to respond forcefully. As a senator, Kerry had voted to authorize the war in Iraq, and during the campaign he had not found a way to criticize it effectively. Overall, Kerry appeared uncertain and indecisive, while Bush succeeded in presenting himself in the campaign as consistent and tough.

After voting in Crawford, Bush okayed a final election day stop in Ohio before Air Force One headed back to Washington in mid-afternoon. On the presidential plane, Karl Rove took a call from Dowd around 3 P.M. as the plane descended through the clouds on its final approach to Andrews Air Force Base in Maryland. The connection broke up but was soon reestablished on Rove's cell phone.

"It doesn't look good," Dowd told Rove, reeling off numbers from the first wave of exit polls—a sampling of voters leaving key precincts. Rove cradled the phone in his neck and tried to scribble on a piece of paper balanced on his knee.

In Mississippi, a linchpin of the solid Republican South, Bush was up by only one percentage point, according to the exit polling. Pennsylvania and New Hampshire were worse. Bush was down 17 and 19 points respectively, where pre-election polling had shown him down by a point or two at most. Other exit numbers put Bush up by a single point in the heavily Republican state of Virginia, and said the race was too close to call in Colorado and Nevada.

"God damn," Rove said. "How can this happen?"

Dowd was trying to answer that question himself. "It's one of two things," he said. "Either these things are totally screwed up, or we fundamentally misunderstood the electorate, and I don't want to say it's the second because that would say that we really didn't know what we were doing." They would be legends, guilty of campaign malpractice.

Rice, who had traveled with Bush for the last four days of the campaign, saw that the exits had her home state of Alabama listed as "plus-1" for Bush. Alabama was one of the most reliable Republican states, and Bush was up by only one point? Polls had put him ahead comfortably by double digits in Alabama. She walked out of Bush's cabin so she wouldn't have to see the president, and headed toward the back of the plane.

"I didn't want to be in the same room with the president at that moment," she later told colleagues. "I just didn't."

Rove walked in the opposite direction, toward the front cabin, as Air Force One touched down.

"I've got numbers," Rove told Bush, "and they don't look good." He read them off. He was being factual and careful, but then he added, hedging, "Some of them just don't make sense."

"I don't believe it," Bush said. "What do you make of it?" he asked when he'd caught his breath.

"I don't know," Rove replied, adding that he had not gone through the exit poll data in detail. "I've got to wait until we get to the White House and look at the numbers. It's the first wave. They are generally unreliable but something's—either we're going to get blown out or something's fundamentally flawed with these numbers."

"Well," Bush said coolly, "let's see what happens. We've been through this before." He didn't have to mention the 36 days of turmoil after the 2000 campaign, before the Supreme Court settled the election in his favor. Victory in Florida had been by only 537 of 6,138,765 votes cast in 2000. "I'm going to tell Laura and the girls," the president said.

One of his twin daughters burst into tears when he told her the news.

"Look, I want you to have faith," the president said to his family. "Let's everybody get a smile on their face. The night's not over."

As they flew by helicopter from Andrews to the White House, Bush realized the media had seen the same exit poll data. The cameras would be looking for the live action shot of faces betraying anguish or defeat— the killer photo or film telegraphing the raw emotions of bad news.

"Everybody put their game face on," the president directed.

AT THE WHITE HOUSE, Chief of Staff Card had also seen the same exit poll data, and he and a few other staffers were waiting to go out and greet the president as he got off the helicopter.

"There are smiles on all our faces," Card told the others as they stepped outside.

"Great to see you," Card said to the president. Card had the biggest, most over-the-top smile on his face. "Great day. What a great day!"

"Did you see the numbers?" Bush asked as they went inside.

"Yes," he said, "I've seen the numbers. I don't believe the numbers. And not only that, you don't believe the numbers. So we are well positioned."

"What's going on?" Bush asked. "What's going on?"

Card and Rove went off to huddle, and the president followed. Card said again he didn't think the numbers were credible.

"Don't worry about it," Card told Bush. They would try to learn more. "Don't get your mind in this game. It'll be all right."

The president said he didn't want people around. "I'm going upstairs," he said, meaning the White House residence. He and Laura had invited a dozen friends and family members to spend the night at the White House. Blair House, the auxiliary guesthouse across Pennsylvania Avenue, was filled with other friends. Local hotels were stuffed. He didn't want to see them all yet. "I'm not ready," he said. "I'm not ready."

RICE WENT STRAIGHT from the helicopter to her West Wing office suite. Hadley was shocked at her appearance. He had seen Rice about 20 times a day, almost every day for four years, through 9/11, the Afghanistan War, the Iraq War. Through good times and bad times, she had always seemed to live up to the nickname her staff had given her—the Princess Warrior—and always seemed to have it all together. But now Rice looked as bad as Hadley had ever seen her. She even had a slight break in her normally near-perfect posture. Hadley, who was marvelously clueless about political Washington and had few media contacts, didn't know about the exit polls. He followed Rice into her office and closed the door.

"Condi, what's wrong?" he blurted.

"We just saw the early polls, and they're not good," she said. They were really alarming, in fact, pointing toward a blowout win for Senator Kerry.

THE PRESIDENT'S PARENTS, former President Bush and First Lady Barbara Bush, were among those staying at the White House for the night. One of the longtime Bush family friends found Barbara Bush.

"Look, we are so thrilled to be here," the friend said, "but I know the kind of tension this night is. They need their privacy."

Barbara Bush seemed to agree. She reported that her husband, the former president, now 80, was so nervous his stomach was flaring up.

At 5:10 P.M., the elder Bush dropped by to see Rove. What was happening? he wanted to know.

Rove said the exits did not seem right at all. The exit poll firms were polling a greater percentage of women than were actually voting, Rove said, and they were accounting for more late deciders than there actually were. At 5:18, the president called Rove, interrupting his briefing.

Rove repeated his conclusions.

"Well," Bush said, "we'll see soon enough."

No, no, no, thought Rove. Everything, every argument and analysis he could make told him these numbers had to be wrong, really wrong. But no matter how methodical his thoughts, he couldn't quite stamp out the doubt. It made no sense to him, but who could know? The numbers could be right. He realized if he was ever in his life going to have a heart attack, it would probably come in the next few hours.

At 5:20, the older Bush left to wander about his former residence and offices. Six minutes later, Rice popped in.

"Bad, bad, bad!" Rove exclaimed. "I'm so pissed off I can't see straight."

MICHAEL GERSON, the president's speechwriter, was sending e-mails to some of the top people in the Bush campaign at around 6:30 P.M., asking what had happened. Gerson, a 40-year-old evangelical Christian who had majored in theology at evangelist Billy Graham's alma mater, Wheaton College in Wheaton, Illinois, had written all of Bush's memorable post-9/11 speeches, including the one he gave at Washington's National Cathedral on September 14, 2001—"This conflict has begun on the timing and terms of others. It will end in a way, and at an hour of our choosing"—as well as his remarks before a joint session of Congress on September 20, 2001: "Americans should not expect one battle but a lengthy campaign." Gerson had written Bush's 2002 State of the Union speech identifying Iraq, Iran and North Korea as an "Axis of Evil" connecting terrorism with weapons of mass destruction, and had also come up with the intellectual and historical roots for Bush's "preemption" doctrine speech, delivered at West Point in June 2002—"The war on terror will not be won on the defensive." He knew it was his duty not only to have Bush's victory speech ready, but also to have ready what he called "the second speech." The contingency concession to John Kerry was designed to be gracious. Gerson was very proud of the first line in his draft. Bush was to say, "I just received a call from my opponent who is no longer my opponent. He is president-elect of the United States."

AT 7:35 P.M., with the polls beginning to close in the East, Rove moved to the high-tech campaign War Room set up in the Old Family Dining Room on the first floor of the White House residence. Five large flat-screen TVs dominated one wall. Rove installed himself at the end of a large table in the center of the room. He had a large map of the United States on his computer screen. All he had to do was hit a state and up would pop the latest Bush and Kerry numbers. Next a map of that state would appear. He could hit any county in that state and retrieve the numbers flowing from campaign aides and local Republican officials in county courthouses and election centers throughout the country.

Bush senior arrived in the War Room at 9:14 P.M. He was nervous.

We're leading in Ohio and Florida, Rove reported. He'd just been on the phone with Florida Governor Jeb Bush, who reported they were beating their targets in his state. With the polls closed everywhere but six Western states, Rove surfed on his computer, tapping into the key counties around the major cities. Rice was there, working as a kind of clerk, consulting Rove's book of goals and the 2000 performance in the counties as he called them out.

"Time to spin," Rove declared. He called various key TV reporters about Ohio. "We're outperforming the percentage of vote in every city from 2000, and they're underperforming," Rove said.

The president came down, and Rove took him through the numbers in the main counties that showed he was winning Ohio. Bush left, but at 9:50 P.M. Rove called him again.

"We're going to win Ohio," Rove reported confidently.

"Keep looking at it," Bush ordered.

About an hour later, just before 11 P.M., Card phoned Kerry's campaign manager, Mary Beth Cahill, to see if he could give the Kerry campaign a nudge.

"I don't know what your numbers are showing, but our numbers are showing that we're going to win. And if your numbers are showing that, we should probably think about scheduling a phone call. Do your numbers show that?"

"No," Cahill said politely. She made clear the Kerry campaign's numbers didn't show that.

"Okay, I am not pushing," Card said. "I am not pushing. That's it."

At 11:29 P.M., the president, wearing slacks and a shirt without a necktie, came back into the War Room.

"The election that will never end," Bush said. He said he was "so tired," and he looked it. The night lacked the kind of hard-count clarity he wanted. The network performance was particularly outrageous, he said. No one had called Florida for him even with 95 percent of the precincts reporting. Almost unbelievable.

At 11:40 P.M., ABC News called Florida for Bush. Rove's War Room erupted with cheers.

At 12:29 A.M., Bush's anxiety flared. "When will it end?" he asked Rove. He wanted to go to the Reagan Building, where his supporters were gathered, and declare victory. When could he go?

"Maybe within the hour," Rove said. Less than 10 minutes later he said that Ohio was now assured. But the networks still weren't calling it.

At 12:51 A.M., Card decided that the numbers were sufficiently clear and overwhelming. "Congratulations," Card said, turning to Rove, "we just won the election." He and Rove hugged. Rice and Rove hugged too.

After 1 A.M., Card called Cahill again.

Cahill said the Kerry campaign felt confident.

Card was caught a bit off guard. "Okay. Do you think we're going to do— Is there going to be a phone call?" He meant a concession call from Kerry to Bush.

"We won't be calling you," Cahill replied. She seemed to be half asking whether Bush would be calling Kerry to concede.

Among the close Bush friends at the White House was Mary Matalin, 51, Queen of the Republican Sound Bite and the outspoken longtime communications expert for the Bushes going back nearly two decades. Most recently she had been the communications director for Vice President Cheney for several years. Both the former president, 41, and current president, 43, hugged and embraced her when she arrived.

Matalin is married to James Carville, a Democrat who had been chief political strategist for Bill Clinton in 1992. He was not directly involved in the Kerry campaign but was still very plugged in. She called him.

"Look, I know this is hard for you," she told him sympathetically.

Carville told her he had some inside news. The Kerry campaign was going to challenge the provisional ballots in Ohio—perhaps up to 250,000 of them. "I don't agree with it," Carville said. "I'm just telling you that's what they're talking about."

Matalin went to Cheney to report.

What? the vice president asked. Federal law required that provisional ballots be provided to people who showed up to vote but whose names could not be found on the registration rolls. They could be checked later in a close election. If there were really 250,000 provisional votes, they might change the result in Ohio or at least tie the result up for days or longer.

"You'd better tell the president," Cheney told her.

Matalin and Cheney located Bush and the three went off to sit down in a corner.

"They're going to contest it," Matalin said.

"What does that mean?" the president asked. He had his note cards with talking points in hand, ready to go over to the Reagan Building to declare victory.

Matalin said somebody in authority needed to get in touch with J. Kenneth Blackwell, the Republican secretary of state in Ohio, who would be in charge of any challenge to the provisional votes.

At 1:30 A.M., Mary Beth Cahill released a statement. "The vote count in Ohio has not been completed. There are more than 250,000 remaining votes to be counted," she said, referring to the provisional ballots. "We believe when they are, John Kerry will win Ohio."

At the White House it looked like Carville had given Matalin good information. While two major networks, NBC and Fox, had called Ohio for Bush, the obvious implication was that it was not over.

By 1:49 A.M., Rove was on his cell phone with the Nevada secretary of state's office. A Bush victory in the state would be announced in 20 minutes. Barring a contested election in Ohio, Nevada would put Bush over the top.

Rice was listening in. A Bush win seemed surer than ever. "Congratulations," she said to Rove, "after all we did to screw it up."

ABOUT 2 A.M., Jim Francis, who had been chairman of Bush's two successful races for Texas governor, was alone with the president off to one side on the second floor of the White House residence. They had been friends for 34 years, beginning in 1970, when Francis had been the 21-year-old scheduler for Congressman George H. W. Bush in his unsuccessful run for a Texas Senate seat.

"George," Francis said to the president, "I've just got to tell you, you're the toughest son of a bitch I've ever seen. No president has ever had so many guns lined up at him. The 527s"—the independent campaign organizations that financed massive TV advertising—"the national press, the diplomatic corps, every Democratic interest group, plus the Democratic National Committee, plus the Kerry campaign. The whole world was trying to take you down. And you beat them all."

Bush mumbled a thank-you. Tears welled in his eyes, and he threw his arms around Francis in a bear hug. Francis realized that it was the way George W. Bush saw himself: tough and resolute, standing strong against the world.

Bush was soon on the phone again with Rove. It seemed to Rove that the president was calling every two or three minutes now. If it was true that he had won, Bush wanted to know, why wasn't the rest of the world—television, Kerry—abiding by reality?

Rove promised to get back to the president after he matched more hard numbers with his expectations in key counties and states. "He's going insane," Rove said to Susan Ralston, his assistant, who dutifully recorded the remark in her notes at 2:16 A.M.

Bartlett talked with one of the vice presidents at Fox News Channel, the conservative cable television outlet whose ratings were soaring and whose CEO, Roger Ailes, had been Bush senior's media consultant. Ailes was being careful this night not to talk with the White House directly. But the network official Bartlett spoke with was relaying a message from Ailes for Rove. In 2000, Fox had been the first network to call the contested state of Florida, and thus the election, for Bush. This time, the message from Ailes was "You don't want me to be the first one to call it."

Matalin and Scooter Libby were talking about sending Cheney with Bush over to the Reagan Building, where their supporters were gathered for the expected victory party. He'd have to be alert and ready to speak.

"Go get him somewhere where he can sleep," she said. "Don't send him home."

Cheney went into his office to sleep, while his wife, Lynne, went to rest in the White House doctor's office.

"Keep me apprised," Libby requested of Matalin when she went to the War Room.

"Just come down and keep yourself apprised," Matalin replied. "Because this has a lot of moving parts."

Bush came back down to the War Room, pacing about and waiting. At 2:35 A.M. he was watching Dan Rather on CBS. In September, Rather had reported in a *60 Minutes II* segment that Texas National Guard documents showed Bush had received favorable treatment when he had joined in 1968. The documents turned out to be apparent forgeries.

"CBS is horrible," Bush said.

At 2:43 A.M. someone noted that Bush was ahead 3.8 million in the popular vote nationwide.

"If the popular vote made it," Bush said snidely to Rove, "I wouldn't be here."

"We're ahead in the electoral vote," Rove reminded the president.

Bush took a call from British Prime Minister Tony Blair. It was morning in London, and Blair had gone to bed thinking Bush was going to lose. He was frankly stunned that Bush was still in the race, let alone a likely winner.

"Latest I've been up since college," Bush told Blair. "I need one more state."

Rove reported that they would get a proposed statement from Blackwell in Ohio within the next half hour. Blackwell, a former black-power-saluting student leader who had shifted to the Republican Party, was a lone ranger who shunned party discipline.

"I'm the president of the United States," Bush said fuming, "waiting on a secretary of state who is a nut."

He paced the room, hands in his pockets, chewing nervously on his cigar. Rove said that the Associated Press was going to call Nevada for Bush.

"Can I get my coat?" Bush asked sarcastically.

In Ohio, Blackwell reported there were likely no more than 175,000 provisional ballots, making it almost impossible for Kerry to overcome Bush's lead of about 140,000 votes. But Blackwell still wouldn't call it.

Reports came in that the networks wanted to go off the air without calling the race for either candidate.

Rove shouted, "They can't go off the air!"

At 3:36 A.M., a very sensitive communication from the Kerry camp was relayed to Rove and Bartlett at the White House. Mike McCurry, Clinton's former White House press secretary and a last-minute addition to the Kerry campaign, had e-mailed Nicole Devenish, the Bush campaign communications director, an off-the-record congratulations, advising that the Bush team should not try to force a resolution now. Don't pressure Kerry, McCurry said. In the end, he believed Kerry would do the right thing.

Bartlett and others told Bush about the e-mail, summarizing the message as "We'll do the right thing at the right time." They could trust that McCurry would be in a position to know what the Kerry campaign was thinking, Bartlett said, but they had to be careful not to put too much stock in it. At least we know there are people in the Kerry camp giving rational advice, Bartlett said.

Bush again declared that he was tired. "I'm not going to stay up all night," he said. "Come and wake me when you know what's going on."

"What should we do?" Rove asked Card at 4:24. "Networks won't announce."

Card said they should declare victory. He was worried about a vacuum, about another Florida. This was a battle being fought on many
fronts, and second only to the hard numbers was the perception battle.
"We know we won. We should declare it."

They woke the president and got him on a speakerphone with the War
Room.

CARD AND JIM FRANCIS made it clear they thought the president should
go to the Reagan Building and give his victory speech. It would be a kind
of preemptive strike. Otherwise the media would peck the situation to
death. They had to fill the vacuum. Provide the news. Make the headline
"Bush Declares Victory!" The declaration would become reality.

Francis weighed in strongly. "The Democrats are going to attempt to
turn Ohio into Florida, and act like it's a 500-vote difference instead of
150,000 votes." They could not let it wind up in limbo—litigation, re-
counts, court fights. The margin of 140,000 to 150,000 votes in Ohio
was not a landslide, but it was a lot more than 537—the deciding margin
in Florida in 2000.

Rove had earlier been in favor of making the victory speech, but now,
at about 4:30 A.M., he reconsidered. What was the point? Who was the
audience? The people in the Reagan Building? Everyone else was asleep.

Matalin, who had been sleeping on the floor in the War Room, woke
up about 4:40 A.M. Within five minutes she joined the debate.

"What's the pivot?" she asked. If Bush went out now and declared
victory, the press would wonder what had changed in the last hour or
two. They would ask, "Why now and not an hour ago?" The media might
latch on to it. The absence of a reason could become part of the story
line. What would they say?

Steve Hadley had been summoned to the War Room from the Roosevelt Room, where he had been waiting and watching, occasionally running up to Rove's office to check in. Usually a model of caution, Hadley
weighed in. A preemptive declaration of victory would be the worst
thing the president could do, he said. Don't jam Kerry. Don't pressure
him. Over the next two or three hours the numbers that Rove had seen
would be clear to Kerry. The margins were sufficient, even big, in Ohio.
"If you jam him, the lawyers will go and it's a mess."

Bartlett agreed. It was exactly the advice they'd received from
McCurry. The president should stay put. The validation of victory had

to come from either the media, preferably television, or even better from a Kerry concession. Bartlett then threw up a giant cautionary flag.

"John Kerry, for seven hours or so, was president of the United States in his mind," Bartlett said, "and was being treated like it and acted like it, I'm sure."

"Don't jam him," Hadley repeated.

"He's right," Matalin interjected. "He's absolutely right."

Jim Francis continued to argue passionately for an immediate declaration of victory. They had to leverage the 150,000-vote lead. Two TV networks found it sufficient. Another legal hell had to be avoided. Don't jam Kerry? That was exactly what they needed to do. They had done it throughout the campaign. Why stop now? The act of having the president of the United States declare victory would carry its own weight, and make things more difficult for Kerry.

Soon Francis and Bartlett were in a heated debate.

"There's a box in the corner of every television set in America," Bartlett said, "that doesn't say the requisite number of electoral votes." He needed 270 to win and the networks showed only 269. "People are going to think it's presumptuous for us to do this." He suggested they all take comfort in the knowledge they had won. There was no debate on that point. "We know it. Let's be patient."

No, Francis repeated, the reality was the Florida precedent, the prospect of legal skirmishes, lawsuits all over again. They had to do anything and everything to head that off. "They're going to have lawyers on the tube at 7 A.M., talking about how they're going to milk this, stop the clock, and they're going to run the show. *And they're going to take it from us.*"

Over the speakerphone Bush was mumbling, apparently in agreement. Bartlett knew all too well that the suggestion that someone was going to take something from Bush would bring out the fighter.

Several in the War Room thought they could almost hear Bush putting on his coat.

Bartlett fired off the most powerful ammunition he could muster. "You cannot go out there and put the crown on your own head," Bartlett finally summarized. "You just can't do it."

There was a second or two of silence.

"Laura thinks the same thing," Bush replied over the speakerphone. "Laura doesn't think I ought to go out either."

Card was still pressing at 4:59 A.M.

"Let's do it tomorrow," Bush finally said.

Hadley believed it had been Bartlett's finest moment, holding off the cascade. If Bush went it might have forced a confrontation, with legions of lawyers and a huge mess.

Of his own small role in arguing against the stampede to the Reagan Building, Hadley later joked to a colleague, "That may be the most useful thing I did in four years."

IF BUSH WASN'T GOING to declare victory, Card felt somebody at least had to go and say something, especially to the crowd at the Reagan Building. He was nominated. He reached the Reagan Building at about 5:30 A.M.

"We are convinced that President Bush has won reelection with at least 286 electoral college votes," Card told the thin crowd that had stuck it out. "And he also had a margin of more than 3.5 million popular votes."

He offered a careful and deliberate olive branch. "President Bush decided to give Senator Kerry the respect of more time to reflect on the results of this election. The president will be making a statement later today."

KERRY WAS UP BY 7 A.M. talking things over with three of his top campaign aides. He had decisions to make.

First, he could mount a challenge in Ohio based on the provisional ballots. But the number of provisionals was roughly equivalent to Bush's lead in the state, so Kerry would have to take virtually all of them.

Second, he could challenge Ohio based on allegations of voting irregularities.

The third option Kerry had to consider was the most dramatic. His campaign had a dossier that showed how people in Democratic precincts in Ohio waited three, four, five and seven hours to vote. In Republican precincts there were no lines, it seemed, and voters went through in five minutes, even three minutes. Eight voting machines in some Republican precincts, and only one or two in Democratic precincts, that kind of thing. There was a real disparity.

It could be unbelievably powerful, Kerry thought. He could fly to Ohio with his full press entourage, and stand with a whole bunch of people who had been disenfranchised. He could literally camp out in

Akron, perhaps, with his running mate, Senator John Edwards, in Columbus. They would say, "This election was a fraud in Ohio and the United States of America deserves a president of the United States who is properly elected. And we're going to court to challenge under the due process clause of the Constitution. People's right to vote was not accorded to them. And we want, one week from now: Ohio votes for president."

Bush and the White House and the Republicans would have been in a huge moral morass, Kerry believed. What could Bush do? Fight having a fair election for president?

But the biggest impact on Kerry was the number of provisional votes. There just weren't enough provisionals that he could overcome on the numbers.

Kerry realized that fighting would mean leaving the country in disarray for the second presidential election in a row. It was a decision he would have to make himself. He decided to accept the result. "To do otherwise," he said later in an interview, "would have been personal. It would have been venal. It would have been just the wrong thing to do when you're running for president of the United States. It's just what my gut told me. It just said to me, 'Look, this is the presidency.' And as much as I fought for it and as much as we care about what we fought for, there are larger interests that you've got to think about." Ironically, though he would not become president, he said, "It was sort of the kind of presidential moment if you will, and I felt the right thing to do at that point was not prolong the agony and not put the country through it no matter how personally invested in it we all were."

He added, "Based on the numbers we had, you would have had to challenge the underlying foundation of the election. And as strongly as I feel that it is flawed, deeply flawed, I made just the fundamental decision that that was the wrong thing to do."

AROUND 10:30 A.M., November 3, Kerry called Cahill to say that he was not going to challenge the election in Ohio or anywhere else. He would call Bush and concede. "What's the telephone number?" he asked her.

An assistant at the White House put Kerry through to Bush. Rove, Card, Hughes, Bartlett and Gerson were in the Oval Office.

"Congratulations, Mr. President," Kerry said.

"You were a very, very tough opponent," Bush said. "You really gave us a run for it. I hope you are proud of the effort you put in. You should be."

"Mr. President, this is really a moment for the nation to come together. People are yearning for it. And I hope you'll take advantage of this to speak to the nation and bring people together and really reach out. I'm prepared to work with you to try to do the things we need to do."

Bush said Laura and he wished Kerry and his wife and family the best. Both men made a few more benign but warm comments, and said goodbye.

The president put down the phone and started to cry, a deep, convulsive cry. As he tried to compose himself, he went around and hugged each of the people in the room with him—Rove, Hughes, Bartlett, Card and Gerson.

"Congratulations," Rove mumbled. He teared up and couldn't say anything more. Gerson cried also.

"This is a wonderful gift you've given your dad," Card told the president.

Bush then led them out of the Oval Office and down the corridor to Cheney's office. But the vice president was in the Situation Room, so Gerson called him to say the president had news.

Cheney came up and they met in the hallway, where Bush told him about Kerry's call.

"I know you're not the hugging kind," Bush said. He shook his vice president's hand.

32

B USH MET WITH HIS CABINET the next morning, Thursday, November 4.

"This election was not won by country club Republicans," he said. "I don't know if they exist. There are only country club Democrats. This election was won by people that carry lunch pails to work. I think that if it had just been policemen and firemen voting in this election, I would have won most—you know 90 percent of the vote."

Bush had tapped into a new group of lower- and middle-class voters concerned about security. After 9/11, he believed, many more people were primarily worried about terrorism, afraid of the next attack. Before the invasion of Iraq, Bush had used the fear to the fullest, intimating that Iraq might launch a nuclear strike. "We cannot wait for the final proof—the smoking gun—that could come in the form of a mushroom cloud," Bush had warned. At other times he had talked of an attack by Iraq that could "kill untold thousands," and "bring a day of horror like none we have ever known."

In the campaign, the Bush reelection team had dramatically framed the issues to make the voters' fear of terrorism as palpable as possible. The starkest, most direct suggestion that reelecting Bush would save America but electing Kerry would lead to the country's utter demise had come from Cheney on September 7. "It's absolutely essential that eight weeks from today, on November 2nd, we make the right choice," Cheney warned. "Because if we make the wrong choice, then the danger is that we'll get hit again, that we'll be hit in a way that will be devastating from the standpoint of the United States."

The Bush campaign had marched purposefully up to the line of fear mongering, and the record showed that they had crossed it. The election results showed that it had worked.

TWO DAYS AFTER ELECTION DAY, Bush and the first lady flew to Camp David. Card, his wife, Kathi, and Rice went along.

As chief of staff for a newly reelected president, some of the reflected glory of the triumph fell on Card. He was in a powerful position. After all, something had gone right.

But Card knew other things had gone wrong, seriously wrong. The intelligence showing that Saddam Hussein had stockpiles of weapons of mass destruction had been wildly off the mark. He had sat in the Oval Office three months before the invasion and listened to the CIA's presentation on Iraqi WMD. It was weak and unconvincing, and he had worried that there might be no "there there." But then he had been comforted by Tenet's assurance that the WMD case was a "slam dunk." Card wondered if he had done enough. He prided himself on the quality of the information flow to the president but this information had been flat wrong.

The president had already talked to Card about making a lot of changes for the second term—some new cabinet officers, some new senior White House staff. Change was good, Bush had indicated, although Card knew that change ran counter to Bush's gut. The president liked old, comfortable shoes. His staff had become comfortable shoes.

Bush and Card went into the president's office at Camp David.

"You want to make a lot of changes," Card began. "The best way to signal that you are serious about making changes is to change your chief of staff. If you don't change your chief of staff, everybody else will presume there's no change."

"Are you planning to leave?" the president asked.

"That's the wrong question," Card replied. "That's not the right question. The question is: What do you need to accomplish what you need to accomplish in the second term? And I may not be what you need."

Card knew better than most that such offers to resign almost always were insincere. The offer was often a way of asking, Do you still love me? Given the stakes, Card felt he had to get beyond the personal.

"When you married Laura," Card added, "it was for better or worse. With me it's only for better. If it isn't better, I'm out of here."

"I want you to stay," Bush said.

"You shouldn't," Card said. "You should not ask me to stay. It's a mistake to ask me to stay."

The president was dismissive. He said he wanted to come to closure quickly, and also to relax and play a little bit. Card felt the reelection campaign had been an "emotional burden" for Bush.

"Please listen," Card said. "There are lots of good choices out there. And there shouldn't be a presumption that I would stay, especially if you're talking about you wanting to make changes."

Card produced an 8½-by-11-inch spiral notebook, a half-inch thick with a blue cover. He called it his "hit-by-the-bus" book. On separate pages he had lists of possible replacements for all the major administration posts, including his own. The names were listed in no particular order. Card kept the notebook in his desk at the White House and periodically added or deleted names. He had intentionally used a student notebook, something he had bought himself, so it wouldn't be considered a government document or a presidential record that might someday be opened to history. It was private and personal.

He had a list of 54 replacements for himself as White House chief of staff, divided into three categories reflecting different styles and approaches.

Bush started to get up.

"No, no, no, sit down," Card said gently. He knew this might be a conversation designed more to satisfy himself, not Bush. "Please, listen as I go through these categories and I go through these names."

The first type of White House chief of staff was a micromanager—tight control, someone who would pronounce that no person, no piece of paper could go to the president without the chief knowing and approving. They both knew that the model for this type was former New Hampshire Governor John Sununu, the well-known imperial, blustery chief of staff in Bush senior's first three years as president.

The second type was a prime minister type—a Hill operator, deal-cutter, negotiator and policy person who could handle the Congress, the media and the world.

The third and final type would be a facilitator—doing what the president wanted, keeping the cabinet and staff focused on the president's agenda. That was Card's type.

Bush really didn't want to go through this exercise.

"Josh Bolten," Card continued. Bolten, a 49-year-old bachelor and organization man, had been Card's deputy the first several years of the administration. Now he was director of the Office of Management and Budget. He had impressed everyone with his capacity for hard work.

Bolten was a possible choice, Bush indicated.

"Don Evans," Card read.

No, Bush said. Commerce Secretary Evans was Bush's best Texas friend in Washington. Card agreed the president shouldn't choose his best friend.

"Al Gonzales," Card read, the White House counsel.

Bush seemed to have other plans for Gonzales.

Card read on, not getting any particular reaction from Bush: Harriet Miers, the deputy White House counsel and a Bush favorite, and Scooter Libby, Cheney's chief of staff.

"Larry Thompson," Card suggested. Thompson was a former deputy attorney general, who had resigned in August 2003. Bush seemed intrigued by that possibility.

What about Roland Betts? Card suggested. Betts was Bush's Yale classmate and a big New York investor who had been part of Bush's group that had owned the Texas Rangers baseball team.

"No."

"Jim Francis," Card suggested.

"No."

"Ed Gillespie," Card read. Gillespie was the chairman of the Republican National Committee.

Bush again seemed intrigued, but no name so far had created much excitement. He seemed to like one idea, picking a current or former Republican governor. George Pataki, the New York governor, Frank Keating, the former Oklahoma governor, and John Engler, the former Michigan governor were among the names Card suggested.

"Karen Hughes," Card tried.

Not possible, Bush indicated.

"Karl Rove."

"Couldn't be a chief of staff."

"Condi Rice."

Bush had other plans for her.

Card read some former members of Congress: Chris Cox of California, Vin Weber, Bill Paxon. He also suggested former Senator Fred

Thompson of Tennessee, then starring in the television series *Law & Order.*

"Would you stay?" Bush finally asked.

"You've got a lot that you want to get accomplished in the second term," Card answered. "If you think I can help you accomplish that, I would stay." He reminded the president that his wife, Kathi, was his partner. "If my wife is not a partner in this process, I will not stay," Card said.

"I will talk to Kathi," Bush said.

"A second-term president does become a lame duck," Card said. "The question is when, and what are the consequences?" Bush had to make sure he controlled that as much as possible.

Bush was intent on having a big agenda for the second term.

Recognize that it will be less about your perspective because it is not as relevant anymore, Card said. The media would have a perspective, but that too would be less relevant. It was more about the audience that would have to respond to his call: the Congress, the public and his supporters, his base. The chief of staff would have to make sure those audiences responded. There was some breathing space, Card said. Now reelected with no way to seek reelection again, he would be defined as a statesman for an undeterminable period.

It was about 5 P.M. when they wrapped up their discussion. Soon, people were gathering for dinner. Bush took Kathi Card aside. Afterward, Bush approached his chief of staff.

"Kathi is comfortable," he said.

Trust but verify. Card went over to his wife.

"If this is what you want to do," she said, "and the president wants you, it's okay."

So she was "comfortable" and "okay," far short of an endorsement.

Bush had noticed the Cards talking. As his chief of staff walked into the room where they were to have dinner, the president was standing in the doorway.

"We'll do it," the president said slapping Card on the back. "We'll do it!"

CARD WAS SOON WONDERING if he would look back on that day at Camp David and conclude that it may have been an even bigger mistake for the president to ask him to stay, and for him to accept, than he had initially thought. Could a holdover chief of staff be an agent for change?

It was not long before Card was directly asking the president. How much change was needed? Not change just in personnel, but in policies, and the larger question of where the Bush presidency was going. What decisions needed to be revisited? Was Card too much a part of the past to be part of a changed future? Of course, the biggest part of that past was the Iraq War, the 18 months of follow-on decisions. Who else might be too associated with those past decisions to be part of a changed future?

THE NEXT DAY, FRIDAY, Bush met with Rice in the afternoon. He said he had thought a lot about his second term, and he wanted her to take Powell's place as secretary of state.

"I'm honored that you would think of me in those terms," Rice replied, adding all the right things about the importance of his vote of confidence and trust. She then shifted to what was on her mind. "Mr. President, I really think I ought to go home."

No, Bush said. Look at all they needed to do. The amount of unfinished business was staggering.

Iraq—their war. A Middle East peace—their hope.

"Well," she asked, "are you saying that you're committed to trying to get a Palestinian state in this period of time?" It was one of her favorite topics.

Bush said he was committed, and he drew her into a substantive discussion of other worries and opportunities.

It was late afternoon, and the sun was going down over the Catoctin Mountains. Rice had not planned for such a talk, and she was still exhausted from the campaign. No matter what she decided to do, she said, she thought Steve Hadley was the natural person to succeed her as national security adviser.

Bush didn't say whether he agreed.

"I don't know anybody who is more balanced and dedicated and smarter and more of a problem-solver than Steve," Rice continued. She noted that the president obviously trusted Hadley, and without that trust the president might get the Reagan effect—six national security advisers over two terms.

"You know, Mr. President, you probably need new people," Rice continued. "And you know, not just to move them around. You need new people because we've been through a terrorist attack, the worst terrorist attack in American history. We've been through two wars. You know, maybe you need a new team who can serve you."

"Don't tell me what I need," Bush replied.

"Mr. President, the threshold issue for me is do I stay or not." A lot of people were saying she wanted to succeed Rumsfeld at Defense. "This is not about where you send me. This is about do I stay or not."

They talked for another half hour. Bush tried to steer the conversation back to what they could do in the second term. He had always held the upper hand in their relationship, and Rice had almost always done what he wanted. But he couldn't get her to accept.

"Mr. President," she finally said, "I have to think about it."

"Of course you have to think about it."

At the end of the weekend, Rice told Bush, "Yeah, you know, I'm still thinking about it." But she sensed her own body language was more forward-leaning. By the next day she was very excited about the prospect of becoming secretary of state.

She told Bush she would do it. "Yeah," she said, "if that's what you want me to do."

IN IRAQ, THE WAR WORE ON. Fallujah had turned into terrorism central, exporting car bombs into Baghdad and all over the country. General Casey mobilized a large force of six U.S. assault battalions backed up by as many battalions of Iraqi troops and cordoned off the city. Nearly all of the civilian population emptied out of the city, while the tight cordon kept suspected terrorists trapped inside. The message was that Casey was finally going to take care of Fallujah.

One Sunni delegation after another filed in to see interim Prime Minister Allawi with a single message: "Don't do Fallujah." The message Washington sent was basically: "Please do another Najaf," with a peaceful resolution.

But there was no resolution. With the American presidential election over, and the first Iraqi national election two months away, Casey and Negroponte sent counsel back to the NSC and the president. According to one official the blunt message was: "There is no way you can get this country to an election, either from a standpoint of security or just a standpoint of political belief in what this endeavor is, if you don't do Fallujah and if you don't deal with Moqtada. And you've got to deal with this or else the country is going to disintegrate."

Bush gave Casey the go-ahead to order the attack. Those in Fallujah stood and fought. The U.S. military considered the city a perfect shooting gallery, and killed between 1,000 and 2,000 alleged hard-core insurgents. The U.S. lost 70 troops—about one soldier or Marine per platoon. The Iraqi battalions lost between 20 and 30 each. Though their role was not that significant, the big deal was that the Iraqis hadn't run away. Most of their battalions were ambushed on the way out, but they continued to fight.

In the midst of the battle, Arab and world attention was diverted to Paris, where Yasser Arafat, the Palestinian leader and idol of the so-called Arab Street, was near death. Like most everything involving Arafat, it was a prolonged and orchestrated drama with publicized medical treatment, controversy over the cause of his eventual death on November 11, and the return of his body to Palestine. The Arafat theater dominated Al Jazeera and other Arab media despite the fighting and dying in Fallujah, reducing the story at times to little more than "Meanwhile in Fallujah . . ."

Bush, Rice and Powell tried to explain to the various Arab leaders why the U.S. was convinced the Fallujah assault was necessary and pleaded with them to be on board with the United States. The Arab leaders weren't exactly supporters, but they did not take hard positions against the Americans.

AT THE WHITE HOUSE, the biggest question mark was still Rumsfeld. Should he stay? Card had to approach the issue with delicacy. Rumsfeld had made Card's job difficult. Rice and Card were not in the chain of command—and everyone knew who was—but Card's job was to serve Bush. Iraq was the centerpiece of everything now, and Rumsfeld had been effectively supplanted as overall person in charge, first by Rice in the fall of 2003 when she took over the Bremer account, and then in 2004, when NSPD-36 had made State the lead agency in Iraq. Still, Iraq was mostly about the violence and the 130,000 American troops, which were indisputably Rumsfeld's.

The president was clearly predisposed not to do anything that would disrupt the war effort, and the effect of replacing Rumsfeld was not clear. If Rumsfeld left, what would the impact be on overall momentum and on the morale of those who were doing the fighting? Of course, because Rumsfeld had a virtual monopoly on Defense contacts with the president, there was no way the president could get independent information to answer those kinds of questions.

The biggest voice for change was Powell. In one conversation, Powell had told Card, "If I go, Don should go." But now that Bush had decided to replace Powell with Rice, it was unclear who he wanted at Defense.

There were other, more subtle champions of change at Defense, such as Rice, Hadley and, in the right circumstances, Card himself. The first and best way to present the case to Bush was to argue that he needed a whole new national security team. But Rice had already failed with the new-team argument, and then she had accepted State, undercutting her own suggestion.

Still, Card decided to proceed. Since he had floated several dozen alternatives for himself as chief of staff, he figured he could do the same for Rumsfeld. He got out his "hit-by-the-bus" book.

The list of possible Rumsfeld replacements included some old names, such as former Senator Dan Coats from Indiana, who had been passed over the first time; Fred Smith, the FedEx CEO, who was an old fraternity brother of Bush's but who apparently was not willing to take a government job; Deputy Defense Secretary Wolfowitz; and Deputy Secretary of State Armitage. Card knew that the mention of Armitage at the Pentagon would be coarse sandpaper to Cheney, so he probably was not a real option. He mentioned Senator John Warner, the Virginia Republican who was chairman of the Senate Armed Services Committee; Senator Joe Lieberman, the Connecticut Democrat who had run with Gore as his vice presidential running mate and was a staunch defender of the Iraq War; and Governor Pataki and former New York Mayor Rudy Giuliani. Other possibilities included Arizona Senator John McCain and former California Governor Pete Wilson.

But Card had what he thought was a great idea—a sleeper candidate. The best replacement for Rumsfeld would be James A. Baker III, the former Reagan White House chief of staff and treasury secretary, secretary of state to the president's father and his chief political adviser.

Card floated the names to Bush over the course of several weeks, all the while underscoring the advantages of change. But his focus was on Baker.

"Everyone would say, 'Phew,' " Card said. "No learning curve. Great. Interesting." Baker was 74, only two years older than Rumsfeld. He had served in the Marine Corps. He had been the best modern White House chief of staff, Card thought. He had successfully handled the 2000 Florida recount for Bush. Mr. President, this is my quiet counsel, Card said. Put a diplomat in the Defense Department.

The president seemed genuinely intrigued.

You don't have to rush to make a decision, Card advised.

Card spoke with Rumsfeld, who talked as if he presumed there would be no change. Card had sources inside the Pentagon, even among Rumsfeld's inner circle, and he reached out to them. What did they think? One source said Rumsfeld expected that if there was a change it would come much later, maybe four or five months away. Maybe in March. Then Card heard that Rumsfeld wanted to stay until the budget was done. Then someone said he expected to stay until June. Finally, one of Rumsfeld's minions told Card, "Nothing will happen until the war is over."

Rumsfeld wanted to stay. There was always something on the horizon in Iraq—the coming elections on January 30, 2005, the effort to get the Iraqi security forces constituted, a new wave of violence. Did they want to make a switch at such critical moments?

Karl Rove weighed in. A contentious session with Congress was coming up. As he saw it, the Democrats were in no mood for a honeymoon. With Rice's confirmation hearing and with the expected nomination of White House Counsel Alberto Gonzales as attorney general, would another Senate confirmation overload the system?

"I've got Powell going. I'm going to have to replace Condi," the president told Rove. "Do I have to have some continuity in all of this? I feel more confident at making the change at State because I have Condi, in whom I've got confidence. Where do I have the same confidence level for somebody, particularly in the middle of a war, at Defense?" And, clearly, the conduct of the war in Iraq would be the subject of confirmation hearings for anyone Bush nominated to be the new secretary of defense.

Rove agreed they did not want to do anything that would prompt hearings on the war. Jesus, no.

"If we need to do it, we need to do it. But if we don't need to do it, you know . . ." Bush said, deciding nothing but sounding reluctant to make a change.

Bush talked with Cheney. He came back to Card with questions and speculated about the impact of some of the names on Card's list, especially Baker. But the big decision stayed undecided.

MICHAEL GERSON ALSO WENT to the president to argue for a change at the Pentagon. As a symbol of change, Gerson said, he believed that Rumsfeld should be replaced. Yes, some adjustments to the Iraq policy had been made or were under way and Rumsfeld had been a part of that change, and it might be unfair to him to replace him now, whatever his mistakes. But all the elements of a much more effective Iraq strategy had to be put in place. The president should talk to Lieberman about taking over from Rumsfeld, Gerson recommended. What better symbol of change could there be than to bring in Al Gore's running mate?

Bush said he was still impressed with Rumsfeld's efforts at transformation and his ability to take on the entrenched military interests.

That did not undermine the argument for different leadership, Gerson said. Knowing how important loyalty was to Bush, he said, "Mr. President, it's not disloyal to have someone in for four years, four and a half years, in a job like this, and then for a variety of reasons, many of them not of his own doing, okay, to say that it would be advantageous to have a change."

Interesting idea, Bush said.

Card had known Gerson was going to speak to the president about Rumsfeld, and he had encouraged it. It was part of his campaign plan.

ANOTHER PROBLEM WAS THE CIA. Porter Goss's chief of staff, Pat Murray, clashed bitterly with Deputy Director for Operations Stephen Kappes and his deputy, Michael Sulick, in November 2004. Kappes and Sulick ran the clandestine and covert operations for the agency at the center of the counterterrorism efforts. Both resigned, causing an internal storm.

Card made another appointment to see Goss at Langley. Not everything Card was hearing was bad, but the turmoil was unsettling. It was precisely the kind of shake-up that an institution needing to focus on its work did not need.

Goss insisted he had done the right thing with Kappes and Sulick.

Card spent half a day getting briefings, asking questions, moving around the headquarters building, hoping to boost morale. He attempted to show appreciation and respect to those on the front line in the war on terror. But he left uncertain whether his visit had helped or hurt.

HADLEY, WHO WAS NOW 57, was also thinking about change. He wanted out. As the end of the first term approached, he had a couple of conversations with Armitage about the virtue of leaving.

The worst thing, Armitage said, would be for a deputy to be promoted to the top spot. "Don't do it," Armitage warned.

Hadley said he agreed. The number one and the number two jobs were different, requiring different skills. He also felt that it was important for a second-term president to demonstrate that he was robust and powerful, that he could bring in people even more qualified for the top jobs than the people leaving. He called this the "oh, wow" factor. Finding new, true heavyweights for the top posts would generate its own momentum and credibility.

Hadley also agreed the president ought to replace most of his national security team. They had a lot of baggage, especially the Iraq War. Bush needed a clean start. In the first term he hadn't had the diplomacy of the country harnessed behind his agenda, Hadley believed, and Powell had only carried out a modified version of Bush's agenda. It was often too much Powell, and not enough Bush. Powell was too independent-minded. So it made sense to make Rice secretary of state.

But Rumsfeld was a managerial and bureaucratic lone ranger. No one would call Rumsfeld a team player, and he wasn't going to change. He continued to disparage the NSC and the interagency process on both the largest and smallest matters. Hadley was known to refer sarcastically in private to "the great Don Rumsfeld."

Hadley joined the parade who told Bush he needed a new national security team. But Bush had different ideas, and he asked Hadley to move up to fill Rice's shoes as national security adviser. "I need you to do this," the president said.

The summons—and opportunity—for presidential service at this level could not be refused, at least not by Hadley.

"So it's ironic, isn't it," Hadley later said to Armitage, "that I find myself in this position."

"Yeah," Armitage said. "I don't know whether to congratulate you or offer you condolences."

Hadley said he wasn't sure himself.

THE HARD DUTY OF INFORMING Colin Powell that he was out fell to Card. He phoned Powell and invited him to his West Wing office.

"The president wants to make a change," Card said, delivering the classic line.

"Well, fine. We talked about that," Powell replied.

"The president is likely to name Condi. I'm pretty sure it's going to be

Condi. Obviously something could happen between now and the time it does, but I think it's going to happen, and you should plan on it."

"Okay," Powell asked, "when do you want my letter?"

"If you get the letter to me, I will hold it. No one will know I have it." They would release it only at a mutually agreed-on time.

"There's a lot coming up right now," Powell said. "We've got all the meetings in December, all the ministerial meetings, a lot of other things coming along." There were NATO conferences, an annual summit in Chile, a December gathering of Arab leaders in Morocco. The Iraqi elections would be January 30. "Do you want to wait and let me go through all of that?"

"No," Card replied, and said there were going to be other cabinet changes too. "The president thinks if we're going to do it and we're doing all the others, we ought to do them all at once."

"Is there going to be a change at the Defense Department?" Powell asked.

"I haven't seen any indication of that yet," Card replied. Powell understood. If all the cabinet changes were going to be announced at once, and yet there was no indication of a change at Defense, it meant Rumsfeld was probably staying. Clearly disappointed, Powell became much more emotional than Card had expected.

It suddenly became emotional for Card too. The meeting turned sad. Nobody could have been a better secretary of state for Bush's first four years, Card thought. Bush had come in with no foreign policy expertise or interest, and he picked Powell, who was known and respected in the United States and around the world. Powell was no shoot-from-the-hip Texan. He'd been tested as Reagan's national security adviser and as chairman of the Joint Chiefs. Back in 2001, Powell was already thought of as a statesman, and he had helped Bush clear lots of hurdles. But Card did not think Powell would be right for the second term. Maybe he would go on to be the secretary-general of the United Nations.

Powell was a towering figure, and Card wanted him to leave at the top of his game, but he thought the secretary of state was kind of like a Hall of Fame–bound baseball player who wants one more time at bat. It was sad, but not everyone could be Ted Williams and go out with a home run.

"You've made great contributions," Card said, trying to comfort. "But we're going to another phase."

Afterward, Card gave a full report to the president and recounted the feeling of sadness and how Colin Powell was not Ted Williams.

Bush was impatient as usual. He had picked Rice and she had accepted. He wanted to get it announced. Where was Powell's resignation letter?

Card waited several days and the letter didn't come. He called Powell at home. It was a polite but curt conversation. Where's the letter?

"It's on its way," Powell said.

The letter arrived Sunday, November 14. Two days later, Bush announced Rice's nomination. He praised Powell, and in a single paragraph announced that Hadley would be his new national security adviser.

33

CARD KEPT PUSHING ABOUT RUMSFELD. With Rice at State and
Hadley as the national security adviser, Rumsfeld's unwillingness
to work the interagency process would drive them bonkers. Card found
he'd had to mediate constantly. He once said, "I was frequently the person trying to take sand out of people's underwear, which is a very difficult task if it's not your underwear."

At one point, Card spoke with Cheney about a possible change at the
Pentagon.

No, Cheney said, he was predisposed to recommend that the president keep Rumsfeld right where he was. That was no surprise.

Bush and Cheney were talking in private. For Cheney, the hydraulic
pressures in the Washington political system were well known. Rumsfeld's departure, no matter how it might be spun, would only be seen as
an expression of doubt and hesitation on the war. It would give the war
critics great heart and momentum, he confided to an aide, and soon they
would be after him and then the president himself. He virtually insisted
that Rumsfeld stay.

Card couldn't get a read on what was happening, and all he learned
was that now Rumsfeld wanted to make some changes of his own at Defense. He would be replacing Wolfowitz and Feith. Bush agreed they
were in the wrong jobs. Rumsfeld recommended that the timeline for
those changes be stretched out.

Bush kept talking with Cheney. Bottom line, Cheney said, in the middle of the war the president could not change his secretary of defense without raising all kinds of questions.

In mid-December the president made his final decision. Rumsfeld would stay, he indicated to Cheney and Card. He couldn't change Rumsfeld.

"That didn't mean he didn't want to," Card later said.

In 2006, I told Rumsfeld during an interview that Powell, Card, Rice and Hadley had all recommended to Bush that he get a new national security team.

"I did not get engaged with those people in recommending to the president that he ought to fire somebody else," Rumsfeld said.

"When did the president ask you to stay?" I asked.

"I don't know that he did. I don't recall that he asked me to stay."

"Did you want to stay?"

"I'm here," he replied.

"I noticed."

"I really wanted, and do want, what's best for the country, and what the president feels is appropriate. He's got a tough job and he's got to do it his way."

"But there was never a moment or a meeting where he said, 'I want you to stay'?"

"I don't recall that there was," he said. But on the other hand, he added, laughing, "I'm quite confident there was never a moment where he said, 'I want you to leave.' "

One of the administration's talking points was that 14 of Iraq's 18 provinces were relatively quiet or stable, and that the violence and problems were really contained in only four provinces. Rumsfeld had made the claim himself on November 8.

"Okay," Wolfowitz told Rumsfeld, "but the ones that are relatively stable are not getting more stable. They're getting less stable." It was the dirty little secret they weren't talking about that would put the claim in context—attacks were going up everywhere. Overall, the attacks had spiked again to nearly 3,000 in November—almost a record, according to the classified reports. "Why don't we pay more attention to making the 14 really stable and have them become models for the rest of the country?"

Rumsfeld seemed to like the idea.

Wolfowitz put together a briefing chart with maps showing in the standard stoplight—red, yellow and green—a plan to avoid surrendering part of the county but isolating and eventually surrounding the insurgents in the four most violent provinces.

At Rumsfeld's request, Wolfowitz went through several redrafts. He continued to sell it hard, and once gave the briefing to Cheney, but it was never bought. Almost punctuating the lack of interest and Wolfowitz's waning influence, Bush reverted to the old talking points in a public question-and-answer forum.

"Listen, 14 of the 18 provinces appear to be relatively calm," he said.

CARD LAUNCHED TWO OTHER personnel searches. He had to find someone to be the first director of national intelligence, and someone to replace Secretary of Homeland Security Tom Ridge. Homeland Security had downgraded the "terror alert" from Orange to Yellow on November 10, eight days after the election, and shortly afterward Ridge told Bush that he wanted to resign.

Card got out his "hit-by-the-bus" book. His lists included many of the usual names—former Senator Coats, Senator Lieberman, Rudy Giuliani and Armitage.

Card phoned Armitage again to see if he would be interested in Homeland Security.

"No, thank you," Armitage replied. "The secretary and I are kind of in together, out together."

"Well," Card said, "you could go out one day with him and come in another door the next day."

"No, I think not," Armitage said.

Hadley then called Armitage to follow up on Card's inquiry.

"Did he also ask you about the national director of intelligence?" Hadley asked.

No.

"Well, he was supposed to. Would that make any difference?"

Armitage said it would not, then added what was on his mind. "I just don't know how I can work in an administration that lets Secretary Powell walk and keeps Mr. Rumsfeld."

MOSUL, A CITY OF 1.8 MILLION, erupted. Insurgents raided police stations, stole weapons and spread mayhem. On November 14, they kidnapped a wounded police officer from a hospital and dismembered him.

At least half the city's police walked off the job. Insurgents hit two C-130s with surface-to-air missiles, and American troops and armor poured in. Negroponte flew up to see what was going on but his plane was waved off. He was furious and exploded with a long chain of profanities as they flew 200 miles back to Baghdad.

General Casey and Jim Jeffrey flew into Mosul at night. They were shelled as soon as they landed. By the end of November, with the scheduled January 30 elections 60 days off, there were massive logistical problems. Never mind security at the polling places, which was bad enough, but the Iraqis were planning to import millions of ballots in dozens of wide-bodied aircraft. Though they had the help of the United Nations, Jeffrey wondered how this was going to come together. Overall, he concluded, Iraq was "in deep shit."

The U.N.'s Lakhdar Brahimi was sending messages to Bush pleading with him to delay the Iraqi elections. The minority Sunnis were making it clear they would resist or even boycott the elections, and Brahimi wanted more time to get them to reconsider and actively join in the electoral process. Back in the 1920s, the Shiites had refused to participate in the political process. Popular history held that it had cemented Shiite exclusion for decades. Now the fear was that the Sunnis would be caught in a similar cycle of disenfranchisement, frozen out of a new Iraqi government for all time.

Prime Minister Allawi and others were sending the same message about delay. A lot of Iraqi media said the elections would fuel violence indefinitely. Blind adherence to an arbitrary deadline made no sense.

The lone Iraqi voice saying go ahead with the elections was the Shiite leader Grand Ayatollah Sistani. The Shiites had waited long enough. They wanted democracy. They wanted to exercise their political muscle.

"It's really important to have the election on January 30," the president said at an NSC meeting November 29. Some of the NSC principals were wavering and could have been talked into postponing, including Hadley. But Bush never invited anyone to offer reasons for delaying.

"Everyone is for going ahead, right?" the president said. It wasn't really a question.

There was silence.

"Thank you for being strong," he continued, proceeding as if the silence equaled consensus. "We gain nothing from delay. Sistani is right. Look, here's the situation I'm in. I've got the majority community wanting elections and I'm supposed to say no?"

He also stated, "We're not going to pick winners." Neither the embassy nor the CIA was to assist. "Let the chips fall where they may."

That was a hard order to follow for both the diplomats, who were used to giving support to candidates close to the United States, and the CIA, which favored interim Prime Minister Allawi. However, Tony Blair had sent two British operatives to assist Allawi. He told Bush the British would take care of it.

The elections were yet another matter on which the top military man, JCS Chairman General Myers, did not get a vote. Neither did anyone else for that matter. Myers could feel that when any doubt started to creep into the small, windowless Situation Room, the president almost stomped it out. Whether it was alarming casualties, bad news, the current decision on the timing of Iraqi elections, some other problem or just a whiff of one of the uncertainties that accompany war, the president would try to set them all straight.

"Hold it," Bush said once. "We know we're doing the right thing. We're on the right track here. We're doing the right thing for ourselves, for our own interest and for the world. And don't forget it. Come on, guys."

BUSH HARBORED DEEPER, even grandiose ambitions. The morning of Friday, December 3, 2004, he called in his chief speechwriter, Michael Gerson. Bush's goal now was to dramatically alter the American foreign policy mind-set as radically as it had been changed at the beginning of the Cold War in the late 1940s with policies of containment and deterrence. Bush's speech at West Point in June 2002 had laid the groundwork and justification for the invasion of Iraq. Historian Arthur Schlesinger Jr., who despised Bush, marveled that he could change American foreign policy so significantly into a doctrine of what amounted to "preventive war"—a war to stop a war. "To do this without igniting a national debate shows remarkable leadership skills," Schlesinger said.

When Gerson arrived that Friday morning, the president said he wanted his upcoming second inaugural address to set one idea in stone: "The future of America and the security of America depends on the spread of liberty." That was it. He wanted a liberty-and-freedom inaugural address. He wanted Gerson to find the most memorable and economical way possible to state this for all time, words that would define his policy as it related to the new world they were facing. The terrorist Abu

Musab al-Zarqawi in Iraq and the international jihadists had chosen to fight in Iraq for good reason, Bush said. They knew that an American failure in Iraq would have far-reaching consequences in the Middle East.

"They understand the stakes," Bush said, "and we should too."

Rarely did a speechwriter have such an opportunity to define an age. It was a chance to break down further the traditional barriers between realism and idealism in American foreign policy. The realistic interests of America would now be served by fidelity to American ideals, especially democracy. As usual, Gerson had read lots of old speeches, especially the inaugurals in which Harry Truman had defined the doctrines of the Cold War and John Kennedy had amplified them.

But Kennedy's rhetoric had gone over the top and been too grand, in Gerson's estimation. "Pay any price, bear any burden, meet any hardship, support any friend, oppose any foe to assure the survival and the success of liberty," he had said in his 1961 inaugural. That was the mindset that had led to Vietnam. Gerson did not want something that suggested some wild-eyed, open-ended commitment to full democracy everywhere. The fall of Hosni Mubarak's undemocratic but friendly government in Egypt, for example, would hardly be in the immediate interests of the United States.

Gerson wanted the speech to define realistic elements of democratic reform—not just elections, but the development of democratic cultures in Egypt, Saudi Arabia and Jordan. This would include the rights of women and minorities, religious liberty, more trade and legal reform.

"We are going to define a serious range of policy options that lie between indifference to the fate of others and constant war," Gerson told a colleague. For example, on Iran, there was an option somewhere between the extremes of an outright invasion and doing nothing. Gerson hoped he could come up with the blueprint for a long-term strategy that would be not destabilizing and confrontational but firm and moral.

The speech could thematically bring together everything Bush had done since 9/11. For Bush, 9/11 was the demarcation line between the new century and the 1990s, when Clinton had failed to respond aggressively enough to a series of attacks. The 9/11 attacks were a warning about the kind of strategic circumstance that every president would be facing for the next 50 years.

Hadley had a number of polls of Iraqis that supposedly indicated a significant turn in public opinion in recent months. The surveys showed deep resentment of the American occupation but did not show a distrust of democratic institutions. So trumpeting democracy in the state of the union might appeal to Iraqis.

Gerson was very aware that Bush's foreign policy was not the type espoused by traditional conservatives, who, as William F. Buckley wrote, "stand athwart history yelling, 'Stop!'" Bush was clearly saying "Go," and Gerson believed that Bush was operating more in the tradition of Franklin D. Roosevelt by using government to expand freedom.

Gerson was exuberant, hoping for something equivalent in foreign policy to Einstein's unified field theory of the universe. He was so pumped up that he had a heart attack in mid-December. The doctors told him it wasn't overwork. It was a combination of his genes and stress.

Bush called Gerson at the Alexandria hospital where he was registered under the pseudonym John Alexandria.

"I'm not calling to check on the inaugural," Bush said. "I'm calling to check on the guy who's writing the inaugural."

Gerson recovered. In a few weeks he was back at work on a reduced schedule, focusing on the speech.

ARMITAGE TRAVELED TO IRAQ at the end of 2004.

"What did you find?" the president asked him upon his return.

"We're not winning," Armitage said, and added carefully, "We're not losing. Not winning over a long period of time works for the insurgents." He said that the campaign of intimidation being conducted by the insurgents was unbelievable.

Bush didn't argue. Afterward Armitage called both Negroponte and Casey to tell them what he had told the president because he didn't want them to be surprised. What was surprising was that neither argued with him. It was a terrible mess. He also found that the CIA and DIA analyses were in agreement. The enemy is by and large homegrown. The external forces, Syria and Iran, are important but not critical to the insurgency.

Hadley listened to Armitage's formulation of we're not winning, we're not losing, and felt that it was an execution and implementation issue. They were just not doing it right.

After the violent attacks on Iraqi police stations, Frank Miller once again expressed concern about the way the U.S. military was training police. Various estimates put the number trained at 60,000, but it was hard to know what the number represented. Another estimate said only half of that were really present for duty. In any event, they weren't going to be able to defeat the insurgency with police. This was a war. They needed to focus more on elite combat and paramilitary power.

"There's something wrong with the picture here," he told Rice. "We're building beat patrolmen. Excuse the fact that they're going to work for Saddam-era colonels. There is no station house in the world, I don't care if it's in Los Angeles or New York, that's going to withstand attack from RPGs and heavy machine guns."

Miller had argued unsuccessfully at the deputies committee meetings that the U.S. embassy in Iraq needed to have outposts all around the country. That was one of the few bright spots during the Bremer era, he thought, that they had 18 regional administrators who actually were plugged in to what was going on in the country. But his idea went nowhere. The U.S embassy footprint was basically limited to the Green Zone.

There were simple fixes that Miller thought the embassy in Baghdad should be pushing. Insurgent attacks were shutting down the Iraqi oil pipelines, for one. Miller ordered a study that showed nearly all the attacks were directed at small, vulnerable sections of the pipelines. He suggested the military bury these sections with sand and dirt. But they wouldn't do it. He also failed in an effort to get the military to raise its goal for the availability of electricity.

"How do I make the embassy in Baghdad follow the government's orders?" Rice asked Miller in December 2004. After six months, Negroponte wanted to come home, and they had to decide who would replace him. Rice and Miller started to talk about Zalmay Khalilzad, the Afghan-born American who had been the NSC's point man for the Iraqi opposition and had moved on to become ambassador to Afghanistan. "Zal has turned the embassy in Kabul into an embassy on a wartime footing," Rice said. "He gets things done."

It was the kind of Washington gossip that would not stay secret for long, and in early January, an item from Al Kamen's "In the Loop" column in *The Washington Post* said that Khalilzad would be taking Negroponte's place.

Soon, however, there was a snag. Sensitive intelligence revealed discussions in which Khalilzad told the U.N.'s Lakhdar Brahimi not to worry about the January 30 date for the Iraqi elections because it could be slipped. It was remarkable that one of Bush's ambassadors would tell a foreign official he didn't have to worry about official U.S. policy.

Armitage called Miller. "You've got to see this thing," he said.

Miller went down to the White House Situation Room and asked to see the cables, but they weren't there. He called Armitage back.

"Rich, I can't find it. The SitRoom can't find it."

"Yeah, I know," Armitage said. "They've all been impounded."

That's it, Miller thought.

"Zal, you really blew it," Hadley told Khalilzad in a phone call. "I doubt the president will ever be able to nominate you as ambassador to Iraq, and certainly not now. At minimum a decent interval of several months will have to pass before he can. But maybe never."

BUSH HOSTED A WHITE HOUSE RECEPTION on January 3, 2005, for newly elected members of Congress and their spouses. "Laura and I know how hard it is on a family to be in the political arena," he said. "It's the ultimate sacrifice, really—sacrifice your privacy, sacrifice time with your kids."

It was inappropriate in the extreme given that 1,333 Americans and thousands more Iraqis had made the true ultimate sacrifice. Bush was in a post-election bubble.

Bush made only a passing reference to Iraq. "We've got to make sure that we win the war. We've got to make sure we support our troops."

Two days later, at an NSC meeting, there was a long discussion about how the Sunni participation would be increased in the upcoming election.

"Let's be clever about exploring creative ideas about how we can permit Sunnis to participate notwithstanding the violence," the president said. "How about voting by telephone? How about mailing in ballots? How about getting ambassadors to go to Arab countries and encourage Arab countries to get in touch with Sunnis and encourage the Sunnis to participate in the process?"

As Jeffrey watched Bush from Baghdad on the secure video, he was astonished. Rarely were diplomats or military in the field given such direct, clear guidance from a commander in chief: "You will make it happen." Bush's ideas about voting by mail and phone were impractical, but there was something about Bush's enthusiasm and belief. Bush was saying, in effect, "You really don't have a choice in this one. This is one you can't screw up." As the elections approached, Jeffrey felt a mixture of dread and hope.

At the White House, Hadley watched in some wonder as the CIA came in regularly to brief the president with dire forecasts of civil war.

The elections would not reduce violence and would likely make things worse, the CIA said.

"We're going to hold the election on January 30," Bush replied. Deadlines were critical to progress. No deadline, no progress, and nothing would happen.

The CIA—both orally and in classified written reports—repeated its message. The January 30 date was like pinning a target on all of Iraq—strike that day, hit the polling places. Because the minority Sunnis knew this was an election they were going to lose, it would trigger sectarian violence by both Sunnis and Shiites. The agency again recommended delaying the election.

Hadley went head-to-head with CIA Director Porter Goss and some of his analysts and operatives. He wanted them to be engaged in propaganda operations to support the election. But the CIA's idea of information operations, he thought, was to spread lies.

"Why spread lies?" Hadley asked. "Spread the truth. It's much more powerful. You don't get it. You need to find ways to get out the truth in a way it won't be instantly discredited because it's from us."

America had the loudest voice in the world with its movies, music and television. But, Hadley lamented, every day America was beat on message by the terrorists and Al Jazeera.

At an NSC meeting January 10, 2005, Bush reaffirmed that they would stick to the Iraqi election date 20 days away. "We need to think about the post-election strategy," he said. Success hinged in part on whether the minority Sunnis would see themselves as part of the new government. "We will need to influence the Shia victors so they will make clear to all that the Sunnis will be included. What matters is not as much the vote, but what the government will look like that comes out of the vote."

But which Sunnis? Who had power among that minority? The U.S. invasion had ousted the Sunnis, so how could the U.S. be seen as the honest broker, let alone as outsiders looking out for Sunni interests? Those questions were not addressed and thus were unanswered.

Hadley was getting cold feet. Maybe they should delay.

"We're sticking with the elections," Bush repeated. In private he railed at the lack of forceful leadership in Iraq. Where were the leaders? Why wouldn't they step forward. "Why don't they take charge of their own destiny?"

34

O N JANUARY 18, Rice appeared before the Senate Foreign Relations Committee for her confirmation hearings. Democrats came out swinging. "Your loyalty to the mission you were given, to sell this war, overwhelmed your respect for the truth," accused Senator Barbara Boxer of California, before launching into a litany of Rice's pronouncements about WMD before the invasion.

Rice was clearly taken aback as she responded. "Senator, I have to say that I have never, ever lost respect for the truth in the service of anything," she said. But back at the White House she was clearly down.

"Buck up," Rove said. Republicans controlled the Senate, so her confirmation might be bruising but it would be a formality. It was a cost of doing business in Washington in politics. Winners suffered wounds, but they could survive and even thrive. "You're going to be fine. You're winning."

A week later the Senate voted 85–13 to confirm her.

BY INAUGURATION DAY, January 20, Bush had practiced his address many times. "I can't wait to give this speech," he told Gerson. Though others had some input, it was a speech, and policy, essentially worked out by Bush and his speechwriter. After reading a final draft, Andy Card half joked, "This is not a speech Dick Cheney would give."

After Bush took the oath of office on the Capitol steps, he stepped to the podium and delivered his 2,000-word, 17-minute address. In terms of delivery, it was one of his best performances. He spoke crisply, with neither a stumble, nor a moment of drift nor hesitation.

"It is the policy of the United States to seek and support the growth of democratic movements and institutions in every nation and culture, with the ultimate goal of ending tyranny in our world," Bush declared. He used the words "freedom" or "liberty"—or variations such as "free" or "liberating"—44 times, nine of them in the last two paragraphs.

Gerson usually watched Bush's speeches on television, so he would see them like the average person and be better able to understand reactions. But this time he was on the inaugural platform. He had never had a more palpable sense that they were involved in an important historic enterprise. Every future president, in Gerson's view, would have to take the Bush Doctrine seriously. It would point a way through the coming decades.

"Something big has happened," reported Hadley after getting some international reactions.

For many conservatives, the speech was a big negative. Peggy Noonan, Bush senior's speechwriter, blasted the speech in *The Wall Street Journal*, sticking her finger in the eye of its central principle. "It left me with a bad feeling," Noonan wrote. "It carried a punch, asserting an agenda so sweeping that an observer quipped that by the end he would not have been surprised if the president had announced we were going to colonize Mars.

"It seemed a document produced by a White House on a mission. The United States, the speech said, has put the world on notice." She said the ambition of ending tyranny was laudable, but "This is—how else to put it?—over the top," adding, "The most moving speeches summon us to the cause of what is actually possible."

When informed of the reaction of his father's favorite speechwriter, Bush was dismissive.

Rice thought the speech was soaring, one of the best she had ever heard. But as she sat there listening, she thought, "All right. Now how do we execute it?" She realized it would take years. The question, she told her staff, was: "If people look back 30 years from now and they read President Bush's second inaugural, will they say that American policy helped to deliver on that, or deliver the foundations for achieving that?" As for the criticism, she said, "If the president of the United States can't stand up and say we should look to the day when we end tyranny and that all live in liberty, where else are you going to say it but in an inaugural? That's the time to have a kind of daring dream."

STEVE HADLEY HAD FOUND over the past four years that some of the principals would rather complain about problems than fix them. General Myers once complained to Hadley that he had a problem on coordination on military matters with the Saudis.

"I just fixed that," Hadley replied.

"Well, great," Myers replied. "That's a good example but I got nine other things."

"Send me your list, Dick," Hadley said, "and I'll tick them off one at a time."

On Saturday evening, January 22, 2005, Rumsfeld and Myers cornered Hadley at the annual Alfalfa Club dinner in Washington.

"You know, the interagency's broken," Rumsfeld said, launching right into him. Interagency coordination was Hadley's job. "Dick Myers has a long list. Every day he comes in and bitches to me about the interagency is broken. He has a long list of things he wants done."

"You know, Don," Hadley replied, "I told Dick Myers we needed to do this four months ago. Send me your list, and I'll treat it like a punch list for a home closing."

Two weeks later Hadley was waiting for the list.

RUMSFELD LATER CONFIRMED in an interview that he believed the interagency process was broken. "In the 21st century," he said, "in the information age, we're still functioning with an interagency process and a governmental structure that is in the industrial age in the last century. And it would be like if the DOD tried to function today without the Goldwater-Nichols reform of the JCS, where each service was going to go off and fight the Navy war and the Army war and the Air Force war, and that doesn't work in this world we're in. And it is not a—my comment about the interagency being broken was not in any way characterizing the people that are in it or even the structure that they control. It's a reflection of that fact that the government structure is a leftover from an earlier era. And it is something that I think all of us feel on occasion."

"Have you told the president this?" I asked.

"Sure."

"What does he say?"

"I don't say what he says."

"But that's—that would be something worth fixing, wouldn't it?"

"Indeed," Rumsfeld said. On the wall of his office, right across from his large desk, hung a copy of the old Uncle Sam "I WANT YOU" recruiting poster from World War I. The slogan on Rumsfeld's poster read, "We're at war. Are you doing all you can?" He said he did not think the rest of the government was doing all it could.

"This department is at war," Rumsfeld said. "The other departments are not here for that. They're being asked to do something that they were not organized, trained and equipped to do. And it takes time and it's hard and there's resistance in the Congress. People are attracted to different organizations depending on what their bent is, and the people that are attracted here are the people that are ready to be deployed and ready to go into danger zones. And the people that are attracted in other departments may or may not be. And if they're asked to, it wasn't something they signed up for. And it may not be career-enhancing."

Rumsfeld cited an example from 2001, when he said he'd been unable to get funding to train soldiers in Afghanistan. "Why couldn't we? Well, because the Department of State has the training funds, and they're programmed out two or three years in advance."

Many in the military felt the rest of the U.S. government had not shown up for the war, I told him, and were not doing their fair share.

"Can you share the concern the military people have?" I asked.

"Well, sure. I do! My Lord! Can I share it? I'm here!"

Can you mobilize the rest of the government?

"We've tried and tried and tried," Rumsfeld said.

MILLER WAS STILL ON HIS MISSION to implement the president's order allowing the British and Australians access to the full secret SIPRNET military network. He went to a meeting at the Pentagon with some of the key civilians and Joint Staff officers dealing with the issue. He read both Rumsfeld's and the president's directives to the group.

"You don't mean unfettered access," said one of the three-stars on the Joint Staff.

"If the president or the secretary of defense had wanted to say give them access according to the following limitations, they would have said so," Miller replied, looking straight at the general. "This is an interagency cleared document. Your people signed up to it. Access means access. What about 'access' don't you understand?"

Miller put something together for Hadley to send to Rumsfeld in the president's name, requesting him to fix the SIPRNET access.

"Look," Hadley replied in a friendly tone. "I've got two difficult tasks for me personally. I've got to establish my own relationship with the president, and I've got to change my relationship with Rumsfeld from being a deputy to being a peer. And my first step out of the box will not go well to send a 'Don, your people are screwing it up. Fix it.' "

There was a certain logic to that, Miller recognized. They had a lot more to work on than just this information-sharing issue. But still, it meant they had to work the back channel that much harder to get the president's order implemented. Miller was stunned that everyone at the senior levels—the president, Rumsfeld, Rice and Hadley—seemed to accept the laxness and defiance in the system.

Up in his second-floor West Wing office Karl Rove was at loose ends, almost bouncing off the walls four days after Bush's second inauguration. His real job, getting Bush reelected, was over. What would he do now at age 54?

"Has-been. Downhill from here, bubba," he tried to joke to a colleague. "I don't know what I mean. I like my job and I'll stick around for a while." As Bush's senior adviser he would have a big role in economic and other policy. "My job is to be a good colleague. I stir up a lot of shit without pissing people off."

But Rove was bored. He played with a battery-powered "Redneck Horn" that he had shown the president. Every time he pressed a button on the four-square-inch plastic novelty, suitable for dashboard mounting, it rattled off recorded obscenities and insults in an angry Southern drawl. "Slow down, dumbass! Wal-Mart's open all night," the red toy blared as Rove pressed the button. And again. "Driver's license? You ought to get one, asswipe!" *

The CIA kept up its steady stream of warnings about Iraq's upcoming exercise in democracy. The Sunnis would be excluded and violence would go up, it warned. The alarmist classified briefings were unremitting, and grew in the days before January 30. In Baghdad, Negroponte

---

* The toy had eight other recordings: "Hey, hogneck, who taught you how to drive?" "What the hell was that maneuver?" "What race are you in, shithead?" "Son of a bitch!" "Get the hell out of my way!" "Are you freaking blind?" "Put the cell phone down, dickhead!" and finally, "You're a goddamn moron!"

disagreed with the CIA's view, and the embassy was encouraging the U.N. and the Iraqis to go ahead. He said publicly that security was adequate.

After one CIA briefer presented another warning, Bush chimed in, "Is this Baghdad Bob?" referring to Saddam's propagandist. It was a stunning insult. "I'm not hearing that from anyone else but the CIA," Bush said. "If I take more time there's no evidence the security will get better. I'm depending on the prospect of the elections and an elected government to get the insurgency down and get the security improved."

The election would be for an interim National Assembly that would appoint an acting government and draft a permanent constitution. The constitution would then be put up to a vote of the Iraqi people in a referendum in the fall—nine months away. If it passed, a second national election would follow in two months to choose a permanent government under the new constitution. It was a long, tedious three-step process. But it had been approved by the United Nations and everyone was stuck with it. Bush said again that he did not see how waiting would help.

Finally, at an Oval Office briefing just before the Iraqi election day, after hearing the latest dire CIA predictions, the president suddenly clapped his hands loudly, like a rifle shot, and slammed his briefing book closed.

"Well," he said, "we'll see who's right."

AS THE DATE APPROACHED, violence surged. "I expect something spectacular to occur" either on election day or right before it, warned Major General Peter Chiarelli in Baghdad, who was wrapping up a year as the commander of the 1st Cavalry Division. On January 26, a Marine Super Stallion helicopter crashed in the western part of the country, killing 31 Americans. It was the deadliest single incident for U.S. forces since the invasion.

In his Saturday radio address the day before the Iraqi elections, the president went further out on a limb, if that were possible. "Tomorrow the world will witness a turning point in the history of Iraq," he said. He noted that the al Qaeda terrorist Zarqawi, who was behind many of the car bombings and beheadings in Iraq, had recently called democracy "an evil principle."

Rice woke up Sunday morning, January 30, and turned on CNN. The sound came through before her television's picture warmed up.

". . . an extraordinary day for Iraqis," she heard.

The picture came on, and there were pictures of long lines of Iraqis waiting to vote. Rice called the president.

"You have to turn on the TV," Rice said. "You just have to see this."

"Is it good? Is it a good outcome?" Bush asked.

"It's really amazing. It's amazing to see what those Iraqis are doing."

Some 8 million Iraqis went to the polls. Many waved their purple-inked fingers in the air to signify they had voted. It was a stunning turnout with minimal violence.

Bush thought it was a vindication not only of his Iraq policy but of his freedom agenda. Iraqis were seizing the moment and taking control of their future. Bush gave a brief televised address to the nation.

"The world is hearing the voice of freedom from the center of the Middle East," he said, and Iraqis "have taken rightful control of their country's destiny."

The mood and atmosphere in the White House shifted, Gerson felt, and it was as if a corner had been turned. But the minority Sunnis had effectively boycotted the election, leaving 20 percent of the population out—an important, critical segment that had been the elites under Saddam. The Sunnis were the backbone of the insurgency.

IN BAGHDAD DURING January 2005, the CIA station compiled an AARDWOLF, the name given an overall chief of station assessment. It was an important document saying that the insurgency was gaining strength and Iraq was on the verge of civil war. Despite the excitement over the elections, enemy-initiated attacks had jumped from about 2,000 in December to 3,000 in January. The AARDWOLF was reviewed by Negroponte, who told the CIA division chief, Rob Richer, and the Baghdad CIA station chief to be vocal with President Bush.

"I'm making the same point," he told the station chief.

Negroponte merely told Bush, "We've got some hiccups."

Richer felt this was a classic case of sugarcoating bad news. He later confronted Negroponte for failing to back up the station chief like he had promised.

"I get my message across," Negroponte said.

AS HADLEY TOOK OVER as national security adviser, Bush had one basic instruction: "I'm trusting you to make sure that I have a process where I hear from my cabinet secretaries." The president believed in letting the line managers run their departments. "You can have your own views," Bush told him, "and if I ask you for them, you tell them to me."

From his experience as Rice's deputy, Hadley knew he would be spending lots of time working closely with the president. There would be a way for him to get his thoughts across. But Hadley believed firmly that he and the NSC staff had a limited role. They were not elected, not even confirmed by the Senate. Running programs by committee was to be avoided because no one was responsible.

Success would be to the credit of the president or the cabinet secretaries, Hadley concluded. Failure would in part be his. His job was important but ultimately thankless. It was unthinkable that he try to be a national security adviser in the mold of the globe-trotting, high-visibility Henry Kissinger, who competed with and ultimately dominated the cabinet secretaries. He didn't even want to be as visible as Rice had been. Hadley hoped to be like Brent Scowcroft, national security adviser to Bush senior, who was low-key and operated largely offstage.

As Rice's deputy, Hadley had been the fix-it man, the one to call Armitage or Wolfowitz or someone at the CIA to solve an immediate problem. Now the president told Hadley that he could no longer be Mr. Fix-It. "Hadley," Bush said, "you've got to get yourself a good deputy because you need to help me think up here about what's our overall strategy, and are we organized right, and get it done." At the same time, as Hadley knew only too well, the president's predominant emotion was often impatience. If he wanted something fixed, he would generally assign it to the nearest person. Most frequently that had meant Rice or Hadley. So Hadley would be in some respects retaining his old job, while also getting a new one.

He made an assessment of the problems from the first term.

"I give us a B minus for policy development," he told a colleague on Saturday, February 5, "and a D minus for policy execution."

Hadley knew that nearly two years after the invasion, the basic problems of Iraq had not been solved—security, infrastructure and governance. His assessment was especially interesting because he continually insisted that the NSC had no role in executing policy. So the D minus apparently would not apply to him. It was for the job done by people such as Powell and Rumsfeld.

What did Rumsfeld think of that notion?

"If I were going to do it, I might flip those," Rumsfeld told me in an interview later when I relayed Hadley's assessment. The problem wasn't the execution; it was the policy development. "I think there's been execution in a lot of things that has been very good," he added.

In other words, the problem was the interagency, not him.

35

BANDAR CAME OVER TO THE WHITE HOUSE on February 5 to see
Bush. An Afghani had recently walked into the Saudi embassy in Is-
lamabad, Pakistan, and said he knew where Osama bin Laden was hiding. He could point out his location if they gave him a map, he claimed.
Since he'd be putting himself and his family at risk, he wanted the Saudis
to promise to take them to the Kingdom and let them live there for the
rest of their lives.

The Saudis did some preliminary evaluations and the walk-in in-
former looked interesting, so the Saudis promised asylum. He had
located a spot on a map that seemed plausible.

Bandar said the Saudis planned to send a military or intelligence unit
to the spot and get bin Laden. "We're not going to go through a trial,"
Bandar explained. "We get him, we kill him. Get it over with."

"Go ahead," the president said. "I could care less."

Bandar asked if the CIA could assist in evaluating the source, and
Bush gave his approval.

Bandar did not get along with Porter Goss, so before he left the White
House, he called Rob Richer, the CIA Near East and South Asia division
chief.

"We're going to Pakistan," Bandar said.

"I can't take orders from you," Richer objected.

But almost instantly, Richer got his orders through regular channels.
He went to Bandar's mansion, and soon they and another expert from
the CIA were on Bandar's plane.

Once they arrived in Pakistan, they started an evaluation of the walk-in. Ah, Jesus, the CIA men soon realized. The walk-in was a known commodity to both the CIA and the British MI6 intelligence service. He had tried the scam before.

Why hadn't the Saudis and the CIA been able to figure that out before going to the president and sending a mission to Pakistan? "Because nobody ever shares sources with anybody," said one of the people involved. "That is standard modus operandi. He was a fabricator. He was looking for money basically."

The message was relayed to Bush: no bin Laden.

IN EARLY 2005, Rumsfeld sent retired General Gary E. Luck to Iraq for a sweeping review. Luck, a former head of U.S. forces in South Korea, was an adviser to General Franks during the 2003 Iraq invasion.

Luck, who has a Ph.D. in math, was to examine strategy, troop levels and training programs. He found that the training of the new Iraqi army was totally screwed up, a disaster. In some cases it consisted of not much more than handing the recruit a rifle, giving him three days of training and calling him a member of the New Iraqi Army.

Luck told General Myers, "You know we have underestimated the effect Saddam Hussein and his regime had on the spirit of the Iraqi people. Nobody got any credit for showing any initiative under Saddam Hussein. Now we're asking them to show all this initiative and they don't know how to do it."

Rice didn't need the Luck report to tell her the training of the Iraqi army was a disaster. But the report did make a good point, she thought, that they couldn't just train individual soldiers; they had to train entire units.

Rice hired Philip Zelikow, an old friend, as the counselor to the State Department, a powerful but little-known top post that would leave him free to undertake special assignments for her.

Zelikow, 50, a lawyer with a Ph.D. in history, headed the Miller Center at the University of Virginia, which studied the modern presidencies. He and Rice had co-authored a 1995 book, *Germany Unified and Europe Transformed*, the only book former President Bush and Brent Scowcroft said they used in writing their memoir. The end of the Cold War and the collapse of the Soviet Union had left Rice and Zelikow optimistic. It was possible to get foreign policy right.

Zelikow, who could be taken for a well-groomed banker, had also co-authored books on the Cuban Missile Crisis, and served on the President's Foreign Intelligence Advisory Board. Most recently he had been the executive director of the 9/11 Commission, forcing Rice to testify in public and raising serious questions about the administration's pre-9/11 response to al Qaeda. He had also supervised the writing and editing of the final 9/11 Commission report, a widely praised best-seller with exhaustive, groundbreaking details about the origins, planning and execution of the attacks.

Rice dispatched Zelikow and a small team to Iraq. She needed ground truth, a full detailed report from someone she trusted. Zelikow had a license to go anywhere and ask any question.

On February 10, Rice's 14th day as secretary, Zelikow presented her with a 15-page, single-spaced MEMORANDUM TO THE SECRETARY OF STATE. The report was classified SECRET/NODIS, meaning "no distribution" to anyone else.

The January elections that had so buoyed the White House had been a landmark success, Rice read, "but we are still at a tipping point."

"At this point Iraq remains a failed state shadowed by constant violence and undergoing revolutionary political change," Rice read. This was a shocking notion—"a failed state," after two years, thousands of lives, and hundreds of billions of dollars. "Failed state" was about as low as it got in geopolitics, and Rice later wanted to remember it differently, as if Zelikow had said it was only in danger of becoming a failed state. But he had said it was already there.

It was ugly. The insurgency was "being contained militarily," but it was "quite active," leaving Iraqi civilians feeling "very insecure," Zelikow said.

Conditions for U.S. officials seemed to resemble those of the Bremer era, locked down in the Green Zone. "Mobility of coalition officials is extremely limited, and productive government activity is constrained."

Because the Shiites and Kurds had dominated the election, there was a "danger of a backlash from the disaffected Sunnis," she read.

The evidence of this backlash was available daily. Two days earlier, for example, a man had walked into a crowd of Iraqi army recruits in Baghdad and blown himself up, killing 21 of the recruits and wounding 27 others. Insurgents had killed 168 Iraqis in the ten days since the January 30 election. The astonishing fact was that there had been 3,000 attacks in January—about two thirds on coalition forces and about one third on Iraqi security forces and civilians—but that information was kept classified.

Zelikow criticized the Baghdad-centered effort, noting "the war can certainly be lost in Baghdad, but the war can only be won in the cities and provinces outside Baghdad." He urged that the coalition empower provincial and local authorities to improve security and intelligence, and proposed the creation of Regional Security Teams of military and coalition civilians. This would replace the current patchwork of people from military headquarters, regional embassy offices and State Department teams.

She read that Zelikow had met and been impressed by Major General Peter Chiarelli, the commander of the Army's 1st Cavalry Division, who was a proponent of what the military called "full-spectrum operations," meaning that his soldiers didn't just do typical infantry tasks like killing insurgents, but they also did civil projects that helped the local population. Chiarelli had his infantry soldiers out hooking up houses to the local sewer lines. Zelikow said it was one of the best briefings he had ever heard from a general.

"Everyone stressed to us that movement on this civil dimension of government performance is now key to solving their military problem. We recommended that the US take the lead to set strong targets for much greater distribution of electricity and fuel across the country within the next six months." In the last six months, the availability of electricity and fuel had decreased.

The memo also noted that it would be hard to get more reconstruction money, critical police training was lagging, Kirkuk, the Kurdish city that sits astride major oil fields some 200 miles north of Baghdad, was a powder keg, the banking system was a mess, the agriculture system was a Soviet relic, and a real Iraqi justice system was needed, so high-value detainees could get fair trials.

Overall, Rice read, the United States effort suffered because it lacked an articulated, comprehensive, unified policy.

Zelikow's memo was depressing, but Rice was not one to be discouraged.

"I've been working on this for years," Rice said. She felt a strong sense of responsibility, not just because of her current government position. She'd been at the White House when Bush decided to invade, and was one of only two people whose opinions he'd asked beforehand. "I own Iraq," she said. "I have to operate that way. I was part of the team that made the decision." Clearly the State Department effort was inadequate. Not enough attention was being paid to the political side of the counterinsurgency fight. They had to make a concerted effort to win hearts and minds at the local level in Iraq.

Rice had visited Iraq only once, very briefly, going along with Bush on his surprise Thanksgiving Day 2003 trip. It was only a photo opportunity. She was eager for a real visit.

"Not the right time," Jim Jeffrey told her, but she insisted and arranged a trip for March 1. Her senior assistant, Jim Wilkinson, told the State Department reporters about the planned trip in confidence. "You can't report it. It's for planning purposes only," he said. Wilkinson, 35, had been director of strategic communications for Rice at the White House NSC and then for General Tommy Franks during the buildup and the invasion of Iraq. In his memoirs, Franks wrote that the youthful public relations man "looked a little like Tom Sawyer, without the fishing pole."

Despite Wilkinson's admonitions, e-mails started flying. Rice was the rock star of the Bush administration, the face of a new active diplomacy. "Condoleezza Rice's Commanding Clothes" was the headline of a *Washington Post* Style section story in late February, focusing on her "sexy" knee-high boots. Soon news of her pending trip to Iraq was reported in the press.

Rice received multiple death threats every week from extremists along the entire political spectrum, from right-wing white racists to left-wingers accusing her of selling out African Americans. Wilkinson and Rice's head of security realized that knocking off Rice would be a sensational coup for Iraqi insurgents. A quick, surprise visit was the best security. Now that was impossible. It was too dangerous. They told her she couldn't go, and she was furious. "How did this happen?"

"Frankly," Wilkinson told the State Department press corps, "the next time she goes you're not going to know about it. You're just going to wake up and Condi Rice is going to be in Baghdad. Sorry."

BUSH WAS TRYING TO FIND a director of national intelligence. He wanted someone who would bring the perspective of a president to the job, someone who had been a consumer of intelligence, knew the importance of producing intelligence for policy-makers to make decisions. He wanted someone who would ask what would be the best way to take the intelligence to the president. And he needed someone who would not be captured by one of the bureaucracies—State, Defense or one of the intelligence agencies. Most important, they had to find someone who would ensure, at any and all costs, that there would be no more WMD-style intelligence fiascoes.

Card called Negroponte in Iraq. Negroponte said he was interested, and that he would come to the White House to talk about it. On the plane from Baghdad, he read the new 262-page law.

"What does the job mean?" he asked Card when they met. The DNI would have some authority over the Pentagon intelligence agencies but really couldn't manage them and have full control over the personnel. There was lots of so-called dual hatting, with the head of the National Security Agency reporting to both Rumsfeld and the new DNI, for example. The FBI would remain part of the Justice Department. It was out of the DNI's control but was nevertheless a key counterterrorism intelligence agency.

"It's new," Card said. These are all good questions. He didn't have the answers. You get to invent it, create it, he said. "Isn't it better? How you mold it is likely how the director 20 years from now or 15 years from now is going to be doing the job. How many chances do you have in the U.S. government to build an institution?"

Negroponte met with the president. "This will be the capstone assignment for your career," Bush said.

There weren't a lot of people lined up for the job, and Negroponte wanted to leave Baghdad. Bush needed somebody who was hard-nosed, and instead of a killer angel, he would be getting one of the smoothest, least confrontational old-school diplomats around.

Bush announced Negroponte's appointment on February 17, 2005. The problem now was what to do about replacing him. The only real choice was Khalilzad, and both Rice and Hadley were eager to get him to Baghdad, although first they had to rap his knuckles about contradicting the president on the date of the Iraqi elections. They couldn't name him right away as a result. More than two months passed after Negroponte returned before Khalilzad took over in Iraq.

IT WAS AN UNEASY TIME for Vice President Cheney. He had been the most active and influential vice president in history. But the center of gravity on Iraq had shifted out of the White House—first to Defense and now to State.

He felt like he was being pushed aside on the Iraq decision making. "Who do they think they are?" Cheney said to Prince Bandar on February 28. "I was reelected too."

Rice was determined to be actively engaged in managing Iraq on a daily basis. The sort of "senior officials hands off; let Baghdad handle it" approach was over. NSPD-36 put State in charge.

The leading candidate to become interim prime minister after the January 30 elections was Ibrahim al-Jafari, a Shiite who had been part of both the Bremer-era Iraqi Governing Council and the temporary government after the transfer of sovereignty. Negroponte found him incredibly difficult, the only person he had ever met who could talk for an hour and make only one point. In one such hour-long talk, Jafari said that Talabani, a Kurd, should not hold the largely ceremonial post of president. He was trying to reach out to the Sunnis and it would be awful to have a Kurd. Then, in the last two minutes, Jafari said, well, if it was necessary he could accept Talabani.

After Negroponte left Baghdad for Washington to begin his confirmation hearings as the first director of national intelligence, Jeffrey became the head of the embassy as chargé d'affaires. Rice began bombarding him with calls saying that she was coming to Iraq.

"No," he advised again. "Not the right time."

Okay, Rice said. After the January 30 elections, the formation of the new government was going too slowly. "Who do we call?"

Jeffrey dreaded her request. First, he figured he could handle the Iraqis himself. Second, Rice—and Bush, Cheney and Hadley for that matter—had only the most general understanding of the situation on the ground and the personalities involved. The officials in Washington couldn't compete with the wily Iraqis.

Talabani was sworn in as president of Iraq on April 7. Minutes later Jafari was named prime minister. The next task was to pick other officials to fill out the government.

Rice wanted to participate in applying the pressure to get the government set up. She insisted on calling Talabani, who had been engaged in these survival negotiations for decades.

"How's it going, Mr. President?" Rice asked Talabani in an April 22 phone call.

Everything was great, he said, even when she asked about the need to include Sunnis in the new government. "Oh, I'm telling your man Jeffrey that every day. I'm cooperating and consulting fully with him and we believe we're moving forward."

Jeffrey realized Rice didn't want any call to go badly. Talabani was saying good things, not arguing, and Rice didn't want to interfere with the good vibrations. Jeffrey feared that Talabani would slip in some idea or solution that had been rejected days earlier, and Rice would say it sounded encouraging or say she would order Jeffrey to go along with it. Jeffrey was relieved that no damage was done in the call. He saw Rice was all over the problems. She was not going to go away, so he changed course and encouraged her to come to Iraq for serious discussions. That way he could sit next to her when she met with the leading Iraqis and whisper in her ear, "That's Plan C, which you zilched at an NSC meeting three weeks ago."

Jeffrey attended the NSC meetings via secure video, and a pattern was very clear. Hadley said that Iraq was like "an abused child," and the U.S. would have to continue to act as its caretaker. Rumsfeld said strongly and repeatedly, the Iraqis need to be given the chance to fail and fall on their faces, and only then would they pick themselves up, dust themselves off and come up with solutions. He used the analogy of a parent trying to teach a child to ride a bike. They had to take off the training wheels and remove their hand from the back of the seat or they'd wind up with a 40-year-old who could not ride a bicycle. Rice was between Hadley and Rumsfeld, once remarking, "Let's let them try to pedal on their own, but we better be there to catch them."

When Card heard this, he thought to himself that the bicycle seemed to be moving forward, upright and momentarily stable. But he knew there were no pedals.

36

IN EARLY MAY, Jeffrey broke out the champagne and whiskey in Baghdad. He had been pressuring the Shiites nonstop to let more Sunnis into the new government process. These are the guys doing the insurgency, he had argued. Include them. The Shiite leaders finally agreed, adding nine Sunnis to the government process.

Then, 36 hours before Rice was to arrive in Iraq for her long-anticipated but secret visit, it all fell apart.

Jeffrey realized he hadn't convinced the Shiites of anything. They didn't get the larger points, about reconciliation, outreach and inclusiveness. They were initially compliant because he had been in their faces saying, "You must do this."

They were right back where they had been two months earlier when Negroponte had left. Rice would be arriving on May 15. Jeffrey was furious.

Rice traveled in General Abizaid's airplane, with a private cabin in the back. From a security standpoint it was probably the best aircraft to use to avoid attracting attention, because it was going into and out of Iraq all the time. She first flew into Irbil, 200 miles north of Baghdad in Kurdish territory, to meet with Kurdish leader Massoud Barzani. It was kind of an insult to interim Prime Minister Jafari to see somebody other than the head of government on the first stop, but the Kurds were key to reconciliation.

Rice told Barzani how important it was to President Bush that everyone make compromises. The Sunnis had to be included. She voiced concern about the meddling of both the Syrians and especially the Iranians in Iraq.

They're both enemies, Barzani said. There's the stupid enemy, Syria, and then there is the smart enemy, Iran, which is the long-term problem.

Rice agreed.

The flight to Baghdad was 45 minutes. In her next meeting, with Jafari, she toughened her stance.

"You don't get it," Rice told the prime minister. "This is about inclusiveness." True, she acknowledged, the Sunnis had not participated in the January 30 election. Either they were intimidated or had boycotted it. "Now we're asking you to put that aside and effectively grandfather them into the political process." It might be the most difficult thing to do, she added. "But you need to do it, because if they're not part of the political process, they can destroy your ability to govern."

Everyone else in Rice's group was nodding off after the 20 hours of travel. She really amazed some of the people traveling with her, as she sat there, not a hair out of place, catching every word, a real machine.

Jafari was his own machine—a fog machine. It was very depressing, but Rice put the best public face on it later and gave seven-minute interviews to four U.S. and two Arab media outlets. Her message was persistence. "If you think about it, this government has been in power a very, very short time," Rice told a reporter from NBC. "In fact, it's been less than a year since they actually transferred sovereignty to the Iraqi people. And so there are going to be ups and downs. Things are not going to happen overnight."

Afterward Rice went for an unpublicized visit to the military's Combat Support Hospital in Baghdad. Some of the soldiers had their digital cameras and asked for pictures with Rice.

After speaking with the doctors and nurses, she visited a 19-year-old Iraqi woman who had been part of Jafari's security detail. She had thrown herself on a bomb as a human shield. The bomb partially exploded, and the teenaged Iraqi had lost her leg.

"You're a very brave young woman," Rice told her. "You're one of the people who's already sacrificed for your new democracy."

The Iraqi woman quietly said thank you. It was one of the first times Rice had encountered a personal sense of the sacrifices Iraqis were making.

Trying to keep her visit low-key and as unobtrusive as possible, Rice walked down a hallway, and wound up in a room with a single patient inside. He was an American soldier, in terrible shape, his face bandaged, on life support, barely alive.

Rice was staring firsthand at the human toll—the real and personal costs of war, a war she had advised the president to wage.

RICE LATER TOLD SEVERAL of her staff, "I have to be able to look at those young soldiers and ask myself honestly if I think what they're going through was worth it, and are we making it worth it. And so these are not toy soldiers that somebody sent in, you know, little toy soldiers. These are real, living human beings.

"If there were some way to win wars and secure countries without sending young people to either circumstances where they may be killed or where they might be maimed, we'd all do it.

"But wars have costs. And nothing makes me angrier than when I hear people say, 'Well, George Bush wanted to go to war. He was looking for a reason to go to war.' You know, you can't know this president, or any president, and what they see and what they feel when they know the implications of their actions, that they're just anxious to go to war. I think it's a completely outrageous statement."

JEFFREY WENT TO WORK on the Sunnis. They wanted 30 representatives on the Constitutional Committee, which was the next milestone on the road to democracy. Why 30? he asked. The argument was that the Sunnis were at least 30 percent of the population, probably 40 percent.

"Well, no, you're not," Jeffrey replied, "you're 20 percent of the population."

Back and forth it went. The Sunnis had won only two of the 55 committee seats. Some 10 days after Rice's visit, the Shiites agreed to expand the Constitutional Committee to include more Sunnis, and after several weeks of negotiations settled on 15 full Sunni members and 10 Sunni advisers.

ZELIKOW WENT BACK TO IRAQ for Rice in May 2005, to focus on how the U.S. was training Iraqi police—the local solution to the security problem. She had discharged the bureau head in the State Department responsible for such training. In a word, it was broken. He traveled outside Baghdad to places such as Mosul. The U.S. had set up an Iraqi police training academy and even staffed the school. A little training, a uniform, a pistol and the message "Go forth and be policemen." It was the same old story. The sole metric of progress was numbers trained. Zelikow found that no one knew if the newly minted policemen even showed up for their assignments. There was no follow-on training in the field—as critical for police as for military training.

Several hundred International Police Liaison Officers had been hired, mostly from the U.S., to do field training, but they did not expect to work in a combat zone. They visited Iraqi police stations, inventoried the guns, and did routine inspections rather than training. They were not embedded in the Iraqi police units, where Zelikow was sure they could be more effective.

He also discovered how closely the police and intelligence issues were linked, including the quality of intelligence and the degree to which anyone could find out about the insurgency or its plans.

Zelikow found that the CIA was focused on al Qaeda and effectively used the technical side of intelligence—communications intercepts and overhead photography—but was not actually involved in the major aspects of counterinsurgency intelligence at the local level.

Though more specific, these findings echoed the failure to engage the local Iraqi police that Frank Miller of the NSC staff had identified for Rice more than a year before, following his inspection trip to Iraq for her. The more Zelikow got down into the weeds, the more obvious it was that these liaison officers needed to be embedded, live on operating bases and interact more fully with the Iraqi police.

But the State training of police was only one third of the effort. General Petraeus had another third of police training. The final third belonged to the basic U.S. military divisions, which had military police who were used in their battle space or particular areas of the provinces or cities.

Zelikow recommended that all three be combined, and essentially given over to the U.S. battalions and brigades running the military operations and the foot patrols in particular regions. He had studied insurgencies, and realized all they were doing was discovering the lessons that others had learned: Politics is local, even during an insurgency. It was also the ancient problem: unity of command. Several people were responsible so in the end no one was.

CHENEY WAS ON CNN's *Larry King Live* on May 30. "I think they're in the last throes, if you will, of the insurgency." It was a total denial of reality and of the trend. The overall insurgent attacks in April had been about 1,700, and 52 Americans dead. In May, the attacks went up to 2,000, and 82 Americans had died.

SENATOR CHUCK HAGEL, 58, a short, serious-minded Nebraska Republican, didn't get a lot of invitations to the Bush White House. Though he had voted for the resolution authorizing the war, he had become an outspoken critic of the handling of the postwar phase. The White House had to include him in the invitation for all Senate Republicans to have their weekly Tuesday policy lunch at the White House June 21, 2005.

Hagel had been a decorated Army sergeant during the Vietnam War and he understood that the use of military force was the most important, defining decision for a president and for a nation. Months before the Iraq invasion he had publicly asked questions such as "Who governs after Saddam?" and "Have we calculated the consequences?" In his speech on October 9, 2002, favoring the war resolution, he said he recognized the solemn obligation involved and added, "We cannot do it alone. . . . How many of us really know and understand Iraq, its country, history, people, and role in the Arab world. I approach the issue of a post-Saddam Iraq and the future of democracy and stability in the Middle East with more caution, realism and humility." A month before the war he said, "First, a post-Saddam transition in Iraq must focus on security, economic stability and creating the conditions for democratic change. We should put aside the mistaken delusion that democracy is just around the corner."

Bused to the White House before the luncheon on June 21, the senators went through the buffet line at noon, and Bush arrived at 12:30.

The president spoke for about 25 minutes on Social Security, spending, deficits—everything except the big elephant in the room.

Senator John Warner, chairman of the Armed Services Committee, took the floor, said some nice things about Bush, and addressed the elephant. "I had dinner with my former boss when I was secretary of the navy," Warner said, referring to former Secretary of Defense James Schlesinger. "My former boss is very concerned about Iraq because he sees some very eerie parallels developing with Vietnam."

Bush then launched into his defense—9/11, the continuing threat of terrorism, his conviction that Saddam was a threat. Nothing new.

Senator Ted Stevens, the chairman of the Appropriations Committee, then said, "I want to echo part of what John Warner has just said. I think there are some serious issues here."

Bush fell back on his standard rhetorical flourish that it was the right thing to do, that they had to stick it out.

After the lunch Hagel walked out with Bush and they went off to a corner.

"Mr. President," Hagel said, "let me ask you a question. I believe that you are getting really bubbled in here in the White House on Iraq. Do you ever reach outside your inner circle of people, outside your national security council?" Then he added the obligatory softening. "This is not a reflection on, in any way, or an assertion of inadequacy. That's not my point here. I think it's important for presidents, especially in a time of war, to get some other opinions—of people that maybe don't agree with you, or you don't agree with. Call them in. Sit them down. Listen to them. Do you ever do that?"

"Well, I kind of leave that to Hadley."

"I know that your national security adviser talks to people, but do you talk to people?"

"Well, maybe I should talk to Hadley about that."

"I think this is very important, Mr. President, that you get some outside opinions here. Just to test your theories and how you're doing." Hagel mentioned themes from histories and biographies he had read. "When a nation's at war, the president is under tremendous pressure. You go deeper into that bunker, and I don't think it's good for you." There, he had said it.

"That's good advice," Bush said.

Hagel went back to the Senate. About two hours later Hadley called.

"The president told me about the conversation," Hadley said. "Do you want to come talk to me?"

"That really wasn't the conversation, Steve," Hagel said. The issue was new or dissenting voices. "You know what I'm talking about."

"I know what you're talking about," Hadley said.

Hagel offered to provide lists of people the president should talk with and said it didn't have to include him. Nonetheless, Hadley invited him down to the White House several days later. Hagel, who is an earnest student of foreign policy, sent Hadley copies of several long memos he had given to Rice. When he got to Hadley's office it was crowded with NSC staffers. "Do we really need everyone here?" Hagel asked. Apparently so. For an hour, Hagel made his pitch that Iraq was a much bigger mess than they were acknowledging, and the administration should be doing more on security, training, governance and infrastructure.

He left unsatisfied and gave an interview to *U.S. News & World Report* saying, "Things aren't getting better; they're getting worse. The White House is completely disconnected from reality."

Hadley and others at the White House were angry, but Hagel thought it was one of the clearest things he had ever said. His private assessment was worse: The administration had no strategic thinker. Rice was weak. The military was being emasculated and severely damaged by uniformed sycophants.

ON JUNE 21, Zal Khalilzad was sworn in as ambassador to Iraq, and Jim Jeffrey returned to Washington to become senior adviser to Rice with the title of coordinator for Iraq policy. He would work side by side with her on the dominant issue.

In July 2005 the agenda items for many of the deputies committee and principals committee meetings had headings such as "Infrastructure Security" that included debates on oil pipeline and electrical plant security. They were talking about utility issues like a local government public works committee. One day Baghdad had only six hours of electricity.

"Isn't that where we were 15 months ago?" Hadley asked.

Rumsfeld, General Casey and the military did not want to expend resources on static guard duty at pipelines or electrical power plants, and they resisted. It was finally agreed that the new ambassador, Zal Khalilzad, would take responsibility for addressing the infrastructure security issue, including protection for thousands of miles of aboveground pipeline. But, of course, he did not have the security resources—so it would be almost impossible to do.

ON JULY 7, 2005, four suicide bombs ripped through buses and trains in London, killing 52. It was the deadliest bombing in London since World War II.

In Washington two days later, Rihab Massoud, the aide to Saudi Ambassador Prince Bandar, got a call from Riyadh telling him to go through the files and look at an intelligence memo dated December 14, 2004, that had been shared with both the CIA and British intelligence.

When Massoud found the four-page interrogation memo, he had to read it twice. In December, the Saudi government had arrested one of its nationals at the airport in Buraydah, in north-central Saudi Arabia. The man, whose first name was Adel, had entered the country from either Iran or the United Arab Emirates on a fraudulent passport. He was taken into custody and under interrogation revealed that in six months there would be a multifaceted operation in London, using explosives from Bosnia, and said it would specifically include the area around "Edgewood Road." Massoud knew that one of the four London suicide bombers had detonated his explosives on a train at the Edgware Road Underground station.

"Within six months . . ." Massoud read again. Adel supposedly knew Abu Musab al-Zarqawi, the Jordanian-born head of al Qaeda in Iraq. At that point he claimed that $500,000 was still needed to fund the London operation. Four people would be carrying it out. He did not know their names, but he gave their rough ages, rough heights, descriptions, and said one of them had tattoos on his fingers. He also said the coordinator of the group was a Libyan businessman in London who was to help them to move around, find safe houses and automobiles.

After getting the $500,000, Adel was to call a phone number in Syria to get further instructions. In February 2005, Massoud read, the Saudis had made a second report to British and American intelligence, this time giving better descriptions of the individuals who were to execute the plan. In addition to the four, Adel said there were also "British British" and "German Germans," meaning European-looking Caucasians, as opposed to Arabs. In the February report, the Saudis had said that Adel claimed that the four would be coming from different countries.

After the July 7 attacks, the British immediately asked to interrogate Adel themselves. The Saudis agreed. On July 11, Massoud checked in with the CIA, which told him that they'd received the Saudi memo but hadn't found anything to back it up. They'd checked out the telephone number in Syria but it amounted to nothing.

Massoud then called Fran Townsend, the president's deputy national security adviser for homeland security, and told her about the memo.

"The president needs to know about this," Massoud told her. Bandar was out of the country.

"I think you need to come in," Townsend said.

Massoud went to the White House and Townsend took him to see Bush.

"Look, Mr. President, here is a copy of the memo," he said, holding the Arabic-language Saudi memo in his hand but reading an English translation.

Bush wanted all the details. The CIA and British intelligence investigated as fully as they could. It soon looked like another fabricator, and clearly should have been handled at a much lower level. But President Bush, still on edge about al Qaeda, had become his own intelligence coordinator.

BUSH STILL ENJOYED FRAT-BOY PRANKS. In July 2005, Ben S. Bernanke, the chairman of Bush's Council of Economic Advisers, who would soon succeed Alan Greenspan as chairman of the Federal Reserve, wore tan-colored socks to a meeting with the president. The socks stood out among a sea of conservative, dark socks, and the president commented on them. Within days, the president had another economics meeting, and everyone else, including Cheney, showed up wearing tan-colored socks. All had a good laugh.

Bush and Rove in particular dwelled on "flatulence"—passing gas—and they shared an array of fart jokes. The son of one senior White House staffer had a small toy with a remote control that produced a farting sound. The staffer brought it to the White House and placed it under Rove's chair for the morning senior staff meeting on July 7. But when they learned about the terrorist bombs in the London subways and buses that morning, the prank was postponed.

Several weeks later on July 20 the device was placed under Rove's chair and activated during the senior staff meeting. There were multiple activations and it took Rove several minutes to locate the toy. Everyone laughed. They needed the humor, one of Bush's top advisers recalled.

37

ROUND THIS TIME, General Jim Jones, the NATO commander, paid a call on his old friend General Pete Pace, the vice chairman of the Joint Chiefs. It was virtually certain that Pace was going to move up to replace Myers as chairman.

Two people, two Marine generals, could not be more the same and yet so different. They had been in Vietnam at about the same time, a searing and formative experience for both, and then served side by side as first lieutenants in 1970 at the Marine barracks in southeast Washington.

Pace, a thin, attentive, 1967 Naval Academy graduate, had spent four years as vice chairman, the number two ranking officer in the U.S. military. Jones, a tall, outgoing Georgetown foreign service graduate, spoke French fluently and had lived at the barracks as commandant from 1999 to 2003 before Rumsfeld moved him to NATO.

Theirs was a professional friendship that extended about as far as it could in the American military among active-duty officers—more than three decades.

Jones expressed chagrin that Pace would even want to be chairman. "You're going to face a debacle and be part of the debacle in Iraq," he said. U.S. prestige was at a 50- or 75-year low in the world. He said he was so worried about Iraq and the way Rumsfeld ran things that he wondered if he himself should not resign in protest. "How do you have the stomach for eight years in the Pentagon?" he finally asked.

Pace said that someone had to be chairman. Who else would do it?

Jones did not have an answer. "Military advice is being influenced on a political level," he said. The JCS had improperly "surrendered" to Rumsfeld. "You should not be the parrot on the secretary's shoulder."

His concern was complete. When Senators John Warner and Carl Levin, the chairman of and ranking Democrat on the Senate Armed Services Committee, visited him at his headquarters in Belgium, Jones told them about all the problems. He said they needed new legislation, a kind of Goldwater-Nichols II, to reempower the service chiefs or make some kind of sense of the crazy system.

"The Joint Chiefs have been systematically emasculated by Rumsfeld," Jones said.

Pace later said that he and Jones have had many discussions about the problems in the interagency process. There is inadequate coordination, he said, "because there's nobody below the president who has the authority to tell people what to do." He flatly denied that Jones had told him that Iraq was a debacle or that Rumsfeld had systematically emasculated the Joint Chiefs. "He's a good friend. He was in my wedding," Pace said, noting they had known each other for 36 years. "If Jim felt that way he would tell me."

I called Jones at NATO headquarters in Belgium. He said that he had made all those comments to Pace in their meeting in 2005. "That's what I told him," Jones said.

AFTER PACE WAS CONFIRMED AS CHAIRMAN, he asked Admiral Vern Clark, who had just retired as chief of naval operations, to stop by.

"Vern, give me a sense of this," he asked him.

"Okay," Clark said. "You're going to give four years of your life to the country and this job. When you leave, what do you want them to say about your time here? I challenge you to sum up in two sentences what was accomplished when previous chairmen were here. You name one. Pick 'em. Go back. Pick one."

Pace was silent.

"I'll make it easy for you," Clark continued. "Start with Colin Powell, a guy like that. What did he accomplish as the chairman?"

Pace remained silent.

"We'll give him that he put the policy of overwhelming force in place."

The irony was obvious. Rumsfeld had discarded Powell's overwhelming force doctrine in the Iraq invasion.

"So let's go to Hugh Shelton," Clark said. "Summarize all of Hugh's accomplishments here. Now describe it in two sentences."

Pace did not respond.

"I'll give him this," Clark said. "He really created an understanding that we had to pay more attention to the Special Forces." Shelton had been the commander of Special Forces before he became chairman.

"Shalikashvili?" Army General John Shalikashvili had been chairman from 1993 to 1997. Clark waited for a response from Pace. "I can't think of anything either." He said he would not be so unkind as to ask Pace to sum up how Dick Myers had done. "You figure it out. You lived up here with him."

Clark said he believed in his five years as CNO he had brought dramatic change to the Navy. "Now here's the question for you, Pete. What do you want them to say about your time as chairman?

"Fundamentally," Clark continued, "this job will eat you up day to day doing the inbox and it deserves better than that." The job definition had to go beyond what Rumsfeld decreed or wanted. The few authorities under the law given to the chairman, including a requirement that the Chairman's Program Assessment be sent directly to Congress, had been neutered by Rumsfeld. Though it was just one report, it was symbolic. Rumsfeld had refused to let it go to Congress for over a year.

Clark said that Pace should reassert his legal responsibility as chairman. "You should have something to say about it when the guy sitting one deck up refuses to forward your assessment to the Congress for 13 months. This is fundamentally not just a breakdown in the system. That is a breach of faith."

Pace said thank you, and Clark left.

Later Pace said that he recalled the meeting and Clark's question—"When you leave, what do you want them to say about your time here?"

"That was a great question to ask," Pace said. It sounded "about right," he said, that Rumsfeld sat on the Chairman's Program Assessment for 13 months. "Not to my knowledge," he said, did Clark say the delay was a breach of faith. "The conversation I had with Vern Clark was very relaxed, no angst, no anger."

BY THE SUMMER OF 2005, Dan Bartlett was exerting more and more pressure; it was constant, within the White House and on the president, about the need to change their communications strategy on Iraq. The language of resolve was no longer working. They were losing more and more credibility and the only way to regain some of it was to acknowledge that there had been mistakes along the way. There was power in acknowledging mistakes. It would convince people they were willing to adjust and alter their policy by first admitting that some things had to be changed. This was consistent with the goal of communicating that the president had a flexible strategy.

The other point Bartlett made to the president was the need to show that he was listening to critics. Where their intentions were good, he recommended, the president should say so. The resolve and determination were coming off as pigheaded.

All of this flew in the face of Bush's natural tendencies. His primary message to Americans and Iraqis had to be that he would not be shaken. The Sunnis, in particular, were playing both sides. American steadiness would help encourage them to participate, the president believed. Any American steps back would feed the Sunni insurgency, and make them optimistic for a post-American future in which there might be an ultimate sectarian war, from which they could wrest control of the country again.

Bush did not outright disagree with Bartlett that some message adjustments would have to be made. But it would take time to wean the president from his zero-defect proclamations.

FORMER SECRETARY OF STATE Henry Kissinger had a powerful, largely invisible influence on the foreign policy of the Bush administration.

"Of the outside people that I talk to in this job," Vice President Cheney told me in the summer of 2005, "I probably talk to Henry Kissinger more than I talk to anybody else. He just comes by and I guess at least once a month, Scooter and I sit down with him."

Cheney had worked closely with Kissinger in the Ford administration, when Cheney was deputy and later chief of staff. Kissinger at first had been both secretary of state and national security adviser, an arrangement that every subsequent secretary of state had envied. Kissinger's ego was monumental, but Cheney found his hard-line advice useful after 9/11. They shared a worldview that international relations were a matter of military and economic power. Diplomatic power derived from threatening to and then actually using that power. In its rawest form, using the military sent a useful message to the world: It's dangerous to be an enemy of the United States.

The president also met privately with Kissinger every couple of months, making the former secretary the most regular and frequent out-side adviser to Bush on foreign affairs. Bush, according to Cheney, was "a big fan" of Kissinger. Of the Bush-Kissinger meetings, Rumsfeld said, "I helped set it up." The president, who generally discounts the importance of outside advisers, found his discussions with Kissinger important, ac-cording to Cheney, Rumsfeld and others in the White House.

Card and the president's personal office staff knew that Kissinger was one of the few nonfamily outsiders with a standing invitation to call whenever he was coming to Washington to see if the president was avail-able. By Card's calculation about half the meetings were just the presi-dent and Kissinger. Either he or Rice attended the other half.

No one in the American foreign policy establishment was more con-troversial or carried more baggage than Kissinger, then 82 years old.

Vietnam was like a stone around his neck and the prism through which he saw the world. After Lyndon Johnson, Richard Nixon and Robert McNamara, probably nobody else was so associated with that war. He had been the architect with Nixon, and later Ford, of U.S. for-eign policy from 1969 to 1975. In his writing, speeches and private com-ments, Kissinger claimed that the United States had essentially won the war in 1972, only to lose it because of weakened resolve by the public and Congress.

If Kissinger felt he had something to say, he generally wrote about it, often in opinion pieces in *The Washington Post*. He had lots of thoughts about Iraq and Bush. He supported the war. Though he had little prob-lem with Bush's second inaugural urging the spread of democracy and the end of tyranny, Kissinger would have been more modest in applying it. "We cannot abandon national security in pursuit of virtue," he had written in his 1999 book, *Years of Renewal*, on the Ford presidency. The United States "must temper its missionary spirit with a concept of na-tional interest and rely on its head as well as its heart in defining its duty to the world."

In a practical sense, Kissinger was not at all certain that Iraq was ready for democracy, and he had reservations about using American combat troops in a massive effort to train a foreign military. In addition, since most Iraqis identified first and foremost with their tribal or reli-gious sectarian background—Sunni, Shiite or Kurd—the question was how to encourage the development of a national Iraqi identity. Closely related was the crucial question of who the Iraqi army would fight for.

Kissinger liked Bush personally, though he told colleagues that it was not clear to him that the president really knew how to run the government. One of the big problems, he felt, was that Bush did not have the people or a system of national security policy decision making that ensured careful examination of the downsides of major decisions.

Kissinger sensed wobbliness everywhere on Iraq, and he increasingly saw it through his Vietnam prism. For Kissinger, the overriding lesson of Vietnam is to stick it out.

His column in the *Post* on August 12, 2005, was entitled "Lessons for an Exit Strategy." It was almost as long as Bush's second inaugural address. In the key line, Kissinger wrote, *"Victory over the insurgency is the only meaningful exit strategy."* He then made the rounds at the White House with Bush, Cheney and Hadley. Victory had to be the goal, he told all. Don't let it happen again. Don't give an inch, or else the media, the Congress and the American culture of avoiding hardship will walk you back. He also said that the eventual outcome in Iraq was more important than Vietnam had been. A radical Islamic or Taliban-style government in Iraq would be a model that could challenge the internal stability of the key countries in the Middle East and elsewhere.

Kissinger told Rice that in Vietnam they didn't have the time, focus, energy or support at home to get the politics in place. That's why it had collapsed like a house of cards. He urged that the Bush administration get the politics right, both in Iraq and on the home front. Partially withdrawing troops had its own dangers. Even entertaining the idea of withdrawing any troops could create momentum for an exit that was less than victory.

Rice understood that Kissinger's message reinforced a conviction that the president already held.

IN EARLY SEPTEMBER 2005, Mike Gerson went to see Kissinger in New York City.

"Why did you support the Iraq War?" Gerson asked him.

"Because Afghanistan wasn't enough," Kissinger answered. In the conflict with radical Islam, he said, they want to humiliate us. "And we need to humiliate them." The American response to 9/11 had essentially to be more than proportionate—on a larger scale than simply invading Afghanistan and overthrowing the Taliban. Something else was needed. The Iraq War was essential to send a larger message, "in order to make a point that we're not going to live in this world that they want for us." He said he had defended the war ever since. In Manhattan, this position got him in trouble, particularly at cocktail parties, he noted with a smile.

Gerson understood that Kissinger viewed Iraq purely in the context of power politics. It was not idealism. He didn't seem to connect with Bush's goal of promoting democracy. "What did you think of the second inaugural?" Gerson asked him.

"At first I was appalled," Kissinger said, carefully covering himself because that was what he had told others, and continued to say in private. On reflection, he claimed, he now believed the speech served a purpose and was a very smart move, setting the war on terror and overall U.S. foreign policy in the context of American values. That would help sustain a long campaign.

On Iran, Kissinger said it was absolutely critical that Iran not be allowed to gain nuclear capability and nuclear weapons. If it does, he said, all the powers in the region—Turkey, Egypt, Saudi Arabia and the others—would go nuclear. "That would be one of the worst strategic nightmares that America could imagine," he said. That could dwarf the uncertainties of the Cold War.

Returning to Iraq, Kissinger told Gerson that Bush needed to resist the pressure to withdraw American troops, repeating his axiom that the only meaningful exit strategy was victory. "The president can't be talking about troop reductions as a centerpiece," Kissinger said. "You may want to reduce troops." But troop reduction should not be the objective. "This is not where you put the emphasis."

He then gave Gerson a copy of his so-called salted peanut memo, written during the first year of the Nixon administration. In the memo to President Nixon, dated September 10, 1969, Kissinger warned, "Withdrawal of U.S. troops will become like salted peanuts to the American public; the more U.S. troops come home, the more will be demanded." The policy of "Vietnamization," turning the fight over to the South Vietnamese military, Kissinger wrote, might increase pressure to end the war because the American public wanted a quick resolution. Troop withdrawals would only encourage the enemy. "It will become harder and harder to maintain the morale of those who remain, not to speak of their mothers."

For Kissinger, Iraq was the Vietnam sequel. He replayed for Gerson his version of the end of the Vietnam War. The public, the Congress, the Defense Department and the military had all lost their will. At one point, he said, he had proposed to President Nixon a major ultimatum to the North Vietnamese with dire consequences if they did not negotiate peace. But it didn't happen, the former national security adviser said wistfully. "I didn't have enough power."

NOW IN WASHINGTON, as the Iraq policy coordinator, Jim Jeffrey told Rice he saw some serious problems with General Casey's "Campaign Plan," the classified outline of the goals for the U.S. and other coalition forces in Iraq.

In short, the massive document said the Multi-National Force–Iraq, which Casey commanded, had two goals: first, to defeat the terrorists, which meant killing Zarqawi and neutralizing the insurgency; and second, to stand up, train and equip the Iraqi armed forces. There were also six other missions called "lines of operations." *

War was no longer just the application of lethal firepower from guns, artillery and bombs. The larger task and the more enduring one was the concerted effort to win the hearts, minds and support of the Iraqi people. That meant not only solving the immense security problem. It meant improving the daily lives of average Iraqis. It meant that it would take much more than physical security to win the war, and the political and economic conditions would be decisive to get to the peace.

The problem was execution. Zarqawi was still alive and the insurgency was not being neutralized. Casey had been up front about that in classified reports and briefings. "They are containing the insurgency," Jeffrey said. That was "containing" in the sense that the Soviet Union had been contained during the Cold War. The Soviet Union remained a powerful threat, and was never neutralized until it collapsed.

The Iraq insurgency posed a similar, devastating threat. "Attacks have crept up over the last two years," Jeffrey said. Though the American casualty rate was about the same, the Iraqi security forces were being harder hit. "They're losing 2 to every 1 of ours," Jeffrey said. "And thus the effects of the insurgency are about the same or maybe just a little bit greater. It isn't going to go anywhere.

"It's still capable of tying us in knots on the electricity," Jeffrey said,

---

* The lines of operations included: assist Iraqis in governing and developing a democracy; help to provide essential services such as electricity, water, sanitation and schools; help to strengthen the economy; assist in strengthening the rule of law and civil rights; increase international support; and communicate to Iraqis and promote "free, independent and responsible Iraqi media."

"killing lots of people, sparking sectarian violence, generally being a pain in the ass. They're not going to overrun the country, but they're not going away and they're not allowing themselves to be neutralized."

Rice understood that she needed to move more out of her lane and into Rumsfeld's. It was creating noticeable friction with the secretary of defense.

Rumsfeld pushed back, countering regularly that the lack of progress on the political and economic front, Rice's areas, was impacting negatively on the security. Publicly he insisted that they needed progress on all three fronts.

The Rice-Rumsfeld conflict was soon focused on the Iraqi economy. The classified "National Strategy for Supporting Iraq" (NSSI), a massive document of some 500 pages brimming with color-coded charts, outlined how some $21 billion in U.S. aid to Iraq would be spent— refurbishing schools, building massive electrical power plants and reconstructing the oil infrastructure. Most of the State Department money and personnel in the field were directed at this, as was much of the U.S. military effort.

But it was not going well, and the reasons had to do with the same infrastructure security problems that Frank Miller on Rice's NSC staff and others had identified for her years earlier.

BANDAR HAD BEEN ILL and out of commission for months, even spending some time in a hospital. Now he was going to leave the United States after nearly 22 years as ambassador. The Saudi king was going to create a National Security Council modeled after the U.S. version, and Bandar was going to be secretary general of the council, a post equivalent to the American national security adviser.

He paid a farewell call on President Bush on September 8, 2005. There was no real discussion of politics or policy. Bandar gave the president a silver medallion engraved with a dove and his initials and those of his wife, Princess Haifa. In a photo with Bush, Bandar looks worn and distant.

38

ZELIKOW FLEW BACK TO IRAQ in September 2005 for another inspection tour, nine days this time. He traveled fairly light with six people—a staff assistant, a colonel from General Casey's command, a State Department security officer and three soldiers. He visited four cities and Baghdad twice. When he came back he wrote a 23-page SECRET/NODIS memorandum for Rice dated September 26, 2005.

He first noted there had been major progress on security over the past year, but the insurgency had adapted. They had improved their tactics and were now using more effective improvised explosive devices (IEDs). Their choice of targets and how they hit them was very troubling, especially considering that they had more lethal weapons now. The disappointing reality was that the insurgents could operate freely in many parts of the country and U.S. forces were spread thin.

Momentum after the January 30 election had substantially dissipated, Zelikow reported, and the transitional government under Jafari was generally underperforming. One of the most dramatic findings was that the Iraqi Ministry of the Interior, which oversaw the police forces, was "operating a shadowy system of extrajudicial detentions and killings."

On the two other pillars for postwar Iraq—economic development and governance, the two that State was responsible for—the report was grim: "Not visibly advanced and some areas had moved backwards." In the areas of electricity, oil and water, the U.S. was expending a huge effort just to stay in the same place. Then came the killer line: "Iraqis had exaggerated hopes about what we would do in their country and the general failure of public services has hurtled [them] into profound disillu-sionment about America."

Zelikow asked the ultimate question: "Are we on the right track? Suc-cess in Iraq is hard to define once you get past the platitudes. What does success mean?"

He laid out some measurable goals or milestones that would mean success:

First: "An insurgency broken and neutralized enough so that an Iraqi government can contain it without large scale US help. In other words, the US would not need a corps-sized commitment of US ground forces beyond, say 2008." That meant no more than 40,000 to 50,000 U.S. troops in Iraq by the last year of the Bush presidency.

Second: "An independent Iraqi government, able to maintain enough public order so that Iraq is not a significant base for Islamist terrorism against the United States, and is not an open field for violent revolution-ary Iranian subversion and interference with world oil supplies."

Third: "An Iraqi government that demonstrates some positive poten-tial for democratic processes in the Arab and Muslim world."

Fourth: "An Iraqi government turning the corner fiscally and econom-ically to the point that there is a sense of economic hope and a visible path towards financial self-sufficiency."

Zelikow concluded, "Failure is a condition where you don't get that by the time the administration leaves office"—January 2009. "Cata-strophic failure" could be said to occur "if the center doesn't hold and Iraq's experiment at truly national government has collapsed."

Despite the specifics, Zelikow realized that everyone in Washington would really want him to answer one basic question: "How's it going?" Answering that was extremely difficult. He was a lawyer, and he felt he was at the point where he could fluently argue the upbeat case, or just as easily and convincingly argue the downbeat case.

"I'm uncertain," Zelikow concluded. That was the bottom line. But, he wrote, "In the best case, on a good day, I could tell the president, 'We believe our effort in Iraq will probably succeed.' " He had carefully used the word "probably." "Indeed, if pressed, the odds of success are as good as, say 70 percent. Again, that means at least a 30 percent risk of failure, and a significant risk of catastrophic failure."

Zelikow noted that he had not found anyone who believed there was more than a 70 percent chance of success. "Even in the upbeat assess-ment," he continued, "we might optimistically judge that our efforts are probably just enough to succeed. Not much room to spare, but hopefully just enough."

Of course, "just enough" really meant "nowhere near enough." The president had declared that failure in Iraq was not an option. Zelikow agreed, and that meant the current risk of failure was unacceptably high. They needed a plan and strategy that was more than enough to succeed. They had to "win going away," he wrote. His intended audience was Rice, the diehard NFL football fan, so he described the goal in those terms. We need to win by two or three touchdowns, Zelikow said.

There was too much barely coping, just getting by, and making incremental improvements. They needed to make a major effort to prevail. Outside of a few components of the Defense Department and the military, few were going all out.

"We should try to then make 2006 a turning point year, setting the new government that will win or lose the war on a positive path."

Under "U.S. Force size and critical infrastructure protection," he said the forces were spread thin, but he did not advocate a massive infusion of U.S. troops. General Casey needed to accept that one of his core missions was infrastructure protection. The Iraqi infrastructure battalions were a bust, and the lack of security was getting lots of people killed. "We need to treat key pipelines and electricity pathways with the same regard as we treat MNF's own main supply routes"—the military term for highways—"and devise a security plan accordingly with a mix of Iraqi and coalition forces."

Again, he noted that the degree to which insurgents were using more lethal IEDs, which accounted for the majority of American military deaths, was especially troubling. There was strong evidence that starting in mid-2005, there had been a flow of advanced IED components coming into Iraq from Iran. The designs weren't revolutionary, but by shaping the charges and causing the explosives and projectiles to travel in a straight line, as opposed to a large, undirected explosion, the newer IEDs concentrated their force and could penetrate armor. They were very lethal—at least four times more lethal than what Iraqi insurgents were capable of producing themselves—and capable of killing everyone inside an armored Humvee.

The Pentagon had a $3.3 billion plan to come up with effective defenses against IEDs. But this was really a multifaceted problem. It was no longer just the lethality of the weapons that was important, but the significance that the weapons were coming from Iran. Some evidence indicated that the Iranian-backed terrorist group Hezbollah was training insurgents to build and use the shaped IEDs, at the urging of the Iranian Revolutionary Guard Corps. That kind of action was arguably an act of war by Iran against the United States. If we start putting out everything we know about these things, Zelikow felt, the administration might well start a fire it couldn't put out.

Rice recognized Zelikow's use of a standard academic model of risk assumptions, and she realized that he was questioning whether they were giving themselves enough margin for victory given the enormous stakes. But her considerations had to be practical. On the surface, Zelikow's calculation that there was a 70 percent chance of success might lead to a conclusion that overwhelming force was required because, in the tradition of the Powell Doctrine, they had to guarantee success. But a little deeper, it was not clear that overwhelming military force was how to beat an insurgency. An insurgency, Rice believed, would not be defeated principally by the military. It had to be defeated politically. So her focus had to be on the State Department's role. Did she need to change the structure of how she used her people? How could she get the very best people out to Iraq? What incentives could she offer to get the right people to go? How could she put her department on more of a war footing?

She was all too aware that Rumsfeld had persistently argued to reduce Iraqi dependencies on U.S. assistance and insisted that it was time to get the American hands off the back of the bicycle seat.

"I think it is true that people will hold on to dependencies as long as they can," Rice said. "But it's also true that if you take the hand off the bicycle and it goes over a ravine that's not a very good thing either. So it's a balance. How do you judge that they're really capable enough? I think you do it by doing it pretty gradually."

ON SEPTEMBER 29, 2005, I went to the Senate to have breakfast with Senator Carl Levin, 71, of Michigan, a 26-year Senate veteran and the ranking Democrat on the Armed Services Committee. Often and accurately described as "rumpled," Levin peered theatrically over his tiny glasses. In the Rumsfeld Pentagon they frequently referred to Levin as "the prosecutor" because he was always after them. Before the war, he had believed that Saddam had WMD but he didn't think that was a good enough reason to invade.

Levin voted against the war and he had pounded hard on the CIA, convinced that they had not shared all the suspected WMD sites with the United Nations inspectors. That meant they hadn't all been inspected before Bush ordered the invasion. But this information from the WMD Master Site List was classified.

"I tried in 10 different ways to get that declassified," Levin said, "because if we could have brought out in advance of the attack that we had not shared with the U.N. all of the sites that we were suspicious of, it would have put a chill on the decision to go to war."

I remarked that the WMD Master Site List had been based on lots of five-year-old intelligence, and that the military intelligence people on the ground had had little confidence in it.

Levin said the inspection process was incomplete, not thorough. It could have delayed war, he believed, but not stopped it. He complained about "all of the shadings, exaggerations, and hype" about WMD by Bush and Cheney and said it "showed the most willful and purposeful intent" to create a deception.

"I've never thought that Bush was dumb at all," Levin said, lightly rapping on the table for emphasis. "But I think he's intellectually lazy and I think he wants people around him who will not challenge him but will give him the ammunition which he needs or wants in order to achieve some more general goal."

I said I thought Powell was in anguish about what had happened in Iraq, with 130,000 American troops still stuck there, facing an ever-growing insurgency.

"I don't want to hear about his anguish," Levin said, nearly exploding in anger. "I don't have the stomach to hear his anguish. He is so smart and his instincts are so decent and good that I can't just accept his anguish. I want more than anguish. I expected more than anguish."

"What did you want?" I asked. "An apology?"

"Honesty. I wanted honesty. I don't want to read a year later or two years later saying that this is the worst moment of his life or something. He had problems with this along the way. I had hoped for a George Marshall type." In World War II, General George Marshall had kept his distance from President Roosevelt, telling him at one point, "Mr. President, don't call me George."

"Powell had the potential to change the course here," Levin continued. "He's the only one who had potential to."

How could he have done that? I asked.

"If he told the president that this is the wrong course," Levin said. "I don't think he ever realized what power lay in his hands, and that's an abdication. I think Powell has tremendous power." He said Powell had a number of things he could have done to slow down if not possibly stop the war. He could have threatened to resign or insisted that the U.N. weapons inspectors be allowed to continue, Levin said. When Bush asked Powell in January 2003 if he would be with him in the war, Levin said, Powell was at the peak of his influence.

"Can you imagine what would have happened if he'd said, 'I've got to give that a little thought'? Can you imagine the power of that one person to change the course? He had it."

BUSH HELD SO-CALLED BIG FIVE MEETINGS with the top leaders in Congress—the majority and minority leaders in the Senate and the House of Representatives, plus the speaker of the House. The meetings generally started promptly at 8 A.M., and Bush would deliver a 45-minute monologue, mostly on foreign policy. There would be 10 or 15 minutes for questions or comments, and the meetings always ended at 9 A.M. There was never anything important enough to go longer.

Senator Harry Reid of Nevada, the Democratic minority leader in the Senate, a 65-year-old former boxer who had been chairman of the Nevada Gaming Commission, found Bush nice, even friendly, at these meetings. But the partisan divide was so great that Reid told his staff, "I just can't stand him." He found it unbearable to watch most of the president's nationally televised speeches. Instead, members of his staff would watch and then brief him on what Bush had said.

On Iraq, there was little common ground between the two parties. Real communication had virtually broken down.

THE SENATE FOREIGN RELATIONS COMMITTEE, once a powerhouse in national foreign policy debates, had been clamoring for nearly a year for Rice to testify about Iraq. Her ducking was humiliating for the senators, many of whom thought she was just trying to avoid being tarred with the prolonged war. She finally agreed to testify in the fall.

Rice conferred with Zelikow and others on her staff, hoping to come up with a definition of success for her testimony. She went back to Zelikow's September memo, where he had said success would include breaking and neutralizing the insurgency, keeping Iraq from becoming a significant base for terrorism, demonstrating some democratic process, and turning the corner fiscally and economically. She decided to incorporate his benchmarks almost verbatim. But her planned testimony lacked a cohesive, understandable, headline-grabbing summary.

Zelikow had been reading *A Better War*, a 1999 book by Lewis Sorley about a "clear and hold" strategy that Sorley claimed had led to some success in the Vietnam War after the "search and destroy" strategy had been discarded.

In Zelikow's view, "clear and hold" was not enough. It needed another pillar that was positive, more declarative. Holding was too passive. He came up with the notion of "clear, hold and . . . build."

Rice made it the centerpiece of her testimony before the Senate committee on Wednesday, October 19. It was the first time any senior administration official had come to the committee in more than a year and a half specifically to talk about Iraq. She told the senators, "Our political-military strategy has to be to clear, hold and build: to clear areas from insurgent control, to hold them securely and to build durable Iraqi institutions."

Much of this was a military mission, and Rumsfeld was furious. As far as he was concerned, it did not convey what they were really trying or should be trying to do: get the Iraqis to shoulder more of the burden. It was wrong to say that the United States' "political-military strategy" was all about what the U.S. would do and not what the Iraqis would do. They had to get their hands off the back of the bicycle seat, had to lose the training wheels.

According to Rumsfeld, Rice "felt that a bumper sticker was needed" to explain what the State Department was doing in Iraq.

"I didn't need one," he told me later in an interview. "We've got our job to do. We're doing it. And they had to fashion something like that. And they're right. If you're going to communicate with multiple audiences, including ours—our Congress, our public—the Iraqi people, then they want to know, 'Well what are you doing? Do you have a strategy? Do you have a plan?' The answer is we do have a plan.

"But the question was, clear is one thing, and my problem was I wanted—if that is our strategy for the United States, then I worried about it because in fact I wanted—we've got what, 263,000 Iraqi security forces? I wanted them clearing. And then holding. And I didn't want the idea to be that it was just us. And so that was my concern, because that is grabbing ahold of the bicycle seat and holding on for dear life."

•   •   •

ON FRIDAY, OCTOBER 28, 2005, Scooter Libby was indicted in the CIA leak case on charges of perjury, obstruction of justice, and making false statements to the FBI. He resigned that day. White House security officials came to his office, took away his passes and told him he had to leave immediately. Libby had broken a bone in his foot and did not have a car. He was literally put out on the street, hobbling away on his crutches. Later, when he saw a copy of the indictment, *United States of America versus I. Lewis "Scooter" Libby,* he broke into tears. He later told friends he was reading Kafka.

ONE NIGHT THAT FALL, Brent Scowcroft sat next to Senator John McCain at a dinner. McCain, who had campaigned hard the previous year with Bush for the president's reelection, said that he had grown to like Bush.

"Does he ever ask your opinion?" Scowcroft asked.

"I don't believe in giving my opinion when I'm with him campaigning," McCain answered. "These guys come up. They get two minutes with the president and they try to tell him how to run the country. I don't."

"That's not what I asked," Scowcroft said. "Has he ever said, 'John, what do you think about . . . ?' "

"No, no, he hasn't," McCain said. "As a matter of fact he's not intellectually curious. But one of the things he did say one time is he said, 'I don't want to be like my father. I want to be like Ronald Reagan.' "

That burned Scowcroft, who was feeling increasingly hopeless. He concluded that the administration was doing the unthinkable, repeating the mistakes of Vietnam. Few people knew more about Vietnam than Scowcroft, who had worked on Vietnam for Presidents Nixon and Ford. He felt there was even less of a chance of building an Iraqi army that would fight than there had been three decades earlier when they were trying to build up the South Vietnamese army, which had existed as a powerful, even almost autonomous force in Vietnam its own right. In Iraq, the armies were all connected one way or another to the Shiites, the Sunnis or the Kurds. It was a political catastrophe.

Scowcroft was increasingly disappointed in the performances of those he had worked with and mentored. He considered Hadley, who had been on his NSC staff in the early 1970s, a dear friend. But Hadley would not stand up to anyone—not to Cheney or Rice, and certainly not to Rumsfeld. He wouldn't even stand up for his own opinions.

Even the president's father had confided that he was unhappy with Rice. "Condi is a disappointment, isn't she?" the former president had offered, adding, "She's not up to the job."

From his military contacts, as far as Scowcroft could tell, General Myers, the outgoing chairman of the JCS, was a broken man, a puppy dog. General Pace was worse. Pace had watched Myers with Rumsfeld for four years, knew exactly what he was getting into, and accepted it anyway.

Cheney was the worst, Scowcroft felt. "What's happened to Dick Cheney?" all the old hands were saying to him, the people who'd known him for years. "It's a chorus. 'We don't know this Dick Cheney.' "

Rumsfeld was behaving as he always had, going back to the Ford administration—"enigmatic, obstructionist, devious, never know what his game is." To Scowcroft, Rumsfeld was a wholly negative force.

Most tragic, Scowcroft felt, was that the administration had believed Saddam was running a modern, efficient state, and thought that when he was toppled there would be an operating society left behind. They hadn't seen that everything would collapse, and that they would have to start from zero. They hadn't seen the need for security, or that probably 90 percent of the Iraqi army could have been saved and used. So Iraqis now felt overwhelmingly insecure. Without security there was little opportunity to give people a stake in their society, little reason for them to have a positive attitude. It seemed to Scowcroft that the Iraqis were in despair.

But the administration wouldn't reexamine or reevaluate its policy. As he often said, "I just don't know how you operate unless you continually challenge your own assumptions." Most distressing to Scowcroft was to see his good friend and former leader Bush senior, "41," as Scowcroft called him, in "agony," "anguished" and "tormented" by the war and what had happened afterward. It was terrible. The father still wanted his son to succeed. But what a tangled relationship! In his younger years, Scowcroft thought, George W. couldn't decide whether he was going to rebel against his father or try to beat him at his own game. Now, he had tried at the game, and it was a disaster. Scowcroft was sure that 41 would never have behaved this way—"not in a million years."

39

U.S. INTELLIGENCE AGENCIES were conducting polls in Iraq measuring the favorable/unfavorable ratings of some of Iraq's leaders and figures.

From November 11 to 18, 2005, the person with the highest standing in Iraq was Sistani, with 61 percent favorable, 39 unfavorable.

Former Prime Minister Allawi was close behind, with 59.7 percent favorable, 40.3 percent unfavorable.*

Those were the kinds of approval ratings Bush could only dream about in the United States. A poll by NBC News and *The Wall Street Journal* on November 10 had him at 38 percent favorable, 57 percent unfavorable.

RICE WANTED TO ESTABLISH some concrete State Department presence in Iraq outside the Green Zone. She took seriously Zelikow's criticism that the civilian agencies were not deployed enough beyond Baghdad, and she wanted to develop Provincial Reconstruction Teams involving political and economic experts, aid workers and engineers who would go into the 18 provinces, set up outposts, and help in the rebuilding. Khalilzad had established similar PRTs in Afghanistan when he was ambassador there. Rice and Rumsfeld got into another dispute because he

---

* Others in the Iraq polls had high negatives. Chalabi was at 34 percent positive, 66 unfavorable. Saddam Hussein was at 22 percent favorable, 78 percent unfavorable. The lowest ratings were for Izzat al-Duri, Saddam's former vice president, who had never been caught by the U.S., who had a 20 percent favorable rating, and 80 percent unfavorable.

wanted the State Department to hire private contractors to provide security for the teams, at a cost of hundreds of millions of dollars. Rice, of course, wanted the military to provide the security. Back and forth it went.

On November 11, Rice made her second trip to Iraq, arriving first in Mosul, the primarily Kurdish city about 225 miles northwest of Baghdad, to announce the inauguration of the first PRT. Three other teams, which she felt were worth their weight in gold, were established in three other Iraqi cities. But funding, staffing and security issues delayed some of the others, and a couple of hundred people in the field were not going to make a measurable difference in a country with a population of 25 million.

ENEMY-INITIATED ATTACKS had hit an all-time high of more than 3,000 in October, according to the classified reports.

On Veterans Day, Bush was scheduled to give a speech at the Tobyhanna Army Depot in Pennsylvania, a giant military repair and maintenance facility. A draft of his speech was circulated among the principals, and Rumsfeld noticed that the president was planning to endorse Rice's "clear, hold and build" language as "our strategy."

Rumsfeld called Card about a half hour before the president was scheduled to speak.

"Take it out," Rumsfeld said. "Take that out."

"It's the centerpiece to the speech," Card replied. More than that, it was the centerpiece of their whole strategy.

"I recommend that we take it out," Rumsfeld persisted, noting that "clear, hold and build" just was not happening. The "clear" part was fine, he said. "Clear, we're doing." He meant the military. "It's up to the Iraqis to hold. And the State Department's got to work with somebody on the build."

Rumsfeld confirmed to me in an interview that he had asked that the phrase be removed. It might sound good at the moment but come back to haunt them. "It's not just us clearing, it's the coalition. And the holding is increasingly them and not us. And the building is, we want to help create environments that they can reconstruct their own country."

Rumsfeld lost that particular battle. The president said, "Our strategy is to clear, hold and build."

Gerson didn't understand Rumsfeld's objections. It was the only effective bumper sticker to explain their counterinsurgency strategy.

The other, bigger message in Bush's speech, however, was that the White House was going to come out swinging at anyone who claimed Bush and Cheney had misled the country before the war. The effect was to equate criticism with undermining the troops.

"While it's perfectly legitimate to criticize my decision or the conduct of the war, it is deeply irresponsible to rewrite the history of how that war began," Bush said, prompting applause from the audience of troops and veterans. "The stakes in the global war on terror are too high, and the national interest is too important, for politicians to throw out false charges," he added, to more applause. "These baseless attacks send the wrong signal to our troops and to an enemy that is questioning America's will."

On November 16, Cheney gave an address to a conservative organization called the Frontiers of Freedom Institute, and amplified Bush's challenge. The accusation that they had lied was "one of the most dishonest and reprehensible charges ever aired in this city," he said, adding, "The saddest part is that our people in uniform have been subjected to these cynical and pernicious falsehoods day in and day out. American soldiers and Marines are out there every day in dangerous conditions and desert temperatures—conducting raids, training Iraqi forces, countering attacks, seizing weapons, and capturing killers—and back home a few opportunists are suggesting they were sent into battle for a lie. The President and I cannot prevent certain politicians from losing their memory, or their backbone—but we're not going to sit by and let them rewrite history."

That day, the White House released a 5,000-word, point-by-point rebuttal of a 913-word *New York Times* editorial that was sharply critical of Bush's prewar WMD rhetoric, and the more recent administration "claims that questioning his actions three years ago is a betrayal of the troops in battle today."

The next day, Congressman Jack Murtha, a Pennsylvania Democrat, introduced a resolution in Congress calling for American troops in Iraq to be "redeployed"—the military term for returning troops overseas to their home bases—"at the earliest practicable date." Murtha, a former Marine Corps drill instructor and the first Vietnam veteran elected to Congress, had excellent sources among the armed forces. No one had better credentials as a supporter of the military than the 73-year-old

Murtha. Murtha had voted for the October 2002 resolution authorizing the president to use military force in Iraq. A four-time visitor to Iraq, Murtha made weekly trips to the military hospitals to visit wounded Iraq veterans.

"The war in Iraq is not going as advertised," Murtha said. "It is a flawed policy wrapped in illusion." The military was suffering, he said on the House floor. Choking back tears, he added, "Our military has done everything that has been asked of them. It is time to bring them home." Many of the troops had become demoralized and were poorly equipped. Two years after the war, their very presence in Iraq was impeding Iraq's progress toward stability and self-governance.

This was shocking and House Republicans knew it had to be met head-on. The next day the House had one of its most emotional and raucous debates. Speaker Dennis Hastert asserted that Murtha and other Democrats had "adopted a policy of cut and run. They would prefer that the United States surrender to the terrorists who would harm innocent Americans."

House Armed Services Chairman Duncan Hunter, a California Republican, introduced a resolution that cynically twisted Murtha's proposal for a pullout "at the earliest practicable date." Hunter's resolution called for an immediate troop pullout. Murtha himself could not and did not vote for it. It was defeated, 403–3.

Later that day, the president's press secretary, Scott McClellan, issued a statement. "Congressman Murtha is a respected veteran and politician who has a record of supporting a strong America. So it is baffling that he is endorsing the policy positions of Michael Moore* and the extreme liberal wing of the Democratic party. The eve of an historic democratic election in Iraq is not the time to surrender to the terrorists. After seeing his statement, we remain baffled—nowhere does he explain how retreating from Iraq makes America safer." The upcoming December 15 election in Iraq McClellan referred to was to elect a permanent assembly, which would select a prime minister to serve for four years.

Murtha's was a voice from deep inside the soul and conscience of the American military. Informed military officers knew he was speaking for many more than himself.

---

* Moore made the controversial anti-Bush documentary film *Fahrenheit 9/11*.

. . .

CARD TRIED TO HAVE A PRIVATE, candid session with Laura Bush about every six weeks to hear her concerns. He set aside an hour and a half for each meeting. Sometimes it took 30 minutes, sometimes the full hour and a half and on occasion two hours.

The first lady was distressed about the war, but Card knew that she was not aware of the classified intelligence or information on Iraq. Nonetheless she often pressed him for information.

"I can't talk about that," Card said.

"Well, he won't tell me either."

The first lady was worried that Rumsfeld was hurting her husband, and her perspective seemed to reflect Rice's concern about Rumsfeld's overbearing style and tendency to dominate. Card knew that the first lady and Rice often took long walks together on the Camp David weekends.

"I agree with you," Card said. On one level he was trying to educate and explain, but he was also lobbying. So he outlined his problems with Rumsfeld and how he believed it was time for a change.

"Well, does the president know about that?" she asked. Was he being candid with her husband?

Card said he was. "That's why I'm arguing." He said, however, that so far his advice on the Rumsfeld situation had been considered and rejected.

"He's happy with this," the first lady said, "but I'm not." Another time she said, "I don't know why he's not upset with this."

FOR MUCH OF THE YEAR the president had been working out how he might explain the strategy to win in Iraq. In Nebraska on February 4, 2005, he had said, "Our strategy is clear. We're going to help the Iraqis defend themselves. We'll accelerate training. . . . We'll help them stand up a high-quality security force. And when that mission is complete, and Iraq is democratic and free and able to defend herself, our troops will come home with the honor they deserve."

The problem was that training Iraqis and building Iraqi defenses is not a strategy for classic military victory—the "kinetics" of bombing and engagements with other military forces. Generals Abizaid and Casey realized that the goal of "neutralizing" the insurgents as outlined in the classified "Campaign Plan" had not been realized. In a practical sense the military had adopted a transition strategy to shift the problem to the Iraqis, as opposed to a strategy to win. "Neutralizing" or even defeating the insurgency was too hard. The plan was to train the Iraqi security forces to do it.

The key was to make the transition strategy sound like progress. In an address to the nation from Fort Bragg, North Carolina, on June 28, 2005, the president said, "Our strategy can be summed up this way: As the Iraqis stand up, we will stand down."

Abizaid went before Congress and later appeared on television on Sunday, October 2, 2005. "We've got close to 200,000 Iraqi security forces in the field, we've come a long way," the general told NBC's Tim Russert. "I'm optimistic."

Indeed the number of Iraqi security forces had been going up steadily while the number of U.S. forces had remained constant. But the classified reports showed that over the previous eight months the enemy-initiated attacks had gone up pretty steadily to 2,500 in the month of September 2005.

Abizaid kept in touch with a bunch of old Army buddies—many from West Point and mostly retired, including retired Army General Wayne Downing and Jim Kimsey, a founder of America Online. They were worried that Iraq was slowly turning into Vietnam—it would either wind down prematurely or become a war that was not winnable.

Some of them visited Abizaid at his headquarters in Doha and then in Iraq. Abizaid held to the position that the war was now about the Iraqis. They had to win the war now. The U.S. military had done all it could. It was critical, he argued, that they lower the American troop presence. It was still the face of an occupation with American forces patrolling, kicking down doors, looking at the Iraqi women, which infuriated the Iraqi men.

"We've got to get the fuck out," he said.

Abizaid's old friends were worried sick that another Vietnam or anything that looked like Vietnam would be the end of the volunteer army. What's the strategy for winning? They pressed him.

"That's not my job," Abizaid insisted.

No, it is part of your job, they insisted. Abizaid was the articulate one. He could talk for an hour and it sounded great, better than anyone.

No, Abizaid said. Articulating strategy belonged to others.

Who?

"The president and Condi Rice because Rumsfeld doesn't have any credibility anymore," he said.

• • •

HADLEY HEARD SIMILAR COMPLAINTS that there was no strategy. He wanted to launch a public relations offensive. He assigned his NSC director for Iraq, Meghan O'Sullivan, to comb through the classified documents that he thought outlined their strategy, and see what could be made public.

In June 2005, Hadley had recruited Peter Feaver, 43, a Duke University professor of political science and Navy Reserve officer who had worked on the Clinton NSC, to the NSC staff. Feaver had studied the impact of war on public opinion and concluded that the public was more tolerant of combat losses than politicians or senior military officers. He felt that Clinton came close to almost questioning his authority as commander in chief to order someone to his death. This had cascaded down so that the political and military leadership during his presidency had virtually no tolerance for casualties.

Feaver's survey work suggested that the public would tolerate casualties if they believed the war policy was reasonable, aimed at winning. O'Sullivan and Feaver worked on a strategy document that would depict a reasonable path to victory. Feaver believed the document they came up with showed mixed progress, and did not mindlessly declare a necessity to stay the course.

Hadley sent the draft out to the principals. Rumsfeld had numerous comments, carefully hedging. The final document said, "We expect, but cannot guarantee, that our force posture will change over the year." In other words, there was no timetable for withdrawing forces.

The document was given the title "National Strategy for Victory in Iraq." It was right out of the Kissinger playbook—the only meaningful exit strategy would be victory.

Bush approved and the plan was to put out a 35-page "Strategy for Victory" in September. But on August 29, Hurricane Katrina devastated New Orleans and the Gulf Coast, and caught the Bush administration flat-footed. The rollout had to be delayed.

CARD'S RELATIONSHIP WITH RUMSFELD was always difficult. A vast majority of the times, Rumsfeld accepted Card's word that the president wanted certain things done and gave the chief of staff the benefit of the doubt when he passed on an order. But a handful of times Rumsfeld balked.

In the days after Katrina, Bush had decided more National Guard troops were needed, and asked Card to relay the message to Rumsfeld.

"You know, I don't report to you," Rumsfeld said.

"I know you don't report to me," Card replied. "You report to the president. But believe me, he would like you to do this."

"I'm not going to do it unless the president tells me," Rumsfeld told the chief of staff. Too many strains and obligations were being placed on the Guard.

Card protested that he had just talked to the president, who had made an absolute decision.

"Then he's going to have to tell me," Rumsfeld said.

"Hey," the president said to Card later, "Rumsfeld called me up. I thought you were going to handle that."

"I did," Card said dryly, "but he wanted to hear it from you, I guess."

After Thanksgiving, Card made another concentrated effort to get the president to replace Rumsfeld. He didn't want the president to have blinders on. Rumsfeld's assault on "clear, hold and build" was only one example. Many of the Republican and Democratic leaders were telling Card privately that they just could not deal with him. He was more arrogant and unresponsive than ever. Card was also hearing from members of the old foreign policy establishment connected to the president's father—the "Gray Beards," he called them—who were complaining more and more. A focus was Rumsfeld.

"Who's going to do the job?" the president asked Card.

Card again mentioned Jim Baker. "How do we get Roger Clemens back into the game?" Card asked, comparing Baker to one of the all-time great pitchers. Clemens had retired from the New York Yankees in 2003, only to come back for another year with his hometown Houston Astros. "He can still pitch," Card said about Baker.

Bush reminded him that they were at war. Rumsfeld was transforming the military, hadn't been insubordinate, and needed to get the new Pentagon budget approved. Replacing him would be disruptive to the upcoming Iraqi election December 15. "Interesting," the president said nonetheless. "Interesting."

Card could see that the point was sitting in Bush's mind. Maybe it would come out. But the president would not even authorize Card to send out feelers or to enter into any discussion with Baker.

THE 35-PAGE "NATIONAL STRATEGY for Victory in Iraq" was finally released on November 30, 2005. "No war has ever been won on a timetable and neither will this one," the executive summary said. U.S. forces would be withdrawn "as the political process advances and Iraqi security forces grow and gain experience. While our military presence may become less visible, it will remain lethal and decisive, able to confront the enemy wherever it may organize. Our mission in Iraq is to win the war. Our troops will return home when the mission is complete."

Part of the plan was for Bush to give four speeches on Iraq, starting with one that day at the Naval Academy in Annapolis, Maryland. Dozens of large "Plan for Victory" signs hung in the background. Bush used the word "victory" 15 times, insisted he would not compromise, and maintained his upbeat tone. He conceded a few mistakes, saying that the training of Iraqi security forces, for example, had not always gone smoothly, but said that lessons had been learned. "We changed the way the Iraqi police are trained. Now, police recruits spend more of their time outside the classroom with intensive hands-on training in antiterrorism operations and real-world survival skills."

BUSH'S WAR POLICY had not changed, but the news coverage suggested he was being more explicit and comprehensive. From Iraq, *The Washington Post* reported that day, violence was no mere abstraction. "On the streets of Baghdad, such optimistic rhetoric contrasts sharply with the thunder of suicide bombs, the scream of ambulance sirens, the roar of racing police cars bearing men with masks and machine guns, the grim daily reports of assassinations, murders and hostage-taking.

"On the same day Bush spoke, nine farmworkers were killed when gunmen opened fire on a bus near Baqubah, snipers fired on the office of a National Assembly member in the capital, and three Iraqi army officers were wounded when a bomb went off near their patrol. In Fallujah, 20,000 people marched in a funeral for a Sunni cleric shot while leaving prayers."

The violence on the ground had not changed. But a dispatch from Baghdad by two respected *New York Times* correspondents, John F. Burns and Dexter Filkins, went the furthest, noticing a change in the president. Headlined, "For Once, President and His Generals See the Same War," they called Bush's speech a "watershed," because it acknowledged the immense difficulties in training Iraqis and getting Iraqi army and police battalions to the point where they could hold their own against the insurgency.

• • •

ON DECEMBER 7, the president flew to New York City to address the Council on Foreign Relations for the second of four planned speeches on Iraq.

"Today we mark the anniversary of a fateful day in American history," he said, and compared Pearl Harbor with 9/11. It was still his main theme.

Later that afternoon in Washington, Bush invited the Republican House leaders, including the 15 deputy whips who were the core organization of the Republican Party in the House, to the White House. These were the ambitious Republicans that Bush wanted to hold close. Cheney, Rove, Card and Bartlett attended the meeting in the Oval Room of the White House residence.

The president acknowledged that he had been off his game since Hurricane Katrina. There had been a lull in the political momentum, he said, no doubt. But now in Iraq, he said, they were doing things differently than they had two years ago. He would not withdraw troops until the conditions for victory were right.

"We're not leaving if Laura and Barney are the only ones who support me," Bush said.

Representative Roy Blunt, the Missouri Republican who was acting majority leader, said that when Democrats like Murtha proposed getting out of Iraq, people realized the only acceptable alternative was what Bush was doing. They all agreed that forcing the issue with the vote in the House had been a great tactical victory.

"I know I make long and boring speeches, but my advisers say it's necessary," Bush said.

Several congressmen encouraged the president and said he needed to make long, single-topic speeches because it forced the news media to cover them. Who cared if the media were annoyed? It was a matter of attempting to control their coverage.

40

THE NEXT DAY, December 8, 2005, Bush and Cheney held a video teleconference with Ambassador Khalilzad and General Casey.

How long would it take to stand up the new, permanent government after the elections for the National Assembly that would select a prime minister? Bush asked.

Last time it took about 90 days, Khalilzad said, but this time he hoped to do it in about half that time, six weeks after the upcoming December 15 elections.

Bush gave his third Iraq speech in Philadelphia on December 12. This time he answered questions from the audience, ordinary members of the public who had not been screened.

The first question was pointed: "Since the inception of the Iraqi war, I'd like to know the approximate total of Iraqis who have been killed. And by Iraqis I include civilians, military, police, insurgents, translators."

"How many Iraqi citizens have died in this war?" the president responded. "I would say 30,000, more or less, have died as a result of the initial incursion and the ongoing violence against Iraqis. We've lost about 2,140 of our own troops in Iraq." The numbers were telling, as was the fact that Bush had almost the precise death toll for Americans, 2,144, right on the tip of his tongue.

THE DEFENSE POLICY BOARD, the outside senior group of advisers for Rumsfeld that included Kissinger, Newt Gingrich and Ken Adelman, met at the Pentagon for two days of closed-door briefings on December 8 and 9. During the first day, Ryan Henry, a top Rumsfeld deputy, briefed on the Quadrennial Defense Review, the detailed strategy for the U.S. military over the next 20 years. Rumsfeld thought this was one of his greatest accomplishments—a blueprint for the future. Midway through a long PowerPoint briefing with slides and charts, Henry paused. "The good news is that not one defense program had to be cut," he said.

"Well, why is that good news?" Adelman interrupted. It was unusual to break in. "A strategic review for four years since the war on terrorism began, since 9/11 happened, since the world is different and there wasn't one program that you could eliminate?"

Henry said that everyone in the building—civilians and those in uniform—had decided nothing had to be cut.

"I'm sorry I interrupted," Adelman said, "but I just find it incredible."

The next day, the board met with Rumsfeld, who was proud of the in-depth review, which included plans to increase Special Operations Forces by some 15 percent and to add sophisticated programs to fight terrorism and to deal with weapons of mass destruction.

"I think Ken has a different view on that," said Chris Williams, a defense contractor and lobbyist who was the board chairman. Dissent was unusual.

"What's that?" asked Rumsfeld tartly of the man he had wanted to run his presidential campaign 20 years earlier.

Adelman, exasperated, said that after four years of work, after 9/11, and after all the efforts at transformation, with Rumsfeld spending maybe a quarter of his time on the QDR, and the deputy up to half his time, "I find it incredible that nothing is going to be cut."

"Who told you that?"

Adelman at first didn't want to single out Ryan Henry, so he said maybe he had misunderstood.

"Who said that?" Rumsfeld pressed.

"Ryan Henry sitting right there told us that," Adelman said, pointing to Henry, who was sitting in the back, off to the side.

"The review isn't over," Rumsfeld said.

"Oh, I'm sorry. I thought it was going to the printer."

"Well, the president hasn't signed off."

"If it's going to the printer," Adelman said, "whether the president's signed off or not, it seems pretty far along."

"All right," Rumsfeld challenged. "Supposing it doesn't have any cuts."

"I think it's astonishing," Adelman said. "The whole world has changed. This was supposed to be the new Pentagon."

Rumsfeld gazed at Adelman, clearly furious. He said that everyone in the building had agreed. "We all get along," he added. "Sometimes you don't need to cut and there was no reason to cut."

An hour later the policy board was talking about the briefing they had received from Abizaid and Casey. Both had said they were making progress in Iraq and things seemed to be going well.

"Again I think Ken has a different attitude," Williams said.

"What's that?" Rumsfeld inquired.

Adelman said that Casey had reported that military personnel—officers and enlisted—were being rotated out of Iraq about every nine months or less, on average. "When you look at history, I don't know of any counterinsurgency that's won by a country that rotates people out every six to nine months."

"We're not rotating all the people out," Rumsfeld said. "We have Casey there."

"I'm not talking about that," Adelman said. "I'm talking about the people."

"Let me tell you the reason for that," Rumsfeld replied, describing Army and Marine recruiting and promotions.

"I'm not talking about what the Army wants to do and what the Marines want to do," Adelman said. "What I'm talking about is winning the war. I don't know any counterinsurgency that wins on a strategy like that."

"Well, I think you've got it wrong because a lot of the soldiers go back in the theater for a second tour," Rumsfeld said.

"What do you mean by theater?" Adelman asked.

"The CENTCOM theater."

"Oh, so they go back to Afghanistan. That's not what I'm talking about."

"Well, some of them go back to Iraq."

"Okay, but do they go back to the neighborhood they were in? What are the chances of that?"

"Almost never," the secretary answered honestly.

"Well, that's my point."

"What's your point?"

"They have to know who to pay off," Adelman said. "They have to know whom to deal with. They have to know whom to maneuver. And that's tough sledding. That takes time. Six months, they know nothing. Nine months?"

Rumsfeld screwed up his face. He cited a recent study showing that most of the casualties came in the first months.

"That reinforces my point," Adelman said.

"It does," Rumsfeld conceded.

GINGRICH SAID EVEN THOUGH a fortune in executive manpower had been spent on the QDR strategy review, "None of that matters."

Rumsfeld looked at him uncomfortably.

"Only Iraq really matters," the former speaker continued. He said that the measure of seriousness was the 132 days it took to go from Ambassador Negroponte to Ambassador Khalilzad. Iraq was only "the most important country in the world that all of American foreign policy hinges on," he added sarcastically.

After the meeting, Adelman ran into Rumsfeld in the Pentagon hallway. Rumsfeld indicated he wanted to talk further.

"See you," said Adelman.

BEHIND THE SCENES, on December 13, the NSC principals approved a classified paper of some 10 rules or guidance to apply to forming the new Iraqi government. The ministers in the new government should have no affiliation with militias or external powers such as Iran or Syria. New ministers must have a clear record of competence. The new government should be formed quickly but not at the expense of quality; the minister of oil, for example, should have a history in that industry.

In other words, the United States would still be vetting the government in sovereign Iraq.

In his fourth Iraq speech the next day, December 14, at the Woodrow Wilson Center in Washington, Bush said, "When the history of these days is written, it will tell how America once again defended its own freedom by using liberty to transform nations from bitter foes to strong allies."

IN IRAQ ON ELECTION DAY, December 15, some 11 million voted for members of the National Assembly, who would sit for four-year terms. It was about a 70 percent turnout, much larger than in most Western democracies.

"There's a lot of joy," the president said.

The next day the headline on the front page of *The New York Times* was: "Iraqis, Including Sunnis, Vote in Large Numbers on Calm Day." Bush was thrilled. During a meeting with the Iraqi ambassador to the United Nations, the ambassador stated, "I think it was a turning point," and added extravagantly, "and the beginning of the end of terrorism in Iraq."

But the violence continued, with more than 2,500 insurgent attacks throughout December, according to the classified reports.

At a meeting in the Situation Room, Rumsfeld noted, "We don't have any more elections."

THREE DAYS AFTER THE ELECTIONS, on December 18, the president gave a prime-time TV speech from the Oval Office. After highlighting the apparent success of the elections, he recapped his history of the war, starting with the decision to invade, the toppling of Saddam, and on the question of WMD admitting flatly that "we did not find those weapons."

As the war continued, he acknowledged, many people were arguing that the U.S. was "creating more problems than we're solving" by remaining in Iraq. He rejected the notion. "Defeatism may have its partisan uses, but it is not justified by the facts," Bush said, adding, "To retreat before victory would be an act of recklessness and dishonor, and I will not allow it."

Toward the end of the speech, Bush added a message he said was intended for "those of you who did not support my decision to send troops to Iraq: I have heard your disagreement, and I know how deeply it is felt. Yet now there are only two options before our country—victory or defeat. And the need for victory is larger than any president or political party, because the security of our people is in the balance. I don't expect you to support everything I do, but tonight I have a request: Do not give in to despair, and do not give up on this fight for freedom.

"Americans can expect some things of me, as well. My most solemn responsibility is to protect our nation, and that requires me to make some tough decisions. I see the consequences of those decisions when I meet wounded servicemen and women who cannot leave their hospital beds, but summon the strength to look me in the eye and say they would do it all over again. I see the consequences when I talk to parents who miss a child so much—but tell me he loved being a soldier, he believed in his mission, and, Mr. President, finish the job.

"I know that some of my decisions have led to terrible loss—and not one of those decisions has been taken lightly. I know this war is controversial—yet being your President requires doing what I believe is right and accepting the consequences. And I have never been more certain that America's actions in Iraq are essential to the security of our citizens, and will lay the foundation of peace for our children and grandchildren."

He had rarely sounded so somber.

At the NSC meeting December 21, 2005, the paper on rules for forming the new government was presented to the president. "It's one thing to influence voters in an election," Bush said, referring to his clear decision not to try to influence the results of the December 15 election. "And it is another thing to influence government formation." He made it clear he wanted to weigh in heavily and looked to Ambassador Khalilzad, who was participating on secure video from Iraq. "Zal, we need to work with the Brits not to dictate outcomes or choose personalities, but to shape an outcome." That outcome was to be consistent with the principles. It was a fine distinction—shape an outcome but not dictate it. After more than two and a half years it was clear that Bush and the others were not going to let power in Iraq slide to someone unacceptable to them.

The discussion turned to the caliber of people who would be available in Iraq, and general frustration was voiced once again about the absence of a Washington or Jefferson, let alone a John Adams or lesser lights. There was so much corruption. It was a major obstacle. They agreed that lack of corruption should be included on their list of rules for Iraq. They had to find ministers who did not have a history of being on the take.

"Okay," Bush said, "add corruption to this list of principles and then, Zal, use your influence to make it happen."

The problem was fully in the ambassador's lap. The president was his case officer.

"You need to be clever about this, Zal," Bush continued. "You need to be figuring out some things that are enough for the Sunnis to declare the process successful without being so stressing to the Kurds and the Shia that it fractures the process."

It was another tall order. Bush wanted hard-nosed negotiations. Zal could threaten to cut off U.S. assistance, whatever he needed. Just fix it.

Hadley's NSC staff prepared a situation report each morning for the president and invariably the first item was Iraq and the casualties. In November, 88 American troops in Iraq had been killed; December was less at 67. There was also a situation report available to Bush at midday and a third one at night.

But the ebb and flow of the rate of attacks, probably the best measure of the level of violence and threat, was hard to predict. In October it had been 3,000. It dropped to 2,100 in November, and then shot back up to 2,500 in December.

ON NEW YEAR'S DAY, January 1, 2006, Bush visited Brooke Army Medical Center in San Antonio, Texas, where doctors and nurses had treated 2,300 casualties from Afghanistan and Iraq. It was the 34th time Bush had gone to visit the wounded.

He encountered a young soldier whose body was about 99 percent burned, and stood speechless for perhaps 30 seconds. Later, Bush told his aides, "I didn't know what possibly, as the most powerful man in the world—There's not a thing I could say." He then sat and prayed with the soldier's family, thanked them for their service and left, stunned by the family's spirit.

Afterward, he spoke to a group of reporters. He had a minor gash on his forehead from clearing trees on his ranch, and he inappropriately drew attention to his wound.

"As you can probably see, I have injured myself, not here at the hospital but in combat with a cedar. I eventually won. The cedar gave me a little bit of a scratch." A military doctor asked if he needed first aid, Bush said. "I was able to avoid any major surgical operations here."

The office of the White House physician, Dr. Richard J. Tubb, a one-star general in the Air Force Medical Corps, kept track of the wounded the president had met so he could send personal notes or make calls. Not long afterward, Tubb sent word to Bush that the soldier he had seen at the San Antonio hospital had died.

It hit the president hard. Dan Bartlett, his communications director, could see Bush's anguish. But Bush and the others in the White House tried hard to avoid conveying publicly that the president felt any torment. They believed such a disclosure would suggest he had doubts.

But in the visits with the wounded, a number of times family members confronted the president.

"See?" said a relative, pointing to a maimed soldier in a hospital bed. "It's not worth it."

"You can stop this," said another.

"Only you can stop it," said someone on a third occasion.

"I can understand why you feel that way," Bush responded.

"YOU CANNOT HELP BUT come out of there—" Rumsfeld said in an interview, recalling his own visits to military hospitals, "I'll put it in priority order: Inspired. And strengthened. And you are because the wounded there are—an enormous percentage are—anxious to get back to their units, proud of what they've done, confident that they'll be able to survive the injuries in one way or another. In a case with a leg off, go back to jump school and qualify first in the class and get back over to Iraq. So you come out inspired and strengthened, to be sure. You also cannot help but look at those wonderful human beings and see the damage that's been done to their bodies, and not understand the difficulty of tying a tie or putting a shirt on or the simple things."

"So do you feel anguish?" I asked.

"Oh sure."

"At those moments?"

"Sure. My goodness. You—no one could do that and not feel that, in my view," he answered. "You come out and you get in the car and you talk about the experience of the people you've met, the soldiers and sailors and Marines, the families, and how inspiring they are and how different they are in their personalities and yet how almost predictable they are in their pride of their service. And we are so lucky to have people like that."

Had he ever been challenged by the wounded or their families, the way Bush had, I asked.

"Sure. Sure."

"What have they said?"

"I don't think I want to discuss the private conversations," Rumsfeld said. "But they have indicated their disagreement with the conflict in Afghanistan or the conflict in Iraq. Personal disagreement."

What do you say to them? I asked.

"My goodness. They're going through a period in their life where something that they loved and cared for and nurtured is damaged, and in a way that they never anticipated. And so you can certainly understand the fact that any person in that circumstance is going to go through some swings of emotion, and it depends on where you hit them and where they are when you're there."

"Does that give you any swing of emotion yourself, where you kind of go, Why do I have this job?" I asked.

"No," Rumsfeld said. "There are things that raise that question in my mind. But not that so much."

"What are those things that raise it?" I asked.

"I'm not going to get into that," he said uncomfortably.

Visiting the wounded at military hospitals is part of the job of secretary of defense, he said. "I understand that historically. I understand it from my prior service here. I understand it today. So I do not go away and think, Gee, this is something that I ought to toss in the towel or something."

41

On December 23, 2005, the International Monetary Fund approved $685 million for Iraq. Almost as important as the money was the fact that the IMF had determined that the Iraqi exchange rate was stable, inflation was low, economic growth was estimated at 2.6 percent, and its overall medium-term outlook was "favorable." It was great news, though the IMF required that Iraq reach certain benchmarks on revenue and other matters.

Before long, though, in January 2006, Bush and the NSC faced a new crisis. Iraqi oil exports, the country's cash lifeline, were down about 20 percent from a year earlier. The drop meant that the Iraqi government was looking at a $2 billion to $3 billion revenue shortfall for the first quarter, even with rising oil prices. The shortfall would immediately jeopardize their IMF status, and potentially set off a chain reaction.

At the NSC staff, Meghan O'Sullivan examined the numbers in detail. They were so bad that the very viability of the government would be called into question. Not only was Iraq losing the revenue from the oil it wasn't exporting, but it now had to import fuel to make up the gap. It was like importing sand to the desert. Oil was Iraq's cash crop, but the insurgent attacks and the infrastructure decay put the country on the edge of an incredibly negative economic cycle. Despite all the talk about earlier "turning points," they were at a true tipping point. Everything could collapse.

O'Sullivan and Jeffrey's Iraq steering group met, as did the deputies committee. Finally, Andy Card joined the discussion at a principals meeting. The causes of the drop in oil exports included spotty maintenance at the refineries, poor weather in the south, inadequate storage capacity, attacks by the insurgents and criminal networks within the Iraqi ministries.

The Iraqis really have to take responsibility, Rumsfeld argued. If we do it for them, they will let us, once more expanding the mission. The plan was to give the Iraqis more responsibility. And how could the U.S. military protect thousands of miles of pipeline?

Rice disagreed. A key part of our counterinsurgency strategy, she said, involves protecting Iraq's economic lifeline—the oil flow. That in turn affected electricity. Baghdad was now often down to two to three hours a day of electricity.

There was also corruption. Oil was being stolen. The Iraqi Oil Ministry was paying many times what it should have paid for pumps and other oil equipment, and the difference was being pocketed. Add to this the targeted insurgent attacks on pipelines and other oil facilities, plus the decrepit condition of the infrastructure with its leaky pipes and broken pumps, and it was a mess. In at least one case it looked like Iraqis guarding a pipeline had attacked it themselves, or at least allowed it to be attacked, so they could get a bigger contract to protect it.

Lieutenant General Gene Renuart, now the director of the plans and policy division at the JCS, said, "If you want the electrical lines and the power plants, it's corruption. That's the problem. There's too much corruption!"

Rice stiffened. "You know that country has seen corruption for thousands of years," she said. "It'll probably see corruption for thousands of more years. I can't fix corruption, but you can fix some of this security."

There was a deadly silence. So there it was on the table. Where was the security? What kind of country were they fixing?

The military was aggressively raiding insurgent hideouts and strongholds, and had some 15,000 detainees. The principals discussed whether the raids were really accomplishing much. There was no conclusion after a long debate.

Card was struck by the tension between Rice and Rumsfeld. It was not new but it had a sharper edge. He was inclined to agree with Rice. Yes, they should turn over as much to the Iraqis as possible, but they could not let the economic lifeline of the country be further jeopardized. The oil resource could not be squandered.

As always, the debate turned to the perennially unanswered ques tions: What is the U.S. role here? How much do we leave it to the Iraqis? How much do we help the Iraqis? How much of it is our responsibility? The president had never made a decision, though the debate had raged for three years. What model applied to Iraq and the U.S. mission? Was it Hadley's abused child? Or was it Rumsfeld's Darwinian, American corporate model of allowing the Iraqis to fail? Should Rice's middle view prevail? Was there a strategy?

BUSH ATTENDED AN NSC MEETING on the Iraqi oil export issues. Rumsfeld argued once again that this was the Iraqis' job. They can do it, he said. Let's just tell them go do it. But there was no specific security training for pipeline and other oil infrastructure, so it would take months to get the Iraqis in a position to take control of infrastructure security.

No, Rice said, there was no time to dilly-dally. Security was so vital to everything they were attempting in Iraq that it had to be made an explicit part of the American military's mission.

Bush later expressed his frustration to Card that he was getting sucked into the details of this issue.

Rumsfeld couldn't have agreed more. "This isn't presidential," he told Card. "You don't have to take a lot of his time on this thing. We can work it out."

Still Rice pressed. She was down in the weeds on this thing, and she wanted the president with her. That was where he belonged. Besides, if Bush would not get involved it pretty much gave Rumsfeld carte blanche.

The president attended another NSC meeting, a briefing on Iraqi oil infrastructure security that included General Casey and Khalilzad. At the end, the president addressed Khalilzad on the video screen. "Look, we all have to agree that this is just unacceptable."

That was the one part everyone did agree on.

"Zal," the president continued, "I need you to come up with a plan to help the Iraqis fix this problem. I don't know what the right answers are but I need you to think differently. We need to fix this."

Khalilzad and General Casey said they would assume responsibility for a new plan.

Hadley and O'Sullivan took the president's directive to heart. They needed to "think differently" too. What they had been doing was not working. But it hadn't been working for nearly three years, and there had never been any prohibition on creative thinking. Instead, at this moment in February 2006 everyone went into crisis mode.

A series of video conferences was set up so Hadley could talk at length with Baghdad—the embassy and General Casey's command. He got into so much detail, drilled down so far, and had to pull out so much information that the conferences were often not with Casey or Khalilzad but with their deputies. The national security adviser became, in effect, the mission manager for Iraqi oil production quotas.

Card saw how awkward it was for Hadley to try to bridge Rice's and Rumsfeld's views. He was not sure Hadley could succeed. After weeks of work, Hadley came up with a plan that, at least on paper, looked integrated with the six main parts. The new part was a proposal to create rapid repair elements that could quickly fix almost any damage inflicted by the insurgents, an idea the government of Colombia had used in its battle against FARC insurgents.

These repair units would be called Strategic Infrastructure Battalions and would be comprised largely of Iraqi tribal-based forces that lived near the pipelines. Since there was some evidence that these battalions had been complicit in the attacks, a whole new retraining and vetting effort would be undertaken. In addition, U.S. forces and regular Iraqi forces would be embedded or partnered with the tribal units to increase their effectiveness and monitor them.

The other elements included: physically hardening the pipelines; building resilience and redundancy in the pipelines, including some secondary pipelines that would run alongside the primary; ferreting out corruption in the oil and electrical ministries; and improving intelligence coordination. They would ask for $250 million in the supplemental budget to fund it all.

Hadley asked that Rice and Rumsfeld be briefed separately. The plan was presented as what one official called "a fully coordinated, fully integrated, fully vetted, multi-pronged strategy to help Iraqis address this problem."

Rumsfeld seemed satisfied because the plan involved helping Iraqis get an Iraqi solution. "We can't solve this for them, although we can help them solve it."

Nearly three years after the invasion and two years after the transfer of sovereignty, the administration was addressing the same issues.

• • •

GENERAL CHIARELLI, who had been commander of the Army's 1st Cavalry Division in 2004–05 and who had impressed Rice's State Department counselor, Philip Zelikow, had become the biggest uniformed advocate for using less so-called kinetic or coercive warfare with military hardware or troops armed to the teeth.

In a summer 2005 article in *Military Review*, a scholarly journal for the armed forces, Chiarelli said that for three decades in the Army he trained to maneuver large troop and armor units to find the "point of penetration" in the enemy lines. In Iraq now he said the "point of penetration" was to have his troops hook up a sewer line, build a school or oversee a democratic election in Iraq. He envisioned a kinder, gentler presence, shooting and arresting fewer Iraqis and kicking down fewer doors. It sometimes sounded like his soldiers were functioning as Peace Corps workers.

Chiarelli was given his third star and in January 2006 made commander of all U.S. ground forces in Iraq. He argued convincingly that Iraq had a culture of revenge and honor. The brazen killing and even capturing of suspected or real insurgents had alienated Iraqis, who then joined or supported the insurgency. As Thomas E. Ricks, a *Post* colleague who has studied the Army and counterinsurgency, said in his book *Fiasco*, "The people are the prize." The American military was coming to realize that—at least on paper.

ON THE MORNING of Wednesday, February 22, 2006, bombs leveled the golden dome of the Askariya Mosque in Samarra, about 65 miles north of Baghdad, leaving it in ruins. The attack on one of the holiest Shiite shrines had been carefully planned. Shiite militias, especially those aligned with Moqtada al-Sadr, poured into the streets, and in retaliation fired grenades and machine guns into at least two dozen Sunni mosques in Baghdad. Three Sunni imams were killed and a fourth was kidnapped. Tens of thousands rioted. A daytime curfew was imposed in Baghdad. Prime Minister Jafari condemned the violence but did not publicly criticize Moqtada, who had been one of his early supporters.

Bush appealed for calm.

Intelligence indicated Zarqawi was responsible. General Casey had an additional problem. Rumsfeld liked to have a list of things that could go wrong, and Casey, with the help of the embassy, had put together a list of possible catastrophic events. It included an invasion by Iran or by Syria, a cutoff of oil exports, and the assassination of Sistani. The list included religious shrines though the Askariya Mosque wasn't on it. That meant it hadn't been guarded. The bombing was almost the breaking point for the Shiites and their most prominent leader, Sistani. Rice thought it unlikely that Iraq could withstand another such attack.

For Card, it raised the Rumsfeld question again. It was not clear to what extent Defense had planned to protect against sectarian violence and this was a classic case of sectarian violence. Iraq seemed on the brink of civil war.

IN MARCH 2006, Rumsfeld invited six of the Pentagon's outside advisers to be briefed by General Richard A. Cody, the vice chief of staff of the Army, who had just returned from Iraq. After the briefing, the six would meet with Rumsfeld. Among the six were Ken Adelman, whose relationship with Rumsfeld was nearly over, and James Dobbins, of RAND.

Adelman asked Cody, a husky 1972 West Point graduate and master aviator with 5,000 hours of flight time, what they were measuring to see how the war was going. "What are the metrics coming back that you would say were needed to identify so we know if we're winning or losing?"

"I'd say three," Cody replied. "Number one is the number of Iraqi civilians that are killed by these insurgent attacks. Number two is the number of usable, important bits of information we get from the Iraqi people—the actionable intelligence. And number three is the number of competent Iraqi police and military." He stayed away from a body count and the number of enemy-initiated attacks.

Shortly after, Rumsfeld entered. "Let's take some questions," he said.

Adelman asked him the same question he'd asked Cody. "What metrics would you use for success in Iraq? You know, for winning the war?"

"Oh, there are hundreds," Rumsfeld replied. "It's just so complicated that there are hundreds."

Dobbins pressed Rumsfeld on the number of Iraqi civilian casualties.

Rumsfeld said he didn't think the numbers were relevant. "The country's not in civil war," he said. "If it was in civil war, there'd be a large number of refugees."

Dobbins quoted the president's statement that 30,000 Iraqis had died in the last three years. It seemed about right based on the classified numbers they'd all seen. That was about 200 a week.

"Allowing for the fact that Iraq is 15 times smaller than the United

States," Dobbins said, "Iraqis for the first three years suffered the equivalent of a 9/11 attack every week. You can imagine the traumatic effect a
9/11 attack being repeated weekly would have on American society.
Don't you think it's having a similar effect on Iraqi society?"

Rumsfeld dismissed the notion.

"Wait a minute," Adelman insisted. "A former boss of mine always
said identify three or four things, then always ask about, get measure-
ments and you'll get progress or else you'll never get any progress." The
former boss was Rumsfeld himself, who had driven the point home to
Adelman 35 years before, when he worked for Rumsfeld at the Office of
Economic Opportunity. What are they? Adelman insisted.

Rumsfeld said it was so complicated that he could not give a list.

Adelman believed that meant there was a total lack of accountability.
If Rumsfeld didn't agree to any criteria, he couldn't be said to have failed
on any criteria.

"Hundreds," Rumsfeld insisted.

"Then you don't have anything," Adelman said. He left as disturbed
as ever. No accountability. When he had been Rumsfeld's civilian assistant in the Ford administration, all Rumsfeld had to do to be a great secretary of defense was to bitch about Kissinger. It became his main
occupation, along with bashing the Soviet Union and stopping SALT II,
the treaty for strategic arms limitations.

Now, Adelman thought, Rumsfeld's task was of greater strategic and
historical meaning. The Pentagon, Rumsfeld and Bush—to say nothing
of the very age in which they lived—would be remembered for either
winning or losing the Iraq War.

THE PRESIDENT MONITORED Khalilzad's efforts to put together a new
government. It was slow and tedious. Bush repeatedly reminded his ambassador of the immense frustration in the U.S. People want to see
progress in Iraq, he told Khalilzad, and it's hard to portray progress
when there's so much political wrangling around this new government.

The Iranians started saying openly and emphatically that Jafari was
their candidate. For Washington, Iranian support for Jafari was reason
enough to dump him. Besides, nobody at the NSC could think of a time
when Jafari had taken a decisive stand on anything.

In addition, Jafari's crutch was Moqtada al-Sadr, who had supported
him early in the process.

Bush's frustration boiled. He repeated his mantra to Card: "Where's the leader? Where's George Washington? Where's Thomas Jefferson? Where's John Adams, for crying out loud? He didn't even have much of a personality."

In retrospect, Card wished they had expanded their search to the leaders of the provinces or even the tribes to see if a Thomas Jefferson was hanging around. It was now apparent that most of the Iraqi leadership who had embraced the invasion weren't Iraqis so much as longtime Iraqi exiles living in Europe or the United States. Where were the grassroots political success stories? Card wondered.

In late March, President Bush secretly sent a personal letter to Ayatollah Sistani—his first directly to the Shiite leader. Without personally referring to Jafari, Bush said the United States wanted to work with someone who had the support of all Iraqis. The current situation did not meet that test. Bush said the United States wanted to work with Sistani, who was doing a great job being a calming influence. Normally presidential letters went out only in English, leaving it to the recipient to translate it, but the White House translated it and sent the original in Arabic to avoid ambiguity and to show respect. Word came back that Sistani appreciated the letter and its sentiments.

Given Sistani's reaction, Hadley and Rice concluded that Iran had overplayed its hand by supporting Jafari.

On Wednesday, March 8, before 7 a.m., Andy Card walked the 35 or so paces from his corner West Wing office to the Oval Office for what promised to be one of the most difficult conversations of his life. He planned to talk himself out of his job.

The condition of the Bush presidency was not good. Iraq was a mess. The president's political standing was plummeting, with his overall approval rating below 40 percent and still sinking. Seventeen months earlier, the weekend after Bush's reelection, Card had unsuccessfully pushed for more staff and cabinet changes, including his own offer to resign. Since then he had focused on getting the president to replace Rumsfeld—another failed mission.

The second term was full of setbacks. A plan for Social Security reform had not even gotten out of the box. Hurricane Katrina had destroyed New Orleans and the president's handling of the crisis had become a metaphor for cluelessness. The nomination of White House Counsel Harriet Miers to the Supreme Court had to be pulled when conservatives revolted. Scooter Libby had been indicted for perjury in the CIA leak investigation.

The previous month Cheney had been in the spotlight after he accidentally shot a friend in the face during a hunting foray in Texas, an escapade that landed the shotgun-toting vice president on the covers of *Time* and *Newsweek*. The White House had also fumbled the explanation and policy portfolios on a controversial deal to have a Dubai firm manage several U.S. ports. The only real positive for Bush was that two of his conservative nominees to the Supreme Court had been confirmed and taken their seats—Chief Justice John Roberts and Justice Samuel Alito.

"The drumbeat for change is not going to go away," Card told the president as they talked alone in the Oval Office that morning, "and you should not be afraid to change me." The accumulation of troubles required visible, decisive presidential action.

"No, that's stupid," the president replied. "That's not the way it is."

"Well, you should think about it," Card said. "You owe it to yourself to think about it." A big personnel move was now almost required. "There are only five and a half people that you can change and get any credit. Don Rumsfeld, Karl Rove, Andy Card, Condi Rice, Dan Bartlett." The president would not get a lot of credit for replacing Bartlett because most people didn't know who he was. "And you get a half credit if you change John Snow." Snow was the treasury secretary, who received tepid reviews from almost everywhere. "You won't get credit for removing him. You might get credit for putting somebody else in.

"Karl you can't touch probably," Card said. Rove was under investigation about a discussion with a *Time* magazine reporter in the CIA leak case, and no one seemed to know if he would be indicted. "There's a cloud over him," Card continued, "and since I don't know that the sun is going to shine and I don't know that it's going to rain, you probably can't change Karl.

"Changing the secretary of defense, that's a different set of questions." They both were aware of Card's efforts on this front. "You can't change Condi. She's the star in the administration." But, he added, "You can change me." He spoke with sadness. "And there's no Senate hearing. The change can happen overnight. There's no confirmation. There's nobody being grilled about past policies or future biases. And Dan Bartlett is a very valuable counselor and you wouldn't get any credit for changing him. And the Snow thing is what it is, but that wouldn't represent real change." The White House chief of staff would be real change.

"No, that's absurd. No," Bush said, dismissing his chief of staff. He left for New Orleans for his 10th trip there since Katrina.

Two days later, Friday, March 10, Card again went to Bush, "Did you think about it, because it's the right thing?" Bush again waved him away.

That afternoon the online magazine *Slate* reported that Claude A. Allen, who had been Bush's top domestic policy adviser until he had resigned the previous month, had been arrested by police in the Maryland suburbs and charged in a bizarre case of allegedly defrauding local stores of more than $5,000.

Bush called Card at home around 9:30 P.M., late for the president. He wanted a detailed explanation of what had happened to Allen, 45, a favorite on the staff, a lawyer and born-again Christian. Allen was Bush's highest-ranking African-American White House adviser, and he regularly briefed and traveled with the president. Card said that when Allen resigned the previous month he had told both Card and Harriet Miers that there was some misunderstanding. Bush said he thought the White House had done the right thing, handled it the right way, but he wondered how a senior White House official could be arrested without the chief of staff finding out.

"Well, Mr. President, if this is not comfortable for you, this is a perfect time to lay it all on me. Just lay it on me. This is it. Perfect."

"No! That's—" Bush didn't even finish his sentence. It was out of the question.

The next morning, Saturday the 11th, Card went to the White House early. Bush had his daily intelligence brief, and later met with Rumsfeld and retired General Montgomery C. Meigs, the director of a $3.3 billion Defense Department program to defeat the new, increasingly lethal, advanced IEDs in Iraq. The components and the training for them had more and more clearly been traced to Iran, one of the most troubling turns in the war.

Afterward, Bush and Card talked again. The president said he was troubled by the conversation the previous night about Claude Allen, and troubled by Card's comment.

"Don't worry about it," Card replied. "But seriously, this is the role of the chief of staff. If this wasn't handled the way you think it should have been handled or wasn't handled the way the world thinks it should have been handled, or it wasn't handled, that's the chief of staff's job. So it's perfectly appropriate."

That night both Bush and Card attended the Gridiron Dinner. In his satirical speech, Bush joked that the media had blown Cheney's hunting accident way out of proportion. "Good Lord, you'd thought he shot somebody or something."

Two days later, March 13, Card was alone with the president again. "Have you given this some thought?" he inquired.

"Agh, I don't know what to do," the president said.

"Well, the drums are still beating out there," Card said.

"Is there anything new on Karl?" Bush asked impatiently.

There was not. For practical and legal reasons they couldn't find out much. There were questions that no one in the White House or administration could properly ask the prosecutor, the Justice Department or even Rove about. On March 15, Card continued to press.

"Did you give it some thought?"

"Yeah, I've given it some thought," the president answered. "What do you think?"

"Well, first of all, you shouldn't get advice from me on this. You should get some advice from wise counsel."

"Okay. Well, who do you suggest?"

"You know better than I do, but you're going to see Jim Baker later today. I would get his counsel."

"Yeah, he'll tell me what he thinks."

"He will," Card said. "I think he'll just tell you what he thinks. Ask Jim about it."

"I will. I will."

Normally when Bush met with Jim Baker or Henry Kissinger or one of the old hands, he would either have Card there or right afterward would summarize for Card. But this time there was no recap.

At home later that night in Arlington, Virginia, Card told his wife, Kathi, what had happened.

"I think the president made the tough decision but he doesn't know it yet," he said.

On March 16, General Abizaid was in Washington to testify before the Senate Armed Services Committee. He painted a careful but upbeat picture of the situation in Iraq.

Senator Elizabeth Dole, Republican of North Carolina, blamed the news media for the idea that Iraq was a mess. "Now knowing the great progress that's been made, continues to be made, all the accomplishments in Iraq, it's got to be frustrating to hear accounts from our media that offer sometimes nothing but negativity and pessimism."

Abizaid was tactful, but he said he didn't think the media had any negative impact on morale.

Afterward, he went over to see Congressman Murtha in the Rayburn Office Building. Sitting at the round, dark wood table in the congressman's office, Abizaid, the deputy commander at CENTCOM during the invasion and the top general for the region since July 2003—the one uniformed military commander who had been intimately involved in Iraq from the beginning and who was still at it—indicated he wanted to speak frankly. According to Murtha, Abizaid raised his hand for emphasis and held his thumb and forefinger a quarter of an inch from each other and said, "We're that far apart."

42

RICE HAD WANTED ZELIKOW to go back to Iraq again in February 2006, but the Askariya Mosque bombing and crisis postponed the trip. He made it over finally and wrote Rice a nine-page SECRET/NODIS memo dated March 18.

Iraq is holding together in an uneasy balance, he reported. "The Iraqi Army has been rebuilt and the insurgency has been contained, but the underlying rhythm and scale of insurgent attacks has actually been remarkably steady for more than a year. Neither side has gained decisive edge. The result is a lingering unstable equilibrium." Whatever positive momentum had been built from the December 2005 election was starting to dissipate, and people across the spectrum were worried that the center was no longer going to be able to hold.

To succeed, Zelikow argued, the Iraqis would have to pass three major tests in the coming months: "establish a truly national government, check communal violence and develop a security bargain that can sustain the Shia and Sunni moderates, and get the new government off to a visibly promising start."

Zelikow addressed the question of whether the United States could live with Jafari. Though he wasn't anyone's first choice, Zelikow feared they would start thinking of him as an acceptable second choice. As far as Zelikow could tell, Jafari was incompetent. But he was a shrewd and tenacious back-alley politician who was dramatically prolonging the attempts to form a new government. "We could say we have lost confidence in Jafari's ability to lead the country out of its current crisis, and that if he remains prime minister we would have to fundamentally reevaluate our position and strategy in Iraq because we would no longer be sufficiently confident that our existing strategies could succeed."

In other words, dump Jafari. It would be bold and risky. It was dangerous not to hedge bets in Iraqi politics.

CARD WAS STILL TRYING to get himself replaced, as he went with the president and first lady for a weekend at Camp David. There was the usual gaggle of Bush family and friends. Card tried to get the president alone, without success. It wasn't that Bush was avoiding Card; it was that he was avoiding being alone with him. There were always people around. Bush kept saying, "We'll talk." But every time Card tried to talk to Bush there were other people sitting with them.

On Sunday, Card left Camp David at 5:30 A.M. so he could attend his wife's church service.

"I'm feeling lousy," he told his wife in a phone call from the car. "I'm not going to make it to church. I'm going to go right home and go to bed." He did, and Monday morning he was as sick as a dog. Nonetheless he got to the White House at 5:30 A.M. By about 6:15 A.M., Dr. Tubb, the White House physician, was in Card's office performing a quick exam.

"You've got the flu, and are highly contagious," Tubb said. It was influenza B.

"Then I'm out of here. I'm going home. I don't want to see anybody. I don't want to see the president. I don't want to see anybody." Card packed up some papers and left for home. He stayed there for three days.

"OUR STRATEGY IS GETTING RESULTS," Bush said in his March 18 radio address from Camp David. "Evidence of real progress" was lost in the news reports and pictures of violence. "In the past three years, Iraqis have gone from living under a brutal tyrant to liberation, sovereignty, free elections, a constitutional referendum, and last December, elections of a fully constitutional government." None of these addressed, let alone solved, the security problem, or the basic political and infrastructure problems.

At a press conference on March 21, Bush was asked about the statement of former Prime Minister Allawi that some 50 to 60 Iraqis were dying each day. "If this is not civil war, then God knows what civil war is," Allawi had said.

Bush said he disagreed. Other voices—the Kurdish leader Talabani,

General Casey, Khalilzad—saw it differently, he noted. "The Iraqis took a look and decided not to go to civil war."

That morning in a town north of Baghdad, armed men had overrun a police station and courthouse, killing 17 policemen and freeing at least 20 prisoners. What was his reaction? Bush was asked. "We have a plan for victory," he responded. "I'm optimistic about being able to achieve a victory."

And what about retired Army Major General Paul D. Eaton, who had run the training of the Iraqi military for the first year and in an op-ed piece that weekend in *The New York Times* called Rumsfeld "incompetent strategically, operationally and tactically" and urged his resignation?

"No," Bush replied, "I don't believe he should resign. I think he's done a fine job." The embedding of U.S. troops with Iraqis had "been a success."

On and on he went, 7,484 words, according to the transcript.

Card was back at the White House, Thursday, March 23, but it was not until the end of the day that he found the president alone. The two men walked out of the Oval Office to the Rose Garden. It was overcast and cool. "Mr. President," he said, "the string has run out. You know it and I know it." In one of his more inelegant summations, he added, "And right now the string is flopping around."

"Why? Why do you say that?"

"I know it."

"No. I don't know why you say that."

"Well, the string has run out."

ON FRIDAY, MARCH 24, Card again accompanied Bush to Camp David. Bush finally said what Card knew. The time had come, probably.

It was sad. The end of an era for both.

"Don't worry," Card said, realizing it was emotional for the president. "This is the right thing to do. Just don't worry. It's the right thing," he said almost like a comforting parent. "Don't give it another thought. It's the right thing, and it can happen easily." He too was emotional. "I wouldn't have written the script this way, but it wasn't up to me to write the script."

The decision made, they turned as they had done so many times before to the questions of who should know, in what order, and when and how to tell the world.

They didn't have to discuss the why. Like so many of Bush's decisions, such as the decision to invade Iraq, there was a momentum, the big and the little incremental steps that suddenly converged. Card's resignation might buy Bush a little time. He needed a new direction.

The president said that Josh Bolten, the director of the Office of Management and Budget, had agreed to take Card's place. Though it was Card who had been pushing, it was a jolt to realize that Bush was a step ahead of him. Bolten, who had been Card's deputy for two years before going to the budget office, had a Stanford law degree and had worked for Goldman Sachs before joining the Bush campaign in 1999 as policy director.

"I'd like to have the announcement sooner rather than later," Card said. "As a courtesy I'd like to tell my kids and my siblings and three very close friends."

On Monday afternoon, Card flew to Cincinnati for a Lincoln Day dinner speech that had been long arranged. Before about 600 people, Card focused mostly on what had happened on September 14, 2001, three days after the 9/11 terror attacks, when Bush ordered a change in direction for the FBI, visited Ground Zero in Manhattan, and visited with families of those killed in the attacks.

The next morning, Tuesday, March 28, at 8:30 A.M. the president, Card and Bolten stepped into the Oval Office and announced the changes.

CARD HAD A SENSE of relief mixed with the knowledge that he was leaving unfinished business. One of his great worries was that Iraq would be compared to Vietnam. There were 58,249 names on the Vietnam Veterans Memorial in Washington. One of Henry Kissinger's private criticisms of Bush was that he had no mechanism in place, or even an inclination, to consider the downsides of impending decisions. Alternative courses of action were rarely considered. As best Card could remember there had been some informal, blue-sky discussions at times along the lines of "What could we do differently?" But there had been no formal sessions to consider alternatives to staying in Iraq. To his knowledge there were no anguished memos bearing the names of Cheney, Rice, Hadley, Rumsfeld, the CIA, Card himself or anyone else saying let's examine alternatives, as had surfaced after the Vietnam era.

Card put it on the generals—Myers and Pace in the Pentagon, Abizaid and Casey in Iraq. If they had come forward and said to the president, "It's not worth it" or "The mission can't be accomplished," Card was certain the president would have said, "I'm not going to ask another kid to sacrifice for it."

Card was enough of a realist to see that there were two negative aspects to Bush's public persona that had come to define his presidency: incompetence and arrogance. Card did not believe that Bush was incompetent, and so he had to face the possibility that he himself, as Bush's chief of staff, might have been incompetent. In addition, he did not think the president was arrogant. But the personality and presentation—the *marketing*—of Bush had come across as arrogant. Maybe unfair, unjustified in Card's opinion, but there it was. He was leaving. And the man most responsible for the postwar troubles, the one who should have gone, Rumsfeld, was staying.

"IT'S IRAQ, IRAQ, IRAQ," Card told Bolten. "Then comes the economy." As budget director and earlier as Card's deputy, Bolten had not been involved in Iraq. "You don't have that luxury now."

"I can count on Steve," Bolten said.

"You can't do that. It's not fair to the president. You should take the time to be informed. And you shouldn't be informed by me. It should be a fresh look. I have been involved and I do have biases, but you should give it a fresh look because the president needs to have someone take a fresh look at it."

"I don't want to deal with that," Bolten said.

"You don't have a choice."

In his first days as chief of staff, Bolten called in some of the senior U.S. government officials who knew Iraq.

"Where will Iraq be in six months?" he asked one.

"About where it is today."

SINCE 2005, AS FAR AS Rice's and Rumsfeld's top aides could tell, Vice President Cheney no longer had a visible role in the management of Iraq. At the NSC and other meetings and discussions, he had one message for Rice: "Got to win it." Once he told her, "Do whatever you need to do with whatever resources to win it. It's too important to the war on terror. It's too important to our policies worldwide. This is not something you can do without maximum effort." Rice began calling him a "100-percenter." A 100 percent effort had to be made on Iraq. She and Cheney were in total agreement.

But Cheney was lost without Libby, many of the vice president's close associates felt. Libby had done so much of the preparation for the vice president's meetings and events, and so much of the hard work. He had been almost part of Cheney's brain.

As criticism of the administration's handling of Iraq continued to grow, and as doubt suffused many weaker supporters, Cheney told associates that it was the true test of leadership for Bush. Cheney said there were few politicians, even the great leaders, who could withstand political pressure. Most succumb, but Bush hadn't, and Cheney said he marveled at it.

Cheney relied more on his wife, Lynne, and daughter Liz for advice. They reinforced his sense he was right, and Cheney became increasingly removed from reality, some of his close friends felt. He was even convinced that the administration's two nearly universally accepted missteps—the handling of Hurricane Katrina and the abortive Supreme Court nomination of White House Counsel Harriet Miers—would turn out to be net positives for Bush.

TONY BLAIR WAS GETTING increasing heat for the Iraq War and was in serious political trouble. He proposed to Bush that their top foreign policy people travel together to Iraq to apply pressure to form a new government.

Bush shared Blair's impatience. What could be going on? How could this possibly be taking months? He raised Blair's idea with Rice that she and British Foreign Minister Jack Straw go.

"That's a little much," she told the president. "I don't think that's a very good idea." It could too easily be viewed as a 63-yard field goal attempt in the final seconds, desperate.

Well, they were desperate. It would send a strong message, Bush said. And somebody needed to go talk about their growing impatience.

Rice was in England on April 2 when she and Straw took off secretly for Iraq in her plane. Straw was sick so Rice gave him the one foldout bed and she stretched out on the floor near the burn bags for classified information and slept during the overnight flight. There was a torrential rainstorm when they arrived, so they could not take helicopters to the Green Zone. Rice's staff and the press piled into large Rhinos, a kind of armored Death Star vehicle that is a cross between a bus and a tank. Inside they were required to put on body armor and helmets. It was a little nerve-wracking knowing they were going to travel the BIAP highway—the so-called Highway of Death—into town.

"Don't worry," Jim Wilkinson joked sarcastically, echoing Cheney's famous line, "we're going to be greeted with flowers and sweets."

Rice and Straw rode in an armored Suburban. They promptly got stuck in traffic for half an hour at a checkpoint, and the chief of security's heart raced. As they edged along, Rice and Straw tried to figure out Jafari's state of mind. They were going to push him. His record over the last year had been one of drift. They needed him out. He was supported by the Shiites in the National Assembly by only a single vote—64–63— and he had no other support. The Kurds particularly wanted to get rid of him.

Later that afternoon, Rice and Straw met alone with Jafari. They wanted an intimate setting. It was going to be as tough a meeting as foreign diplomats might have with a leader of a sovereign state. Rice had some Iraqi cartoons that had been published in the Iraqi press ridiculing and mocking the failure to form a government. The Iraqi people are very frustrated, she said. Americans and President Bush are very frustrated and impatient.

"Time to step aside," Rice said bluntly to Jafari. Straw repeated it. The British also have a parliamentary system, he noted, and he explained the importance of forming new governments swiftly because the public would otherwise get frustrated. Did they have a government? Did they have leaders?

Jafari would not commit.

Afterward at a press briefing, a reporter asked Rice what she would do if she didn't see a new government taking shape in five weeks.

"I can assure you that I'm not going to wait for five weeks," she answered.

MEGHAN O'SULLIVAN, Hadley's Iraq chief, had gone on the trip with Rice and stayed behind after Rice and Straw left. Later, she and Khalilzad spent three hours with Jafari. Their message was simple: Under the Iraqi constitution you have to form a government with the support of the other communities—Sunni and Kurd. You don't seem to have that support, so what is your plan for moving forward?

Jafari said he believed he had more support than the public expression in statements and letters.

The problem for the United States and the United Kingdom was that Jafari's support came from the Iranians and the detested Moqtada al-Sadr. After the Samarra bombing on February 22, Jafari did not move smartly to clamp down on Moqtada's attacks on the Sunnis, which had been horrific, especially in Baghdad. The worry was that if Jafari was elected prime minister for four years he would become Moqtada's pawn.

After all the years of effort, such an outcome—a prime minister beholden to a warlord like Moqtada—was unthinkable.

NO MATTER HOW BAD the news might get, few were as good as Rumsfeld at reframing the issues and debate. In April 2006, six retired generals publicly called for his resignation, citing missteps in Iraq, especially the failure to have enough troops. On Tuesday, April 18, 2006, Rumsfeld appeared for one of his periodic press conferences with General Pace by his side. There was much anticipation about his response to the very public critique that was being labeled "The Revolt of the Generals."

"Good afternoon, folks," Rumsfeld began. "One of the interesting things about this city is that there are so many distractions that people sometimes lose track of how fortunate we are.

"It was 64 years ago today that Jimmy Doolittle led the against-all-odds raid on Tokyo during the early days of World War II," he said, and added that it was also "a hundred years ago today that San Francisco was nearly destroyed by an earthquake."

After five minutes of this, a reporter got to ask about the retired generals who had said "that you've been dismissive and even contemptuous of the advice offered by senior military officers."

"I kind of would prefer to let a little time walk over it," Rumsfeld said and added, as if their comments about him were their problem, "I just am not inclined to be instantaneously judgmental about them."

"Mr. Secretary," a reporter tried.

"Coming into work today," Rumsfeld continued with his history lesson, "I did think about something that happened 30 years ago, I think close to this month. I was secretary of defense." He described in detail how he overruled the Army's recommendation for the gun and engine on its M1 battle tank.

"Well, you would have thought the world had ended," he continued. "The sky fell. Can you imagine making that decision and breaking tradition for decades in this country? Can you imagine overturning what the service had proposed for a main battle tank? Well, it went on and on in the press, and it was a firestorm.

"The people involved were good people," he added, "and there were differences of views, and somebody needed to make a decision." For an-

other five minutes, he went on to list all the changes he had made in recent years. Lots of his personnel moves had ruffled feathers, he said,
such as making a Marine like General Jones the NATO commander or
General Pace the chairman. "A Marine as Chairman of the Joint Chiefs of
Staff, for the first time in history—imagine! What a stunning thing to
do!" Rumsfeld said.

A reporter tried to interrupt with a question.

"I was asked a question and I'm going to take all the time I want!"
Rumsfeld said. There was laughter.

"But I think it's important that we recognize that there's a lot of change
going on, it's challenging for people, it's difficult for people." When asked
again about the concerns of the six retired generals, he noted, "We've got
what, 6,000, 7,000 retired admirals and generals . . . Who thinks they're
going to be unanimous on anything?"

In other words it was very hard to be defense secretary with so many
backward-looking forces arrayed against him. After the press conference
Rumsfeld met privately with a group of a dozen retired generals—none
of whom had called for his resignation—and other outside advisers. It
was supposed to be a close-hold, off-the-record session.

He was asked about his thinking on the number of troops used in the
Iraq war plan.

"The final war plan called for a ramp-up to about 400,000," Rumsfeld
said from one end of the table. "That's right, isn't it, Pete?"

"Yes, sir," General Pace said from the other end.

"Then General Franks called me," Rumsfeld recounted, "and said
stop the force flow. He didn't need more." Franks was the combatant
commander on the ground, so, Rumsfeld said, he went with his general's
recommendation.

How convenient, thought one of the retired military men, Major General William L. Nash, who was now a senior fellow at the Council on Foreign Relations. At the press conference, Rumsfeld had presented himself
as the bold, decisive change agent. When it came to one of the most important decisions during the war, Rumsfeld simply acquiesced to General Franks.

43

J AFARI FINALLY STEPPED ASIDE on April 20, and the next day, the Iraqi parliament selected its first permanent prime minister—a stiff but cerebral Shiite named Jawad al-Maliki, 56. U.S. intelligence knew little about him. He had been in exile for 23 years, apparently bouncing between Syria and Iran, a former spokesman for the Shiite Party Al Dawa (The Call), and seemed to say all the right things. But to Western eyes, he was basically one of the faceless Dawa people.

The president spoke with Rice. He was aware of the tension between Rice and Rumsfeld. They were veering out of their lanes—she was looking at the military, and he was looking at the politics. "I think it would be really good if you and Don went over," Bush said. "Show that we've got the military and the political really linked up. And I could hear from both of you. You both get to look at both parts of it and I can hear from you simultaneously."

Four days later Rice and Rumsfeld were in Baghdad. They went over to Khalilzad's residence and met with Maliki at 4 P.M. on Wednesday, April 26. Maliki does not shake hands with women and so he just crossed his extended arm across his chest and heart in a common Arab gesture. Small, balding with a distinctive fluff of hair above his forehead, Maliki wasted no time on small talk. While he understands English, he spoke in Arabic and used a translator.

His first challenge, he said, according to a U.S. note-taker, was to address the sectarian mistrust among the Shiites, Sunnis and Kurds. Second, he said, his biggest challenge was terrorism. "If I succeed at the first," he said, "then this will help the terrorism."

Maliki said he believed that in the first three months he was going to have to demonstrate improvements in services. "The people need power," he said, meaning electricity.

On the security issue Maliki said, "If I'm out on the highway, I'm not so pleased to see the police." He didn't trust the police, and even indicated that he disguised himself.

Rice said she personally understood. As a black child she had been raised in racially torn Birmingham, Alabama, in the early 1960s, she said. "If the police came into my neighborhood, we didn't feel a sense of comfort. We felt a sense of fear." In the 1960s, the city's public safety commissioner had been Bull Connor, a notorious segregationist who had ordered the use of fire hoses and attack dogs on civil rights marchers. "One of the most remarkable things for me was to go back to Birmingham last year and meet the black woman who is Bull Connor's successor. And so these things can change." She did not note that in Alabama it had taken decades.

Maliki seemed to warm to that picture and said he was going to try to reestablish the Ministry of the Interior, which oversaw the police. "There are a lot of those people who are not bad people," he said. "They're just not trained to do the job and we have to work on that." He hoped to have a security plan he was going to call "Take Back Baghdad." If the new government could make the capital secure, he indicated, the rest of the country would follow. As he would be selecting ministers, he said, "Ministers should be ministers for Iraq, not a political party."

Khalilzad was working his worry beads furiously, and Maliki noticed and started fumbling around for his own. He located them, pulled them out and was soon churning through them.

At some point, Rumsfeld said, we need to begin to talk about U.S. forces. It was in the context of patrols. He didn't use the word "drawdown" or "withdrawal" but everyone else, including Maliki, knew what he meant.

The prime minister–designate looked at the American secretary of defense as if he were crazy. "It's way too early to be talking about that," he said.

AT A DINNER THAT NIGHT with the key Iraqis and Americans, Maliki looked around and said, "This is the team that shoulders the responsibility of our country. This team represents all the elements of Iraqi society. We believe in the unity of Iraq and we're going to work on our national security."

"Success depends on competency," he told Rice. During a lengthy discussion of the message they wanted to send, he said, "The world looks at Iraq with two eyes," meaning both violence on television and the high hopes.

Afterward Rice had a one-on-one session with Maliki. "The Iraqi people have had enough," Maliki said to her. "And if we don't demonstrate we can govern, then we're not going to be able to do this. All will be lost if we can't demonstrate we can govern."

Rice was surprised. It was the first time she had met an Iraqi leader who took things upon himself and wasn't immediately asking what the United States would do. She said there was a time when the confidence of the American people was gone as a result of the Great Depression in the 1930s. Franklin Roosevelt's New Deal had created the impression that something was going to be different. The New Deal, she said, didn't make people's lives better overnight. But they felt somebody cared. They felt someone was totally committed and trying to get the job done and get them to work. It was a message of hope that somebody was in charge and that life was going to be different.

What would be the one thing he could do? Maliki asked. Would it be delivering electricity? Would that give people a sense that things were different?

Rice was impressed. She took him over to see Jim Wilkinson, her communications adviser.

"This is the man I was telling you about," Rice said to Maliki. "This is Jim, and I'm going to leave him to help you." Wilkinson had headed government transitions, including hers to the State Department and in places ranging from Mongolia to Palestine. He'd studied Arabic for a year after 9/11, and she said he knew how to help with the management and structural issues of a new office down to the nuts-and-bolts questions of office space and phones. "He looks very young but he has a lot of experience in management and policy and can really help you. And I'm going to leave him here as long as you want."

This came as a surprise to Wilkinson, who had no warning and had brought clothes for only a few days.

"You're the professor, I'm the student," he told Maliki in Arabic. Maliki laughed and gave his new adviser a hug.

• • •

RICE AND RUMSFELD met with American reporters.

"You'll have to fly in secret," a reporter from Bloomberg News said. "What does that say about prospects for restoring security and stability here and the true state of the security situation here?"

It was at the heart of one of the disagreements between Rice and Rumsfeld. Rice turned to Rumsfeld. Security was his portfolio. Ten seconds of silence passed before Rumsfeld spoke, glaring at the reporter.

"I guess I don't think it says anything about it," he answered abruptly. He said he was here to meet with his generals. "But I just don't see anything to your question."

Rice interjected, "Obviously, the security situation will continue to take our attention and the attention of the Iraqis. But we've always said, and I feel it even more strongly today, that the terrorists are ultimately going to be defeated by a political process here."

The next question was about how to diminish sectarian influence in the Iraqi military, police and militias. "Exactly how do you accomplish the objective?"

"I guess the first thing I have to say is: We don't. The Iraqis do," Rumsfeld said. "It's their country. It's a sovereign country. This is not a government that has an interim in front of it or a transition in front of it. Other countries have dealt with these issues and done them in a reasonably orderly way and over a period of time in a manner that was, in many instances, without much violence. So it's possible that these things can get done."

Rumsfeld wrote or doodled with his pen or stared at the ceiling as Rice carried the rest of the press conference.

Rice knew that it was inevitable now that her legacy too would be judged by what happened in Iraq. She briefed Bush about her meeting with Maliki when she returned, saying she was encouraged. This was the first Iraqi leader, she reported, who had said, "This is on me."

WILKINSON WENT TO MEET MALIKI at his office in the international press center. There was no air-conditioning, and it was sweltering. The first order of business, however, was Maliki's personal security. After the three-year struggle to bring democracy to Iraq, the symbolism of the assassination of the new Iraqi prime minister would be too much to bear. Wilkinson introduced Maliki to the Navy SEAL team that would be assigned to guard him around the clock.

"Pick your own management model," Wilkinson suggested. "There's the Iraqi way. There's the American and Western way. And there's a Maliki way of doing business. I urge you to use the Maliki way."

They spent two and a half hours with computerized charts and diagrams—Maliki seemed very technology-savvy—putting together an arrangement to oversee the cabinet ministers, a personal office, and offices for media, finance, protocol and policy advisers. At Maliki's request, Wilkinson wrote job descriptions for each position and came up with a written plan for his first five days in office after he formally took office the next month. He noticed that Maliki had five cell phones.

Wilkinson had to get Khalilzad to intervene to get security for Maliki's offices. Maliki had appointed a spokesman, Dr. Salah Abdulrazzak, who lived ouside the Green Zone with his wife and two young children. Not surprisingly, he feared for their lives. "What can I do?" the new spokesman asked Wilkinson, who took him to the Al Rashid Hotel.

"We need to get this guy a room for tonight—he and his family," said Wilkinson.

Well, that would take a while.

"He's moving in here tonight."

He did the next day.

Maliki's chief of staff and spokesman needed credentials to get into the Green Zone.

"Can you get these guys badges?" Maliki asked Wilkinson.

Sure, Wilkinson was told on his first inquiry, but it will take six to eight weeks. Wilkinson threw a fit and got Khalilzad involved. Maliki's two men soon had permanent badges.

The next days were occupied with the mundane. Maliki's office didn't have computers. Wilkinson found some and had them driven over and installed. "We need phones," Maliki said. So the embassy team installed phones. At one point, Wilkinson had to send over pens and paper.

As his inauguration approached, Maliki said he was going to be able to invite only about 10 percent of the parliament because there was no air-conditioning in the big hall. "Will you look at it?" he asked Wilkinson. Soon new air-conditioning systems were being flown in from all over the Middle East, and the U.S. embassy and military got the big hall air-conditioned.

Maliki did not want a showy or elaborate inaugural. "How can I do that when Iraqis are dying?" he asked.

Wilkinson found that Maliki kept saying all the right things, almost sounded like the U.S. ambassador. An embassy staffer asked Wilkinson for an overall appraisal.

"He's either full of shit, or he's the real thing," Wilkinson replied. From what he could tell it looked like Maliki had a group of about seven people who were making all the personnel and other critical decisions. He realized he had found a way to enter Maliki's system on the management side but he had not found one on the policy side. Maliki was keeping his cards close to his chest. One of the key British advisers asked Maliki if he would like help writing his inaugural address.

Maliki answered with an Arabic version of "Whoa!" It was clear there were boundaries he didn't want crossed. Whenever Wilkinson asked something about policy he could see Maliki's polite but impenetrable glass shield go up.

As WILKINSON TALKED to U.S. military officers at high and low levels, he saw the contradiction. The forces were getting two messages. Bush and Rice were saying, Iraq is the most important thing, central to the war on terror, essential to the stability of the Middle East and the future of civilization. At the same time, the internal pressure in the military was, we've got to get out as quickly as possible.

In the end Wilkinson concluded this was the last chance. If Maliki couldn't show his people why democracy was better, get his government to deliver services and more security, it wasn't going to work.

"I'm not sure what Plan B is," Wilkinson often said.

At times he wondered if George W. Bush's democracy agenda would really work. Did this high rhetoric resonate or not? Had so much of the actual or potential goodwill of the Iraqis been destroyed that they would cease to believe democracy would work for them? The Americans with their ideas and military and promises had once put a man on the moon but they couldn't get the damn electricity to work? He wondered if Maliki was going to be judged by American mistakes, and, in turn, would America be judged by his? And what would break the back of militant Islamic fundamentalism?

And was Bush getting good information? Bush had been told too many times, for example, that the electricity was up or about to be up. It wasn't. For a long time Wilkinson thought the center of gravity was electricity because that was something Rice and the State Department could influence.

But the real issue was security. He watched *Baghdad ER*, the highly graphic, even grisly HBO one-hour documentary about the same combat support hospital in Baghdad that Rice and he had visited the previous year. The documentary was a gripping, gory depiction of the horrors of war visited on those shredded, maimed and killed by IEDs, bullets and mortars. The central character is the soldier's body. Up-close shots inside the ER show legs and arms that had been blown off or must be amputated. Soldiers arrive with bloodied, shrapnel-shredded faces and shrapnel embedded in everything from limbs and chests to an eye. Many of the survivors are medically evacuated to hospitals in Germany or to Walter Reed. The many who die are shown being placed or encased in the black body bags. Blood is endlessly mopped up from the operating room floors.

"I hate this stupid war," one of the hospital staff says. "I think it's the most ridiculous thing I've ever seen. I don't think it's more intelligent than any other war that's ever been fought."

Wilkinson was shaken after he watched it. His brother was an enlisted soldier in Iraq.

"Is it worth his life?" Wilkinson was asking himself.

The whole Iraq situation was really tragic. He could see it was even getting to Rice, who at times seemed demoralized.

Rice had once told him, "I don't like extremists."

Why not?

"Because on some of these issues I don't trust anybody that's that sure," the secretary of state had said.

RICE'S IRAQ POLICY COORDINATOR, Jim Jeffrey, had heard the refrain that Maliki was the last chance for Iraq. He thought it was bunk. The idea of a "last chance" for Iraq was simply unthinkable. Attacks were up, but there had been some success in putting together a government. They were making progress, he thought.

Jeffrey simply couldn't imagine a scenario like in Vietnam in 1975 or Somalia in 1993. There, he thought, the U.S. simply decided it was too hard and not worth it.

If we leave, he thought, Iraq will do one of two things. Either it will descend into complete chaos or it will become a nation dedicated to hatred of the so-called Great Satan, meaning the United States.

Besides, the country was sitting on between a third and a half of the Middle East's oil reserves, depending on which experts you listened to. Iraq was now hugely important. Bush recognized his presidency hinged on success there. Therefore, Jeffrey concluded, the U.S. wasn't leaving. If Maliki didn't work, they'd find a Plan B. Or a Plan C, or D, or whatever it took.

THE PRESIDENT INVITED ten former secretaries of state and defense to the Roosevelt Room on Friday, May 12, so he could hear their views on Iraq. Five months earlier, in January, he had held a similar session with essentially the same group, but he had devoted little time to them and been very defensive.

Powell was given a seat next to Rice, who was on the president's left. Powell had followed the press accounts of the designated new Iraqi Prime Minister Maliki. Suddenly everyone, including Bush and Rice, was embracing him. Who is he? Powell asked himself. This new man was allegedly a more effective leader than Jafari. Why? Having served four years in the Bush administration, he knew there was another important question to ask himself: "Is that true? What do we know about him?" Doing a little reading, research and tapping into his own contacts still in the U.S. government, he was surprised to find that no one from the U.S., including Rice, had previously met him.

"What executive skills does he bring that gets this vote of confidence?" Powell asked himself. Maliki was saying all these things that were so pleasing to everybody. He was pledging to bring the militias under control, reconstruct pipelines, and take care of water.

Bush's main teaching point was Maliki's centrality.

Former Secretary of State Madeleine K. Albright and former Secretary of Defense William Cohen shifted the focus to Iran. Albright also said that the president ought to talk with Prime Minister Badawi of Malaysia.

Powell had met with Badawi the week before. He raised his hand and was recognized by Bush.

"But while I have the floor," Powell continued, "I'd like to offer you caution about Mr. Maliki, because frankly I don't think any of us heard anything about him or knew anything about him until he was announced last week. And we pushed Jafari aside, but he is a deputy of Jafari's out of the Dawa party. And I have to have a little bit of caution about somebody who spent most of the last 20-odd years in Iran and Syria.

"The significant difference between the January meeting we had with you and this meeting is that in January we had a raging insurgency and terrorism. I think things have gotten worse. We have a raging insurgency still. We still have terrorism. But the new element which came out from the bombing of the religious site at Samarra is that we now have sect-on-sect violence and it's serious. And this is a new war. And it's a war that American troops have less and less to do with. I understand that the [CIA] chiefs of station have a somewhat more negative view."

Powell could not resist. He had the president's attention in a way that he rarely had when he was secretary of state. He intentionally did not want to contaminate the discussion by saying Iraq was in a civil war, but he wanted to underscore what he thought was the real danger. "Your strategy is correct in terms of building up the military and police forces and the government," Powell said, "because if you don't have a government that you can connect these forces to, then Mr. President, you're not building up forces, you're building up militias."

Bush nodded to Powell.

Cohen and Albright returned to Iran.

"Mr. President," Powell said, asking for the floor again, "I join in what Bill and Madeleine and others have said about Iran, but the main event is *Iraq and Iraq*. Iraq. This is the one that will determine everything. What we do with Iran, that's important, but you've got to look at the wolf that's eating you."

Afterward, Hadley came up to Powell and said he wanted to call to follow up. Josh Bolten, the new chief of staff, said the same thing. "Let's have dinner," Rice said to Powell. They set it up, but she had to cancel. She had been unexpectedly dispatched to Europe to meet with leaders there on nuclear negotiations with Iran.

MALIKI TOOK OFFICE in a formal ceremony on Saturday, May 20. In a high-security hall inside the protected Green Zone he laid out a 33-point program. The three major challenges, he said, were terrorism, corruption and providing services to the people.

In a speech in Chicago two days later, Monday, May 22, Bush said that progress in Iraq had been incremental and had included some setbacks. "Yet we have now reached a turning point in the struggle between freedom and terror," he said, pouring on the optimism. Iraqis have, he said, "demonstrated that democracy is the hope of the Middle East and the destiny of all mankind."

Bush normally avoided predictions about history and its judgments, but this day he closed by saying, "Years from now, people will look back on the formation of a unity government in Iraq as a decisive moment in the story of liberty, a moment when freedom gained a firm foothold in the Middle East and the forces of terror began their long retreat."

THAT WEEK RUMSFELD was holding three days of closed-door Pentagon meetings with the combatant commanders and top civilians in Defense. Before Rumsfeld, these regular meetings had been run by the chairman of the Joint Chiefs. Rumsfeld now ran the meetings.

General Jones, the NATO commander, told Pace he believed that Rumsfeld so controlled everything, even at the earliest stages, that they were not generating independent military advice as they had a legal obligation to do. Rumsfeld was driving and affecting the debates and decisions "politically." They, the uniformed military, should be worried about the "political spin," he said. He proposed that Pace meet alone with the combatant commanders and service chiefs—without Rumsfeld, without any Defense Department civilians. "I've got issues," he said, that needed to be addressed and debated without Rumsfeld present.

Pace agreed to hold a one-hour meeting one morning that week with just the service chiefs and combatant commanders.

At the meeting, Jones said he wanted to focus on one issue—the value of forward basing. The Marines, Army, Navy and Air Force had bases all over the world so they would be at trouble spots to prevent conflict, secure borders, capture or defeat terrorists. Rumsfeld's idea was to bring as many of the forces as he could back to the United States. Jones argued that this was altering the basic concept and premise of American global presence. They had an obligation to state their views and fight this new theology because it would weaken the position of the United States in the world. A number of those present agreed in principle, but no one seemed willing to take on the secretary of defense.

44

THE NEXT DAY, WEDNESDAY, May 24, the intelligence division of the Joint Staff, the J-2, circulated an intelligence assessment, classified SECRET, that showed that the forces of terror in Iraq were not in retreat. It was a stunning refutation of the president's forecasts, most recently just two days earlier in Chicago. The report was sent to the White House, the State Department and other intelligence agencies.

It put hard numbers on trends that had been reported to Bush all year. Terrorist attacks had been steadily increasing. The insurgency was gaining.

In large print, the assessment said, *"ATTACKS IN MAY WILL LIKELY SURPASS APRIL LEVELS, WHICH WERE THE HIGHEST EVER RECORDED. THE SUNNI ARAB INSURGENCY IS GAINING STRENGTH AND INCREASING CAPACITY DESPITE POLITICAL PROGRESS AND IRAQI SECURITY FORCES DEVELOPMENT."*

Next to this statement was a bar graph showing the average number of daily attacks in the first five months of the year. It showed a steady increase:

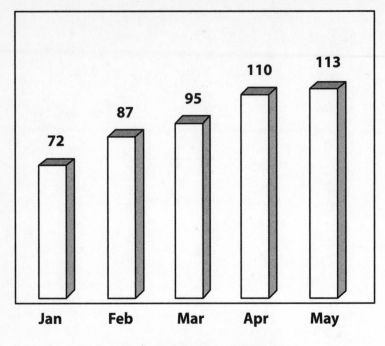

Jan 2006 - May 2006
Average Attacks Per Day

That meant the attacks were now averaging 600 to 700 a week. Every IED that was discovered—whether it detonated and caused damage or casualties or was identified and disarmed before it could do any damage—was still counted as an attack.

A graph measuring attacks from May 2003 to May 2006 showed some significant dips, but the current number of attacks was as high as they had ever been—exceeding 3,500 a month.

The assessment also said, *"INSURGENTS AND TERRORISTS RETAIN THE RESOURCES AND CAPABILITIES TO SUSTAIN AND EVEN IN-CREASE CURRENT LEVEL OF VIOLENCE THROUGH THE NEXT YEAR."*

The picture could hardly have been bleaker. Though the United States had about 130,000 troops—about 80 percent of the height of 160,000—the Iraqis had steadily added security forces and now had some 263,000 military and police. Maybe half of those were in the lead, running security operations throughout Iraq, although even they each had U.S. military advisers working with them.

The SECRET assessment had a pessimistic report on crude oil production. The Iraqi government had set 2.5 million barrels a day as the

SECRET

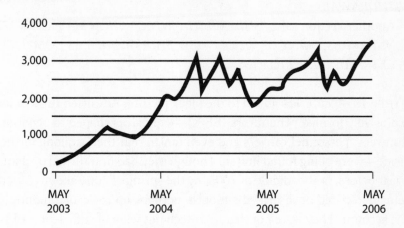

ENEMY INITIATED ATTACKS AGAINST
COALITION AND IRAQIS EACH MONTH FROM
MAY 2003 TO MAY 2006

target for June 2006. It was a high goal and probably unrealistic. It was averaging 2.1 million a day.

The SECRET report said: *"ASSESSMENT: CONTINUING SECURITY AND SABOTAGE DIVERT RECONSTRUCTION FUNDS TO TRIAGE RE-PAIRS AND FUEL IMPORTS. PRODUCTION UNLIKELY TO MEET 2006 MINISTRY OF OIL TARGETS WITHOUT INFRASTRUCTURE REHABILI-TATION, ENHANCED SECURITY AND EXPANDED FOREIGN INVEST-MENT."*

On electricity: *"ASSESSMENT: DESPITE ADDED CAPACITY THERE HAS BEEN LITTLE NET GAIN IN GENERATION SINCE PRE-OIF [OPERA-TION IRAQI FREEDOM]. BEYOND IMPROVED SECURITY, IRAQ NEEDS A STRATEGIC APPROACH TO SECTOR REHABILITATION, DEVELOP-ING LARGE SCALE PLANTS IN CENTRAL SOUTH THAT UTILIZE DO-MESTIC FUELS."*

On the political front the news was not much better. The fight for control of the ministries between the Shiites and Sunnis was critical.

"MINISTERS WILL BE POLITICALLY LOYAL TO THEIR RESPECTIVE PARTIES AND SOME MINISTRIES ARE LIKELY TO BECOME HAVENS FOR THE POLITICAL PARTIES WHO CONTROL THEM," the report said.

"THREATS OF SHIA ASCENDANCY COULD HARDEN AND EXPAND

SHIA MILITANT OPPOSITION AND INCREASE CALLS FOR COALITION WITHDRAWAL."

Another section said, *"SHIA MILITIA INTEGRATION MAY ALIENATE SUNNI ARABS, MANY OF WHOM VIEW SHIA GROUPS AS COMPLICIT IN EXTRAJUDICIAL KILLINGS."*

OTHER INTELLIGENCE added to the bleak picture. Advanced IEDs called explosively formed penetrators (EFPs)—explosives shaped to penetrate Humvees, personnel carriers and even tanks, that then explode further inside—were being found in Iraq. Though they had first turned up about a year before, in the middle of 2005, by the spring of 2006 about 15 were being detonated or disarmed a month, perhaps up to 40 one month by one account. They were not that high-tech but were of sufficient sophistication that they couldn't have been homemade. The high-quality machining and the higher-quality triggering devices had been traced to Iran. Some were triggered by passive infrared devices that could overcome U.S. countermeasures. The EFPs were about four times as lethal as the conventional IEDs. In one study, one person was killed for every two conventional IEDs, but each advanced EFP killed an average of 2.2 people. There was at least one example of an EFP penetrating the heavy armor of a large Abrams tank.

The radical Iranian Revolutionary Guard Corps had asked Hezbollah, the terrorist organization, to conduct some of the training of Iraqis to use the EFPs, according to U.S. intelligence.

If all this were put out publicly, it might start a fire that no one could put out. First, questions would immediately arise about the quality of the intelligence. Was this potentially another WMD fiasco? Second, if it were true, it meant that the Iranians were killing American soldiers—an act of war. The chief premise of a Republican foreign policy had been toughness—no more weakness, no more Carters or Clintons and their pathological unwillingness to use force. Where would that lead them in dealing with Iran now?

There was a third problem. The EFPs were being fed into the Shiite groups in the south and some in Baghdad, but comparatively speaking, the level of EFPs was not all that high. Suppose the Iranians put their minds and energies to it and started giving the technology, know-how and equipment in large numbers to the Sunni Arab insurgency, as well as the Shiites? That would be an entirely different matter.

Polling showed that about 50 percent of the Sunnis had a positive attitude toward the insurgency. Since Sunnis were about 20 percent of the overall population, that meant at least 10 percent of Iraqis—over 2 million people—had a favorable attitude toward the insurgents.

IN JULY 2006, I TOLD RUMSFELD that I understood the number of attacks was going up.

"That's probably true," he said. "It is also probably true that our data's better, and we're categorizing more things as attacks. A random round can be an attack and all the way up to killing 50 people someplace. So you've got a whole fruit bowl of different things—a banana and an apple and an orange."

I was speechless. Even with the loosest and most careless use of language and analogy, I did not understand how the secretary of defense would compare insurgent attacks to a "fruit bowl," a metaphor that stripped them of all urgency and emotion. The official categories in the classified reports that Rumsfeld regularly received were the lethal IEDs, standoff attacks with mortars, and close engagements such as ambushes—as far from bananas, apples and oranges as possible.

"THE ATTACKS ARE UP," JCS Chairman General Pace confirmed, "because folks want that place to be ungovernable so that when it is ungovernable we would walk away so they could then take over." He then got wound up, adding, "So you can expect the attacks to stay up because every day that Prime Minister Maliki and his parliament meet and make decisions is a bad day for those who are creating those attacks. . . . They're on the ropes . . . if this parliament continues to function and this prime minister continues to function."

"Okay," I said, "but are they on the ropes?"

"Wrong word," Pace said.

"You're going to sound like Cheney," I said. "You want to retract that?"

"I do," he said. "I would like to retract that. Thank you. I appreciate that. I appreciate the courtesy."

I asked about victory and how it might be achieved, and he said that would require more than security in Iraq. There would have to be self-government and the physical reconstruction of the country—all the "lines of operation" in Casey's war plan.

"Is this going to happen in your lifetime?" I asked.

"Yes, it is. Well, I hope, yeah. I don't know," he said. "I should retract that line. It can happen in my lifetime."

"Do you have any doubts this was the right decision to invade Iraq?

"I have no doubts at all," he said. "None. Zero."

"Isn't the process, though, you always have to have doubt?" I said. "I live on doubt."

"I'm sorry for you," the Marine general said.

"Don't be sorry for me," I replied. "It's a wonderful process."

"I do not have doubt about what we've done," he said. "We did not do this. When we were sitting home minding our own business, we got attacked on 9/11."

There it was: "We did not do this." There is a deep feeling among some senior Bush administration officials that somehow we had not started the Iraq War. We had been attacked. Bin Laden, al Qaeda, the other terrorist and anti-American forces—whether groups or countries or philosophies—could be lumped together. It was one war, the long war, the two-generation war that Wolfowitz's Bletchley II group had described after 9/11.

"You sure it's the right war at the right time?" I asked Chairman Pace.

"Yes."

"Right place?"

"Yes, absolutely," Pace said. "Fundamentally, yes. I said that before we started. And I'll say that today. It may not surprise you to understand that taking my country's battles to my country's enemies on their playing field is where I think we should be. To protect my country, to do my oath to my country, and to protect my kids and my grandkids and your kids and your grandkids, I have zero doubt that we have done the right thing."

ON MAY 26, two days after the SECRET intelligence assessment, the Pentagon released a public report to Congress entitled "Measuring Stability and Security in Iraq." It was a quarterly report required by law. Though there was a chart buried in the middle of the 65-page document showing that average weekly attacks were up to over 600, the document put the most positive spin on stability and security.

The four-page introduction was all happy talk. "Anti Iraqi forces—extremists and terrorist—continue to fail in their campaign to derail the political process . . . and to foment civil war," the report said, omitting any mention of how the security picture was significantly worse.

"More than 80 percent of terrorist attacks were concentrated in just four of Iraq's 18 provinces," it said as if violence had gone down. Those four provinces, including Baghdad, had 37 percent of the population.

The report defined "Iraqi Rejectionists" as former regime loyalists, Saddamists and terrorists, including al Qaeda. "Rejectionist strength will likely remain steady throughout 2006," the report said, which was consistent with the SECRET intelligence assessment. But the Pentagon report went on to say that the Rejectionist "appeal and motivation for continued violent action will begin to wane in early 2007." The Pentagon report flatly contradicted its own secret assessment two days earlier that said the insurgents and terrorists retained the resources and capabilities to "sustain and even increase current level of violence through the next year."

JOHN NEGROPONTE had been director of national intelligence for over a year. He had access to everything, and saw the president almost daily. He was one of the few who knew the most about the U.S. involvement in Iraq. From the beginning of the insurgency in 2003, he believed, the administration had underestimated its size and miscalculated its motivation. Worse, they were still doing it.

The sectarian violence, particularly Shiites killing Sunnis and Sunnis killing Shiites, was migrating down lower into the community to the local blocks and neighborhoods. This was a startling new phenomenon. In March, after the bombing of the Samarra mosque, there had been more than 450 violent sectarian incidents with 1,800 Iraqi casualties. The next month it had gone down to about 330 incidents with some 1,300 casualties—still incredibly high.

The key was that Zarqawi, the Jordanian thug who had become the al Qaeda leader in Iraq, had been successful in getting people pissed off at each other. In some respects it was like throwing a fist at someone in a crowded bar that happened to be filled with permanent enemies. The indiscriminate attacks on Iraqis and long-nurtured sectarian hostility had fueled a chain reaction. Iraq was now much more fertile ground for sectarian violence. Zarqawi had created that fertile ground.

Negroponte was not surprised that the Pentagon would put out optimistic reports. It was natural. He had seen it in Vietnam. The generals and civilians would sugarcoat things, praising their people and insisting that there was light at the end of the tunnel.

But sugarcoating was not his job. Now there was so much sectarian violence in Iraq that the U.S. military or intelligence agencies might not even know about it or be able to measure it, Negroponte concluded. The real problem was how blind the coalition, the U.S. and the intelligence agencies were in Iraq.

Who is the enemy? Negroponte asked, posing the same question that Deputy CIA Director John McLaughlin addressed nearly three years earlier, when he concluded it was a mix of former Baathists, foreign fighters such as Zarqawi, Iraqi nationalists and tribalists offended by American aggressiveness. Negroponte came up with some of the same answers—Saddamists, troublemakers and Zarqawi, who obviously was more important. But overall he found it hard to get anywhere on this. The reason was that the human sources that the CIA had recruited reflected the polarization of Iraq. Everyone had taken sides, and it was hard to find unbiased Iraqi sources. When it was all sorted and analyzed, the mystery for him had deepened.

Negroponte went around telling an old joke about an admiral who asks a scientist how to deal with the threat posed by submarines. "Figure out how to boil the ocean," the scientist says. "That will solve the submarine problem. I'll leave the implementation to you."

Overall, he concluded, it had all been downhill in the first six months of 2006. Clearly now, in early June, he could see the U.S. Iraq policy was in trouble. It was time to face facts. The Shiites were already the winners. They would prevail. The only question was how the United States could help shape things—which was different from determining them. It was time to take American hands off.

"If we had 10 years, then we could do it another way," Negroponte said privately. "I'm with Rumsfeld on the training wheels now. We're just going to have to take them off."

RICE BELIEVED THEY HAD to be careful about reducing forces. At the same time she wanted to be flexible with a political solution that would bring in the insurgency and get them involved with the government. But that could not include compromises or any kind of outreach to those with American blood on their hands. As the insurgency grew stronger and the attacks increased, that became more and more difficult. It was almost impossible.

Rice had always been the superachiever, undeterred by impossible odds. "Our obligation is to get this right," she said. The word "obligation" loomed large for her. "The obligation is to work our way through the thicket of problems that are there."

She was regularly challenged about the administration's claims of progress. "What I found hardest to say," she said, "what I honestly believe, was that side by side you had progress and chaos, all right? And that was hard for people to accept. They would think you were spinning." But it was truly a mixture of progress and chaos, she felt. That was the paradox.

In Rice's analysis, the Iraq invasion had challenged the old authoritarian structure and foundation of the Middle East. Now the old Middle East was destroyed, and they had to put a new order in place. She reminded people that not so long ago, it was sort of taken as a given that France and Germany would always be fighting with each other. Nobody now believed that France and Germany would ever fight again. The two world wars had changed the fundamental pillars. That too could happen in the Middle East, but it would take time. The president and his war cabinet would have to show how the new foundation was going to be built.

Part of her seemed to long for the day when it might be over, when she would be out of government.

"I'm sure that in seven or eight years I'll come visit you in Crawford," she told the president. "And we'll think, 'We should have done this or we should have done that.' Or maybe we'll all look really good in retrospect, the way things do when you're getting older."

45

C LASSIFIED REPORTS BORE OUT exactly what the Joint Staff's intelligence report in May had grimly predicted—still higher levels of insurgent attacks in Iraq. During one week in May 2006, enemy-initiated attacks soared to 900, a new record. In June, attacks went down to about 825 one week but then spiked up again.*

It was even worse considering that the level of violence existed after two years spent training, equipping and funding 263,000 Iraqi soldiers and police. The cost had been $10 billion, and American teams had been embedded with most of the Iraqi units for over a year. At an equivalent time in 1971, after several years of Vietnamization, the trend lines of insurgent violence had been down, not up. The simple conclusion was that the Iraq strategy was not working, and the insurgency was strong and sustainable.

---

* The classified report on weekly security incidents for the week of June 16 to June 22, 2006, divided the approximately 825 attacks that week into five categories:

A) Undetonated, discovered or disabled improvised explosive devices—nearly 200.

B) Exploded mines, IEDs, other modified ordnance and vehicle-borne IEDs (car bombs)—more than 200.

C) Close engagements—small-arms fire, ambushes, drive-by shootings, snipers, rocket-propelled grenades and standard grenades—about 175.

D) Standoff attacks—mortar, artillery and multiple rocket launcher barrages, surface-to-surface missiles, surface-to-air missiles—about 100.

E) Attacks on Iraqi authorities—about 150.

A note on a graph showing the escalation of violent attacks said the incidents did not include insurgent "reactions to Coalition-initiated actions such as sweeps, safehouse raids, weapons seizures or high-value target captures."

• • •

STEVE HERBITS WENT to have a sandwich with Rumsfeld at the Pentagon on Wednesday, June 14.

The most important op-ed piece of the year, Herbits told him, was probably the one in *The New York Times* the previous month by Senator Joseph R. Biden Jr., the Delaware Democrat and ranking member of the Senate Foreign Relations Committee, and Les Gelb, the former president of the Council on Foreign Relations.

Rumsfeld began taking notes.

Biden and Gelb had proposed an option between staying the course indefinitely and bringing the U.S. troops home on some kind of timetable, Herbits noted. This would be done by establishing three largely autonomous regions, one each for the Kurds, Shiites and Sunnis, who would make their own domestic laws and be responsible for security in their regions. The central government in Baghdad would control border security, foreign affairs and oil revenues. Iraq was already heading toward partition and this loose federalism of three ethnic states was developing on its own.

Herbits said that the current concept of an integrated national police was not working at all, and the sectarian militias were increasingly powerful and violent. Tens of thousands of Iraqis were migrating on their own to their ethnic regions already, he said, and the voting by foot was more important than any of the highly touted elections. Events were already taking Iraq in this direction and it might be impossible to stop. U.S. policy could effectively embrace it. This, he noted, was the conclusion in a forthcoming book by Peter W. Galbraith, an expert with two decades of experience with Iraq, called *The End of Iraq*.

Rumsfeld continued to take notes, expressing neither agreement nor disagreement.

Set up an A Team and a B Team on the possibility, Herbits proposed. Have each give you a 30-minute argument so you become familiar with the language and issues on each side because it was likely to become the focus of debate.

"It is an exit strategy," Herbits told the secretary, and the administration frankly did not have a viable one. "It would be something this administration could adopt in the name of freedom and self-determination. And they could call it victory."

• • •

THE U.S. WAS STILL keeping score and releasing body counts. Inside Iraq, evidence of the Great American Killing Machine and the trumpeting of its latest body counts became recruiting tools for the insurgents. The ground reality was that since the insurgents didn't wear uniforms and lived and blended into the population, some of those killed, possibly a significant number, were innocent civilians. Body counts also reminded Iraqis that they were living in an occupation. Counterinsurgency experts say that body counts offer a false measure of winning, and cite the Vietnam War when the North Vietnamese, the winning side, lost about a million, compared to the United States, which had 58,000 killed but lost the war.

But President Bush loved to keep scorecards. Notes of the NSC meetings in the days after the 9/11 terrorist attacks show Bush repeatedly asking for a "scorecard" as a way to measure the war on terror. On October 10, 2001, Bush went to the FBI headquarters and personally unveiled a list of the 22 "Most Wanted Terrorists," which included Osama bin Laden. He took a classified version of the list with photos, brief biographies and personality sketches of the 22 and slipped it into a drawer in the Oval Office. When one on the list was killed or captured, he personally drew a big "X" through the photo. With pride, Bush displayed his terrorist scorecard during an Oval Office interview December 20, 2001. During an interview at his Crawford ranch on August 20, 2002, he said, "The scorecard is important because I want people to know there is progress."

So during the Iraq War it was difficult for the president to restrain himself. Rumsfeld, Rice and Card had cautioned him on body counts, but he wanted to know, wanted the tally sheet for what he saw as a series of separate battles. "They killed three of ours. How many did we kill of them?"

It bled into his public statements. In an October 1, 2005, radio address, for example, he noted that one sign of success was that "hundreds of insurgents and terrorists have been killed."

Rumsfeld too did not resist, ignoring his own advice. On July 11, 2006, in a press conference with Afghanistan President Karzai, the secretary of defense said, "If you look at the number of terrorists and Taliban and al Qaeda that are being killed every month, it would be hard for them to say that the Coalition forces and Afghan security forces were losing."

Nine days later I went to interview General Pace, the chairman of the

Joint Chiefs. He confirmed that body counts were a red line for him. But despite his strong, absolute feelings that body counts are a false measure of success, President Bush still asks for them. "The president has asked on occasion to get a flavor for the give-and-take about enemy killed," Pace said, adding that on the secure videos, Generals Abizaid or Casey "have given him a number for that battle."

"The president wants to know, are we damaging the other guy. That's really how it comes up. But it's not frequently. . . . It's not inappropriate for the leadership to know on occasion that we are giving a whole lot better than we're getting." He said that Abizaid agrees with him that body counts should not be used. "John and I totally agree," Pace said. "He's a good soldier and he understands exactly the same thing."

But well into the summer of 2006, the president was still asking. "I am satisfied that the president knows exactly where I am on body counts," Pace said.

Three days after I interviewed Pace, for example, Casey's headquarters put out a report, "Coalition, Iraqi Troops Kill 15 Terrorists." Pace's caution about body counts was just another example of advice that was rejected. It was another argument the number one military man in the United States had lost even though it raised the ghosts and anguish of Vietnam. Meeting the president's emotional and political needs was apparently more important.

IN JULY 2006, I interviewed Rumsfeld on two successive afternoons. Asked about the battle with the Iraq insurgency, he said, "It could take eight to 10 years. Insurgencies have a tendency to do that." Overall, he said, "Our exit strategy is to have the Iraqis' government and security forces capable of managing a lower-level insurgency and ultimately achieving victory over it and repressing it over time. But it would be a period after we may very well not have large numbers of people there."

I said I understood that General Casey had reported that the insurgency had not been neutralized—a key goal of his campaign plan—but only contained. After some typical verbal jousting, I was able to ask directly, "Do you agree it has not been neutralized?"

"Oh, clearly not," Rumsfeld answered.

"Only contained?"

"Yeah," he said. "Thus far."

I then read from the May 2006 assessment that said the "Sunni Arab insurgency is gaining strength and increasing capacity." I asked him, "Does that sound right to you?"

Here was one of the central questions in any war. Was the other side "gaining strength and increasing capacity"? Casey, the Joint Chiefs' intelligence staff, and the CIA had all categorically said the insurgency was gaining. Certainly Rumsfeld knew that. I had also quoted from the assessment on a list of 29 sample questions I had submitted in advance, and I know he had spent at least one hour the day before preparing for the interview.

"When was this?" Rumsfeld asked.

Six weeks ago, I answered. The question on the table was whether he agreed or not that the insurgency in the Iraq War was gaining. I was ready for a pure Rumsfeldian moment, and I was not disappointed.

"Gosh, I don't know," the secretary of defense replied. "I don't want to comment on it. I read so many of those intelligence reports"—I had never said it was an intelligence report—"and they are all over the lot. In a given day you can see one from one agency, and one from another agency, and then I'll ask Casey or Abizaid what they think about it, or Pete Pace, 'Is that your view?' And try and triangulate and see what people think. But it changes from month to month. I'm not going to go back and say I agree or don't agree with something like that."

He was right that there might be some changes month to month, but, as he knew, the overall assessment and trend was visibly, measurably and dramatically worse.

I NEXT QUOTED from a speech that Rumsfeld had given earlier in the year at the Truman Presidential Library in Independence, Missouri, when he told some stories about Truman as a leader standing up to the Soviet foreign minister. Could he recall any moments showing Bush as a wartime leader that were important?

"What I try to do with him is to put myself in his shoes and say, 'What would I want to know?' " Rumsfeld said. He then went on to describe himself as a wartime leader—not Bush—working with General Franks to keep the president informed about the factors used in deciding on what targets to bomb in Iraq. Though the question was about Bush, Rumsfeld described how all this care in selecting targets would make the president comfortable and show that Rumsfeld and Franks "had an approach that was rational and as humane as possible but as effective as possible in terms of saving American lives."

Can you recall any moments of Bush leadership in the postwar period? I asked.

He then went on to describe how he had sent "three or four assessment teams"—one every six months or so—to Iraq to "take a look at how are we doing."

"I drive back at this point," I said, "the president as a wartime leader, because that's the issue here."

"He's a good one," Rumsfeld said. "He's a very good one. You watch him and I don't know quite how he does it. Here in this department we move across a full spectrum of maybe 180 degrees. He moves 360 degrees. He'll go from stem cell research to immigration to 15 other things in a given day. And the stuff we bring to him on a regular basis is complicated. It's new. And he has a very effective technique. . . . He just keeps pinging question after question after question."

I was getting a description of the Rumsfeld style.

"He's getting to know the people and taking their measure," Rumsfeld continued, "and seeing how they handle those questions and how they answer them and how much they know and who they rely on for answers to things. And he ends up coming away with a confidence level, and he develops an ability to know how much—how long a leash he wants different people to be on."

"How long's your leash?" I asked.

"Oh, goodness gracious," he replied. "Don't ask me."

"I am."

"No. I have no idea," he said.

Rumsfeld certainly knew that Bush gave him a very long leash.

"Do you feel a tug sometimes?"

He declined to answer.

What about the notion that Cheney is the all-powerful vice president who controls the president?

"That's nonsense," Rumsfeld said. "Clearly they have a good relationship. You can feel it in the room. But the president is *the* president, and let there be no doubt about it. The vice president isn't even slightly confused on the issue. His handling of issues when the president's in the room is, in my view, just perfect in the sense that he does not take strong positions when the president's in the room that could conceivably position him contrary to the president. . . . He asks good questions. But he doesn't put the president in a corner or take away his options."

It was a revealing comment. I wondered how Cheney's questions or comments could put the president in a corner or take away his options. Presumably if it was nonsense that Cheney was all-powerful he would be in no position to do either.

Rumsfeld said that he believes Cheney is completely candid with Bush in private. "He knows that one of the prices of proximity to the president is the willingness, the burden that goes with that is the burden of having to tell him the truth."

I ASKED RUMSFELD what was the best, most optimistic scenario for a positive outcome in Iraq.

"This business is ugly," he replied. "It's tough. There isn't any best. A long, hard slog, I think I wrote years ago. We're facing a set of challenges that are different than our country understands. . . . They're different than our Congress understands. They're different than our government, much of our government, probably understands and is organized or trained or equipped to cope with and deal with. We're dealing with enemies that can turn inside our decision circles." The enemy can move swiftly, he said. "They don't have parliaments and bureaucracies and real estate to defend and interact with or deal with or cope with. They can do what they want. They aren't held accountable for lying or for killing innocent men, women and children.

"There's something about the body politic in the United States that they can accept the enemy killing innocent men, women and children and cutting off people's heads, but have zero tolerance for some soldier who does something he shouldn't do."

"Are you optimistic?" I asked.

Rumsfeld looked through me and continued. Three of his aides who were sitting with us at the table in his office could not help but register surprise as Rumsfeld plowed on without answering.

"We're fighting the first war in history in the new century," he continued, "and with all these new realities, with an industrial-age organization in an environment that has not adapted and adjusted, a public environment that has not adapted and adjusted."

Among other matters, Rumsfeld was obviously upset about the Supreme Court decision a week earlier in the *Hamdan v. Rumsfeld* ruling that the Bush administration in effect had to respect the rights of terror suspects held at Guantánamo Bay, Cuba, to have lawyers and trials. Rumsfeld felt they should be interrogated and kept in detention to keep them off the battlefield. The court's decision was a major blow to the Bush administration's ideas about fighting the war on terror. In the 5–3 decision, the High Court said that the administration had to adhere to due process.

Several months earlier, on May 1, Rumsfeld had circulated a six-page secret memo proposing some fixes, entitled "Illustrative New 21st Century Institutions and Approaches."

It was almost the latest version of the "Anchor Chain" memos he had written in his first months as secretary in 2001—a cry from his bureaucratic and managerial heart. Not only was the Defense Department tangled in its anchor chain but so was the rest of the U.S. government, and the world.

Like Andy Card, Rumsfeld was sensitive to the charge of incompetence. He dictated, "The charge of incompetence against the U.S. government should be easy to rebut if the American people understand the extent to which the current system of government makes competence next to impossible."

AT THE END OF THE SECOND INTERVIEW I quoted former Secretary of Defense Robert McNamara, "Any military commander who is honest with you will say he's made mistakes that have cost lives."

"Um hmm," Rumsfeld said.

"Is that correct?"

"I don't know. I suppose that a military commander—"

"Which you are," I interrupted.

"No, I'm not," the secretary of defense said.

"Yes, sir," I said.

"No, no. Well . . ."

"Yes. Yes," I said, raising my hand in the air and ticking off the hierarchy. "It's commander in chief, secretary of defense, combatant commander."

"I can see a military commander in a uniform who is engaged in a conflict having to make decisions that result in people living or dying and that that would be a truth. And certainly if you go up the chain to the civilian side to the president and to me, you could by indirection, two or three steps removed, make the case."

Indirection? Two or three steps removed? It was inexplicable. Rumsfeld had spent so much time insisting on the chain of command. He was in control—not the Joint Chiefs, not the uniformed military, not the NSC or the NSC staff, not the critics or the opiners. How could he not see his role and responsibility?

I could think of nothing more to say.

ON DECEMBER 11, 2003, I had interviewed President Bush and got a taste of his style and habit of denial. It was eight months after the invasion and WMD had not been found.

"On weapons of mass destruction," I asked.

"Sure," the president said.

One of my bosses at *The Washington Post* had suggested I ask, "Was the president misled—"

"No," Bush said.

I continued the question, "—by the intelligence, or did he mislead the country?"

"No."

"No, okay," I repeated his reply.

"The answer is absolutely not."

"What happened?" I asked.

"What do you mean what happened?" Bush asked, sounding as if he had not been the one who gave all those speeches about WMD.

"In terms of weapons of mass destruction," I explained. "And the 'slam dunk' case."

The president said that weapons inspector David Kay's initial report supported the idea that Saddam had weapons programs. "I think that it's way too early to fully understand the complete history. This is intelligence," he pointed out.

"I understand," I said. "Not fact."

"It was intelligence, hard-enough intelligence for the United Nations to pass several resolutions. Hard-enough intelligence for President Bill Clinton to make a military decision on this" by ordering the bombing of Iraq's suspected WMD sites in 1998.

"But we have not found any weapons of mass destruction," I said.

"We have found weapons programs that could be reconstituted."

"Could be, I agree."

"A weapon could come very quickly. And so therefore, given that, even if that's the very minimum you had, how could you not act on Saddam Hussein, given his nature," Bush said.

I mentioned that I'd spoken with Americans as I traveled around the country who thought that after 9/11 he had been the voice of realism by saying it had been a catastrophic attack, that the terrorists were killers, and that America was in for a long battle. His unwillingness to acknowledge that no WMD had been found was making him less the voice of realism.

"I disagree with that, that construct," Bush replied.

"Fair."

"Saddam Hussein had weapons, he used weapons."

"No question."

"And he hid weapons. He hid systems. He had plans," Bush went on. "And so therefore—the voice of realism just lays out where we are. That's a realistic look."

"And include in there, We haven't found them yet," I said.

He chuckled. "From my perspective, I don't want people to say, 'Aha, we told you so.' I want people to know that there is a process that's ongoing in a very dangerous part of the world. And so, frankly, I haven't heard one person say that to me, but you run in different circles than I do. Much more elite."

I said the people I was talking about were business people.

"The realism is to be able to understand the nature of Saddam Hussein, his history, his potential harm to America."

"Clearly we haven't found bubbling vats," I said.

"Well," the president chuckled.

"But the status report, for the last six or seven months, is we haven't found weapons. That's all," I pushed one more time.

"True, true, true."

It had taken five minutes and 18 seconds for Bush simply to acknowledge the *fact* that we hadn't found weapons of mass destruction.

"The person who wants the president to stand up and declare that publicly is also the person who wants to say, Shouldn't have done it," Bush said, adding, "I'm probably sounding incredibly defensive all of a sudden."

I said I would deal with what he said in my book about the decision to invade, due to come out in 2004.

"Why do you need to deal with this in the book?" he asked. "What's that got to do about it?"

I said I had to deal with it because it was an important issue.

Later he wanted to be sure that I understood the terms of the interview—his comments were for the book and not an article in The

Washington Post. "In other words, I'm not going to read a headline, 'Bush Says No Weapons.' "

I said I would wait.

I VIVIDLY REMEMBERED how he had told me in an earlier interview, "A president has got to be the calcium in the backbone." His rhetoric on postwar Iraq was right out of that "calcium in the backbone" script. All the perpetually upbeat talk and optimism—from "Mission Accomplished," through "stay the course" and "when they stand up, we'll stand down," his proclamations that he'd stay on the same path even if only the first lady and his dog supported him, the talk about turning points and turned corners, and the barbs that suggested anyone who questioned his strategy in Iraq did not support the troops and instead wanted America to "cut and run" or "surrender to the terrorists"—it was the same play, over and over. His strategy was to make repeated declarations of optimism and avoid adding to any doubts.

In researching and reporting for a newspaper series in *The Washington Post* and my two previous books on Bush's war decisions, I interviewed him four times—December 2001, August 2002, and finally twice in December 2003. The transcripts for the combined seven and a half hours of interviews run hundreds of pages.

Those were the days when Bush was a popular president—post-9/11, and later during the first nine months after the Iraq invasion. As the war dragged on, as Americans and Iraqis continued to die, and as Bush's approval ratings dropped dramatically in 2005 and 2006, so did my chances of getting another interview with him.

I asked repeatedly for the opportunity to talk with Bush. In February 2006, Dan Bartlett said he and Hadley would continue to help me but the president probably would not be interviewed. I interviewed key members of the administration many times and reviewed thousands of pages of documents. By the summer of 2006, Rumsfeld had talked with me on the record for two afternoons, but Bartlett and Hadley had gone radio-silent and would not return my phone calls.

As early as 2005, I had learned, Hadley was leaning against further White House cooperation. He knew the issues and events I was pursuing and the kinds of questions I was asking: What is the strategy for victory in Iraq? Didn't anyone at the White House notice that the actions being implemented on the ground in the months after the invasion were almost diametrically opposed to the plan that had been briefed to Bush?

What was Rumsfeld telling Bush? What was Cheney telling Bush? What did Bush decide? What did he neglect? When did the administration begin to realize that they were dealing with a monumental task, and that major combat was not over? When did they realize that there would likely never be weapons of mass destruction found in Iraq? Are things really as good in Iraq as the top civilian and military officials in the U.S. government keep insisting publicly?

"What's going through my mind is this is just going to be great," Hadley said sarcastically to a colleague in October 2005. My book on postwar Iraq, he said, would be published in 2006, after Jerry Bremer's book. "So, let's see, this is going to be an issue. So we will go into the '06 congressional elections with a raging debate on everybody who will say politically, 'I was with the administration. I wouldn't have gone into Iraq but I recognized how important it was. And if the administration had had a plan and if they had any competence at all I would have stayed with them. But as it is they clearly didn't have one. This is an incompetent administration. Iraq is the most important issue. I support the troops. I understand the importance of the mission, but given the incompetence of this administration, as demonstrated by the Bremer and the Woodward books, we have no choice but to throw the Republicans out and bring the troops home.' I mean, this is really going to be awful."

Hadley sighed. Later, he picked up the theme again, telling his colleague, "I've got to help this president get through what is going to be a really rugged three years. And if the Democrats take over the House and the Senate it's going be unbelievable after 2006."

The president's national security adviser understandably wanted to win the 2006 congressional elections. Having the president answer questions about Iraq was conspicuously inconsistent with that goal. The strategy was denial.

With all Bush's upbeat talk and optimism, he had not told the American public the truth about what Iraq had become.

A NOTE ON SOURCES

NEARLY ALL of the information in this book comes from interviews with President Bush's national security team, their deputies and other senior and key players in the administration responsible for the military, the diplomacy and the intelligence on the Iraq War. Officials serving at various levels of the White House staff, the Defense and State Departments, and the Central Intelligence Agency, with firsthand knowledge of the meetings, documents and events, were also primary sources. Most of these interviews were conducted on background, meaning that the information provided could be used but the sources would not be identified by name in the book.

Several former and current officials, such as Secretary of Defense Donald H. Rumsfeld, spoke on the record. President Bush and Vice President Cheney declined to be interviewed for this book. Past interviews from which I drew material for this book are noted.

In addition, critical information came from documents including memos, official notes, personal notes, letters, talking points, briefing summaries, e-mails, chronologies and calendars.

Most sources were interviewed multiple times, by me or my assistant Bill Murphy Jr. I interviewed several sources a half-dozen or more times. Nearly all allowed us to record the interviews so the story could be told more fully and accurately, with the exact language they used.

When thoughts, conclusions and feelings are attributed to a participant, I have obtained them from that person directly, from the written record, or from a colleague whom the person told.

PROLOGUE

The information in this chapter comes primarily from background interviews with two knowledgeable sources.

xi   In late December 2000: For descriptions of President Bush's meetings with Coats and Rumsfeld, see especially Eric Schmitt and Elaine Sciolino, "To Run Pentagon, Bush Sought Proven Manager with Muscle," *The New York Times*, January 1, 2001, p. 1; see also Thomas E. Ricks, "For Defense, Cheney's Mirror Image; Pentagon Will See Elder Statesman and Power Player in Rumsfeld," *The Washington Post*, December 29, 2000, p. A1; and Eric Schmitt, "Defense Secretary Chosen; Held Same Post Under Ford," *The New York Times*, December 29, 2000, p. 1.

xii   There was another dynamic: See George H. W. Bush, *Looking Forward: An Autobiography* (New York: Doubleday, 1987), pp. 157–59.

xiv   "Get it right": Author's discussion with Secretary Rumsfeld, March 4, 2001. Later confirmed by Vice President Cheney.

CHAPTER 1

The information in this chapter comes primarily from background interviews with five knowledgeable sources.

2   When Michael Deaver: See also David B. Ottaway, "Saudi Lobby Losing Strength; Defeat of Arms Sale Contrasts with Earlier Success," *The Washington Post*, May 10, 1986, p. A1.

3   I interviewed President Bush on December 11, 2003, and asked him about Prince Bandar's 1997 visit to Austin:

Q: Do you remember when you were thinking of running for president, when you were governor, and you talked to Prince Bandar. You went, he came to Texas, you stopped at his plane.

President Bush: Yeah.

Q: And had a discussion. And he kind of, your dad had said he knows a lot about foreign affairs. And he kind of did a tour around the world.

President Bush: Is this Bandar telling you this? What did he say? I can't remember.

Q: This is a fascinating moment. He said that there are people who don't like Saudi Arabia, who didn't like your father, who might not support you. And you kind of have to make peace with them. And you bristled at that.

President Bush: Sounds like Saddam Hussein. [laughter] Go ahead.

Q: No, no, wasn't—you know, that there are enemies out there.

President Bush: Yeah, sure.

Q: People who didn't like your father, don't like Saudi Arabia. And he's saying to you, make peace with them. And you're saying "No, I don't want to do that. That's not straight and honest," and he said to you, in the big boys' game it is cutthroat. It is bloody.

President Bush: [laughs] I don't remember that. But I do remember it with Bandar.

7   The campaign autobiography: George W. Bush and Karen Hughes, *A Charge to Keep* (New York: William Morrow, 1999).

8   "I will defend": Transcript of Governor George W. Bush's speech at The Citadel, September 23, 1999, printed from www.georgewbush.com.

CHAPTER 2

The information in this chapter comes primarily from background interviews with five knowledgeable sources.

10   Among the Vulcans was another veteran: See also James Mann, *Rise of the Vulcans* (New York: Penguin, 2004).

11   Bush had no problem: Author interview with President George W. Bush, August 20, 2002.

11   On February 28, 1999: FDCH Federal Department and Agency documents, March 3, 1999, "Bush Tells Gulf Vets Why Hussein Left in Baghdad."

14   He and the elder: George Bush and Brent Scowcroft, *A World Transformed* (New York: Alfred A. Knopf, 1998).

CHAPTER 3

The information in this chapter comes primarily from background interviews with eight knowledgeable sources, as well as with retired Rear Admiral J. J. Quinn, who was interviewed on March 22 and 23, and May 3, 2006.

17   In his first: Author interviews with Secretary Rumsfeld in 1988 and 1989.

24   On Thursday, March 15, 2001: Bandar's meeting with Bush and his assessment come from official Saudi notes and were confirmed by an American source.

25   Rumsfeld was trying: Copies of four "Anchor Chain" memos, other documents and snowflakes obtained by the author; author interviews with Secretary Rumsfeld, July 6 and 7, 2006.

CHAPTER 4

The information in this chapter comes primarily from background interviews with six knowledgeable sources and with retired Rear Admiral Quinn.

33 On April 25, 2001: ABC News transcript, *Good Morning America*, April 25, 2001.

CHAPTER 5

The information in this chapter comes primarily from background interviews with seven knowledgeable sources and documents obtained by the author.

45 Twelve days later: DOD transcripts of Secretary Rumsfeld's speeches: www.defenselink.mil/speeches/2001/s20010528–secdef.html; www.de fenselink.mil/Speeches/Speech.aspx?SpeechID=368.

45 At his Senate testimony: FDCH Political Transcripts, Senate Armed Services Committee hearing, June 21, 2001.

45 In May, Crown Prince Abdullah: Roula Khalaf, "Regal Reformer: Crown Prince Abdullah, Regent to Saudi Arabia's King Fahd, Has Spearheaded Diplomatic and Economic Change," *The Financial Times*, June 25, 2001.

45 On June 1: Lee Hockstader, "Bombing Kills at Least 17 at Tel Aviv Clubs; Suicide Blast Hits Young Crowd," *The Washington Post*, June 2, 2001, p. A1.

46 Israeli military units: Deborah Sontag, "As Emotions Boil Over, Arab-Israeli Violence Rages On," *The New York Times*, May 20, 2001, p. 4.

46 The previous year: Lee Hockstader, "Israel Steps Up Battle with Rioters; Army Firepower Boosts Death Toll; Albright to Meet with Barak, Arafat," *The Washington Post*, October 3, 2000, p. A1; also see http://news .bbc.co.uk/2/hi/middle_east/952700.stm.

47 On June 16: President Bush described his conversation with Ensenat to me in an interview on August 20, 2002.

47 Bush's first mention: "Branding Rite Laid to Yale Fraternity," *The New York Times*, November 8, 1967, p. 80.

CHAPTER 6

The information in this chapter comes primarily from background interviews with seven knowledgeable sources, and documents obtained by the author.

50 Two weeks earlier: See Richard A. Clarke, *Against All Enemies: Inside America's War on Terror* (New York: Free Press, 2004), p. 235.

52 Philip Zelikow: Philip Zelikow and Condoleezza Rice, *Germany Unified and Europe Transformed: A Study in Statecraft* (Cambridge, Mass.: Harvard University Press, 1995).

53 "I sat there": Author interview with Secretary Rumsfeld, September 20, 2003.

CHAPTER 7

The information in this chapter comes primarily from background interviews with six knowledgeable sources.

61 H. R. McMaster, *Dereliction of Duty: Lyndon Johnson, Robert McNamara, the Joint Chiefs of Staff, and the Lies That Led to Vietnam* (New York: HarperCollins, 1997).

CHAPTER 8

The information in this chapter comes primarily from background interviews with five knowledgeable sources, as well as with General Richard Myers on January 9, 2002.

68 Later I asked Rumsfeld: Author interview with Secretary Rumsfeld, July 7, 2006.

69 About four days: Rowan Scarborough, "Admiral Called Front-Runner for Joint Chiefs; Clark Is Said to Impress Bush," *The Washington Times*, August 11, 2001, p. A1.

69 On August 24, 2001: Presidential Documents, August 24, 2001: http://frwebgate.access.gpo.gov/cgi-bin/getdoc.cgi?dbname=2001_presi dential_documents&docid=pd27au01_txt-15.

69 Rumsfeld had told: Author interview with Secretary Rumsfeld, July 7, 2006.

71 He had been truly surprised: Vernon Loeb, "A Pilot's 'Good Hands' Near Joint Chiefs' Helm," *The Washington Post*, August 24, 2001, p. A1.

CHAPTER 9

The information in this chapter comes primarily from interviews with 10 knowledgeable sources, and with Christopher DeMuth on March 10, 2006.

75   Over the summer: Deborah Sontag, "Quest for Mideast Peace: How and Why It Failed," *The New York Times*, July 26, 2001, p. 1; Lee Hockstader, "Middle East Cease-Fire Breaks Down; Fresh Clashes Test Viability of Truce Brokered by Powell," *The Washington Post*, July 3, 2001, p. A12.

81   After 9/11, Bush's approval rating: Gallup Poll, "Bush Job Approval Highest in Gallup History," September 24, 2001.

81   On November 21: Author interview with President George W. Bush, December 10, 2003.

81   The Iraq war plan: See Bob Woodward, *The Commanders* (New York: Simon & Schuster, 1991); and Bob Woodward, *Plan of Attack* (New York: Simon & Schuster, 2004).

82   In Franks's memoir: Tommy Franks, *American Soldier* (New York: HarperCollins, 2004), pp. 329–31 and 342–44.

82   memoirs by Powell and Schwarzkopf: General H. Norman Schwarzkopf, *It Doesn't Take a Hero: The Autobiography of General H. Norman Schwarzkopf* (New York: Bantam, 1992); Colin Powell, *My American Journey* (New York: Random House, 1995), p. 487.

83   Bletchley Park: I asked Secretary Rumsfeld about Bletchley II in an interview on July 7, 2006:

Q: And Wolfowitz right after 9/11 set up this thing called Bletchley II. Do you remember that?

Rumsfeld: I do.

Q: Chris DeMuth at the AEI.

Rumsfeld: I asked him to. I said, "Look, we ought to get some group going to think about—"

Q: And they wrote a paper, seven pages, called "The Delta of Terrorism."

Rumsfeld: Right.

Q: Meaning the origin of terrorism.

Rumsfeld: Um hm. [affirmative]

Q: And it essentially said we're in a two-generation war.

Rumsfeld: Um hm.

Q: With radical Islam. And we have to do something and we'd better start with Iraq.

Rumsfeld: Yeah. Oh, I didn't remember that.

Q: Yeah, it's—it had a lot of, quite an impact on the president and Cheney and Rice, because it was short and it said two-generation war, that other countries are the real problems but you can't deal with them yet so you better start with Iraq.

Rumsfeld: Interesting. I don't remember that. I remember asking that they gather a group and that we think that through, and discussing it with

Paul . . . I had in mind something different than they ended up with when I participated in the initiation of it.
Q: Which was?
Rumsfeld: More like Bletchley.
Q: Think tank or—
Rumsfeld: Yeah, that you'd end up with a continuing body that would bring together some very fine minds on a highly confidential basis and provide the intellectual content for something that was obviously new and different, and challenging. And that did not happen.

CHAPTER 10

The information in this chapter comes primarily from interviews with six knowledgeable sources.

87   Press Secretary Ari Fleischer: Press briefing transcripts at www .whitehouse.gov/news/releases/2002/02/20020207-6.html; and www .state.gov/s/l/38727.htm.

CHAPTER 11

The information in this chapter comes primarily from background interviews with 10 knowledgeable sources, and with Marine General James L. Jones on December 21, 2005. Additionally, the war diaries of Major General James "Spider" Marks and Colonel Steve Rotkoff were obtained by the author's assistant Bill Murphy Jr.

97   But instead of saying: Presidential Documents, October 7, 2002: http://frwebgate.access.gpo.gov/cgi-bin/getdoc.cgi?dbname=2002_presi dential_documents&docid=pd14oc02_txt-11.

99   Unbeknownst to Marks: Author interviews with Secretary Rumsfeld, July 6 and 7, 2006, and documents reviewed by author. Also on Rumsfeld's list of things that could go wrong were: Number 19, "Rather than having the post-Saddam effort require 2–4 years, it could take 8–10 years, thereby absorbing US leadership, military and financial resources"; Number 25, "The U.S. will learn, to our surprise, a number of the unknown unknowns, the gaps in our intelligence knowledge. For example: Iraqi WMD programs could be several years more advanced than we assess"; Number 26, "Iraqi capabilities of which we were unaware may exist, such as UAVs jamming cyber attacks, etc."; and Number 27, "Iraq may experience epic strife among Sunni, Shia and Kurds."

100   Congress voted overwhelmingly: Vote history for H.J. Res. 114, Authorization for Use of Military Force Against Iraq Resolution of 2002:

www.senate.gov/legislative/LIS/roll_call_lists/roll_call_vote_cfm.cfm?con
gress=107&session=2&vote=00237.

100 Three weeks later: "How They Aced Their Midterms (And Now for
the Big Tests)," *Time*, November 18, 2002.

102 "They were every morning": Author interview with Secretary
Rumsfeld, July 6, 2006.

103 At the Pentagon: Author interviews with Secretary Rumsfeld, July 6
and 7, 2006.

106 The president very reluctantly confirmed: Author interview with
President George W. Bush, December 11, 2003.

CHAPTER 12

The information in this chapter comes primarily from background interviews with seven knowledgeable sources; with retired Lieutenant General
Jay Garner on September 19, 2005, October 16, 2005, December 13, 2005,
and April 22, 2006; and with retired Lieutenant General Jared Bates on December 14, 2005. Garner's documents and notes provided additional detail.

113 On Saturday night: Hank Stuever, "Civics Lesson: Who's Who in
the Alfalfa Club? Jaime Arauz Knows," *The Washington Post*, January 27,
2003, p. C1.

116 Later in an interview: Author interview with Secretary Rumsfeld,
July 6, 2006.

CHAPTER 13

The information in this chapter comes primarily from background interviews with 13 knowledgeable sources, from interviews with General Garner,
and from documents reviewed by the author.

120 Powell was set: FDCH Political Transcripts, Colin Powell Addresses
the United Nations, February 5, 2003.

123 In 2006, I mentioned: Author interview with Secretary Rumsfeld,
July 6, 2006.

127 Back in his office: Interview by the author's assistant with retired
Colonel Tom Baltazar, January 4, 2006.

131 Rumsfeld said later: Author interview with Secretary Rumsfeld, July
6, 2006.

CHAPTER 14

The information in this chapter comes primarily from background interviews with 11 knowledgeable sources, from interviews with General Garner and General Bates, and from documents obtained by the author.

136 **The next day:** Notes of Feith's briefing to the president were reviewed by the author.

138 **"cakewalk":** Ken Adelman, "Cakewalk in Iraq," *The Washington Post*, February 13, 2002, p. A27.

138 **White House spokesman:** David E. Sanger, "U.S. Tells Iraq It Must Reveal Weapons Sites," *The New York Times*, December 6, 2002, p. 1.

139 **Fleischer announced again:** Press briefing transcript: www.white house.gov/news/releases/2003/01/20030109–8.html.

139 **In his weekly radio address:** Presidential Documents, February 8, 2003: http://frwebgate.access.gpo.gov/cgi-bin/getdoc.cgi?dbname=2003_presidential_documents&docid=pd17fe03_txt-3.

CHAPTER 15

The information in this chapter comes primarily from background interviews with seven knowledgeable sources, from interviews with General Garner, and from documents reviewed by the author.

148 **On Tuesday, March 11:** Garner's press backgrounder transcript, March 11, 2003: www.defenselink.mil/Transcripts/Transcript.aspx?Tran scriptID=2037.

151 **Three days before:** NBC News transcript, *Meet the Press*, March 16, 2003.

152 **The war began:** For a more detailed account of the target-of-opportunity strike on Dora Farm and the beginning of the Iraq War, see Bob Woodward, *Plan of Attack* (New York: Simon & Schuster, 2004), pp. 382–99.

CHAPTER 16

The information in this chapter comes primarily from background interviews with seven knowledgeable sources, from interviews with General Garner and General Bates, and from documents reviewed by the author.

159 **The XTF:** Details of the travails of the 75th Exploitation Task Force were obtained from an interview by the author's assistant with Chief Warrant Officer Richard "Monty" Gonzales on April 14, 2006, interviews with other knowledgeable sources, and documents obtained by the author's assistant.

164 "I picked up": The text of Secretary Rumsfeld's remarks are available on the Pentagon's Web site at www.defenselink.mil. The captions and file names of the photographs that were shown to the media are archived at www.defenselink.mil/news/Apr2003/g030411–D-6570C.html.

165 Bush echoed the comment: Presidential Documents, April 13, 2003: http://frwebgate3.access.gpo.gov/cgi-bin/waisgate.cgi?WAISdocID =168461621+0+0+0&WAISaction=retrieve.

CHAPTER 17

The information in this chapter comes primarily from background interviews with nine knowledgeable sources, from interviews with General Garner, and from an interview with former Secretary of State George Shultz on June 18, 2006. Additional details came from documents reviewed by the author.

169 Rumsfeld's recollection is different: Author interview with Secretary Rumsfeld, July 6, 2006.

170 Tutwiler, 52: Peter Slevin, "Iraqis Unhappy with U.S. Signals; Interference from Americans Among Challenges for Post-Hussein TV," *The Washington Post*, May 26, 2003, p. A13.

174 Rumsfeld was a little defensive: Author interview with Secretary Rumsfeld, July 6, 2006.

CHAPTER 18

The information in this chapter comes primarily from background interviews with 11 knowledgeable sources, from interviews with General Garner and Colonel Baltazar, and from documents reviewed by the author.

178 Though technically outside: Federal News Service, American Enterprise Institute briefing, April 22, 2003.

178 Armitage responded: Edward Walsh and Juliet Eilperin, "Familiar Blast, Then Unfamiliar Silence; Gingrich Lying Low After Attack on State Dept. Leaves Some Conservatives Fuming," *The Washington Post*, April 26, 2003, p. A4.

178 "I don't think I would": Monte Reel, "Garner Arrives in Iraq to Begin Reconstruction; Retired General Upbeat Despite Skepticism, Damage," *The Washington Post*, April 22, 2003, p. A1.

181   **A few hours after:** Presidential Documents, April 24, 2003: http://frwebgate1.access.gpo.gov/cgi-bin/waisgate.cgi?WAISdocID=0482 90177664+0+0+0&WAISaction=retrieve.

182   **Bremer had strongly supported:** L. Paul Bremer III, *My Year in Iraq: The Struggle to Build a Future of Hope* (New York: Simon & Schuster, 2006), pp. 6–7.

184   **In his book:** Bremer describes seeing the Mukhabarat memo on pp. 126–27 of *My Year in Iraq*.

185   **Rumsfeld flew to Iraq:** Vernon Loeb, "Rumsfeld Pays Visit to Postwar Iraq; Defense Secretary Meets Commanders, Tells Troops 'You've Rescued a Nation,' " *The Washington Post*, May 1, 2003, p. A1; author interviews with Secretary Rumsfeld, July 6 and 7, 2006.

186   **"I took":** Author interviews with Secretary Rumsfeld, July 6 and 7, 2006.

187   **The *Lincoln*'s crew:** Karen DeYoung, "Bush Proclaims Victory in Iraq; Work on Terror Is Ongoing, President Says," *The Washington Post*, May 2, 2003, p. A1.

187   **Giving the revised:** Author interview with Secretary Rumsfeld, July 6, 2006; Presidential Documents, May 1, 2003: http://frwebgate.access.gpo .gov/cgi-bin/getdoc.cgi?dbname=2003_presidential_documents&docid= pd05my03_txt-27.

CHAPTER 19

The information in this chapter comes primarily from background interviews with 14 knowledgeable sources, from interviews with General Garner, and from documents obtained by the author. Additionally, see Bremer's *My Year in Iraq*.

190   **Jerry Bremer had just over two weeks:** Bremer, *My Year in Iraq*, pp. 9–10.

190   **After 1 P.M.:** Presidential Documents, May 6, 2003: http://frweb gate.access.gpo.gov/cgi-bin/getdoc.cgi?dbname=2003_presidential_docu ments&docid=pd12my03_txt-13.

190   **Four days before:** Bremer, *My Year in Iraq*, pp. 11–12 and 39.

193   The Coalition Provisional Authority's orders are archived at www .iraqcoalition.org/regulations/index.html#Orders.

198   **Rumsfeld later said:** Author interview with Secretary Rumsfeld, July 6, 2006.

199   **"I am the Iraqi government":** Bremer, *My Year in Iraq*, p. 36.

202   **Bremer recognized that the challenges:** Bremer, *My Year in Iraq*, p. 37.

CHAPTER 20

The information in this chapter comes primarily from background interviews with seven knowledgeable sources, from interviews with General Garner, and from documents obtained by the author.

206   **That same day:** See Edmundo Conchas, "Soldier Won't Forget Memorial Day," *The San Antonio Express-News*, April 21, 2004, p. 1H.

209   **"Occupation is an ugly word.":** Scott Wilson, "Bremer Adopts Firmer Tone for U.S. Occupation of Iraq," *The Washington Post*, May 26, 2003, p. A13.

209   **"We found the weapons of mass destruction."** Presidential Documents, May 29, 2003: http://frwebgate.access.gpo.gov/cgi-bin/getdoc .cgi?dbname=2003_presidential_documents&docid=pd02jn03_txt-19.

210   **Unknown to the president:** See Joby Warrick, "Lacking Biolabs, Trailers Carried Case for War; Administration Pushed Notion of Banned Iraqi Weapons Despite Evidence to Contrary," *The Washington Post*, April 12, 2006, p. A1.

210   **A day after Bush's remarks:** Department of Defense news transcript, May 30, 2003: www.defenselink.mil/Transcripts/Transcript.aspx? TranscriptID=2685.

211   **Bush flew to Qatar:** Bremer, *My Year in Iraq*, p. 71.

CHAPTER 21

The information in this chapter comes primarily from background interviews with three knowledgeable sources, from interviews with General Garner, and from interviews with David Kay on October 26, 2004, and February 28, 2006. Documents obtained by the author provided additional detail.

218   **On June 12, 2003:** Walter Pincus, "CIA Did Not Share Doubt on Iraq Data; Bush Used Report of Uranium Bid," *The Washington Post*, June 12, 2003, p. A1.

218   **This ran contrary:** Presidential Documents, January 28, 2003: http://frwebgate.access.gpo.gov/cgi-bin/getdoc.cgi?dbname=2003_presi dential_documents&docid=pd03fe03_txt-6.

219 A few weeks later: Joseph C. Wilson, "What I Didn't Find in Africa," *The New York Times*, July 6, 2003, p. 9.

219 Eight days after that: Robert Novak, "The Mission to Niger," *Chicago Sun-Times*, July 14, 2003, p. 31.

220 In 2006, I asked Rumsfeld: Author interview with Secretary Rumsfeld, July 6, 2006.

220 After their discussion: Department of Defense news transcript, June 18, 2003: www.defenselink.mil/transcripts/2003/tr20030618–secdef 0282.html.

220 Afterward, Rumsfeld and Garner: Garner's meeting with Bush was described by Garner. Details were confirmed by Rumsfeld and another knowledgeable source. In an interview with the author's assistant on June 29, 2006, Malcolm MacPherson confirmed details of Garner's meeting with "Darth Vader" in Iraq.

224 Later, I asked: Author interview with Secretary Rumsfeld, July 6, 2006.

CHAPTER 22

The information in this chapter comes primarily from background interviews with six knowledgeable sources and from interviews with David Kay.

228 On Sunday, June 22: Patrick E. Tyler, "2,000 at Rally Demand Islamic Supervision of Elections," *The New York Times*, June 22, 2003, p. 11.

229 Sistani refused: Bremer, *My Year in Iraq*, p. 165.

229 Bush appeared: Presidential Documents, July 2, 2003: http://frweb gate.access.gpo.gov/cgi-bin/getdoc.cgi?dbname=2003_presidential_docu ments&docid=pd07jy03_txt-18.

230 In Saddam's Iraq: The description of Iraqi television and the so-called Lebanese cooking channel comes from the author's assistant's interview with a knowledgeable source.

230 At a White House press conference: Presidential Documents, May 25, 2006: http://frwebgate3.access.gpo.gov/cgi-bin/waisgate.cgi?WAISdoc ID=42074832524+4+0+0&WAISaction=retrieve.

232 "Knowing all we know now": Walter Pincus, "White House Backs Off Claim on Iraqi Buy," *The Washington Post*, July 8, 2003, p. A1.

232 On Friday, July 11: Walter Pincus and Dana Milbank, "Bush, Rice Blame CIA for Iraq Error; Tenet Accepts Responsibility for Clearing Statement on Nuclear Aims in Jan. Speech," *The Washington Post*, July 12, 2003, p. A1.

232 His long statement: www.cia.gov/cia/public_affairs/press_release/2003/pr07112003.html.

233 The next morning: Walter Pincus and Dana Milbank, "Bush, Rice Blame CIA for Iraq Error; Tenet Accepts Responsibility for Clearing Statement on Nuclear Aims in Jan. Speech," *The Washington Post*, July 12, 2003, p. A1.

233 Eleven days after: White House news release: www.whitehouse.gov/news/releases/2003/07/20030722-12.html.

234 In July 2003: Rajiv Chandrasekaran, "Appointed Iraqi Council Assumes Limited Role," *The Washington Post*, July 14, 2003, p. A1; Rajiv Chandrasekaran, "Tape Hails Hussein Sons as 'Martyrs'; Ex-President's Bodyguard Captured; Council Chooses 9 Leaders," *The Washington Post*, July 30, 2003, p. A1.

239 Kay went to Congress: FDCH Political Transcripts, Senator John Warner's media availability with David Kay, July 31, 2003.

CHAPTER 23

The information in this chapter comes primarily from background interviews with nine knowledgeable sources, from interviews with David Kay, and from an interview with Newt Gingrich on December 12, 2004.

240 Al Kamen's popular: Al Kamen, "Now Playing: The Replacements," *The Washington Post*, July 9, 2003, p. A25.

244 In the summer doldrums: Glenn Kessler, "State Dept. Changes Seen if Bush Reelected; Powell and Armitage Intend to Step Down," *The Washington Post*, August 4, 2003, p. A1.

245 In a brief session: Presidential Documents, August 6, 2003: http://frwebgate.access.gpo.gov/cgi-bin/getdoc.cgi?dbname=2003_presidential_documents&docid=pd11au03_txt-7.

247 He flew: Presidential Documents, August 22, 2003: http://frwebgate3.access.gpo.gov/cgi-bin/waisgate.cgi?WAISdocID=93122724065+0+0+0&WAISaction=retrieve.

247 He added in a radio address: Presidential Documents, August 23, 2003: http://frwebgate.access.gpo.gov/cgi-bin/getdoc.cgi?dbname=2003_presidential_documents&docid=pd01se03_txt-2.

248   Though no one: Documents reviewed by author; Government Accountability Office report, "Rebuilding Iraq: Governance, Security, Reconstruction, and Financing Challenges," GAO-06–697T, April 25, 2006.

248   At a small dinner: Bremer, *My Year in Iraq*, p. 156.

248   David Kay had: See Dana Priest, "Rumsfeld Is Muted on Weapons Hunt; Secretary Tries to Avoid Issue During Trip," *The Washington Post*, September 9, 2003, p. A12.

248   If there was: DOD transcript at www.defenselink.mil/transcripts/ 2003/tr20030908–secdef0656.html.

248   Bremer was making: L. Paul Bremer III, "Iraq's Path to Sovereignty," *The Washington Post*, September 8, 2003, p. A21.

249   "Those people couldn't": Bremer, *My Year in Iraq*, p. 171.

249   On September 24: Bremer, *My Year in Iraq*, pp. 174–76.

CHAPTER 24

The information in this chapter comes primarily from background interviews with nine knowledgeable sources, and from interviews with David Kay and with General Pace on July 20, 2006.

256   In two interviews: Author interviews with Secretary Rumsfeld, July 6 and 7, 2006.

258   A memo creating: David E. Sanger, "White House to Overhaul Iraq and Afghan Missions," *The New York Times*, October 6, 2003, p. 1.

258   Bremer read the story: Bremer, *My Year in Iraq*, pp. 186–87.

258   At a news conference: Department of Defense transcript: www .defenselink.mil/Transcripts/Transcript.aspx?TranscriptID=3544; see also Mike Allen, "Iraq Shake-up Skipped Rumsfeld; Confidential Memo Was First Alert, Defense Secretary Says," *The Washington Post*, October 8, 2003, p. A10.

262   Afterward, Bush invited Bremer: See Robin Wright and Glenn Kessler, "Rapport Between Bush, Bremer Grows," *The Washington Post*, November 23, 2003.

265   On November 7, Bremer: Bremer, *My Year in Iraq*, pp. 222–24.

265   Bush gave a luncheon speech: Presidential Documents, November 11, 2003: http://frwebgate.access.gpo.gov/cgi-bin/getdoc.cgi?dbname=2003 _presidential_documents&docid=pd17no03_txt-12.

267 Later, Rumsfeld: Author interview with Secretary Rumsfeld, July 6, 2006.

CHAPTER 25

The information in this chapter comes primarily from background interviews with 12 knowledgeable sources, from interviews with David Kay, and from an interview with Newt Gingrich on December 10, 2004. Documents reviewed by the author provided additional detail.

270 It worked: The meeting is described in Bremer's *My Year in Iraq*, at pp. 226–27. See also Rajiv Chandrasekaran, "Iraqis Say U.S. to Cede Power by Summer; Town Meetings to Set Process in Motion," *The Washington Post*, November 15, 2003, p. A1; Susan Sachs, "U.S. Is to Return Power to Iraqis as Early as June," *The New York Times*, November 15, 2003, p. 1.

273 On December 6, 2003: Bremer, *My Year in Iraq*, p. 245.

274 Rumsfeld later confirmed: Author interview with Secretary Rumsfeld, July 6, 2006.

274 He gave an interview: John Barry and Evan Thomas, "Dissent in the Bunker," *Newsweek*, December 15, 2003, p. 36.

274 Gingrich then went: NBC News transcript, *Meet the Press*, December 7, 2003.

275 For Rumsfeld: Author interview with Secretary Rumsfeld, July 6, 2006.

275 On December 13: Rajiv Chandrasekaran, "U.S. Forces Uncover Iraqi Ex-Leader Near Home Town; Detention Could Lead to Trial on Charges of War Crimes, Genocide," *The Washington Post*, December 15, 2003, p. A1.

275 "Ladies and gentlemen": Text of L. Paul Bremer's news conference, Associated Press, December 14, 2003.

275 "We've got to really": Bremer, *My Year in Iraq*, p. 260.

275 The violence continued: Documents reviewed by author; Government Accountability Office report, "Rebuilding Iraq: Governance, Security, Reconstruction, and Financing Challenges," GAO-06–697T, April 25, 2006.

275 On January 16: Department of Defense News at: www.defendamer ica.mil/iraq/update/jan2004/iu012104.html.

275 Rice's frustrations with Rumsfeld: Author interview with Secretary Rumsfeld, July 7, 2006.

277 **Classified reports:** Documents reviewed by author; Government Accountability Office report, "Rebuilding Iraq: Governance, Security, Reconstruction, and Financing Challenges," GAO-06–697T, April 25, 2006.

277 **He referred not:** Presidential Documents, January 20, 2004: http://frwebgate.access.gpo.gov/cgi-bin/getdoc.cgi?dbname=2004_presi dential_documents&docid=pd26ja04_txt-10.

277 **That night a reporter:** Tabassum Zakaria of Reuters, "Top U.S. Arms Hunter Resigns; David Kay, who led the search for Iraqi weapons, said he now believed there were no stockpiles. An ex-U.N. inspector will take over," *The Philadelphia Inquirer*, January 24, 2004, p. A1.

278 **Kay testified publicly:** FDCH Political Transcripts, Senate Armed Services Committee hearing, January 28, 2004.

281 **Powell went to *The Washington Post*:** Glenn Kessler, "Powell Says New Data May Have Affected War Decision," *The Washington Post*, February 3, 2004, p. A1.

281 **So Powell had to go back:** Powell remarks at the State Department, February 3, 2004: www.state.gov/secretary/former/powell/remarks/28788 .htm.

CHAPTER 26

The information in this chapter comes primarily from background interviews with seven knowledgeable sources, with Judge Laurence H. Silberman on September 7, 2005, and from documents obtained by the author.

285 **House Minority Leader Nancy Pelosi:** Dana Priest and Dana Milbank, "Intelligence Panel Will Cast Net Beyond Iraq," *The Washington Post*, February 3, 2004, p. A1.

286 **"It goes to the core":** David M. Halbfinger, "The 2004 Campaign: The Massachusetts Senator; Gephardt Throws His Support to Kerry," *The New York Times*, February 6, 2004, p. 19.

286 **The president was not:** Presidential Documents, February 6, 2004: http://frwebgate.access.gpo.gov/cgi-bin/getdoc.cgi?dbname=2004_presi dential_documents&docid=pd09fe04_txt-20.

286 **The members of the Silberman-Robb Commission were:** Judge Laurence H. Silberman, co-chairman; Charles S. Robb, co-chairman; Richard C. Levin; Senator John McCain; Henry S. Rowen; Walter B. Slocombe; Retired Admiral William O. Studeman; Charles M. Vest; and Judge Patricia Wald.

287 **Representative Henry Waxman:** Mark Matthews, "Diverse Group to Examine War Data; Misinformation on banned weapons led to Iraq fight; 'Determined to figure out why,' " *The Baltimore Sun*, February 7, 2004, p. 1A.

287 **Senator Harry Reid:** Eric Lichtblau, "Panel's Finances Will Stay Private," *The New York Times*, February 15, 2004, p. 1.

288 **Bremer had folded:** Bremer, *My Year in Iraq*, p. 288.

291 **Attacks had climbed again:** Documents reviewed by the author; Government Accountability Office report, "Rebuilding Iraq: Governance, Security, Reconstruction, and Financing Challenges," GAO-06–697T, April 25, 2006.

CHAPTER 27

The information in this chapter comes primarily from background interviews with six knowledgeable sources.

296 **On Wednesday, March 31, 2004:** Sewell Chan and Karl Vick, "U.S. Vows to Find Civilians' Killers; Marines Move to Seal Off Fallujah; Army Steps Up Patrols in Baghdad," *The Washington Post*, April 2, 2004, p. A1.

297 **"We still face thugs":** Presidential Documents, March 31, 2004: http://frwebgate.access.gpo.gov/cgi-bin/getdoc.cgi?dbname=2004_presi dential_documents&docid=pd05ap04_txt-9.

297 **Bremer promised:** Sewell Chan and Karl Vick, "U.S. Vows to Find Civilians' Killers; Marines Move to Seal Off Fallujah; Army Steps Up Patrols in Baghdad," *The Washington Post*, April 2, 2004, p. A1.

297 **Sanchez grew up poor:** Sig Christenson, "South Texan Has a Tall Order to Fill; Coalition's Commander Has Beaten Odds Before," *San Antonio Express-News*, June 23, 2003, p. 1A.

297 **In 2006, Rumsfeld acknowledged:** Author interview with Secretary Rumsfeld, July 7, 2006.

304 **A year after *Plan of Attack*:** Tenet spoke at a public forum at the Universal City Amphitheatre in Los Angeles, California, on April 11, 2005.

CHAPTER 28

The information in this chapter comes primarily from background interviews with 10 knowledgeable sources, from an author interview with Judge Silberman, and from documents obtained by the author.

305   In late April: CBS News, *60 Minutes II*, April 28, 2004.

305   Seymour Hersh: Seymour M. Hersh, "Torture at Abu Ghraib," *The New Yorker*, May 10, 2004; Seymour M. Hersh, "Chain of Command; How the Department of Defense Mishandled the Disaster at Abu Ghraib," *The New Yorker*, May 17, 2004; Seymour M. Hersh, "The Gray Zone; How a Secret Pentagon Program Came to Abu Ghraib," *The New Yorker*, May 24, 2004.

305   Rumsfeld stated publicly: Department of Defense Transcripts, May 4, 2004: www.defenselink.mil/transcripts/2004/tr20040504–secdef1423 .html.

305   Myers, on one: ABC News transcripts, *This Week with George Stephanopoulos*, May 2, 2004.

305   "Bush Privately Chides Rumsfeld": Robin Wright and Bradley Graham, "Bush Privately Chides Rumsfeld; Officials Say Pentagon Resisted Repeated Calls for Prison Changes," *The Washington Post*, May 6, 2004, p. A1.

306   The next day, May 7: FDCH Political Transcripts, House Armed Services Committee Hearing, May 7, 2004.

306   The next day: Elisabeth Bumiller, "In the Balance: Rumsfeld's Job," *The New York Times*, May 8, 2004, p. 1.

306   Just before noon: Presidential Documents, May 10, 2004: http:// frwebgate.access.gpo.gov/cgi-bin/getdoc.cgi?dbname=2004_presidential_ documents&docid=pd17my04_txt-12.

306   "I submitted my resignation": Author interview with Secretary Rumsfeld, July 6, 2006.

309   Rumsfeld said: Author interview with Secretary Rumsfeld, July 7, 2006.

310   In largely overlooked: FDCH Political Transcripts, House Armed Services Committee Hearing, June 22, 2004.

313   Transfer of sovereignty: The early turnover and the conversation between Bush and Blair were described to the author's assistant in an interview with a knowledgeable source. See also Bremer, *My Year in Iraq*, pp. 388–95.

CHAPTER 29

The information in this chapter comes primarily from background interviews with 12 knowledgeable sources, from an author interview with Judge Silberman, and from an interview with General Pace on August 25, 2003.

316 **On July 15, 2004:** Document obtained by author.

317 **The June 4** *Washington Post***:** Dana Priest and Walter Pincus, "Tenet Resigns as CIA Director; Intelligence Chief Praised by Bush, but Critics Cite Lapses on Iraq War," *The Washington Post*, June 4, 2004, p. A1.

317 **Eleven days later:** *Final Report of the National Commission on Terrorist Attacks upon the United States* (2004).

318 **One of the most inexcusable:** It wasn't just in Iraq. A Royal Navy ship that was helping the U.S. on a counternarcotics mission in the Caribbean couldn't get its orders directly and in real time because its captain could not access the SIPRNET.

320 **In August 2004:** See also Josh White and Scott Higham, "Army Calls Abuses 'Aberrations'; Report Cites 94 Detainee-Mistreatment Cases in Iraq and Afghanistan," *The Washington Post*, July 23, 2004, p. A1; Amy Argetsinger, "Arabic Language a Tough Assignment; More Student Speakers Try to Fill Need," *The Washington Post*, July 3, 2004, p. B1.

325 **I had explored:** Author interviews with President George W. Bush, December 20, 2001, and August 20, 2002.

325 **"I know it is hard":** Woodward, *Bush at War*, pp. 256–59.

326 **In particular:** David McCullough, *1776* (New York: Simon & Schuster, 2005), p. 110.

327 **But the reality:** Documents reviewed by the author; Government Accountability Office report, "Rebuilding Iraq: Governance, Security, Reconstruction, and Financing Challenges," GAO-06–697T, April 25, 2006.

CHAPTER 30

The information in this chapter comes primarily from background interviews with 12 knowledgeable sources, and from author interviews with David Kay.

329 **David Kay testified:** FDCH Political Transcripts, Senate Select Committee on Intelligence hearing, August 18, 2004.

331 **In August 2004:** Documents reviewed by the author; Government Accountability Office report, "Rebuilding Iraq: Governance, Security, Reconstruction, and Financing Challenges," GAO-06–697T, April 25, 2006.

336 **In the days and weeks:** Documents reviewed by the author; Government Accountability Office report, "Rebuilding Iraq: Governance, Security, Reconstruction, and Financing Challenges," GAO-06–697T, April 25, 2006.

336   In Diyala Province: Karl Vick, "Insurgents Massacre 49 Iraqi Recruits; State Dept. Official Killed in Attack at U.S. Military Base," *The Washington Post*, October 25, 2004, p. A1.

336   "We have a strategy": Presidential Documents, September 23, 2004: http://frwebgate.access.gpo.gov/cgi-bin/getdoc.cgi?dbname=2004_presidential_documents&docid=pd27se04_txt-31.

CHAPTER 31

The information in this chapter comes primarily from background interviews with 15 knowledgeable sources, from an interview with Senator John F. Kerry on October 27, 2005, and from notes obtained by the author. This chapter also draws on media reports about election day, such as newspaper and magazine articles, and transcripts of the broadcasts from NBC, Fox News, CBS, ABC and other networks.

345   At 1:30 A.M.: Lois Romano and John Wagner, "Clinging to Hope as Long Journey Nears Conclusion," *The Washington Post*, November 3, 2004, p. A22.

347   At 3:36 A.M.: "You've got it right," Mike McCurry said in an interview on August 11, 2006, when asked about the e-mail he sent to Nicole Devenish. "I can confirm that."

350   "We are convinced": Congressional Quarterly Transcripts, November 3, 2004.

CHAPTER 32

The information in this chapter comes primarily from background interviews with 12 knowledgeable sources.

353   "We cannot wait": Presidential Documents, October 7, 2002: http://frwebgate5.access.gpo.gov/cgi-bin/waisgate.cgi?WAISdocID=2148 05110712+0+0+0&WAISaction=retrieve.

353   At other times: Presidential Documents, January 28, 2003: http://frwebgate.access.gpo.gov/cgi-bin/getdoc.cgi?dbname=2003_presidential_documents&docid=pd03fe03_txt-6.

353   The starkest, most direct: FDCH Political Transcripts, September 7, 2004.

CHAPTER 33

The information in this chapter comes primarily from background interviews with 11 knowledgeable sources.

368 In 2006: Author interview with Secretary Rumsfeld, July 6, 2006.

368 One of the administration's: Presidential Documents, September 23, 2004: http://frwebgate3.access.gpo.gov/cgi-bin/waisgate.cgi?WAISdoc ID=218281882+0+0+0&WAISaction=retrieve.

368 Rumsfeld had made the claim: Department of Defense transcript: www.defenselink.mil/Transcripts/Transcript.aspx?TranscriptID=2091.

369 "Listen, 14": Presidential Documents, January 7, 2005: http://frweb gate4.access.gpo.gov/cgi-bin/waisgate.cgi?WAISdocID=2160625206+5+ 0+0&WAISaction=retrieve.

369 Mosul, a city: Karl Vick, "Trouble Spots Dot Iraqi Landscape; Attacks Erupting Away from Fallujah," *The Washington Post*, November 15, 2004, p. A1; Karl Vick and Jackie Spinner, "Insurgent Attacks Spread in Iraq; 'Hard Fighting' Expected in Mosul in Coming Days," *The Washington Post*, November 16, 2004, p. A1.

371 Historian Arthur Schlesinger Jr.: Schlesinger spoke at the Robert F. Kennedy Book Awards in Washington, D.C., on May 24, 2005.

372 "Pay any price": Transcript of President John F. Kennedy's inaugural address, January 20, 1961, www.jfklibrary.org.

374 It was the kind: Al Kamen, "Skipping the After-Dinner Cordial," *The Washington Post*, February 23, 2005, p. A17.

375 Bush hosted a White House reception: Presidential Documents, January 3, 2005: http://frwebgate.access.gpo.gov/cgi-bin/getdoc.cgi? dbname=2005_presidential_documents&docid=pd10ja05_txt-13.

CHAPTER 34

The information in this chapter comes primarily from background interviews with seven knowledgeable sources.

377 On January 18, Rice: Congressional Quarterly Transcripts, January 18, 2005, Senate Foreign Relations Committee Hearing.

377 A week later: Charles Babington, "Rice Is Confirmed amid Criticism; Democrats Assail Iraq War Policies Before Senate Approves Nomination," *The Washington Post*, January 27, 2005, p. A3.

378   **"It is the policy:** Inaugural address, Presidential Documents, January 20, 2005: http://frwebgate.access.gpo.gov/cgi-bin/getdoc.cgi?dbname =2005_presidential_documents&docid=pd24ja05_txt-13.

378   **For many conservatives:** Peggy Noonan, "Way Too Much God," *The Wall Street Journal*, January 21, 2005; www.opinionjournal.com.

379   **Rumsfeld later confirmed:** Author interview with Secretary Rumsfeld, July 6, 2006.

382   **As the date approached:** James Glanz and Thom Shanker, "Anti-Vote Violence in Iraq Is Widespread and Intensifying, Latest Surveys Show," *The New York Times*, January 27, 2005, p. 14.

382   **On January 26:** Josh White, "In Hawaii, Time to Grieve Yet Again; Crash in Iraq Is Latest Setback for Military Town," *The Washington Post*, January 27, 2005, p. A12.

382   **In his Saturday radio address:** Presidential Documents, January 29, 2005: http://frwebgate.access.gpo.gov/cgi-bin/getdoc.cgi?dbname=2005_ presidential_documents&docid=pd07fe05_txt-3.

383   **Some 8 million Iraqis:** Dexter Filkins, "Iraqis Vote Amid Tight Security and Scattered Attacks," *The New York Times*, January 30, 2005, p. 1, and "Defying Threats, Millions of Iraqis Flock to Polls," *The New York Times*, January 31, 2005, p. 1; Anthony Shadid, "Iraqis Defy Threats as Millions Vote; Mood Is Festive; Turnout Appears Strong Despite Deadly Attacks," *The Washington Post*, January 31, 2005, p. A1.

383   **Bush thought it was:** Presidential Documents, January 30, 2005: http://frwebgate4.access.gpo.gov/cgi-bin/waisgate.cgi?WAISdocID=0920 0627764+0+0+0&WAISaction=retrieve.

383   **Despite the excitement:** Documents reviewed by the author; Government Accountability Office report, "Rebuilding Iraq: Governance, Security, Reconstruction, and Financing Challenges," GAO-06–697T, April 25, 2006.

385   **"If I were going to":** Author interview with Secretary Rumsfeld, July 6, 2006.

CHAPTER 35

The information in this chapter comes primarily from background interviews with 10 knowledgeable sources.

387   Zelikow, 50: Philip Zelikow and Condoleezza Rice, *Germany Unified and Europe Transformed: A Study in Statecraft* (Cambridge: Harvard University Press, 1995).

390   In his memoirs: Tommy Franks, *American Soldier* (New York: HarperCollins, 2004), p. 411.

390   Rice was the rock star: Robin Givhan, "Condoleezza Rice's Commanding Clothes," *The Washington Post*, February 25, 2005, p. C1.

391   Bush announced Negroponte's appointment: Presidential Documents, February 17, 2005: http://frwebgate.access.gpo.gov/cgi-bin/getdoc .cgi?dbname=2005_presidential_documents&docid=pd21fe05_txt-13.

392   Talabani was sworn in: Ellen Knickmeyer and Caryle Murphy, "Iraqis Pick Kurd as New President; Shiite Set to Be Named Prime Minister," *The Washington Post*, April 7, 2005, p. A1; Ellen Knickmeyer, "Talabani Offers Amnesty to Insurgents; New Iraqi President Reaches Out to Sunnis, Names Jafari as Prime Minister," *The Washington Post*, April 8, 2005, p. A22.

CHAPTER 36

The information in this chapter comes primarily from background interviews with eight knowledgeable sources.

396   "But wars have costs.": Rice told her staff it all reminded her of an old episode of the science fiction TV show *Star Trek*. "Death, destruction, disease, horror—that's what war is all about," Captain Kirk tells an alien leader in the episode. "That's what makes it a thing to be avoided." (*Star Trek*, "A Taste of Armageddon," first aired February 23, 1967.)

397   Cheney was on CNN's: CNN transcript, *Larry King Live*, May 30, 2005.

398   "Who governs after Saddam?": NBC News transcript, *Meet the Press*, July 7, 2002.

398   "Have we calculated": David S. Broder, "The Hagel Doctrine," *The Washington Post*, September 18, 2002, p. A29.

398   "We cannot do it alone.": Congressional Record, October 9, 2002: http://thomas.loc.gov/cgi-bin/query/F?r107:7:./temp/~r107411eL7: e98605.

398   "First, a post-Saddam transition": Landon Lecture at Kansas State University, February 20, 2003.

400   He left unsatisfied: Kevin Whitelaw, Ilana Ozernoy, and Terence Samuel, "Hit by Friendly Fire," *U.S. News & World Report*, June 27, 2005.

400   On June 21: Tyler Marshall and Borzou Daragahi, "The Conflict in Iraq; 80 Countries to Weigh Solutions for Struggling Iraq," *Los Angeles Times,* June 22, 2005, p. 7.

400   On July 7, 2005: Glenn Frankel, "Bombers Strike London at Rush Hour; At Least 37 Killed on Trains, Bus," *The Washington Post,* July 8, 2005, p. A1.

CHAPTER 37

The information in this chapter comes primarily from background interviews with nine knowledgeable sources and from an interview with General Peter Pace on July 20, 2006, and from an interview with General Jones on July 27, 2006.

406   Former Secretary of State Henry Kissinger: Author discussion with Vice President Dick Cheney, July 14, 2005.

407   "We cannot abandon": Henry Kissinger, *Years of Renewal* (New York: Simon & Schuster, 1999), pp. 1074–76.

408   His column in the *Post*: Henry Kissinger, "Lessons for an Exit Strategy," *The Washington Post,* August 12, 2005.

CHAPTER 38

The information in this chapter comes primarily from background interviews with six knowledgeable sources, and from an interview with Senator Carl Levin on September 29, 2005.

418   Zelikow had been reading: Lewis Sorley, *A Better War* (New York: Harvest/HBJ, 2000).

418   Rice made it: Senate Foreign Relations Committee, October 19, 2005, State Department transcript at www.state.gov/secretary/rm/2005/55303.htm.

418   According to Rumsfeld: Author interview with Secretary Rumsfeld, July 6, 2006.

CHAPTER 39

The information in this chapter comes primarily from background interviews with 11 knowledgeable sources, and an interview with Congressman Jack Murtha on June 8, 2006.

422   Enemy-initiated attacks: Documents reviewed by the author; Government Accountability Office report, "Rebuilding Iraq: Governance, Security, Reconstruction, and Financing Challenges," GAO-06–697T, April 25, 2006.

422   Rumsfeld confirmed to me: Author interview with Secretary Rumsfeld, July 6, 2006.

423   The other, bigger message: Presidential Documents, November 11, 2005: http://frwebgate3.access.gpo.gov/cgi-bin/waisgate.cgi?WAISdocID =10490720041+0+0+0&WAISaction=retrieve.

423   On November 16, Cheney gave an address: Congressional Quarterly, FDCH Political Transcripts, November 16, 2005.

423   That day: Editorial, "Decoding Mr. Bush's Denials," *The New York Times,* November 15, 2005, p. 26; White House statement, "Setting the Record Straight: *The New York Times* Editorial on Pre-War Intelligence," November 15, 2005.

423   The next day: Eric Schmitt, "Fast Withdrawal of G.I.'s Is Urged by Key Democrat," *The New York Times,* November 18, 2005, p.1; see also Library of Congress records at http://thomas.loc.gov.

424   Later that day: Statement by the press secretary on Congressman Murtha's statement, November 18, 2005: www.whitehouse.gov/news/ releases/2005/11/20051118.html.

425   For much of the year: Presidential Documents, February 4, 2005: http://frwebgate.access.gpo.gov/cgi-bin/getdoc.cgi?dbname=2005_presi dential_documents&docid=pd07fe05_txt-13.

426   In an address: Presidential Documents, June 28, 2005: http://frweb gate.access.gpo.gov/cgi-bin/getdoc.cgi?dbname=2005_presidential_docu ments&docid=pd04jy05_txt-8.

426   Indeed the number: Documents reviewed by the author.

428: The "National Strategy for Victory in Iraq," November 30, 2005: www.whitehouse.gov/infocus/iraq/iraq_strategy_nov2005.html.

429   Part of the plan: Presidential Documents, November 30, 2005: http://frwebgate.access.gpo.gov/cgi-bin/getdoc.cgi?dbname=2005_presi dential_documents&docid=pd05de05_txt-9.

429   Bush's war policy: Doug Struck, "In Baghdad, Reality Counters Rhetoric; Violence Remains Everyday Pattern," *The Washington Post,* December 1, 2005, p. A21.

429 **But a dispatch:** John F. Burns and Dexter Filkins, "For Once, President and His Generals See the Same War," *The New York Times*, December 1, 2005, p. 22.

430 **On December 7:** Presidential Documents, December 7, 2005: http://frwebgate.access.gpo.gov/cgi-bin/getdoc.cgi?dbname=2005_presidential_documents&docid=pd12de05_txt-9.

CHAPTER 40

The information in this chapter comes primarily from background interviews with six knowledgeable sources.

431 **Bush gave his third Iraq speech:** Presidential Documents, December 12, 2005: http://frwebgate.access.gpo.gov/cgi-bin/getdoc.cgi?dbname=2005_presidential_documents&docid=pd19de05_txt-5.

434 **In his fourth Iraq speech:** Presidential Documents, December 14, 2005: http://frwebgate.access.gpo.gov/cgi-bin/getdoc.cgi?dbname=2005_presidential_documents&docid=pd19de05_txt-8.

434 **In Iraq:** Dexter Filkins, "Iraqis, Including Sunnis, Vote in Large Numbers on Calm Day," *The New York Times*, December 16, 2005, p. 1.

434 **"There's a lot of joy":** Presidential Documents, December 15, 2005: http://frwebgate.access.gpo.gov/cgi-bin/getdoc.cgi?dbname=2005_presidential_documents&docid=pd19de05_txt-14.

435 **After a meeting with the Iraqi ambassador:** Presidential Documents, December 16, 2005: http://frwebgate4.access.gpo.gov/cgi-bin/waisgate.cgi?WAISdocID=11873431240+0+0+0&WAISaction=retrieve.

435 **But the violence continued:** Documents reviewed by the author; Government Accountability Office report, "Rebuilding Iraq: Governance, Security, Reconstruction, and Financing Challenges," GAO-06–697T, April 25, 2006.

435 **Three days after:** Presidential Documents, December 18, 2005: http://frwebgate.access.gpo.gov/cgi-bin/getdoc.cgi?dbname=2005_presidential_documents&docid=pd26de05_txt-10.

437 **But the ebb and flow:** Documents reviewed by the author; Government Accountability Office report, "Rebuilding Iraq: Governance, Security, Reconstruction, and Financing Challenges," GAO-06–697T, April 25, 2006.

437 **On New Year's Day:** Presidential Documents, January 1, 2006: http://frwebgate.access.gpo.gov/cgi-bin/getdoc.cgi?dbname=2006_presidential_documents&docid=pd09ja06_txt-4.

438 **"You cannot help":** Author interview with Secretary Rumsfeld, July 7, 2006.

CHAPTER 41

The information in this chapter comes primarily from background interviews with 10 knowledgeable sources, and with Congressman Murtha on June 8, 2005.

440 **On December 23, 2005:** International Monetary Fund Press Release, December 23, 2005: www.imf.org/external/np/sec/pr/2005/pr05307.htm.

444 **General Chiarelli:** Major General Peter W. Chiarelli and Major Patrick R. Michaelis, "Winning the Peace: The Requirement for Full-Spectrum Operations," *Military Review*, July–August 2005.

444 Thomas E. Ricks, *Fiasco* (New York: Penguin, 2006), p. 318.

444 **On the morning:** Ellen Knickmeyer and K. I. Ibrahim, "Bombing Shatters Mosque in Iraq; Attack on Shiite Shrine Sets Off Protests, Violence," *The Washington Post*, February 23, 2006, p. A1; Robert F. Worth, "Blast at Shiite Shrine Sets Off Sectarian Fury in Iraq," *The New York Times*, February 23, 2006, p. 1.

448 **The previous month:** Evan Thomas, "The Shot Heard Round the World," *Newsweek*, February 27, 2006, p. 24; *Time*, February 27, 2006, cover headline reads, "Sticking to His Guns."

449 **That afternoon:** Rachel Shteir, "Former Bush Aide Charged in Felony Theft," *Slate*, March 10, 2006, www.slate.com.

450 **On March 16:** Congressional Quarterly, FDCH Political Transcripts, Senate Armed Services Committee Hearing, March 16, 2006.

CHAPTER 42

The information in this chapter comes primarily from background interviews with 11 knowledgeable sources.

453 **"Our strategy is":** Presidential Documents, March 18, 2006: http://frwebgate.access.gpo.gov/cgi-bin/getdoc.cgi?dbname=2006_presidential_documents&docid=pd27mr06_txt-4.

453 **"If this is not civil war":** Michael A. Fletcher, "Bush Still Upbeat on Outcome in Iraq; On Third Anniversary of Invasion, President Foresees 'Victory,' " *The Washington Post*, March 20, 2006, p. A1; Presidential Documents, March 21, 2006.

454   And what about: Paul D. Eaton, "A Top-Down Review for the Pentagon," *The New York Times*, March 19, 2006, p. 12.

455   On Monday afternoon: Jennifer Edwards, "Bush's Chief of Staff Rallies Butler Co. GOP," *The Cincinnati Enquirer*, March 28, 2006, p. 2B.

455   The next morning: Presidential Documents, March 28, 2006: http://frwebgate.access.gpo.gov/cgi-bin/getdoc.cgi?dbname=2006_presi dential_documents&docid=pd03ap06_txt-9.

455   There were 58,249 names: From the National Park Service as of August 1, 2006, www.nps.gov.

457   Tony Blair was getting: Mary Jordan, "Britons Feeling 'Tired of Tony'; Former Fans Call Blair Out of Touch," *The Washington Post*, April 16, 2005, p. A1; Kevin Sullivan, "Blair Reshuffles Cabinet After Election Losses; Foreign Secretary Dismissed in Overhaul," *The Washington Post*, May 6, 2006, p. A11.

458   Afterward at a press briefing: Transcripts of Secretary Rice's comments: www.state.gov/secretary/rm/2006/63994.htm.

459   No matter how bad: David S. Cloud and Eric Schmitt, "More Retired Generals Call for Rumsfeld's Resignation," *The New York Times*, April 14, 2005, p. 1.

459   On Tuesday, April 18, 2006: Department of Defense News Briefing, April 18, 2006: www.defenselink.mil/Transcripts/Transcript.aspx?Tran scriptID=1253.

CHAPTER 43

The information in this chapter comes primarily from background interviews with six knowledgeable sources.

461   Jafari finally stepped aside: Nelson Hernandez and K. I. Ibrahim, "Top Shiites Nominate a Premier for Iraq; Al-Maliki Opposed Hussein and the U.S.-Led Invasion," *The Washington Post*, April 22, 2006, p. A1.

464   Rice and Rumsfeld: Transcripts of Rice's and Rumsfeld's press conferences in Iraq: www.state.gov/secretary/trvl/2006/64876.htm.

466   He watched: Directed by Jon Alpert and Matthew O'Neill, *Baghdad ER*, Home Box Office, 2006.

468   The president invited: Elisabeth Bumiller, "This Time Around, Bush Lets Former Secretaries Speak," *The New York Times*, May 13, 2006, p. 9.

469 Maliki took office: Nelson Hernandez and Omar Fekeiki, "Iraqi Premier, Cabinet Sworn In; Sectarian Bickering over Unfilled Posts Interrupts Ceremony," *The Washington Post*, May 21, 2006, p. A1.

469 In a speech in Chicago: Presidential Documents, May 22, 2006: http://frwebgate.access.gpo.gov/cgi-bin/getdoc.cgi?dbname=2006_presi dential_documents&docid=pd29my06_txt-12.

CHAPTER 44

The information in this chapter comes primarily from background interviews with four knowledgeable sources, and from an interview with General Pace on July 20, 2006.

471 The next day: Documents reviewed by the author.

475 In July 2006: Author interview with Secretary Rumsfeld, July 6, 2006.

476 On May 26: Full report can be obtained from the Pentagon's website: www.defenselink.mil/news/Jul2005/d20050721secstab.pdf.

CHAPTER 45

The information in this chapter comes primarily from background interviews with five knowledgeable sources, and from an interview with General Pace on July 20, 2006.

480 Classified reports: Documents reviewed by the author.

482 But President Bush: Author interviews with President George W. Bush, December 20, 2001, and August 20, 2002.

482 On July 11, 2006: Transcript of Secretary Rumsfeld's press conference, July 11, 2006: www.defenselink.mil/Transcripts/Transcript.aspx? TranscriptID=47.

483 Three days after: News release from Multi-National Force-Iraq: www.mnf-iraq.com/index.php?option=com_content&task=view&id= 1179&Itemid=38.

483 In July 2006: Author interviews with Secretary Rumsfeld, July 6 and 7, 2006; document reviewed by the author.

488 On December 11, 2003: Author interview with President George W. Bush, December 11, 2003; see Bob Woodward, *Plan of Attack*, p. 422.

ACKNOWLEDGMENTS

T HIS BOOK is based almost entirely on my own reporting and interviews, but the very large group of reporters and authors who have
come before and written about the Iraq War have provided important information and added immensely to my understanding. I thank them all,
especially those who have reported from Iraq. These men and women
have endured hardships and risked their lives to keep a steady stream of
information coming to the rest of the world. More than 70 reporters
from *The Washington Post*, and probably thousands from other news organizations, have filed from Iraq. They, and all the Iraqis who have as-
sisted them, have my respect and deep appreciation.

Post reporters whose work from Iraq was of great help include but are
by no means limited to Rajiv Chandrasekaran, Anthony Shadid, John
Ward Anderson, Karl Vick, Jackie Spinner, Ellen Knickmeyer, Nelson
Hernandez, Scott Wilson, Ann Scott Tyson, Caryle Murphy, Josh White,
Vernon Loeb, Barton Gellman, Peter Slevin, and Doug Struck.

Simon & Schuster and *The Washington Post* once again supported me
completely as I reported and wrote this book, my 14th. Alice Mayhew,
who has been my editor at Simon & Schuster for the past 34 years, once
again was the skillful and devoted guide and counselor, helping me at
every stage and making sure we found the story.

The remarkable team at Simon & Schuster of Carolyn K. Reidy, the
president, and David Rosenthal, the publisher, were at their very best on
this book—engaged, prodding and thoughtful. They treat their authors
as family, keeping the bar high, but bestowing on them full attention and

devotion. They know how to publish a book right and as fast as 21st-century technology permits.

Thanks to Roger Labrie, the editor, for help in so many areas—words, photographs, deadlines and overall coordination. Roger is one of the unsung heroes of publishing, making sure that everything lands at approximately the same time. I also thank Jack Romanos, the president and chief executive officer; Elisa Rivlin, senior vice president and general counsel; Victoria Meyer, the executive VP director of publicity; Tracey Guest, director of publicity; Jackie Seow, art director and jacket designer; Irene Kheradi, executive managing editor; Allison Murray, associate managing editor; Serena Jones, associate editor; Linda Dingler, director of design; Lisa Healy, the senior production editor who took charge and so skillfully managed one of the tightest fast-track schedules in book publishing; Jaime Putorti, who worked on the photo layout and design; Nancy Inglis, director of copyediting; Lynn Anderson, proofreader; and Chris Carruth, indexer.

A special thanks to John Wahler, associate director of production, for his care and expertise with all details—small, medium and large.

Bill Murphy, Christine Parthemore and I have much gratitude for master copy editor Fred Chase, who again came from Texas to join our garrison in Northwest Washington. This is my fourth book with Fred. He is great company, knows the world and language, and offers unmatched expertise, good sense and mature advice.

Leonard Downie Jr., *The Washington Post*'s executive editor, and Phil Bennett, the *Post*'s managing editor, provide the foundations for in-depth, book-length projects that are on the news. Len calls it "accountability reporting," and this effort has been undertaken with that important idea very much in mind. Don Graham, the *Post*'s chief executive officer, is unique among media owners and top executives. Don is a pillar of independence and he even tolerates employees who declare their independence from him. Bo Jones, the *Post* publisher, is a true friend of journalism. Bill Hamilton, an assistant managing editor at the *Post*, has a keen eye for the essential and used it wisely for the excerpts from this book for the *Post*.

I am certain that I have used material that sources have told me about or information reflected in records that has appeared earlier in some form in another publication or news account or book. I have not done the archaeology to see who should be given credit for first reporting on various episodes or issues, but the endnotes give specific citations for material that was used.

My colleagues at the *Post* provided much assistance, not only in their excellent daily coverage but informally with many suggestions and ideas. Those reporters and editors include Jeff Leen, Peter Baker, Thomas E. Ricks, Walter Pincus, Karen DeYoung, Al Kamen, Susan Glasser, Steve Luxenberg, Robert Kaiser, Charles Babington, David Broder, David Ignatius, E. J. Dionne, Jim VandeHei, Carol D. Leonnig, Dana Priest, Bradley Graham, Glenn Kessler, Eugene Robinson, Liz Spayd, Michael Abramowitz, David Hoffman, and Joby Warrick. They have always been gracious and accepting of a lone ranger in their midst. Much significant background and understanding was also provided by *The Washington Post* foreign and national staffs.

Special thanks to Joe Elbert, Vanessa Hillian, Erica Lusk, Michel duCille and the rest of the *Post*'s wonderful photo staff.

I was also helped immeasurably by the reporting and analysis in *The New York Times*, *The Wall Street Journal*, *Newsweek*, *Time*, *U.S. News & World Report*, *Los Angeles Times*, *The New Yorker*, *The National Journal*, the Associated Press and dozens of other news organizations.

The books I have found most useful include *Fiasco* by Thomas E. Ricks, *My Year in Iraq* by L. Paul Bremer, *The Assassins' Gate* by George Packer, *Rise of the Vulcans* by James Mann, *No True Glory* by Bing West, *The UN's Role in Nation-Building* by James Dobbins et al., *Rumsfeld's War* by Rowan Scarborough, and *American Soldier* by General Tommy Franks.

Robert B. Barnett, my agent, attorney and friend, again provided steady counsel beyond the lawyerly skills he so ably brings to any task. His wife and daughter call him the Waukegan Warrior, because he was raised in that Illinois town. Wherever his origins, he is a real warrior—the good kind, 100 percent on your side but aware of the bigger picture in the tradition of his mentor, Edward Bennett Williams. Because he represents prominent Democrats such as former President Bill Clinton and Senator Hillary Rodham Clinton and prominent Republicans such as Lynne Cheney, he was not consulted on the contents and he did not see this book until it was printed.

Thanks again to Rosa Criollo and Jackie Crowe, who keep life sane and orderly.

Tali, my older daughter, spent four days reading the manuscript and brought a keen eye and good sense to the task, reminding me that not everyone knows what the "J-5" does on the Joint Chiefs of Staff. Diana, our 10–year-old, brought much good cheer and, more important, real affection during the reporting and writing.

Love, gratitude and admiration to Elsa Walsh, my wife and best friend. Elsa bears up well under the hours of private discussions we have about politics, wars and books. She graciously helps with the story development and the editing. Elsa remains the solid rock on which we all depend. Wise, joyful and cool under any pressure, Elsa has solved most of life's dilemmas and helps her family and friends as we stumble through our own.

INDEX

PHOTOGRAPHY CREDITS

Luis Acosta (Getty): 9

Susan Biddle *(The Washington Post):* 8, 18

Courtesy of the Cohen Group: 10

Kevin Coombs (Reuters): 6

Charles Dharapak (Associated Press): 16

Larry Downing (Reuters): 29

Eric Draper (The White House): 27, 28

Sean Gallup (Getty): 3

Gerald Herbert (Associated Press): 22

Mian Kursheed (Reuters): 25

Ray Lustig *(The Washington Post):* 26

Melina Mara *(The Washington Post):* 24

Courtesy of James "Spider" Marks: 11

John McDonnell *(The Washington Post):* 19

Larry Morris *(The Washington Post):* 12

Paul Morse (The White House): 14

Scott Nelson (Associated Press): 13

Lucian Perkins *(The Washington Post):* 17

Robert A. Reeder *(The Washington Post):* 21

Dayna Smith *(The Washington Post):* 7

Susan Sterner (The White House): 15

Helene C. Stikkel (Department of Defense): 23

Courtesy of the United States Navy: 4

R. D. Ward (Department of Defense): 1, 5

Jim Watson (Reuters): 20

Courtesy of The White House: 2